P9-BIS-077

The Life and Letters of St. Paul

An Exegetical Study

by

J. W. Shepard, M.A., Th.D.

Founder of Rio Baptist College and Seminary
and formerly Professor of New Testament and Greek
in the
New Orleans Baptist Theological Seminary

Author of
The Christ of the Gospels

WM. B. EERDMANS PUBLISHING COMPANY
GRAND RAPIDS MICHIGAN

Fifth Printing, October 1967

PHOTOLITHOPRINTED BY CUSHING - MALLOY, INC.
ANN ARBOR, MICHIGAN, UNITED STATES OF AMERICA

Dedicated to
the Progress of the Gospel of Christ
and to the Furtherance of Universal Peace

FOREWORD

The purpose of the author in undertaking the stupendous task of the preparation of this treatise on Paul, the Apostle to the Gentiles, was to apply the same method of historico-grammatical exegesis which was employed in writing the preceding companion volume, *The Christ of the Gospels.* In that work the results were gratifying, and the author entertains the hope, in seeking to clarify Paul's interpretation of the Christ, that the extensive writings of the Apostle be made a little plainer to the understanding of the less instructed, and that possibly the searcher after the truth, so extensively set forth in Paul's not-too-well understood epistles, may be helped. Paul was an original thinker and made a vast contribution as the best of all interpreters of the Christ, to whose authority as the founder of Christianity he ever held his own interpretation subservient. The preparation of this treatise, based on forty odd years of research, has cost the author several of the most laborious years of his life-work in the normal and systematic processes of its writing. He earnestly hopes that it may follow the former treatise on Christ in a long and useful career in the service of the kingdom.

CONTENTS

PART III — Paul's Prison Experiences and Letters

CHAPTER PAGE

INTRODUCTION

How to Interpret Paul's Epistles

INTRODUCTION

How to Interpret Paul's Epistles

I

A VITAL interpretation of Paul and his letters, avoiding the temptations to pure intellectualism, to super-profuse emotionalism, and to mere humanitarianism, is a task of tremendous pretension, calling for the keenest spiritual perception, the deepest religious experience, and nothing less than extreme devotion to Christ and complete dependence on the guidance of the Holy Spirit. It was such qualifications as these that Paul himself possessed in the highest degree for the interpretation of Jesus, the Christ and his Lord and Master, and yet he did not profess to measure up.

Baur, and a long line of critics, following in his train, gave a wrong orientation to the study and interpretation of Paul and his writings, by the elaboration of their speculative systems, which for a time eclipsed Paul's interpretation of the Gospel. This was due to their desire to theologize his writings and the result was Paulinism.

1. The best and really only way to interpret Paul's message concerning Christ is to follow the common-sense method of a historico-grammatical exegesis of Acts and of each letter or epistle in its own 'life-situation'. It is impossible to fit Paul into a preconceived system of theology. He was dealing with vital problems in the churches in all of his epistles. For example, the circumstances of the inroads of the Gnostic teachers in the church in Colosse gave occasion to the writing of such an epistle to the Colossians as dealt with that particular problem. The Pauline doctrinal teaching administered in the solution of that problem is applicable in dealing with problems of the same type and character today. He was dealing with the Christian way of life, and one who seeks to understand his teachings must take them in their own vital context historically and grammatically and study the real meanings with which the author invested them. The jealous rivalries over preachers, the irregularities in conduct, the irreverent behavior at the Lord's supper, the jealousies about spiritual gifts and their exercise in the church assemblies, together with some other problems gave occasion for the writing of First Corinthians, one of the longest of the epistles. In just the same way, disturbances raised in the churches in Galatia by the Judaizers called forth the Galatian letter. Almost every letter of Paul was brought forth by problems in the churches or some other vital need.

To properly understand each of these letters, the interpreter must get a close-up view of the writer, together with all his experiences in his missionary activities, his victories and successes, his antagonisms and defeats, at the time of the writing.

2. If we wish to get the living message from Paul as he got his message from Jesus, we must have his understanding of the true attitudes of an interpreter. Paul considered himself a bearer of the revealed message of the living Christ. With him immediate contact with the risen Lord and with the Holy Spirit in unbroken communion was the thing of greatest importance. In his period of communion in Arabia and in the Cilician ministry of several years, Paul was receiving into his heart, directly from the Lord, the understanding of the new life and vocation into which he had been called. It is for us to try and penetrate as far as possible into the comprehension of the fundamental doctrines which he there and then found to be vital and germane to the needs of men, as had been proven by his own experience. *His approach was through the door of experience.* For example, Paul's experience with legalistic traditional Judaism had been that it did not give him internal peace and joy. He had with great zeal and sincere earnestness sought to live up to the requirements of the Pharisaic legal standards, but he, like the Rich Young Ruler, had felt that there was something lacking. We make the same mistake Judaizers made when we endeavor to lay down a system of Pauline theology as a plan of salvation, and declare that by means of the intellectual acceptance of it one may be saved. The experience of union with Christ is central in repentance, faith, forgiveness, justification, regeneration, and every vital Christian experience, and apart from the realization of communion, there is no reality in any of the experiences denoted by these theological terms. For example, forgiveness is attended with joy and peace. For Paul the real marks of orthodoxy were love, joy, peace, access, longsuffering (Raven), and other spiritual experiences of like character.

3. Some of the greatest expositors of recent times, seeking to interpret Paul's epistles, have followed the clue of "word pictures" in working out true interpretations of the Pauline and other New Testament writings. Paul used many words which present graphically[1] concrete mental pictures, illustrative of the great redemptive transactions. In the "triumphal train" of Christ, Paul was glad to be one of those who was "led captive" in the glorious ministry; and in the acts of worship, he gloried in being a priestly "censer-bearer" as if in the temple, to scatter sweet smelling perfume of prayer and praise.[2] But it is easy for the interpreter to read inaccurately, even into these word-pictures, things not found in the actual historical experience of the apostle. Paul's heart was open to the vision, as that of W. M. Poteat, when discussing the Incarnation: he paused suddenly in a flight of eloquence and exclaimed, "Oh

1. Robertson's *Word Pictures* and Vincent's *Word Studies* are examples.
2. II Cor. 2:14.

the wonder of it!" Such was his facial expression at that moment that the picture of the speaker was eternally graven in the memory of the hearer.

4. To interpret Paul, one must have an intimate acquaintance and sympathy with his inner life. He experienced in a most marked degree the *grace of God in Christ* in his conversion. He had followed out his own righteousness under the law to the utmost endeavor and it had failed him. In utter desperation, when well-nigh all the ideals of his Messianic hopes had faded into a starless night, the sun of God's righteousness in Christ, the real Messiah, burst on his vision and flooded his soul with the eternal light and love of a new life, a new humanity, and a new world. This experience sent him forth as the greatest herald of the Christ in the Christian era in which we live.

Luther and other great interpreters had to rescue Paul's message centuries later by unearthing it from beneath the accumulated debris of systems of man-made theological creeds and formulations of belief. It was when Luther was on his knees, ascending the stairway of the shrine of *a too theological Christianity*, hoary with ages of traditional legalistic interpretations, that a vision of the real meaning of Paul's most fundamental Christian experience, "The just shall live by faith," came home to his seeking, hungry heart, and he arose and returned home to be the incomparable evangelist of this recovered truth, which like a star of the first magnitude has since shed its effulgence over our benighted world.

5. Paul is in truth the greatest interpreter of Jesus. He was utterly devoted and loyal to His Lord and ever considered it his highest honor to be His confessed bond-servant. There never was any "gulf" between Jesus and Paul. To Paul it was given to be the refutation of the apparent defeat of the Galilean by victorious Phariseeism at Calvary, when, as the brilliant Pharisaic leader of the persecution against the humble disciples of the crucified Nazarene, he went down before Jesus in capitulation and utter commitment to Him. As a beacon light, his conversion stands forth as the greatest example of the power of the Gospel of Jesus to completely and suddenly change a great man's whole life and thereafter mould all his thought after the Christian model. He reflects as a mirror the glory of the Lord more powerfully than any other man in human history. His life was the most perfect example of the influence and the most dramatic illustration of the power of Jesus.[3]

Paul's experience in communion with Christ is the starting point and basic element of all the concrete truths of the doctrinal revelations of his epistles. Reflecting on his experience in conversion, he revealed his conviction of God's grace, born from the love-light which he beheld in the face of Jesus. Reflecting on the appearance of the majestic defender of His humble flock in the Damascus Way, he fell at His feet calling him Lord and offering himself as His obedient slave. Reflecting on the effect of that commitment of himself and its instantaneous results, he testified to the truth that *forgiveness* is immediate, and peace and joy fill the soul the very moment one repents and

---

3. Stewart, James S. *A Man in Christ*, p. 20

accepts the Lord.[4] Paul's spiritual intuition was keen and his vision became always the basis of reflection and careful expression of the vivid experiences with the Lord. Experience must ever be the basis of thought, but it is equally true that thought should be the logical outcome of experience. Some of the great apostles were more heralds of the Gospel than expositors of its theological implications. Paul was a great preacher of the Gospel but also a sublime teacher of its real transforming power. When the Apostle prayed to Jesus, and had the assurance and the realization of the answers to his prayers, he understood that Jesus was the Son of God and that at His name every knee must bow in reverent worship and recognition of His deity. (Phil. 2:1-10). *Paul was a great thinker, and much of the incomparable service he rendered to Christianity as its protagonist is to be found in his trained ability for reflective thought.* It was his to interpret to Christians their own experiences. He appealed to Christian experience many times in his defense of the Gospel. In the vindication of his apostolic authority before the bar of the experience of the Galatian Christians he asks, "Did you receive the Spirit by doing what the Law commands or by believing the Gospel message?"[5] So it is true that the Christian worker who reflects, like Paul, on his own experience with Christ, in the miracles of his grace, cannot but realize the verity of the power of Christ to change the heart of man. Paul prayed for the Ephesian Christians that the eyes of their hearts might be enlightened by the Spirit, that they might understand the hope God had in calling them, the wealth of God's glorious heritage in his saints and the surpassing greatness of the power working in believers, the same which operated in raising Christ from the dead,[6] and in making him to sit down at the right hand of the majesty as the head of creation and redemption. Paul in the Ephesian letter reaches the sublimest peak in his reflections on the nature of Christ and Christianity and the duty of the Church and every individual member of it to recognize the Lordship of Christ and the call for complete commitment to his plan of the ages. This is "high thinking" for which we should be devoutly grateful! Truly Paul was 'apprehended by Christ.' The epistle to the Romans was, by the expression of Jullicher, Paul's "Confession of faith." It is experiential and of the character of a personal letter rather than a formal treatise and should be so interpreted.

6. In his use of terms Paul does not follow rigid definitions; for the measuring of a word varies according to the context. He did not envisage the construction of a doctrinal system, but considered himself a *witness* whose business was to report what he saw, heard, and experienced in communion with Christ in His Word, His work, and His world. In his delineation of sin he uses a half dozen or more words to picture the character, nature, and consequences of this "ancient wrong."[7]

---

4. Romans 5:1-3.
5. Gal. 3:2.
6. Eph. 1:18-20.
7. Dodd, E. Harold: *The Meaning of Paul for Today*, Chap. V; cf. Robertson, A. T., *Word Pictures* for meanings in context of Greek words.

In spite of the apparent incongruities and even inconsistencies in doctrine with which Paul is accused, it will be found that his passion for truth was his constant guide in the midst of the stormy seas of cross-currents and under-currents, of the fierce antagonisms he had to encounter. For him Christ was the center of unity in all his thought and activities and the secret of the integration of his experiences and unifying of his doctrinal expressions.

II

1. The character of Paul's writings: Most of Paul's epistles were written when he was moving to and fro in the midst of intense activities in preaching and teaching. In spite of this fact his epistles have been "among the mightiest intellectual forces of the world" (Stalker). Paul was the greatest thinker of his age, if not of any age. He far surpassed any of the great missionaries of all Christian history in his ability to think deeply and express clearly the great eternal truths about God and man, and his words have stirred mankind as no other words, except those of Jesus Christ.

His epistles were letters revealing their writer and his eager desire to serve God and man. They were not models in style but throb with emotion, and in many places, from the very excellence of the ideas they bear, run into a style of expression almost poetic in form. At times his style also becomes a very torrential mountain stream irresistibly leaping from cascade to cascade; sometimes broken in *anacolutha* as it tears onward in formless precipitation. From the vast masses of ideas and thoughts which stream forth from his fertile brain, men have constructed whole systems of theology. He wrote under inspiration of the Spirit of God, with all his powers of mind and heart ablaze with the fire of an incomparable genius.

In his epistles we see the man standing forth self-revealed. But he was greater than all his combined epistles and sermons. In the words of Weiss: "Paul is able powerfully to move, but also to lift up and comfort; high moral earnestness is always associated in him with depth of religious feeling, which often finds vent in inspired utterance. He is not without passion; he lashes the weaknesses and errors of his readers without pity; he is able mortally to wound his opponents, and does not even despise the weapons of irony and satire; the ebullition or righteous anger (at times) softens down to the most touching expression of heart-felt love; he can speak the language of deeply wounded love as well as of the most ardent longing; of exulting gratitude as well as of suppressed pain."

Paul's modes of thought are of great value in the interpretation of his epistles. He makes frequent use of personification, as for example, of *Sin* as a *ruler* on the throne. (Rom. 5:12; 3:9). Mystical realism is a characteristic mode of his thought as in the identification of unregenerate humanity with Adam the natural head of the race and of believing humanity with Christ. Paul also uses the legalistic mode of thought, as for example, in speaking of himself as the bond-servant of Christ, or Christians as the adopted sons of

God. Finally, he frequently uses the parallel, as illustrated in Rom. 5:12-21 comparing and contrasting Christ and Adam in their relationships to the race.

2. Paul's attitude toward and understanding of the Christian traditions: In lieu of the Apostle's vision on the Damascus road he believed in a historical Jesus, who was incarnated, and as the God-man, dwelt in our midst and founded Christianity, *which is a historical religion.* There is a Christian mysticism which holds to revelation in Jesus Christ. Paul was a Christian mystic of that type, and his mode of thought as already observed before was many times cast in the mould of mystic realism. The Gospels are historical documents. The Christian religion did not evolve from mere thought or imagination but is based upon facts and events. Jesus Christ was a real person, God incarnated in the flesh. In the Gospels we have the record of the mighty acts of God, in the consummation of the plan of redemption in the eternal purpose of God (Eph. 3:11). The sinless life, atoning death, and supernatural resurrection constitute the solid basis of the Gospels.

The Pauline epistles, written for the instruction and guidance of the early Christian communities, reveal a great variety of the activities and many aspects of the thought of these communities. All of Paul's teachings hark back to the authoritarian pronouncements of Jesus, whom he held to be the Christ, (Messiah) of the Jewish prophecies. Paul did not attempt to lay any other foundation than that which was laid which was Jesus the Christ (I Cor. 1-4).

The epistles of Paul contain apparently few direct citations of the Gospel traditions because the traditions had not crystallized completely when he wrote. But he used the Gospel tradition as a frame of reference, and to Paul, Jesus was the sinless, incarnate Christ, who was pre-existent[8] but who in this life subjected himself to human limitations.

To Paul, as to John, the Word of Christ was ultimate authority.[9] Although Paul recognized his own teaching as Spirit-inspired, his independent teaching is "subordinate and derivative."[10] He got his authoritative statement about the last Paschal Meal and his First Supper from the Gospel Traditions (I Cor. 11:23-26). He was acquainted with the circumstances of Jesus' death as well as His life and character.[11]

Among the Christian traditions, the one which held the Central place in the preaching of the primitive church was the ***Passion story.*** In Peter's great sermon at Pentecost the death of Jesus, a crime committed by the Jews, was declared to have been the predetermined plan and purpose of God (Acts 4:27, 28). In the Psalms (Ps. 2, etc) and prophecies it had been foretold that God's plan for the salvation of the race would be through the vicarious suffering and sacrifice of his Suffering Servant (Isa. 53), which prophecies were fulfilled in Jesus the Messiah. The Christian conceptions of the *sufferings* and *death* and *resurrection* of *Jesus*, as recorded in all the Gospels

8. Phil. 2:5-11.
9. I Cor. 7, 10, 12, 25, 40.
10. Dodd, C. H.: *History and the Gospel,* pp. 57, 58.
11. II Cor. 11:1; Phil. 2:7,8; Rom. 13:14.

(Luke 24:46-47), Paul expressly sets forth as the very core of the evangelical message of good news to the world. In the name of this Messiah Sufferer was to be proclaimed repentance and remission of sins. Jesus himself had foretold His suffering, death, and resurrection to His unbelieving disciples. He was to suffer for them that they might have forgiveness of sins. Paul states this Gospel most completely in his first letter to the Corinthian church,[12] the letter next in chronological order following the Thessalonian letters.

---

12. I Cor. 15:1-5.

The Life and Letters of St. Paul

Part I

THE CHRISTIANITY THAT FOUND PAUL

CHAPTER I

The Christianity of the Christ

THE Christianity of the Christ is that which was seen in Him. His kind of Christianity is revealed in the inspired records of what He did and taught. The very abbreviated narrative of the Gospels gives us a limited account of those things. It would have taken a world of books to record all that He did and said. That was all a shining page of absolute perfection, the only one of human history. He alone taught only what He did, and practiced only what He taught. His Christianity is unattained, has never been realized completely in the experience of any Christian that ever lived because mere man has never come to perfection. This is the kind of Christianity that could be presented only by the perfect sinless Christ as a model and standard for all mankind to strive toward if never to fully reach it, in this human life. To admit that Christ was less than perfect would be to compromise the whole truth of His redemption of humanity. The acceptance of His deity, is the very foundation upon which the whole eternal structure of Christianity is built. It was this Christianity that found Saul of Tarsus because the risen and ascended Christ, exalted at the right hand of God, arrested him on his way to Damascus.

Jesus did not complete his earthly ministry until after He rose from the grave and, had begun His eternal reign at the right hand of the Father. Through the Holy Spirit, He gave the final command to the apostles whom He had chosen for the world-campaign of the Gospel, while He was yet present with them, in the post-resurrection period.

During the forty days between His resurrection and ascension, the Lord Jesus showed Himself alive after His suffering and death on the cross and His burial in the tomb of Joseph of Arimathea, (who was reported to be His uncle). His ten appearances to the apostles and disciples, (not to the unbelievers), were under varying circumstances, in different places and to people representative of all classes among His followers. He was both seen and heard by them. Especially did He speak on the central theme of His preaching, and teaching ministry, which covered approximately three years, and was limited to the small country of Palestine. This great theme was the Kingdom of God to which He Himself was related as its Messiah.

The second important step of the resurrected Christ was to announce the coming of the Holy Spirit in person to conduct the work He had begun, representing Him and carrying out His plan of redemption of the race, in history, to the end of time. He charged the disciples not to depart from Jerusalem, as they might be tempted to do, until the Spirit, promised by the Father, about whom He had spoken to them, had come. They must be ready in a few days to receive his indwelling and be immersed within the influence of his presence and power.

The inspired historian, Luke, sets down in the briefest essential narrative possible the activities of the Lord just before His ascension. One of the important facts that he revealed was that the disciples were even yet held fast by the traditional idea of a temporal Messianic Kingdom. Tradition has ever been one of the greatest barriers to progress through real experience. The traditional interpretation of the Old Testament prophecy about David's greater Son, as the Messianic King, was literal and wrong. It had always proven a blind to the real truth and was even retained by these disciples, who asked their resurrected Lord whether He was going to restore again at that time the Kingdom of Israel. Jesus brushed the question to one side, revealing to them that the important thing for them to know relative to the Kingdom was not 'times and seasons' but how to get equipped with the power of the Holy Spirit in order to serve as witnesses in the evangelization of the world. They would not be able to do the vast work of this global campaign in their own strength at all. It was too stupendous to be encompassed by their imagination, much less to be accomplished by the body of workers, even counting on its rapid and enormous growth. They must begin with the evangelization of Jerusalem and expand their working force to spread rapidly, in spite of the most difficult obstacles of race prejudice, to Samaria, and then to the whole Gentile world! And with this final command their Master-Teacher made His surprising exit while they looked with amazement, as He floated up from them into a cloud which received Him out of their sight. Two men clothed in shining garments awakened them from their rapture saying, "Men from Galilee why do you remain standing, looking up into the Heaven? This very Jesus who was received up from you into the heaven thus shall come again in the same manner as you saw Him proceeding into the heaven." Such was the departure of the risen Christ and such the promise of His return again to earth.

The picture of the primitive apostolic Christianity which Saul of Tarsus first encountered and which touched his life and changed it into that of Paul the Apostle to the Gentiles, is portrayed in the first twelve chapters of the so-called Acts of the Apostles and in the earliest Christian traditions, mostly oral, in existence when he was converted.[1]

The book of Acts, written by Luke, is taken up with the narrative of those activities of the Holy Spirit, who came to inaugurate his leadership at Pentecost, and carry out the Christian program of "things which Jesus began to do and to teach" while in His earthly ministry. Luke's "first treatise," (*protos logos*) narrated the gospel of early Christian traditions, carefully compiled

1. The Sinaitic MS gives the name of "Acts" only.

by the learned doctor of medicine from the Markan and other written and oral sources such as the logia of Matthew and especially from "eye witnesses who had been in the service of the proclamation of the Gospel message from the beginning." Of this he informs us in his classical preface to the third Gospel (Luke 1:1-4).

The purpose of the masterly historian in drawing up in order that narrative, as many others had assayed to do, was that Theophilus, probably a Roman friend of his, who was a 'God-lover,' might know accurately (*epignōs*) the absolute certainty of the truth of the doctrines he had been taught. In his second treatise (*deuteros logos*), Luke continued the same historical narrative of the kingdom activities, but now of the risen and ever-living Lord, in and by His apostles, through the agency and power of the Holy Spirit in them.

I. Before Christ's ascension, His disciples received the charge to carry forward the work of the practical program of propagation of the Realm[2] of God, which He had inaugurated in the days of his incarnation. Those things that Jesus began to do and teach were the content of their message. His earthly ministry terminated on the day of the ascension, when He issued His orders, through the Holy Spirit, under whose leadership they were to carry forward to completion the same kind of doings and teachings as those He had begun, in His name, through the Holy Spirit. (Acts 1:1-3).

1. A glance into the world in which Christianity was planted shows an environment of dire need and urgent opportunity for the entrance of the Good News.[3] The Graeco-Roman world was so situated socially and religiously as to be in divinely ordained preparation for the coming of the Gospel message. The same God, who gave Christ to the world, has been working in human history, preparing the world for His advent. The contact of the new leaven of the Gospel with the old mass of a pagan civilization was one of contrast in character, as that of light with darkness. This is not to say that paganism did not possess and nurture certain valuable ideals before Christ came. Even paganism, darkened as it was with error and sin, had some sages, philosophers and religionists, who groped after higher things (Acts 17). The Christian religion was to enter into the world as a force for changing the world's darkness into a new light and for substituting in the place of its moral weakness a spiritual strength.[4] In the providence of God, the world-civilization corrupted by sin must be purified by the Gospel of Christ, and humanity must be regenerated and made new before it could come to that "one far-off divine event toward which the whole creation moves." The resurrected, living Christ entered upon his historical activities which continued to go on at the time of His ascension and now. He is working out the redemption of the race to the end of time.

2. The natural religion of mankind, by the testimony of W. M. Ramsay, is,

---

2. Cf. James Moffatt's *Translation*, in loco.
3. Cf. Angus, *Environment of Early Christianity*, Ch. I.
4. C. H. S. Angus, *Environment of Early Christianity* Ch. I.

"that wherever evidence exists, with the rarest exceptions, the history of religion among men is seen to be a history of degeneration." Even Christianity, dating from its first uncorrupted beginnings, soon became a contaminated religion in the process of its historic developments. But, as a stream casts down its silt in a sediment, Christianity has been a self-purifying current down through the ages, ridding itself largely of contaminations due to contacts with its world environment, while at the same time slaking the thirst of the perishing multitudes of mankind. *Even in the glimpses we have into the life of the first Christian community we do not find the reflection of the true force of the Christ uncorrupted, except in its projector, Jesus, who worked always toward the regeneration of men.* We do find that the primitive Christians were conscious in their experience of the resurrection and ascension of Jesus and of the presence and power of the Holy Spirit in them. They had really seen the Lord and walked with Him during forty days after his resurrection, receiving from Him instruction and His final orders, to bear the Gospel to the whole world. This was not a matter of hallucination or of apparitions. Out of their experiences there arose quickly a Christian community, proceeding from the united, holy brotherhood of one family which had formed itself around Jesus, as illustrated at the time of the first Supper. Glimpses of this primitive Christian community we have in the first chapter of the Acts. It was composed of regenerated men, constituting a new type of humanity, prophetic of a new heaven and a new earth in which dwelleth righteousness.[5]

II. The origin and development of Christianity among the Jews and its entrance among the Gentiles is sketched in the first twelve chapters of Luke's second treatise, the Acts. The remaining sixteen chapters deal with its expansion among the Gentiles. In the first general section (Chs. I-XII) the author deals with: (1) The ascension of Christ and related matters in a general introduction (Ch. I), followed (2) by the founding of the church community in Jerusalem (Chs. II-VIII:1) and (3) its expansion through Palestine into Antioch of Syria (Chs. VIII:2-XII:23). The second main division narrates the expansion from Antioch of Syria to Asia Minor in the first missionary journey of Paul with Barnabas and John Mark (XII:25-XV:39); then in the second missionary journey with Silas, Timothy and Luke into Macedonia and Greece (XV:40-XVIII:22); and following this in the third missionary journey to Ephesus and the surrounding regions during three years (XVIII:23-XXI:16). Finally, there follows the narrative of Paul's prison experiences and other events which brought him to Rome (XXI:17-XXVIII:31), where he ended his labors. Our immediate concern in this section of our interpretation is with the discussion of Christianity as revealed in the first twelve chapters of Acts,[6] the Christianity that found Paul and converted him and the Christianity that Paul found and interpreted.

1. In the introduction of his second treatise Luke points out, as we have seen, the connection between his Gospel and the Acts, in which he presents

5. E. F. Scott, *The Nature of the Early Church.* pp. 49-67.
6. Cf. James Moffatt, *Introduction to the Literature of the New Testament.*

the continued story of the *things which Jesus had begun both to do and to teach,* now to be continued by the Holy Spirit representing Him (1:1-3). The disciple-workers had in their possession already the common traditions, oral and written, about the deeds and teachings of Jesus, but they needed to receive power from on high through the coming of the Holy Spirit before they should launch the campaign of world-evangelization. In the passion narrative, received by Luke through eye-witnesses orally, and in sermons and writings of the apostles, he learned that Jesus charged the disciples *not to depart from Jerusalem,* but to keep on waiting there for the promise of the Spirit's[7] coming. He reminded them that John had baptized them symbolically in water but that *they would be immersed* or baptized in the Holy Spirit not many days later (1:4, 5).

Jesus committed to the disciples on the occasion of the ascension the responsible work of the propagation of the kingdom through witnessing (1:6-11). They needed in preparation for their great Kingdom work to become "clothed-upon" with spiritual power and to come to the right understanding about themselves as the "chosen people," in their relation to God. These disciples were facing a great task. After their baptism in the Spirit they would have a spiritual understanding of the Kingdom and their part in its program. It was a work which would meet the local needs of a complete transformation of individuals and society, but it was to meet the needs of the whole wide world also. *They were to be witnesses in Jerusalem, Judea and Samaria, but also in the whole world and in all times.*

The ascension commission was given to the small group of a hundred and twenty disciples on the Mount of Olives, and even while He was speaking the unforgettable words, His feet parted from the ground and He floated upward and was soon enshrouded in a cloud.

Reminded by two men dressed in white, *in obedience to the remembered command of Jesus* (Luke 24:52) *the disciples returned with joy to Jerusalem* from the place of the ascension, somewhere on the Mount of Olives, *and entered the upper chamber* (Cf. Luke 22:12), probably the place where they had celebrated the last paschal meal with the Lord. In this house, which was likely that of the mother of John Mark (Acts 1:12f), *they were either abiding continually as guests or more probably coming day after day for prayer and fellowship with the apostles and other disciples, who were awaiting the coming of the Spirit, according to the promise.* The names of the eleven apostles are mentioned in the list of this notable prayer-group. Along with them, all of Jesus' half-brothers were there. They must already have been converted after His resurrection. In company with them also were the faithful women, who had supported the Lord and His apostle-group while in the strenuous Kingdom campaign, during His earthly ministry. The name of Mary the mother of Jesus is delicately singled out for honorable mention by Luke. James, the oldest of the Lord's natural half-brothers, became an outstanding apostle

7. Subjective genitive, the promise given by the Father, (Robertson) *Word Pictures.*

and pastor in the Jerusalem Christian church-community later. In this protracted prayer-meeting they were "giving their strength persistently in unity of mind or spirit to prayer." The hundred and twenty who were waiting, in obedience, for the coming of the Spirit, were continually in the temple blessing God (Luke 24:53), but evidently had their special and separate Christian sessions in this private home, for prayer, for the fulfillment of Jesus' promise of the Spirit (vv. 12-14).

III. While they were waiting here for the Spirit's advent they turned their attention to the resolution of a problem of organization (1:15-26).

1. *Incipient but permanent principles of organization and government of the churches are here beginning to appear.* We see the functions of the individual members recognized in their participation in the group activities. We do not see yet a fully organized local church, but we do sense a corporate Christian community dealing with a vital fundamental problem of organization.

This assembly of a hundred and twenty disciples was one of the first meetings of the Body of the ascended Lord and one of the most significant ones of all Christian history. It was natural that Peter with his alert and impulsive nature should appear as the leader in the meeting, though it was doubtless by common consent of the brethren.[8] The apostles were expected to take the leadership, though the assembly was a democratic voting-body. The voice of the people was heard but only after committing in prayer the decision to the Lord's will. The Jewish device of casting lots was here employed but, as it seems, for the last time in Christian assemblies.

The problem was the choice of one who had been an eye-witness, from the beginning, of the ministry of Jesus, to succeed Judas in the school of the twelve apostles. The names of the two proposed persons were inscribed on small cubes of wood or other material and placed in a bowl which was put in whirling motion until the cubes were thrown out. The name on the first cube cast from the bowl was the name of the one chosen. Matthias was thus chosen, but he and Joseph (Barsabas) had previously been recommended in the assembly as fulfilling the requirement "from the beginning." *And it was after prayer that the Lord might make known which* of the two should be indicated into the the service and apostleship, *that the Christian body* or assembly *had taken a popular vote of its members and cast the lot.* All of this was after Peter's explanation of the necessity of electing someone to fill the place of Judas. The tragic end of the traitor who deserted and sold his Lord is pictured in livid colors, as well as is the memorial of his dastardly act which was the field of blood (*Alcedama*) which remains to testify until today. The name of Matthias does not appear again in the New Testament record, but for that matter eight of the Twelve do not figure in Luke's narrative any more.[9]

2. *Jesus "created the movement of Christianity out of His own knowledge of God." The primitive church arose spontaneously out of the life, work and*

8. Cf. W. O. Carver, *Acts of the Apostles*, p. 19 f.
9. Ibid. p. 22.

teachings of the Master.[10] Its members tried to put into effect and practice what they had learned from Him. The first stage of the church in its history was comparatively uncorrupted, being guided by the instruction of Jesus himself. It had no set order or government, but operated under the control of the Spirit. It had its task marked out for it, and its members were to press to the goal set for it by the Lord. Luke preserved the fundamental facts about its beginning. *The ideas and beliefs habitual among the first disciples are described in his brief narrative of the Acts. The atmosphere of the church's life is also sensed in his record.*

The Epistles of Paul are another source of our knowledge of the primitive churches, a good many of which he founded. He was conversant with the Christian traditions, both oral and written, of the early churches. The teachings of Jesus, many of which were recorded in the synoptic gospels and John's later account, were accepted as the final word of authority for the teaching and practice in the churches. The central theme of the Kingdom had been magnified in His teaching. *The primitive church was given the task to tell the world what it believed and had experienced in Jesus, as the Messiah, and now the way of life.* It was inseparably bound up with the life, teachings and work of Jesus as its cause and source. Luke's "former treatise" dealt with the life of Jesus on earth; the second with his larger invisible life in all subsequent time. In the study of Christianity, the theory of *development* does not help, because Christianity was purer in its origin than in its later development; was more divine in its earliest days than it could be afterwards.[11] In Jesus the founder, perfection is found, but in Him alone. The churches founded by Paul later, demonstrated in the life and example of their members, many imperfections.

3. *It is true that the history of the church is a resultant of two forces: the Christianity exemplified in the Christ; over against the forces of evil in the world, contaminating the stream of* pure Christianity *with their* muddy confluents *of secularizing influences and elements.*[12] The message of Jesus is not impracticable but simply has not been preached and applied. The cry "Back to Christ" is practicable. If His ideals are unattained they are yet the attainable goal of all true endeavor.

> "What I aspired to be
> And was not, comforts me"—Browning.

The primitive church appears, in the first chapter of Acts, in action. It had existed before as an organism and now is seen advancing toward organization. Jesus had instructed His disciples and they naturally follow out now His principles long since presented informally. This democratic fellowship, not yet a church, is working now to complete the group of apostles (Acts 1:15-26). This

---

10. E. F. Scott, *The Nature of the Early Church*, p. 13.
11. E. F. Scott, *The Nature of the Early Church*, p. 13.
12. J. W. Shepard, *Os Actos Dos Apostolos*, (in Portuguese), Comm. in loco.

body of a hundred and twenty members now appears as the core of the larger body of believers in Palestine, *as the outcome of the personal ministry of Jesus.* They were passing from mere discipleship into apostleship. The church was to become the most fundamental of all, the human-divine institution, whose office and work would be to revolutionize and reform continually all other institutions, and also itself, by its divine mission and message. Its democracy must be that of redeemed personality, and its mission the bringing in of a new humanity and a new world, 'in which dwelleth righteousness.'

CHAPTER II

The Founding of the Christian Church in Jerusalem

(Acts 2:1-8:1)

THE WORK of the Kingdom campaign was to begin in Jerusalem. Here the workers received their spiritual equipment for the task in the baptism in the Holy Spirit and initiated the campaign. The story of this work Luke may have received, as it seems, from Aramaic written sources, and orally from eye witnesses.

Section I

The Holy Spirit in Christianity

True Christianity is preeminently a spiritual religion.

I. The coming of the Holy Spirit and inauguration of his work was at Pentecost. Acts 2:1-47.

Jesus was crucified at the time of the feast of the Passover; the Spirit came on the occasion of Pentecost, fifty days later. This was the beginning of the broader evangelization of Jerusalem, covering some three years, from A. D. 29-32. (Acts 2:1-8:1). Jesus came and wrought redemption; the Holy Spirit's mission was to apply it in the conversion of the nations.

1. The outward manifestation of the Spirit's coming, when the disciples were assembled, was first that a sound or echo as a rushing and mighty wind which filled all the house (vv. 1-4). A second thing was the appearance of a fiery sheet which separated into tongues as of fire, one tongue reposing on each of the hundred and twenty disciples present. The sound symbolized power, the fiery tongues the power of purification and the many languages the universality with which the message of the gospel would be proclaimed. The fact recorded by Luke is that the disciples on whose heads these tongues rested "were filled with the Holy Spirit and began to speak in foreign languages, *as the Spirit granted them to utter divine things.*" The Feast of Pentecost was the celebration of the giving of the Law at Sinai. The laws of God were to be put into the minds of the people and written in their hearts, (Jer. 31:31f). This fact of the miraculous manifestation of supernatural power is one which has never been nor could be explained away either by antagonists or critical friends of Christianity, either as ecstatic speech or as *glossalia,* such as Paul later defined and restricted. Luke's "second treatise" is "*an account of the Acts of the Holy Spirit*" (1:2, 5, 8) performed through

some of the apostles,"[1] and here the manner of his advent is narrated. The "unlettered" Galilean fishermen-apostles were speaking in various dialects the wonderful works of God. This was something new in the history of religion, but is linked up, as a continuation, with prophetic inspiration of the Old Testament. It had been foretold by John the Baptist and promised by Jesus. It was a power from the outside which laid hold of these Christians and worked through them (Matt. 3:11; Luke 24:49). The supernatural power gave them utterance to speak the message of God and wonderful results followed. It was, significantly, at the time of Pentecost, *the feast of the harvest,* (Lev. 23:17), symbolic of the releasing of the redemptive power of Christ for the spiritual harvest among men in all future time. Here is the dynamic which makes valid the ethic of Christianity. This extraordinary manifestation was to meet an emergency and special need, in the initiation of the new faith, which was to be not a mere continuation or revival of current Judaism but a distinctive new departure in the economy of God.

2. The sensational impression on the large cosmopolitan group which had rapidly gathered in the locality of the Temple was one of amazement and perplexity, and finally, in some, of scorn and ridicule (vv. 5-13).[2] Among those who witnessed this remarkable demonstration of the humble Galilean fishermen speaking in various foreign tongues, which hitherto these speakers had never known, were Jewish proselytes from various national groups. It was no unintelligible jargon they heard but dialects familiar to these visitors, (a) from Eastern babylonia (Parthians, Medes, Elamites and Mesopotamians), (b) from Syria, Judea, Cappadocia, Pontus, Asia, Phrygia, Pamphylia. (c) from Egypt, Libya and Cyrene, (d) from Rome, (e) from Crete, and (f) from Arabia. They were in a state of perplexity, and wholly at a loss to explain this marvelous thing. Other observers made a joke of it, saying; "They are tanked up to capacity with new wine."[3] This was the "reasonable" but not the true explanation, these superficial onlookers proposed. The stubborn fact remains that those primitive disciples were given audible and visible manifestations as a special dispensation of Providence in the initiation of the new faith, and they had experienced the baptism of the Spirit announced by Jesus. They were possessed or endued with power and used by the Spirit in speaking the great and wonderful things of the Gospel of the risen Christ.

3. The first sermon of the new order by Peter and its result (2:14-47):(1) The explanation of the phenomenon by Peter (vv. 14-21), backed up by the eleven who stood up with him, served as an introduction to Peter's great sermon which followed (vv. 22-36), which had marvelous results in the conversion of three thousand souls, followed by various permanent manifestations of Christian life. Peter explained the phenomenon first by refuting the accusation of drunkenness by superficial critics, who should understand that this early morning hour of prayer (9 a. m.), especially on this feast day of the

---

1. Moffatt, James, *Introduction to Literature of the New Testament,* p. 284.
2. Conner, W. T., *The Faith of the New Testament,* p. 193f.
3. Imperfect middle denoting a continuing status.

Jews, was entirely against such a supposition. His own explanation, over against that of the rationalistic superficial critics, was based on their Old Testament prophecy of Joel (2:28f). According to Joel, in the last days, which would be days of judgment, God would pour forth his Spirit upon all mankind, without distinction as to age, sex, or social standing, resulting in the seeing, preaching and testifying of a new era of prophetic activities.

(2) Peter then enters upon the first sermon (vv. 22-36) of this new era, addressing himself politely to the permanent dwellers and also to the visitors in Jerusalem and adducing the evidence and arguments to the fact that Jesus was the Messiah and fulfillment of all these Messianic prophecies (2:22-36). This was the characteristic line of argument Jesus had suggested in his talk to the two disciples on the way to Emmaus after His resurrection. It was the same general line Paul later followed, as in his discourse in Antioch of Pisidia. (a) The first argument was based on the life works of Jesus, which had been evidently approved among them by God, by miracles, wonder-works, and signs (v. 22). (b) The second argument went to the core of the matter by presenting the resurrection of Jesus (vv. 23-32). This same Jesus who was manifestly divinely approved, in accordance with the pre-determined plan of God, had been betrayed by these very men of Israel and turned over to the wicked Romans to be crucified. But now he, Peter, and the eleven apostles, besides a great crowd of eyewitnesses in all parts of Palestine, were ready to testify that God raised Jesus up, by loosing the pang of physical death, which could not hold Him. David had spoken of this fact (Ps. 16:8ff), referring to Jesus the Messiah and not to himself. *Jesus had been exalted to the right hand of God, the Father*, according to David, and had received authority to send the Holy Spirit, which was the very thing Peter's hearers were witnessing now. He winds up with the conclusion: "*Let all the descendants of Israel understand* (beyond the shadow of a doubt), *that God has made this Jesus whom ye crucified both Lord and Messiah* (Christ)." (c) The third argument, he based on the present manifestation of the Holy Spirit sent by the exalted Christ (vv. 33-36). In proof of this he cites Ps. 110:1, where David again spoke about the Messiah. This Psalm had been cited by Jesus in the Temple on Tuesday of the Passion Week, when He met and confounded His enemies (Matt. 22). He had declared there, by implication, His Messiahship. The Jewish leaders had previously set themselves in opposition against their covenant-God, several times in history, and this crucifixion of Jesus, his anointed one, was the climax of all their opposition. The terrible fact of this antagonism now stared Peter's hearers in the face. What would they do about it?

(3) The results of the sermon (vv. 37-41). (a) In conviction of sin (v. 37). The hearers were pierced to their hearts and cried out to Peter and the other apostles: "Brother-men! What shall we do?" Peter gave them instruction as to how to be saved (vv. 38-40). "*Repent* quickly,"[4] was the first thing they should do. They must be sorry for their sins. The second thing to do was

4. Aorist Imperative of metanoeō, to change one's mind (quickly).

to *be baptized* or immersed, on the ground of their faith in the remission of sin through the redemption in Jesus. Baptism sets forth pictorially the death to sin and resurrection to the new life and points to that change or regeneration which has already taken place in the life of the one being baptized. The third thing to which he directs them is, the *infilling of the Holy Spirit for service in witnessing for Jesus.* While Peter continued testifying and exhorting them with many other words, three thousand presented themselves for baptism, on repentance and confession of their faith in the Lord Jesus. Another result was the general outcome and ordering of the Christian life. They applied their strength to the *teaching* (*didachē*) of the apostles, to the *fellowship* or partnership in salvation in the blood of Christ, to cooperation in the work of the Gospel (Phil. 1:5), in contributing to the *work* of the Gospel (Gal. 6:6) and to the aid of the poor brethren in the church (II Cor. 8:4; 9:13). Their activity probably covered all these phases of the common fellowship, including also that in the *love feasts* (I Cor. 10:16). Another manifestation of their new life was seen in frequent celebration of the *Lord's Supper* to commemorate his death until his eagerly hoped-for return. This ordinance was a symbol of the sustenance for the new life itself. *Prayer* was emphasized both in private life in the homes and in public worship in the temple and religious gatherings such as this in the "upper chamber."

A glimpse of the new order, particularly its impression on the world about it, its care of its poor, and other activities of its service and worship. (vv. 42-47). A reverent fear 'kept on coming' on all when they witnessed the continued *miracles, causing wonder* (*terata*), and the *sign-miracles* (*sēmeia*), testifying to God's manifestation of his power through the apostles. All the Christians united in making a general plan to take care of the abnormal material conditions of *transient* members and those who were poor. This was done by voluntary sales by individuals of their property from time to time, and the dedication of the proceeds to the general welfare in a community of goods. There were various contributing causes for the abnormal economic conditions prevailing in the Christian community in Jerusalem at this time. Besides a large number of visiting brethren, there was a general economic disorder of depression, and some of the disciples looking for an early return of the Lord had come to regard any economic arrangement as relatively unimportant. Paul had to correct this error among some of the early Christians in Thessalonica. There was no rash disposal of all salable property but voluntary donations of available means as the need arose. Common meals were served in various homes and this fraternal generosity impressed the environing community in Jerusalem. The Christians were in the temple worshipping daily. No breach or estrangement had come between Christianity and Judaism as yet. There was spiritual unity in the worship in the temple, and the Christians had special meetings also in their homes, which were used as worship places. All of these religious services and worship hours went on continually, and there was gladness in the common meals, and hearts united in worship-praises to God. All of this blessed fellowship impressed the Jerusalem public well, and the believers found favor with all the people. Many were attracted to the new Christian community, and, as they were saved from day to day, they were added to the assembly of the church.

Section II

The Spirit's Leadership of the Apostles

I. The Spirit's work through Peter and John in Jerusalem arouses opposition. Ch. 3:1-4:31. Christianity performs miracles of grace through its apostles in the name of Jesus the Christ. It is irresistible and invincible before all antagonizing forces of the world, including wrong or error in church or state.

The development of Christianity in Jerusalem following the coming of the Spirit at Pentecost, resulting in a great initial manifestation of His power in the conversion of three thousand souls in one day, naturally would soon meet with opposition from the enemies of Jesus who had brought about His condemnation before the Jewish authorities, through their demand that the Romans approve their sentence in His crucifixion. This kind of opposition the apostles Peter and John encountered, as seen in the narrative of Luke in Acts 3 and 4.

1. The miraculous cure of the lame man at the temple gate (called Beautiful) by Peter and John creates a fresh sensation. Chap. 3:1-11. This is one of the episodes wisely chosen by Luke to show a turning point in the history of primitive Christianity. There was a great increase in the disciple-group at Pentecost and immediately afterwards, and the new departure in religion was taking root rapidly in spite of the latent enmity of the enemies of Jesus, which like a smouldering fire was destined to break out soon. As yet there had been no break with Judaism, and Peter and John went up to the temple, as did all the other Christians, to attend the worship services at the stated hours (3:1). Many wonder-miracles and sign-miracles were taking place currently.[5] Luke chose one of these — the cure of the lame man — as marking the turning point in an outburst of opposition on the part of the *Sadducees*, who bitterly opposed the doctrine of the resurrection. This miracle took place a year, more or less, after Pentecost. The two leading apostles came at three o'clock in the afternoon, and as they were about to pass into the Temple they were addressed by the lame beggar, who was customarily laid at this gate daily. He began to beg[6] and kept on begging them for an alms. Peter and John both having set their eyes on him said, "Look at us!" The man eagerly fixed his eyes on them, gazing intently at them, expecting to receive something. Whereupon Peter said: "Silver and gold I do not possess, but what I do have, this I give to you. In the (authoritative) name of Jesus, the Messiah, a Nazarene, get up

5. Acts 2:43.
6. Inchoative imperfect.

and start walking." But the beggar made no effort to rise. So Peter laying hold of his right hand pulled him up. Immediately, his feet and ankles grew strong, and leaping up[7] he stood, and then, immediately kept on walking, coming into the temple with them, walking around and leaping spontaneously and praising God. All the people in the temple by this time saw him walking and praising God, and as they continued looking, they began to perceive and came to understand fully that he was the very same beggar who was accustomed to sit at the Beautiful Gate of the Temple daily, begging alms. They were now filled with amazement at what had happened to him. The Holy Spirit went before these two apostles, as he goes before every Christian worker now, and opened up the opportunity for them to encounter this lame man, cure him in the name and by the authority of Jesus, and follow this up with the preaching of the message about Jesus Christ as the Messiah. Peter and John knew how to make use of the opportunity. Peter did not "have control"[8] of money but he could draw on the spiritual resources and supernatural power of Jesus, the Messiah. Mark must have had from Peter himself the dramatic description of that apostle's action in "grasping the right hand of the man" to help his faith. The man responded to this act of Peter eagerly at first and cautiously afterwards until he fully realized that he was cured, then burst into almost violent emotional expression of his gratitude until all the people were convinced of the amazing cure, which almost sent them into ecstasies. Many of those who had witnessed the cures by Jesus during the years of His public ministry were surprised to find that His apostles had the same kind of power to work miracles but now they have "accurate knowledge"[9] that the lame beggar, well-known to them, had been completely cured.

2. Peter explained to the people that the miracle was due to the power of Jesus and took advantage of the opportunity to preach Christ to them until he was interrupted (Chap. 3:12-4:4). When the cured man held on to Peter and John begging not to be sent away, the people all ran together to the apostles at Solomon's porch in the temple. The true cause of the miracle, Peter declared, was Jesus who was crucified. The apostles had performed the miracle in the name of Jesus, in whose power the lame man was led to trust. Peter tactfully and politely addressed his Jewish hearers and declared to them that he and John deserved no credit for the cure but that the God of their forefathers had glorified in this miracle His Servant Jesus, whom they had betrayed and disowned before Pilate, after that ruler had decided to release Him. With severity he brings home to them the charge that they had asked, that Barabbas, a murderer and destroyer of life, be given them in liberation, instead of the Holy and Just One. They themselves had killed the Prince of life. Afterwards God had raised Him up from the dead and Peter and his fellow-Christians here declared themselves as witnesses of this fact. The cured man

---

7. Present middle participle, the subject acting for himself now.
8. Greek verb, huparchei.
9. *Epignosis.*

was completely whole through faith in Jesus. This cure of the body resulted in leading him afterwards to spiritual salvation. (3:11-16).

Peter next made a conciliatory explanation saying that 'they,' the Jewish leaders, 'had acted in ignorance.' (3:17-21) Anyway it had been in the plan of God that the Messiah should suffer, as the prophecy of Isaiah revealed. This they had not understood. Peter now calls on them to repent, turning their backs on past offenses, that their sins might be erased or wiped away. *They must change their purpose, but also their conduct, else they could not expect 'restoration for the Jews.'* They had expected a new era of restoration, but their idea had been a mistaken one of materialistic character. Repentance must precede a real spiritual restoration, when the 'Prophet like Moses' should appear. At that time there would be utter extirpation from Israel of any soul disobedient to the real Messiah. (3:22-26). At this juncture the enemies of Jesus interfered, and the chief priests and leaders of the political and rationalistic party of the Sadducees, who did not like the apostles to preach the doctrine of the resurrection, came down upon them and had them arrested and imprisoned until the next day. But many who had heard the word preached by Peter at Pentecost believed, and the number of converts in Jerusalem was increased to five thousand. The purpose of the miracle had been gained, which was, first, to help the man; then to make use of the opportunity, when the people were stirred up, to preach Jesus; and finally to win many, including the man himself, to Christ. The opposition had come but not early enough to defeat the work. (4:1-4).

3. In the trial before the civil authorities on the following day, Peter explains the case, defends the cause, and preaches Jesus the Christ to the court. (Chap. 4:5-12). This miracle, followed by its explanation, had put Christianity in the spot-light in the Temple court. The opposition of the old enemies of Jesus could not be avoided longer now, and the leading apostles were called in before the Sanhedrin. The persecution was doubtless most bitter by the Sadducees, who had hoped perhaps that the "new sect" started by Jesus would wither up and disappear gradually. But it was evident now that such a hope was ill-founded. These apostles were preaching the resurrection of Jesus, and the people were accepting their message. They must be stopped, or else Sadduceeism would suffer a great reverse. A session of the Sanhedrin was called, including the twenty-four Saddusaic rulers, with Annas, the venerable but astute ex-high priest, and John, and Alexander, as their leaders; the twenty-four elders who were of neither sect; and the twenty-two Scribes, usually Pharisees. Before this official court of their people, Peter and John were placed in the center of the semicircle. Caiphas, the official high priest, chosen by the Romans, asked Peter and John "by what power or in what name they did this *cure*." The High Priest did not attempt to deny the miracle but hoped the apostles would confess to some power of exorcism. The prisoners, under fire, must have known that they were in the hands of this court, authorized by the Roman government to deal with all religious matters of their people. (1) Peter took the lead in the explanation and defense of the cause of the young

Christianity before the court. He must have remembered in that hour what Jesus had promised, when his disciples should fall into persecution and be called before the courts. They were "to fix it in their hearts not to be anxious about what they should answer" on such occasions, because "the Holy Spirit would teach them in that hour what they should say" (Matt. 10:20). The Spirit did give Peter words to answer, which would be a defense of the cause and a witness to Jesus. With respectful address to the Rulers of the people and Elders, he defined skilfully the charge as he understood it, and they did not deny his statement of the case. The Apostles were, in fact, being prosecuted because of an act of benevolence done to a poor, helpless, infirm beggar and with regard to the means by which this man had been entirely cured in body and saved in spirit permanently in a complete transformation of his heart. Peter's answer to the charge was direct and courageous. "It was in the name and by the power (*dunamis*) of Jesus," the Nazarene Messiah, "that this man had been made permanently whole."[10] (2) Peter then proceeds to assume the role of *prosecutor* and lays out the charge against these men who were guilty of the blood of Jesus. They had crucified Jesus, but God had raised him from the dead. In accord with Messianic prophecy, "the stone which they, the builders of the national religion, had rejected, had become the head of the corner" in God's new building, Christianity (Psalms 118:22). (3) In him and no other there was salvation, "for there is no name under heaven which has been given by God among men whereby we must be saved." Peter included his hearers, who were antagonizing God, among those who could now find salvation in Jesus by repenting and turning to Him. His statement is absolute for then and now. There is no name in the world, no saving power for men anywhere, save in Jesus. This message was given. There was no answer possible from his enemies. His hearers were convicted. They interrupted the speaker and would not allow Peter and John to speak further.

4. The decision of the Sanhedrin was reached after a brief secret session of consultation, and Peter's answer was then heard. (4:13-22). In the secret session they thought to dismiss this difficult case on the ground of the ignorance[11] of these men. They were amazed at the courage and readiness of speech of the apostles. They found and recognized[12] in them some of the unaccountable things they had encountered in Jesus. After all, it might be better to let this "new sect" simply die down. The miracle could not be denied, and that was the difficulty. There was no answer to that. The best thing they could do was to threaten these men and if possible stop their mouths. So they called the prisoners back before them and charged them *"not to speak at all, nor teach in the name of Jesus any more." This was their decision and it must be obeyed.*

Peter and John joined in their reply, which Peter expressed for both: "If it is right that we hear and obey you rather than God, judge ye, for we cannot

10. Acts 4:9, Perfect tense *sesōstai.*
11. *Idiōtai.*
12. Took accurate knowledge of them that they had been with Jesus.

fail to speak the things we have seen and heard." The Sanhedrin could do nothing more about this matter on account of the people, so they threatened the apostles further and turned them loose. To retain them in prison would be dangerous because the people were glorifying God for the marvelous cure of the lame beggar, who was of mature age and had long suffered with this infirmity.

For primitive Christians, the Kingdom was mostly opposed in its principles to the secular state, as that has always been organized and conducted in the existing world-order. Christianity must stand for true liberty of conscience in carrying out the kingdom program. This is what Peter and John did when they refused to keep silent in the matter of testifying for Christ. "We must obey God rather than men," they said, "for we cannot fail to speak the things we have both seen and heard." This is what they understood by "*liberty in religion.*" The highest interest of the Kingdom is liberty and such should be the greatest end of the state, but the secular state almost universally corrupts this standard and transgresses this ideal. This is true also of every institution of man. Christ had to redeem institutions and regenerate society by redeeming and regenerating individuals. In the secular state there should be a spiritual purpose but this ideal is corrupted and violated almost always.[13]

5. How the apostles and disciples turned the persecution to account (Chapter 4:23-31). These Christian leaders gave a good example of how to deal with opposition and persecution by civil authorities. They came to their brethren and fellow-workers and after full explanation of all that the high priests and elders had said, they resorted to united and earnest prayer to God, *appealing through prayer to his sovereign power and care.* The records of this prayer and of the speeches Peter made were doubtless preserved by John, who was an eyewitness, and later transmitted them to Luke. It is nothing short of pagan to think that Luke would put a prayer into the mouth of the Christian leaders as some *pagan writers* were accustomed to put speeches into the mouths of their *dramatis personae.*[14] The prayer they offered was an appeal to a Sovereignty above that of all earthly rulers. "O Despot [Absolute Ruler], Thou who madest the heaven, the earth and the sea and all that in them is, Thou who didst speak by the mouth of our father David, Thy servant: 'To what purpose did the nations stamp around in rage and the peoples conspire vain things; The Kings of the earth set themselves in array and the rulers came together united against the Lord God and against His Messiah.' For in this city, of a truth they met against Thy Holy Child, Jesus, whom Thou didst anoint, Herod and Pontius Pilate, with the heathen and the peoples of Israel, to do all the things that Thy hand and Thy plan had predetermined should take place. As to the present situation, Lord, give attention to their threats and help Thy bond-servants, with perfect courage to continue to speak Thy message, and by stretching out Thy hand to cure people and to perform signs and wonders by the authority of Thy Holy Servant Jesus."

---

13. Scott, E. F., *The Nature of the Early Church.* pp. 220ff.
14. Scott, E. F., *The Literature of the New Testament,* p. 100f.

When they thus had prayed the place where they were assembled was shaken as by an earthquake and they were all filled with the Holy Spirit and went on speaking the Word with boldness. So the Saddusaic attempt to suppress the Christian movement was a failure and Peter and John declared their purpose to continue their work in the Temple area as true Jews, but Christians. They were dismissed from the court with boastful threats but the Sanhedrin stood condemned and intimidated, fearing the people, who praised God for the great miracle and honored those who had performed it. Later the Sadducees came back with a determined effort to exterminate Christianity, and of that we have a record in Acts 5:17-42, where the wise counsel of Gamaliel turned the scales in favor of the Christians. *But persecution would not cease until the consummation of the ages. Of this Christians should always be sure.*

Section III

An Internal Problem in this Primitive Church

The problem cited from the experience of this primitive church illustrates church problems of all times and sets forth many principles and methods universally applicable in the resolution of such problems.

I. The internal condition of the primitive Christian community is portrayed and illustrated in its dealing with the problem of Poverty in the new order. (Chapters 4:32-5:10). Luke showed, in the section preceding this, how the primitive Christian community dealt with persecution by the civic and religious authorities and made clear their understanding of their relations to the secular state. He shows in this section (4:32-5:10) the method of resolving the problem of poverty among the poorer brethren of their group in Jerusalem. The example of Barnabas was cited in illustration of individual Christian benevolence and liberality in contrast with that of the perfidy of Ananias and Sapphira and the peril of judgment to be expected upon such abuse and deception. 1. The Christian spirit portrayed in its dealing with the problem of poverty in the Christian church community. Illustration of Christian liberality and benevolence in the example of Barnabas (Ch. 4:32-37).

There existed among the Christians a spirit of complete harmony and unity of "heart and soul," based on a common faith in Jesus and evidenced in a fraternity and fellowship that was real in its expressions. In this example of Christian fellowship we find eternal basic principles of Christian fraternity and stewardship. *Man's ownership of material properties and goods is against the eternal principle of God's ownership of everything. Along with this is coupled mans temporary possession and administration of material possessions for God's glory.* The duty of stewardship and responsibility of administration under God cannot be disregarded. The local need of the poorer brethren of the church community was an occasion for putting to the test the spirit of Christian liberality and fraternity. The wealthier brethren did not allow any member to be in want, but different individuals voluntarily sold their property and pooled the results to be used in meeting the needs of the poorer brethren. The apostles went on giving, with great energy of the Spirit, their testimony to the resurrection of Jesus, the very doctrinal teaching which had caused their first arrest by the Sadducees. Their testimony met with great popular favor.

This was not the form of communism found in many parts of the world today, but among Christians there should always exist such a spirit of fraternity that no poverty-stricken brother would be allowed to suffer. *But to place all property in the hands of the state, negating, for the most part, individual stewardship, would be wholly different from the principle here exemplified in primitive Christianity.*

The example of Joseph, nick-named Barnabas (Son of encouragement), is cited, who sold his estate in Cyrus and brought the proceeds to be used by the Christian church community under the leadership and administration of the apostles. This Barnabas was the "helpful" friend who later on introduced Paul, after his conversion, to the Christian church in Jerusalem, and later worked with Paul in the evangelization of Antioch of Syria and also accompanied him on the first missionary journey. He was a Hellenistic Jew. His fine example of benevolence was held in high esteem by the brethren in Jerusalem. He was a "brother who could be called on in need and who visited others in order to find out and help meet their needs."

2. A deceptive double role in the pooling of properties was illustrated in the example of Ananias and Sapphira (5:1-10). They deliberately planned to gain the distinction of being large contributors without paying the price, by selling a property and hypocritically keeping back part of the money. When Ananias professed to bring his contribution, having kept back part of what he had professed to give, Peter tore off the mask of his hypocrisy and revealed his Satan-inspired deception, practiced against the divine Holy Spirit, third person in the Trinity, who had suggested these sales and gifts. Ananias did not have to sell his property. Even after he sold it he was not obliged to give the whole price to the church. The deception was in trying to get credit for whole-hearted liberality which in reality he had not practiced. When the mask of his hypocrisy was torn off, the consciousness of the terrible act against God was so acute that Ananias, shocked, fell down in a swoon and expired, and was, according to custom of early burying in Jerusalem due to ceremonial defilements, immediately borne out by the younger men, whose office it was to care for such situations in the temple.

Sapphira, who had conspired in the deception, as *particeps criminis,* came in, three hours later, ignoring the fact of the death of her husband, and met the same fatal and tragic end. In the case of Ananias, Peter had pronounced no judgment; but in the case of the wife, he did speak for God the sentence of judgment. The effect of these tragic deaths was that a reverent and wholesome fear fell on the whole church and on all who heard about it.

To summarize the causes of the extreme poverty of the Jerusalem saints as a group we note (1) general economic destitution in Palestine due to excessive population, famines, and sometimes to the operation of religious prejudices in dealing with Gentiles, (2) difficult relations with and the attitudes of revolt toward the Roman government, (3) persecution and boycott by anti-Christian Jews, (4) mistaken expectation of an early return of the Messiah, leading to under-estimation of economic obligations. These conditions prevailed increasingly until the revolt of A. D. 66-70, making necessary that the Christian leaders should resort to charitable support of the poorer brethren.

To clarify the method and motive in meeting this abnormal condition of poverty we summarize: (1) the community of goods through voluntary occasional sales of property by devoted individual Christians, as pressing necessity recurred,[15] (2) the outpouring of the Spirit which brought about a spiritual unity and fraternal fellowship which could not permit a brother to suffer want. Religious revival brought a recognition of spiritual stewardship and a fraternal community of material interests. Barnabas was an outstanding example of this spirit of helpfulness and won the merited esteem of his brethren by his liberality. Ananias and Sapphira practiced diabolical dishonesty, deception and hypocrisy in a fraudulent effort to win the same kind of honor and popularity under false pretense, and both became tragic examples of the fatality of tampering with divine things. This was a necessary and sobering lesson, indispensable to correct such misuse and abuse of the Spirit-inspired principle of Christian stewardship, which even until now is so woefully disregarded.

Section IV

The Christian Community Becomes the Church

Rapid progress followed the purification of the Christian community, and it came to be called for the first time the called-out-assembly (*ekklēsia*) or *church.* Christ spoke but once of building His church.[16] The central theme of His preaching was the kingdom. He defined the attributes[16] of the kingdom subjects and their privileges and responsibilities.[17] The messianic kingdom ideal is perfection.[18] The kingdom is the rule of Christ in the hearts of men. Christ said it was within the disciples and therefore was of the present. But He taught the disciples to pray for its coming, and its consummation is therefore in the future. The church arose out of the fellowship[19] of the Christian community and had its origin with Jesus. He was the cause. It was a new creation and did not partake of the character of the congregation of Israel.

15. Iterative imperfect tenses denoting repeated recurrence.
16. Matt. 5:1-13.
17. Ibid. 5:13-16.
18. Ibid. 5:48.
19. Koinōnia — sharing, fellowship.

It did not copy the Jewish institutions but was a result of the mission of Jesus, a new creation of His. Jesus made a new man, a new society, a new humanity, a new order. The church was not an evolution. It was better in its initial stage than ever after.

I. Rapid progress and development in evangelistic activities was attended by divine approval, as a consequence of the spirit of reverence due to the miracle of judgment. (Ch. 5:11-42). 1. In increased evangelistic activities. (Ch. 5:11-16). This purge of the miracle of judgment, operated through the convicting power of the Holy Spirit, working through Peter and the other apostles and the guilty persons, brought about such a spirit of reverent fear upon the disciples themselves and upon outsiders, both rulers and others, that the latter were now afraid to press into the fraternal community to get material help or honor through false profession. The assembly of the Christian community by this drastic judgment was set apart and defined as something divine *and for the first time the word church*[20] *appears in the narrative of Acts.*

Christ spoke of the church (Matt. 16:18) as the whole body of believers and later (Matt. 18:17) as the local body. We find in Acts 7:38 the word used of the whole congregation of Israel, while in 19:32 of the public assembly in Ephesus. In Acts 8:3 it is used of the church in general which Paul was persecuting in their homes when not in assembly. Already the fear of persecution was becoming a distinct and, may we say, a beneficial factor in the formation of the church.

A great burst of miraculous power by the hands of the apostles now began and went on continually, showing God's approval on the apostles through *signs* (*sēmeia*) and many miracles, producing *wonder* (*terata*) in the people. The approval of the Lord upon Peter in miraculous demonstration shows that there was nothing in the conduct of Peter, in his role of apostle, in the whole experience with Ananias and Sapphira, out of accord with the conduct of a true disciple of Jesus. The purpose and conduct of Peter were in accord with the Holy Spirit who was making use of this primitive miracle in the death of the irreverent and hypocritical couple, guilty of a daring dishonesty. It saved the cause of the primitive church-community from a corruption which would have defeated its mission.

Until now all Christians continued to worship in the temple, holding their meetings for preaching in Solomon's porch.[21] There had been as yet no sharp separation between Judaism and Christianity. The Christians were also united in mind and purpose as they had been just after the advent of the Spirit at Pentecost (2:46) and later. (4:24; 7:57; 8:6; 12:20; 15:25; 18:21; 19:29). The people, but not the rulers, magnified the apostles, and a great multitude of both men and women kept on being added to them. The apostles were not set apart in a separate class of those 'whom the people feared.'

---

20. Chapter 5:11. Cf. also Matt. 16:18; 18:17; Acts 7:38; 8:3; 19:32.
21. Cf. Acts 3:11.

The result[22] of the manifestation of great supernatural power in many signs and wonders was, that many brought their infirm out into the broad streets and placed them on little beds (diminutive) and pallets (Mark 2:4, 9, 11) in order that, when Peter should come by, his shadow might fall upon some of them. That was a faith bordering on superstition, like that which we find in a number of instances, where the Lord honored, in His ministry, a weak and imperfect faith. (Matt. 9:20; Mark 6:56; John 9:5; also Acts 19:12). The faith of many Christians is mixed with superstition more or less. A multitude of those from towns around Jerusalem kept on coming in to bring their sick and those troubled by foul spirits and all of them were healed one by one.[23] When the purity of the church is secured, there is progress and supernatural power, and great numbers are added.

2. Progress and development brought on fresh opposition from the political and religious authorities (5:17-42). (1) The Sadducees now extend their determined persecution by having all the apostles arrested. (vv. 17, 18). This shows that Christianity was now making rapid gains. The Sadducees were filled with a boiling-over spirit of jealousy and envy and laid their hands on all the apostles, placing them in the public prison until they could call together the Sanhedrin. (2) The apostles freed by the angel of the Lord were told to take their stand in the temple and go on preaching the full message of this resurrection and eternal life which the Sadducees deny (5:19-25). A little before dawn they were there, ready to enter when the temple doors opened, and they immediately began their teaching. When the high priest and those with him arrived later, they called the Sanhedrin and the Senate, composed of the elders of the people of Israel, and sent to the guard house where the prisoners had been left bound for safe-keeping. The head temple officer did not go in person, but sent the temple police, who were his subordinates, to conduct the culprits before the court. These leaders were greatly perplexed when the temple police returned and informed them that they found the prison doors shut tightly and securely.[24] The sentinels also were standing at the doors and when they opened the doors they found no one. It is no wonder the chief officer of the temple and the high priests were in a state of perplexity as to what would come out of these things if the apostles were allowed to go on.[25] This seed of Christianity was growing with amazing rapidity! (3) At this very instant, a person came reporting that the apostles were there near them in the Temple, and had stationed themselves boldly, and had been seen already teaching the people without fear. They were immediately sent for and brought solemnly before the court (5:26-28), led by the chief officer, without any use of violence, because the Temple police and rulers feared lest they themselves should be stoned by the people. Leading them in, he placed them in the midst

---

22. *Hoste*, with present infinitive to express result.
23. Imperfect, of repetition.
24. Perfect participle.
25. Conditional sentence of fourth class with condition unexpressed, undetermined with less likelihood of determination.

of the Sanhedrin. Then the high priest asked them with a contemptuous gesture: "In charging, did we not charge you[26] *not to teach in this name*: and behold you have filled Jerusalem with your teaching and wish to bring down the blood of this man upon us." These rulers had agreed to that responsibility, of His blood, in the trial of Jesus before Pilate (Matt. 27:25). (4) Peter's defense of the cause and his effective Spirit-indicted testimony to the resurrection, with its result. (vv. 29-33) In this defense Peter was speaking for all the apostles and what they all said was what he and John had said before, in effect: "It is necessary to obey God [as ruler] rather than men." Then he added their testimony about the resurrection and charge against the rulers:

"The God of our Israelitish fathers raised up Jesus to life [who was the fulfillment of Israel's historical mission], when you rulers laid your hands upon Him and slew Him on a wooden cross."

'This very man,' to whom the high priest referred contemptuously, even now God had exalted by his right hand (instrumental) to the place of power on high, (locative) for the purpose of giving the privilege of repentance to Israel and the remission of sins. His testimony, and that of the apostles to these things of the resurrection, is backed up by the manifest approval or testimony of the Holy Spirit. God raised this Jesus up to be the Leader and Savior, and, *the Holy Spirit*, God also since had granted to those who obeyed Jesus as ruler. The members of the Sanhedrin who heard these things were being literally cut, by their rage, to their very hearts, and were plotting and planning to kill right there and then these apostles. Peter and John had disobeyed the Sanhedrin, but that was not a capital offense for which they might be stoned. What were they to do with them? They were on the point of committing a grave judicial blunder.[27] Gamaliel intervened with his counsel.

(5) The wise counsel of Gamaliel cited the historical example of rash revolt (vv. 34-39). This outstanding teacher, the grandson of Hillel, later to be the president of the Sanhedrin, was a Pharisee and an honored and popular doctor of the law. He was a man of judicial temper and, though he spoke as a Pharisaic opportunist, this teacher of Saul of Tarsus did counsel in favor of a temporizing policy. He first ordered that the apostles be taken out of the court for a little while and then he made a speech. It is probable that Saul of Tarsus was present when this speech was delivered, and years later, after his conversion, gave Luke the report. Standing up in the Sanhedrin to speak, Gamaliel said: "Gentlemen Israelites![28] Give careful attention to your own interests in what you are about to do to these men." Then, to reenforce this counsel, he cited the example of Theudas, who had risen up in revolt, making profession to be somebody, to whom about three thousand men gave a willing ear. Josephus later cited three men of the name of Theudas who were "instigators of rebellion." It is possible that this man referred to by Gamaliel was one of

26. Hebraism.
27. Quoted in Robertson's *Word Pictures* on Acts, p. 67.
28. Hackett: *Commentary on Acts*, in loco.

those and not the Theudas of A. D. 44, in the reign of Claudius. To accuse Luke of inaccuracy or compare his accuracy, as a historian, with that of Josephus, would be out of the question. The Judas, founder of the party of Zealots, cited by Gamaliel, led a revolt against the Roman government in A. D. 6. The party of some four hundred men led by Theudas was dispersed and their leader slain. The revolt of Judas suffered a like fate. Finally, on the basis of these recognized examples, the orator made his appeal (v. 38b) that they follow the safe policy of "hands off" and leave these men (apostles) alone. He cites his twofold reason: first, if this plan or this work had its origin merely with men, it would be overthrown.[29] He does not say whether it was or was not from men. On the other hand, "if it is from God you will not be able to destroy it,"[30] because then you might even be found to be "God-fighters." In this argument he *assumes* that the Christian movement is from God, though he does not affirm it. This was a very favorable argument to the apostles and would show an apparent inclination of Gamaliel to favor Christianity. (6) The flogged and threatened apostles, rejoicing to be honored in suffering for Jesus, return to their work in the temple-square and homes of the city. The name of Jesus was already reverenced as that of God. The apostles were willing to suffer shame for Him. They did not heed the threats of their accusers, but continued to preach Jesus as the Christ.

To summarize the second effort of the Sadducees, to suppress the apostolic message and the Christian movement, which continued to grow in influence in Jerusalem and the surrounding regions, we note:

(a) The growth of the opposition in the number of those who opposed, and their increased hatred and determination to exterminate the Christian heresy by arresting all the apostles.

(b) The frustration of the effort through providential means, as for example, the advocacy of a very powerful Pharisee, Doctor of the Law, who was a real, historical person and the famous head of the school where Saul studied. He must have had a wise insight into the character of Christianity, and he got in some good work for the Pharisees in their longtime antagonism against the Sadducees, by advocating a very cautious handling of the case of the apostles with special regard to the interests of the Sanhedrin itself. Luke did not have to "put this speech into the mouth of Gamaliel," since Gamaliel's favorite student of recent classes must have been present when the speech was delivered and could report it very well to Luke after his conversion to Christianity. Such a procedure as this was practiced by pagan writers but would not consciously be adopted by a Christian writer at all and surely not when the Spirit was "bringing to his mind the things relating to Jesus."

(c) The abortion of this effort through the division within the Sanhedrin itself, also along the line of the cleavage of sectarian antagonism between the Pharisaic and Saddusaic sects.

---

29. Third class general condition.
30. First class condition according to fact.

(d) The supernatural power manifested increasingly in the protection of those who gave themselves expressly to the leadership of the Spirit.

(e) The rapid growth of the cause of the persecuted faith and increased popular favor and respect through the miracle of judgment on Ananias and Sapphira.

To conclude our brief treatment of the first five chapters of Luke's second treatise, we note that the writer had a practical end in view: to inform Theophilus and any "friend of God" more completely concerning the things he had been informed about in part — "the things Jesus began to do and teach." These first five chapters were based probably in part on an Aramaic document or documents of the Jerusalem tradition and in part on the testimony of eyewitnesses. Having the practical end of furthering Christianity, Luke chose wisely certain episodes which would portray the origins and early development of primitive Christianity. The two opening chapters set forth the glorification of the risen Lord, the advent of the Holy Spirit with the beginning of his permanent work, and the universality of the message and character of the new faith. Following this, chapters III-V present a series of episodes of the work in Jerusalem, illustrating the rising antagonism and persecution from the secular environment under the political patronage and leadership of the enemies of Jesus, particularly of the Sadducaic sect. The character of Christianity is demonstrated in the handling of these problems arising from contact with the outside world but also of the standing problem of poverty among the "saints" or members of the new Christian community. The pooling of financial resources on a voluntary basis, the cultivation and use of Christian liberality illustrated in Barnabas, the drastic discipline of abuses of this method illustrated in the case of Ananias and Sapphira, in an artistic and skillful portrayal by the historian, *give the reader a clear-cut though diminutive picture of infant Christianity.* This picture is invaluable because it is the only one we have of the primitive form of Christianity and it presents a Christianity with all the innate character of a universal religion, motivated by a force and power which would conquer the entire world and leaven the whole of humanity in the end.

CHAPTER III

Expanding Christianity Finds Saul

SECTION I

Institution of the Diaconate

THE RAPID progress in the growth of the cause in Jerusalem made necessary the broadening of the program of the church by increased organization. The work of local beneficence, in taking care of the poor in the Christian community, overburdened the apostles, who must meet the growing demands in the wider activities of the ministry of the Word in evangelization. Spirit-led apostles foresaw that the nature of the program of Christianity would call for a permanent role of ministry supplementary to that of the ministry of preaching and teaching the Word and prayer in its various pastoral and ministerial uses. The Spirit-led Church in Jerusalem led the way in the election of seven specially endowed men for this service (*diaconia*), and they were called deacons. These men were elected and ordained to meet a permanent need.

A problem of Internal dissension was thus resolved by better organization, *effected through the leadership of the Holy Spirit* (Ch. 6:1-7:60).

I. The choice of deacons (6:1-6) was followed by greater progress, extending even to the winning of some of the priests. It is always necessary in studying the history of the church to remember that the secular influence on the human side of the church makes its history a resultant between the two forces; the spiritual on the one hand and the secular influence on the other. Even in the primitive church there were abuses, as in the case of Ananias and Sapphira. But *in primitive Christianity, which we see pictured in the first chapters of Acts, we find the nearest approach to the purity of the Christ, in conduct and doctrine, because of the novelty of the faith, the ardor of its Spirit-led representatives, and the nearer view of its Founder.*

The community of properties as an economic method[1] of meeting the problem of poverty in the primitive church did not break down in its fundamental principles of stewardship, in which God is the sole owner and Christians are merely stewards. *It did break down on the human side of ambition, selfishness, greed, and racial prejudice.*

In the section to be treated now, (Acts 6:1-8:1), we have the further permanent development of the organization of the church under the leadership of Spirit-led Apostles. *The permanent needs of a larger, more elaborate organiza-*

1. Cf. Lake, Kirsopp, *An Introduction to the New Testament*, p. 72.

tion for a growing church community called for additional roles of service and their proper definition. On the human side, the occasion, for this elaboration was the complaint[2] that the widows of the Hellenists or "Grecian Jews" from outside Palestine were being neglected[3] or overlooked in the daily ministration of the common fund (Acts 4:32-37). A line of cleavage existed between the Hebrew or Aramean Jews and the Hellenists. This was the first serious disturbance in the life of the primitive church. The leadership in this ministration or "deaconing" had been in the hands of the divinely constituted apostolate until this time. This leadership, which had become burdensome from the material side due to the growing number of Christians in Jerusalem, called for more men, who would share this work with the Twelve. We notice here that the general membership of the church was consulted and the voice of the people was heard. The apostles called the multitude of the disciples and said: "It is not pleasing to the Lord or fitting for the people that we should leave the teaching of the Word of God to minister in the growing service of the common meals in the homes and in that of the periodic and frequent celebration of the Lord's Supper" (Acts 2:43-47). The word ministration (*diakonia*) is used of the service of the apostles, and no discrimination is made in the kind of work these new "ministers" were to perform. But it was the predominantly material nature of the service that gave rise to the character of the new role and led to the peculiarly different and definite role of "deacons" in the church at that time. Their role was to take care of the "tables" or distribution of food and of the ministration of material help to the poverty-stricken saints in the church. This need was of course abnormal in the Jerusalem church community, but the work of benevolence in the local churches was to be a permanent one and so the peculiar character of the role of deacon was the occasion of the creation, by popular vote of this Spirit-led group, of this new role of deacon. This was done under the leadership of the divinely constituted apostolate. The necessity for additional "servants" or deacons was the normal growth of the work of the ministry of benevolences. The apostles, like Moses of old who was counseled by Hobab, must "look out some men" to take special responsibility in this function. It was necessary that there should be men specially fitted for this responsible service in a growing church community and this for the reason that a large local church has need for a larger number of deacons than a small one does. The church must take care to look out these men and choose only those who are properly qualified.

The qualifications of deacons were: first, a good reputation; then they must also be good "witnesses" by past experience and go on giving the right testimony in their daily conduct while they continue in this role. There is nothing said as to the permanency of the role. The choice of the church by popular vote would govern[4] the formal appointment of these seven men needed for this service in the large Jerusalem church. These men were also to be spiritual or

---

2. Murmuring, *goggusmos*.
3. Impefect passive of *paratheōreo*.
4. Future indicative, *katastēsomen*.

full of the Holy Spirit and they must be wise or full of wisdom, for the administration of the practical affairs of the church. Under the Spirit-led suggestion and indication of the apostles, these seven men were chosen by the church, and ever since then the Spirit-led churches and pastors have gone on choosing specially qualified men to take care of the practical side of the work of the ministering. There is nothing indicated as to a special divine call for this service as in the case of the apostles, who took care of another role in the "ministering." Nor is there any discrimination made in the qualification necessary for both the roles of the general service of ministering. The special role of the apostles calling for a "steadfast continuation" was in the sphere of prayer and the ministry of the teaching and preaching of the Word.

This word of leadership of the apostles was "pleasing" and it seemed fitting to the multitude as a whole. They chose the seven Grecian Jews or Hellenists: Stephen, a Greek proselyte to Judaism, who was mentioned especially for his being full of faith and the Holy Spirit; and Nicholas, a Gentile proselyte from Antioch, being among the number. The church picked out for itself[5] these seven men, all of whom bore Greek names and were doubtless Hellenists. This was evidently to show no disposition toward partiality on the part of the church in the distribution of help from the common fund. The Hellenists had been the ones to complain, and not their widows. They were appointed formally by the apostles with the symbolic laying on of hands with prayer. This was a ratification of the choice of the apostles and a symbol of the impartation of the gifts and graces, for which the prayer was offered. This prayer did not guarantee such an impartation, but, on the contrary, the qualifications they had demonstrated in their daily living would indicate that God had already imparted to them special gifts for this practical service. This symbolic act would impress the men chosen with the responsibility of the service.

The role for which these men were chosen did not look to higher orders, nor did it militate against their ministry in other roles to which the Lord might call them. Two of these "deacons," Philip and Stephen, became notable preachers. Philip later became outstanding as an evangelist (Acts 21:8) and Stephen became the first preacher-martyr of the cause (Acts 7:1-53). The role became a permanent one in primitive Christianity, being mentioned in the writings of Paul about churches in various places (Phil. 1:1; I Timothy 3:8ff). Seven deacons seem to have been able to care for a membership of more than ten thousand in the Jerusalem church, though they may have had many helpers in the work of serving.

In this incident we find (1) the leadership of the apostles in suggestion of what was to be done, (2) a popular voice and vote of the church in the choice (for themselves)[6] of these men, (3) special qualifications in the men which were evident to the church as a whole by their daily witness in character, conduct and service. (4) Hellenistic names did not indicate that all were neces-

5. Middle voice.
6. Middle voice in Greek.

sarily Hellenists, as many Jews in Palestine might give their children Greek names. It would indicate Hellenistic sympathy.[7]

Divine approval was evidently upon this development in the organization of the church. The Spirit's administration was manifesting itself in palpable form, with apostolic leadership serving as the point of human initiative and the popular democratic vote of the church as one of its principal vehicles. The number of disciples greatly increased, and inroads were made into the exclusive and hitherto hostile group of the priests. "A great company of priests," some of whom must have been from the persecuting Sadducees, obediently heard the gospel and accepted its Savior. But the apostles did not yet go outside the city of Jerusalem to evangelize.

Some of these deacons, notably Stephen and Philip, became leaders in new missionary and evangelistic enterprises. Philip, who initiated the work in Cesarea, had four daughters who were prophetesses. He came, as did James the Lord's brother, to be called an apostle. Prochorus is the name attached to an apocryphal *History of the Apostle John*, a late work. Both he and Philip were said to have been among the seventy sent out by Jesus. There was no fasting but only prayer and the laying on of hands in the ordination of the seven, three of whose names (Nicanor, Timon and Pomenas) never appear again in history.

Christianity which began so humbly in Galilee was plainly destined, because of its universalism and missionary character, to spread rapidly and conquer the world in the end. Luke wrote his second treatise to set forth the work of the Gospel Christianity proclaimed by Jesus and the apostles. It was not, as Gibbon and others would have it, the product of a 'natural fortuitous conjunction of elements and circumstances,' such as the Greek philosophy and Oriental mysticism. From the beginning, Christianity had to wage a mortal combat for its very existence against the hostile secular environment. "It was originated among the later Jews, and its founder was executed by the Roman government as a criminal." But it had within it a new and strange power which was irresistible in its working.

The picture that Luke gives us of the primitive Christian community, in which "no one accounted anything to be his own," where there was an ardent spirit of brotherhood, and all were filled with the Spirit and with faith, is one which strikes conviction to all hearts, of the verity of its supernatural character. This manifestation was not the result of a naturalistic evolution but of a supernatural intervention.[8] Proof of this is that in subsequent generations a decline came in the spirit of enthusiasm, in the purity of Christian life in the historic church, and in the contagious growth and rapid extension which characterized its development in its apostolic period.

We agree with those who find in Jesus the true founder and builder of the church (Matt. 16:18). According to the clearest and soundest exegesis the Kingdom of heaven was right at hand when both John the Baptist and Jesus

7. Dana, H. E., *Jewish Christianity*, p. 46.
8. Cf. E. F. Scott, *The Nature of the Early Church*, in loco.

proclaimed it. By many expressions in the teachings of Jesus, His Kingdom was a rule within the heart of his disciples and all believers of all times. It was present in this world in the hearts of his servants then, while He was in His active ministry; and is in the midst of the world of unbelievers, now *though not in them anywhere,* if we are to take numerous phrases in the Gospels and entire New Testament introduced by the preposition *en,* used with the locative case, to mean what such phrases have been found to mean in the Koinē-papyri. According to the teaching of Jesus one must be a citizen of the invisible Kingdom before he becomes a member of a visible local church of the Kingdom; but he might, on the other hand, even be admitted to the membership of a local church without being a member of the Kingdom at all. Jesus created and goes on building His church on the basis of a vital faith in Him and the regeneration of heart which follows. He never intended that his church should conform to the secular environment, losing its pristine purity, its primitive devotion, and its spiritual enthusiasm. He did not desire or contemplate accommodation to the world in the compromise of its ideals or its standards of purity and excellence. The primitive believers acknowledged no other control than that of the Spirit. The church was different in character from secular societies. (Luke 22:25, 26). It was composed of men who by a new-birth regeneration had come into the Kingdom and pertained to a new humanity. Such a church could not desire or seek to integrate itself with the secular order. It could properly have laws or principles governing its activities, but its members enjoyed perfect liberty. All must be subject to the "perfect law of liberty," but love was the fulfillment of the Christian principles of law and order. The will of the Master and of His only true vicegerent on earth, the Holy Spirit, was supreme.

In the beginning the leadership of the church was in the hands of the Twelve who were chosen and ordained by the Master in person; but as time passed these apostles must of necessity disappear and the Spirit indicated others to take the place of leadership, such as James, the half-brother of the Lord Jesus, and Paul the apostle to the Gentiles (Acts 13). James became the president of the meeting of the Conference in Jerusalem which debated and decided the question of Gentile liberty. He had a gift for organization and did much toward organizing the Jewish Christian Community in Jerusalem.

The increase and growth of the church made necessary a more elaborate organization. Paul was a great organizer of Christian congregations in various strategic centers of Asia and Europe, but, while he "became all things to all men," *he never compromised a single principle of Christianity in doing so.* He had discipline and order of the right kind but never at the expense of the free motion and spontaneity of the Spirit. The church never gave up its claim to its supernatural origin, character, and mission. Its members belonged to a higher brotherhood and possessed mysterious privileges, having part in the heavenly order. A true church is not just an earthly organization with a divine sanction. It does not have to submit to the world's conditions, nor does it confess the demands of Jesus to be impracticable. It must take its stand on ideal principles and not be willing to compromise, and it must stand for the kingdom and not keep step with the world. (Matt. 5:48)

Organization was necessary to the permanence of the church and to its efficiency in the execution of its program. As an organized institution, it was able to maintain itself against persecution and other opposing forces, as in the times of its hiding in the catacombs of Rome. But when the church attempted to integrate itself with the world, as in the time of Constantine, it lost most of its spiritual character and supernatural power. The church is the divine organization of the Body of Christ and not a mere human organization. It must hold always before it a guiding ideal which is beyond its power to fully attain.

Its reach must always exceed its grasp. A more complete and elaborate organization was necessary for the growing work of an expanding Christianity and a permanent addition was made to this phase of its equipment by the Holy Spirit before the new faith entered on its wider mission in the regions round about. This came about in the divinely guided church, in the institution of the diaconate.

SECTION II

Stephen, the First Christian Martyr

It took the martyrdom of the great evangelist-deacon Stephen to pierce through the heart of the fiery zealot of Judaism, the brilliant Saul of Tarsus, leader of the persecution, and convict him of the sin and folly of his madness against Christianity. When dragged before the Sanhedrin, Stephen bravely stood his ground, and in one of the most brilliant missionary sermons of all sacred history made his apologetic defense, while his whole personality was radiant with the light of heaven. The keen intellect of Saul could not but be convinced of the truth of that deliverance. Its missionary vision, later, worked in the conscience of Saul and finally became the light that illuminated his darkened and confused mind and prepared him through the troubled hours of his meditations to face the risen Christ, on the road of reckless persecution in the way to Damascus. There he would surrender to his future Master and Lord. As he stood outside the gate, later called Stephen's Gate, and directed the maddened fury of the blood-thirsty mob, as they hurled themselves upon the helpless missionary, precipitating upon him a shower of cruel stones; he saw clearly the light of heaven in Stephen's face and heard his last words of witness uttered distinctly above the melee of fury. He was made cognizant of the presence of Jesus, whom Stephen saw at the right hand of God, and Saul would never more have peace in his soul until he should surrender to that same Jesus.

I. The work and witness of Stephen, first mentioned of the seven deacons. Ch. 6:8-8:1. The expanding work in Jerusalem was already reaching out in its influence in the towns round about Jerusalem and people were bringing in their sick to Peter and the other apostles to be cured (6:7). But the

Twelve had given their strength mainly thus far to the solidification of the work in the great center, Jerusalem. It was natural for some of the newly appointed deacons, who were Hellenists and had wider connections with and perhaps a broader sympathy for the work among alien peoples, to begin the work in Samaria and press out later to other countries beyond Palestine. Stephen was a Gentile proselyte and would find it easier to interpret the universalism of the Old Testament prophets than would the apostles of Jewish Christianity. It is not strange therefore that we find one possessed of these advantages and withal full of the Spirit and faith, early demonstrating great activity and leadership in the missionary enterprise of the church. The more complete organization now, with the election of the seven deacons to take over the duties and responsibility of the administration of the practical material affairs of the church, as well as to help in the work of evangelization, had ironed out the difficulties of the community benevolences and brought back peace, harmony, and an abounding evangelistic activity, resulting in the addition of many new converts to the church, including even "not a few of the priests."

The zeal of Stephen aroused the learned Scribes. At first the Christians had carried on their preaching services in Solomon's porch in the Temple and naturally had to meet the opposition of the Sadducees who dominated the Temple. This opposition was weak, but the Pharisees were less tolerant once they had been stirred up. Their intolerance manifested itself when Stephen and other Hellenistic workers began to preach in the synagogues. Pharisaic persecution began now. (6:8-15).

The newly appointed Gentile-proselyte deacon, Stephen, was full of *grace*,[9] not only being favored in his rich God-given natural endowments but being so gracious in his words and ways that he greatly attracted the people. He was also full of supernatural power[10] to perform miracles and his ministry in miracles produced wonder in the people, and also his sign-miracles brought a conviction of the approval of God upon his work. He was a veritable whirlwind of power in the midst of the people.[11] He went on with[12] this ministry of great and notable miracles and signs day after day. But such activity could not fail to bring antagonism. Certain ones of the learned Scribes from the synagogue of the so-called Libertines or Jewish freedmen[13] probably from Rome, and the Cyrenians and Alexandrians, and some others who had come from the provinces of Cilicia and Asia, stood up against[14] him. These were Jews of the Diospora, from Rome, Cyrene and Alexandria in Egypt, and from Cilicia, including Saul of Tarsus, and from Asia Minor. The official worship

9. *Charitōs* (not pisteōs)
10. *Kai dunameōs.*
11. Locative case.
12. Imperfect tense, continued action.
13. There were possibly five of these synagogues for Hellenistic Jews, though some think one, two or three.
14. Constative aorist, during a period of time.

of the Jews in Jerusalem was conducted in the Temple but the synagogues were used for prayer, preaching, and the discussion of the law.

Certain of the learned Hellenistic students of the law, among whom Saul was probably outstanding, rose up against Stephen and in the synagogue meetings continued disputing with him. But they did not have the strength[15] to withstand his practical and experiential understanding and wisdom in the debates, and, especially could they not stand against the Holy Spirit with the help of whom[16] he kept on speaking from day to day. So these ambitious young theologue-lawyers, being defeated in debate, had recourse to a plan to silence this powerful young deacon-speaker, who was introducing a dangerous and seductive heresy[17] into their Hellenistic synagogues. They found and suborned some men who would serve as false witnesses against him, just as the Jewish leaders had done in the trial of Jesus before Caiaphas. The charge of these false witnesses was, that "They had heard Stephen speaking blasphemous words against Moses[18] and (what was less important by their statement) against God." They went further and "shook the people up,"[19] stirring their emotional prejudices. These were Pharisaic leaders, the Scribes, who were stirring up the mob spirit, and Stephen did not have a Gamaliel to step in and counsel moderation to help in his critical situation, because the Pharisees were the attacking party now. Scribes and Elders joined with the excited mob, rushing upon Stephen in fury and seizing him, as he would have attempted peaceably to withdraw from the synagogue. Leading him forth to the meeting of the Sanhedrin which had doubtless been convened in the temple quietly for this very purpose, they put the false witnesses forward, who gave their testimony saying: "This man does not cease speaking words against this holy place and the law," for we heard him saying that Jesus, 'that contemptible Nazarene,' will destroy this holy place and change the customs which Moses delivered to us." Stephen had doubtless referred to the universal Christ of Christianity in his speeches in the synagogues. He had rehearsed probably some things Jesus had said about the changes which must come in the Temple worship and about His interpretation of the law. The circumstances of the trial of Stephen were similar to those of Jesus' trial but Jesus did not speak, while Stephen did in his trial. When Stephen stood before the Sanhedrin and heard the false charges, tying him up with Jesus in the suffering of injustice his face was lighted with a supernatural effulgence which impressed all the members of the council, "as it had been the face of an angel." This was a part of the report Paul must have narrated to Luke, of the experience he had

15. Imperfect *ischuon*, did not have the strength in these debates which continued possibly in various synagogues.

16. Instrumental case of relative pronoun, *hēi*.

17. The 'foreign-mission' heresy!

18. Josephus said that the Essenes whom he greatly admired would endure any torture rather than blaspheme their lawgiver (Moses). For this same reason Christians, according to Pliny, were called on to "curse Christ".

19. *SuneKinasan*, stirred them up by appeal to their emotions of fear using the false witnesses to do so.

that memorable day, as a member of the Sanhedrin. Saul would never be able to forget that look, try as he might!

II. Stephen's speech in apologetic reply to the high priest's demand of a confession of guilty or not guilty (Ch. 7:1-53). In his speech Stephen replied to the charges made against him, but rather by implication. He pressed to the main point along positive arguments based on the history of Israel: that God's purpose in the redemption for Israel and through them for the whole world had *usually* been missed by the Jews through their rejection of God's true representatives sent to them from time to time. The two-fold charge brought against Stephen (answered by implication), was (1) that he claimed that his Master, Jesus of Nazareth, would destroy the temple and (2) that Stephen repudiated the Mosaic code.

The general context of this speech is to be found in the deacon's foreign mission ministry in and around Jerusalem. Hitherto the Christian propaganda by the apostles had been confined to Jerusalem. They had not gone out to Judea, Samaria and beyond, and now that expansion had begun through Stephen and Philip rather than through the Twelve. The appointment of the Seven deacons brought in Hellenistic contacts and sympathy, and with it, leadership for the evangelistic expansion. Stephen became the first martyr for the cause through his vigorous attacks upon the historically founded Jewish unbelief (6:8-7:60), and, due to the persecution which followed the outburst of Pharisaic opposition under the leadership of Saul of Tarsus, the new missionary enterprise in Samaria was begun by Philip (8:1-40). The conversion of Saul was linked up also with the martyrdom of Stephen (7:58; 8:1-3; 9:1b). He was confronted by the resurrected Jesus, while on his way to Damascus to stop this new enterprise of missions to the Jews of the dispersion which had been greatly accelerated on account of the persecution in Jerusalem. Paul himself was converted and became a missionary to the Gentiles, whose evangelization was included in the program of Stephen in this first missionary speech delivered before the Sanhedrin. Peter was also led later by the Spirit to the work outside of Jerusalem, and though he was the apostle to the Circumcision, became, under the leadership of the Spirit, the first to open the door officially for the Gentiles to enter the Christian fold. The first place was in the home of the Roman Centurion Cornelius in Cesarea. (9:32-11:18). In the light of this general context we can better interpret the speech of Stephen as he must stand before the Sanhedrin to give account of his recent ministry in the synagogue of the Jewish Dispersion in Jerusalem.[20] In view of this general background, the character of Stephen's address, showing the progressive dealing of God in his revelation to the Jews through history and their backwardness in accepting his unfolding revelation of his universal salvation destined for the whole human race, is seen. The apparent escape from persecution at this time of the apostles who were more exclusively Jewish is to be explained in the light of subsequent history, also. We have to look forward

20. Cf. Moffatt, James, *Introduction to the Literature of the New Testament*, pp. 291, 292.

only a little to find the ultra-conservative elements of the Jerusalem Christian church in open antagonism toward the work of Paul in the synagogues and among the Gentile proselytes of the Dispersion (Diaspora).

The election of the seven deacons brought the Hellenistic Jews to the front and at least two of these seven, Stephen and Philip, were of liberal mind and missionary passion. Stephen turned from the use of the Temple as an exclusive place to preach and entered into the synagogues of the Hellenistic Jews, in his work of carrying the alms to the Hellenistic widows but also in his presentation of the message of the gospel. It was in this ministry in the synagogues where he found not only some Jews of more liberal mind, but some ultra-conservative elements also of those who had come back to Jerusalem to escape the life of isolation among the Gentiles.

Stephen introduced his history-making speech based on Israelitish history, in a most polite and dignified manner, bespeaking a man of culture (7:1). He laid the foundation of his address in a general view of the history of Israel, in which God's dealing with his people was of the type of a progressive revelation. The great epochs of Jewish history compose the main divisions of his discourse. The first division extends from Abraham to Moses (7:2-16). This was the period of the patriarchs, before the nation existed. Abraham did not enter into Canaan in a short time but after many tests. The covenant of the circumcision was not given him until almost at the end of his life (v. 8). His posterity received the promise only after approximately four hundred years, during which these Hebrews suffered the horrible bondage of Egypt, learning by experience the evil of the dealing of the patriarchs with Joseph their brother. All that the immediate offspring of Abraham received of Canaan was a grave which Abraham himself purchased with money (v. 16).

The point implied all along in Stephen's address is the comparison of the way the people of Israel blindly destroyed God's representatives with the way the Jewish leaders had recently rejected and crucified Jesus. Some of the critics seem greatly disturbed over minor inaccuracies they think they see in Stephen's historical narration. These foibles loom up so great before their eyes that they fail to see the main issues involved in this most remarkable and epoch-making speech. The purpose of the speech was inclusive of a number of important points of emphasis. Stephen was making a fearless apologetic address for Christianity before its enemies, and some of his main issues were impressed by implication, until the closing words when he arraigned the Sanhedrin in no uncertain terms.

The temple, as the exclusive center and place of God's revelation of Himself, was not final and must be superseded. It was a holy place but not the only holy place. God had appeared to Abraham in Mesapotamia with his call and Abraham's seed sojourned in a strange land. Joseph had his whole God-blessed career in a strange land and Moses was born and reared in a foreign land. In another heathen land Moses found God at the burning bush; in Egypt he wrought his signs and wonders; and at the Red Sea and in the wilderness God blessed him along with Israel. Even the Ten Words were received in foreign territory. The conclusion was obvious: God could be served elsewhere than in the Temple of Jerusalem.

The second main division of the speech presented an analysis of the history of the deliverance of Israel from the bondage of Egypt (7:17-43). In this analysis there is couched an implied comparison between Moses and Jesus. The speaker did not use the name of Jesus at all, nor make any reference to Him until the end of his speech, and then by title. The Jewish council would sharply perceive the comparison and drift of the argument. Young Moses, who was instructed in all the wisdom of the Egyptians, could not succeed at first as a messenger of peace to his people. His violent intervention in their fratricidal quarrels led to crime and his flight for refuge to Midian, a foreign land. There he was a refugee for forty years and it was in that foreign land that he found God (vv. 30-34). Stephen made clear the fact that by the rejection of the intervention of Moses, the Israelites delayed their deliverance forty years. But God later made this same Moses the redeemer of Israel (vv. 35, 36), and it was he who told Israel that God would raise up later a "prophet like Moses." The Jewish leaders had heard Peter at Pentecost identify this promised "prophet like unto Moses" with Jesus (Acts 3:22). *The fact that remained more and more potent at every turn of the argument in Stephen's speech was that Israel had been a consistent loser in all her history by the rejection of God's representatives.* They had rejected Moses' leadership in the wilderness and "made a calf," for which idolatry God punished them (v. 42, 43). Their repeated murmuring against Moses and faithlessness toward God left the bones of that generation to bleach in the desert.

In a third point in his speech Stephen made an interpretation of the Israelitish history of the period of the prophets (7:44-50). The temple was not the exclusive place for the approved worship of God. His people had worshipped in the wilderness before the temple was built and until the days of David. Even he was not allowed to build a temple but that work was left to Solomon. The speaker cited Isaiah in the thought that the "Most High dwelleth not in structures made by hands." He is independent of temples, and his worship would have to be mainly apart from the temple. True worship is invisible and spiritual and was not to be limited to the temple in Jerusalem. Stephen evidently knew the teaching of Jesus about the universality of worship (John 4:24).

Chrysostom thought that the purpose of Stephen in his speech was to show that the promises of God were more important and before the law and the law before the temple. Long before the temple existed God manifested himself in the tabernacle and had given his people his revelation in strange countries. To be sure Stephen meant to establish the fact that God's gracious purpose in salvation was never limited just to Israel, in spite of the fact that they were the chosen people. The obstinate opposition of the Israelites to revelation through Moses, God's leader, was repeated now again in the rejection by them of Jesus. But Moses brought the greater revelation of "living oracles" even if Israel did rebel and go into idol worship (vv. 35-43). Again, those who came after Moses were not content with the tabernacle which was God's pattern, but must have a temple, which called down the cutting words of Isaiah's prophecy[21] (vv. 47-50). It was Moses himself who predicted the coming of a "prophet like unto Moses." These Jews addressed by Stephen were now much concerned about "Stephen's repudiation of Moses", the same Moses whose leadership was rejected by their fathers.[22]

In his conclusion Stephen made a direct and vehement application of the arguments of his discourse to Jewish leaders and their adepts (7:51-53). By their appearance these members of the Sanhedrin were furious and did not intend to allow him to go much further with his invective against the disobedient Jews. So he knew he must conclude quickly, and he seized the final moments to bring a severe arraignment of these leaders of Israel. He accused them of being stiff-necked, stubborn unbelievers and of resisting the Holy Spirit. "Which of your prophets did your fathers fail to persecute?" he asked. "They slew the ones who announced beforehand the coming of the Righteous One," he added, and "because you have done worse than they, the betrayers and murderers of God's Just One!" They knew that he meant Jesus. He did not need to call His name! "And you," he concluded with cutting words of irony, "are those who profess to have received the law by the hand of angels, are the very ones who have not obeyed it!"

III. The testimony and martyrdom of Stephen, stoned by his enemies. (7:54-8:1). When Stephen neared the end of his discourse, he thus responded to the accusation by a counter thrust. He knew his adversaries well. He had no hope of softening or convincing them. He followed the example of Jesus, in His last encounter with the Scribes and Pharisees in the temple on the last day of His public ministry, in fierce denunciation of their hypocrisy and obstinacy. This precipitated the fury of the Sanhedrin and their adepts. They were literally sawed through their hearts by the rasping words of judgment pronounced upon them by Stephen, of being "betrayers and murderers of the Just One" as their fathers had been of the ancient prophets. But they were not repentant in their hearts as were the auditors of Peter at Pentecost, when he preached against their sin and revealed their guilt in crucifying Jesus. Stephen's enemies, boiling with a mounting rage, began to gnash their teeth and went on madly in this audible token of their hot anger against him.

Stephen, on the contrary, being full of the Holy Spirit, looking steadfastly into the heavens, saw as Moses had, the glory of the Lord, the same God of Glory about whom he had spoken in the first words of his discourse. He also saw Jesus, standing as if to witness all and receive His servant. The Lord Jesus was standing at the right hand of God the Father in the place of honor and power. In his rapture, Stephen spontaneously burst forth in words of testimony: "Look!" he said, "I see the heavens opened and the Son of Man standing at the right hand of God."[23] These very members of the Sanhedrin were

---

21. Isaiah 56:1, 2.
22. Cf. *Exp. Greek N. T.* (Knowling) p. 204b.
23. Perfect tense denoting permanent status for him.

doubtless reminded by these words of what Jesus had spoken on the cross, and were stricken in their conscience. (Luke 22:39).

But they cried out with an uproarious shout in order to drown out Stephen's words, while at the same time stopping their ears so as not to hear "his blasphemy." With a common impulse they now suddenly flung themselves upon him, not waiting to pass a formal vote of condemnation by their Jewish law nor to seek any approval from the now intimidated Pilate or of the Roman government for the act of violence they intended to perpetrate. That the blood of this blasphemer might not contaminate their sacred temple or their city, they hurled him forth[24] from the city gate, and there outside began to rain upon him a shower of stones, the suborned witnesses being the first to take part in this dastardly cruel crime. (Deut. 13:10; 17:7). Thus the first criminal witnesses (martyres) who had falsely testified against the first Christian witness (martyr) for Jesus, had met victorious argument with brute strength, the way of reason with the way of violence. Luke must have been requested by Paul (from whom he probably received this vivid report) to note the fact (for him very important) that those men (witnesses) were directed by himself to lay their capes at his feet, while carrying out the bloody scene, (for Saul most probably was in charge of the stoning).

These members of the Sanhedrin and their adepts kept on throwing stones while Stephen was calling on the Lord Jesus. He was heard saying: "Lord Jesus, receive my spirit!" Then falling on his knees in the attitude of prayer he cried out with a loud voice, audible to all above the melee and fury of the mob and almost in the exact words of Jesus while on the cross, "Lord, do not lay this sin to their charge!" "And when he had said this he fell back in the sleep of death." Under the hail of murderous stones he went to sleep in the arms of Jesus!

Saul's part in this criminal act is significantly mentioned by the historian, his friend. "And Saul was consenting[25] unto his murder." That brilliant "young man" had been outmatched in argument and had chosen to meet it with stones. But he could never get away from the things he saw that day, and years afterward the Christian apostle Paul would pronounce himself the "chief of sinners, less than the least of all the saints" and "not worthy to be called an apostle because he had persecuted the Christian church." The picture of the martyrdom of Stephen would be "a goad, pricking in his conscience" from this time on until he should meet the risen Lord in the road to Damascus! Some of the words of Stephen's defense of Jesus that day before the Sanhedrin would find echo in Paul's first recorded Christian sermon at Antioch of Pisidia, years later, while on his first missionary journey.

---

24 *Ekballein,* to cast forth.

25. Periphrastic imperfect, giving his approval with pleasure, cf. Acts 22:20.

CHAPTER IV

The Conversion of Saul of Tarsus

(Acts 9:1-31)

IT WAS SAUL'S plan to exterminate Christianity. But the Christians suffered to the death without recanting. Both men and women were bound and committed to prison by the persecutor, who was commissioned by the Sanhedrin to stamp out the heresy. As the persecution continued, many were put to death and others fled to various parts of Judea, to Samaria, and others to more distant places. Saul had done his cruel work thoroughly in Jerusalem. The Lord did not intervene then in that center, but when Saul started out to check the work in outside regions to which His disciples had been scattered, divine interference by none other than Jesus was quick and effective. The Christians had borne their message to various countries from Jerusalem after Pentecost, and planted the Word in the islands and in such centers as Antioch in Syria, in Rome, and probably in Damascus, in Phoenicia and in other countries, and the light of the Gospel, like tiny beacons, began to illuminate the darkness in many a place. The persecution begun some time before had intensified and the Christian flock was scattered abroad. Many found refuge in places where small groups had already been formed and others became pioneers in new places.

I. The Risen Lord meets the zealous persecutor on his way to Damascus. (9:1-9). Saul had taken a superintending part in the martyrdom of Stephen and recorded himself as in favor of the murderous execution by casting his vote against the hated heretic (Acts 26:10). The apostles were left unmolested in Jerusalem for reasons consistent with the leadership of Providence but Saul had gotten his first taste of blood and his zeal led him on to make a thorough job of the purge of the heresy from the city and elsewhere (I Cor. 15:9). This he did in his blind zeal for Pharisaism, forcing himself to think that it was a real service to God, a thing which he deplored in subsequent years (Gal. 1:13; I Tim. 1:13). The death of Stephen had been illegal and so was that of many a Christian in Jerusalem in the period following, until almost the whole membership of the church in that city had been exterminated or driven out. *Still* the persecutor was not satisfied and even while *yet breathing in*, as his natural breath, threats and murderous slaughter toward the disciples of the *Lord* Jesus, he had received information that some Christian fugitives had found refuge in the ancient Syrian city of Damascus. "Exceedingly mad against them" he resolved to pursue them thither. So, making use of the Sanhedrin's religious jurisdiction over Jews in the synagogues in most cities of the Roman Empire,[1] he asked from the high priest for himself[2] letters unto the synagogue authorities in Damascus, that if he might find there certain persons pertaining to this Christian 'Way'[3] of life, men and even women, that he might lead them away helplessly bound[4] to Jerusalem (v. 2). Damascus probably ruled over by Aretas of Iradis at this time, was about a hundred and forty miles to the Northeast of Jerusalem, and Saul set out with his letters and an attending group of Sanhedrin officers of the temple police, probably on foot, by the nearest route through Perea and Batanea — a journey of about seven days.

In Luke's characteristic phrase, "in his journeying" through a desert way, Saul had much leisure to think. He had been in a disturbed state of mind, though he thought "he was doing God service in extinguishing this conflagration of heresy in Jerusalem and the regions round about." Seven days of reflection upon the bloody scene of Stephen's martyrdom, followed by a succession of other similar scenes, brought no rest to his soul. The warning by Gamaliel, his beloved teacher, to the Saddusaic leaders, to wisely leave the Apostles alone "lest they be found fighting against God" also had sunk into his zealous but now reflecting soul. And he could find no explanation for the angelic light on the face of Stephen, when that witness spoke to the Sanhedrin, nor for the prayer he uttered for his enemies while they were stoning him. Many other Christians had followed in the same kind of example with inexplicable serenity, courage, and utter fearless devotion to their Nazarene leader. The arguments of Stephen in proof of the Messiahship of Jesus yet rang in the ears of the persecutor. As he went further in the journey, his thoughts were ever more gloomy and his heart more deeply disturbed.

Finally the journeying group came in the way, to the traditional place of the murder of Abel by Cain, and the old city of Damascus loomed up in the distance, some ten miles ahead. Soon they would enter the city and the persecutor could begin the work of his mission there and find relief from his gloomy thoughts. But it was not to be so. The little band of Christians in Damascus had doubtless heard about the coming of the "Wolf" who had ravaged the flock in Jerusalem. They had prayed that his course might be arrested by the great Shepherd of the sheep, and their cry for protection was not unheeded. Suddenly at midday, "a light from heaven flashed around Saul and his companions like a streak of lightning."[5] In his speech in the Tower of Antonia before the murderous mob years later, Paul called it a "great light, about noon" (Acts 22:6), and in his speech before Festus and Agrippa (Acts 26:13) he said it was "above the brightness of the sun" and that of a Syrian sun at midday[6]. He and all his companions fell to the ground (Cf Acts 22:7; 26:14).

1. Robertson, *Word Pictures*, Vol. III, Acts p. 113.
2. For middle voice, *Eitēsato*, force of middle voice, 'for himself'.
3. The Way of the Lord, of the Gospel: (Cf. Acts 19:9, 23; 22:4).
4. Perfect passive participle, in a state of imprisonment.
5. *Periastroptō* — ingressive aorist.
6. There are three accounts of the conversion of Saul in Acts 9:3-18; 22:6-16; and 26:12-20. Luke attaches great importance to Saul's conversion. It was epoch-making in the man and in the history of Christianity. Robertson, A. T., "The three accounts are supplementary and in agreement, some critics to the contrary."

Dazed with the shock, Saul heard the words in Hebrew (Aramaic): "Saul, Saul why persecutest thou me? it is hard for thee to kick against the goads" (Acts 26:14). Jesus had now identified himself visibly with the "little flock" in Damascus in this persecution. Saul had been kicking against the sharp-pointed goads of his conscience in all this horrible work of persecution of the Christians, and was confused and frustrated. "Who art thou, Sir?" he asked as he looked up and saw for the first time the glorious figure of the Risen Christ whom Stephen had said he saw in his dying hour, standing at the right hand of God. "I am Jesus of Nazareth whom thou art persecuting," was the instant reply. The attendants of Saul had fallen to the ground under the shock when Saul did, and they saw the light, but did not catch the articulated words or see the vision of the Lord as did Saul. The horrible fact of his persecuting the Risen Lord burst instantly upon his soul. "What wouldst Thou have me to do, Lord?"[7] was the quick and repentant question of the now surrendered but erstwhile bold leader of the persecution. He saw the real Person of the Risen Christ and immediately capitulated to Him.[8] "Arise and stand upon thy feet and go into Damascus, and there it shall be told thee of all the things appointed for thee to do," the Lord firmly commanded. (Acts 22:10; 26:16) "For to this end I have appeared unto thee, to appoint thee a minister and a witness both of the things wherein thou hast seen me and of the things wherein I will appear unto thee; delivering thee from the peoples and from the Gentiles, unto whom I send thee, to open their eyes, that they may turn from darkness to light, and from the power of Satan unto God, that they may receive remission of sins and an inheritance among them that are sanctified by faith in me." The repentant persecutor got forgiveness and a commission in the same *word*.

Then Saul arose from the ground and when his eyes were now opened,[9] he could see[10] nothing. His attendants taking him by the hand led him and brought him into Damascus. There he rested in the house of Judas of the Synagogue of the Jews for three days without sight, and neither ate nor drank. But from there, after three days of meditation and prayer, he came forth a "new man in Christ."[11]

This was not a mere subjective phantasm, but an actual vision.[12] Years later Paul the Apostle said to the Corinthian Christians, "Am not I an apostle? Have not I seen Jesus our Lord?" (I Cor. 9:1). It was the same sort of manifestation of His glorified Person as that which had been vouchsafed to His disciples during the period of forty days between his resurrection and

7. Acts 22:10 is genuine text not in Acts 9:6 where it was interpolated by Textus Receptus.

8. Robertson, *New Testament Word Pictures*, p. 117.

9. Perfect passive participle of *anoigō* indicating blindness, at least temporary. The result may have had to do with a permanent malady from which he seems to have suffered later (Gal. 4:15).

10. Imperfect tense, continued status of his vision or blindness.

11. *A Man in Christ*, title of a valuable work by James Stewart.

12. Cf. David Smith, *Life and Letters of St. Paul.* p. 51.

ascension. (I Cor. 15:5-8).[13] Jesus here wore the same glorified spiritual body, in which He was seen of the disciples then *and like that which Christians shall wear in the life beyond the grave.* (I Cor. 15:40-44) This body was, under normal conditions, invisible and impalpable to the natural physical senses of touch. But the physical sight and hearing attended by acute spiritual insight and perception soon approach the indistinct border-line between the natural and supernatural.[14] To say this implies no effort to eliminate the reality of Saul's miraculous experience, in the realization of the visible presence of the Person of Christ. Paul claimed to see Jesus and he was later accounted even the chiefest of the apostles. It is not to be wondered at if Paul's attendants neither saw the form of the Risen Lord Jesus[15] nor detected the articulate words which He spoke to Saul, the erstwhile fierce persecutor of His people. Paul did have a personal interview with Jesus after His death, by his own statement, which in the face of much critical antagonism remains unimpeachable. In the interview Jesus had pressed the question of relationship and Saul had surrendered. The light of the knowledge of the glory of God in the face of Jesus Christ had shone into his heart (II Cor. 4:6). Saul in his speech before King Agrippa had claimed to have been "obedient to the heavenly vision" (Acts 26:19). The fact is that a struggle had been going on in his soul for weeks as he "haled men, and even women, dragging them from their house and committing them to prison." He had felt that Stephen was somehow on the right side of the argument. In the vision the powerful but loving look of Jesus melted the soul of the persecutor, already sadly shaken. That vision changed the whole world for Saul. When he had yielded and asked the Lord what he should do, a deep peace came into his heart and a new joy flooded his soul. He could never be the same again. His old burden was gone. A new world opened up before him. He needed the three days of darkness, meditation, prayer to the intensity of fasting, for adjustment in his thinking, ere he ventured to speak forth his confession of the change that had taken place within him.

II. The Lord sends a devout but timid disciple of Damascus, Ananias, to minister to Saul (9:10-19a). Ananias was a devout, reverent man who was very correct in his daily life, judged by the standard of the Mosaic code, remaining faithful to the ancient ordinances. Moreover, he had a good reputation among all the Jews of the colony in Damascus, in spite of the fact that he was a disciple of the Nazarene (Acts 22:12).

Jesus chose to send this humble disciple to minister in the restoration of Saul's vision, to reenforce and further explain to him the fact and character of the special mission entrusted to him by Jesus, to lead him to the experience of the special enduement of the Holy Spirit for service, and to baptize him when he should have confessed his experience of salvation from the Lord to the disciples in Damascus. The purpose of Jesus in sending him instead of

---

13. The same word *ōphthē* is used in I Cor. 15:8 and in the narrative of His appearance to the disciples.

14. Cf. *The Natural and the Supernatural* by J. Oman.

15. Cf. James Orr, *The Resurrection of Jesus* (1908).

one of the apostles ought to be interpreted in the light of the subsequent history of Christianity. Saul did not receive his apostleship through any kind of apostolic succession.

When Jesus appeared in supernatural dealing with Ananias in a dream, the conversation was none the less real and the appeal and order to the timid Ananias none the less positive. Saul was being entertained in the house of Judas and not that of Ananias, as Kirsopp Lake and Silva Lake would have us think. Ananias was to seek Saul, the well-known persecutor of the Christians, in a street called Straight, known even today, though in modified conditions, in Ancient Damascus. He was informed of the reassuring fact that Saul was praying and had seen in a vision a man called Ananias coming and placing his hands upon him that he might have his sight restored.

Timid Ananias answered Jesus: "Lord, I have heard from many (different people) about this man, how many evil things he has done to your disciple-saints in Jerusalem. And even here now, he has in his possession authority[16] from the empowered high priests, to bind all those who are identified with the band of Christian disciples here in Damascus."

The Lord responded to these objections simply by a silencing command: "But" (in spite of these objections) "go, because this man is my chosen vessel to bear my name before the nations[17] and even kings, and indeed before the sons of Israel." Furthermore, "I will go on showing him the many things which it will be necessary for him to suffer on behalf of my name, throughout his life."[18] (Phil. 1:39).

The mission of Saul was made plain to him. Jesus had informed him that he would be told in Damascus "what he should do." Ananias knew from Jesus that Saul was a "chosen vessel." In a fuller sense than any other man, Saul was to know the will of God; and above all he was privileged to see the righteous one, the Risen Lord, and hear His voice. He was to be a witness of the things he had seen and heard, and bear the name of Jesus before the Gentiles and Kings, also before the Jews, to open the eyes of the Gentiles and turn them from darkness to light, as well as the Jews, that they might receive remission of sins. (Acts 25:16). He would go on having other experiences of suffering and of revelation, which would constitute also the ground of his knowledge and teaching of God (Acts 9:16). He was to preach the unsearchable riches of Christ, and understand and reveal the plan of the ages in Christ for universal salvation (Eph. Chs. 2, 3). Paul understood and accepted the challenge of his call. Of this his great activities and marvelous epistles give evidence. All the way through this conversation in Ananias' miraculous dream runs the thread of revelation and of the supernatural, Zeller and other critics to the contrary. These things were realities and not mere illusory beliefs or hallucinations. The report of Luke is a simple historic narrative of what

---

16. *Exousian,* rich word meaning authority, power, prerogative, etc.

17. The chief mission of Paul was to bear the name and message of Jesus to the Gentiles.

18. Constative aorist infinitive covering the whole life-career of Paul.

actually transpired in the supernatural ministry of the Holy Spirit in preparation of the man who is the most astounding, simply human fact in all history. This manifestation of the supernatural was necessary to prepare the group of disciples in Damascus to receive Saul. It was also designed to prepare Saul immediately for entrance on his incomparable apostolic mission, which shines out as the most brilliant testimonial of the truth of Christianity, which is and has been consistently a religion of a supernatural revelation.

That Ananias and others of the disciple-group were prepared by this miraculous dream is evidenced by the manner of his address when he came to Saul in the house of Judas. "Brother Saul," said he, "the Lord has sent me: Jesus, He who appeared to you in the way when you were coming, that you may receive your sight and be full of the Holy Ghost." Saul never knew of the reluctance of Ananias when Jesus assigned him the task of coming. That timid, fearful disciple placed his hands on Saul's head when he entered the room where Saul had been sitting in darkness for three days. Immediately, when he had finished speaking these words, there fell from Saul's eyes as it were skins or scales and he "looked up"[19] and saw this stranger who had spoken. Said Ananias further: "The God of our fathers appointed thee to know his will, and to see the Righteous One and hear a voice from his mouth. For thou shalt be a witness for him unto all men of what thou hast seen and heard. And now why tarriest thou? Arise and be baptized and wash away thy sins, calling on His name." (Acts 22:13-16) The baptism of Saul was a part of the ministration of Ananias under orders from Jesus alone, as far as the record shows, as no local church appears in the picture. There would be no difficulty in the matter of water for immersion, since the (Oriental) Jews had bathing facilities in the court of the home. Saul had made his decision when he surrendered to Jesus and he made no protest when baptism was suggested. Oriental symbolism would sufficiently explain the inversion of the order of regeneration (conversion) and baptism, since the Orientals put the symbols first. But Paul had received the baptism of the Holy Spirit already anyway. (Acts 9:7b)

The narrative of Luke (9:18, 19a) thus completes briefly the scene: "He rose up and was *baptized*[20] and taking food he was strengthened."

III. Responding at once to the heavenly call, Saul initiates his career as a witness to Jesus the Son of God, and follows that up with work about his own development into the apostle to the Gentiles and subsequently the greatest interpreter of Christ (Ch. 9:19b-30). Convinced of the divinely authorized mission entrusted to him, Saul put his hand to the plow at once and never did look back. But he was aware of the tremendous difference this experience of the vision of the Lord was going to make in his understanding of all the Old Testament Scriptures. *He would need some time to make a new and complete examination of those writings and others of the Jewish literature, which he had studied in the years of his course under the greatest teacher of rabbinical lore of his times, the famous Gamaliel.* This was a natural conclusion of the

19. *Aneblepsen*, literally to look up or to see again, Aorist Active Indicative.
20. *Ebaptisen.*

brilliant young student, as he thought now of his new career, marked out for him by his glorious new Lord and Master. He would find time to gather up later the traditions of the new gospel of Jesus from the many eyewitnesses yet living, among whom the apostles were the chief ones; but the most natural course for him to pursue before beginning the work of his public ministry was to make a new examination of the inspired writings of the Jews in Hebrew and in the Septuagint translation, which we know he did use later in his ministry. This would take some time. On reflection, and that he might not precipitate his ministry into hopeless conflict with antagonists before he should be thoroughly equipped for the fray, his best course of action was to make his testimony an independent one from that of the apostles and of the current traditions both oral and written, by making a new study of the Old Testament literature in the light of the Jewish Talmud too, but especially from the standpoint and in the light of the vision of the Risen Lord Jesus, the Son of God. To do this, it would be best to retire, after giving ample evidence of his great change of life, to some place, where, without outside distractions, he might have opportunity to make this new study.

A. The initiation of his work as a witness of Jesus, the Son of God, was in Damascus. For "certain days," an indefinite period, Saul remained in Damascus with and began his first Christian activities in the fellowship of the disciples there. He had been prepared in the school of Gamaliel for public speaking and trained in argument. He began preaching at once in the synagogue and so effectively as to attract much attention. Peter preached much on Jesus as the Messiah of prophecy; Saul proclaimed Him as the Son of God. Jesus had claimed to be the Son of Man (Messiah) and the Son of God. Saul, from his vision of Jesus in his conversion, declared the deity of Jesus from his very first release of the message. The more he preached, the more filled and empowered of the Holy Spirit he became. All those who were attending his experiential testimonies and expositions of the Scripture were beside themselves with amazement and kept on saying over and over again: "Is not this the very same man who played havoc with the disciples in Jerusalem, and all bearing the name of Jesus the Nazarene; and did he not come here for the purpose of leading the disciples in this city away, bound as prisoners, to the high priests in Jerusalem?" But Saul went on with his preaching and testifying, being endued more and more with the power of the Holy Spirit, confusing the orthodox Jews living in Damascus by putting together the Scriptural expositions with experiences of the life of Jesus, proving that this same Jesus was the real expected Messiah, whose coming was foretold in the Word of Hebrew prophecy. This zealous and Spirit-filled preaching would have soon brought great increase in the group of Christian disciples, and along with it that fierce antagonism on the part of the orthodox Jews in Damascus, had not Saul retired for a period to carry out his plan for recasting his theological studies in a retreat somewhere in Arabia. Luke, compressing the limits of his narrative, omits the account of this period of retirement, which we find narrated by Paul in his epistle to the Galatians. (Ch. 1:12-24).

B. The period, "sufficient days," in Luke's account (v. 23) covered the three parts-of-years of retirement and adjustment for Saul (Gal. 1:12-24).

With the revelation to Saul of the person of Jesus Christ at the time of his conversion and Jesus' revelation to him of his mission "to reveal God's Son to the Gentiles, and Kings and also to the Sons of Israel," Saul sought a retreat in Arabia, probably near Sinai. Here he conferred with God, and "*not with flesh and blood*," about what "his gospel" or interpretation of Jesus and the Scriptures should be. Elijah had met God there (I Kings 19:8-18) and later Moses was also forty days in that mount with God, receiving the Law. How appropriate it would be that Saul, who was to be the greatest interpreter of the Christ, should have a long period in the atmosphere and solitude of this awe-inspiring place, bringing to memory constantly the things of the Law, so revered by Saul, who had been the most brilliant and devoted student of the Law in the school of Gamaliel. Here he would pore over each phrase of the Mosaic code and delve deeply into the study of the other Scriptures, motivated by the thrilling mission assigned him by Jesus. Moreover, he would there rethink all his system of theology, learned at the feet of Gamaliel, *making it now Christo-centric.* In that austere atmosphere of the Law near Sinai, he would also recount his experiences with Jesus, in those transforming moments of his vision, and recall also his experiences when under the spell of the dying testimony of Stephen, and of many others whom he, in his zeal for the law, had hounded to the death. There he would meditate on his own inner conflict under the Law, and how it was changed into a peace he had never known before, when he accepted Jesus as his Lord. His difficult mission to the heathen nations had been assigned. He must now adjust his whole thought and life to a new orientation and program. It took months even for the brilliant intellect of Saul to effectively work out this new theology and program which have made Paul, the Apostle, the leading thinker and greatest leader of all Christian history. The root of this new theology was: *God's "revelation of his Son in Paul,"* in order that he might preach Him among the heathen nations (Gal. 1:16).

C. The return of Saul to Damascus for a successful but trying ministry (Ch. 9:23-25). This young preacher had a brief testifying and testing ministry before he went away to Arabia, in which he not only gave evidence of his identity with the cause of the Gospel of Jesus but showed ability and created an extraordinary sensation, attracting many to Jesus the Son of God and the Messiah, meeting criticism and active opposition leading finally toward plans by the Jewish leaders to destroy him.

When he began anew his work in Damascus, after a period of withdrawal to Arabia covering many months, the enemies of this young "renegade Rabbi and turncoat Jew" got themselves busy planning[22] to kill him. But Saul was more seasoned now and tactfully carried on his work, avoiding any unnecessary collision with his enemies. But it is not probable that he spent as much as

---

21. Cf. Galatians 4:22-31.
22. First Aor. (effective) Mid. Indicative of *bouleuō* with the preposition *sūn*, to counsel or plan together for themselves.

two years in his work in Damascus,[23] seeing that he had incurred the ill-will of the Jewish leaders before his period of retirement, which probably was of less than three years duration. These leaders would not have forgotten so soon the keen thrusts they had received from the former champion of the cause of Judaism, who was now for them the renegade Jew and leader of the "new gospel sect." A plot of these alert enemies was soon made known to Saul. They kept watching secretly the gates of the city *by day and by night, that they might kill him.* He had achieved conspicuous success and was already recognized by this time as the champion of the cause of the entire Christian church in Damascus. He had many "disciples" who were studying the Scriptures with him; and the cause would soon have many preachers, if this work were not stopped. His enemies, foreseeing this, had enlisted the sympathy of the tetrarch or governor of the city, which was under the rule of King Aretas, and arranged for him to put guards at the gates to apprehend Saul. But the devoted students of Saul took their beloved teacher (Master) in the night time[24] and lowered him from a window of a house on the city-rampart to the ground outside of the wall, in a large (hamper-like) basket which was made of plaited ropes. These disciples, whom Saul the persecutor had formerly come to Damascus to destroy, risked now their own lives to deliver their beloved teacher from his enemies. Paul, the Apostle to the Gentiles, later remembered his persecution of the church with repentant shame (II Cor. 11:33). Luke probably read later on in that Corinthian letter about this. Saul, the erstwhile persecutor had now to flee from Damascus to save his own life. Under cover of darkness he must have made his way toward Jerusalem, passing in the road a few miles out from the city the place where he had seen Jesus in the vision years before.

D. Fleeing to Jerusalem, Saul remains for a short time and is sent on to Tarsus (9:26-30). A summary of the progress of the church (v. 31).

It has been about three years now[25] since Saul came from Jerusalem with letters from the Sanhedrin, to exterminate nascent Christianity in Damascus. This included naturally an extensive period of retirement and also his shorter time in the ministry in Damascus after returning from Arabia. Now, he has to submit to the humiliating experience of fleeing for his life as a culprit would, stealing out by night, though graciously aided by his student-disciples. This was a testing time for Saul but he had a clear conviction of his mission now and his orders were from Jesus, who had said: "Be ye wise as serpents," and "when they persecute you in one city, flee to another."

Arriving in Jerusalem in about six days, he sought[26] to make the acquaintance and win the friendship of the disciples, but met with a cold reception, at

23. Cf. David Smith, *Life and Letters of Paul,* App. I.
24. Genitive, *nuktos,* expressing the kind of time.
25. Perhaps longer, Cf. David Smith in loco.
26. Imperfect active of conative action, *epeirazen,* was attempting, with present middle unfinitive *kollasthai,* to join himself.

least for a time. They were afraid[27] of him and suspicious of his rumored profession of conversion, for this might be a cleverly devised method of betrayal of them to the Sanhedrin authorities. Saul had come with the noble purpose in mind, of making amends to them for the atrocious acts of violence perpetrated against them three years before, and to join himself to the church, to participate in the common cause of evangelizing the great city of Jerusalem yet more completely. He wanted especially to get acquainted[28] with Peter, the outstanding leader, and doubtless have his understanding approval and that of the other apostles on the work Jesus had commissioned him to do. This seems to have been his main purpose in coming to Jerusalem, instead of starting off immediately to evangelize the Gentiles, the main item in his mission program. He had not come to get official authority from the church in Jerusalem in order to carry out his mission but to make known to the brethren of the church his experience of conversion and humbly acknowledge and confess the grievous wrongs and injuries he had inflicted on them in the lamented persecution. He could not wonder that they were afraid of him and refused to take him into their church at first.

But his confession of conversion was sincere; and when Joseph, surnamed Barnabas, the Cypriote Hellenist, heard about him, he took him to himself,[29] listened to his story, and, being convinced of its sincerity, brought him to Peter and to James, who was also now classed with the Twelve, the rest of whom were out of the city engaged in evangelistic tours about Judea and in other parts. This Barnabas, whose name signifies "son of consolation," was gracious and distinguished, and also an "apostolic" man who had figured as one of the most liberal givers and consecrated workers of the Jerusalem church. He was a "good man" and described by Chrysostom as "sweetly reasonable, gentle, kindly and accessible."[30] He came to Saul's aid and "taking him by the hand" conducted him to the apostles who thus received him into their confidence and entertained him while in Jerusalem, probably in the home of Mary. Mother of John Mark, who was either a sister or niece of Barnabas. Thus began a friendship which resulted in the companionship of Saul and Barnabas in the first great missionary tour in which the gospel was first planted in Asia Minor. Saul greatly enjoyed the fellowship of Barnabas and of James, who was also now prominent in the leadership of the movement of Christianity, especially in Jerusalem. He had time during these two weeks of his visit to hear from the lips of Peter and James, a first-over of the oral traditions of the gospel, afterwards embodied in Mark's original document, the materials for which he derived mainly from hearing Peter narrate the episodes in his sermons and conversations. Peter and Saul both were probably guests in this home during the two weeks of Saul's visit (Furneaux).

---

27. Imperfect middle, *ephobounto*, continued state of mind.
28. *Historasai*, Gal. 1:18.
29. Second Aorist Middle participle, *epilabomenos* (Acts 9:27).
30. John Chrysostom, *In Act. Apost. Hom.* XXI.

When Barnabas set forth fully the story of Saul's conversion to the apostles, including the description of how he had seen Jesus and talked with him (aorist),[31] and had recounted Paul's entire identification with the cause in Damascus through his full testimony in preaching, they received him and recommended him to the disciples. From that time on he moved freely in and out among them, preaching boldly in the synagogues in the name of the Lord Jesus. He went on day after day speaking and disputing in the very synagogues of the Hellenists, where Stephen had preached, and where he had terminated, soon after, his zealous ministry, sealing his testimony with his blood. Saul desired to appeal now to his old associates, who had followed his own leadership, when meeting the irresistible Spirit-filled preaching and discussion of Stephen, in this very Cilician synagogue. Perhaps he might convince them now of the mistake they all together made in stoning Stephen. But all his fine rhetoric and logic, reenforced and made more powerful now by his infilling with the Holy Spirit, were insufficient to convert these hard-hearted Jewish leaders. They responded to his arguments with derision and mockery and went about[32] to kill him. As in the case of Stephen, Saul's enemies, worsted in argument, resorted to the syllogism of violence.[33] It was a joy to Saul to have the intimate story of the life and teachings of Jesus told him graphically by Peter as they went together about the city which was the main scene of His activities, especially during the last days of His ministry. But the visit was to be cut short. Saul would have liked to continue in Jerusalem. What a joy it would be if he could but win the ear of Gamaliel, his old teacher, who was so moderate and humane. He would thus be able to undo some of the mischief he had done in persecuting the church. But this was not to be. The plot of his enemies thickened and their antagonism mounted from day to day against this "turncoat" traitor to their cause. Saul resorted to the temple for prayer and in a trance he again sees Jesus at his side. The Master bids him leave Jerusalem. "Depart," said He, "for I will send thee forth far thence unto the Gentiles" (Cf. Acts 22:21). Before the plot of his enemies could be carried into effect, his brethren escorted him hurriedly out of town and sent him on the way by Cesarea to Tarsus.

How would he be received in his home and his native city? Paul wondered in the short voyage and as he later leaves the ship to make his way to the old home. He did not know then that it would be many years before he would again see Jerusalem. His reception at home could not be very warm. He had been nurtured in a home of rigid Pharisaism and had been sent away to study under Gamaliel in Jerusalem to be a rabbi. Now he returns, a persecuted, fleeing disciple of the hated Nazarene sect. The records about his reception were left in silence and it was better so. In the eyes of his father, a strict Pharisee, he could be considered none other than a traitor to the ancestral faith. Many years later Paul writes his counsels to the Christian families in the

31. Jesus talked with Paul, elalēsen, (Aorist Act, Ind.).
32. Conative imperfect, epecheiroun anelein auton.
33. John Chrysostom, on Acts 9:23

churches; "Fathers, never anger or irritate your children lest they be discouraged, but bring them up in the nurture and admonition of the Lord."[34] In these words we seem to sense a strong emotional note, an echo of the narrow restrictions of youthful days and the bitter reproaches of the experience of the young preacher as he was probably turned out from the paternal home, as one dead to his Jewish kindred!

An outcast from his home, he turned sadly to seek consolation and healing for his grieved and broken heart, in the wonderful ministry and mission entrusted to him by Jesus, for whose sake he had "counted all things else but as refuse!" He began at once his ministry in Tarsus and the province of Syria-Cilicia round about. For nine years he wrought as a master-builder, achieving no small success, the fame of which spread far and wide even to Judea, bringing gladness and strength to the disciples there. During these years he not only spread the gospel over a vast region but also gained much valuable experience and splendid self-development which would serve him marvelously in the later expansion of the gospel to all Asia Minor, Europe and even to Rome. To him were vouchsafed during those years the plenitude of spiritual power for his work and the revelation of the glory of the Lord in heavenly vision. (II Cor. 12:2-4)

A brief statement, summarizing the expansion of the cause in Judea, Galilee and Samaria, reveals the fact of the cessation of persecution of the church with the conversion of its leader and promoter, Saul of Tarsus. Attention was diverted also from the church in Palestine by the effort of the Roman emperor Caligula (A. D. 39) trying to compel the Jews to engage in Emperor worship.[35] The church expanded generally into Judea, Galilee, and Samaria (Gal. 1:22). Peace continued and the evangelistic activities were intensified, the apostles making tours out from the city. The church grew rapidly, being edified, and multiplied by the comfort of the Holy Spirit and the conduct of the Christians, walking in the fear of the Lord.

34. Ephesians 6:4; Colossians 3:21.
35. Josephus *Antiq.* 18:8, 2-9.

CHAPTER V

Saul and the Christian Traditions

CHRISTIANITY was the climax of the activity of the God of history in the redemption of mankind. It is therefore a historical religion, and Jesus Christ its Founder was a historical person. The radical school of criticism in Holland and Germany which years ago questioned the historical character of Christianity and even denied the reality in history of both Jesus and Paul, if not entirely dead, is at least now suffering in its successors from a low vitality.[1]

The Bible is a history of redemption and the New Testament is the fulfillment of the law and prophets and culmination of revelation. "The weak spot in the Quellenkritik, of the end of the nineteenth century, was that it studied the gospels as a literary problem rather than as a reflexion of early Christian life."[2] The New Testament writings were a result of Christian life in the period beginning soon after the crucifixion and resurrection of Jesus. The oral gospel traditions were passed from mouth to mouth, as the cause of primitive Christian missionary activity was developed in the carrying out of the great commission of Jesus. The Gospels were tracts written to produce faith. Christianity did not spring from the confluence of two or more streams of philosophy, but came into being when God in the person of the God-Man, Jesus Christ, broke into history. The Christian religion was not founded by some great human sage reaching up after God but by God reaching down to lift man through the revelation of himself in Jesus Christ, the incarnate Word. There is a Christian mysticism which holds to concrete objective revelation in Christ. Christianity accepts revelation in the realm of material creation and in man's conscience. Man sees in the order of the material world and nature an infinitely powerful and good God, who is the Creator of all and the Redeemer of sinful man. God revealed himself concretely also in the history of his chosen people Israel. The prophets interpreted the events of Israel's history from experience, in which was revealed an immanent and transcendant God.

History is not a uniform field for scientific investigation or for the movement of progress, as claimed in the evolutionary organic sciences, nor a Hegelian dialectical process. A true philosophy of history must start from the Christian evaluation of a particular set of facts in the interaction between man's spirit and the God of history, as in the mighty acts, such as the call of Abraham, the exodus from Egypt, the exile and the *Diaspora*.

---

1. Kirsopp Lake and Silva Lake, *An Introduction of the New Testament*, p. 22f.
2. *Ibid.* p. 18f.

The ethical teaching of Jesus is not the main point of emphasis in the Christianity of Paul and the Twelve. Their preaching and teaching was about **Jesus,** who was the Divine Savior, Author of eternal life, and Judge of the world of humanity.[3] The historical events of the sinless life, atoning death, and supernatural resurrection were the fulfillment of Hebrew prophecy in the consummation of the plan of redemption in the purpose of God, and constitute the solid basis of the Gospels which are not merely religious but historical documents.

In the coming of Jesus Christ, the prophecies of salvation for a remnant of Israel and the redemption of the race through His death and resurrection are realized. In the Gospels we have the record of the mighty acts of God, in the consummation of the plan of redemption in the purpose of God. The historical reality of the events of His sinless life, atoning death, and supernatural resurrection from the dead, constitute the solid basis of the Gospels *which are thus shown to be not merely religious but also historical documents.*

The Gospel Tradition Traced

The annals of peace are not written except on the ostraca and non-literary-papyri, but where they are examined they reveal the life of the common people. There is only an occasional glimpse, from secular history, of the life of the people in Palestine. Tacitus refers to the persecution of the Christians under Nero and writes Trajan about the difficulty with the Christians whose character he depicts in a brief word. The Christian communities spread during the first two and a half centuries until, in the Decian persecution (250 A. D.) this religion, so different from everything in the Graeco-Roman synthesis and from every other religion which had entered into the civilization of the Roman world, went on to conquer, until it became dominant in the secular power, only to be corrupted in turn by its environs.

The writings of the New Testament, produced in the latter half of the first century, came to be widely known before the reign of Constantine, giving a vivid picture of the conditions in Palestine during the time of the early stage of development of primitive Christianity. The Pauline Epistles portray the time of expansion to the Neronian persecution; the Epistle to the Hebrews, the First Epistle of Peter and Revelation reveal the early persecutions to Domitian; and the General Epistles and Acts that toward the end of the century. These Gospels and those Epistles which were written before the Fall of Jerusalem set forth the character, works, and teachings of Jesus and became at once the authority and point of reference for the guidance of the primitive church. The life and thought of the early church in turn became the environ for the shaping up of the Gospel tradition received from eyewitnesses in many stories, teachings and illustrations of the activities of Jesus. The Pauline Epistles, written for the instruction and guidance of the early Christian communities, reveal a great variety of the activities and many aspects of the thought of these communities. Primitive Christianity, at first united in Jewish temple worship,

3. *Ibid.* p. 21

soon broke away and organized its own local churches, because its standards, doctrinal teachings and practices were different. In Paul both dogmatic and apologetic varieties of teachings appear. All his teachings worked back to the authoritative pronouncement of Jesus. He did not establish a new religion but only interpreted Christianity. Nor did the unknown author of the Hebrew Epistle attempt to lay any other foundation than that which was already laid. There was a common tradition and upon that foundation they were content to build.

Two aspects of the central tradition were the (kārugma) preaching or proclamation and (didaché) teaching. The latter followed neither the code form of Jewish Law nor that of the first principles of Greek philosophy but something of the same type as the Wisdom literature of the Old Testament and the Apocrypha. In the Pauline Epistles we find two parts in general: the theological and the ethical, the former being a development of the preaching and the latter the teaching. The Epistles of Paul contain few direct references to the facts of the Gospels because the Gospel traditions were well known and the epistles were written to give instruction in the fundamentals of Christianity, using the Gospel tradition only as a point or frame of reference. Jesus was to Paul the incarnate historical Christ,[4] who voluntarily subjected himself to human limitations. Christianity presents a plan of salvation revealed by God in Jesus Christ. Paul appealed to the Gospel tradition (I Cor. 7:10, 12, 25, 40), in the question of "separation," for his authority in Christ. (Matt. 5:31, 32, 19:9; Luke 16:8). Paul's independent teaching is "subordinate and derivative."[5] The Christian plan of salvation was in contradiction to philosophic systems of Creation and Salvation, as for example the philosophy of the Gnostics and the evanescent idea of Philo's Logos. Saving knowledge in the Christian system is conditioned on the testimony to the historic Christ.[6] To Paul and John the word of Jesus was ultimate authority, although Paul recognized his own teaching as Spirit-inspired.[7] Christianity recognized no spiritual revelation not connected with and referred to the historic Jesus Christ. The tradition embodied in the preaching (karugma) is historical and eschatological. It records events historical but in a history which reaches its divine conclusion in the Messiah in whom the prophecies are fulfilled. The Messianic idea came down from the beginning of time through the Old Testament and the Apocryphal literature and history and culminated in the "last things" of Jesus, the spiritual Messiah.

The historic and spirit-inspired memory of the evangelists, authors of the written Christian tradition, found a correspondence between certain Messianic prophecies of the Old Testament and the life, character and activities of Jesus. They did not find historic correspondence in the case of the reference to the Messiah in the Apocryphal literature. Eschatological references in the Old

4. Romans 8:3; Philippians 2:5-11.
5. Dodd, C. H., *History and the Gospel*. pp. 57, 58.
6. I John 1:1-3.
7. I Corinthians 7.

Testament literature found their fulfillment in the *eschaton* of Jesus.[8] Paul received his authoritative statement about the Last Paschal Meal and the First Supper from the Gospel Tradition (I Cor. 11:23-26). He was acquainted with the circumstances of Jesus' death,[9] as well as of His life and character.[10] In the Hebrew Epistle also we have testimony as to the character, life and death of Jesus.[11] In the Epistles to Timothy and I and II Peter there are also definite references to the Tradition. In the Acts are found various discourses of Peter and Stephen, and Paul refers to the historical tradition of the gospel of both the "preaching and teaching" sections. The Gospels are but the crystallization of the historical tradition in narrative form, and Mark represents primarily the preaching (Kārugma) and (Q) the teaching of Jesus.

How Paul Employed the Christian Traditions

In the midst of the confusion created by many schools of criticism, some have boldly charged Paul with being responsible for leading the world astray from the simple Jesus of the Gospels. He is sometimes called the creator of Christianity or the perverter of the Christianity of the Christ. But Paul, far from assuming any attitude of disloyalty to Jesus, is on the contrary the greatest interpreter of the Christ and true Christianity.[12] Let us therefore examine how Paul employed the Christian traditions in his epistles.

Paul, in spite of his great emphasis on the crucifixion and resurrection of Jesus, did not forget the circumstances of the life of his Lord, as did Harnack in his, *What is Christianity?* On the other hand his testimony to the historical life of Jesus is one of great value. In spite of the fact that it was his vision of the risen Nazarene and his immediate recognition of Him as the Messiah of Hebrew prophecy, around whom he rethought and rebuilt his own gospel (cf. Galatians Chs. 1 and 2:1-10), he was acquainted with the details not only of the incidents of the Passion Week but of His life and teachings in general. These details of the sinless life of Jesus constituted a large part of the foundation and content of Paul's preaching, teaching and Kingdom building.

Much of the information about the life of Jesus he could have received during the visit to Jerusalem to meet Peter and the other apostles, most of whom were absent from the city on the occasion (Gal. 1:18). Contrary to the critical opinion of some, Paul doubtless also knew many among the five hundred eyewitnesses of the ministry, death and resurrection of Jesus, who gathered on the mount in Galilee to receive from Him the Great Commission. The greater part of those brethren were yet alive at the time when Paul wrote the first Corinthian Epistle, near the close of his third missionary campaign while in Ephesus. Furthermore, many of the statements made by Paul in his epistles were based on assertions of Jesus about Himself. Paul's gospel of justification

---

8. I Corinthians 15:11.
9. I Thessalonians 2:15.
10. II Corinthians 10:1; Philippians 2:7, 8; Romans 13:14.
11. Hebrews 2:3; 3:1; 10:5-9.
12. A. T. Robertson, *Paul the Interpreter of Christ*, pp. 13-39.

by faith in the risen Christ did not make him indifferent toward the facts about the historical life of Jesus of Nazareth. He certainly cited a tradition, well understood by the Christians from the time of the crucifixion forth, about the atoning power of the death and resurrection of the Lord (I Cor. 15:3, 4). He had referred to the same tradition years before (I Thess. 5:10 and Gal. 1:4). The same idea was in the tradition later embodied in the earliest Gospel (cf. Mark 10:45), and Paul must have received it from the same source from which Mark, Peter's amanuensis, got most of his information. One of the Gospel traditions most clearly set forth in Paul's first Corinthian Epistle recorded in chapter 11:23-27, which is the tradition of the Lord's Supper, he said he had received from the Lord. He had seen Jesus and recognized him as the divine Lord on the Damascus road.

Paul's letters were more than mere tracts or epistles to be coldly read and studied in churches. They were the effusive and fervent outpouring of a heart yearning for sympathy while ministering to the sorrows and heart-breaks of others. The reference he would make to the traditions about the historical life of Jesus would not be as the account of a biographer but that of a grateful application of balm to the dire spiritual needs of mankind. Weiss sees, in the background of Paul's references to Jesus, a world of information in Paul's consciousness of details of the historic life of his Lord, knowledge of the details of which is assumed to be in his hearers or readers. Thus Paul's dealing with Jesus is not as a historic person in the main but as the exalted and living Lord. This was natural, as we should realize in our experiences as His disciples of today. The living Christ was the foundation of his preaching and source of the salvation which was his message to a lost humanity.

Paul preached Jesus as the Son of God, from his very first release of the Gospel message in Damascus immediately after his conversion. For him the understanding of the deity of Jesus was fundamental and of primary importance. In his first epistle (I Thess. 1:10) he so presented Jesus as the crucified and risen Savior and divine Messiah who would return in the *Parousia.* Paul learned from the teachings of Jesus what He meant by the "Kingdom of God." It was spiritual, not mere meat and drink, but righteousness, peace and joy in the Holy Ghost (Rom. 14:17).

The vast work of Paul, the Apostle to the Gentiles, called for all the information he could possibly obtain from the oral traditions, eyewitnesses, and especially the apostles and outstanding Christian workers. We know that he visited the home of Philip, one of the first seven deacons of the Jerusalem church, who became an evangelist. Paul's visit to his home in Cesarea would be an occasion of the rehearsing of the traditions which had come down from the beginning because he lodged in the house of Manson, one of the disciples who had been present at Pentecost (Acts 21:8, 16). Paul made his first Missionary Journey with Barnabas, an outstanding member of the apostolic church of which James, the Lord's half-brother, was the pastor.

From both of these men the great body of traditions about the life of Jesus, even from his childhood, would have come into the knowledge of Paul. Andronicus and Junias, his kinsmen and fellow-workers, whom he mentions in his Roman epistle (16:7), preceded him in the Kingdom. From them he would learn much. Furthermore, it is impossible to suppose that Paul, having been with Luke in the Cesarean imprisonment and constantly later while the historian was doubtless engaged in writing the Third Gospel and the Acts, or at least gathering materials to that end, should not have been in constant communication with him in the matter of the common body of traditions. The statement in II Cor. 5:16 is many times misinterpreted and simply means that Paul's knowledge of Christ was not an external objective matter after his conversion when he became "a man in Christ" and therefore had internal and experimental knowledge of Him as his Savior. The inside knowledge (gnosis) of the Kingdom is exclusive and not properly or fully understood by the uninitiated, as it is spiritually discerned. He looked on Christ as a mere man before his conversion when he was a student in the school of Gamaliel and probably may have seen Jesus with his own eyes in the midst of His ministerial activities in the porch of the temple or in the streets preaching and healing. But now after the experience of seeing the risen Christ be no longer knew Him (kata sarka) according to the flesh or as a mere human being. He did not understand Jesus, when he, as a brilliant member of the Sanhedrin, took the lead in the persecution of the church and met Stephen in debate in the synagogue and later gave his vote of consent to his stoning outside the city walls. When he saw the risen Christ in the Damascus road the "light of the knowledge of the glory of God in the face of Jesus" whom he now knew to be the Christ, shined into his heart (II Cor. 4:6). This qualified Paul to interpret Christ, and the same light must shine into the heart of any one who would interpret Jesus through Paul to the world today. Paul's vision was as real as that of the apostles in the post-resurrection appearances of their great Teacher (Rabban). It was there that the stream of his new experience overflowed the stream of his old theology and gave him the basis and center for a new theology. Paul had relatively little intimate knowledge of the life of the historic Jesus when he was converted, although he did know that Jesus was the antithesis of Phariseeism and the greatest enemy of ceremonial traditional Judaism. He started out with a small capital in Christian tradition but he made good use of his experiential knowledge of the risen Christ and began to preach Him in Damascus. Later his capital would increase by leaps and bounds.

The necessity was upon him to learn all the fundamental useful traditions of Christianity in order that the two systems of thought of the Old Testament and the Gospel might be reconciled and blended in his mind, enlightened now by the new revelation in Jesus, the Messiah. This new spiritual Messiah called for a new spiritual Israel, where there should be neither Jew nor Gentile, Barbarian, Scythian, bond nor free, but Christ be all and in all (Col. 3:11). Law and grace met together in the love-look and commission given him by the risen Christ. Paul must suffer the shocks from both social and religious prejudice in carrying out that commission, but he would willingly suffer the loss of all things for the Christ of the Damascus way. He must learn the content of

Christian tradition in order to interpret that Christ to doctrinally and religiously antagonistic Jews and racially alienated Gentiles. Like a man without a country, he went about his difficult task, always with the apologetic-defensive attitude, but always with a positive message. The secret of the resolution of every problem in that task was wrapped up in the mystery of the Gospel, long-hidden but now revealed. It was to be fully known not without his *epignosis* or accurate and full knowledge of all the available Gospel traditions. Paul was a pearl-hunter for these pearls of great price, a seeker for the hidden treasures.

In the earliest of the epistles written by Paul, those to the church in Thessalonica, we find a milky way across the firmament, composed of the luminaries of Christian traditions cited by Paul with purpose. In the salutation, the Thessalonian Christians are greeted in God and equally in the divine Lord Jesus, the Messiah. Paul was thankful at every remembrance of their work of faith, labor of love, and patience of hope, all of which grew out of the dynamic connection with Jesus the divine Savior and Son of God through Whom they received power for this service rendered to the living God. It was this Jesus whom God raised from the dead and He is the Son of God and One Who is delivering us "from the wrath to come." These words were written by Paul, a contemporary of Jesus, just twenty-three years after the resurrection of[13] the Jesus whom Paul calls *Lord* more than twenty times in this epistle.[14] Paul gives his salutation of the gracious blessings and divine peace in Jesus Christ as in God; he gave his exhortations and commands through Christ (I Thess. 4:2); they are to find patience and purity in the fellowship and example of Christ; they are to be imitators of the Lord and of Paul as one in Christ (I Thess. 1:6). The tradition embraced in Luke 10:16 is cited in I Thess. 4:8: "He that rejecteth *the Christ, rejecteth not man but God.*" Paul was acquainted with the instruction Jesus gave His apostles when He sent them forth for the campaign (Luke 10:7; cf. I Thess. 2:6; II Thess. 3:8). The denunciations of the Pharisees, Matt. 23:31, are cited in I Thess. 2:14, 15.

The expression of Jesus, "to be counted worthy of the kingdom" Matt. 22:3; Luke 14:16, was in the mind of Paul when he wrote II Thess. 1:5. The Christians in Thessalonica were exhorted to holiness and patience worthy of the kingdom, in the very phrases of Jesus. They had been "called into the kingdom," (cf. Matt. 22:3; Luke 14:16), which was not a material one of "meat and drink, but of righteousness and peace and joy in the Holy Spirit,"[15] like that which Jesus had spoken about as recorded in John's gospel in connection with the miracle-tradition of the feeding of the five thousand (John 6) and also with His parables of the Kingdom (Matt. 13).

The Kingdom is represented as present and future, of the present world and the world to come. This brings Paul to one of the major subjects of the two

---

13. Dr. Sanday on I Thess. 1:10 versus W. B. Smith. Cf. Peter's confession near Cesarea Philippi, with which Paul was conversant.
14. R. J. Knowling, *The Testimony of Paul to Christ* p. 231.
15. Rom. 14:17.

epistles, i. e. the *parousia* or second coming of the Lord Jesus. That "day of the Lord" Jesus, when He would return with His Holy angels on the clouds, would "come as a thief in the night." (I Thess. 5:2) This was a reference to the eschatological prophetic discourse of Jesus as recorded by Matthew. The point of Paul's reference to the sudden coming was as a basis for his exhortation "let us watch and be sober."[16] The word *parousia*, used seven times in the two epistles, corresponded with "the day of the Lord (I Thess 3:13)." In that second coming He will be the Judge of all mankind, separating between the good and the bad as a shepherd the sheep from the goats.[17]

The tradition of the Second Coming referred to by Paul in I Thess. 4:15 was that of the word of Jesus cited in Matthew 24:31, 32. This is also cited by Paul in II Thess. 2:1. It was not a reference to the Apocalyptic literature of the Jews. It might less probably have been one of the *logia* of the Lord not included among those cited by the Evangelists. Jesus was to be the Judge, and Paul prays that his converts may be prepared to receive Him when He comes, I Thess. 5:2. The second advent was not a 'make believe' coming, as that of the legendary return of King Arthur or the vindictive return of the monstrous Nero, believed not to be dead, but a real *parousia* with great glory and divine justice to be meted out to all men "without acceptation or partiality."

These citations of Paul, of the Gospel traditions, transmitted orally by the *memoriter* method, are an illustration of the intimate understanding of Paul of the earthly life, character and activities of Jesus the Messiah, which underlies all of the epistles written by him.[18]

---

16. Cf. The Parable of the Ten Virgins and especially that of the Drunken Steward.
17. A Parable in the prophetic discourse (Matt. 25).
18. Cf. R. J. Knowling, *The Testimony of St. Paul to Christ*, Lecture XI ff.

CHAPTER VI

Militant Christianity on the March

(Acts 8:1-12:25)

IT WAS a militant Christianity that found Saul and a vivacious expanding Christianity that Saul found. The Christianity of the Christ was always universal in its nature and destiny. But like a growing child it had to apprehend gradually its true character and awaken to its innate powers. There were a number of contributing factors which soon led it to break its bonds and like a swollen current overflow its banks. The foundations of traditional Judaism were already potentially undermined by the work of Jesus, the founder of Christianity. The reaction to his iconoclastic work soon brought the tragedy of His death on the cross. But the influence of His signal victory on the cross would soon burst through the levee of Judaistic religious traditions and spread out in a flood which would inundate many sections of Palestine. Persecution of the early apostles, Peter, and John, and of the deacon Stephen, would flare up into a general conflagration resulting in the dispersion of Jerusalem saints from the beloved city, soon to fall by the hands of the Roman legions into utter destruction. The aggressive universalism of Stephen precipitated the antagonism of Jewish leaders to the resurrected Christ and His Christianity. At first the Apostles were not forced to leave Jerusalem, but soon they were definitely led to reach out in their work of evangelism. When the persecution came, they went, following the crest of the wave to various parts of Palestine, and penetrated into centers and places beyond the little country, where Jesus had spent His whole life and ministry. Other factors, which cannot be discussed here, led on to the spread of the conflagration which must yet sometime envelop the whole world.

Philip's Work in Samaria and the South

A. The martyrdom of Stephen marked a great crisis in the history of the early church. The murderers of Stephen returned within the city of Jerusalem and raised up a general persecution against the disciples of Christianity (8:1-4). It was necessary that practically all the Christians should flee for their lives. Saul of Tarsus, the brilliant student of the school of Gamaliel, a robust intellectual leader who had just come forth from his studies of theology and law, an ardent Pharisee in his religious zeal for his sectarian view, assumed the leadership of the movement against the Christian community. When some pious Hebrews had buried Stephen, to whose death Saul had given his consent, it was a signal for that ardent young academic devotee of the strict Pharisaic party to assume the leadership of the persecution in person, and he went all the lengths to stamp out the heresy, by the most violent measures of a thorough purge. He entered into the houses and dragged both men and women who were Christians to the prisons. He had both the Pharisees and Sadducees behind him, in this united effort of these old enemies of Jesus, to erase every vestige of Christianity from their beloved Jerusalem. Only the apostles remained in Jerusalem. This would indicate that their work had temporarily become more or less paralyzed. Jerusalem almost falls out of the picture for a time. But Divine providence was in the movement of persecution, and the disciples fled into all parts of Judea and Samaria, and wherever they went they were found heralding the Word of the Gospel (Ch. 8:4-40). One of the seven deacons of the Jerusalem church, Philip, took up the work of preaching the good news in Samaria. He did a complete job, heralding the Messiahship of Jesus, proving by the Scriptures that the Messiah had come. The Samaritans already believed a teaching Messiah would come. Had not Jesus told the woman at the well near Sychar that He was the Messiah, and had He not assumed that role before them in Sychar? And now Philip, whose name was Greek, was not bound down by the Jewish strictness, but presented the Jesus of the Sychar incident, as the Messiah. He, like the ardent Stephen, who had sealed his testimony to the same universal Gospel, now proclaimed the same message which had brought Stephen to martyrdom. Philip, full of the Holy Spirit, preached with power the Kingdom of God and the name of Jesus Christ.

The people of the capital of Samaria were in a state of confusion religiously. A certain Simon, a sorcerer, had been bidding for the mastery of the minds of the people, who were seeing for spiritual satisfaction, which their Samaritan religion, a mixture of traditional Judaism and of heathen cults, was not able to give them. Philip's message was satisfying and won the victory over the the black art of sorcery. It converted Simon as well as his adepts to give assent to the claims of Christianity (8:5-13).

The fame of the work of Philip spread far and wide and finally reached back to Jerusalem, where the Apostles and a small group quietly awaited the abatement of the fury of the storm of persecution. They were stirred by the news of the reception the Gospel was having in the capital of Samaria. It was an important city and its acceptance of the message of Christianity aroused great interest in the apostolic church. They sent Peter and John to inspect and report back on the work of Philip. These apostles came with open minds to visit the work in Samaria and found the glowing report to be true. Christ had said, His disciples should go into Samaria and they had come and were attended with great success in their ministry among the Samaritans.

One of the important consequences of the visit of these apostles was that they found the new disciples had not experienced the baptism of the Holy Spirit for their service of witnessing. The apostles gave added instruction to the fine evangelistic work of Philip and with prayer and their laying on of hands the Samaritan Christians were led to the experience of the baptism of the Spirit.

Simon the magician had been converted, in that he gave his assent to the claims of the Gospel, but now fell into the temptation to turn to gain his knowledge of the marvelous manifestations of the miraculous power of the apostles, in cures. He offered to buy of them this power, that he might make of it a means of personal gain. When much to his chagrin he was rebuked by Peter and repented, he asked that the Apostles should pray for him that he might be forgiven. When Peter and John returned to Jerusalem, it is wonderful to note, that they themselves preached in many of the villages of the Samaritans as they went on their way. Persecution in Jerusalem had proven to be a blessing in scattering the Gospel in Judea and Samaria, as Jesus had desired and about which He gave command at the hour of His ascension.

B. The notable conversion and baptism of the eunuch in the wider evangelistic campaign of Philip in Judea (8:26-40). There are several things to be noted about this remarkable conversion on the road toward Gaza, a town in Judea: (1) Jesus through His messenger (*aggellos*), the Holy Spirit, spoke in the heart of Philip, saying: "Arise and go down toward the South in the road which leads from Jerusalem down to Gaza, through the desert country." *Specific impressions* directing the willing evangelist were then given, to leave Samaria and broaden the work, extending it into a new unevangelized section of Judea. The preacher obeyed and went. (2) For this evangelist, fresh from a great success in preaching to the crowds in the city of Samaria, the Spirit prepared opportunities for personal evangelism. A strategic person, the eunuch, head treasurer in the court of the Candace or queen of Ethiopia,[1] probably a "proselyte of the gate," had come from that distant land in Africa to worship[2] "in Jerusalem," and was now being driven by his charioteer on his return journey. Seated in his chariot he was engaged in reading[3] the prophet Isaiah. Again Philip had the inner urge from the Spirit and ran forward and "glued himself" to this chariot. Philip was not seeking a ride, but with a prayer for direction and a purpose in his heart he ran and politely begging assent jumped on the "running board" of the traveler's chariot and jocularly asked him in the Greek language: "Ara geginoskeis ha anaginoskeis?" Both the Hellenist Philip and the eunuch who was reading from the Greek (Septuagint) translation knew and used Greek. The ready and playful[4] use of that language produced a good impression on the eunuch and a ready response to Philip's very relevant question: "Do you understand what you are reading?" This was not an irrelevant question from a Hellenistic Jew to a foreigner who might not be much acquainted with the Hebrew Scriptures. Philip saw that the foreigner was interested. He was yet more convinced by the eunuch's response. Inviting Philip urgently to come up and ride with him in the chariot, he replied to his question good-naturedly: "How in the world could[5] I [understand]

1. The queens of Meroe were given the title, Kandakēa.
2. Fut. active participle *proskunēsōn*.
3. Imperfect tense, *aneginosken*.
4. Example of parnomasia in the Greek language.
5. Fourth class condition undetermined, with less probability of determination. (rare)

unless someone teaches me."[6] The eunuch confessed that he needed a guide[7] or teacher, he being little acquainted with these writings. Such a need is almost universal even today, if men would make a frank confession, as the eunuch did. (3) It was not just a matter of chance that the eunuch was reading at that instant from the fifty-third chapter of Isaiah, one of the clearest references to the Messiah, if we are to accept the general thesis of the real title of the second treatise of Luke: *The Acts of the Holy Spirit.* The Spirit had selected the preacher, the person to be instructed, and all the means and occasion of his instruction, going before the preacher and opening the heart of his hearer. *His promised part in the work also included the illumination and reenforcing of the mental powers of Philip and the receptive capacities of the eunuch in the teaching and learning process.*[8]

> *"As a sheep to the slaughter he was led;*
> *As a lamb before his shearer is dumb,*
> *So he opens not his mouth:*
> *By oppression and unjust judgment he was taken away:*[9]
> *Who shall declare the wickedness of his times?*
> *For his life is taken from the earth."* —ISAIAH 53:7, 8.

Here is the best portrait in the Old Testament of the Suffering Servant, bruised and broken, but emerging in triumph. Stopping right in the midst of the reading, the eunuch said: "I beg of you, tell me of whom the prophet speaks this; about himself or someone else?" This was a discerning and pertinent inquiry and gave Philip his opportunity. So, beginning from this Scripture, he preached to him Jesus. This was Philip's interpretation of this Messianic Scripture of which Jesus Himself had claimed to be the fulfillment (Matt. 8:17). This was also the interpretation Philip gave of this mountain-peak passage on the Suffering Servant. He did not preach on the "national servant" of modern critical exegesis, but Jesus as a personal Messiah and Savior. The eunuch was an intelligent hearer and caught the message which Philip had been instructed to preach, including repentance and faith in the atoning sacrifice of Jesus the Messiah, Who was portrayed in the text under consideration. Philip must have urged the personal acceptance of this Savior whose atonement was effected through His death, burial and resurrection, symbolized in baptism. Suddenly they came upon a certain stream or pool and the eunuch turned to Philip and thoughtfully and earnestly said: "Look, here is water: what hinders me from being baptized?" Here was a soul that had been seeking the light. His heart was filled with an eagerness to follow in the way of obedience and identification with the Lord before the world. He ordered the charioteer to stop.

---

6. William's Translation in loco.
7. *Hodēgos,* a guide, to show the hodos, way.
8. Cf. various passages in John's gospel on the work of the Spirit (Chs. 14-16).
9. *Gr. Exp. New Testament* p. 325.

The character of the baptism *requested* by the eunuch, when they came suddenly upon a stream or spring-pool of water on the way, was such as to require that both[10] should go down into the water. The request was a confession of the eunuch's acceptance of Jesus and an eagerness to follow Him now in obedient immersion. Both he and Philip went down *into* the water and Philip immersed[11] the eunuch. They both came up out of and not just from the edge of the stream or pool.[12] There was no need of the interpolation of verse 37 probably by some churchman in the interest of creedal tendencies in the growth of historic ecclesiasticism. It was not a part of the earliest original manuscripts extant. The confession naturally accompanied the request for baptism.

Philip's happy work with this important man of far distant Ethiopia was done and the evangelist was suddenly and miraculously carried away[13] and was found later in Azotus. He afterwards went forward evangelizing as far as Cesarea where he built up a work. Here Paul found him later, as pastor. The eunuch went on his now happy and contented journey homeward with a glad message and happy experience concerning which to bear testimony among his people. He was the first African (Negro) to receive the message of Christianity. "Ethiopia shall haste to stretch out her hands unto God." Psalm 68:31.

Peter's Leadership in Judea

Peter's Spirit-led miracle-activities in Judea open the door for the Gentiles to enter the Christian fold. Chaps. 9:32-11:18. In tracing the expansion of Christianity Luke has followed the chronological order and cited illustrations from the work of various apostolic men. The work had been confined almost exclusively to Jerusalem until the problem of poverty among the Hellenist saints precipitated a forward movement reaching out unto Judea, Samaria, Galilee and even to some places beyond Palestine. The missionary sermon preached by Stephen before the Sanhedrin brought on his martyrdom and the persecution of the disciples in Jerusalem. Philip, another one of the six Hellenist deacons, appointed by the church, was thrust forth by the persecution and instituted the mission to Samaria (8:1-40). The conversion of Saul, which grew indirectly out of the death of Stephen, laid the foundation for the wider evangelization of the Gentiles, to which work he was called (9:1-31). Peter and the other apostles, after the persecution subsided, began to go out into the regions round about and Peter worked down toward Lydda and Joppa and finally up to Cesarea, where he was used of the Holy Spirit to open the door to the Gentile (9:32-11:18). Finally, the outburst of persecution led also to the evangelization of Antioch of Syria (11:19-26).[14]

---

10. Emphasized by repetition in the narrative.
11. Primary signification of the verb *baptizo* is immerse, in accord with the most ancient mode, practiced even today in the Greek Catholic Church.
12. Preposition Ek with ablative of separation, cf. Mark 1:10.
13. Harpazō means seized and carried off.
14. Moffatt, James: *Introduction to the Literature of the New Testament*: pp. 291-292.

A. Peter evangelizes Lydda and the regions around it and cures Aeneas a paralytic (9:32-35). It happened that when Peter was going around preaching among all the people of that region, he came also to the saints living in the town called Lydda. He found there a man called Aeneas, who had been lying bedridden for eight years, being a paralytic. This man was probably one of the humble disciples who had received the gospel through the deacon-evangelist Philip. Seeing his desperate plight, Peter addressed him, saying: "Aeneas, Jesus the Christ heals thee.[15] Get up and take up your bed!" And he stood up at once. This was one of the many miracles performed by Peter as soon as he started from Jerusalem to evangelize the rural regions and small towns around the Judean country. His missionary activities round about brought a new power into his work. He followed right on through the Sharon plain noted for its beautiful flowers in the way that Philip had gone after the conversion of the eunuch. All those who witnessed this remarkable cure of Aeneas, both those dwelling in Lydda and in the plain of Sharon, turned to the Lord.

B. Coming to Joppa, a town on the coast, the apostle raised Tabitha from the dead (9:36-43). This good woman who was also called Dorcas (Greek) which means gazelle, was full of alms-deeds and good works which she was in the habit of doing. Gazelle was a favorite type of beauty in the orient and she must have combined physical and spiritual beauty with youthful activity in the service of the church at Joppa. It happened in those days that she grew ill and died. The sisters of the church prepared her corpse, and, instead of burying her at once as was the custom, they laid her in the upper room of her house, and sent twelve miles to call Peter and beg him to come without delay. They had heard of the mighty works being done by Peter, and doubtless had faith that he might raise Tabitha from the dead as Jesus had raised the little maid in the house of Jairus.

They were not to be disappointed, for Peter at once got up and went with the messengers. When he arrived they took him at once to the upper room where the weeping widows had taken their stand around the body and were showing the garments she had made while she was with them. They expected some wonderful miracle, and Peter lost no time in having them all retire from the room (cf. Elijah and Elisha). Then he prayed, falling on his knees. After prayer he turned to the body and said: "Tabitha, get up!" She opened her eyes and saw Peter and sat up. He immediately took her by the hand and raised her up from the pallet where she had been laid. He then called the saints and some others among the widows for whom she had made garments, who probably were not yet numbered among the disciples, and presented her to them, alive. This notorious miracle resulted in many believing in the Lord and Peter remained many days in Joppa, evangelizing the town and its environs, residing in the home of a certain man by the name of Simon who was a tanner by trade.

---

15. Acristic present mid. Ind, iātai.

C. The Holy Spirit prepares Peter and the church for the entrance of the Gentiles. Acts 10:1-11:18. Cornelius, a Roman centurion, was a volunteer Italian officer at the head of a cohort of a hundred soldiers, sent from Rome for the policial work of guard in Cesarea. This city was built by Herod, and the palace of the provincial Roman government of which Palestine was a part was located there. He was doubtless a Roman citizen serving under Herod Agrippa, and was entrusted with a position calling for a strong disciplinary character and able leadership, in a country where insurrection was not unknown. Religiously he was at least a proselyte of the gate, more probably ranking as full-fledged in proselytism, observing all the ceremonial rites of the Jews. He undoubtedly followed the main idea of the Hebrew religion of a monotheistic philosophy. He might have belonged to a great Roman family, being possibly a patrician or plebeian. Luke's record states that he was "a devout man who feared God with all his household, gave alms liberally to the people, and prayed constantly to God." He was a worshipper in the Hebrew religion as set forth in the Old Testament and as interpreted by the Jews. Cornelius, not only followed this religion himself, but led his household including his children and servants to do the same, keeping the hours of prayer and giving alms liberally to the people.

It was in the hour of prayer at the ninth hour or 3 p. m., the Hebrew hour of prayer, that he saw clearly in a vision an angel of God come in, addressing him, "Cornelius." And he stared at the angel in terror and said, "What is it, Lord?" And the angel-messenger replied, "Your prayers and your alms have ascended as a memorial before God. And now send men to Joppa, and bring one Simon who is called Peter; he is lodging with Simon, a tanner, whose house is by the seaside." When the angel who spoke to him had departed, he called two of his servants and a devout soldier from among those who waited on him, and having related everything to them, he sent them to Joppa. These who were sent, being a part of the household of the centurion, shared his religious beliefs and practices.

Cornelius here appears as a man of rare religious character in the pagan world of the Romans of that time. He had responded to the light of conscience within him and doubtless he had observed in the Jewish people, in their colony in Rome, the peculiarity of their religious beliefs. He may have had some touch with the small group of those Hebrews who were at Jerusalem from Rome at Pentecost, when the Holy Spirit fell upon the hundred and twenty. Apart from all surmise Peter was a man prepared by response to the God-given opportunities, whatever they might be, to be blessed with the fuller revelation of Jesus Christ, the fulfillment of Hebrew prophecy and the "only name under heaven given among men whereby we must be saved." This was in line with the purpose of God and fully justified the supernatural manifestation granted him in the visitation of the angel-messenger. It was God's fulness of time to open the door to a greater part of the human race for entrance into the Messianic Kingdom, whosoever would. Someone prepared must be the first, and

Cornelius was that man. A special vision of God's angel-messenger led him to appeal to Peter (Acts 10:1-8).

In like manner Peter was prepared through a supernatural vision on the house-top of Simon the tanner in Joppa, to heed the appeal of Cornelius (Acts 10:9-16). Peter had said in his sermon at Pentecost that the supernatural demonstration, visible and audible at Pentecost, far from being what some said in derision that it was, the results of drunkenness, was a fulfillment, of the prophecy of Joel about the pouring out of the Holy Spirit *"upon all flesh."* Perhaps the prophets themselves sometimes spoke things the full import of which they did not comprehend. But Peter had been seeing during many days now the spread of Christianity through Judea and Samaria, and had himself experienced the power of the Holy Spirit in the operation of miracles, in a measure far in excess of anything he had personally felt and seen before. The barriers of race had been transcended by the power of the Spirit in the conversion of the Samaritans, and he had personally experienced the fact in his own ministry in Samaria. He had partly relinquished his Jewish strictness in the very act of preaching to the Samaritans. He was doubly impressed, especially when he saw that they were being genuinely regenerated and empowered by the baptism of the Spirit who came upon them as upon the Jews at Pentecost.

But the Gentiles were further away than the Samaritans, who had some belief in the Monotheistic religion and looked forward to the coming of "a teaching" though not "a ruling Messiah." Peter had not understood his own words about "the Spirit coming upon all flesh," when he preached his great sermon at Pentecost.

When the messengers from Cornelius were on their way to Joppa on the day after the vision of Cornelius, Peter went up on the flat-topped roof of the house of Simon to pray, about the sixth hour or at midday. While there in meditation and prayer he became hungry, having fasted perhaps the whole morning. While food was being prepared below he fell into a trance and saw the heaven opened and something descending, like a great sheet, let down by four corners upon the earth. In it were all kinds of animals and reptiles and wild birds. And there came a voice to him, "Rise, Peter, kill and eat." But Peter said, "By no means Lord, for I have never eaten anything that is common or unclean." And the voice came to him again the second time, "What God has cleansed, you must not call common." This happened three times, and the thing was taken up at once to heaven. Many of the creatures in that vision were common and not permitted by the ceremonial law of the Jews for food, and all were unclean by being herded together. The vision was repeated three times to impress it the more upon Peter, who was extremely devoted to the Jewish traditions. He had lodged with Simon, the tanner, who had been made to build his house fifty cubits outside the city to prevent defilement for the people who should pass it. But Simon the tanner was a clean Christian brother and Peter did not feel himself defiled by being in his home, where the smell of the skins was ever in evidence. But Peter still felt that the Gentile must come through the gate of circumcision to get into the fold of Judaism and become a

Christian, while Christianity was yet closely united in the worship of the Jews. Peter had not yet come to recognize that he himself was liberated by Christ from the ceremonies, rites and sacrificial system of the Jews which had been fulfilled in Christ. He did not remember the teaching of Jesus about foods and "that contamination came out of the heart of man and not from foods at all." Christianity teaches the law of health. Nothing must be eaten or done to harm the body. Peter was perplexed as he reflected on the meaning of the vision. In the midst of it all came the clear impression through the Spirit that Peter should go with the men below at the entrance of Simon's house, who had been sent by Cornelius to fetch him. "Behold, three men are looking for you. Rise and go down and accompany them without hesitation, for I have sent them." Such was the message of the Spirit in Peter's heart and he went down and said; "I am the one you are looking for; what is the reason for your coming?" And they said, "Cornelius, a centurion, an upright and God-fearing man, who is well spoken of by the whole Jewish nation, was directed by a holy angel to send for you to come to his house and to hear what you have to say." So Peter called these messengers of Cornelius into the house to be his guests, though they were Gentiles, which he well knew. He even took liberties with his brother Christian, Simon the tanner, and presumed on his hospitality which he knew very well would be proferred. Without doubt he sat at the table with his guests and did not consider them "common or unclean." Peter had understood and rightly interpreted God's message to him in his conscience and heart and forthwith put it into practice, an example which, if followed, would unify all Christendom in one common belief. True exegesis faithfully followed will unite all through the same Spirit whom Peter obeyed in this instance.

Peter kept up the line of obedience to the Spirit and the next day he rose and went off with the three messengers of Cornelius. He foresaw trouble, which would come later, from the reactionary traditionalists of the Jerusalem church, and chose some of the brethren of the local church in Joppa to serve as witnesses to all that might be done or said between himself and Cornelius on his arrival in Cesarea.

On the day after the messengers came to Joppa, the whole party of ten arrived in Cesarea. Cornelius was expecting them and had called together his kinsmen and close friends. When Peter arrived Cornelius met him outside and fell down at his feet and 'did him reverence.' But Peter lifted him up, saying, "Stand up, I too am a man." And as he talked with him, he went on in and found many persons gathered; and he said to them, "You yourselves know how unlawful (according to the Jewish belief) it is for a Jew to associate with or to visit anyone of another nation. But God has shown me that I should not call any man common or unclean. So when I was sent for, I came without objection. I ask then why you sent for me." And Cornelius said, "Four days ago about this hour (3 p. m.) I was keeping the ninth (Hebrew) hour of prayer in my house; and behold, a man stood before me in bright apparel, saying, 'Cornelius your prayer has been heard and your alms have been remembered before God. Send therefore to Joppa and ask for Simon who is called Peter; he is lodging in the house of Simon, a tanner, by the seaside.' So I sent to you at once, and you have been kind enough to come. Now, therefore we are all present in the sight of God, to hear all that you have been commanded by the Lord." Thus did the Spirit make use of the two visions to bring Peter to the home of Cornelius in Caesarea (Acts 10:17-33).

Peter had known from Jesus that Gentiles were to be saved by God's plan for the race. Had not Christ commanded the hundred and twenty, saying that they were to be His witnesses to the ends of the earth? But Christianity was not to be imposed on the heathen. Cornelius came knocking at the door, directed by God to do so. Peter could not impose the Gospel on the pagan Romans. God took the initiative in sending the heathen to seek salvation. Cornelius sent in faith to ask Peter to come to Cesarea. His messengers found Peter prepared to welcome them to his hospitality in the home of his Jewish brother Simon on the basis of equality, sitting at the table with the Gentile messengers on the same social plane without discrimination. He was ready also to accompany them to the home of Cornelius in Cesarea on the morrow. After the rest of the night in the hospitable house of Simon the tanner, his brother in Christ but despised by the over-scrupulous Jews, Peter came to feel that Christianity was the great leveler and no man was common or unclean, after all. The shackles of exclusive Judaism were loosened and about to fall away. He would no more "make common" even the Gentiles who came seeking salvation. And thus he went on his way on the next morning in reflective converse with the three Gentiles and a few of his Jewish brethren wisely chosen as eyewitnesses of the event about to take place.

The busy world about Peter and Cornelius knew nothing about the sublime epic taking place in the humble house by the seaside, pointed out to travelers to-day in Joppa as the house of the tanner. The sound of the waters lapping on the nearby shore continue their musical rhythm as they were heard in the night when Peter, sleepless, lay upon his reflective couch and wondered and prayed. The story of this sublime event, couched in the classic Greek tongue by Luke, the consummate historian, has been rendered in elegant modern English which has been used here in its simplicity to recount the details of this divine drama.[16] The streams of age-long history were converging here to be merged in one vastly swollen stream to be, of God's eternal elective purposes for all humanity.

The dialogue of the *dramatis personae* reveals the intense interest of the group of Jews and Gentiles, assembled for the first time amicably, and now in the orderly home of this cultured Roman official in Cesarea. Peter initiates the fascinating inquiry saying, "I ask with what intent ye sent for me?" Whereupon Cornelius recounted the simple story of his vision of the day before and added, "Now, therefore we are all here present before the face of God, to hear all that you have been commanded by the Lord God of the Hebrews to say" (Acts 10:17-33).

---

16. **The Standard Version has been used in this account.**

Then Peter opened his mouth and said (vv. 34ff). "Truly I am perceiving [getting it down] that God shows no partiality in respect to persons but in every nation any one who is fearing him reverently and habitually works righteousness is acceptable to him." Peter seemed to be embarrassed when he came to this point and informally refers to "the word which [God] sent to the sons of Israel." He assumes that Cornelius and his friends had heard about "preaching peace by Jesus Christ." Peter adds bluntly about Jesus Christ, "This one is Lord of all." He goes on rather informally, "You know the word which was proclaimed throughout all Judea, beginning from Galilee, after the baptism which John preached, how God anointed Jesus of Nazareth with the Holy Spirit and with power; how He went about doing good and healing all who were oppressed by the Devil, for God was with Him. And we [Jews here] are witnesses to all that He did both in the country of the Jews and in Jerusalem. They put Him to death, too, by hanging Him on a wooden cross; but God raised Him up on the third day and made Him manifest, not to all the people but to us who were chosen by God as witnesses, we who ate and drank with Him after He rose from the dead. And He commanded us to proclaim to the people, and to testify that He is the one ordained and set apart by God to be Judge of the living and the dead. Furthermore, to Him all the prophets bear witness that every one who believes in Him receives forgiveness of sins through His name." This brief, simple explanation in an informal kind of way held the group enthralled, as the wonderful door to salvation was swinging slowly open to the millions of benighted souls of the Gentile world (Acts 10:34-43).

The substantiation of this miraculous reality was immediately realized in a repetition of the marvelous far-famed experience of Pentecost, before their eyes and in their hearts. "While Peter was yet speaking the Holy Spirit fell on all who heard the word. And the believers from among the circumcised who had come with Peter were thrown into a state of amazement because the Holy Spirit had been poured out even on the Gentiles. For they heard them speaking in tongues and extolling God."

Then Peter expressed his joy by saying, "Can any one forbid water for immersing these who have received the Holy Spirit, just as we have [at Pentecost]?" And he commanded them to be baptized in the name of Jesus Christ, and they were baptized by Jewish companions from Joppa. Then they (Cornelius and his Gentile friends) asked him to remain with them and also his Jewish companions, for some days. Such fellowship would seal the good will of this great hour and would give opportunity for indoctrinating Cornelius and his friends by conversation and proclamation to an expanding group, of the Gospel of the Lord Jesus (Acts 10:44-48).

Peter well understood that this new departure from the beaten track would bring a radical reaction in the Jerusalem church when he should return. He had wisely provided to meet the contention by taking with him some Jewish brethren from the church in Joppa. They were eyewitnesses of all that transpired in the household of Cornelius. The news had spread widely over all

Judea about Peter's opening the door to the Gentiles and so when Peter arrived back in Jerusalem they that were of the circumcision contended with him, saying, "You went in to men uncircumcised and ate with them." But Peter began and expounded the matter in order and recounted in detail his vision on the housetop in the home of Simon the tanner in Joppa. Then he added the story of his going with six messengers, sent by Cornelius the centurion, in obedience to the order of the Holy Spirit, who made known to him that he should go. Next he told of the vision of Cornelius, who had been directed by God to send the messengers to Joppa (11:13-14), and of the descent of the Holy Spirit upon the group of Gentiles after hearing the word preached to them by him, as God had told Cornelius he would do, that they might hear and be saved. God had thus manifested his approval on the message, and the hearers had believed and were given entrance into the kingdom by the explicit direction of the Lord through the Holy Spirit (Acts 11:15-17). Peter's conclusion was final: "If God gave the same gift to them as he gave to us when we believed in the Lord Jesus Christ, who was I that I could withstand God?" When the contenders for the circumcision heard this they were silent. "Contenders for traditional regularity show remarkable facility for ignoring the essential matters and pitching controversies on side issues that are at once concrete and bound up in strong prejudicies."[17] Their ceremonial regulation had been violated. Peter recited the facts of experience and introduced the six Jewish brethren who went with him as witnesses of the whole incident. The church in Jerusalem could not but accept the report and admit the converted Gentiles to fellowship. This vote was a real majority vote but not unanimous. The stubborn minority would yet be heard from, but the door was open once for all to the Gentiles, and Peter's "good brother Paul" would be on hand to help sustain what Peter had done under the Holy Spirit in this great and momentous event in the history of World-evangelization.

Antioch

Barnabas and Saul

The next step in the militant advance of Christianity was the planting of the gospel in a new center, the great Gentile city of Antioch of Syria (Acts 11:19-30). This was the third greatest city in the world, Rome being first and Alexandria second. It was not only large but wealthy. Heathenism, with its grove of Daphne situated there, was tempting and debasing. The Roman prefect with his court was also located there. The city was described for its centrality of position and its general character as "one of the eyes of Asia." There was a large Jewish colony, but the population of the city was mainly Greek.

When the persecution broke out in Jerusalem after Stephen's martyrdom, the believers went everywhere "taking the word to none except Jews." Some

---

17. W. O. Carver, *Commentary on Acts*, p. 118.

went to Phoenicia, some to the island of Cyprus and some to Antioch, all of which were parts of the Gentile territory. And there were some of them, unnamed men of Cyprus and Cyrene, who began to evangelize the Greeks, who were not Hellenistic Jews but (heathen) Gentiles. They found a ready hearing, and the work of the gospel sprang up among the Greeks. This work resulted from no action of the apostles in Jerusalem. But the church in Jerusalem soon knew about it and sent Barnabas of Cyprus, to examine what was being done. When Barnabas reached Antioch he saw "the grace of God" in spiritual evidences on every hand in those Gentiles who had embraced the gospel. This discerning brother made no opposition to the things being done, but stimulated and "encouraged them" to go forward with their work, "cleaving to the Lord Jesus." Barnabas being a good man and full of the Holy Spirit and of faith, many people were added unto the Lord through his help, not just to the church.[18]

This new work among the Gentiles was one more link in the chain which was to bind the world to Christ. Barnabas found that the work in Antioch was independent, being initiated by some laymen Christians without any official capacity at all. But it was genuine, and Barnabas reported it as such and went off to Cilicia to look up Saul of Tarsus, to get him to come over and help in a continuing work of evangelization in Antioch among the Greeks. Saul came, and he and Barnabas carried on a series of evangelistic activities which resulted in a rapid growth until the congregation there came to be called Christian; because of the central place Christ occupied in the teachings of the two evangelists[18] and in the evident Christ-like character of the converts, members of the church (vv. 25, 26). Such was the freedom and independent growth of this young church, such the liberality in giving, such the warmth of fellowship, that knowing of the needs of the poor of the church in Jerusalem, Saul and Barnabas were sent by the church with a gift to these fellow Christians of the Jews in the Jerusalem church. This act of genuine brotherliness expressed the spirit of a real unity, which constitutes a landmark in the history of primitive Christianity in its expansion into the Gentile world. It was the initiation of this idea, which in the hands of Saul (otherwise called Paul), later in the expanding movement of Christianity became a policy in all the Gentile churches, and proved to be a strong tie to hold the Jewish and Gentile elements in the churches together when Jewish exclusivism threatened to break Christianity up into two great partisan groups. Paul succeeded with this policy then, and but recently the gifts of Christians of America to millions of other Christians of many nations have been but a continuation of Paul's Christian policy which started in the Antioch church. This policy is one of the mightiest forces to open the doors of heathen homes in the world today to the entrance of Christianity and to bring about such good will among the nations that it promises to result in permanent peace, in the realization of the "family of man."

The rapid expansion of Christianity is usually preceded and followed by the intensifying of the persecuting antagonism of the forces of darkness in the

18. Notice the punctuation.

world. It is not strange that when the apostles began to go forth from Jerusalem to evangelize Judea and even Samaria, not only the prejudices of Jewish exclusivism were fanned into a blaze inside the church, seeking to keep the Gentiles out, but also the antagonism of the Saddusaic and Pharisaic elements flared up in a persecution from without by the civil authorities (Acts 12:1-25). This persecution broke out violently during the Feast of the Passover, when Herod Agrippa the grandson of Herod the Great had become sole ruler over all the tetrarchies of Palestine. He became greatly exalted in the favor of the Roman Emperor Claudius in 41 A. D. and assumed the role of defender of the Jewish laws. The Christian apostles were not in favor with the Jewish leaders and representation was made against James on some count unknown to us. Not a few Christians suffered persecution but James, the brother of John and one of the three apostles of the inmost circle of Jesus' companionship, was beheaded, being the first martyr among the apostles. According to tradition, he was betrayed by one of his disciple-brothers, who, when James was being led on the way to his execution came and fell down at his feet confessing to him his act of disloyalty, and was forgiven by his teacher the apostle, and joined him in martyrdom a few moments later. The slaying of James made for the popularity of Herod with the Jewish authorities and so he next seized upon Peter, the leader of the apostolic group, and cast him in prison, pending his trial and execution after the Passover. He was kept under strict guard but "prayer was made earnestly by the church to God for him," and Peter was delivered by the angel sent by the Lord Jesus. After passing by the home of John Mark's mother, a sister of Barnabas, and making known his miraculous deliverance to them, he went on his way. Herod had the guards executed who had been chained to Peter in his imprisonment, and, when he had sought for Peter unsuccessfully, he left Jerusalem and went down to Cesarea, his official capital, and tarried there. It would not be long until Herod Agrippa's course would be ended. He had slain James, one of the intimate group of three who had been with Jesus all the way from the first day of his ministry. Herod met with a tragic death when he had been acclaimed as a God by the people of Tyre and Sidon, in flattery, when they came and sought peace and financial aid for their country. Filled with *ego* at the flattery of being called God, and coming to the end of a beastly life of lust, he was eaten of worms and gave up the ghost.

Luke finishes his narrative of the Jewish Hellenistic Christian movement with a note of prosperity and victory for the church, "And Barnabas and Saul, when they had fulfilled their ministration [of alms] returned from Jerusalem, taking with them John, whose surname was Mark."

Part II

MISSIONARY EXPANSION OF CHRISTIANITY

CHAPTER VII

Initiation of the World Campaign for Christianity

First Mission in Asia Minor

THE SECOND main division of the book of Acts (13:1-29:30) narrates the expansion of Christianity from Antioch of Syria through Asia Minor (13:4b-16:4), through Macedonia and Greece (16:6-19:19), and to Rome (19:21-28:30).

Moffatt analyzes the book of Acts: "*an account of some deeds of the Holy Spirit of Jesus Christ, performed through some of the apostles, notably Peter and Paul,*" citing it as "the triumphant extension of the Christian faith from Jerusalem to Rome." His analysis is interesting as an interpretation of the book. The first part covers chapters one to twelve as follows: First, the description of the origin of the church in Jerusalem (1:1-6:6); second, its expansion through Palestine including Samaria (6:8-9:30); third, its progress from Judea to Antioch of Syria (9:32-12:23). The second part traces the expansion through Asia Minor (12:25-16:4), then through Macedonia and Greece (16:6-19:19), and finally its culmination in the experiences of Paul as representative of the Gentile Christian gospel and his arrival at Rome (19:21-28:30). The main emphasis of this part is on the work among the Gentiles.[1]

A. The Holy Spirit inaugurates the definite plan of the work through the call of two missionaries, Barnabas and Saul, to the world campaign (13:1-4a). These men were not called by the local church in Antioch. A dozen years before this, Jesus had called Saul to the ministry of His word "before the Nations and Kings and also before the sons of Israel." He had also made known to the Twelve that the campaign was to cover the entire world (Matt. 28:19, 20; Luke 24:46-49). The plan was to be one of a widening movement, in geographic concentric circles from Jerusalem into Judea and Samaria and unto the uttermost parts of the earth (Acts 1:8). The start had already been made in Jerusalem, and it had spread out into Judea and Samaria and even beyond, on a limited scale, after Pentecost, reaching Cyprus, Phoenicia, Antioch of Syria and even as far as Rome and other distant places.

But the principle of the universality of Christianity had not been readily accepted even by the Twelve, who in the beginning had been sent out by Jesus, not to go but "to the lost sheep of the house of Israel." This concentration had

1. Cf. James Moffatt, *Introduction to Literature of the New Testament*, pp. 284, 285. The single verses between the subdivisions are summations.

been for purposes of more efficient training of a force of workers, that expansion might be more rapid and thorough at the opportune moment, at Pentecost. The universality of the religion of Jesus was initiated in His life and ministry and when He stood on the Mount of Olives in the hour of the Ascension. He had repeated the already given final order of the world-wide campaign. Already the Apostles had been, even now, out in Judea, Samaria and other places, preaching to the Hellenistic Jews, Jewish proselytes of various types and 'God-fearers' among the Gentiles in the Jewish congregations in synagogues. The Jewish Christians had finally become willing for the Gentiles to be saved if God would do the saving. Even Peter was convinced and used, in preaching to the "God-fearers" like Cornelius, after the experience on the top of Simon the tanner's house in Joppa. He had led in convincing some of the members of the local Jerusalem church, though some had refused to be convinced of the possibility of Gentile conversion. Gradually, to the open-minded, it had become clear that the Gentiles could be saved without becoming Jews. But the churches were not yet ready to launch a campaign for converting the Gentiles. Saul had spent seven years, perhaps nine, of his first years in the ministry, preaching mainly in the Jewish synagogues, first in Damascus, and later in the congregations in Tarsus, Cilicia and Syria. He had twice attempted to work in Jerusalem among the Jews who had stoned Stephen, and finally the Lord had appeared again in vision to him in the temple and given him the positive and final word: "I am going to send you to the Nations!" This was after Saul had experienced a year of work in Antioch with Barnabas, an open-minded, good, apostolic man. They had gone down to Jerusalem, with the contribution raised by the mostly Gentile church in Antioch of Syria, to help the "poor saints in Jerusalem," a good many of whom were Hellenistic Jews. He and Barnabas had become thoroughly accustomed to the fact that the gospel of Jesus could save all kinds of people indiscriminately, without conformity to any ceremonial requirements such as circumcision. They were now ready for the leadership of the world-wide campaign, though Barnabas had received no express call like Saul in his vision of Jesus in the Damascus road and later in the temple.

But the church was not ready for such a world-wide campaign. Indeed the real missionary character of Christianity, and this is true in all Christian churches in many places have never become thoroughly conscious of history even unto the present day. There were a few of the leaders like Barnabas who had come to have a world-consciousness. In the church in Antioch the idea had grown, and after Peter's work in the home of Cornelius in Cesarea a number of the leaders in the Jerusalem church had fully accepted the staggering conception of the world-wide task. But even the local church in Antioch, was not fully committed, and certainly the church in Jerusalem was not ready to take any initiative in such a world-wide campaign, which would from its very scope be destined mainly for the evangelization of the Gentiles. The campaign for the universal evangelization must ultimately count on the back-

2. Cf. Dr. J. A. Broadus, *Three Lectures on Missions,* in loco.

ing of the local churches, but it would always count primarily on the individual Christian,[2] *impressed* by the Lord Jesus through the Holy Spirit, and separated by the local church under the guidance of the same Spirit for this definite work. This was what took place in the experience of the local church in Antioch, including Barnabas and Saul, two of its leaders.

The mission of Barnabas and Saul is narrated by Luke with terse brevity (Acts 13:1-4a). The Holy Spirit "spoke" to the prophets and teachers (leaders) in the local church in Antioch, which was to become now the center of the world-wide campaign, for reasons innate in the situation in both Jerusalem and in Antioch. He had led in the expanding work in Jerusalem, Judea, and Samaria, by the most evident manifestations of supernatural power in and through the apostles, wherever they had yielded themselves to his leadership. Now he speaks definitely, through his impression of these leaders in their hearts and through the providential unfolding of the will and purpose of Jesus in the church. Luke, the historian, notes here a new start in the providential "opening of a door to the Gentiles" (Acts 14:27). "Now there was at Antioch," "along"[3] or among the membership of the church, three leaders, who were especially excellent in the role of prophet or preacher: Barnabas, Symeon called Niger, possibly the one who bore the cross of Jesus to Calvary, and Lucius from Cyrene, one of the original evangelists, not Luke (Acts 11:20). Two were outstanding in the role of teacher: Manaen, foster-brother of the family of Herod Antipas, and Saul of Tarsus. As these were "carrying on the ministry of prayer and worship-service day after day, in preaching, exhortation and the Jewish fasting" (Luke 18:12), denoting intensity in their search for the will of God, in a great emergency they felt to be upon them, the Spirit spoke to their hearts in emphatic command: "Separate me[4] Barnabas and Saul for the work whereunto I have called them." This positive and urgent order was not directed to the church, to constitute these men apostles. Paul was already an apostle from his conversion (cf. Acts 22:17, 21; 26:17). It was a special consecration of these missionaries for a work they would do in the Gentile world, and jointly, for the next three years.[5] This special work which they would do together, would be finished in three years (Acts 14:27), and it was understood they would come back to assume their usual role in the Antioch church. The local church was now to "release" them for that special task of indefinite duration, and bid them "God-speed" in a farewell service. The evangelizing of the heathen peoples was their work, and for their special infilling with spiritual power a service of fasting and prayer was held, followed by "laying on of hands," symbolic of the infilling of the Spirit for that special task. This was a kind of ordination service for the work of foreign missions, a new and distinct departure in the kingdom enterprise. The whole church was doubtless present and witnessed this symbolic act, though some might not give their approval on

3. Kata.
4. Aorist imperative, Acts 13:2.
5. W. M. Ramsay, *St. Paul the Traveler and Roman Citizen*, p. 67.

the plan. At least the church acquiesced.[6] They wished the missionaries well. The church would not put a stumbling-block in the way, though they might not contribute financially to the support of the work. Many local churches even now are ready to contribute their professed approval, but not their real prayers and financial support, in missionary work. These missionaries were not sent forth by the church as their missionaries but were the "sent ones" or apostles of Jesus under the leadership of the Holy Spirit (Acts 13:4). Barnabas and Saul had to finance themselves. Barnabas had contributed most liberally all he possessed in the Jerusalem church, and now he and Saul must depend solely on Jesus who would go with them (Matt. 28:20). They would encounter persecution. Herod Agrippa I had already beheaded James, of the Twelve, but these apostolic men were not afraid.

The Founding of the Cause in Galatia

B. The Spirit directs the work of these two apostles on an extended missionary tour and campaign for three years, mainly through Asia Minor. Chs. 13:4b-14:28. Barnabas was the leader, being the elder and more experienced of the two men. He had already been in the lead in organizing and developing the campaign in Antioch, bringing Saul there from Tarsus to help him. He was therefore the natural leader in this new departure, and his name was put in the first place in order, by the Spirit. It would never occur to Saul to expect any other plan. John Mark accompanied the two missionaries, probably because he was a young man who was interested in missions, and more probably because he was either a cousin or else a nephew of Barnabas. He desired to help in the great adventure of missions, but his conviction was likely not fully settled at that time. He went along as an *attendant* to help in any way he could practically, and doubtless Barnabas had a hope that he would develop into a real missionary, by coming in vital contact thus with the work of missions. This hope was ultimately realized, but not without some severe testing first. He had not been indicated by the Spirit or the church, but was taken along by Barnabas, and Saul was willing. He could help on the tour as an *amanuensis* and could also participate after a time in the work of baptizing, preaching, and other functions. He learned the work of *amanuensis* well, it would seem, and afterwards helped Peter, from whom he must have treasured up the gospel traditions.[7] We must remember too that Mark was the writer later of the first gospel.

1. The work of the First Missionary Journey was begun in the island of Cyprus, the native place of Barnabas (13:4b-12). *"They, therefore, being sent forth by the Holy Spirit, came down to the harbour Seleucia and thence sailed away to Cyprus"* (v. 4). This island was the former home of Barnabas, who had been a landed-proprietor there, and who would naturally have many friends and acquaintances in the place. This would be one of the reasons why the missionary party would start the work in Cyprus first. It was also only a

6. Robertson, A. T., *Epochs in the Life of Paul*, p. 104.
7. Papias in Eusebius, *History Eccl.* III 39.

few hours from Seleucia, the port of Antioch from whence they sailed. Luke's narrative makes it evident that these missionaries were sent out by the Holy Spirit and not by the local church in Antioch, now known and ridiculed in the town, by being called Christian. The ultimate goal for this first tour was probably Asia Minor, beyond where Saul had worked in Cilicia. The route they took, not to pass through Cilicia, as they were to do a new work among the Gentiles, lay through Cyprus. There were many Jews in Cyprus and a few Christians who had received the gospel from the first persecution, but there were also many "God-fearers" who were accustomed to attend the synagogue services. The missionaries might be able to win some of these Hellenistic Gentiles as they passed through, for Gentile evangelization had already been inaugurated there.

"*And when they reached Salamis they began to proclaim the word of God in the synagogues of the Jews: and they had John also as a subordinate.*" Salamis was the spacious port at the eastern extremity of this important island which was a hundred and sixty miles long. Cyprus was possessed of excellent natural resources, both mineral and vegetable. It had been an Imperial Roman province since 59 B. C., having its seat of government in Paphos, a seaport city located on the western end of the island. Old Paphos, seven miles from the city, had been the center of the licentious worship of Venus. Cyprus boasted of intellectual traditions also, having been the home of Aristos the historian, of Zeno the founder of the Stoic philosophy, and Appolonius the physician.

The evangelistic campaign conducted in the island was not a superficial work. They began the work by proclaiming the Word of God in the synagogues of the Jews. There they would have a nucleus of Jews and open-minded Gentiles (God-fearers) who would listen to their message. They visited all the synagogues, zigzagging back and forth as they went in their journey throughout the island, until they should reach Paphos at the other extremity (v. 6). Luke makes the annals of this tour brief because there was not much to be said, except that they made a complete preaching tour of the whole island, preaching in all the synagogues.

When the apostles had gone through the whole island until they came to Paphos "*they found there a certain man, magician, and false prophet, a Jew by the name of Bar-Jesus*" (son of Jesus or Joshua). This man was singled out for mention by Luke because of his being the leader of the false religion of sorcery which prevailed in the island at that time. He also falsely claimed inspiration as a prophet of religion. He had been taken into the circle of personal friends and counselors of Sergius Paulus, the proconsul (not propraetor) at that time described by Luke as "*a man of understanding.*" This magician, whose Greek name was Elymas, had gained the ear of the proconsul, who having found no satisfaction in the polytheistic religion of the Greeks and Romans was seeking the light even among the abounding soothsayers and sorcerers and their false philosophies. But Sergius Paulus had sufficiently tested out the religious quackery of Elymas not to be blinded completely, as were many others, by the dishonest and self-seeking system of magic, illustrated in Elymas (or Etoimas).[8] He showed his intelligence by *summoning to his presence Barnabas and Saul, to hear, from them, the Word of God.* Traveling philosophers were accustomed in those times to pass through cities and give demonstrations of their philosophic knowledge and skill, seeking thus position as teachers in universities.[9] The magician Elymas was alert to the situation, and, not wishing to run the risk of losing his place among the *comites* of Sergius Paulus, "*stood forth against Barnabas and Saul, seeking to divert the proconsul from the faith,*" in which he was already becoming interested. Here is one of the first encounters of Christianity with false science, philosophy, and religion, linked up together. The error of half-truth in science, wedded to false philosophic hypotheses, has often undermined faith in the realities of the supernatural revelation in Christianity. Priests of false religions also have called in superficial science to aid them in exploiting humanity. Such was the case of this magician, false-prophet. Here youthful Christianity had to face error, heavy with age, in mortal combat. It was a challenge that brought the brilliant young Saul of Tarsus to the front. *Saul, otherwise Paul, filled with the Holy Spirit, looked fixedly at the magician and said*: "*O full of all guile and all villainy,*" of the practice of every trick and form of fraud; "*thou son of the devil,*" and not a son of Jesus (Joshua), motivated as thou art by the father of all lies, the devil, whose prophet thou art; "*thou enemy of every form of righteousness*" by thy very nature and character, "*Wilt thou not cease to pervert the right ways of the Lord*" which are straight? As Saul, henceforth to pass almost exclusively under his Roman name Paul, spoke these spirit-filled words of denunciation, his eyes, ablaze with an almost supernatural intensity, bored into the false prophet and made him tremble with fear.

Paul knew that the intelligence of the proconsul had pierced through the mask of the falsity of the magician. Facing the quaking magician he adds; "*And now see the hand of the Lord is upon thee in a curse and thou shalt be blind, not seeing the sun for a season.*" Mist and darkness or dimness of the eyes fell upon Elymas and he "*goes groping around and continues seeking someone to lead him by the hand.*" It was a victory of the supernatural of the gospel over magical superstitions, superficial science, and false philosophy. The blindness came at once and when Sergius Paulus saw what had actually taken place[10] he began to believe, being convinced of the truth of Christianity. Whether he became more than a "secret disciple" is left to conjecture. He was astounded at the teaching about the Lord Jesus, and it seems that the probable name of a member of his family was later found in a Christian cemetery in Rome. At any rate, the magic art of sorcery had met its fate in the Christian leaders, as it did in Philippi and Ephesus later.

Saul, the Hebrew teacher, turned out to be *Paul, the Roman Citizen,* and in the mission work among the Gentiles in the Roman empire he would be consti-

---

8. Ramsay, W. M., *St. Paul the Traveler and Roman Citizen,* p. 75.
9. Ibid., p. 75.
10. Perfect participle, *to gegonas,* neuter acc. with article.

tuted naturally henceforth the leader of the *teaching, preaching and healing mission.*

Paul and his company sailed from Paphos. He and Barnabas addressed the Gentiles in Antioch of Pisidia and disputed with the Judaizing party at Antioch of Syria on their return. It was Paul who laid out the plan and policy of the work from this time on in "opening the door to the Gentiles." The divine approval was given on this new leadership when Saul faced Elymas and supernatural power left the sorcerer in physical blindness. This change of name is no indication of double authorship of the book of Acts, Weisacker to the contrary.[11] Paul's denunciation checked the sorcerer's career "for a season" and probably ended his favor with the proconsul entirely. At least he was deeply impressed with the teaching about the Lord (v. 12).[12] Paul's natural leadership had worked out naturally, and Barnabas was not jealous. The change was called forth by the needs of the Gentile field, and God's manifest approval was upon it.

2. In Perga, John Mark leaves the missionary party and returns to Jerusalem (13:13). *"Paul and his company set sail from Paphos and came to Perga in the province of Pamphylia, and John* (Mark) *departed from them and returned to Jerusalem"* (13:13). Paul is now in the lead and henceforth will take the initiative in working out the plan of the campaign. He will soon manifest statesmanship in the selection of strategic centers in the empire which will be embraced in his vision and plan for the gospel. He will have to do with the plan, to so conduct the work as to plant it in these strategic places and nourish the small beginnings gradually into vital churches, from which the light will irradiate to the surrounding regions. *He will plan his work in terms of provinces of the empire* to be evangelized from the strategic cities as centers.

The first province to be entered was Pamphylia, in the lowlands of Asia Minor, up the coast from Cyprus a hundred and seventy-five miles. Paul had work in the adjoining provinces of Cilicia and Syria; and Pamphylia, being the nearest province to the west was the logical territory to cover next. The capital of this province was Perga, which was the center of the worship of Diana, having a temple to this goddess on a neighboring eminence.[13] This capital city, six miles from the sea, would be the strategic place to begin the work of the gospel. The province was a fertile country well-watered by several streams, and there were other towns which would be evangelized from this capital. Moreover, the population embraced a considerable percentage of Jews, some of whom were in Jerusalem at Pentecost, returning with the Gospel, which then would be known here at least by some already. Passing the port Attaleia at the mouth of the river Cestros, their boat proceeded six miles up stream to Perga, where the missionary group disembarked in the enervating humid heat of a lowland climate. Paul had passed through the experimental effort in Cyprus, and the outcome of the work had not seemed to be very gratifying or

---

11. Ramsay, W. M., *St. Paul the Traveler and Roman Citizen*, p. 86.
12. Objective genitive.
13. Smith, David; *Life and Letters of St. Paul*, p. 87.

fruitful. The first impression of Perga led him to pause and evaluate the situation carefully, and he was soon led spiritually to the conclusion that they should go forward to the province of Pisidia, further to the interior. This was doubtless not decided without the full consent of Barnabas, after consultation and prayer together. It is here that Luke sets forth the fact without comment that John Mark left them and returned to his mother's home in Jerusalem. *"But Paul and Barnabas, passing from Perga through*[14] the northern section of Pamphylia, *came to Pisidian Antioch."*

While Luke did not cite any reason for the sudden decision of John Mark to leave the missionary group and return at this time, we are not left wholly in the dark. Paul specifically charged Mark later with the desertion of his post (Acts 15:39).[15] There have been various conjectures as to his abandonment of the work. That he was a young man of real worth we cannot doubt by the final results of his life. Perhaps he was not pleased with the change in the leadership of the missionary group. His uncle Barnabas was a great and good man. The new policy of Paul called for greater sacrifice than he had forseen. Barnabas might have remained in Cyprus had he continued in the superintendency, but Paul planned to go forward by the perilous route through the Taurus mountains where there were many robbers to be faced and swollen mountain torrents to be crossed. Some have suggested that with a brief stay in Perga Paul had contracted malaria, which made it necessary to seek relief from the mosquito-infested lowlands of the coastal regions by going to the higher altitudes of Pisidia. Evidences of this malaria are traced by some in his chronic malady later referred to as his "thorn in the flesh." Whether this theory be true or not, the fact remains that Paul and Barnabas decided to go forward and Mark did not continue with them. Later Paul will not consent, when Barnabas desired to take Mark along on the second missionary tour. Mark would have to prove himself a good soldier, ready to endure hardness and privations, before Paul will deposit his confidence in him again. But Mark did regain the confidence of Paul and became 'useful' to the old hero of the cross in his last years of incomparable service. Such a young man would have a better reason for returning than a mere trivial homesickness, even if he did merit the sharp reproof of Paul for considering too lightly the seriousness and the high privilege of fellowship in a great kingdom task. But a young man's mistake is excused when he overcomes afterwards.

Antioch, Capital of Pisidia

3.The experiences of success and trial in Pisidian Antioch recounted by Luke, with the first specimen of Paul's preaching (13:14-52).

a. When Paul and Barnabas left the low coastal region of Pamphylia to go to Pisidian Antioch, whose altitude was 3600 feet above sea level, they did not tarry, but simply hurried across the irregular and perilous country of the

---

14. *Dielthontes,* passing through.
15. Robertson, A. T., *Word Pictures,* p. 185 (Acts).

Taurus Mountains (13:6), and pressed on to Antioch in the Roman province of Galatia. Antioch was a city of the Phrygian region or district in Southern Galatia.

The population in the city of Antioch was mainly Greek, but the Jews had been granted citizenship by the Roman government in 6 B. C., and there was already a large Jewish community in the city. The southern part of Galatia was densely populated, a veritable bee-hive, and Antioch was its most important center. Southern Galatia embraced part of Phrygia, Pisidia and Lycaonia. The northern part or Galatia proper was the old home of the Celts (Gauls). The term Region of Galatia (16:6; 18:23; Gal. 1:2) may include in the language of Paul both the northern and southern parts. One would like to think that the work of Paul covered the northern region, including the cities of Ancyra, Pessino, Tavium, and others. But it seems more probable that Luke used the term Galatia in the ethrographic sense, as Pisidia, Lycaonia, Phrygia and Mysia. This would seem to be Paul's usage also, as he thought of his work in terms of the provinces. This South Galatian theory seems to cover the natural way of interpreting the usage of both Paul and Luke.[16]

Paul states in his letter to the Galatian churches later that it was because of his physical infirmities that he made his first visit to Galatia.[17] It is altogether within reason that he contracted malaria in Cyprus, which had been aggravated soon after by the enervating atmosphere of the lowlands of Pamphylia. Moreover, the strain of the work in Paphos had left him in a condition that he could not with advantage prosecute the work in Pamphylia at this time. At any rate, Pisidian Antioch would be a center from which he could reach the city of Perga and the towns of the coastal region of Pamphylia later, and in Antioch he would recover from the distressing attacks of the periodically recurring infirmity of malaria, which incapacitated him for the strenuous work of his campaign among the Gentiles.

The Galatians proved to be sympathetic and did not despise nor reject Paul's physical infirmity, but "received him as an angel (messenger) of God" (Gal. 4:13). It was one of the greatest blessings that ever came to Paul when he met here Doctor Luke, a Greek physician, who was according to tradition a proselyte to Judaism, probably a "God-fearer" or "proselyte of the gate," who was attracted by the pure ideals of the Jewish religion and shared in its worship, without submitting to the ceremonial rites of the Mosaic law! He was probably Paul's physician in Antioch and became one of his earnest disciples and dearest friends in subsequent years.[18]

Paul had experienced a trying journey through the mountains (II Cor. 11:26) and when he arrived in Pisidian Antioch he had need of rest for several days before renewing his strenuous missionary activities. But with Doctor Luke's help he reacted rapidly and was soon on foot again, ready to meet the first intense effort to effect an entrance among the Gentiles.

---

16. Robertson, A. T., *Epochs in the Life of Paul*, pp. 110, 111. Cf. W. M. Ramsay, *Paul the Traveler and Roman Citizen*, in loco.
17. Ramsay, W. M., *St. Paul the Traveler and Roman Citizen*, p. 92.
18. Smith, David: *Life and Letters of St. Paul*, App. IV, in loco.

Nothing is said by Luke as to just how long it was before Paul preached his first sermon in the Synagogue in Antioch. It would not be like these zealous missionaries to remain very long in the city without seeking contact with the Jewish leaders in the synagogue worship. It might have been as much as a fortnight, not more, before they made their first appearance in the synagogue.[19] Luke, who in after years reported it in his Second Treatise (Acts 14:16-43) was probably present and heard sympathetically the sermon, which left so deep an impression on all who were present.

Paul and Barnabas came into the Synagogue on the Sabbath day and took their places unostentatiously among the worshippers. But they did not enter unobserved nor was their presence unknown in the city. Doctor Luke and Barnabas would have made known, through acquaintances already formed, that the visitors would be present in the worship service of the following Sabbath.

b. Paul's Sermon, Acts 14:16-43.

After the reading, in the assembly, of the Scriptures from the Septuagint, one passage from the Law (Deut. 1:31-39), and one from the Prophets (Isaiah 1:2) the Rulers of the Synagogue sent to the apostles, saying: *Gentlemen, Brethren, if*[20] *there is in you a word of encouragement or exhortation to the people, say on."* It was customary for the rabbis to sit while speaking in a special chair at the front, destined for the speaker. But Paul stood, while speaking, after the manner of the Roman orators. This would attract the special attention of his Gentile hearers. He based his address (vs. 16-41) on the passages of Scripture read Deuteronomy 1, naturally suggesting the historical retrospect, and Isaiah 1, the promise of the remission of sins. Luke dramatically describes the attitude of the speaker, who claimed the attention of the people by a characteristic wave of his right hand. This was not an artificial, made-up discourse, which was put in the mouth of Paul by Luke or someone else,[21] but the record of a real sermon by a dynamic speaker. Luke might have taken notes himself from the address on that same occasion, or he might have had Paul's own notes which would certainly be preserved by the speaker. We know that Luke made "accurate" use of all the veridical documents he could lay hands on in writing his first and second treaties of the gospel of Jesus (Luke 1:1-4). We should be grateful for this *bona fide* report of the first sermon of Paul as he projects the great work of evangelization in this important Galatic Region or District.

The *theme* of the sermon presents the same doctrinal understanding as the first preaching of Paul in Damascus (Acts 9:20). He here proclaimed Jesus as the Son of God and speaks of His resurrection (13:30). The Messiahship is also proven by the testimony of the resurrection (32, 34). Around this theme he built up his arguments.

---

19. Smith, David: *Ibid*, Appendix I.
20. First class condition indicating invitation to speak.
21. This is after the manner of some critics of the school of Form Criticism.

The analysis of Pauls address shows a skillful exposition of the texts, which were read customarily by the Jews at that particular time each year. Deuteronomy 1:31-38 refers to the history of Israel, and Paul, like Stephen, in the first division of his address, reviews the history from Moses to David, proving that Jesus was the Messiah, sprung from the Davidic line (vs. 17-22). In the second main division referring to remission of sins (Isaiah 1:2) he sets Jesus forth as the Savior for Israel (vs. 23-37), who is the fulfillment of prophecy. Finally he winds up with an appeal, in a word of encouragement, (which had been suggested in their invitation to him to speak), and with a warning against the rejection of the message, which had begun to be apparent in the attitude of the Jewish leaders (vs. 38-41).

Paul began his address in terms both polite and conciliatory. There were two classes to whom he must direct his words: the Jews, whom he tactfully put in the first place, and the "God-fearers" or proselytes of the gate, who could be found in almost every Jewish synagogue of the *Diaspora.*

Dealing with the historic division of his address, he observed first that God chose a nation, exalted it, and delivered it from Egypt (v. 17); second, that he provided for them during forty years in the desert and finally brought his people into Canaan (vs. 18, 19); third, that he gave them judges and prophets and at last a King when they demanded it (vs. 20, 21); finally, he raised up David, a King after his own heart, from whose seed the promised Messiah-Savior should come (v. 22). This was the line of argument that Stephen had followed, but the point of view and emphasis in the interpretation of Stephen was that of the ingratitude of Israel toward God and their interference, opposition, and revolt; while in Paul's discourse the Messianic promise and its fulfillment is emphasized.[22]

In the second main division of his discourse, Paul proved that Jesus was the fulfillment of this Messianic promise in David, being the great Deliverer and Savior. This he argued first from the testimony of John the Baptist who was the forerunner to prepare the way, according to prophecy, for the coming of the Messiah-Savior (vs. 24-25). His second argument showed the fulfillment of prophecy in the rejection of Jesus the Messiah (vs. 26-29), resulting in His sufferings and death. The mention of the *burial* is characteristically Pauline, being essential to his ethical conception of faith and baptism (Rom. 6:3, 4). The third and final argument was based on the witness of the resurrection to the Messiahship. In this argument, Paul cited Psalms 2 and 16 and Isaiah 55, as also the testimony of eyewitnesses of the resurrection, who were yet alive (vv. 30-37).

In the third main division of his discourse, he encouraged his hearers, reminding them that there is for them remission of sins, impossible through the Law of Moses but guaranteed now through the atoning death of Jesus, through whom they may receive justification by faith. His closing word is a passionate appeal and warning based on Heb. 1:5 (vs. 30-41).

---

22. Sabatier, A.; *The Apostle Paul,* p. 100.

When the discourse was concluded, many requested that the discussion should be continued on the next Sabbath. When the synagogue service closed and the congregation began to scatter, many Jews and devoted Gentile proselytes followed Paul and Barnabas out of the synagogue, begging them to continue the exposition of these doctrines on the following Sabbath. These apostles, recognizing the delicacy of the situation, continued conversing earnestly with them by repeated words of counsel to remain steadfast in the sphere of God's loving favor (vs. 42, 43).

In this masterly sermon, showing his skillful adaptation of the message to the delicate situation, Paul left a deposit of some of the fundamental doctrines, which would be elaborated later in his great epistles to the Galatians and Romans. The identification of the spiritual Messiah with the Savior, who was for both Israel and the Gentiles; the relationship between the law of Moses and faith, in the justification of men; the fundamental place of the atoning death and the resurrection of Jesus in the plan of man's redemption, through the remission of his sins; the germ-seed of these and other great doctrines were surely planted in the hearts of the people through this sermon. We shall find the same doctrines repeated and developed more and more in Paul's other speeches at Lystra, Athens, in the tower Antonia in Jerusalem, before Felix and Agrippa, and in Rome: briefly recorded in Luke's inimitable record of the Acts. Paul's sermon was beyond measure successful, and stirred the people deeply. The Jewish leaders were on hand on the next Sabbath to protect the traditional faith.

c. The apostles are rejected by the Jewish leaders and turn to the evangelization of the Gentiles (vs. 44-49). These new doctrines produced such a sensation that "almost the whole city was gathered together to hear the word of God." The issue was joined at last. Paul and Barnabas were offering in the gospel of Jesus salvation to the Jew and Gentile alike, on the same identical terms of faith in Jesus. The Jewish leaders were concerned about this attitude toward the Law of Moses. They were not pleased when the Greeks and representatives from other Gentile nations crowded into their synagogue and were received on equal footing with the Jews. Filed with a jealous "zeal," they openly contradicted the preacher in his teachings, interrupting his sermon, railing at him, and accusing the apostles of blaspheming.

When things reached this crisis, Paul and Barnabas joined in a bold declaration, that they were under the orders of Jesus to preach first to the Jews the Word of God, but since they had Jewish leaders who deliberately thrust it aside and had not judged themselves worthy of eternal life, they would now turn to the Gentiles. They quoted the authority of the prophecy of Isaiah (49:6) in justification of this decision: "I have set thee, Christ,[23] for a light of the Gentiles, that thou shouldest be for salvation unto the uttermost part of the earth." The Jewish leaders did not know this Scripture but the preacher knew it and was justified in this far-reaching decision.

23. Interpretation.

d. Persecution of the missionaries Paul and Barnabas, and their departure to Iconium, leaving joy and the Holy Spirit in the disciples (vs. 48-52).

The announcement of this drastic decision might bring some anxiety to the apostles, but Jesus would take care of the results. It was the talk of the town. The fanaticism of the Jewish leaders was thoroughly aroused. Those among the Gentiles, who had been elected, believed and were filled with gladness and glorified God (v. 48b). The evangelization of the region, mainly among the Gentiles, went forward rapidly. This successful outcome of the work angered the Jewish leaders more and more and they went about to stop the apostles by securing the cooperation and arousing some of the women of high social and political connections, who were accustomed to attend the synagogue worship, that they should get the civil authorities to intervene in the matter. The result was the apostles were driven out of this section of the region. They protested against such treatment by the method recommended by their Master (Mark 10:14b). When they were escorted to the gates of the city and cast forth, they left the indelible impression on their persecutors of their protest by the solemn act of shaking off the dust of their feet as a testimony against them (v. 51). But the disciples they left behind were full of joy and the Holy Spirit, whose presence was manifested in their bold testimony and prosecution of the work. When they were hurled off the borders of the region of Antioch, they came to Iconium.

Iconium

4. Great success in Iconium through the extraordinary power of the Holy Spirit in the Apostles is met by strong opposition and persecution by the Jews and Gentiles (14:1-6). It was a distance of about eighty miles that the apostles had to travel to reach the ancient but then growing city of Iconium, which in the time of Hadrian had become a Roman colony and had been honored later by Claudius with the title of Claudiconium. It was in the same region as Antioch,[24] located on the southern margin of the dreary land of Azylus, cold and barren, and on the east of the highlands which reached up to the Taurus, whence flowed abundant streams which watered the region around the town. It was dealt with kindly by nature and has been compared to the ancient city of Damascus in respect to its luxuriant physical environs. The apostles would travel thirty-five miles on the royal road constructed by Augustus from Antioch to Lystra and then continue by a less commodious road the rest of the way to Iconium.[25] The modern Turkish town of Konya has little to remind one of the ancient city of Paul's time, when it was a strategic center of industrial life. The apostles did not enter a new region when they came to Iconium, a town smaller than Antioch, which was the largest city and administrative center of the same province. It was on the border of Lycaonia and was populated by a Gentile people who spoke mainly a native tongue, although many of the inhabitants understood Greek.

---

24. Ramsay, W. M.: *St. Paul the Traveler* etc., p. 109.
25. Smith, David: *Life and Letters of St. Paul*, p. 97.

On arrival in the town, Paul and Barnabas found their way to the synagogue of the Jews. The same experiences happened to them here as in Antioch.[26] They spoke in the synagogue in so winsome a manner, telling the people the wonderful message of good news about the Christ who came to welcome all men without class, nationality, or legal righteousness into His brotherhood of love, that a great crowd of both Jews and Greeks believed. But many jealous, hard-hearted, unbelieving and stubbornly disobedient Jews stirred up and embittered the souls of some of the Gentiles against the brethren, a group of whom already existed in the city (v. 81, 82).

Because of this very success and especially of the opposition too, Paul and Barnabas remained there a "sufficiently extended length of time,"[27] probably six months or more, speaking boldly upon the subject of the Lord (Jesus), who, on His part, went on bearing witness as always to the Word or doctrine about His grace, by granting signs, the seals of His approval, and wonder-miracles which produced amazement in the people, which were performed by their hands (v. 3). These supernatural manifestations of divine approval and power gave the apostles a hold on a good number of both Jews and Gentiles and were the occasion of a division of loyalties in the midst of the Gentile group. Here is the first time Luke called Paul and Barnabas apostles (v.14). This title was afterwards applied by Paul to a number of brethren besides the Twelve, among them James, the Lord's brother, Silvanus, Timothy and a few others, when their spiritual activities became such as to warrant it.

The Jewish leaders were busy and intent on their purpose, and finally, they succeeded in getting enough of the Gentiles on their side to risk bringing the antagonism to a show-down. The opposition of the bad elements, from both the Jews and Gentiles, thus united, was on the verge of breaking out in an onset of insulting insolence and that with the intent of stoning the missionaries. But Paul and Barnabas became aware of the danger of mob violence, and using discretion, withdrew from the city, passing quietly across the borders into the province of Lycaonia and thus out of the jurisdiction of the local authorities of Iconium and Antioch (v. 6). The city authorities did not allow the onset to come to extreme violence; nevertheless, determined Jewish leaders thought they had gained the victory because the "brethren" had to flee. They had carried their point for the time, but the seeds of the gospel had been deeply planted in the hearts of some and would spring up in a new church community later. Paul, Barnabas, and "the brethren," some of whom seem to have gone with them, fled to the cities of Lycaonia, Lystra and Derbe, and the region around these. Paul did use the Roman province as a basic unit in his work. Luke presents the facts about this policy very briefly and leaves the principle of organization to shine through them, according to his usual method.[28]

---

26. *Kata to auto.*
27. Hikanon mēn oun kronon.
28. Ramsay, W. M., *St. Paul the Traveler and Roman Citizen*, pp. 112b.

Lystra

5. The miracle in Lystra was misunderstood and a fickle populace stoned Paul (14:7-20a).

(a) Lystra, which was about twenty miles to the south of Iconium, the terminus of the royal road, was a fortified town and military colony established by Augustus. It was located on the banks of a stream flowing through a pleasant valley, which, like those which watered the environs of Damascus and Iconium, having no outlet to the sea, lost itself in the marshes, here located eastward.[29] Its population consisted of the Roman garrison and mainly of the native peoples who spoke their own dialect, though they understood the Common Greek.[30] There was little commercial activity and no Jewish colony or synagogue there. Paul and Barnabas went to Lystra and remained in the city,[31] working among the Gentiles. There was only one family of Jews, so far as the record goes, living in the town. It is probable that Paul and Barnabas were guests in the home of this family of Eunice, mother of the young man Timothy, whose grandmother Lois also resided with them. The "brethren" who fled with the "apostles" from Iconium, when pelted with stones, carried on the work of evangelization in the region (Chōra) surrounding the Lycaonian cities of Lystra and Derbe, and the entire population was moved at the teaching. The husband of Eunice, apparently long deceased, had been a Gentile; consequently, Timothy had never been circumcised. But both Eunice and Lois were devout Jewesses and had trained Timothy up in their faith, while respecting the loyalties to the Gentile husband.

(b) The cure of the cripple and its results (vs. 8-13). The account of the miracle of Jesus, of the cure of the cripple through Paul, is brief, but a good illustration of Luke's brevity but accuracy in style (Acts 13:6). *"There sat a certain man impotent in his feet, a cripple from his birth, who never walked."* (v. 8) Luke here states five things about the man which leave you completely convinced about his condition. This was a definite (certain) man who was accustomed to having friends[32] bring him and place him in a convenient spot, probably in the market place or near the gate of the town, where many people passed. His purpose naturally was to receive alms because he was impotent in his feet. He had been a cripple from his birth and had never walked.[33]

The preaching of Paul and Barnabas was probably done in the market place or streets of the city near the gates and happened to be near where this cripple was sitting. The apostles had among their transient auditors in this street meeting some Greeks and Romans, but mainly native Galatians of the tribes of fickle heathen peoples of Lycaonia, who, ordinarily, spoke their own peculiar

---

29. Smith, David: *Life and Letters of St. Paul,* in loco.
30. *Koinē*
31. Codex Beza quoted by Ramsay in *St. Paul the Traveler* etc. pp. 113, 114. Difficulties in the text of Acts, which was considered inspired by this ancient document, explained.
32. Imperfect middle, *ekathēto.*
33. First aorist, act., *periepatēsen* with *oudepōte,* statement of a fact about his whole existence or life.

dialect. Paul noted the persistent attention of this cripple.[34] The Bezan text bears a tradition that the man was "in the fear of God" and that he had probably heard through the Jews something about the miracles of Jesus. It is not improbable that Paul himself was preaching at this time about the work of Jesus and especially the divine approval on it in miraculous cures. The preacher, noting in the man an eager interest, fixing[35] his eyes on him intently for some time while preaching, came to the conviction that the cripple demonstrated a strong initial faith and opportune acceptance of the message of the Lord. At a certain moment, the preacher, with his eyes fixed on the man, shocked him by crying out with a loud voice of command: "Get up and stand on your feet, straight!" Immediately "he leaped up with a single bound and began to walk around."[36]

The effect on the heathen population was instantaneous. The traditional Greco-Roman myth of Philemon and Baucis was localized in this neighborhood. According to this legend Jupiter and Mercury, the Greek and Roman Gods, had come down to earth disguised as poor mortals and were turned away by all men save an old couple called Philemon and Baucis[37] at Tyriaeum on the borders of Phrygia and Lycaonia. The story goes that, after the appearance and rejection of the gods, a flood submerged the plain and all those who had turned Jupiter and Mercury from their doors perished, except the old couple who were carried away in safety, their humble dwelling being converted into a temple, in which they afterwards became priests.[38] The natural reaction of this ignorant rabble of the Lycaonian Roman colony was to make sure not to turn away the gods this time. These heathen people, seeing what Paul did, lifted up their voice in the Lycaonian tongue saying: "The Gods have taken the form of men and have come down to us" (v. 11). They took Barnabas, the larger man, stately and of benevolent mien, to be Jupiter, the King of gods and men; and Paul, the interpreter of gods to men, to be Hermes, with the winged feet of a messenger.

They did not wish to incur the disfavor of the gods and bring judgment upon themselves, as in the myth, and so went about to make an offering in honor of the apostles at the gates of the temple of Jupiter in Lystra. In Asia Minor the great God was regularly called by the worshippers, "the God." To the Greeks and Romans "the God" was Zeus or Jupiter. These ignorant heathen peoples of Lycaonia had mixed the Greek and Roman with their own religion and substituted the names of the Greek gods in the place of their own. The priest of the temple of Zeus went about to arrange for a sacrifice to the "visiting gods," and, with the throng of people, came with bulls and garlands, with the desire to offer the sacrifice, outside the city before the temple.

(c) It was at this juncture that Paul and Barnabas, who may have retired after the cure of the cripple to the home of Eunice, became aware of the pur-

34. *ēkouen*, imperfect, continued attention in hearing.
35. *atenisas* aorist active participle.
36. Second aorist middle indicative of hallomai with inchoative imperfect of *peripateo*.
37. Ovid, *Metamorphoses*.
38. Morton, H. V. *In the Steps of Paul*, p. 231, 232.

pose of the crowd, and immediately rushed to the scene, tearing their garments, in the Jewish manner, as a token of their horror, and shouting their remonstrance, said: "*Sirs, what is this that you are doing? We, also, are merely men with natures like your own, who are bringing you the glad news to turn from these vain ones to the true God, the living God, who created the heavens and the earth and the sea and everything in them.*" These "messengers of good news" would have the people turn from their idols and heathen gods to the true God Who is above and "*who in bygone generations had left all the nations to go on in their own ways.*" "Yet he had," in the mercies of nature's provision, "*not left himself without a witness among them,* in that he did good to them, "*giving from heaven rains and fruitful seasons,*" "*filling their hearts with food*[39] *and gladness.*" God is behind the physical world (Furneaux).[40]

When the missionaries reached this point in their explanations, it became difficult for them to restrain the multitudes from doing sacrifice unto them. These were not the Roman colonists, but ignorant heathen peoples of the Lycaonian tribes of barbarians. They could not understand the language well, though they knew something of the *Koinē* Greek in which Paul was speaking to them.

There is no wonder that, disappointed as they were in their disillusionment, they should fall an easy prey to the enemies of Paul, who had arrived at this juncture on the scene from Iconium and Antioch. These Jewish agents came and stirred up the disappointed rabble, and fanned disappointment into a flame of persecution. They persuaded the people and led them personally in stoning Paul, who was the central and more aggressive figure. It looked as if Paul had come to the end of his career now. When he had been struck down and lay senseless, and, to all appearances dead, the instigators of the mob tried to conceal their crime from the Roman authorities by dragging the victim's body away, outside the town. They left him there, thinking that he was dead. When the storm of fury had passed and night drew on, the disciples found out where the mob had placed the body and mournfully and fearfully gathered around the spot where it lay. But they were to receive a joyful surprise, for Paul was not dead but only knocked senseless and left bruised and bleeding from the stones of the mob. Even while they were gathering, grief-stricken and horrified around the body, suddenly Paul recovered his consciousness and sat up. Instantly, young Timothy and Barnabas took him in charge, helped him to his feet, and under cover of the darkness[41] took him to the house of Eunice. The criminal mob would not molest him now, for fear of the Roman authorities. Next morning the apostles, guided by young Timothy and other disciples, departed quietly at an early hour for Derbe, a town located near the border of the Kingdom of Antiochus and Paul's native prov-

---

39. Zeus (Pluvius) was the God of rain but the "great God" was he who gave the rains. (Furneaux)
40. Mercury as the god of merchandise was also the dispenser of food. Paul attributed this to the true and living God.
41. Sahidic version.

ince, Cilicia. Here they would be able to escape the pursuit of their Jewish enemies and rest from the strenuous months of the campaign.

Derbe

6. Many disciples were made at Derbe (20b, 21a). This town on the border of the Roman Empire was some forty miles distant from the pass of the Cilician gates, on the way to Tarsus. Bruised and shaken, Paul made his way slowly, with the assistance[42] of Barnabas, on the way to Derbe, the next day after the terrible experience of stoning. He knew now how Stephen must have felt in Jerusalem when he was being stoned by the Jews, and could recall the vivid scene in which he had played an important but regrettable role. He would remember this experience in Lystra after years, and, when an old man, would write: "once I was stoned," and again, "I bear in my body the marks of the Lord Jesus."

The apostles carried on quietly the work of evangelism in Derbe for a considerable time. Their work was successful and they made many disciples or learners. Luke's account of the work is brief. The city was evangelized. We know that one of the converts was Gaius, who proved to be an active and helpful worker and companion of Paul in the work (Acts 20:4). They had reached the end of their missionary tour in this border city of Derbe. Months had elapsed and it was time to return home. Which way to return was now the question.

The Return Home

7. The return homeward, visiting and strengthening the new churches on the way and reporting on their work to the home church in Antioch of Syria, was perilous, but would be fruitful (vs. 21b-28). Paul and Barnabas might have returned by way of Cilicia and Tarsus, visiting the churches founded there by Paul years before. That would have been the nearest and quickest way; but the new churches of Southern Galatia needed the strengthening and confirmation of their faith, and encouragement to continue firm and faith-filled in the work. In the midst of persecution, their families were subjected to difficult conditions in many places, and the brethren needed encouragement and exhortation to persist faithfully. It must be explained to them why those who believed in Christ must pass through many tribulations in order to come into the full realization at last of the reign of God on earth. The work of the apostles had been terminated suddenly in each of the three strategic cities where they had wrought, on the way out. Now that there had been time for new magistrates to have come into office, in the cities where their persecution had taken place, it was not so likely that they would be molested[43] on their return.

Another phase of the work in those cities, which sorely needed the attention of the apostles, at this stage of development, was that of the better organiza-

---

42. Instrumental case.
43. Ramsay, W. M.: *St. Paul the Traveler and Roman Citizen.* p. 120.

tion of the work of the new churches (v. 23). To this phase they gave special attention on the return journey. Elders or bishops were appointed by public vote of each local church in its respective center. The vote was by show of hands,[44] being a democratic vote, which accurately defines what was the procedure of the apostolic churches (II Cor. 8:10, 19).[45] The seven deacons in Jerusalem were first selected by the church by show of hands and then appointed by the apostles. This same method was used in the selection of elders or bishops (Titus 1:5). It is to be noted that these new churches were Gentile churches and could not or did not use the Jewish synagogues for their worship services. These elders, selected by the churches and appointed afterwards by the apostles in solemn assembly of the local church in each case with prayer and fasting, put the seal of the apostles' approval on them as the responsible pastors, or leaders. These men who were selected were recognized by the churches as peculiarly qualified for the work of the pastor and preacher. They had trusted in Jesus (II Tim. 1:12) and Paul and Barnabas now commend, commit or entrust them to Jesus with confidence.[46]

The journey homeward was comparatively rapid. A well-organized church, with elders or pastors, was left in each city where they had worked, with a season of prayer which was protracted and characterized as to its intensity by fasting. In these final sessions with the brethren, the apostles committed them to the keeping of the Lord in whom their faith was anchored.

After leaving Antioch of Pisidia, their route ran southward to the coast. They passed through the region of Pisidia preaching, and evangelized Adada probably, as they had not tarried there on the way up from Perga when going to Antioch, more than three years ago. The passage of the Taurus mountain fastnesses was attended by perils of swollen rivers and by robbers, which Paul remembered later (II Cor. 11:25). Arriving at Perga they "spoke the Word," perhaps for a short stop, and hastened on to the large port city Attaleia, which they probably evangelized,[47] while waiting for the boat on which they were to sail to Antioch. They had been gone eighteen months and they sailed direct, leaving out Cyprus, eager to get home and give a report of the work to the church in Antioch, for which they had been committed to the grace of God and which they had now completed.

In their report to the church at Antioch, they had a thrilling story to tell. The Jews had not responded to their message but God had "opened the door to the Gentiles" (14:27). God's blessing was manifest on the Gentile churches they had founded. The Jerusalem church had been convinced years before this, that "God gave to the Gentiles repentance for life" (11:18). The conversion of the Gentiles was the large item in their report. It was not an official report they made in Antioch and they made no report at all in Jerusalem

44. *Cheirotonēsantes.* (v. 23).
45. Ramsay, W. M.: *St. Paul the Traveler,* p. 122.
46. Robertson, A. T.: *Word Pictures,* on Acts 14:23.
47. Codex Bezae (D)

until later and then as a mere matter of informing the brethren (15:4). Their missionary cause would contribute to the unity and harmony between the local churches in various parts as it will always do. This church heard from the thrilling accounts of these two missionaries, who took plenty of time to give details, that the new enterprise of missions among the Gentiles had been a real success. These brethren in Antioch had prayed for the work and were more deeply interested henceforth and more convinced.

CHAPTER VIII

The Struggle for Christian Liberty

A Doctrinal Crisis (Acts XV)

THE STORY of the struggle for Christian liberty constitutes one of the most thrilling episodes of all time. It is a continued narrative not yet ended, but building up to its climax and finale at the end of human history. The book of Acts, the Gospel of the Holy Spirit, written by a great missionary historian, companion of Paul, the supreme missionary of all Christianity, is the first chapter in the history of missions, God's message of redemption to mankind.[1]

The scope and aim of this book is to set forth the triumphant extension of primitive Christianity, beginning in Jerusalem, its first great center, and fanning out in concentric circles embracing Judea and Samaria, then Asia Minor, then Greece including Macedonia and Achaia, and finally culminating in Rome,[2] where Paul, its great protagonist, sealed his testimony with his blood in a martyr-death.

Barnabas and Paul had initiated the world campaign of Christian Missions, especially for the Gentiles, starting from the new center, Antioch in Syria, approximately nineteen years (48 A. D.) after the crucifixion of Jesus. They had completed their first missionary journey, covering the rapid evangelization of Cyprus, and central Asia Minor, especially the province of Galatia. Returning home in 49 A. D., they resumed their evangelistic activities in connection with the Antioch church, which had ordained and sent them on the evangelistic tour more than two years before. In their work on this brief tour they had founded a number of important churches in the strategic cities: Antioch of Pisidia, Iconium, Lystra and Derbe, besides evangelizing many other towns and regions. In their work of founding the churches, they had admitted into the membership the Gentile converts, on no other condition than that of faith in Christ. Peter had preceded them fifteen years in opening, under the leadership of the Holy Spirit, the door to Gentile converts on that same basis; God showed his approval and that he had "granted repentance and life to the Gentiles" (Acts 11:18), sending upon the Gentiles the Holy Spirit in Pentecostal manifestation, in the home of Cornelius in Cesarea. This act of God was the unanswerable argument, in Peter's later report to the Jerusalem church, which as a whole accepted it as the final and God-ordained order. But time proved that not all of the Jews were in favor of this decision.

---

1. W. O. Carver, *How the New Testament Came to be Written*, p. 27.
2. James Moffatt, *Introduction to the Literature of the New Testament*, pp. 284, 285.

1. *The origin of the Conference in Jerusalem.*

A considerable time had elapsed since the return of Barnabas and Saul, now Paul and Barnabas, when "certain persons came down from Judea and taught[3] the brethren in Antioch saying, "*except*[4] *ye be circumcised after the custom*[5] *of Moses ye cannot be saved*" (Acts 15:1). These brethren were of a partisan group in the Jerusalem church. They had sent Barnabas up to Antioch when the work had sprung up there just after Pentecost and the persecution following the stoning of Stephen, but he did not return with a report against the work of accepting Gentile converts. On the contrary he remained there and joined in the evangelistic activities, summoning Paul of Tarsus, who had been for nine or ten years a successful and growing evangelist in Cilicia, his home province. This was following Paul's remarkable conversion and his subsequent short visit in Jerusalem, where the good Barnabas, had befriended him (Acts 9), by commending him, the former persecutor, to the Jerusalem church. The Judaizers, who were racially super-zealous and fanatically and narrowly nationalistic, maintained that the Gentiles could not be saved without first becoming proselytes to Judaism. They had fostered the partisan spirit inside the Jerusalem church, creating a Pharisaic party (Acts 11:2; 15:5), which brought on the first schismatic cleavage in primitive Christianity. They were more Pharisaic than Christian, exalting ceremonialism over against spirituality.

Paul and Barnabas had arrived at the opportune moment to meet the subverting, persistent, and progressive campaign to lead this Gentile church astray, for which Paul and Barnabas had labored much before going forth on their missionary journey through Asia Minor. "When these apostles had no little dissension and questioning with them, the church arranged that the missionaries, with certain other brethren of the church, should go up to Jerusalem to consult with the apostles and elders (pastors) about this question" (v. 2). It was not an easy problem to solve. The missionaries could not silence their Judean opponents, who were members of the Jerusalem church. These claimed that the Scriptures were on their side, and argued that God had positively ordered, through his servant Moses, circumcision for the Jews (Gen. 17:14). Moreover, they said neither Jew nor Gentile coming into the fold of Christianity was ceremonially exempt, because the patriarch Abraham administered circumcision to his household, including Ishmael and every male. In previous history the Jews had been the exclusive chosen race and Gentiles must come into Judaism as proselytes, if at all, submitting to the rite of circumcision and all the Law. Now these distinct religious racial customs, though heavy to be borne, yet had come to be considered a badge of superiority, and thus created aristocratic pride in the Jewish people.[6] Furthermore, they expected their Messiah to come and reign over them victoriously, delivering them from their enemy-oppressors.

---

3. Imperfect tense edidaskon, continued action.
4. Ean mē in a third class condition.
5. Associative instrumental case, ethēi.
6. James Stalker: *Life of St. Paul*, pp. 115 ff.

The Christians up to this time had continued to worship in the Temple and synagogues, and the Jewish Christians yet followed out the custom of circumcision and other ceremonies and customs, including those of discrimination in foods and dress. There were also other rules governing their daily lives. Pride and race prejudices are very difficult to overcome, as well as is traditional doctrinal teaching.

Paul had been a zealous Pharisee, going all the lengths in sacrifice and devotion to the Law, but had not found in Judaism the inward peace and joy which he did find when he met Christ in the way to Damascus and learned that He was the Messiah and Savior. He understood full well now that Christ was the sole and only Savior and way of life, freedom, and joy. Now, he must make the choice. If circumcision should be required of the Gentile Christians, his life and the work of the Gospel were doomed to failure. He must defend the independence of the Gospel and Gentile liberty, which had been approved already by the Church in Jerusalem when Peter opened the door to Cornelius. But this former decision of the church must be maintained; otherwise, all his work with Barnabas in the first missionary tour would be lost, and, what was more important, the future freedom of Christianity would be doomed.

2. *The parallel records of the Conference.*

It is necessary to inject here a word of explanation about the two records of Acts 15 and Galatians 2:1-10 which relate to one and the same incident. Dr. A. T. Robertson agrees with Findlay, Art., Paul, in Hastings' *D. B.*, that the above statement is still the position of most scholars. Luke gives the story of the general aspect and Paul of the private dealings with leaders in the conference. Paul was led by special revelation in making this visit. Luke says that they went up by appointment of the church to consult with the apostles and elders. The two accounts are simply supplementary. Paul's account, defending his apostolic authority (Gal. 1 and 2), adds that on this occasion he presented to them a statement of the doctrines of the Gospel, which he, customarily was preaching[7] among the Gentiles, but privately on this occasion, to those of high reputation, probably James, Peter, and John, to ascertain "whether perchance he is running or has run in vain" (v. 2). Paul had no doubt of the truth of his gospel, having received it, as he did, by special revelation from Jesus. But in deference to the leaders of the work in Jerusalem he sought to have their opinion and their understanding approval. He would not submit to the partisan group in the Jerusalem church, which demanded that the Gentile Christians be circumcised, as they had already, in the case of Titus, the Greek. He knew his ground very well, but would the leaders in Jerusalem stand by Gentile liberty which they had voted already, or would they submit to the demands of the reactionary party and return to the beggarly elements of ceremonial Judaism? The Apostle saw the issue clearly and would make the fight to the end in favor of *Christian liberty*.

Paul had not left himself without certain provisions. He had brought Titus, a Greek brother, along, and in going up to Jerusalem he had boldly presented,

7. Historic present tense of Karussō.

in Phoenicia and Samaria, information about the conversions of the Gentiles at Cesarea, Antioch and in many places in the first missionary journey with Barnabas. This caused great joy among these peoples. The silence of Luke about Judea is eloquent of the fact that in Judea, such a report as that of the acceptance of the Gentiles without circumcision, would not be joyfully received by the Jews. Paul did not want to see any schism in Christianity, but he was not willing to purchase Christian unity through the compromise of freedom in Christianity. The weight of the Jerusalem church in this decision would be great. Paul was anxious to have the full approval of the mother church, of which all the apostles were members.

3. *The first public meeting, with the church assembled* (Ch. 15:1-5).

In the first meeting of the Conference, the visiting missionaries from Antioch were accorded the courtesy of presenting, first in the program, their report on the work they had been doing in Asia Minor. The speeches, first of Barnabas, who had been one of the outstanding members of the Jerusalem church previously, followed by that of Paul, once the persecutor of the Christians,[8] but now the most active missionary of the Christian advance movement, were thrilling and convincing, at least to the great majority of the church members in this full assembly.

But the Pharisaic brethren were present and immediately raised the question of circumcision saying, "It is necessary to circumcise them, and to charge them to keep the law of Moses (Acts 15:5). This was the determined attitude and final word of the Judaists and Dr. A. T. Robertson's laconic observation is that the moderator James quickly 'adjourned for dinner,' a convenient parliamentary device to gain time for reflection before further discussion.

It would have been unwise to continue the discussion of this issue in a public debate before a Jerusalem audience composed principally of Jews. The Judaizers were more Jews than Christians, and their boldness is seen in their demand that the Gentile converts also be circumcised, which flew in the face of the previous decision of their church as well as of the teaching of Paul and Barnabas, that the Gentiles should be accepted on the basis of faith alone and without circumcision. These legalists knew that the work of Paul and Barnabas was destined to make Christianity Gentile, within a certain period of time, and consequently render traditional Judaism obsolete. These false brethren had sneaked in, "the heresy-hunters," to spy out the liberty[9] of Paul and Barnabas in Antioch. They did not really agree with the decision of the church in Jerusalem, made several years ago, when the conversion of Cornelius was considered. Paul had provided a test case by bringing his Greek brother Titus along, and the plan proved effective. The false brethren would show Paul and Barnabas that they could not flout this insult in the faces of the Jerusalemites. They had it fully in mind to subject these missionaries in bondage to the ceremonial system (Acts 15:4) by obliging Paul to have Titus circumcised. But Paul and Barnabas had stood up for Gentile liberty and a spiritual Christianity in Anti-

8. *Epochs in the Life of Paul*, p. 127.
9. Galatians 2:4.

och, and they were not afraid to stand for it again. The crisis was precipitated, and Paul accepted the challenge of the Judaists.

Stephen had shown that Christianity was universal in its scope and mission in his speech before the Sanhedrin just before he was stoned.[10] He had declared that it was not limited to the Jerusalem Temple or any one place. Paul understood that the issue before him was the universal and final character of Christianity. It must not continue to figure as a mere sect of Judaism. With him and Barnabas it was not Christ plus circumcision and the Law, but Christ alone.

The Judaizers argued that Christ himself was a Jew and kept the whole Law of Moses. Should Christians not follow Him in this example? Furthermore, the Old Testament had foretold the coming of a Messianic Kingdom, and both Jesus and John, his forerunner, had said that the Christian movement was the Messianic Kingdom. The Christians, including the apostles of Jesus, had until now followed out the ceremonial system of the Jewish worship in the Temple and synagogue services, as well as in circumcision and the keeping of the Law. Was not 'this new idea of Paul and Barnabas' a mere innovation anyway; and did it not imperil the whole Jewish religion and the very existence of the nation? The Judaizers seemed to have much sound argument on their side.

On the other hand, Paul was sure that Jesus had commissioned him to go to the Gentiles and that the divine approval had been gloriously manifested on the ministry of Barnabas in Antioch, where he had assisted him in the work among the Gentiles, as well as in their recent campaign, through Asia Minor. He had received also doubtless from the oral traditions through eyewitnesses, that Jesus had commissioned the disciples to evangelize the whole world (Matt. 28:19, 20). The teachings of the Old Testament about the Messianic reign, bore to Paul's understanding now, a note of universalism. Even recently the apostles in Jerusalem were expanding their work to include Samaria and other regions beyond the borders of Palestine. Christians going back to their homes after Pentecost, and also those scattered by the persecution which grew out of the work of Stephen, were meeting with success in the conversion of the Gentiles in various places. Paul was wholly convinced. The question was, how to wisely meet this crisis so as to avoid a schism in Christianity. They had decided with the church in Antioch that the best plan was that of a deputation, and they had been appointed and had come to meet this very hour of crisis. The church in Antioch had helped with the expenses of their journey to that very purpose. The previous decision about Gentile conversion was in their favor and had been voted years ago by the Jerusalem church. They had not come to Jerusalem now to debate that question afresh, but, taking that as a starting point, to fight for the liberty of the Christian Jews from the bondage of the legal system. The Judaists did raise the question about Titus, demanding that he be circumcised, as Paul had foreseen. To their demand Paul stoutly objected and, "did not yield for an hour (a moment) in subjection to them

---

10. Acts 7.

(Acts 15:5), in order that the truth of the gospel might remain to you," (all generations to come).

4. *A private meeting of the leaders* (v. 6).

A meeting of the apostles and the elders, leaders of the church in Jerusalem, was called to examine this matter. Paul may have requested the calling of such a meeting in order to avoid a heated public debate with the Judaizers. He would talk things over with these leaders in private. He made a full exposition of the doctrinal message he had preached among the Gentiles (Gal. 2:2). These apostles, James, Peter and John, knew that Paul had given the right interpretation of the Christian message because they had heard it from the lips of Jesus Himself. Paul had received the message from Jesus personally on the Damascus road in the vision. He had not come up to Jerusalem to be told what to preach by those who were of high reputation (seeming to be something). Whatever they were, it mattered not to him — God accepts not a man's person — for to Paul those of high reputation communicated nothing to him, but, on the contrary, saw that he was entrusted with the gospel of the uncircumcision just as Peter with that of the circumcision, for the same God who worked in Peter for the apostleship of the circumcision also wrought in Paul for the nations. Paul was not depreciating the person or work of the apostles, but simply asserting, as one item in his argument in defense, the independence of his apostolic authority. So he adds as further evidence of their acceptance and agreement to that independence: "also James, Cephas, and John, knowing the grace given to me, even those (apostles) who are considered to be pillars gave to me and Barnabas the right hand of fellowship as a pledge of their confidence," in order that we should go unto the Gentiles and they to the circumcision. The "only" thing they suggested was; "that we might remember the poor (brethren), which very same thing I made haste to do."[11] Thus ended the private session with the leaders of the Conference, in perfect harmony and agreement as to the unity and cooperation of the sister churches in Jerusalem and Antioch, in their program of work. To this plan Paul gave his consent, that any threatened cleavage or schism in Christianity might be avoided. They were now ready after full democratic discussion among the leaders and unanimous agreement in the end of the session, to call together the Conference, for a final full meeting of the assembly, for the intelligent conclusion of the whole matter. The pillar apostles had admitted the justice of his contention.

5. *The third and final session of the Conference and second public meeting* (Acts 15:7-29).

Paul won a victory in the first two sessions of the Conference. In the final and second public meeting the Judaizers, although wrong in their opposition to the spirituality and universality of Christianity, had a free and full opportunity to discuss and vote as they thought. The discussion was heated and prolonged with equal rights accorded to all in frank and democratic discussion.

At length when the subject had been fully considered from all sides by the brethren, in general, Peter got the floor and presented his views: "Gentlemen

---

11. Galatians 2:6-10.

brethren," said he, "you know that from the early days (of the cause of Christianity) God chose among you, that through me the heathen nations should hear the message of good news and believe it. And God, who knows men's hearts, testified to them by giving them the Holy Spirit, just as He did to us, and in this way He made no discrimination between us and them, because He cleansed their hearts also by faith. Why then do you now go on trying to put God to the test, by placing on the neck of these disciples a yoke, which neither our Jewish forefathers nor we have been able to bear? But, as a matter of fact, we certainly do believe that we are saved through the generous favor of the Lord Jesus in the same manner as they also" (vs. 7b-11).

This speech of Peter's made a deep impression. It took the wind out of the sails of the legalists. Peter was an outstanding aggressive leader of the twelve and a powerful speaker. His opinion was weighty and his personal leadership was such that few would dare to confront him on the floor. The argument he presented was based on personal experience, and the event cited had been observed by eyewitnesses present in this assembly. The fight for the acceptance of Cornelius without circumcision was a matter of past history already. The Judaizers themselves surely recognized from their own experience that the yoke of traditional Judaism was unbearable, and the Gentiles should not be obliged to become Jews in order to enter the brotherhood of Christianity. After all, the common salvation offered to everyone was through the means and intermediate agency of the gracious favor of the divine Lord Jesus Christ. That was the glorious fact for both Jew and Gentile.

The almost painful pause after the speech of Peter showed that the batteries of the opposition had been silenced. The tenseness was broken by Barnabas, who, at this opportune moment arose, and with all the geniality of his attractive and reconciling personality, recounted in tactful language some of the glorious hours of the campaign in Cyprus and Asia Minor, some of the great victories of the grace of the Lord. He knew how to pour oil upon the troubled waters, and when he concluded, Paul with a masterful eloquence rounded out the report of Barnabas by summing up the arguments cogently and tersely, so as to drive home yet more the conviction of a universal, missionary Christianity. The speaker had but a year before been stoned for the cause he was now representing before them. He bore visible marks in his body of the stoning at Lystra. Who could face such an argument, and so touching an appeal (vs. 12, 13).

James, the brother of Jesus, converted after the resurrection of the Lord, who had also been honored by Jesus in a special appearance after He came from the tomb, had become an outstanding leader and a great organizer of the work in Jerusalem. He was classed already with the apostles, and probably at this time had become the pastor of the Jerusalem church. Whether he or John was the presiding officer in this session of the church is incidental, but he was at least the pastor-host and of great influence. His place as a thoroughgoing Jew and leader in the church in Jerusalem would make his opinion of great weight and especially with the Judaizers. James believed in "the law of liberty," and wrote about it during this very year when this Conference met in session (i. e. 50 A. D.).[12] When he rose to speak, there was a tenseness in the eager attention of the legalists in his congregation. The pastor knew them more intimately and sympathetically than anyone else. He began his speech deliberately, begging earnestly their careful attention to what he had to say (vs. 13-21). "Brother men listen to me," he began, Simeon (Simon) has just rehearsed to us how God graciously looked upon and provided for the heathen nations, in order to take from them a people to bear his name. The words of the prophets are in accord with this." He then quoted Amos' declaration about the "rebuilding of David's dwelling" so that "the rest of mankind might earnestly seek God and the chosen ones should come to be saved." On the basis of this agreement of the prophets he sums up in his own inimical way the work of the session, in a suitable declaration to be put in writing. This would offer opportunity for reconciling the brethren of the opposition. It was a fine stroke of the right kind, of a true and tactful policy, and at the same time a constructive measure and real contribution to the content and method of a harmonious Christianity. He laid down here a great principle and method used today. As the pastor of the church, whether in the presiding chair or not, he could exercise a calming and reconciling role in the assembly, and he took full advantage of the opportunity. Starting from the authorities of the Scriptures which he had cited from the Prophets, who were the interpreters of the Jewish Law, he said:

Wherefore I give it as my opinion, we ought not to put difficulties in the way of the Gentiles who are turning to God, but should write them to abstain from all the things which are contaminated by idols, from sexual immorality, from the meat of strangled animals and from the eating of blood. For Moses from ancient generations has had those who preached his doctrines in every town, which on every Sabbath have been read aloud in the synagogues.

Setting his approval on the speech of his good Jewish brother Simeon[13] and on the Law through its prophetic interpreters, he brings to bear the witness of the prophets and ties that up with the Scriptures. and in a beautiful expression with the Apostle of the circumcision in a fine way. They ought not, in his judgment, to lay burdens on the Gentile brothers (v. 17), but in a letter addressed to them individually and in their churches, offer them some counsels and warnings about four certain things which should be avoided by all Christians alike. All four of these things were condemned in the code of Leviticus.[14] This was a wise stroke and appeal to Jewish feelings and the sympathy of the opposers. There was real peril to the new converts, in the Gentile world, of contamination from the idols and prevalent sins of certain types. The restrictions mentioned referred to the moral code. which was to be effective in all Christians alike. Also the Christians were yet worshiping in the Jewish synagogues in many places, and there were opportunities to make many contacts

12. Epistle of James.
13. Aramaic form to make it more Jewish.
14. Leviticus, Chapters 17, 18.

with the "God-fearers" there. This was an important consideration to be remembered. The Gentiles did not have to become Jews by observing these moral restrictions; this fact must be conned by the Jewish brethren if they were to learn the universal character of Christianity.

So, the apostles and elders led the church in passing a resolution which was adopted democratically, if not unanimously (vs. 22-29). Judas and Silas, two members of the Jerusalem church, were chosen by that body to accompany Paul and Barnabas, members of the church in Antioch, to bear the letter, expressing the decision of the joint conference of the two churches, to the churches in Syria and Cilicia.

The letter was not to be a decree or ecclesiastical command, but it contained such counsels as "seemed good" to the members of the united assembly of the two churches to send to Cyprus and the recently founded Gentile churches in Asia. The letter conveyed the approval of the council on the work of Paul and Barnabas, (v. 25) and disclaimed responsibility for the intervention of the Judaizing brethren in Antioch or elsewhere. Gentile liberty was apparently secured, and the Gentiles could become members of Christian churches without conforming to Jewish ceremonies. It was a real victory for Paul, but he would have to pay for it in persecution by false-brethren in many places in his fields of labor in years to come.

Luke, the careful historian, in spite of the usual brevity of his narrative, thought it important to include here, the exact wording of the letter to be sent, which was as follows: "The apostles and presbyters (elders), brothers, send greetings to the brethren, those from the Gentile (group), throughout Antioch and Syria and Cilicia. Since we heard that certain ones from among us troubled you with words, unsettling your minds (souls), quite unauthorized by us (to whom we gave no commandment), we have decided unanimously to select some of our number (it seemed good to us having come to one accord to choose out men) and send them to you with our beloved Barnabas and Paul who have risked their lives (men that have hazarded their lives)[15] for the sake (name) of our Lord Jesus Christ. We have therefore commissioned Judas and Silas who themselves shall tell you the same things by word of mouth. For it seemed good to the Holy Spirit and to us to lay upon you no greater burden than these necessary things: that ye abstain from things sacrificed to idols (Cf. I Cor. 8) and from (the tasting or eating of) blood and animals strangled, and from fornication (sexual vice), from which if you keep yourselves, it shall be well with you. Fare ye well."[16]

With the letter and commendation of the united Assembly the messengers from Antioch and the two brethren, Silas and Judas, appointed by the church in Jerusalem to represent them in the work of communication of the deliberations of the Assembly, went down to Antioch, and assembling the church there,

---

15. The rendering in parenthesis that of the Revised Version, along with Moffatt's translation.

16. Three translations, A., R. V., and Moffatt have been used in a paraphrastic combination.

delivered to them the letter. The brethren in Antioch received gladly the report as well as the verbal account given by the prophets (evangelists), Silas and Judas. They discharged their representatives and informed Silas and Judas they were exonerated from the responsibility of their task.

6. *Peter's defection and Paul's consequent rebuke of him in Antioch.*

This account of Paul's public remonstrance administered to Peter is given by the Apostle in his argument to prove his apostolic independence of all human authority, as stated in the Galatian epistle (Gal. Chs. 1, 2). A statement of his claims to his divine commission (1:11-24) is followed by an account of his visit to Jerusalem to consult on a democratic basis with the apostles and elders of the church there, taking certain other brethren along with him, including Barnabas and Titus. The brief account of the Conference (2:1-10) is followed in time by the account of his rebuke of Peter for his defection in Antioch (2:11-21).

The narrative about the defection is placed by Paul in its logical connection, following the account of the Conference, which was brought on by the free Gospel preached by Paul and Barnabas on their first missionary journey. On the return of the missionaries to Antioch the question became acute and previous reports about their liberal views and liberty, demonstrated in receiving the Gentile converts on the basis of faith alone, brought some of the Judaists to Antioch on a spying mission, to verify the existence of heresy in the work of Paul and Barnabas. Their antagonism was the occasion of the Antioch church's sending Paul and Barnabas and some others to Jerusalem for the Conference. As we have noted, these missionaries were successful in securing the approval of the Apostles and leaders of the Jerusalem church on the work they had done in Asia and on Gentile liberty in the entrance to Christianity through faith alone and without becoming Jewish proselytes, submitting to circumcision and other ceremonies of the Jewish religion. Ramsay presents some strong arguments[17] for placing the defection of Peter before the Jerusalem Conference, but many other authorities prefer what seems to be the more logical and better attested order as given in Paul's narrative (Gal. 2:11-21).

It must have been quite some time after the Conference and return of Paul and Barnabas to Antioch, when Peter, who was heading the mission to the circumcision or Jews, hearing doubtless of the rapid progress of the work in Antioch, decided to go there for a friendly visit. The relationships between the leaders of the two churches in the Conference wound up in the most pleasing and amicable way, with the understanding that there would be a kind of policy of comity observed in their work of missions. In the brief space of this Conference there was little time for mature reflection and earnest seeking for the leadership of the Spirit, and churches in session can fail thus to come to the complete mind of the Spirit in their deliberations and policies. It was doubtless true that the policy for the division of the work along the lines of racial cleavage was lacking in maturity of reflection and in a secure divine

17. W. M. Ramsay: *Paul the Traveler and Roman Citizen*, pp. 155-166.

guidance. The Christianity of the Christ provided for a complete spiritual unity and unalloyed parity of privileges and prerogatives in the constituent elements, without any regard at all for respect of persons, classes or races. When Peter arrived in Antioch he was highly pleased at what he found. Paul seems not to have been present when Peter arrived, and that Apostle was received by the church with a warmth of fellowship which greatly impressed him. The Jewish and Gentile members, with the sincerest fraternity and greatest of enthusiasm, went about their work in a fellowship which it was a blessed privilege to experience. Peter had been the first among the Christian leaders to receive Gentiles into the church on the exclusive faith basis, and he entered into the spirit of liberty and fraternity with the heartiest good will, "eating with the Gentiles" as did Barnabas and Paul. He had received the Gentile messengers from Cornelius into the house of Simon the Tanner in Joppa and ate with them there and in the home of Cornelius in Cesarea (Acts 10:28; 11:3). Now his impulsive, good-natured disposition and true Christian sentiment carried him still further, and the news of this "eating with the Gentiles as Gentiles eat," disregarding any discriminations as to foods, soon came to the ears of the Judaists in Jerusalem. Those enemies of Gentile liberty seized the opportunity to hasten to Antioch and raise again the question of Gentile freedom, which was proving to be a menace to Jewish exclusiveness. The social side had not been emphasized in the Jerusalem Conference. The leaders of that conference had wisely emphasized the religious side, leaving the social side to adjust itself in the process of time. The social side is always the more difficult in dealing with race relations, and social adjustment should be a logical outcome of true religious life and complete understanding of Biblical doctrine.

The Judaists, before leaving Jerusalem, by raising the subject of racial relations between Jews and Gentiles, elicited and possibly secured some expression about the racial relations from James, their pastor, unfavorable or at least ambiguous, which might be quoted in a critical way so as to embarrass Peter on their arrival in Antioch. They had James' approval and were sent by him doubtless to verify some reports that had come back from Antioch. They at least came from James. But there is no record of any message sent by James. On the other hand that apostolic man had agreed with Paul in the Conference, both about Gentile liberty and also especially on the policy of comity. Furthermore, the apostles, including James, had disclaimed any responsibility in connection with the work of "those of the circumcision" who had been disturbing the believers in Antioch (Acts 15:24). The emissaries did actively champion now the cause of circumcision, against Peter in Antioch, and so embarrassed Peter that he began to withdraw gradually[18] from the practice of "eating with the Gentiles as Gentiles eat," disregarding as they did any discrimination in foods, and particularly that which had been previously offered on idol altars. He was unable to resist the argument that Christians should follow the example of Jesus and the Twelve in keeping the whole law and in "living as the Jews."

18. Imperfect tense, inceptive.

The Jewish brethren of the Antioch church withdrew with Peter, and even Barnabas, for the time, was swept from his moorings by their hypocrisy. Evidently Peter and Barnabas had not at first grasped the full import of the teaching of Jesus and only thought of His example in living in full obedience to the Law as a Jew. Now they were abandoning the universality of Christianity, and the evident tendency was to oblige the Gentiles to live as the Jews, observing the whole law. When Paul saw the defection of Peter and the result of his example, bringing schism in the church, he stood up boldly and rebuked him face to face (Gal. 2:14). He did this tactfully, calling attention first to Peter's former participation socially in the Gentile meetings before the Judaist emissaries had arrived. Peter had put aside all racial prejudices and social disequality in this warm fellowship between Jews and Gentiles. He had forgotten in his eagerness and good will all the superficial rules and discrimination about foods, and lived as the Gentiles lived, finding it a most satisfying experience. In fact, by the unanimous judgment of the leaders of the Jerusalem Conference, circumcision, and with it all the ceremonial law of the Mosaic code, had been declared, by implication at least, non-essential in salvation. The fact that Gentiles were being saved in many places without circumcision established this fact, whether they had thought the matter through to its conclusions or not.

But now that the Judaizers had arrived from Jerusalem, Peter had, from fear of the consequences of his eating with the Gentiles, timidly and gradually[19] withdrawn and in an almost imperceptible way left off with practice of eating with the Gentiles and "living in freedom as they lived." This example had already brought on a partial disruption of the Christian unity in the church, when Paul returned and sensed the situation in time to prevent the division. This tendency, he knew, if carried out logically, would wholly destroy the unity in all the Gentile churches where the two races were at present living together in harmony. It would make it necessary for the Gentile converts to be circumcised and obey the whole law if they were to have religious and social fellowship in the church.

Paul grasped the situation and handled it in a masterful way. Turning to Peter, after referring to his spontaneous example before the Judaizers came, he asked; "How is it that thou dost constrain the Gentile Christians to live," (eating) after the Jewish manner in regard to restrictions about foods, thus "compelling them to Judaize," or become Jewish proselytes? (Gal. 2:14). Paul knew that Peter and those who followed him "were not walking in a straightforward way in relation to the truth of the Gospel." The pertinent aim of Paul, which was apparent to all, was to secure Gentile liberty, to maintain the Christian unity in the church in Antioch, and to lay down the conditions which would secure the same unity in all the Gentile churches everywhere. Peter's agreement in the Conference to a policy of comity had been violated by this mistaken example he had set, in withdrawing from the fellowship of the Gen-

---

19. Imperfect tense denoting the effort to cover up his action by a gradual imperceptible withdrawal.

tiles, thus forcing them to Judaize. It was an intrusion into Gentile territory and furthermore it was inconsistent with Peter's speech in the Conference as well as his commitment to the policy of comity. Paul treated Peter with courtesy and Christian consideration, though firmly and boldly. He thus gained his fellow-apostle, and also Barnabas, for the cause of Christian freedom.

Weisacker well said that, "the day in Antioch leads further than the day in Jerusalem."[20] Unity had been secured between the Jews and Gentiles in the Gentile churches. *This would lead ultimately to liberty and freedom for the Jewish Christians also, from all the ceremonial restrictions of the Law.* In the Jerusalem Conference it was implied that Jewish Christians could continue to observe circumcision and all the statutes of the Mosaic code. At the same time it was recognized that none of the restrictions, ceremonial or otherwise, were essential to salvation. Thus the Conference had cut away, without being wholly conscious of the full import of their action, all the supports for the Law as a way of salvation in itself. Paul had years before tried the law out for himself as a devoted and zealous Pharisee and had found it "unable to make man acceptable to God." This stroke in the fight for Christian liberty in Antioch laid the way to open the final action which was already obvious, — to make universally valid this same principle for the Jewish Christian. Paul stated the case in the remaining part of his argument directed later to the Galatians (Gal. 2:15-21), defending his complete apostolic independence, due to the revelation given unto him directly by the personal appearance of Jesus to him as the resurrected and exalted Messiah. The most important part of the incident in Antioch is Paul's address to Peter (2:14-21), which turns into a general review of the relation between the Jews and Gentiles.

---

20. Das Apostolische Zeitalter: p. 169: Cf. Gal. 2:14-21; G. H. Gilbert: The Students' Life of Paul, p. 105.

CHAPTER IX

The Introduction of Christianity into Europe

AFTER returning from the first missionary journey, which covered approximately two years and four months, Paul and Barnabas spent a year in Antioch and surrounding regions, including the visit to Jerusalem. Soon after coming to Antioch, the conflict with the Judaizers was precipitated, leading up to the Conference in Jerusalem nearly a year later. After they returned from that successful conference, they remained for a short time (Acts 15:36) engaged in preaching and teaching, with many others (Gal. 2:11; Acts 15:35). The rapid growth of the work, with the new basis of Gentile liberty confirmed and reinforced, attracted the attention of Peter, who came on a visit and freely entered into the fellowship of the brethren in Antioch without respect of persons or foods. The Judaists in Jerusalem soon learned about this and, "sent by James," came down to verify this irregularity in the conduct of their Jewish leader. Peter, embarrassed by their presence, withdrew his fellowship from the Gentiles in the church and suffered a consequent rebuke, tactfully but firmly administered by Paul, which won both Peter and Paul's good fellow-missionary Barnabas back to the straightforward attitude and conduct relative to the truth of the gospel.

Meantime Judas and Silas had been duly discharged after visiting the churches of the Phrygio-Cilician region in their role of members of the Committee from the Conference. Judas returned to Jerusalem, but Silas chose to remain, after being discharged by the brethren with their peace from his obligation as member of the Committee.[1]

1. *The Inception of the European Tour.*

It must have been with Paul's understanding and consent that Silas remained. The Apostle to the Gentiles had been impressed with the fact that Barnabas was swept by the influence of Peter from his former stand for Gentile liberty. In any case, he would not fail to provide for a good worker, who was a Jerusalem Jew but a stout protagonist of Gentile liberty and one who possessed also the admirable qualification of being, as Paul was, a Roman citizen. Barnabas had lost to Paul the leadership of the missionary party in the first missionary journey, at Paphos, and the young nephew[2] of Barnabas, John Mark, who had been taken along with the uncle as an attendant, turned back from Perga,

---

1. The Bezan Reviser includes v. 34 which is omitted by the great MSS, and many modern editors.
2. Some undertand that Mark was a cousin of Barnabas, instead of a nephew.

playing the role of an apostate for reasons which have been the object of varied speculation of many commentators ever since. He may have disliked the change of leaders of the party, and that is an additional conjecture. It is likely that Barnabas was with Mark in the home of John Mark's parents during the Conference, and, if so, it would furnish a good opportunity for Mark to confess to his uncle his mistake and Barnabas to condone the past and revive the hope of his yet being associated with them in another tour which was in contemplation.

2. *The Second Missionary Journey.*

James Stalker says in his incomparable *Handbook on the Life of St. Paul,* "Indeed this journey was not only the greatest he achieved but, perhaps, the most momentous recorded in the annals of the human race."[3] Paul's restless missionary soul, filled with the inner urge of new fields and greater conquests, coupled with paternal anxiety for the welfare of the Galatian and other churches, proposed to Barnabas his "good" friend that they should visit the churches already established (Acts 15:36). Paul cherished no grudge against Barnabas, whose momentary vacillation in the question of social relationships between the Jews and Gentiles was forgiven, when the "good man" and unselfish friend swung back into line along with Cephas, on the basic principle of social equality and the discarding of racial prejudice. Friendship had been renewed and Paul's invitation to his fellow-missionary of the first tour was whole-souled and sincere.

3. *The Separation of Paul and Barnabas* (Acts 15:36-39).

"Barnabas was minded to take with them John also, who was called Mark (v. 37)." This was a natural suggestion for him to make to Paul, the leader of the missionary party; but Barnabas was a kinsman of Mark; and Paul had been keenly sensitive to that young man's grave fault of deserting their mission at Perga on the first journey and his unwillingness to go to the work in the face of privation and peril. There was no record yet to show that he had recognized his mistake or would prove a persistent and courageous worker in the difficult tasks that faced the missionaries in the present campaign. Barnabas was assured that Mark had the making of a great missionary in him, and insisted on giving him a second trial; but Paul was positive and refused to experiment with him again until he had revealed his worth. The contention became sharp[4] and irritating by the insistence of one and the protest of the other, so that they parted asunder from one another. This was the result[5] of their discussion and disagreement.

Barnabas took along with him his young kinsman, now chastened by the strong reproof of Paul and perhaps stimulated the more to make good in the benevolent companionship of his understanding uncle and loyal friend. They

---

3. James Stalker, *Handbook on the Life of St. Paul,* p. 73.
4. Paroxusmos, irritating contention.
5. Hoste, with the infinitive expressing result.

sailed away from the near-by port from which they had sailed once before, destined again to the port of Salamis on the eastern coast of Cyprus, the old home of Barnabas. The two great missionaries, who had made such a fine record together on the first missionary journey, would never more be associated intimately in the work; but they agreed to disagree and the one missionary stream was separated into two, destined to refresh the souls of many thousands with the water of life. Tradition[6] says that Barnabas remained in Cyprus till his death, and that the Jews burned him outside the gate of Salamis and threw his ashes into the sea.[7] Luke drops Barnabas from his narrative at this place, showing that the sympathy of the Antioch church was with Paul. The stream of missionary history follows in the trail of the Apostle to the Gentiles. "But Paul chose Silas and went forth, being commended by the brethren to the grace of the Lord, and he went through Syria and Cilicia confirming the churches." He seems now to have come to the full consciousness of a complete understanding of his mission to the Gentiles. One of the characteristics of a great missionary leader is his ability to understand men. Paul chose Silas because of his ministry in Antioch, demonstrating his character, preparation and ability to do the work of missions. How to deal with the social question between races was a test to which he was submitted in the Antioch church, and doubtless he was successful. Silas was a Hebrew (Acts 15:22) and a Roman citizen (Acts 16:37). Paul was wise in his choice of such a worker, as the history of the youthful Christianity later proved. His Latin name Silvanus appears in the salutation of the Thessalonian letters. Paul took the initiative in leadership, and Silas was ready to follow this great and highly efficient missionary. The variation between the use of the singular and plural of the verbs indicates the careful training Paul gave Silas, entrusting to him a larger initiative as he went on demonstrating his ability and his loyalty to the plans and methods of the genius of the movement of Christianity (Acts 16:4; 17:2).[8]

The gentleness and sympathy of Barnabas proved a great comfort and at the same time a stimulus to John Mark. Paul himself owed much to Barnabas for his confidence and sympathy which opened the door of friendships to the hearts of the fearful and timid believers in Jerusalem, as they looked upon the erstwhile persecutor of the church when he was being pursued, now by his enemies and theirs, as he fled for his life from ancient Damascus (Acts 9:26, 27). Paul held no grudge against Barnabas, as we may see from kindly references to his old friend in his subsequent letters (Cf. I Cor. 9:6). After the death of Barnabas, Mark appears again and is an example of how a young minister, less often also an older one, may retrieve a fault, recover from a blunder, and become not only efficient and useful in the ministry but win again the good will and confidence of the greatest Christian leaders. Mark later became an efficient amanuensis and helpful companion of Peter[9] and also of

6. Periodoi Barnabae.
7. Acts Barnibae XXIII.
8. W. M. Ramsay, *Paul the Traveler and Roman Citizen*, p. 176, 177.
9. I Peter 5:13.

Paul, who commended him to the Colossians "as a kinsman of Barnabas." Time and God welded the friendship of Paul and Barnabas into the recovery of Mark for a distinguished ministry, in the superlative achievement of giving to Christianity its first and perhaps its greatest source of documents of the Gospel traditions, which both Matthew and Luke, as well as John, used more extensively than any other in the composition of their Gospels. In this most extraordinary service, Mark[10] reincarnated the very spirit of the dynamic personality, terse style, and vivacious message and delivery of Peter, with whom he was intimately associated for many years in the work in Babylon. Both the severity of Paul, and especially the generosity, tenacious sympathy and persistent love of Barnabas, save Mark from turning back permanently, and gave to the world the writer of the first Gospel, and also in the end of Paul's career, one whom he was proud to call his "fellow-laborer, profitable to the ministry" and a minister of comfort to the aged veteran-founder of the Gospel in Asia and Europe, who had so severely reproved him for his role of apostasy.

4. *Visiting the Churches in Galatia* (Acts 15:40-16:5).

Paul with Silas, who took the place of Barnabas, commended to the grace of God by the church in Antioch, set forth with the purpose of visiting the churches already founded, and strengthening the brethren. They did not go by way of Cyprus, as the missionaries had gone in the first missionary journey, because by mutual agreement with Paul, Barnabas was to take that field, with the help of John Mark, as his responsibility. They went therefore by the land route along the picturesque road leading up through the Syrian Gates and across the range of hills down to the port of Alexandretta. Following the shore a few miles, they came to the town of Issus, where Alexander with his small army of Greeks met the Persian hordes and defeated them in a decisive battle, which opened the way for Western (Greek) culture to enter Asia. Paul by the same road was on the way back to Europe to take the triumphant Gospel from the East to the West.

The narrative of Luke passes rapidly over the visit to the churches of Syria and Cilicia, which together constituted a single Roman province. There Paul had labored during some seven to ten years following the date of his conversion (Gal. 1:21). He would meet in this region (Chora) many old acquaintances,[11] and pause long enough to strengthen the brethren of the churches. Judas and Silas had but recently borne the news to these churches, in a letter from the Jerusalem Conference, with reference to Gentile Liberty. Paul would confirm their report and indoctrinate the churches with added explanations. One could wish to know how long he tarried in Tarsus, "no mean city", where he was born and reared, and how he was received there by the church and the people of the town. Doubtless he personally carried the Gospel into not a few homes of that important and strategic center.

10. Philemon 24; Col. 4:10; II Tim. 4:11.
11. Conybeare and Howson, *Life and Epistles of the Apostle Paul.*

But the narrative[12] of Luke is silent on the details of the visit in Cilicia and we hasten on with the missionaries from the sunny plains of Cilicia across the Taurus mountains by the Cilician Gates to Derbe where the first tour had ended. Luke notes Paul as the principal actor in this great drama of Christian history, saying, "*He came also to Derbe and to Lystra and behold a certain disciple was there named Timothy, the Son of a Jewess which believed, but his father was a Greek.*"[13] These two cities, Derbe and Lystra, which constitute a region of the Province of Galatia, had been evangelized by Paul and Barnabas. In the latter, Paul was stoned and almost lost his life.

There is no record of the work of the visit in Derbe. Paul would naturally present the letter, directed by the Jerusalem Conference to the Churches of Syria-Cilicia, but which would be useful here also to define more clearly the relationship between Jews and Gentiles, a question which might disturb the membership of the Galatian Churches later. The Jews had been very antagonistic in Antioch of Pisidia and had followed Paul and Barnabas on to Iconium in the first missionary journey. Paul made known to them that the Christian Jews who believed that salvation was by faith alone might observe, if they desired, the rites of Moses, which had already been fulfilled in Christ. But this constituted no obligation nor rendered any valid help in salvation. On the contrary, he emphasized Gentile liberty and Christian freedom from any obligation to observe the law. This was a hard doctrine for the Jews to receive, even the Jewish Christians.

In Lystra, Paul found another worker and companion for his labors, young Timothy, who was converted when Paul and Barnabas had been there on the first memorable visit to the home of Eunice, Timothy's pious mother, who was a Jewess. The missionaries had doubtless been guests in this home and met Lois the grandmother and possibly Timothy's father who was a Greek. Since then Timothy had developed into a good evangelist whose reputation had spread from Lystra to Iconium, another town closely associated with Lystra in a commercial way (Acts 16:2). Timothy was converted under the ministry of personal evangelism and the influence of the great missionary who suffered such cruel treatment at the hands of the pagan Lycaonians (Tim. 1:1, 2). They wanted to make Gods of him and Barnabas, and when the missionaries protested "that they were but men," these pagans turned upon them and, centering their attention on Paul, the principal actor in the evangelical drama, they stoned him and dragged him forth from the town, leaving his bruised and bleeding body for dead, half concealed in the garbage dump of the town. There the young man Timothy and friends of the family of Eunice found him unconscious, and, under cover of the kindly darkness of the dusk, ministered to him, and, when he revived and was conscious, got him back to the protection of the house. At the approach of dawn, they spirited him away to a distance, whence with the aid of Barnabas, he could make his way to Derbe. This town was located a safe distance from the border of the Region of Lycaonia, from

12. David Smith, *Life and Letters of Paul,* p. 224.
13. Acts 16:1.

whence he might flee to the Regium Antiochi if pursued further by the Jews, who had followed them from Iconium, and had been the prime movers in inciting the mob against the missionaries in Lystra.

In the light of this background of the first visit there, we can understand why Paul on inviting Timothy took Timothy and had him circumcised,[14] to go forth with his missionary party to the work just before them in Iconium and Antioch of Pisidia thus confirming his sincerity in the report on the Jerusalem Conference, that the way was left open to the option of the Jewish Christians for the observance of circumcision and the other ceremonies and rites of their cherished Jewish fathers. His principle of expediency was rightly applicable in this procedure, and there was no inconsistency between this act and that of the refusal to have Titus, a Gentile, circumcised in Jerusalem during the visit at the Conference.[15] In fact, Paul was standing for Gentile liberty there; and here, on the contrary, laying foundations for assuaging the Jewish antagonism in the Galatian towns just ahead, where he had been so bitterly persecuted a few years before. Timothy had not been circumcised earlier, after the usual custom of Jewish families, because his father was a Greek. There were many cases of other marriages of the Jew in the Diaspora and the children sometimes were circumcised, when the Gentile parent might be a proselyte; but other times this rite, administered usually on the eighth day after birth, would be neglected, as it seems it might have been in the case of Timothy.

It was important for the presentation of the Gospel in the region where Timothy was well known to the Jews, that the companion of the one who made it his policy to give the Gospel "to the Jew first," should not himself be an uncircumcised pagan.[16] This act of circumcising Timothy was not one of compromise on the one hand or mere expediency on the other. It was not hypocritical at all, but a piece of consummate statesmanship on the part of one who understood the obstinacy of Jewish race-feeling and who foresaw the damage which the Judaists from Jerusalem might work among the churches of Galatia. Paul was a wise master-builder and made full use of his opportunities to lay down broad and secure foundations in Christ (I Cor. 3:11). His exposition of the "resolutions" of the Jerusalem Conference, which was not a law-making ecclesiastical assembly, but a purely cooperative conference of the two churches, represented by their leaders and other members, was clear; but his time for delay in each place where they stopped was too brief for a thorough indoctrination. The rite performed on Timothy would be more effective than many words, in convincing the Jews everywhere that Paul respected their ancient faith, but that Christianity, far from being a mere sect of Judaism, was the universal and absolute religion for the whole human race. "The Law was

---

14. *Perietemēn*, it is not necessary to interpret this second aorist tense to mean that Paul himself performed the rite on the young man Timothy, though the Jew could, like Abraham, perform the rite. Paul could have had it done by someone in the local synagogue, which seems logical.

15. Conybeare and Howson, *Life of the Apostle Paul*, pp. 228-229.

16. Conybeare and Howson, *Life of the Apostle Paul*, p. 230.

good," but only a preparatory element in salvation, revealing sin and its curse. Salvation was solely through faith in Christ the Redeemer.

Paul had started out to visit the churches which he and Barnabas had already founded, and so he must have gone on to Iconium and Antioch of Pisidia, although neither of these towns is mentioned by Luke's brief notes, probably due in part to the fact that Luke did not join the party, officially at least, until they had come to Troas.[17] Ramsay thinks that Paul fully intended to go forward into the Province of Asia, which was the western part of Asia Minor, surrounding Ephesus its capital; and so it would seem, for the missionary party traversed the Phrigio-Galatic region in that direction. The fact that Iconium and Antioch of Pisidia were not mentioned by Luke might indicate that there was little of special note that took place there, due to Paul's haste to get on to Asia. But it also might be interpreted that Paul found some conditions existing there, in which the better part of wisdom would indicate the policy of not delaying much in these towns for the time. Still, the point of view which doubtless received great emphasis now in Paul's thinking was the vision of a greater work reaching out into other regions yet untouched.[18]

This point of view is borne out by the fact that the Apostle had his eyes fixed on Ephesus, the greatest strategic center of Western Asia Minor. Ramsay has the better argument in holding to the South Galatian theory, though there are strong advocates of the other view.[19]

We know of Christianity in North Galatia in the second century through Pliny. Most of the references of the Galatian epistle apply easily to South Galatian conditions. It seems more natural that the prohibition of the Holy Spirit would come just as Paul was leaving the South Galatian field at Antioch Pisidia rather than in Lystra, unless for some Providential reason it was better that he should not delay in Iconium and Pisidia due to the possibly continued hostility of the Jews, instigated afresh through the intervention of the Judaizers from Jerusalem.

The best exposition of the narrative in the Greek text is that, when Paul finished his work in the Region of Lycaonia, he planned to go on to the Roman Province of Asia, of which Ephesus was the capital; but when the Holy Spirit forbade that he should go to that Province, he turned to the north-west through the Phrigio-Galatic region.[20] Ramsay says that Paul spent little time in the regions of Iconium and Antioch so as not to antagonize the Judaists who were already stirring up trouble when he arrived there. This is also Findlay's explanation which yet leaves the way open for a work "in parenthesis" in north Galatia. Ramsay states that Paul never entered North Galatia at all and that his letter was directed to the South Galatian churches. It is another question about which there has been much discussion, composed mostly of conjecture. Luke hurries over this part of the tour to get to the campaign in Europe. Paul,

17. Weiss on Acts 16:2.
18. Galatians 4:13.
19. Gal. 4:8; 3:3, 4. This condition might apply to the church in Lystra also.
20. A. T. Robertson, *Epochs in the Life of Paul*, p. 143.

when forbidden to go on to Ephesus, turned to the North to enter Bithynia, but again the "Spirit of Jesus," the Holy Spirit, intervened. Paul was determined to enlarge the Campaign in Asia, but God wanted him in Europe. So he "made progress," pressing on through Asia, being forbidden to preach there; and with a still more positive order of the Spirit of Jesus from ever "setting foot in Bithynia" to the north, he turned and pressed forward through Mysia, again not tarrying, with the sole exception, according to tradition, of starting a work near the town Artemaia, sacred to the Goddess Artemis, whose worship he would later combat in Ephesus on the third missionary journey. In all these regions of his passage across Asia Minor, the same expression Luke uses, of "making progress" or hurrying on. The "inner urge" was strong and the supernatural leadership of the Holy Spirit sent by Jesus was evident, whether revealed in the providential happenings, as experienced, for example, in the lives of apostolic missionaries of modern times in the work of Carey, Judson, Livingstone, Hudson Taylor and a host of others; or, as is likely, in visions such as Paul surely had in Troas.

In the statement, "They passed through the Phrygian and Galatic country" (Acts 16:6), we have the geographical recapitulation of the journey implied in verses 4 and 5 preceding. There is no reasonable explanation of this narrative in Acts 16:6-10 that lends itself to the theory of a tour through North Galatia. "The South-Galatian theory follows the test of modern critics and translates it according to the meaning of the documents of the time."[21] Three entire years are required as the maximum time element of this theory, by the most reasonable calculation of most writers on the period. This would not give sufficient time for a work in North Galatia whose principal towns Ancyra, Tavium and Pessinus are far removed the one from the other, in black "uplands, hot and dusty in summer and covered with snow in winter." The argument, based on the syntax of Acts 16:6 and following verses, through the most natural interpretation, places the intervention of the Holy Spirit on the border between the Phrygio-Galatic region and Asia. There Paul turned northward to go into Bithynia; but forbidden to enter that region which was not strategic for the spread of the Gospel, he was led on to Troas where he could see in the distance across the Hellespont, Europe, his divinely chosen destination.

5. *Directed by the Holy Spirit to Europe.*

This strange tour across Asia Minor from Antioch of Syria to Troas on the Hellespont, looked at as a whole, reveals several facts about the work of Paul which are important as bearing on his whole life and ministry. First, that little is revealed as to the work of revisiting the churches already founded, which was proposed as one of the chief aims of the campaign. Would this indicate that the initial effort of Paul and Barnabas had not taken deep root in the hearts of the Galatians? Paul testifies that at first "they had run well." But, Jewish antagonism, which broke out in Antioch of Pisidia on the first visit and

21. W. M. Ramsay, *The Church in the Roman Empire*, p. 83.

had followed them to Iconium and Lystra, had been at work during the years that had elapsed. Second, the work of the missionary party is summed up briefly, as dealing principally with the delivery of the resolutions (decrees) which had been voted by the joint Conference of the two churches, in Jerusalem. Third, it is merely noted that the churches were strengthened in the faith and increased in number day by day (v. 5). Probably the conclusion of Ramsay, that "nothing striking or important occurred in either Iconium or Antioch of Pisidia," is correct. Ramsay was led to insert in his masterly treatment of Luke's brief narrative at this point an account of the desertion of the Galatians, on the theory that the Judaizers followed Paul's party soon and inculcated a wrong interpretation of the "resolutions," "that those Jewish Christians who observed the Law were a grade better and higher than the Gentile Christians and also than Jewish Christians who did not observe it." The Judaizers also attacked Paul's apostolic authority and his character, saying that he diverged from the real apostles, the Twelve, and that he had been inconsistent in circumcising Timothy when he had refused to allow Titus to receive the same rite. But Paul had faithfully delivered the message of the resolutions and it would seem somewhat premature to find the Galatian churches thus strengthened, deserting so soon after Paul's visit, with the skilfully prepared though briefly administered personal indoctrination. Would this call for the writing of his letter to the Galatians before the third missionary tour? It must be admitted that there are some arguments which favor this view as over against weighty evidences of the priority in time of the Thessalonian and Corinthian epistles. No doubt the Judaists would make the best of their opportunity to dog the footsteps of the Apostle and undermine his work wherever it was possible.

The direction of the Holy Spirit in Paul's expanding thought about his mission to the Gentiles was, mainly, in setting bounds to his hopes and plans at this time. He pressed forward, "making progress" in diligent search for wider opportunities for the Gospel, while strengthening the work already planted. But when he came to the boundary of Asia and in sight almost of Ephesus, coveted center of all Asia Minor, where he most desired to station himself in the main stream of commercial and other activity flowing from Europe to Asia, he was instructed by the Holy Spirit, whether through providential measures or a new inner light shed in his heart and mind, or both, not to preach in the Province of Asia. David Smith, following rather the idea of a providential dispensation,[22] thinks that Dr. Luke, who had probably ministered to the missionary recently come to Antioch of Pisidia, from the malarial districts of Cyprus and Pamphylia on the first missionary journey, was instrumental in the hands of a protecting Providence in counseling Paul against the sultry climate and malarial hotbed of the valley of the Lycus and Menander, especially at the season when Paul reappeared in that city. When Paul arrived, he judged it a divine prohibition against his previously conceived plan to go

22. Cf. David Smith, *Life and Letters of St. Paul,* in loco. This explanation not adequate to the clear exegesis of the text. (Author)

to Ephesus, and turned to the North. There at least he would find a more suitable climate, and possibly Dr. Luke offered to attend him on his way and minister to his body, already fatigued by the strenuosity of the work and the travel by foot across from Lystra. On the trip to the North they passed through a region sparsely settled, and this missionary yearned for the multitudes. Coming to Mysia, without finding a strategic field, he turned toward Bithynia, but it proved to be stagnated and unpromising as a place suitable for the strategic dissemination of the Word. The Spirit of Jesus, the Holy Spirit, as director of the activities of a true evangelism such as that of the Master, forbade entrance to that out-of-the-way border Province. It must have come home to the heart of the Apostle, at last, what the mind of the Spirit was, and he turned his face to Europe. It was hard to see why he should be destined to leave Asia, only very partially evangelized, but such was the will of God. Passing through[23] Mysia he came to Troas, full of the historic memories of Europe.

6. *Vision of Paul and Call of Macedonia* (Acts 16:6-10).

At last, in his quest for the field of divine appointment, Paul faced Europe. He had experienced many revelations of various kinds. At every crisis of his ministry, we find that God came to him in a special revelation, sometimes in a vision, other times in a dream. The border-line of the supernatural was always close at hand, and he was sensitive to the leadership of the Spirit in every phase of his life and ministry. In a vision in the night in Troas, he saw *"a certain man, a Macedonian, standing and exhorting him and saying, 'Come over into Macedonia, and help us.' And, when I saw the vision, immediately we sought to go out from Asia into the Province of Macedonia assuredly gathering that God has summoned us to bring the good news to them."* These words of Paul were impressed indelibly on the memory of Luke. He became here or earlier an integral[24] member and part of the missionary party, and notes this fact in his first use of the plural pronoun "WE" in referring to the group of workers. Luke may have come with the party from Antioch, but now he was of the working force. He continued from this time on to be identified with Paul's work as a personal witness. Paul had been led and driven on to Troas.

There in a vision he saw a certain definite man, a Macedonian in his attire and nationality, standing by him and exhorting him. A merely naturalistic interpretation here will not suffice. To say that Luke had connections with Philippi and was the man of Paul's dream may be a half-truth, but this vision was, according to the plainest interpretation, the phraseology, comporting with the extraordinary circumstances and purpose of God in introducing Christianity into Europe, a real vision, as supernatural as that of where Paul saw Jesus on the way to Damascus and came to know that He was the Messiah. *"So on the next day* (v. 11), *we set sail from Troas, and made a straight course to*

---

23. Bezan Reviser (v. 8) "Making a progress through Mysia."
24. Acts 20, 21, 27; W. M. Ramsay, *Paul the Traveler and Roman Citizen*, p. 201.

Samothrace and the day following we came to the harbour Neapolis and thence to Philippi which is the leading city of its division of Macedonia and having the rank of a Roman Colony; and we were in this city tarrying certain days." This account of the crossing over of Luke reveals his love for the sea voyage. It also shows that Paul took his workers into his confidence. Luke became a valuable member in the working force of the Apostle to the Gentiles now and later. He was with Paul and was his ablest interpreter, apart from the autobiographical notes that Paul had. He was the great church historian of the primitive Christianity.

7. *Christianity planted in Philippi* (Acts 16:11-40).

For Paul and his missionary party, the work in Europe was not undertaken with doubt as to the outcome but as a tremendous task in which they depended upon God whose spirit had led them there. Such an attitude relieves mission work from any feeling of uncertainty as to the final result. The tasks of the Kingdom can count on the infinite resources of God, whether in the pioneer work of missions or in the commonplace tasks of the cause anywhere. Paul's leadership under the spirit pressed on immediately upon landing in Neapolis, to Philippi, located ten miles up the river Gaggites.

Philippi, the leading city of its division of Macedonia, had the first place in rank as a Roman colony, not in the mere opinion of Luke who might probably have been a native of the city,[25] but it did actually appear clearly in the preeminence later in history over its rival Amphipolis. That city in the opinion of Paul, also did not rank in strategy with Philippi for the work of the Gospel. Philippi had been made a Roman colony by Octavius (Augustus) with all the regalia of Rome, in the privileges of its citizens, and the autonomous rule by its own chief magistrates called rulers, and its officers the (stratagoi) or lictors. It was a city that reveled in its local pride and in privileges accorded it as a Roman colony. It was situated on the famous Egnation Road, a Roman highway made of cobble-stones, stretching from Dyrrachium to the Hellespont. Its population included Romans, native Greeks (Macedonians), and Asiatics or Orientals, including a small colony of Jews.

Paul tarried for certain days in the city with fellow missionaries, seizing up the situation, before they should launch their missionary campaign (v. 12). It may have been on the first Sabbath day after crossing over into Europe, that, following their accustomed policy of "first to the Jews," they sought out the "place of prayer," outside the gates of the city by the riverside, where a small group of Jewish women were meeting. The fact that there was no Jewish synagogue was indicative of the relative smallness of the colony of Jews in the city. For the convenience of their ablutions, they met beside the river Gaggites. Here Paul and his companions found the small group of women,

25. The evidence that Luke may have been a resident of Antioch of Pisidia, but a native of Macedonia from Philippi, seeking his fortunes in a foreign land seems to the author the most plausible conclusion. Cf. Eusebius, cited, David Smith, Appendix IV. *Life and Letters of St. Paul.* Cf. Ramsay, *St. Paul, Traveler,* pp. 200-9.

among whom one of the leading spirits was a certain Lydia who was a saleswoman from Thyatira, a city of Asia Minor, famous for its dyeing. She was a first-class dealer, judging by her royal purple garments and tapestries, and probably represented some firm of Thyatira having a basaar in Philippi. She was evidently a woman of means and owned her own home, being thus a permanent resident now of this her adopted town. She was probably a widow, since her husband is not mentioned. In Macedonia women were socially accorded special privileges and authority. Coming to the *proseuche* or place of prayer, Paul made himself and his companions known, and opened the conversation about the gospel, in familiar discourse, to those who came. From the first this woman, who had originally come from the Province of Asia, just where Paul had recently planned to take the Gospel when he was forbidden by the Holy Spirit, gladly heard[26] the message, and, through the work of the Holy Spirit, after some days of hearing Paul, her heart was opened to accept the message of salvation. The seal of God was thus placed on the work of Paul in Europe. The conversion of this woman and her household, including doubtless persons of her own family and also employees of her business, was the small but significant nucleus in the founding of one of the most loved of all the churches which owed their origin to the ministry of Paul.

The evidence of the reality of Lydia's heart-change was in her wish to go forward in obedience to the Lord in the ordinance of baptism (immersion).[27] Others of her household followed in her example of profession of faith and also in the symbolic act of baptism, picturing the death, burial and resurrection of Jesus, about which Paul had preached. Another practical evidence of the reality of her regenerated heart was that she threw her home open to receive into its Christian hospitality the entire missionary party, for as long as they should continue in Philippi in their evangelistic activities. Her home became also the temporary meeting place in the city for the little church, the first to be organized in Europe. This church became in many ways the loveliest and dearest of all his churches to the apostle's heart, as is set forth in the wonderful and beautiful message, found in his epistle to it, written when he was in the Lamertine prison when he was already at the sunset hour of his incomparable life. There he felt himself in a strait betwixt two, "to depart and be with Christ which would be far better, or to remain in the flesh which was far more needful for the sake of his dear people in the church."[28]

Christian history in Europe opens with the story of a group of women who were seeking spiritual satisfaction in the worship of the Jews beside the river. Luke preserves in his narratives about Christianity more about women and their relation to Christianity than all the rest of the New Testament writers put together.[29] The Gospel of Paul and Jesus makes no difference between male and female and is not as the Jewish liturgy where "men worshipers offer thanks

26. Imperfect tense of akouō. (v. 14)
27. The primary meaning of the Greek verb baptizein is, to immerse or dip.
28. Phil. 1:23.
29. B. W. Robinson, *The Life of Paul,* p. 121.

that they were not born women." Christianity begins at once to raise the estate of womanhood in Macedonia, when Lydia and her household of children, kindred, and employees became a unit and first nucleus for the formation of the first church planted there. It was not long before another remarkable illustration of this fact so important for Christian history and the world today occurred, in the case of the demonized girl, who was rescued from a life of slavish degradation (Acts 16:16). Luke recounts the incident saying, *And it came to pass, as we were going to the place of prayer, that a certain slave-girl, possessed of a spirit python,* that is a ventriloquist, *met us, which brought her masters* (owners) *much gain by soothsaying* (v. 17). *The same following after Paul and us, kept crying out saying, "these men are the slaves of the God the highest, which announce to you the way of safety* (v. 18)." *And this she did for many days. But Paul being sore troubled turned and said to the spirit, "I charge thee in the name of Jesus the Anointed*[30] *to go out of her." And it went out that very moment.*

Paul's work in Philippi had continued without interruption for many days at the meeting place for prayer in the daytime and perhaps in the home of Lydia at night. Euodia and Syntyche were converted.[31] Then occurred the incident of the divining maid who came under the influence of the Gospel. On the way to the meeting one day Paul and his group of workers were observed by this girl who was possessed of a spirit of divination, connected with the Pythian Oracle of Greek Mythology at Delphi, in which prophetic messages were said to issue from the mouth of the cave of a python. She may have been a ventriloquist, but was probably used by one. A ventriloquist was thought then to act under superhuman influence, attended by power to foretell future events. But this was a case of real demon possession, as truly as those which occurred in the ministry of Jesus, when He addressed the demons in men, and on the same occasion the men who were possessed and possessing the demons by holding on to devils by choice. Paul ordered this demon, which lead captive the demented spirit of the girl, to go out of her. She was a slave to the greed of men and brought much gain to her charlatan masters. When the girl came under the power of the preaching of Paul, she followed him and his fellow-missionaries in the streets and kept on crying out:[32] "These men are preachers, servants of God, the Most High, and are teaching the way of Salvation." When Paul turned to her and cast the demon out by the power of Jesus, the girl, once demented and enslaved to superstition and vice, was freed, and abandoned her owners and their money schemes, which of course brought down their wrath upon the Christian missionaries.

The first conflict of the Gospel in Europe was, thus, with the "vested interests" of a degenerate and godless commercialism, such as has always enslaved humanity and today is exemplified in lotteries, saloons, and gambling-hells, houses of vice, and the militaristic dictatorships and classes of war. Paul

---

30. W. M. Ramsay's rendering, *St. Paul the Traveler and Roman Citizen*, p. 215.
31. Hart, *Judaistic Christianity*, p. 89. Cf. Phil. 4:2.
32. Imperfect tense conveying the idea of repetition.

and Silas, being the outstanding leaders of the Christian group, were "dragged" before the rulers (*archontes*) or magistrates (*praetores*). Whether the girl's masters were Romans (Italians), which is more likely, or Greeks, who outnumbered in population in Philippi, they prided themselves in their (Roman) superiority and austerity. They posed as patriots and stirred up the populace against Paul and Silas as hated Jews. They did not mention their private grudge.[33] The Archons did what the popular voice dictated. Stirred by the demagogues, they ordered the prisoners to be flogged and committed to the inner prison and stocks (v. 21). The charge made before the magistrates (duumviri) was that of preaching a new illegal or unauthorized religion and strange customs. The praetors, "tearing off the garments[34] of Paul and Silas bade the lictors to beat them (v. 23). And when they had laid many stripes on them, they cast them in prison, charging the jailor to keep them safely (v. 24). And he having received such a charge, cast them into the inner prison, and made their feet fast in the stocks." This was the climax in the work of the missionaries in Philippi. The successful campaign of missions leads up to Calvary. Success comes in that way, and no other. Neither Luke nor Timothy was arrested, and so the narrative of Luke drops the use of the first person until Acts 20, when he is again with Paul. He evidently remained in Philippi because of his being able to support himself as a medical man and carry on the work of the Gospel unobtrusively but effectively.[36] But Luke did not own a home in Philippi, as is evidenced in his being with the party in the hospitality of Lydia.

Paul and Silas were suffering too much to be able to sleep, with their backs bruised and bleeding from the terrible Roman scourge. But they could praise God in song and thank him in prayer, for the privilege of suffering for Him. The prisoners were listening to them, in this unaccustomed experience, in a place where the only noise they ever heard was that of the Jailor's voice, full of cruelty or of bitter hatred, and that of cursing by the resentful prisoners (v. 26). "Suddenly the earth shook violently with a great earthquake so that the very foundations of the prison-house were shaken; and immediately all the doors were opened, and everyone's fetters were (shaken out) loosed." No naturalistic explanation will suffice or account for this occurrence. Such an earthquake as could loose the fetters from every prisoner and open every door is beyond interpretation apart from the supernatural. "There was an intelligent use of the earthquake,"[37] and that is only adequate explanation of this miraculous event. Such an earthquake would overawe an oriental or any other people, and the prisoners linked the earthquake up with the prayers of Paul and Silas to God. They did not flee and Paul knew why.

---

33. A. T. Robertson, *Epochs on the Life of Paul*, p. 151.

34. R. V. the garments of Paul and Silas, versus Ramsay, their own garments in holy horror.

36. Ramsay, *St. Paul the Traveler*, p. 219, Luke won a high place as evangelist in all the churches, II Cor. 8:18.

37. W. O. Carver, *Commentary on the Acts of the Apostles*, p. 170.

Then occurred an extraordinary event, which, coupled with the hymns and prayers at midnight in an old Roman jail, have come down the centuries with a message of great hope and good cheer. "*When the jailor was aroused from his sleep, seeing the prison doors open, he drew his sword, and was about to kill himself, considering that the prisoners had escaped* (v. 25). *But Paul cried out with a loud voice, 'Do thyself no harm, for we are all here'.*"

Paul quieted the fears of the jailor and made himself responsible to him for the security of his panic-striken, superstitious, cowed prisoners, when he announced that not a one of them had fled. Paul, now was master of ceremonies, because they believed rightly that he had some connection with the powers above such an earthquake. No ordinary earthquake had ever done such things. How did Paul know the prisoners were all there, or that the jailor was just on the verge of killing himself? There were no lights in the prison and Paul was in a cell of the inner subterranean part with no window or opening except toward the larger outer prison. Of course we know well that the Roman jailor would be responsible for securing his prisoners, and if they should escape would pay for it with his own life. We can hardly agree with the Bezan text of verse 30 which says that "the jailor first attended to the securing of all the prisoners and then went to Paul and Silas." The narrative of Luke says (v. 29): "*and calling for lights, he ran hastily in and trembling for fear, threw himself before Paul and Silas,*" showing that he connected them and their God with the earthquake. He evidently had heard Paul preach salvation, either before at the (*proseuche*) place of prayer or more likely in the darkness of the prison that night. He brought Paul and Silas out of the inner cell and said; "*Sirs, what must I do to be saved?*" And they joined in their testimony and explanation saying, "*Believe* quickly[38] now *on the Lord Jesus Christ and thou shalt be saved, thou and thy household, all who believe*" (v. 32). "*Then they spoke the word of the Lord to him, with all that were in his house.*" While suffering pains from his wounds, Paul preached them a sermon.

Their vital faith brought the change here which expressed itself practically in providing for the two preachers a bath, so much needed for the cleansing of their bodies, cut and bruised by the scourging at the whipping post. Following this, they were guests at the jailor's table, while the whole household joined with the jailor in joyful praise for the fact of their new faith in God, a permanent faith, which brought joyful hearts full of assurance of salvation. They were guests now in the brother jailor's home[39] and not prisoners in his custody. He kept them safely, as his guests, and joined their church and was baptized with all his believing household that very hour.

When day was come the praetors who had been disturbed in their consciences and especially when the strange earthquake occurred, sent the lictors with the message to the jailor, "*Let those men go*" (v. 36). And the jailor reported the message to Paul "*The praetors have sent orders that you be set free. Now, therefore, go forth and take your way in peace.*" The Bezan Reviser added here

38. Aorist Imv., rapid action.
39. W. O. Carver, *Commentary on the Acts of the Apostles*, p. 171.

an explanation, attributing the sending of the message as due to the superstitious fears of the praetors on account of the earthquake, which Ramsay says was not in the narrative style of Luke, who does not give explanations but simply facts. The reasons assigned, however, for the superstitious fears of the praetor were probably near the truth of the facts. Luke makes evident in his narrative the contrast of attitude in these Roman officials, in the evening when the sentence was passed and executed, and in the morning when quietly they send orders to see if they might spirit these prisoners away, without suffering themselves the evil consequences of castigating Roman citizens — a grave offense which called for severe punishment. *The praetors came and begged them,* when Paul's reply demanded public recognition of their Roman rights, on the part of the officials, *"that the apsotles avoid further peril to themselves, by departing peacefully."* They were willing for the innocent prisoners to suffer injustices and Paul exposed this fact when he said that "they had been submitted to a public scourging, when they had not been condemned." These officials wished[40] to shift the blame from themselves to the rabble and get rid of the troublesome situation of embarrassment in which they found themselves. So they played up the hypocrisy of assuming to protect the prisoners from some worse thing that might befall them if they should not depart.

Paul did not wish to exact from these minions the justice due the missionaries, which would have meant humiliation before the public for these officers. He did wish to guarantee such protection as might be possible for the young church, and this he did, first, by suffering without protest the cruelty of a public scourging, when he might have prevented it by making known at the hour of the arrest that he and Silas both were Roman citizens. When the praetors ordered them scourged and imprisoned, they became themselves amenable to the law and were now cowed before Paul and willing to satisfy his request that they be exonerated at least before the group of the friends of the church and the officials who were responsible before the Roman government for this grave irregularity in the maltreatment of Roman citizens. These officers would be careful not to molest the little group of disciples which Paul and Silas afterwards left under the care of Luke the beloved physician, entrusted with the pastoring of the flock. Paul's firm refusal to be spirited away without a public recognition of their rights gave him a dignified position of protector over the little church he had founded. The officers would see to it that the members of the church should not be molested. This was a protection which cost much but remained as a constant cause for gratitude and loyalty in the hearts of the Philippian Christians. No wonder they loved Paul so, through subsequent years.

Content with this conclusion of their vindication, and happy over the protection thus guaranteed, the two missionaries returned quietly to the home of Lydia, where they bade the congregation there assembled, doubtless for prayer, a fond farewell, and then they took their departure by the Egnation Road for Thessalonica. Luke remained behind to pastor the church until 57 A. D., when he rejoined Paul on his way to Jerusalem after the third missionary

40. W. M. Ramsay, *Paul, the Traveler and Roman Citizen*, pp. 223, 224.

journey and the Apostle's ministry of three years in Ephesus. He continued with him from that time on, until Paul finished his career in his martyrdom in Rome (Acts 20:5).

On the way to Thessalonica the missionaries passed through Amphipolis, thirty miles from Philippi, and through Appolonia, thirty miles farther on toward Thessalonica; but they did not stop in either place, due to the fact that the Jewish colony was small in each.

Thessalonica, the largest city in the second division of the province, they found to be the largest city also of all Macedonia, situated in a favorable position at the head of the Thermaic Gulf, a free city, more than three hundred years of age, and an admirable strategic center for the planting of the Gospel of the Kingdom, where it would easily spread out over a vast region round about.

CHAPTER X

The Founding of Christianity in Europe

Thessalonica

Founding of the church in Thessalonica, Acts 17:1-9.

LUKE does not give as much space as he did to Philippi to the founding of the work in Thessalonica, Paul's second church in Europe. But the fact is that it was a far larger city and more important center for the spread of the Gospel than Philippi. When the Macedonian power began to overshadow all the Greek-speaking countries, this city received the name of a half-sister of Alexander the Great, Thessalonica. It was, at first, the capital of one of the four divisions of Macedonia, but later when these divisions were united by the Roman government, it was made the metropolis of the whole province. Strabo says it was the most populous town of Macedonia, and it became in history, before the founding of Constantinople, virtually the capital of Greece. This city, the modern Salonika of today, has had a remarkable history, due largely to its advantageous location at the head of the Thermaic Gulf and on the coastal margin of a vast alluvial plain, well watered by four rivers, making of it thus a natural mercantile emporium, which it has continued to be through the changing scenes of its history of the centuries. Salonika is next after Constantinople in size in the European Turkey of today.

It is not strange that the statesmanship of Paul chose this capital as one of the most strategic centers from which the Gospel would "sound forth like a trumpet, as it did, not only in Macedonia and Achaia but in every place." The annals of this city in Christian history substantiated the wisdom of Paul's choice. Its Christianity did become contaminated with the superstitions of the heathen environment, and Demetrius its patron saint overshadowed Paul and his pure Gospel and "the work of faith and labor of love and patience of hope" of the primitive church to which Paul addressed the two Letters to the Thessalonians. The Jews were strong in Thessalonica, and the first scene of Paul's work there opens in the crowded synagogue-assembly of Jewish worshippers (Acts 17:1-4). *"And Paul, accompanied by Silas, came to Thessalonica, where there was a Synagogue of the Jews."* So goes the record of Luke. The inference would seem to be that there were no synagogues in Amphipolis and Apollonia, which towns they passed through on the long three days journey of a hundred miles by the Egnation Road from Philippi. Coming into the city late in the day, the weary missionaries found lodging in the house of Jason (Joshua or Jesus), a Hellenistic Jew. (v. 2) *And, as was customary with Paul he went in to address them,* (*the Jews* at the synagogue) *and for three Sabbaths he reasoned with them from their Scriptures.* Tired from their journey and bearing the marks of their sufferings experienced in Philippi, to which Paul referred incidentally in a subsequent letter to the Thessalonian church later founded there (I Thess. 2:2), they were invited, as in Antioch of Pisidia, to speak. To these fellow-Jews Paul spoke earnestly about Christ, using the Jewish Scriptures as the basis of his preaching (v. 3). There were three points in the argument of Paul's sermons as he opened the meaning of their Scriptures of the Old Testament to them. He quoted the Scriptures to prove "*that it was proper that the anointed one should suffer and* He should *rise again from the dead*" *and* that "*this same anointed one is this* man the *very Jesus whom I am proclaiming to you.*" He showed them by their Scriptures that "He who was foretold in prophecy was to be a suffering Messiah and not to be a temporal King, as the current belief among the Jews had been." Furthermore, "that after death He was to rise from the dead again" and finally, "that the crucified and resurrected Jesus of Nazareth was indeed 'the Messiah to come'."[1]

Only the premises and conclusions of Paul's general argument are recorded by Luke, and no word is given about the incidents of individual conversions, as in the narrative of the work in Philippi, due probably to the fact that Luke was not with them there in Thessalonica. A general statement is made summarizing the results.

(v. 4) "*And some of them* (the Jews) *were persuaded; and there were in addition gathered to Paul and Silas many of the 'God-fearing' proselytes and a great multitude of the Greeks, and of the leading women not a few.*"[2] The message of Paul was favorably received, "interest of the novelty predominating over the seriousness of the conviction." The hearers of Jesus in the first Nazareth sermon were affected in the same way but soon changed their attitude from attention to cavilling, as it also proved in this case later. The humiliation of the Messiah through suffering has always been a hard doctrine for the Jews. Paul preached the coming of the Messianic Kingdom, for which he was later accused of the treason of proclaiming another King than the emperor. Paul did not tolerate Emperor worship and his enemies sensed this fact and basely used it against him (cf. II Thess. 2:37). He exhorted the Thessalonian Christians to walk worthily of the Kingdom (I Thess. 2:12) and suffer afflictions for it, under the "man of sin" (II Thess. 1:5). The coming of the Kingdom was emphasized in Paul's preaching and in the two epistles and bred a deep conviction in the believers as to the nearness of the second advent (I Thess. 5:2). A misunderstanding arose about the lot of those Christians who should die before the *appearance* (Cf. II Thess. 2:2). Paul corrected their misconceptions and exhorted the idlers to work (II Thess. 3:16). There was a type of

1. Conybeare and Howson: *Life and Epistles of the Apostle Paul*, p. 271.
2. Ramsay's text here used, agreeing with many MSS and Versions, recognizes three classes of hearers besides the Jews. The Approved Text on the other hand unites the God-fearing and the Greeks making two classes, besides the Jews. The great multitude of Jews were not proselytes. Codex Beza agrees with Ramsay.

piety that sprang up in Thessalonica that made some of the believers unfit for work. Paul said that such as did not work should not eat (I Thess. 4:11). Paul, like all religious teachers, was sometimes grossly misinterpreted in his teachings, like that of the Second Coming. He had heresy-hunters, as Jesus did, who took his words and twisted them to mean something else (cf. II Thess. 2:3b).

The work of founding the Thessalonian church was monumental. Among the Jews who were gathered to Paul and Silas in the three week's evangelistic campaign in the synagogue were Aristarchus, who appears later on, and Jason his host, who was haled before the Politarchs by the mob later in Paul's labors. Segundus is also mentioned (Acts 20:4). Then there were a good number of "God-fearers" who were Gentile proselytes. Ramsey says the "multitude of the Greeks" was the largest class of converts, being the Gentile element reached by the revelation of a universal Gospel, received now for the first time here, which also occasioned the jealousy that sprang up immediately in the hearts of many of the leading Jews and especially the rabbis. Not a few of the leading women, making use of the liberty socially accorded them in Macedonia, were numbered among the hearers and converts who were by a correct reading of the text Acts 17:4 and also by the subsequent happenings, wives of leading citizens of the city.[3] One is reminded of the chief women in Antioch of Pisidia turning against Paul. The ministry of Paul and Silas was mainly, in its results, Gentile in this city, and Paul refers in his letters subsequently to the fact that the Jews did not want him to preach to the Gentiles.

The success of the initial ministry among the Jews and other classes aroused great Jewish prejudices. They secured certain toughs from the market-place, hangers-on, and raised up a mob which terrified the city, and then set upon the house of Jason where the missionaries were guests, to bring them out before the mob under the badge of its being a democracy. Paul and Silas were protected from the violence by being absent from the house or concealed by the hospitality of the homes of friends, and the mob vented its rage on Jason and certain brethren, dragging *them* before the magistrates (politarchs).

The Jews were under the ban of the Roman authorities at this time for having raised a tumult in the metropolis, Rome, at the instigation, as was alleged, of one Chrestus or Christus. The provincial city was glad to show its loyalty to Rome by throwing off the blame of the disturbance from themselves and upon the Christians, under the name of the hated Jewish race. Thessalonica was a free city, made so through its loyalty to (Octavius) Augustus, in the recent war against Brutus and Cassius. So the politarchs or magistrates would find it an urgent act of loyalty to deal with any revolt now, against the Emperor, the offense of *lèse majesté*. But the ministry continued for a considerable time, estimated from the final results obtained, amounting to an organized church. It was not the work of three weeks but of several, perhaps five months or more.

3. Cf. Cod. Beza. (D) which has gunaikōn te tōn protōn, wives of the chief men.

The politarchs,[4] who knew less than the accusing Jews about Paul and Jesus, were perplexed. They were well-disposed toward the Christians, from what they had received of information from the women converts, and saw little ground for the accusation that "these who had turned the inhabited world upside down were now in Thessalonica and Jason had taken them under his patronage."[5]

This charge against the missionaries was dangerous. The suggestion of treason covered up the secret grudge of these Jewish rabbis and leaders and exposed the victims of their strategy to the gravest of penalties. The politarchs had not only to take notice of it but to act rapidly in the suppression of any revolt against the emperor in case there were such. They used the measure which seemed most prudent, "*binding the accused over in security, that peace should be kept.*"[6] This security of the peace was exacted from Jason and his associates, the leading Christians of Thessalonica. This measure, in effect, amounted to the banishing of Paul and Silas from the city, for they would not consent to remain silent, being commissioned to preach; and even to appear in public would be perilous to their friends, Jason and others, who had deposited money against the security of the peace, which might easily be broken by an attack on Paul or Silas in the street by their enemies, without any real cause.

Paul understood the severity of the measure, which had been thrust like a wedge between him and the young church he so much loved. The Apostle later wrote longingly of his desire to come to them again and added, "but Satan hindered us." He knew that so long as the same magistrates remained in office and maintained their same attitude he could not return, nor was it probable that they would change their policy which would endanger their own positions. The use of the term "Satan" to mean action taken by the governing power against the message from God is in accord with the figurative use of the term in the whole of the New Testament.[7]

Paul and Silas had to depart from Thessalonica but the church founded there would be a great asset to the cause of Christianity from its very beginning. Paul's *apologia* (I Thess. 2:7-12) praises the brethren there and tells them of his consolation and joy. He recounts the pastoral experiences he had with them through many days, laboring with his hands at night that he might spend the days visiting them personally. He had pointed out to many of them in particular the absurdity of serving idols, and urged these Gentile friends to forsake their false gods and turn to the living and true God and to His Son Jesus, who had not only died for their sins but had been raised from the dead "in order to become the indwelling power unto righteousness and the earnest of a blessed felicity in the not distant future when Jesus the rescuer from the com-

4. This title given by Luke accords with the best results of modern research (Cf. Inscription at the arch in Salong).
5. Cf. W. O. Carver: *Com. Acts*, p. 174.
6. Cf. W. M. Ramsay: *Paul the Traveler*, p. 230.
7. W. M. Ramsay: *Paul the Traveler*, p. 231.

ing wrath would appear and gather all believers unto an eternal fellowship with Himself (I Thess. 1:9, 10; 4:9, 10; II Thess. 2:13, 14)."[8]

The little church became very dear to the apostle's heart. He had cherished its members "as a nurse-mother cherishes her own children," giving them not only the Gospel of God but his very own self, urging them to walk worthily of God who called them unto his own Kingdom (I Thess. 1:6-12). Many of the members were poor artisans, and he worked with his own hands in order that he might not be a burden upon them. The church in Philippi sent material help to him twice while in his intense work in Thessalonica. These brethren endured persecution bravely, and the fame of their faith went forth from this city of many contacts, through commerce by land and sea, to all the regions around far and wide.

It is no wonder that Paul had a great pride in this church which cost him so much but was such a great joy to his heart. It was just like a true father's love for his own children, from whom by some untoward circumstance he has been unwillingly separated, and to whom he is prevented by inseparable difficulties from returning.

Beroea

Acceptance of the Gospel in Beroea. Acts. 17:10-15.

After a few months stay in Thessalonica, it is not surprising that the work of the Gospel had gained a wide acceptance in the circle of the Gentile (Greek) population of the city, bringing on the acute jealousy of the synagogal leaders. Paul and Silas had to leave by night to avoid any further contacts and complications with the Thessalonian Jews, and they were escorted by the brethren outside the city and sent on under cover of the night with protection to Beroea, sixty miles distant. Such was the solicitude of these brethren for the safety of their missionary friends. This was a prudent flight, which went forward according to a policy recommended by Jesus of avoiding the perils of imprisonment or violence in order to embrace the opportunities of freedom and the prosecution of the work of the gospel.

Beroea took its name from Pheres, its founder. The Macedonians had difficulty in pronouncing "ph" and transformed it from Pheroea into Beroea which reverted in part to the Ancient Greek in the modern Verria, a town about forty miles from Salonika. It is an agricultural town located on a ledge of Mt. Bermius, six hundred feet above the marshy plain. There are more than twenty Byzantine churches "hidden away from the Turks"[9] in this town, to which Paul and Silas came in primitive times with the pure gospel.

When Paul and Silas arrived early in the day, following their departure from Thessalonica, they lost no time in making themselves known, and probably on the first Sabbath as their custom was, went into the synagogue of the Jews (v. 10b). They found the Jews in Beroea more noble in that they were

8. James Everett Frame: *I. C. Com.*, Thess., pp. 3-7.
9. Morton, H. V., *In the Steps of St. Paul*, in loco.

not filled with jealousy when the gospel was offered to the (Gentile) Greeks as freely as to themselves (v. 11). Their superiority in nobility was in their openmindedness to receive the word "with favorable inclinations," applying day by day the test of the Scriptures, verifying by their own critical "readings" *whether these things taught* by the apostles "*were thus*" (v. 12). The logical outcome noted by Luke was that "*many believed;*" as did also not a few of the high-born Greek ladies and also of the Greek gentlemen. Here we see also that a wider circle in the Gentile population of the town is distinctly noted by Luke. The Jews took the sermons of Paul and Silas and examined their arguments about the suffering Messiah, who died and was raised from the dead according to the prophecies of the Old Testament, Jesus Christ, the Nazarene. The good will of the Jews gave opportunity for a systematic work in the Synagogue, but the apostles widened their evangelism to include the Gentile populations. So, during a period which covered possibly several months, with the additional aid of Timothy, who had joined them here, they were able to do a substantial work in this town perhaps as large as the modern Verria with its population of more than twenty thousand souls.

(v.13) So prosperous a work could not escape long the detection of the Jewish leaders in Thessalonica, and "*when they learned that in Beroea also the word of God was preached by Paul, they came there also, exciting and disturbing the multitudes.*" They may not have gotten "hoodlums," as they had in Thessalonica; but they stirred up and troubled the multitudes, *and "the brethren had to send Paul on toward the sea*" to avoid peril of violence for him. He left Silas and also Timothy, who had rejoined them here in Beroea, to take care of the work. The brethren who attended the lonely missionary went all the way to the harbour "at Methoni," where he arranged passage for Athens. Paul had given Silas and Timothy instructions before leaving to join him speedily at Athens, where he would wait for them (17:16) to bring him news from Thessalonica and Beroea. Timothy did rejoin Paul at Athens and was sent back to Thessalonica.[10]

Paul's work in Macedonia thus terminated with his departure from Beroea. He had been driven from each of the three cities in which he had worked by persecution. He did some work outside of these cities, preaching in some places even as far as Illyricum; but he had planted the gospel in three strategic centers of the province and from these it would spread to the contiguous regions, as it actually did, through the zeal of his converts (I Thess. 4:10).

Athens

Paul in the University City of Athens, Acts 17:15-34; I Thess. 2:17-3:5; I Cor. 1:16; 16:15.

Driven out of Macedonia, Paul was accompanied by Silas and certain brethren to the port of Methoni near Beroea. "His sense of thoroughness and keen perception of the true strategy of missions made him loath to leave a

10. G. H. Gilbert's *Students' Life of St. Paul*, pp. 124, 125.

ministry interrupted in the midst by his enemies, just when many people were accepting the Gospel. Exhausted from the strenuosity of the campaign to plant the cause firmly in this strategic province, he provided through his fellow-laborers for pastoral care for the small congregations left in the chief coastal centers, and was escorted by a band of brethren to a port near Beroea. There he embarked with some of these solicitous brethren, who went on with him in the voyage of four days to Athens. Anxious about the persecuted Christians in Thessalonica and other places, the apostle left urgent instructions (an order or command) for Silas and Timothy to rejoin him speedily in Athens when things were in a more settled condition in Beroea. They were to bring him news about conditions in Macedonia, and it seems they did, (I Thess. 3:1). But the report they did bring him, particularly about Thessalonica, was anything but favorable.[11]

This caused the apostle to send Timothy back to Thessalonica, where the antagonism of the Jewish leaders who had pursued him and Silas to Beroea had grown more intense, rather than to die down as Paul had hoped. Fearing that it might spread to Philippi also, he sent Silas, as it seems, to be with Luke, who had been carrying on there for several months alone. Paul had a great longing in his heart to return, especially to Thessalonica, but Satan had hindered him; and Silas also could not return to that city for the same reason. Timothy had not been identified as they with the trouble in Thessalonica, and so it devolved on him to undertake the difficult mission of 'establishing' the Thessalonian brethren and ministering comfort and encouragement. He exhorted them to stand by with their faith in Jesus. He was to interpret for them their Christianity and show the abundant resources in it when passing through afflictions which it was their appointed lot and privilege to suffer. Timothy also would find out if they were standing firm against the temptation to give way and recant or compromise their professed belief in Christ. They were beset by unscrupulous and ruthless enemies, who were bent on separating them from the faith by threats or by cajolery.

When the overworked and bitterly persecuted apostle, depressed physically and psychologically, saw his two fellow laborers depart, he was sensitively conscious of the fact that he was alone in Athens, the greatest center of culture of the world.[12] Achaia, of which Athens was the capital, the Roman province, which embraced all of Southern Greece, was the very "paradise of genius and renown." Here Paul was in sight of Mt. Olympus, seat of the Grecian gods. On his voyage down from the port, Methoni, his vessel had skirted the coast of Greece, passing near Thermopylae and the island of Salamis, where, by two great victories, the valorous sons of Greece had saved their country from being overrun by the Persian hordes. When he disembarked at the port, miles distant from the famous city of Athens, he could faintly see the Acropolis. As he traveled by land and drew near, the far-famed Parthenon and other build-

11. Cf. W. O. Carver; *Commentary on Acts*, p. 175.
12. Carver, W. O.: *Commentary on Acts*, p. 175.

ings celebrated in poetry and history now became visible, and the thoughtful apostle was thrilled at the sight. His versatility compassed the knowledge of the language and letters of the Grecian University in Tarsus, one of the greatest rivals of the University of Athens.

Four hundred years had elapsed since Athens was at the peak of her literary glory and possessed more men of genius than ever lived in any city before or since in the history of the human race. At the time of the visit of Paul, the philosophy of Socrates, Plato and Aristotle had already degenerated largely into *sophistry*, the oratory of Demosthenes into formalistic rhetoric, and Athens looked back to her golden age of the time of the epics of Homer. But it was yet a great center of philosophers of different schools and students and teachers of a wide range of subjects. It yet boasted of its University, which was perhaps the greatest of four outstanding Grecian institutions of that type in the world.

The picture of Paul, alone in Athens, before Silas and Timothy came, is one of marked and almost pathetic interest, tired and depressed as he was, and now in the midst of the depressing realities of a city full of idols and all that flows out of such religious conditions. "*His spirit was provoked within him*" (Acts 17:16). After his fellow-laborers departed on missions which would take weeks, perhaps months to accomplish, the apostle, disappointed in his hope and plan to return to Macedonia for a more complete work in a field difficult but promising, turned his attention to the task providentially thrust upon him and (v. 17) so he sought out on the Sabbath and "*reasoned in the Synagogue with the Jews and the* God-fearing *proselytes, and* also *in the market place every day with the chance-comers.*

As Paul wandered through the streets of Athens, viewing its architectural beauty and its extraordinary statuary of the Grecian gods and goddesses, his soul was stirred when he saw how enthralled the populace was to a blind, senseless, idol-worship, so incongruous with the mental stature of the past and present of the people, possessed of great intellectual talents and university culture. There were, in spite of the undermining influence of the reasoning of Greece's highest philosophers, more gods in Greece now than ever in her history, Athens alone possessing more than thirty thousand. Indignation burned in his heart and it soon found expression. We are not informed whether the apostle was welcomed or repulsed in the Athenian synagogue. His main attention in Athens naturally had to do with paganism and not Judaism.

He decided to attack the tremendous problem of bringing Christianity to this great capital, however impossible might seem the task. So he went first, as his custom was always, to the Jewish synagogue. Unlike the record of the work in the synagogue in the cities of Macedonia, we find no mention of any convert in the work in this synagogue, where he reasoned with them from the Scriptures about the Messiah. Paul probably did not stay in Athens more than six weeks and it may have been even a shorter time.[13] Only the principal

---

13. Paul's departure from Athens was an enforced one, Cf. W. M. Ramsay: *St. Paul the Traveler and Roman Citizen*, p. 241.

event of his sojourn in that city is given by Luke's brief account — his speech in the Areiopagus. Another method Paul used currently was to go into the (agora) market-place and talk to individuals, and also in public discourse with the populace. This had been the method of Socrates. Paul reasoned with all classes daily in the *agora,* dealing with those who happened along and would stop to listen. He was just one more among many popular lecturers who presented themselves in this center of intellectual culture. It may be that Paul's debate with the Epicurean and Stoic philosophers began on a visit in the lecture halls of the great university. Paul was taking for himself a tremendous task to give the philosophers, and the chance-comers in the market-place the gospel, in a mixed audience of all classes. But he would not let the opportunity escape to "be all things" to the "intellectuals" also in the halls of their boasted university, where liberty would be given for a hearing in democratic Athens. Demosthenes said, "that the bane of the Athenians was that they were always seeking to hear and discuss the latest political or metaphysical question."

In matching his wits with the Stoic and Epicurean philosophers, whether it was in the halls of the university or in the market-place, we get glimpses of the extraordinary versatility of the apostle. Stoicism, not like the philosophy of Socrates and his great contemporaries, Plato and Aristotle, justified the popular polytheism, their philosophers being themselves pantheists. Matter was inseparable from deity. They knew no personal Creator and Preserver of the Universe. The soul of man was corporeal and not immortal, but destined to be reabsorbed in God. The resurrection of the body, for them, was irrational. Their ideal was to live in austere unemotional indifference to all change, without regard to pleasure or pain. Pride was the end of education, in acquiescence to an iron destiny. In its full development, Stoicism was wholly opposed and contrary to all the fundamental conceptions as to God and man, as taught by Christianity.

Epicureanism was virtually atheism, being but a system of materialism. The world was formed by an "accidental concourse of atoms," and not in any sense created or modified by Deity. The gods were mere phantoms, convenient, but exercising no influence on the physical world or human life. The universe was a great accident and sufficiently explains itself without any reference to Deity. There is by this system no creator or governor and no resurrection, the soul not existing without the body. So their motto was: "If the dead rise not, let us eat and drink, for tomorrow we die." Pleasure was the chief end of life, whether by sensual indulgence or by a tranquil and indifferent life. So Paul must meet the Stoic philosophers, whose Painted Porch was adjacent to the Agora, and also the teachings of the Garden of the Epicureans not far away, with their subversive ideals of pride and pleasure. How well would he succeed in the few moments of one brief address, delivered in the presence of their Council of the Areiopagus, *that was the question that faced him in this crucial experience in this capital of the culture of the world.*

Socrates had turned the trend of the thought of mankind from speculation as to the material universe, to the study of man. Plato had soared aloft in the search for truth in the plane of abstract thought and with many noble ideals. Aristotle systematized the methods of thought and expression in logic. He was prolific in the study of science and neglected the field of religion. Zeno and Epicurus called back to a practical view of life. One sought the conquest of evil in self-control, leading to pride and pantheism; and to despair, leading justifiably to suicide. Epicureans were atheists: light-hearted, flippant, selfish; and their system exalted pleasure as the chief aim in life.[14]

Paul came in contact with these philosophers of both schools, Ramsay thinks, in the lecture halls of the great university. He had been preaching *Jesous,* (masculine) and *anastasis,* resurrection, (a feminine noun), and these sophists thought he was announcing a new and strange god and goddess. But the popularity of Paul was a challenge in the open forum of the market place; and the two groups of philosophers, both finding their doctrines imperiled, seemed to have combined forces,[15] as the Pharisees and Sadducees did against Jesus. "*Certain also of the Stoic and Epicurean philosophers engaged in discussions with him.*" probably after hearing him in the market-place, that "intellectual exchange" where every novel doctrine was always welcome. After recognizing his ability in discussion, they came to look upon him as an invader of their domain, and some sneering at him said: "*What would this babbler* (spermologos) *wish*[16] *to say.*" In their opinion he was a mere ignorant plagiarist. They sought to ridicule him by calling him a "seed-picker," a sparrow picking up the "crumbs of learning" (Farrar) or in the slang of Athens (Ramsay) a *spermologos* who "aped the ways and words of philosophers." This ridicule would be most appropriate in the mouth of Epicurean philosophers who were atheists. Others, probably of the group of Stoic philosophers added: "*He is apparently an exponent of foreign divinities.*" Paul was preaching Jesus and the resurrection, a god and goddess, and they would with tolerance hear of these new *daimonia*[17] (demons or divinities) which he was introducing among the multitudes of Athenian gods and goddesses. They took a more serious view, a more liberal attitude toward the new-comer with his new religion.

To bring in a new religion was a grave offense.[18] Socrates had been condemned in part because he laughed at the gods of Athens and "corrupted the youth by his democratic teachings." The court that had sat in judgment on Socrates had been the Council of the Areiopagus. One function of this august ancient court was "to regulate the education of the young and control the introduction of novel forms of worship."[19]

(v. 19) *And they took hold of him and brought him before* the Council Areiopagus saying, "*May we learn what is this new teaching spoken by thee?*

---

14. A. T. Robertson, *Epochs in the Life of Paul*, p. 158b.
15. David Smith, *Life and Letters of St. Paul*, p. 143.
16. Optative mood of thelō expressing a wish.
17. Diminutive, small divinities or gods.
18. W. M. Ramsay: *St. Paul the Traveler and Roman Citizen*, p. 243.
19. Plato, Apol. 24B., Xen. Mem. I:1:1., cited from David Smith.

(v. 20) *for thou bringest some things of foreign fashion to our ears; we wish therefore to learn what is their nature.*" This action of the philosophers in taking hold of Paul was hostile.[20] They took him before the Council "which was the most awful court of judicature, which from time immemorial had sat to pass sentence on the gravest of criminals and decide the most solemn questions connected with religion." The judges sat in the open air, upon seats hewn out in the open rock, on a platform to which one ascended by a flight of stone steps immediately from the Agora. Even in the political decay of Athens this spot and this court were regarded by the people with superstitious reverence. No place in Athens was so suitable for a discourse upon the mysteries of religion. But we are not to regard Paul's discourse on the Areiopagus as "a formal defense in a trial before the court."[21]

Paul stood in the midst of the Council, as Peter in the midst of the Sanhedrin (Acts 4:7), which was not friendly; but Paul was not on trial, except through the jealousy of the philosophers who feared for their prestige and emoluments. There were judges present, but there was also a throng of curious spectators, anxious as the whole crowd of Athenians and resident strangers who formed the audience, *interested only in saying or hearing something new and smart.*

Paul's address in the Areiopagus (Acts 17:22-31) marked a memorable and crucial hour in the history of Christianity. It was an occasion frought with the most important consequences, when the Apostle, with all the earnestness of his soul, stood on Mars Hill to proclaim the certain truth and awful meaning of the gospel, in comparison with the prevalent worthless polytheism, and that in plain view of the temples, statues and altars of the idol-worshipping masses of the earth's most intellectual capital city.[22] Close to the spot where the apostle stood in the midst of the court of the Areiopagus, was the temple of Mars and the sanctuary of the Eumenides (Fates). Immediately in front of him was the Parthenon, of the goddess Minerva. Here the preacher of the gospel was to make the assertion, that: "in Temples made with hands the deity does not dwell." Standing almost within the shadow of the brazen colossus of Minerva, armed with spear, shield and helmet, the guardian champion of Athens, this missionary of Christianity was to thunder forth the clear ringing declaration that Deity was not to be likened either to that of the work of Phidias or to other forms of gold, silver, or stone, "graven by art and man's device," which at that moment could be readily seen by every soul who cared to look. Objects of devotion, temples of idols, shrines to unnumbered gods, filled the horizon of their vision, in a city *wholly given to idolatry*. With an ardent and enthusiastic eloquence, in an oration regulated by his tactful prudence, the apostle poured out the emotions which welled up in his soul.[23] In

20. W. M. Ramsay: *St. Paul the Traveler and Roman Citizen*, p. 245f cf. Acts 21:30: 18:17.
21. Conybeare and Howson, *Life and Epistles of St. Paul*, p. 308.
22. Cf. Conybeare and Howson; *The Life and Epistles of St. Paul*. p. 309f.
23. Ibid. pp. 309-311.

his discourse he became "all things to all men, if by any means he might lead some into salvation."

(I) His introduction was most conciliatory and tactful (vv. 22, 23). *"Gentlemen Athenians!"* his voice rang out on the Council of the Areiopagus, *"I observe that in all respects you are more reverent than others toward what is divine."* He passes thus a compliment on their religiosity, evidenced in a thousand ways easily perceived. He passes over the worship of idols in order to call attention to one altar among the thousands he had observed in their city, dedicated to the *unknown God* (v. 23). He had not come as some might suppose to introduce a new religion, a procedure which would be illegal, but to present this unknown God whom they were already worshipping without knowing him. He was not unfaithful to the truth in so stating his mission as he purposed to present the eternal God, and His Son to them, as he did. *Going through your city and surveying the monuments of your worship, I found also an altar with the dedicatory inscription. To AN UNKNOWN GOD.* That divine nature, *then, which you worship, not knowing* what it is, *I am setting forth to you.* (II) The relation of this unknown God to all created things and man (vv. 24-27). Waiving aside the worship of idols. with no denunciatory word, he represents the unknown God as *"the God that made the* material *world* (cosmos, universe) *and all things therein, He, Lord* as He is *of heaven and earth, dwelleth not in shrines made with hands, neither by human hands is served as though needing anything, since He Himself giveth to all life and breath and all things."* He thus presented God as the living personal God, as the source of life and maker of all things. He created the cosmic order and all things in it. With one stroke Paul sweeps away the innumerable gods of polytheism and unites all their special imaginary functions into one vital relation embracing all the needs of mankind. (v. 26) This all-creating and all-sustaining God *"made out of one stock every nation or racial section of men, to dwell on all the face of the earth and* determined or *fixed the prearranged* or defined *times and bounds of their habitation."* The plan of God in creation covered the needs of national and racial life and well-being geographically and in historic times or epochs. (v. 27) And this plan had in view the real purpose of God in the creation of men,*"to seek God, if indeed they might feel after Him and find Him, being as indeed He is not far from each one of us."* Epicurus had ascribed the origin and preservation of the universe to a blind chance of "a fortuitous combination of atoms." The Stoic learned from Paul that the cosmos was ruled not by blind Fate but by the providence of a personal God. The Epicureans ridiculed religion, but declared if there were gods they were far away and indifferent to ministration in human affairs. (III) Relative to the nature of the true God (vv. 28, 29) and His relations to men, Paul declared, *"for in Him we live and move and are or have our being or existence."* We are wholly sustained, as truly as we were surely created by Him. Paul appeals to certain of the Grecian poets, as Aratos, a Cilician who said, "For we are also his offspring." (v. 29) Paul then argues from the nature and dependence of man on God back to the nature of God who cannot be a mere creation of man, who was himself created by God. The worship of God should not be material, a matter of images and idols.

"*Being the offspring of God, we ought not to think that the divine nature is like unto gold or silver or stone, graven by art and device of man.*" Thus Paul repudiates their idols. Man can rise no higher than the god he makes. These idols were the creation of men. They were but exaggerated humans, created by man's hands moving under the direction of his imagination, and had no real existence. The true God was above all His creation and the creator of everything. (IV) God's moral government over men (vv. 30, 31) is the apostle's next step in the argument based on the history of mankind. Paul gives the Athenians the benefit of the doubt in judging their great number of idols or objects of devotion to bespeak an earnest search after God.[24] He did not paint the picture of idol worship in the lurid colors in which it is presented in his epistle to the Romans (1:18-32), where the tendency of heathendom is unmistakably and clearly depicted. The pagan might have seen God in nature and in conscience, manifested in his power, wisdom and beneficence in the creation and orderly government of the world. But he refused to have God in his thoughts and went about to make for himself gods, exalting the creature above the creator. The knowledge the heathen had did not save them, as man does not follow the right in conduct because he knows what is right in his intellectual understanding. As Browning says, "It is one thing to know and another to practice." Greek philosophy followed by Herbart and other philosophers yet more modern, erred in thinking that, if a a man knows what is right he will practice it. Paul cited the exceptional pagan, like Socrates, and a long list of sages of the ages who were "seeking after God, if haply they might feel after Him and find Him." Many great religious heathen as the Buddha (Siddartha) reached up after God; but in Christianity God reaches down to save man in a religion of revelation of Himself to them. Paul presents the seeking heathen and says, "*Now, indeed, during the times*[25] *of ignorance God overlooked.*" That was in the times and case of individual pagan men who really searched after God, and the apostle would have it applicable in the lives of these Athenians in their past history if possible, as it was in the lives of some of their philosophers, who pointed to the "necessity of One who would come and be able to guide the frail bark of man across the unknown sea of existence (Plato)."

"*But* now a new era of human history had come and *at present he* (God) *chargeth all men everywhere to repent,* (v. 31) *inasmuch as he hath set a day on which, in* the person of *the man whom he hath ordained, he will judge the world in righteousness; and he hath given all a guarantee by raising him from the dead.*" Paul had appealed to their age-long yearning and seeking after God, illustrated in the purer spirits of some of their poets and philosophers. But now, when he announces a new era in which men must repent of their evil deeds, when judgment will be meted out by a just and personal God, some of

---

24. W. M. Ramsay: *St. Paul the Traveler and Roman Citizen*, p. 250b.
25. Accusative touschrorous, representing, duration of time.

the philosophers met the announcement of the resurrection with ridicule and scoffs, while others, more courteous, lightly postponed consideration saying, "*We will hear thee concerning this yet again.*" They did not have time now for such folly. And so the sermon was ended abruptly without any ceremony. The case, if such, might have been laughed out of court. (v. 33) "*Thus Paul went out from the midst of them.*" He was not run out of Athens; he was frozen out. Ridicule is a keen instrument. There was no fault to find with the sermon, as some critics think. Paul did not acknowledge his sermon to be a failure (cf. I Cor. 2:1ff). It was a skillful and great sermon but it was "not mixed with faith in those who heard." The very core of the gospel was in the sermon. It had condemned idolatry and all sin in the most skillful way. It had presented the necessity of repentance, the certainty of judgment and the sureness of salvation in One whom God sealed by raising Him from the dead.

"The outcome was disappointing but not fruitless."[26] The philosophers went away joking over the occasion "*but certain men clave unto him* (Paul) *and believed, among whom also was* one of the members of the Council of the Court, *an Areopagite* by the name of *Dionysius.* There was also *a woman named Damaris* (perhaps Damales, heifer) *and others with them.* Women of good name lived in seclusion in Athens and some suppose that this woman was of the courtesan class, like Mary Magdalene. If so the power of the Gospel to reach and redeem such individuals and make of them shining saints, receives one more demonstration. Paul had preached this power in the cross of Christ, which might be foolishness to the Greek and a stumbling block to the Jew but was still the power of God and the wisdom of God. He had, with a most wonderful skill, matched the philosophy of the Greeks with a philosophy more profound. In a single hour he had cut the tap roots of the current philosophic systems of Greece and presented the true philosophy about God and the Cosmos, in germ. He did a masterful job of it, but when he goes to Corinth later he will preach the simple message of "Jesus Christ and Him crucified."

"Paul left Athens a despised and lonely man. And yet his visit was not in vain. He founded no church in Athens; but, there — it may be under the fostering charge of the converted Areiopagite, Dionysius, — a church grew up."[27] In the second century it furnished Christianity martyr-bishops. In the fourth century St. Basil and St. Gregory of Nazianzus were trained in its Christian schools. Yet Athens was one of the last cities of the Roman Empire to abandon idolatry, and it never took a prominent place in Christian history. But its myriads of deities later took their flight into outworn creeds, and her tutelary goddess Minerva resigned her place of honor to the virgin mother of the Lord. But its religion continued to be a sort of baptized paganism, of worship to the ancient Greek genius, instead of a Christianity of the Christ, as has been the case in many other parts of the world, where Christianity has taken over

---

26. W. O. Carver: *Commentary on Acts,* p. 181.
27. F. W. Farrar, *Life and Epistles of St. Paul,* Vol. I, p. 521, 522.

much of the pagan life, thought and ideology, in the desire for a progress which has not been thorough — not a true Christianity of the Christ.[28]

Corinth

The Establishment of Christianity in Achaia. Acts 18:1-21.

a. The entrance and work of Paul at Corinth, 18:1-11. The most important strategic center for the founding of the work in Achaia, the second of the two Roman provinces of Greece, was the great commercial city of Corinth. Stalker compares the two cities of Athens and Corinth to Edinburgh, the intellectual capital of Scotland, and Glasgow, its principal commercial center. Paul left Athens, never to return to it; he entered Corinth "with much weakness and fear and trembling." Athens was full of nationalistic pride. Its population was composed of pleasure-loving and flippant people, light-hearted and gay. Paul had become used to persecution but not much to scorn and indifference. He was entering now an ancient pre-war Paris, luxurious and given to sensuality. Would he be able to meet the sophistry and intellectual hauteur of Corinth better than he did the ridicule of the Epicurean Garden and the pride of the Stoic Painted Porch of the philosophers of Athens?

Corinth, which was destroyed by the Romans two centuries before Paul's time, was rebuilt and had now become one of the great commercial cities of the world. A Roman colony founded by Julius Caesar, it was now the capital of the province of Achaia. It was located on the isthmus connecting the Peloponnesus with the main land and was about fifty miles west of Athens. It is not improbable that Paul, following his long adopted policy, would have thought of this great commercial city with its many contacts, and its flowing population as the most strategic center from which the gospel, when once firmly planted, would spread into many other surrounding towns and cities of the province, to other places around the coasts of the Aegean Sea, and to ports of the Mediterranean with which this emporium sustained commercial relations. The isthmus called by Pindar "the bridge of the sea" was the center of the activity of the Greek race. Xenophon spoke of it as "the gate of the Peloponnesus." A fortified wall was built at the time of the death of Leonidas across the neck of the Isthmus to keep out the hordes of the Persians.

The Acrocorinthus or citadel of Corinth, rising two thousand feet above the level of the sea, with space for a whole town on its summit and its sides precipitous like the rock of Dumbarton, constituted an impregnable citadel, with the wall across the Isthmus, a strongly fortified defense against invasion. In a military sense Corinth was thus the "eye and acropolis of Greece." It was near enough to be visible from Athens. The city of Corinth is built on a low table-land, joined to the Acrocorinthus on its northern side. At the edge of this table-land are the harbours which made Corinth the "emporium of the richest trade of the East and the West."[29] The ports of Cenchreae on the east

---

28. Cf. Schaff's *History of the Christian Church,* Vol. I, p. 325.
29. Conybeare and Howson: *Life and Epistles of St. Paul,* Ch. XII, p. 337ff.

and Lechaeum on the west and a third smaller port, Schoenus, received the trade from all the surrounding ports of the Mediterranean, a trade which was the cause of Corinth's commercial greatness and fabulous wealth.

After the destruction of the city by Mummius in the Roman conquest of Greece, Julius Caesar placed a strong colony of Italian freemen there. The greater part of the population of the city harbour was Greek, and there was a considerable community of Jews who had been attracted by the commercial possibilities to make Corinth their home.

This city, which Paul entered "with weakness and much fear and trembling," was dominated, like Athens, by idolatry. The great temple of Aphrodite stood forth silhouetted constantly before the eyes of all the populace, planted as it was upon the Acrocorinthus, more than a thousand feet above the general level of the city. Connected with its worship were a thousand "consecrated prostitutes" or courtesan votaries, who enriched this temple with their nefarious trade in "sanctified vice."[30] A considerable part of the temple of Apollo, which had survived the sack of the Romans, was already six hundred years old when Paul arrived there. Seven columns, nearly 25 feet high and 6 feet in diameter at the base, remain even today as vestiges of the ruins, to mark the location of the temple to this god.

The new city, which within a hundred years before Paul came had sprung up into vast wealth, had become a byword for every form of vice that flows forth from idolatry. The word "Corinthianize" was proverbial of an evil life.[31] The "notorious Lais, whose tomb was surmounted by an effigy of a lioness clutching her prey" was symbolic of the immorality of the thousand courtesan priestesses who plied their trade, chiefly among the shipmates and commercial traders who visited this great center of the world's sin. There was a proverb that "not every man could afford a voyage to Corinth." Such shameless vice, brazenly manifested on every hand, struck despair into the soul of Paul, as he contemplated the newest field of his missionary endeavor.

Along with the evils of the acquisition of sudden wealth by this flourishing metropolis, leading into luxury and vice, were coupled those of a false culture. Arrogant intellectuality and false philosophy are generally scornful in their attitude toward spirituality and true religion, and Corinth's philosophy was mainly one of sophistry. Still there was more of a spirit of freedom and less of domination by the critical atmosphere of the University than in Athens.[32] Moreover, Corinth excelled in statescraft and art, painting, statuary and bronze work.[33]

When Paul left Athens after his experience with the philosophers and a period of waiting in the city for the coming of Timothy and Silas from Macedonia, "*he came into Corinth.*" Apparently he did not expect to remain long there at that time, hoping and praying that he would yet find it possible to

30. W. O. Carver: *Commentary on Acts*, p. 181f.
31. H. V. Morton: *In the Steps of St. Paul*, pp. 341, 342.
32. A. T. Robertson: *Epochs in the Life of Paul.*
33. David Smith: *Life and Letters of St. Paul*, p. 150, cf. Strabo. pp. 369-381.

return to Thessalonica.[34] But in the unfolding of the plan of Providence he was to remain there for a year and a half in a varied, difficult but successful ministry (Acts 18:1-11). On reflection, after making a close study of the strategic character of the city, from which the message of the gospel would be carried by sailors and travelers both westward and eastward to every port of the Mediterranean, he must have been convinced that it was, in spite of the unfavorable moral conditions, the best center in Greece to capture for Christ.

For a prolonged stay it was necessary that he should find a home and work by which to support himself. So in pursuit of this end, as the record of Luke goes, "*finding a certain Jew named Aquilla, a man* of (native to) Pontus on the Euxine in Asia Minor, *recently come from Italy with Priscilla his wife, when the Jews were expelled from Rome by the edict of Claudius*" on account of Jewish disturbances, he came in with them.[35] These disturbances, according to the record of Suetonius, were due to the action of Chrestus, the leader of the Christians,"[36] (49 A. D.). Aquilla thus arrived in Corinth six or seven months before Paul (in 50 A. D.) and took up his abode there, establishing himself in the work of tent-making.

There were Jews from Pontus in Jerusalem on the day of Pentecost and some of them likely bore the message of Peter's sermon back to their province. It is not stated that Aquilla and Priscilla, his gifted wife, were already Christians, but it is likely that they had heard and accepted the gospel either in Pontus, from the fact cited above, or in Rome, where they were involved in the edict of expulsion by Claudius. At any rate "*on account of his being of the same craft, he abode with them and they began* to *work* together, *for they were tent-makers by trade.*" So while Paul was waiting for the coming of Silas and Timothy from Macedonia, he carried on, either employed or sharing the business with these new and valuable friends, fellow-Jews, and, due to no mention of their conversion later, probably fellow-Christians. (v. 4) *On every Sabbath he* customarily *discoursed in the synagogue and went on trying to persuade*[37] *the Jews and Greeks,* proselytes or God-fearers. (v. 5.) *When* at length the Apostle's *helpers, Silas and Timothy, came from Macedonia,* bringing good cheer from the saints in Thessalonica (I Thess. 2) and gifts from Philippi (II Cor. 11:9; Phil. 4:15), it became possible for him to leave off his manual labor and "*he was constrained by the word, giving thorough testimony to the Jews that Jesus was the Messiah.*" His effort was greatly intensified and the effects began to be manifested in conversions, arousing the consequent antagonism of the Jews. The antagonism of the Jewish leaders grew rapidly with the continuous and energetic testimony of Paul, and soon organized itself. (v. 6) "*And when they* (the Jews) *began to form a faction and blaspheme*"

---

34. I Thessalonians 3:11.
35. W. M. Ramsay: *St. Paul the Traveler and Roman Citizen,* p. 254, cf. Suetonius.
36. Tertullian says that "Chrestus" was used for "Christus." The conflict was probably between the Jews and Christians about Jesus being the Messiah and both Jews and Christians were expelled.
37. Conative imperfect tense.

against the name of Jesus, whom Paul announced as the Messiah and Son of God, "*he* (the apostle) *symbolically shook out his outer garments*" (*himatia-cape*), an act of denunciation of their blasphemy against the Lord "*and said unto them, 'Your blood be on your own head!'* "[38] He thus "turned them over to death," solemnly charging them with the responsibility by declaring; "I on my side am clean! Clear of any responsibility, "*I henceforth go unto the Gentiles*" in this city. Ramsay says Paul was not very conciliatory in this instance and that the shaking of the garment was a "very exasperating gesture." (v. 7) "*He changed*" his place of meeting for those who had already become Christians and those who were interested in his teachings, "*and went into the house of a certain man named Titius Justus, one who was a 'God-fearer'* or proselyte *whose house joined hard to the synagogue.*" This man Titius Justus was, by his name, a Roman or Latin, pertaining probably to the colony of Italians, maintained by the Roman government in Corinth.[39] This was a key man and an open door for the gospel to the better class of people in that extensive section of the population of Corinth. It does not appear to us to have been very tactful to establish his place of meeting next door to the Synagogue; but it might have been justified, on the ground of being the only place available at that time where they could meet. It might have been wise on another ground quite different, in order to attract those already interested in the Gospel of Jesus. Paul would not have done it for spite. *The ruler of the Synagogue Crispus*, himself was one such who *believed in the Lord Jesus with all his household.* Customarily there were two rulers in a synagogue, but it seems there was only one in this one in Corinth.[40] This produced a bitterness, like that when the pastor of one denomination joins the church of another next door.[41] The success of the work intensified and the interest deepened, bringing on an ever mounting wave of antagonism on the part of the Jews. (v. 8) "*And many of the Corinthians* from outside the circle of the synagogue *were accustomed to hear* and *were continually* accepting or *believing and professing* their belief by *being baptized.*"[42] Paul baptized personally Stephanus, who was won to Christ in Athens before Paul came to Corinth; Crispus, the ruler of the Synagogue; and another Latin, Gaius, from the Italian colony, a man of considerable means and of generous hospitality. These were the only ones Paul baptized, that function being left ordainarily to be performed by his helpers, Timothy and Titus, who were absent at the time it was done. The bitterness and resentment of the Jews soon grew to the point that the life of the apostle was endangered.

It was in the midst of this vexation and disturbance of his equanimity that "*the Lord* Jesus came, and *in the night in a vision said unto Paul, 'Be not afraid but speak on, and hold not thy peace* (v. 10) *because I am with thee,*

38. W. M. Ramsay: *St. Paul the Traveler and Roman Citizen*, p. 255.
39. Ibid. cf. Acts 18:7.
40. The Bezan Text discriminates between the archons, two in number in the synagogue and the archisynagogoi, the chief rulers of the synagogue.
41. A. T. Robertson, *Epochs in the Life of Paul*, p. 165.
42. Imperfect tenses of progressive and continued action, in the verbs.

and no man shall set on thee to harm thee, because I have much people in this city. ' " The resentment of his enemies had grown so strong that Paul had reason to fear an assault at any time. He might be driven out of this city as he had been from some of the cities of Asia and Macedonia. But just at this juncture came the revelation of God's will that he should remain. This brought assurance, and he "set himself" definitely to stick to his job there until the Lord should reveal some other plan. (v. 11) "*And he settled down and stayed a year and six months, teaching among them*[43] progressively day after day *the word of God.*" The work of indoctrination went on and the work of evangelization was expanded more and more, until the word sounded out from the great church Paul built there throughout all the province of Achaia,[44] of which Corinth was the political capital. A church was also founded at Cenchreae,[45] the principal sea-port town on the side of the Aegean Sea. The period of Paul's residence in Corinth was at least eighteen months and probably two years or more in all.[46]

---

43. Locative case.
44. I Thessalonians 1:7f.
45. Romans 16:1.
46. Acts 18:11, 18.

CHAPTER XI

The Thessalonian Missionary Epistles

Introduction

THE first of Paul's two epistles written to the Thessalonian church was the earliest of his epistles, and was probably written before any of the Gospels were compiled from notes and oral traditions in their present form. Paul was already in the middle of his Christian career as a missionary and preacher. His ministries in Tarsus and Cilicia, followed by his work in Antioch of Syria with Barnabas and their three years missionary journey in which they founded the cause in Cyprus and in large areas of Asia Minor, were already recorded history.

On this second missionary journey going forward from Philippi, Paul passed, by the Egnation Road, through Amphipolis, and Apollonia, neither of which had a Jewish Synagogue, and came to Thessalonica (modern Saloniki) a free city and self-governing democracy, approximately a hundred miles from Philippi. Into this important capital, with a population of nearly 100,000, and, later in the beginning of the 10th century, about 200,000, the apostle quietly entered unheralded, with the Gospel message burning in his heart.

The wider ministry of Paul and his fellow-missionaries covered two or three months or longer, including the three weeks in the synagogue before the break with the incensed Jews. The missionaries had turned to the Gentiles at that time and had gained many converts. During all this time Paul labored strenuously, watched and spied upon by the malicious eyes of his fellow-countrymen. Heroically, the apostle carried on, visiting from house to house, preaching the goods news, "with Silvanus and Timotheus."

The Church

The fine character of the church founded here was the outgrowth of the nature of earnest work of the missionaries in its founding. It was composed more largely of the Gentiles than Jews, because the apostles turned to the Gentiles when they were rejected by the leading Jews. The work among the Gentiles was largely personal and individual evangelism. They manifested courage in their work, reliance upon the leadership of the Holy Spirit, and conviction in their teaching. From this kind of ministry grew up a church full of spontaneous and intense religious life and experience (I Thess. 5:21, 22). The church, which began its history in the home of Jason, must have been small in the beginning, but must have grown rapidly enough (II Thess. 3:7).[1] Paul's diligence in self-support would appeal to the working class of skilled labourers, but there were some from the higher social class, chiefly of the Gentile women. Paul gave himself tenderly to the infant church 'as a nurse cherishes her own children,' giving them much individual and tender care, warnings against evils, instructions as to faith, hope, love, hospitality and brotherly love, endurance in trial, and joy in the Holy Spirit. Their consecration to God must be linked to a moral life. The indwelling Christ was guarantee against worry about their salvation. The Lord was to return, and when He did, would save them from the persecution which they must patiently endure for the time. They must be diligent in their work and exemplary in their lives.

I Thessalonians

It was soon after Silas and Timothy came back from their special missions to Philippi and Thessalonica, that Paul, relieved by the monetary aid from the Philippian church, and cheering news from Thessalonica, that the brethren had stood firmly in the midst of persecution, wrote his First Epistle to the Thessalonians. The oral report of Timothy had been reenforced and supplemented by a letter from the brethren of the, as yet, small but substantial Thessalonian church, which made known other conditions and problems, for the resolution of which they requested the help of the apostle. Paul laid hold on the *epistle* — an instrument popularly used in his age — to encourage, stimulate, inform, indoctrinate and warn the believers in the churches he had founded in various places, about the life of a Christian and a church in the midst of an evil world. Some of Paul's letters were of a more personal character, as that to Philemon; others were formal and stately, being designed to be read in public assemblies for "indoctrination, reproof, correction and instruction in righteousness."

Paul wrote some letters less important than others, as several references in his extant letters seem to indicate. Compare II Thessalonians 2:2, a warning against forgeries; and 3:17 how to tell a genuine letter of his (Robertson). The usual and what seems the most reasonable chronological order, is: I and II Thessalonians; I and II Corinthians, Galatians, and Romans; Philippians, Philemon, Colossians, Ephesians; I Timothy, Titus, II Timothy.[2] Paul seems to allude to a letter which was lost (cf. I Corinthians 5:9).

The Thessalonian Epistles were probably written during the period 50-51 A. D. The fundamental principles of Paul's theology, as preached by him until the time of the writing of these two epistles, are recorded in them. The gospel of God, (I Thessalonians 2:13; Acts 13:46) was also the gospel of Christ who is its (Savior) content, I Thessalonians 3:2; and the gospel of salvation: I Thessalonians 2:16; Acts 13:26, because that is the end and purpose of it.[3] Paul's main argument in this early missionary preaching was to prove by the

1. Cf. Deismann, *Bible Studies,* in loco.
2. Cf. A. T. Robertson, *Epochs in the Life of Paul,* p. 166.
3. Cf. A. Sabatier, *The Apostle Paul,* p. 112ff.

Scriptures that Jesus was the Messiah. In Paul's letters may be traced a spiritual and doctrinal development. Experience always precedes theory. The ecclesiastical nature of the epistle did not overshadow the personal and pastoral experiences. On the contrary the letters grew out of concrete circumstances and cannot be correctly interpreted apart from the historical background.

In these first two epistles, which are so personal, dealing with life situations, we find the seeds of all the principal doctrines, expounded more fully by Paul later in the more lengthy epistles. Some of them are: the love and grace of God in Christ; the death of Christ on the cross, for man's sin; justification by faith; redemption; obedience; judgment; and the second coming,[4] which last was greatly emphasized. Paul came to the conclusion, through experience with the gospel in Thessalonica, as he came into contact with the Roman officers and government, that emperor worship was the greatest foe of Christianity.

Analysis and Paraphrastic Exegesis

Address and Salutation I Thess. 1:1.

Paul and Silas or Silvanus (Roman name) *and Timothy*, his associates in the work in Thessalonica, address this letter *to the church* or called out assembly *of Thessalonians*, characterized as being *in* the sphere of fellowship and union with *the* true *God* of Israel, the *Father*, Creator of all men but Father in a peculiar sense of the Christian, and to them equally, as *in* union with *the Lord Jesus*, the *Messiah*, whom he had preached to them as risen from the dead, and Who is therefore the living Lord of Christians forevermore. His salutation to them, simple but combining the richness of the Greek (charis) *grace*, the sum of all spiritual blessing that man receives and experiences in God's love and favor to the undeserving, together with (eirēnē), the Hebrew *peace*, which is not only the absence of hostility and disorder but the health, harmony, tranquility and spiritual well-being, or blessings of the Messianic Kingdom, to be realized only through the grace of God in Christ.

I. Paul reminds them of his recent experiences with them on the occasion of his visit to them with Silas and Timothy.

CHAPTERS I-III

1. Their *thanksgiving* for the Thessalonian Christians and reasons for it. 1:2-10

v. 2 *We* (the apostle, with Silas and Timothy, his associates in the work in Thessalonica), *give thanks to God at every time concerning all you* Thessalonians, Christians, *making mention* specifically and constantly of you *at our prayer times.* The reasons for this constant thanksgiving is: first our

v. 3 *remembering your work growing out of faith,*[5] your activity in the labor[6] of the Kingdom to the point of fatigue, which comes from *love,* and

4. A. T. Robertson: *Epochs in the Life of Paul,* p. 168.
5. Ablative of source.
6. Fatiguing toil.

your faithful *patience* or endurance, remaining under the burden, having its origin and motive in your *hope* based on *our Lord Jesus Christ, in the presence of God our Father.*

v. 4 Furthermore, this kind of life in the Thessalonian Christians had convinced the missionaries of their election: *because we know,*[7] *brothers beloved by God* with a permanent and abiding love,[8] that *your election* is a fact.

v. 5 (*because*) *our gospel* which we preach *did not come unto you in word only* or as a matter of hearing merely or of logical argumentation on our part, *but in* the sphere of real divine power, *even in* the sphere of *the Holy Spirit and* through His instrumentality,[9] making use of our preaching which was accomplished *with much* conviction or *assurance.* Another reason for their thanksgiving on behalf of the Thessalonian Christians was the character of their conversion under trying circumstances.

v. 5, 6 *Just as you know what kind of men we* missionaries *became in your midst,*[10] *on your account* or for your sakes, *and* knowing our lives and conduct *you became imitators of* us *and of the Lord, receiving the word* we preached *in* the midst of *much affliction* caused by persecution, *with* genuine *joy from the Holy Spirit.*[11] A fourth reason for thanksgiving was found in the result of such conduct on their part in the effective scattering of the gospel message everywhere.

v. 7, 8 *So that you became an example* or model community of Christian life and conduct, *to tell the believers in Macedonia and in Achaia. For, from you has sounded forth* in a complete way[12] *the word of the Lord, not only in Macedonia and Achaia* but *in every place,* the news of *your faith toward God has gone forth, with the result that there is no need for us to say any thing* about you. The fifth reason cited for thanksgiving was the notorious story of the conversion of the Thessalonians to the Gospel and the consequent transformation in them which it had, producing a profound effect far and near.

v. 9, 10 The people everywhere *themselves are reporting about us*[13] missionaries[14] *what kind of access we had to you* on our visit there, *and how you turned to God from your pagan idols, to serve the* only *living and true God and await His Son from the heavens,* in His second advent (as we all expect), *whom He raised from the dead,* as I revealed unto you in my preaching, even *Jesus the one who is delivering us from the* anger or *wrath* of judgment *which is coming.* Paul points thus to the judgment which comes consistently and always upon every transgression but in a special way in the day of the great Assizes, the judgment day.

---

7. Second perfect participle, *eidotes,* Paul and his associates come to know completely and were not at all in doubt about the reality of their conversion.
8. Perfect participle, *agapamenoi* denoting a love which abides.
9. Case of the noun may be locative or instrumental here.
10. Locative case.
11. Ablative of origin — or source of the joy.
12. Perfect tense.
13. Betald, *humōn* easier reading but *hēmon* better for what follows (Frame) ICC.
14. Second perfect *esxowev.*

2. Paul's reference to their work in Thessalonica as missionaries, by way of defense of his conduct, 2:1-12.

Paul was being attacked personally by his enemies in Thessalonica. This was reported to him by Timothy his devoted son in the faith and by the loyal brothers in Thessalonica in their letter sent by Timothy to him. In his reply to the letter he refers especially to his own conduct and also to that of his fellow-missionaries who followed his example, saying,

Ch. 2:v. 1 *You yourselves know brothers*, the character of *our entrance* or visit *to you, that it has not become*[15] or proven to be vain or *empty*. This he proceeds to show by various considerations, citing their courage, purity, love and fidelity, as marks of their Christian genuineness.

(1) The courage of the missionaries in the midst of the conflict of their work in Philippi, which they had made known to their hearers in Thessalonica.

v. 2 *but having suffered before and having been shamefully* (insolently) *treated just as you know in Philippi*, a treatment by the magistrates, of scourging and imprisonment, which Paul and Silas, who were Roman citizens, resented but bore courageously. In spite of this recent experience of injustice, he says, *we waxed bold*,[16] became emboldened in our confidence, *in our God to speak to you the gospel in* the midst of *much conflict*, both outward, due to real dangers, and inward due to anxiety, in the beginning of the work in Thessalonica. Herein was a strong evidence of the genuineness of their work and integrity of their motive. This was a courageous power inspired by God.

(2) Another evidence of the genuineness of the missionaries had been their sincerity and freedom from any personal ambition. Paul's Jewish enemies had insinuated, as soon as they had succeeded in expelling him from Thessalonica, that he was a self-deluded, sensual renegade, full of deceit. "His message was one of error and ignorance," they said, "one of flattering words motivated by selfish greed, one of deceit seeking the honor of men." Paul responds to these insinuations, speaking for himself and his associates, saying,

v. 3 *For our exhortation* or appeal *is not out of error* or self-delusion, from ignorance of the truth, *nor* does it spring *from* sensual *uncleanness*, conscious of moral impurity and guilt. On the contrary his motives were pure from unselfishness and private gain and he was conscious of integrity. Nor did his work originate from deceit done *in guile*.

v. 4 *On the contrary, just as we were approved by God* being tested out by him *to be entrusted with his gospel*, even *thus we go on speaking*[17] *it, not as being pleasing to men, but to God who* is *the one who constantly tests our hearts. For neither did we ever once come* to you *with word of flattery, as you know, nor with a pretext* springing *from* but covering up selfish *greed, God is my witness; nor seeking glory* or honor *from men, neither from you nor from others,* although *we were able to be in* a position of *weight* or burden,

15. Second perfect, *gegonen.*
16. Ingressive first aorist middle, *eparrasiasametha.*
17. Present tense of customary or progressive action.

as apostles or missionaries *of Christ,* either in the matter of finance or honor (Robertson).

(3) Another evidence of their genuineness, as missionaries, was their gentleness and tender affection toward the Thessalonians.

v. 7, 8 He continues, "*But*" contrary to such conduct "*we* (Paul and his fellow-missionaries) *became* (gentle) *babes in the midst of you.*" instead of imposing ourselves as burdensome missionaries,[18] but *as a nurse cherishes her own children.*

v. 8 *Even so being affectionately desirous of you, we were well pleased*[19] *to impart to you not only the gospel of God but our very selves* as well, (for) *because you had become*[20] *very dear* (beloved) *to us.* The affectionate nature of Paul is here confessed in the extreme and most beautiful figure of a "mother-nurse who suckles and nurses her own children" (Lightfoot). What could express more completely the tender and gentle affection of the great-hearted apostle!

(4) Paul calls to their memory his arduous labors and holy, righteous and blameless conduct.

v. 9, 10 *You remember* of course *brothers our* fatiguing *toil and our* difficult moil or *labor, working* for our living *by night-time,*[21] rising before dawn and working until after dark, *and* also in the *day-time,* to the extent, *not to burden anyone of you,* so *we preached unto you the gospel of God.* This was a strong evidence of sincerity, unselfishness and self-sacrifice of the missionaries. *You are witnesses* (*martures*) *and God also, how piously* toward God, *and righteously* toward men, *and blamelessly to you* the *believers we became* in our conduct and daily life.

(5) The apostle reminds them finally of the fidelity of the preaching, teaching and spiritual help of their missionaries.

v. 11, 12 *Just as you know, as a father,* deals individually with *each one of his own children,* we were both *encouraging* or consoling you, and *witnessing* or testifying, that *you* should *walk worthily of God, the one who is calling*[22] *you into his own kingdom and glory.*

In these few strokes of his pen the apostle depicts the pastoral ideal, strokes that build up in a shining picture, which will remain incomparable in its beauty and attraction for all the aeons of time and eternity. In it we see the individual marks of boldness and courage, purity and truthfulness, fidelity and loyalty to God, unselfishness, love, the gentleness of the mother-nurse, altruistic disinterestedness, strenuous self-sacrifice, longing evangelism, affectionate treatment of the new converts with a fatherly pastoral care, with other numerous lines which intertwine and overlap in a mesh of marvelous beauty. What a picture of the ideal minister-missionary and the pastor-preacher![23]

---

18. J. E. Frame, *ICC,* p. 91.
19. Imperfect indicative.
20. Aorist passive *gegonen.*
21. Genitive case expressing kind of time.
22. Present participle, progressive action.
23. Cf. Walter F. Adeney, *The Century Bible,* p. 33.

3. Thanks to God for their welcome extended to the gospel, while in persecutions by the Jews, 2:13-16.

The Thessalonian believers had welcomed the gospel while in the midst of severe persecutions, and while the missionaries were also under fire from their common enemies, the Jews.

(1) Paul and his associates are progressively and increasingly thankful to God for this welcome.

v. 13 On account of this other thing, *also we go on giving thanks* to God *without ceasing, because when you received from us the word, which you heard, you welcomed it not as a word* (message) *from men, but as it really is, a word* (message) from *God,*[24] *who also operated*[25] *in you who believe.* Paul was conscious of preaching God's message and he was not in doubt about its being God's divinely inspired word. It did not grow out from error or ignorance but it came from God to men, and the evidence of this fact was to be seen in its energizing effects in those who were believers.

(2) Those results or effects he next points out: v. 14 *you became imitators brethren of the local churches of God which are in Judea,* being Christian churches *in* the sphere of the belief in and mystical communion with *Christ* the Messiah, who was *Jesus the Nazarene.*

Their complete fellowship with these churches in Judea in suffering was evidenced, *because you suffered the same things by your own countrymen* in Thessalonica, incited as they were by the persecuting Jewish rabbis who stirred them up, exactly *as these* Judean churches, *by the Jewish leaders* in Palestine.

(3) In a brief digression, the apostle denounced the violence of the Jewish persecutors.

v. 15, 16 *who put to death the Lord Jesus and,* even before him, in their historical antagonism to God's will, *the prophets, and drove us,* his missionaries *out* of Thessalonica, and *not pleasing God* thus, as they think, *and are contrary to all men.*[26] This hostility of the Jewish rabbis in Thessalonica was seen in their trying to *hinder us from speaking to the gentiles in order that they might be saved.* Paul declared that "Satan had hindered him," and doubtless it was through these same Jewish persecutors who did not desire that he should preach to the gentiles in Thessalonica and arranged by a slick method to drive the apostle and Silas out and keep them out, by putting Jason and the church under bond. All this Paul said was to wind up, for these persecutors, *in the filling up to the full their sins of all time,* an hereditary accumulation from the sins of their forefathers until they came to their culmination in the death of God's Son on the cross. *The wrath* of judgment *is come* already *unto completion* or climax and rests *upon them* (these offenders) now.

4. Paul's present relations to the Thessalonian saints and his prayer for them. 2:17-3:13

---

24. Ablative of origin *anthropōn* and *theou.*
25. Middle Voice Perfect Tense, *energetai,* showing the vitality in the message itself.
26. Tacitus, History, V, 5. He says 'the Jews are *adversus omnes alios hostile odium.*'

The cruel enemies of Paul and of his associated missionaries, shut them out of Thessalonica, so that Paul and Silas might never return, and later added insult to injury, by declaring to his newly made disciples in Thessalonica, 'that Paul did not desire to return to them nor had ever had any such intention.' Paul presents his apology and explanation now, for his failure to return. He had just expressed his thanks to God for them and given the reasons for such; he now explains his present feelings about them and his plans for a future visit. Now, he speaks (1) of his great desire to revisit them and the thwarted attempts he made to do so (2:17-20). (2) He states how he sent Timothy when it was impossible for him to come (3:1-5). (3) He expresses his satisfaction with the report of Timothy, on his return (3:6-10).

(1) His intended visit (2:17-20).

To remove any doubt as to his intention and desire to revisit them, Paul states that, contrary to the calumny of his enemies, he and his fellow missionaries had intended and greatly desired to return but were hindered. (v. 17) *But we* missionaries, *brethren, when we had been* torn away from and *bereaved of you* (lit. orphaned) *for a short season* of an hour, *in presence, not in heart, endeavored the more exceedingly to see your face, with great desire.* Paul had felt a mental anguish, when he was separated from his new converts in Thessalonica, similar to that which a father feels, when forcibly separated from his own children, as in the dastardly emergency caused by war. As soon as the separation came, he had a passionate desire to return, and had attempted to work out a plan to do so.

v. 18. *Because, we did wish to come to you, certainly I, Paul, did once and again;* (ofttimes); *but*[27] *Satan* cut in our path and *stopped us* by *cutting us off* through his wily devices. He is a great interceptor of the plans of missions! Paul asserts warmly his love for the Thessalonian (saints) believers, over against the insinuation of his enemies to them that he did not care for them. (v. 19) *For what is our hope or joy or crown of glorying? Are not you* (as also other churches) our chaplet to boast of *in the presence of our Lord Jesus at his coming*, in his expected second advent.

v. 20 *For you* yourselves really *are our glory and our joy.* These exuberant words of a hearty and genuine confession of his love for them, were convincing, and had a ring of no uncertain sound.

(2) The sending of Timothy (3:1-5).

In view of the above facts Paul passes to reveal the plan he adopted to meet the frustration which Satan had introduced to defeat him, by sending Timothy to them.

v. 1 *Wherefore* since *we intended no longer to forbear* (cover up our feelings about) the separation, *we thought it well to be left in Athens alone,*

v. 2 *and we sent Timothy our brother and God's minister in the gospel of Christ,*[28] *to strengthen* or establish *you and encourage* or comfort *you on be-*

---

27. Adversative use of kai.

28. Codex B, the best of the Greek MSS, reads simply, "our brother and fellow-worker in the gospel of Christ."

half of, or in the furtherance of *your faith, that no one of you be moved in the midst of these afflictions.* Temptation often comes in the midst of trial. *For you yourselves know that we* believers *are appointed unto this* temptation of the beguiling effect of tribulations, which we must resist.

v. 4 *For verily when we were with you, we were accustomed to tell you beforehand,* that[29] *'we are about to suffer affliction,' even as it came to pass and as you know.*

v. 5 On this account, I too *when I intended no longer to forbear, enduring the separation, sent him to get a knowledge*[30] *of your faith,* fearing *lest by any means the Tempter had tempted you* even *to the extent that our labor should turn out to be in vain.*

(3) Timothy's return with a good report (3:6-10).

Timothy returned with a good report on the favorable conditions religiously of the saints in Thessalonica and their good attitude toward Paul. This greatly encouraged the apostle, who was himself in the midst of a trying work in Corinth. He would like to be in Thessalonica to confirm yet more their faith, faithfulness and love in the midst of their bitter persecutions.

v. 6 *But when Timothy came even now to us from you and brought the good news*[31] *to us with* respect to *the Christian faith*[32] *and the love,* which *you* retain hardy in the midst of persecutions, *and that you continue to hold a kindly memory of us*[33] *at all times, and have continued to long for us to see us just as we also* to see *you.*

v. 7 *For this reason, brothers, we* (Paul and Silas) *became* comforted or *encouraged* by *you,* to face *every kind* of *necessity* of the nature of *our* privation or distress *and affliction* and this *through* the influence of *your faith.*

v. 8 *because now, we live, if you go on standing fast in the Lord* as Timothy's report positively declares you do.[34] Paul's life was so wrapped up in the church that when the "good news" came it gave him a great relief and released new energies for the work in Corinth.

v. 9 *For what* adequate *thanksgiving are we able to give back unto God concerning you for every kind of joy wherein we rejoice on account you in the presence of our God, and therefore sincerely*

v. 10 *by night and by day beyond measure exceedingly begging to see your face and make up the deficiencies of your faith?* The insinuations of Paul's

---

29. *Hoti,* here has the value of quotation marks, Cf. Dana and Mantey, *New Testament Greek Grammar,* in loco.

30. *Stegōn, from stegō* to cover up, here as in papiri, to endure, Cf. Moulton and Milligan's *Vocabulary.*

31. Perf. middle participle of *evaggellizō,* to evangelize or bring good news.

32. *Pistin — agapēn.* Verbal accusatives of 'specification.' Cf. Dana and Mantey, Robertson, N. T. Greek Grammar.

33. *Hēmōn,* Paul always associates his workers with himself in these references to the relationships with the church. It is not the editorial use but rather the fraternal use of the plural pronouns. Silvanus was with Paul already as also Timothy who brought the report.

34. *Ean* with first class condition indicating reality.

enemies that he did not care for his converts in Thessalonica are met by these exuberant expressions of his feelings of affection and pride toward them and his delight in knowing of their spiritual well-being and loyalty to their missionaries. He and his fellow-missionaries had given the Thessalonians good news and now they are receiving "good news" back in Timothy's report. The Apostle Paul inserts tactfully and wisely in the midst of his warm expressions of thanksgiving to God for them and loving appreciation and personal regard for them, a sincere reference to the perils of their situation and the necessity that they should persist in their faith and love. At the same time he expresses his deep interest in seeing them again and being of real help in the *perfecting of their faith.*

5. Paul's prayer for the Thessalonian saints 3:11-13. From thanksgiving for the persevering faith and love of the Thessalonian believers, Paul passes into prayer for them. He prays in the night time and day time for them that the deficiencies of their faith and faithfulness may give way to a more perfect development, *the things lacking being supplied or made up.*

v. 11 Now may *God himself both our father and our Lord Jesus* also, *direct*[35] *our way to you.*

v. 12 And *may the Lord make you to increase* and *abound in* the sphere of *love, toward one another* as brethren, *and to all men,* unbelievers as well, *just as we* in our love *also toward you,*

v. 13 That *he may strengthen your hearts* so that they may be *blameless in holiness* and that *in the presence of our God and Father in the appearance of our Lord Jesus with all his saints,* at the second coming. The apostle still hopes to visit the believers and prays *that they may be perfected and secure in view of the 'parousia' of Jesus.*

II. Instructions and exhortations 4:1-5:22.

These exhortations are specific in view of the conditions and needs of these believers, who were passing through severe persecutions accompanied by temptations which were incident to and reenforced by the heathen environment. The Thessalonian church had doubtless written for advice concerning various things about which the apostle naturally speaks in his letter to them. He deals especially with the problem of love of the brethren; the dead in Christ; and the times and seasons,[36] with particular reference to the second coming; and the need of watchfulness and sobriety; concluding with various practical exhortations.[37]

1. Exhortations about moral purity and consecration of life, 4:1-8; brotherly love 4:9-10a; and idleness 4:10b-12. The things that were lacking to perfect their faith and character, in view of the second advent of the Lord, leads

35. First aorist optative of *kantenthunō* expressing a wish in prayer, make straight, direct our way to you, note accute accent instead of circumplex.

36. Cf. J. E. Frame, *Int., C. Crit. Com.,* p. 140 and W. F. Adeney, 34.

37. Ibid. in loco,

the apostle to administer a lesson on Christian morals suited to instruct and also to stimulate them in their struggle.

(1) Moral purity and consecration of life, 4:1-8.

v. 1 For the rest, or *finally then, brothers, we beg you* and *exhort* (encourage) you *in* the sphere of *the Lord Jesus, in order that just as you received from us how it is necessary that you walk* or conduct yourselves *and* in a manner *to please God,* even *just as you are also* already *walking, in order that you may go on abounding more* in the same conduct.

v. 2 *For you know what kind of charges* (precepts, commands) *we gave you* in our instructions *through the Lord Jesus* our authoritative leader and teacher. After this *introduction* (4:1, 2) the apostle proceeds to instruct them as to chastity and the true sanctification of the body (v. 3-8).

v. 3-5 *For this is the will* (thelēma) *of God* even *your sanctification* or consecration, namely *that you abstain from fornication,*[38] *that each one of you know* or learn the habit of purity, how *to possess*[39] *his own vessel in* holiness or *sanctification and honor, not in the passion of lust.*[40]

v. 6 *even just as the gentiles who know not God, that no man transgress,* overreach or go beyond, *and wrong his brother in the matter*[41] of moral conduct in the relationships with other men's wives (or husbands), *because the Lord is an avenger in all these things,* of sexual immorality *just as we predicted to you and solemnly testified* or affirmed.

v. 7 *For God did not call us* Christians *for impurity* but *in* the sphere of *progress consecration*[42] of life, wherefore (consequently) *the rejector* of this principle *rejects not man but God even the one who puts his Spirit, the Holy* consecrating *Spirit, into you.* Paul's divine admonition about sexaul purity is based on a divine reality of the gift of the Holy Spirit to indwell the Christian and God is the avenger in case of any disrespect of this principle.

(2) Exhortation to brotherly love (4:9-10).

v. 9, 10 *But concerning brotherly love,* about which you asked in your letter, *you have no need that I should write you. For you yourselves are God-taught to love one another; for you are already doing this very thing* in your relationship *to all the brothers in the whole of Macedonia. But we exhort you, brothers, to go on and abound yet more* in this virtue and practice.

They had the proper instruction about brotherly love, which is so fundamental in the progress of the Kingdom work, and they had manifested this love which extended toward all the brethren in all Macedonia but it only reached into the midst, only touching some personally and not all. Paul delicately reminds them that they need 'to abound more' in this love so that their love may not be one with respect to certain persons and discriminating against others. God loves all and Christ taught his disciples to love all mankind.

---

38. Ablative of separation, *apō tēs norneias.*

39. This calls for sexual purity whether in the married or unmarried. Chastity is required in both husband and wife, man or woman, no double standard.

40. Marriage cannot be for purposes of sexual indulgence.

41. Paul is delicate in his treatment of this wrong.

42. Sanctification.

(3) Exhortation relative to idleness (4:11-12).

Paul urges against the serious fault of some, who in view of the second coming which they thought to be imminent had neglected their occupational duties and activities, that they work quietly with their hands attending to their own business.

v. 11 And we exhort you *to make it* an earnest *study* or "ambition"[43] *to be calm* and *to make it a practice to* do or *attend to your own things* or business, and not to be meddlesome as idlers are, restless busybodies, attending to the affairs of others with little interest in your own proper tasks. And this habit of life will require you *to work with your own hands,* not just those of employees as half the world of unregenerate mankind does, *just as we charged you.* All of this has in view the purpose: *in order that you may walk around* in a manner or conduct, becomingly to your Christian calling, in the presence of and *toward*[44] those who are *without* the fold of the kingdom, *and* that you *may have need of nothing,*[45] of material help from the brotherhood. Thus Paul corrects an evil of meddlesome and 'pious' idlers who are the cause of disturbances in the brotherhood, like dogs that snap and bite the hand that feeds them. People on the "outside" have a right to watch the conduct of professing Christians in business, domestic life, social life and politics (Robertson). Therefore there is a responsibility on the individual Christian to walk "in a manner worthy."[46] If the man outside looks to the example of the "pious idler" in the church, he will turn away and be lost, on his own responsibility, but his blood will be upon the Christian whose example proved a stumbling block to his brother-man "without."

In Paul's epistle there is always a doctrinal and an ethical or practical part. In the ethical part are to be found the positive statements and full explanation of what human conduct should be and must be "inside," in the Christian fold. The motivation of moral conduct is based on the regenerated heart, and there is little to appeal to in man apart from that condition. Mere instruction in the right, apart from the power of the indwelling Spirit to reenforce the human will in practicing the right, has never proven a success. The objective truth of the Word of God alone is sufficient, as a basis for a Christian civilization, and should be taught effectively in all educational institutions of humanity. Ethical subjectivism will never save civilization from suicidal strife.[47] Paul's positive explanations of the great principles of the Hebrew traditions, embodied in the Ten Words, are detailed and effective, if made known to the Christian Brotherhood, which is itself the fundamental hope of a regenerated social order. Only the *Christian* religion furnishes this moral basis and there is no other. To depend on anything less than the evangelization of the social, economic, political and religious life of mankind is futile!

---

43. *Philotimeisthai,* ambition to be quiet, the right aim for the right kind of ambition, not one that uses the good and evil both (ambo) to accomplish one's purpose (Robertson).
44. *Pros,* toward.
45. Neuter gender, not masculine.
46. Cf. Phil. 1:27f.
47. Elton Trueblood, *Foundations for Reconstruction,* Chs. I-III.

2. Instruction and exhortations as to the Second Coming of the Lord Jesus 4:13-5:11.

The most important subject and instructive feature in the "Epistle of the Christian Hope,"[48] is the Coming of the Lord Jesus. In the midst of the bitter persecutions, during the period of the founding of this church the apostle must have emphasized this subject much in his thought and preaching. It appealed powerfully to the imagination of his hearers, beset as they were by fears; and his preaching was potent in inspiring hope in them. In the minds of many Christians, who had been eyewitnesses to the post-resurrection appearances of Jesus and some who had been present at the memorable hour of the ascension, the promises of the Lord himself and also that of the angelic messengers, "that He would return," must have bred in them a hope that it would be soon. Paul himself was heir to this Christian tradition, passed on from mouth to mouth. Had Jesus not said that it would be "before that generation should pass away"? At least many had interpreted literally His statement to them. "The coming of our Lord Jesus Christ with all His saints" was therefore an "object of intense desire and fervent "anticipation," of the apostle himself. This hope was the strongest support of his appeals and warnings when he was in the midst of the newly made and persecuted disciples in Thessalonica. The doctrine of the final judgment was also adopted to rouse the Greeks from their levity and moral indifference. Paul had later used this doctrine in his sermon in the Areopagos in Athens (Acts 17:30f). He surely must have made vivid this doctrine in his preaching in Thessalonica, judging from the results (I Thess. 5:2; II Thess. 2:6). In his entrance into Europe, and even before the Roman Empire had greatly impressed the apostle and led him to visualize the coming Kingdom of the Lord Jesus, already reigning as He was on the Messianic throne in the heavens, Paul looked ardently for the appearance of the Lord (parousia.) The Kingdoms of this world must some day, from their very nature, pass away. Then the Messianic Kingdom would take their place.[49]

Paul's teaching about this Kingdom had been misunderstood and there were also some new questions, raised by the deaths of believers in Thessalonica. Some fainthearted (*oligopsuchoi*) believers were concerned about their dead (4:13-18) and also about their own salvation (5:1-11). Paul hoped that the Lord might return while he himself was alive. But he had not ignored the teaching of Jesus about "no man knowing the day or the hour." The misunderstanding and misinterpretation of his teaching, now made necessary some explanation, and it gave rise to his writing the classic passage (4:13-18) of this Epistle on the subject, which has been of such incomparable comfort to homes visited by the hand of death and to bereaved hearts, for the many centuries since Christ taught that the death of the Christian disciple is but a sleep and Paul added "that Christians are to sorrow not as those that have no hope."

---

48. R. D. Shaw, *The Pauline Epistles*, p. 31.
49. Geo. G. Findlay, *The Cambridge Bible*, Thessalonians, pp. 18-21,

(1) Concerning them that fall asleep — the dead in Christ (4:13-18).

Paul had been in his career for seventeen years, but few Christians relatively had died in that time. The question of the status of the dead in Christ, in comparison with the saints alive, at His appearance had not been raised until now, although Jesus had intimated that some would die before He should come (Mark 9:1). This expression of Paul is the first we have by him as to the resurrection of believers.[50] He places the survivors and the dead in Christ on the same level in the Second Coming (hama sun).

v. 13 *But we do not wish to have you go on in ignorance, brothers, concerning them who are falling asleep*[51] in death from time to time, *in order that you may not sorrow just as the rest that have no hope.*

v. 14 *For if we believe that Jesus died and rose again even so also God will* lead on or *bring through Jesus those who already fell asleep,* together *with him.*

So Paul bids the brethren who had loved ones and brethren who had died in Christ, to be assured (1) that their departed fellow-believers would not be at a disadvantage or disparity with the living saints when Jesus should appear in His second advent (vv. 13, 14). (2) He goes on to reveal further that the deceased in Jesus will have the first place in the assembly of the saints at His appearance (parousia).

v. 15-17 *For this to you we say, by the word of the Lord,*[52] *that we who are alive, who are left to the* time of the *coming of the Lord shall not precede* those who fell asleep. v. 16 *Because the Lord himself will descend from heaven* as a Conqueror *with a command, with a voice of an archangel and with a trumpet of God and the dead in Christ shall rise first, then* afterwards *we the living* believers *who are left shall be caught up* (siezed up) *at the same time with them,* (hama sun, autois), the dead who have, been raised, *in clouds,*[54] *to meet the Lord in the air; and thus we shall be always*[55] *with the Lord.*

v. 18 *So, comfort one another with these words.*

Paul did not mean to assert that he expected to be living when the Lord should return; nor did he declare that he would not, when he wrote: "God will also raise us up by his own power" (I Cor. 6:14). The apostle was not mistaken about Jesus' work as Messiah on earth, nor did he profess to know when Jesus would come. To have done so would have been to contradict what Jesus said in His prophetic discourse.[56] Furthermore the apostle was not discussing

---

50. Lake, *Expos,* 1907, pp. 494ff.

51. Present passive (or middle) participle (koimonenōv). Greeks and Romans used sleep as figure of speech for death as Jesus did.

52. Either instrumental or else locative case logō kuriou by the word or in the words of the Lord (quoting His authority). Paul always put Christ first as his authority when he could quote his words or his teachings in traditions.

53. Second aorist active subjunctive with negative. Robertson, *N. T. Greek Grammar,* p. 929. Cf. *Word Pictures* in loco.

54. Locative case, (nefelais) sphere within which, rather than instrumental.

55. Pantote, at every time, always, forever.

56. Cf. Matt. chapters 24, 25 in loco.

the general resurrection in I Thess. (4:13-18) but reaches the climax of his thought in (v. 17) declaring that, in His appearance, all his saints will be received by Him into His presence "always." This is enough to know about those who sleep in Jesus and those who are in Him in life now. The status of those who died out of Christ is not discussed. Paul sets at rest forever the saints in Christ, about their deceased fellow-believers. The survivors are not to sorrow for their departed friends, as the unbelievers who have no hope.[57]

(2) Paul's reply to the Thessalonians, as to the times and seasons, in relation to the Second Coming (5:1-11).

The important subject of the Second Coming of the Lord Jesus was discussed (4:13-18), as related to those who had fallen asleep in the Lord; the same subject is dealt with (5:1-11), as related to the saints who were alive. In view of the uncertainty of the time (vv. 1-3), the living saints[58] are to be always ready for the event (vv. 4-9). Some of the faint-hearted brethren in Thessalonica were concerned not only about their deceased fellow-believers but also about their own salvation. They were stirred up by Paul's emphasis on the subject of the Second Advent, fearing lest the sudden coming of the Lord "like a thief in the night," as Paul cited it from Jesus' parabolic teaching on that subject,[59] might catch them morally unprepared. Paul replies that they need no further instruction on the suddenness of His coming (vv. 1-3), but rather encouragement; and stimulates them to be prepared always (v. 4-5a). They would not be overtaken by surprise as the unbelievers who will not accept the warning and repent, but will be aware, if they are really acting the part of "sons of the light and of the day," as they should be. (v. 5) He incorporates himself with them in the exhortation to all to be sober and alert, armed with faith, love, and the hope of salvation (vv. 5b-8). There is no cause for anxiety, as the indwelling Spirit of Christ is the convincing assurance of their salvation.[60] (vv. 9, 10)

(a) The suddenness and uncertainty of the time of His coming (vv. 1-3).

v. 1 *Concerning the times and seasons, brothers, you have no need that anything be written unto you.* The implication is that the Thessalonians had been writing Paul about "the times and seasons."

v. 2 *For you yourselves know accurately that the day of the Lord shall come just as a thief in the night, suddenly and unexpectedly.*[61]

v. 3 *Whenever they may say peace and safety, then sudden destruction comes upon them even as the travail pain upon the woman with child.* The suddenness and certainty of the event are declared along with the uncertainty of the time; and the character of the time is here depicted,[62] *and they shall not escape.*[63]

(b) It should be different with them (vv. 4, 5).

---

57. Some Christians do so grieve, but should not, Cf. subjunctive mood, v. 13.
58. Cf. Geo. G. Findlay, *Cambridge Bible*, I Thessalonians, Chap. 4:13-5:11.
59. Matthew 24, 25 in loco.
60. Cf. J. E. Frame, *ICC*, in loco.
61. Matthew 24:39; Luke 21:34, 35.
62. Boise's *Notes on the Epistles of Paul* (Wood), p. 488.
63. Aorist Subjunctive with ***hōtan.***

v. 4, 5 *But you, brothers, are not in the darkness that the day* of the Lord's coming *should overtake you as a thief. For all of you are sons of light, and sons of day.*

(c) *We Christians are not of night nor of darkness.* Thus would Paul identify himself with the faint-hearted brethren and help them to a clearer understanding of their position in the Christian life as sons of the light.

v. 6 *So then let us not sleep as do the rest* (unbelievers), *but let us watch and be sober.*

v. 7 *For it is during the night that sleepers sleep and in the night-time that drinkers drink.*[64]

v. 8 *But we, since we belong to day, let us be sober, putting on the breast-plate of faith and love, and as a helmet the hope of salvation.*

(d) But there is no need of anxiety (vv. 9, 10).

v. 9 *For God did not appoint us unto wrath but unto the obtaining of the salvation, of a victorious life through the agency of our Lord Jesus Christ*[65] who is our Savior.

v. 10 *Who died for us, that, whether we wake or sleep we should live together with him.*

v. 11 *Wherefore exhort one another, and build each other up, even as also ye are doing.*

3. Instructions and exhortations for the sanctified Christian life. 5:12-22.

Paul enforces, in this final section of the ethical part of his first letter, the virtues which the believers need to cultivate, in order to live the life of consecration to God and the cause of Christ. These instructions were given for all the members of the church and not just to the Elders as some have understood. The indwelling of the Holy Spirit was presented in the general exhortation as the reason, basis, and means of a consecration of life. The exhortation, there, is to a holy life, which begins in the consecration or setting apart of life in the initial act of acceptance of Christ. The practical life of consecration cannot be desecrated by fornication. Every man must know how to avoid fornication. In the common terminology and the (konion) common law, the wife was spoken of as the vessel. The consecrating power is God (I Thess. 5:23); Christ (I Cor. 1:2, 30); the Holy Spirit (I Thess. 5:8; II Thess. 2:13 cf. Rom. 15:16). The meaning of *hagiasmos* in I Thess. 4:3, 5 is the 'process of consecration' but the state of consecration I Thess. 4:4, ct. Frame *ICC*, p. 147. The word in the title above refers to the work of the Spirit as the motive power of a pure life. In I Thess. 5:23, the implication of the prayer for a full sanctification implies imperfection and incompleteness in the believers, calling for progress.

(1) Exhortations relating to the social duties and relations in the church in leadership and in following the leaders. (vv. 12-15)

(a) Spiritual laborers (vv. 12, 13).

---

64. Cf. Frame, *ICC*, in loco.
65. *Dia* with the genitive of agency.

v. 12 *But we beg you, brothers to* get acquainted with and *know those who are toiling* in the work among you as your missionaries *and those who are over you in the Lord,* your leaders in the Lord, both presbyters or bishops and deacons, *and those who admonish* you having the task of putting some sense into the heads of some of the people.

v. 13 Esteem them very highly in love on account of their work. *Be at peace among yourselves.* These instructions refer to leadership and the relations of the believers to their spiritual leaders.

(b) Paul had referred to the three classes of meddlesome idlers, (4:11, 12; 5:12, 13), those concerned about their dead (4:13-18), and about their own salvation (5:1-11) and those who were weak being tempted to unchastity (4:3-8). He adds now about the same classes:

v. 14 *Furthermore we exhort you brethren, admonish* or warn *the disorderly* idlers and "put some sense into their heads" (Robertson); *encourage the faint-hearted* (or little-souled brethren); cling to or *support* with your helpful counsel *the weak* who are tempted to sin; have patience and seek to hold on to them and help to get them straightened out, *be long-suffering toward all.*

These functions of nourishing, encouraging and admonishing were not a monopoly of the leaders, though the exhortations were applicable to them. They refer to all the brethren of the church in their social relations one with another and between the leaders and those who follow.

v. 15 *See that none render unto anyone evil for evil* in retaliation, but keep up the chase and *follow after the good.*

(2) The religious duties (v. 16-22). (a) Of a general character (v. 16-18) and then in relation to the gifts of the Holy Spirit in the church (v. 19-22).[66]

(1a) General exhortations to joy, prayer and thanksgiving (v. 16-18). Christ in the believers is the source of joy, prayer and thanksgiving for he gives the power to carry out all these injunctions.

v. 16 Begin to *Rejoice* (and keep on rejoicing) *always;* begin to *pray* (and keep on praying) *without ceasing* or leaving it off.

v. 17 begin to *give thanks,* and go on in thanksgiving *in everything, for the will of God is this in* the sphere of *Christ Jesus for* (into) *you.*

(1b) Exhortations relating to the gifts of the Holy Spirit (vv. 19-22).

v. 19, 22 *Do not quench* (stop quenching)[67] the fire of *the Holy Spirit.* The exercise of these special gifts must be in decency and in order and not for show (I Cor. 14:26, 40; Rom. 12:6-9). Christians should avoid the extremes in relation to these gifts. The fire of spiritual fervor should not be put out nor allowed to run to wild excess. *Despise not prophesyings.* Stop despising them if you have done so. Prophesying or forth-telling (not foretelling) is the main gift of the Spirit. But some Christians do not like preaching and ridicule the preachers.

---

66. G. G. Findlay, *Camb. Bible for Schools and Colleges,* Thess. Epistles, p. 1116.
67. Aorist Imperative with negative *mē*,

v. 21 *Prove all things* putting them to the test. Even the preaching and preachers must be tested out in order to avoid error. *Hold fast* (keep on holding down) *to the good,* and morally beautiful.

v. 22 *From the* very *appearance of any kind of evil hold yourself aloof.*

4. Prayer 5:23, 24.

And the God of peace himself, whose nature is one of peace and who himself gives peace to others, *sanctify* each of *you, wholly,* every part of you, full grown, complete and perfect through and through, *and may your* eternal and immortal *spirit, your* human mind and heart or *soul* the earthly manifestation of your spirit, *and your* physcial *body be preserved entire* (holoklaron)[68] *blameless at* the Second Coming or appearance (parousia). *Faithful is the one calling you, who will also* certainly *do* this very thing.

5. Final requests 5:25-27.

v. 25 *Brothers, keep on praying for us,* also just as we are praying for you as just now expressed.

v. 26 *Salute all the brethren with a holy kiss* as a token of our sincere friendship and brotherly love.[69]

v. 27 *I adjure you* (put you on oath) *by the Lord that this epistle be read unto all the brethren.*[70]

Benediction (v. 28).

v. 28 *The grace of the Lord Jesus Christ be with you.*[71]

---

68. Singular adjective denoting unity of man's nature, spirit, soul and body, not necessarily trichotomy as opposed to dichotomy elsewhere in Paul's writings (Robertson, *Word Pictures*).

69. This was a customary salutation for Jewish rabbis, Robertson, *Word Pictures.*

70. An indirect command that this epistle was for the church and must be so used.

71. II Thessalonians same with addition of "all."

CHAPTER XII

Second Thessalonians

Analysis and Paraphrastic Exegesis

Salutation 1:1, 2.

THE salutation of the Second is very much like that of the First Epistle. Paul associates *Silas* (Silvanus) *and Timothy* with him in the salutation. They were present when he wrote this letter in Corinth, about a month after the writing of the first. Timothy had carried the first letter to Thessalonica, and, after observing its effect, had returned and reported to Paul. The error, in the interpretation of his preaching on the Second Advent, had not been corrected by the first Epistle. The enthusiasts, who were proclaiming the Day of the Lord as imminent, grew more rampant, and the meddlesome idlers increased yet more in number. But Paul begins his letter to them with the same salutation of, *Grace to you and peace* and adds, *in God our Father and the Lord Jesus Christ,* putting Jesus in the same category with God, the Father.

I. Thanksgiving and prayer for these believers who have been faithful under persecution 1:3-12.

We owe it to God to be giving thanks always for you, brothers. His reasons for spontaneous thanksgiving and earnest prayer for them are expressed in the warmest words.

A. For the growth of the church in faith and love resulting in assurance of salvation 1:3-10.

v. 3 *Just as it is worthy,* meet, or fitting *because your faith grows exceedingly,* and *the love* of *each one* of *you all toward one another aboundeth* progressively.[1]

v. 4 The result (hōste) is *that we ourselves glory in you,* boasting of you *in the churches of God on behalf of* (for) *your patience* or stedfastness *and your faith* and faithfulness *in the midst of all your persecutions and* the *afflictions which you bear.* Paul sees in these afflictions and persecutions a token of God's righteous judgment which will be effected at the coming of the Lord (vv. 5-10). In their endurance of persecution there was proof of the future salvation of those who were faint-hearted.

v. 5 *A manifest token of the righteous judgment of God, to the end that you may* be *accounted worthy*[2] *of the Kingdom of God,* (This was the test of their worthiness; let them stand it well!) *on behalf of which you are suffering.*

---

1. Present active indicative, progressive or linear action.
2. Aorist Pass. Articular Infinitive *Kataxiōthēnal* with Genitive, and expressing end or purpose.

v. 6 *If indeed it is a righteous thing* (as it certainly is)[3] *in God's sight* for God *to recompense affliction to those who afflict you.*

v. 7 *And to you who are afflicted rest with us* who are being persecuted and afflicted here in Corinth, *at the time of the revelation* or apocalypse of *our Lord Jesus from heaven with His angels.* They, who are afflicting you will have to pay for all they are inflicting upon you and also for their refusal to accept the gospel of Christ, when He returns in His second coming, with His angels, *of His power with fire of flame.*

v. 8 *Rendering vengeance to them that know not God and to them that obey not the gospel of our Lord Jesus.*

v. 9, 10 *Who shall suffer punishment even eternal destruction from the presence of the Lord and from the glory of His strength, when He shall come, to be glorified in His saints and to be wondered at by all those who are believers, because* our *testimony to you was believed, in that day.* Thus Paul assures the faint-hearted and strengthens all to endure afflictions and points them to the assurance of their salvation, evidenced by their patience in the midst of the afflictions.

B. Prayer for their progress in righteousness (vv. 11, 12).

vv. 11, 12 The apostle adds a prayer on their behalf that his readers may receive the blessedness to which their sufferings are intended by God to lead them. *To which end we pray always for you, that our God might count you worthy of the calling* into the Christian life *and fulfill* bringing to completion *every desire* (good will, choice) of *goodness, and work* resulting *from faith* with *power, that the name of our Lord Jesus might be glorified in you and you in Him, according to the grace of our God and of our Lord Jesus Christ.*

A summary of this point of Paul's views of the Second Coming or Advent would clarify our understanding of the important teachings of these two epistles. The Christians of Thessalonica expected an immediate advent. It does not appear whether they believed, according to Jewish traditions, that the Messianic Kingdom would be established in this world as a temporal kingdom, an idea which the disciples of Jesus harbored before His crucifixion and for some time after His resurrection, which was not approved by Jesus, but to which they clung. The Thessalonian Christians would find it harder still to dispense with the idea of an earthly Kingdom, and in consequence of their expectation, excitement was rampant, the church was thrown into confusion and idleness, and disorder reigned. Hence Paul's counsel that they study how to be quiet, attend each to his own business and work with their own hands (I Thess. 4:11, 12; II Thess. 3:9-13). Some were anxious about their deceased friends and Paul allayed their distress (I Thes. 4:13-18) by explaining the equality and preeminence of those who had died in Jesus.

The fact is that Paul's teaching about the Second Coming had been misinterpreted in Thessalonica by some, who assumed to teach that the Day of the

---

3. Conditional clause of first class, according to reality.

Lord, spoken of in prophecy, was *at hand*. They circulated, either a spurious letter or a false interpretation of a letter received from Paul, whether the first Thessalonian epistle or some forgery (II Thess. 2:1, 2), and thus disturbed the minds of the brethren. Paul had directed the believers while in Thessalonica to look for the coming of the Lord as their Judge and Messianic Deliverer from persecution. It is unquestionable that he taught them that Jesus would descend from heaven, with a trumpet of an angel of God announcing His coming, and with a fire of flame and accompanied by His holy angels. The two angels at the Ascension of Jesus had said: He "would return in the same way" in which He went away. The believers should be in a state of watchfulness and readiness to receive Him when He should come. This was Paul's instruction to them.

In his first epistle Paul never asserted that he would be alive when Jesus returned; much less did he declare that he knew anything about when Jesus should come. It would be sudden and unexpected by the people of the world. He did not misinterpret or go beyond the Lord Jesus in his statements in the prophetic discourse he delivered when he said: "no man knows, not even the Son of Man" when the second advent shall be. The question of what would happen when He did come was limited by Paul to the assertion, that all the believers, the living and the dead in Christ, would, at that time, be assembled together with the Lord in a state of conscious blessedness forever.

The second epistle to the Thessalonians definitely represses the erroneous belief of the Thessalonian Christians in the immediate coming, and also the curiosity about when the Lord would return. Paul neither taught that he himself would be alive or that he would be asleep in the Lord, when the second advent should transpire. The state of sobriety, expectancy, watchfulness and readiness for His return were all emphasized (cf. Matt. 24:42, 44). It was hard for the Thessalonian Christians, as it is for us, to understand all the expressions of Jesus in his great prophetic discourse about the two topics discussed in it: the destruction of Jerusalem and the second advent. The state of the world when He should return, as described in that discourse, conforms vividly with the conditions of our present age and so the great message of these epistles to watch and be ready is very applicable to every worker in His glorious vineyard today!

II. Instructions and exhortations about the second coming (parousia) 2:1-12.

Paul's epistles spring out of actual historical circumstances and meet immediate and pressing needs. They were vibrant with life then as now. These two letters grew out of his preaching and other experiences with the Thessalonians. The second advent was the subject which received the greatest emphasis because it was of all the teachings of Jesus the subject, which fit into Paul's mood and the church's needs best, in the midst of the pressure of persecution. It was not understood in his preaching, by the unlettered majority of the synagogue circle, due to their illiteracy. This appears from the rough style and lettering in the superscription which was over the door of the synagogue, to be seen today on the block preserved in the Museum at Corinth. This is evidence of the fact that the Jews were not the aristocrats of the city.[4] There were among the Christians there "not many wise after the flesh, not many mighty, not many noble" (I Cor. 1:26). So Paul had to write a second letter to correct false interpretations. Thus, the principal emphasis in the second epistle is the same as in the first, but for a different purpose. He had to reveal to them that the great apostasy must come first and the man of iniquity be revealed and destroyed before the final coming of the Lord which would, on this account, be delayed.

A. Why the day of the Lord is not present (vv. 1-7).

vv. 1, 2 *Now* (de, metabatic) *we beg you brethren, on behalf of* the instruction given by inspiration of the Holy Spirit, relative to *the* (parousia) *appearance* in the second advent *of our Lord Jesus Christ and also our gathering together unto Him, to the end that you be not quickly shaken from your mind* (unsettled) *nor yet be troubled* or nervously wrought up, *neither by* statement made by those who claim to be *spirit-led*, nor by *word* (of false teachers or interpreters) *nor by* any letter or *epistle, as if* it were *from us* (a forged letter possibly), claiming by this forgery or false interpretation of what I have said or written in my first epistle, *"that the Day of the Lord is just at hand"* (stands in sight).

Some of their teachers were declaring that the "Day of the Lord" was *already come*[5] and that Paul had written to this effect (vv. 1, 2). The apostle meets this by giving them an 'omen of the Second Coming.' Before the Second Advent there must be: first a supreme manifestation of evil (2:3-12) producing in the church *apostasy*, and, second the revelation of the "man of lawlessness of sin," in whom the sin of humanity will be consummated in Satanic character. This personage was afterwards called Antichrist by John. Paul speaks of a "withholding" influence which delayed the appearance of Antichrist. The lawlessness was already actively at work and would reach its climax (vv. 6, 7) in this person or persons in history.

v. 3 *Let no man beguile* or deceive *you in any wise* or any way whatever, for the Second Coming of Christ will not be, *except*[6] *the* apostasy or *falling away*[7] *come first*[8] *and the man of sin* or lawlessness *be revealed*, who is the *son of perdition.* Both the Christ and the adversary of Christ will be revealed because there is mystery about each and both make divine claims (Robertson cf. I John 2:18). The son of perdition is not Satan, but someone who is doing the work of Satan.[9]

---

4. B. W. Robinson, *The Life and Letters of Paul*, p. 135.
5. Perfect act. Ind. of *enestēmi*.
6. Negative condition of the third class *ean mē* undetermined with prospect of determination (Robertson).
7. *apostasia*, the 'falling away,' on which Paul had instructed them orally while in their midst, which had been predicted by Jesus (Matt. 24;25).
8. *prōton*, first, before the Second Coming (Advent), in comparison of two events only.
9. A definite person. Cf. definite article used (Robertson).

v. 4 *But he that opposeth and exalteth himself*[10] *against all that is called God*[11] *or* that is *worshiped, so that he sitteth* or attempts to sit *in the temple of God and proclaims* (attempts to proclaim) *or sets himself forth as God* (that he is God.)[11]

v. 5 *Or do you not remember that when I was yet with you I used to*[12] *tell you these things?* The Thessalonian Christians had the advantage of Paul's preaching, to help them to understand whether he was referring to one (*to katechon*) or more individuals, or an evil principle, as the Antichrist. John referred to "many Antichrists" (I John 2:18). Paul may show a little impatience here in his question to the Thessalonians. They should have been able to remember (Frame, I. C. C., II Thess. in loco).

v. 6 *And now* as to the logical fact or reality, *you know that*[13] *which restrains,* "the impersonal principle or power, whether manifested under personal form or not." (Milligan). "This was Satan's Messiah, an infernal caricature of the true Messiah" (Moffatt). The Thessalonians knew what Paul was talking about, but we do not. Some think the 'man of lawlessness' was the power of the Roman Imperial line with its "rage for deification" (cf. Warfield), and that the 'Jewish state' was the 'restraining power.' But it might have been the restraining power of God which they knew about, since, for Christians, God overrules human history and His ultimate purpose is finally wrought out. *To the end that in His* (God's) *own season, He or it may be revealed.*

v. 7 *For the mystery* or secret *of lawlessness is already set in operation* (working), *only* (the apostasy will not come and the man of lawlessness (*ho anomos*) will not be revealed) *until the person*[14] who is now detaining *him may be taken out* of the way. So long as the 'restraining' influence working in a person (*ho katechōn*) exists the lawless one will go on working secretly but whenever this personal influence may be removed there will be a revelation of this secretly working man of lawlessness (Gloag).

B. The destruction of the lawless one, first v. 8.

v. 8 *And then the lawless one* (hō anomos),[15] the man of sin, the man of perdition *shall be revealed, whom the Lord* (Jesus) *shall slay by the* (word) *breath of his mouth.* The mere breath of the Lord Jesus will destroy his archenemy *and bring* him to *naught by the manifestation of His* own *coming.* The very appearance (parousia) of Christ will destroy His adversary (the lawless one), the Antichrist.

---

10. Direct middle of *huperairomenos,* to lift one's self above others.
11. Caligula claimed to be God. Emperor worship might be meant here (Lightfoot), in the reference of Paul's language, as an illustration of the character of the Antichrist. But "Paul does not identify the Deception with the Emperor worship, Cf. Moffat, *Ex. Gr. Test."*
12. Imperfect of customary action, elegon, Imp. Ind. Active of *legō.*
13. Neuter gender of present active participle katechon refers most naturally to a principle or person embodying a principle as God's restraining power in history. The imperial power had been a protection to Paul in his ministry but this would break later.
14. **The masculine gender here naturally refers to a person or persons.**
15. The masculine gender here most naturally refers to a person or persons.

C. The Appearance (*epifaneia*) of the lawless one (*ho anomos*), only for the doomed (2:9-12).

vv. 9, 10 *Whose coming* (that of the lawless one) *according to the energy of* (or inspired by) Satan, *attended by every kind of power and signs and wonders, having their origin in falsehood*[16] or falseness *and by every kind of decit proceeding from unrighteousness for them that perish*[17] *because* (for that) *they received not the love of the truth* (the Gospel) *to the end that they might be saved.*

v. 11 *And on account of this God* as a righteous judge *is sending*[18] *to them a working* or energy of *error,* working in them *to cause them to believe the falsehood* of the *anomos.*

v. 12 *In order that they all might be judged who did not believe in the truth, but consented to the unrighteousness* of the (*anomos*) lawless one.

God is shown here to be in supreme control over history and human experience working out His moral purposes in the individual and in society. He sends the gospel but when it is rejected it becomes a savor of death unto death to those who have chosen the way of error. Paul resorts here to the use of the apocalyptic language to express his religious faith and set forth the future of Christianity. For Paul, Christ was not a national political Messiah but a world-redeeming personal Savior. He was the personal embodiment of the wisdom of God over against the Anomos who was the personal embodiment of the principle of evil and unbelief. In Paul's concept God is above His world and the principle of right embodied on the Messiah will prevail. The restraining power and influence of the Roman Empire in the hands of God in history would be removed as evil should go on developing, until the supreme manifestation of the principle of lawlessness embodied in those in authority, the rulers, kings, emperors and dictators who assume that the power over humanity belongs to them and not to God, grows up into the Antichrist in a universal and overwhelming manifestation. In this manifestation there will figure every kind of Satanic power and trickery and naturally such a sway of evil will call many in the Christian churches to fall away from the faith, in an apostasy, when "the faith of many shall wax cold." But this power of evil embodied in many persons of Satanic character will be self-destructive and will destroy those who embrace or consent to it. The judicial God will abandon men of Satanic character to their own sins and self-destruction and when the true Messiah appears in His Second Advent, God will be recognized as supreme and the Anomos will be destroyed.

Paul speaks of the mystery of lawlessness (v. 7), as known to his Thessalonian brethren and present to the minds of the readers of his epistle. He is called the (v. 8) "lawless one." Paul emphasizes the principle of lawlessness

---

16. Ablative of source.
17. Dative of personal interest or in this case disadvantage. Present middle participle *apollumenos*, the process going on.
18. Futuristic (prophetic) present referring to the time when the lawless one is revealed (Robertson).

which is the outstanding attribute of the whole system of evil and sin of which *ho anomos,* or the lawless one is the impersonation. The Gentile world known to Paul had cast off all moral restraint, (Rom. 1:18-23) and the same lawlessness of spirit was truly characteristic of the Jewish people (Rom. 2:1, 17-19). The church, corrupted by its world-contacts, becomes an apostate church which hastens and prepares the way yet more for the advent of the Antichrist of an atheistic world power. Here we have the revolt against God by an atheistic world-power along with the revolt against Christ by the Antichrist. The prophecy of Daniel speaks of two powers (Dan. 8:23). The antagonism of the spirit of lawlessness embodied in the "lawless one" is against God and all that is truly religious, its aim being to abolish true religion of every form. This man of sin, man of perdition, who is the adversary,[19] exalts himself above measure (Cf. Dan. 8:25; 11:36, 37). He desecrates the temple, as Antiochus Epiphanes, who did it with the intent to crush the religion of Israel. The same lawless one was embodied in the Roman Emperors who persecuted Christianity and in the Gentiles, who were incited to persecute Paul and Silas in Thessalonica and elsewhere. The Anomos not only seeks to abolish the true religion but would substitute his own worship, the reverence of mankind for himself, in its place, as illustrated in Emperor-worship.

III. Further thanksgiving, exhortation and prayer, 2:13-17.

Paul again expresses his thanks to God for the Divine call of the Thessalonians, exhorts them to stedfastness and prays that they may be cheered and strengthened.

A. Assurance to the faint-hearted of their salvation (vv. 13, 14).

v. 13 *But we owe it, to go on giving thanks to God at all times concerning you, brethren beloved by* the Lord (*Christ*), *that God chose you, from the beginning*[20] *for salvation,* in *sanctification* of the (Holy Spirit) and by faith in the truth.[21]

v. 14 *Into which also he called you, through the agency of our gospel*[22] *into the* secure obtaining or *possession of the* shekina *glory of our Lord Jesus Christ.* This beloved and elect but faint-hearted brother should have no fear about the future, about the Day of the Lord.

B. Exhortation to stedfastness, holding fast to instructions. (v. 15)

v. 15 *So then, Brothers,* stand fast and hold on constantly to *the gospel traditions which you were taught either through the word orally or by means of our epistle.* Remembering the instructions received orally by his preaching, or written, through his first epistle, they should stand firm.

C. Prayer for encouragement and righteousness (vv. 16, 17).

vv. 16, 17. *Now, our Lord Jesus Christ Himself and God our Father, the one who loved us and gives eternal encouragement and good hope in grace, comfort and stablish your hearts in every kind of good work and word.*

---

19. *anti-keimenos,* adversary, equivalent of the Hebrew word for Satan.
20. Reading Aleph D. L., (ap'archēs), from the beginning correct, not (*aparchen*) first fruits.
21. Objective genitive (*aletheias*).
22. (*euaggeliou*) genitive of means or agency with preposition, (*dia*) usual construction.

IV. Final request for prayer and expression of confidence in them with warnings, and a command for discipline for the idlers, 3:1-17. Paul asks for their continued prayer on behalf of his work that it may be fruitful and that he and his fellow-missionaries may be delivered from unreasonable and evil opponents.

A. Final double request for prayer (vv. 1, 2); and expression of confidence (vv. 3, 4); and prayer for them (v. 5).

vv. 1, 2 *For what remains,* finally brethren, *keep on praying*[23] *for*[24] *us, that*[25] *the word of the Lord may go on running* (in a victorious race) *and may continue being glorified just as* it is *with you* (in your fellowship) (Cf. John 1:1). And (pray with another purpose also) *that we might be delivered*[26] *from unreasonable and evil men* (opponents), (Adeney, *Cent. Bible*), *for not for all is the Christian faith* (Frame, *ICC*) Paul had opposing teachers in the church, who were not in truth Christians, from whom he would be delivered through the effective prayers of the true brethren.

vv. 3, 4 *But faithful*[27] *is the Lord, who will make you firm and guard you from the evil one*[28] (the devil and his temptations which are brought to bear in the testing times). The Lord can be counted upon for this deliverance if we ask Him. (v. 4) *And so we have* unshaken *confidence*[29] *in* the sphere of *the Lord touching* (toward) *you, that the things which we are commanding, you are* already *doing and will* continue to *go on doing.*

v. 5 Paul's wish for them. But it is needful *and* may *the Lord direct*[30] *your hearts* in a smooth and plain road *into* the God-kind[31] of *love* and make it a ruling principle there *and into the Christ-like*[31] *patience;* which will also make you patient to wait for Christ.

B. Command and exhortation to idlers (3:6-15).

Paul is dealing here with the clear case of pious idlers who were disorderly, refusing to work with their hands and claiming help and support from the church while at the same time they were busybodies, stirring up trouble. Paul cited his example of working hard for his support at Thessalonica, urging that these idlers should do the same. Anyone who should refuse to do this should be disciplined by being shunned but still admonished kindly as an erring brother (Adeney, *Cent. Bible*).

v. 6 *Now we command you, brothers, in the name* and authority *of our Lord Jesus Christ, to keep away from* or shun *every brother who is walking disorderly* (out of ranks) in idleness *and not according to the* Christian *tradition* or instruction *which you received from us.*

---

23. Pres. Middle linear action.
24. Peri almost equal to huper in this case.
25. *hina* with present subjunctive in both verbs expressing continued action of content and purpose (Robertson).
26. Effective first Aor. passive.
27. *Pistos,* faithful, in place of emphasis.
28. Reminiscent of the Lord's prayer (Robertson).
29. *Pepoithamev,* Perfect tense, are convinced, in the Lord.
30. First Aorist Act. Opt. *katemthunai.*
31. *Agapēn,* spiritual love and Christ-like patience, (*hupomonēn*).

v. 7 *For you yourselves know how it is necessary* or due *for you to imitate us.*

v. 8 *For we walked in order* (rank) *among you* not in idleness *nor did we eat bread, free of charge, from anyone, but in toil and hardship by night and by day working that we might not be heavy upon anyone of you* in the matter of material support.

v. 9 *Not because we did not have a right* to free support *but in order* that *we may present ourselves to you* as a type or example *to the end that you imitate us.*

v. 10 *For also when we were with you we used to command you:*[32] *"If anyone does not wish to work neither let him eat."*

v. 11 *For we hear* and are informed *that there are certain ones among you who are walking in disorderly fashion* in idleness *not working for themselves but being busybodies,* 'doing nothing but going around' (Robertson). The first persecution of Paul in Thessalonica had been done by "loungers of the market place' (Moffatt), incited by the Jewish leaders.

v. 12 *Now to such as these we command* (as apostles) *and exhort in the* name and authority of the *Lord Jesus Christ* (as brothers and ministers), *that with quietness they work, and eat their own bread* contrary to their present conduct and manner.

v. 13 *But you, brethren, do not grow tired* of *doing the* right and *beautiful thing.*

v. 14 *In case, however, anyone is disobeying our word* expressed *in this letter, designate to that man, not to associate* intimately *with him, that he may be made ashamed.*

v. 15 *And do not think of him as an enemy but admonish* or nourish *him as a brother.*

c. Prayer 3:16.

Now, may the Lord of peace Himself give you peace continually in every circumstance. The Lord be with you all (Frame. *ICC* II Thess.). Paul realizes that the command and counsel not given in prayer will avail nothing in the restoration of peace and harmony within the brotherhood.

d. Salutation and benediction (vv. 17, 18).

The salutation of Paul (myself) *in my own hand-writing, which is the* mark or invariable *token* (of genuineness) *in every epistle.* It is *thus* that *I write. The grace of our Lord Jesus Christ* be *with you all.*

32. Imperfect of customary repeated action.

CHAPTER XIII

Paul's Ministry in Western Asia Minor

Third Missionary Campaign

THE third missionary journey of Paul covered most of the territory of the other two. (Acts 18:22-21:16.) The Bezan text retained the allusion to the Feast in Jerusalem in v. 21 and of the visit of Paul v. 22 which seems to be more in accord with the purposes of the apostle, when he assumed the vow in Cenchreae and hurried on from Ephesus, to get to the Feast in Jerusalem. The expression "went up" was customary in speaking of going to Jerusalem and "went down" in going out from that city.[1]

The call of his mission to the Gentiles would not let the apostle tarry long in Antioch. He *made* or spent *a certain time* there, as some think, writing a letter to the Galatian brethren. It is more probable that Paul would want to make a careful investigation personally of conditions in the churches founded with the help of Barnabas on the first missionary tour, rather than to write a letter, as important as the Galatian epistle is known to be, on the sole basis of the report of even so valued a helper as Timothy, on the assumption of such a visit[2] by that evangelist on the return journey from Corinth.[3]

Paul was quite aware of the temperamental character of the populations of the Phrygio-Galtic region and quite as alert to the racial prejudices and ambitious schemes of the judaizers in Jerusalem. They were beaten in the Jerusalem Conference but not completely subdued. So the Apostle was anxious to tie the Gentile churches of Galatia firmly on to the Jewish churches in Judea. No more opportune or better method could be found than to encourage the Gentile brethren of the Galatian churches to contribute to a general fund to help the large group of destitute members in the churches in Jerusalem. The Antiochene church had sent Paul and Barnabas with gifts some years earlier and the effects had been salutary in the relief of distress and the cultivation of fraternity. General conditions in that city had not altered, and there was opportunity now to broaden the plan to include the Galatian churches in this fraternal Christian cooperation, in a work both laudable and beneficent. The Antiochene church, through the tactful counsel of Paul, took the initiative and appointed Titus who had been with Paul and Barnabas on the similar mis-

---

1. W. M. Ramsay: *St. Paul the Traveler and Roman Citizen*, p. 264.
2. Timothy is believed by some to have returned to Lystra for a brief visit at the time of Paul's return to Jerusalem after the 2nd missionary tour.
3. This likely theory is ably presented by David Smith, *Life and Letters of St. Paul*. p. 191 following Ramsay's *St. Paul the Traveler*, pp. 182ff.

sion before, when the question about his circumcision arose, and became the occasion for Paul's clarifying his attitude as to the exemption of the Gentile Christians from circumcision. The idea of the relief fund, which originally was motivated purely by fraternal loyalty, came to serve later as an aid in the promotion of doctrinal purity.

1. The record of the visit of the apostle in the Galatian churches is very brief, a characteristic of the Lucan account. (v. 23) *He departed and went through the region of Galatia and Phrygia in order, establishing all the disciples.* It is not impossible that Paul had not thought through in the most thorough way the line of argument found in the epistle directed to them later. Many think he sent the letter ahead of him so that on this third visit he would be able to clinch the matter and squelch once for all the efforts of the judaizers to instill their views of a mixed gospel in these churches. Whether the letter was written before or after, in Antioch before his departure or in Ephesus soon after his arrival there, is incidental. The fact is that the apostle succeeded in "making firm" the Galatian churches on the basis of the unalloyed spiritual gospel of salvation by faith alone.

2. Luke's special mention of the work of Apollos in Ephesus. Acts 18:24-28. The importance of the work of Apollos is given recognition by Luke in logical connection, in order that this account may the better fit into the framework of the great ministry of Paul. Immediately on his arrival in the city the Apostle had found his way to the home of his old friends Priscilla and Aquilla whom he had left there on his way to Jerusalem,[4] and had the account from them of the brief ministry of Apollos there, in the interval of Paul's absence. (v. 24) This learned Alexandrian Jew was a remarkable person, trained in the philosophy of Alexandria, being an orator, and powerful in the Scriptures. *He was instructed* orally *in the way of the Lord, was zealous in spirit and when he arrived in Ephesus he began and carried on a work of talking about Jesus and teaching accurately the things pertaining to Him.* But he *only knew the baptism of John* and was not acquainted with the baptism of the Holy Spirit. His theory was good as far as it went.[5] (v. 26) *He began to speak*[6] *boldly in the synagogue. And when they heard him Priscilla and Aquilla took him and expounded to him more accurately the way of God* There had been a question between John's disciples and those of Jesus about baptism.[7] There was a difference between the baptism of John and that of Jesus. The baptism of John was one "of repentance," calling for repentance and confession of sins, looking toward the coming of the Messiah and also symbolizing a complete moral cleansing of the people in preparation for that event. Many of the professed disciples of that time never got further than the message of John, which heralded the coming of the Messiah. This was particularly true of the thousands from far and near who heard John's preaching before

4. Cf. I Cor. 16:19 for the fact that Paul lodged in the house of Priscilla and Aquilla.
5. W. O. Carver, Commentary on Acts p. 188.
6. Inceptive aorist middle.
7. Cf. the Gospel records in loco when Jesus left Judea to go into Galilee.

Jesus the Messiah appeared for baptism at the Jordan and was identified by John with the Messiah which was to come. A few of John's disciples followed Jesus, but for a while the great majority continued to loyally attend on the ministry of their great prophetic leader. They had received the baptism of John and had never received Christian baptism, which was based on actual faith in Jesus as the Messiah already come. Apollos was a catechumen or pupil of some disciple of John who belonged to the earlier group of John's disciples. He had learned the traditional facts about Jesus but had not come into personal appropriation of those facts in a vital faith. Priscilla and Aquilla added this knowledge and a consequent vitalized experience of the Messiah Jesus and the baptism of regeneration in the Holy Spirit, when he came to embrace personally the Christianity of the Christ.

The kind and tactful but frank dealing of Priscilla and Aquilla, in complete sincerity and confidential privacy, gained the heart of the noble Alexandrian and he entered the Christian ministry to do a great work in Corinth and elsewhere later (Acts 18:27; 19:1), where he "watered that which Paul had planted" (I Cor. 3:6). (v. 27) *And when he was disposed to pass into Achaia, the brethren wrote, exhorting the disciples to receive him, who when he was come helped them much who had believed through grace.* He had evidently come to experiential understanding of the plan of salvation by grace through faith at that time. He knew Jesus now as Paul did. the living reigning Messiah at the right hand of the Father. The reason for our conclusion is found in the statement of Luke, *For he mightily convinced the Jews.* and *that publicly, showing by the Scriptures* of the Old Testament *that Jesus was the Christ.* His ministry in Corinth was needed sorely and he met the antagonism of the Jews eloquently, showing before the admiring populace that the Christian view of Jesus was based on the truth. There was great gain to the cause in saving Apollos to the gospel ministry, in spite of the fact that his popularity as a speaker was the cause of his being unwillingly held up as a rival in Corinth, of the apostle Paul himself. But Apollos was loyal to Paul and found excuse to avoid a return to Corinth later when pressed by Paul, his grateful friend, to do so (I Cor. 16:12). When he first went to Corinth with some brethren who had been visiting in Ephesus. he bore with him, a letter of commendation, spontaneously offered him by the little church in Ephesus, initiation to which had been given by the evangelistic message of the Apostle when he passed on his way to Jerusalem. It is probable that Epanaetas was converted in that meeting and that Priscilla, Aquilla and he nurtured the little beginning, and drew Apollos in to help them when he arrived soon afterward. It was thus that Apollos was won and came to the knowledge of the truth.

3. Paul's ministry in Ephesus, Acts 19:1-20:1.

Ephesus, the greatest city of Asia Minor was the preeminent strategic center of that territory. It was for that reason that Paul, being the statesman that he was, desired to strike for that capital even from the very beginning of his campaign in Asia.[8] On his first missionary journey, his physical disabilities — perhaps a combination of malarial infection with a weakness of his eyes — led him to strike along the great thoroughfare through that most accessible Phrygio-Galatic region and untrammeled, liberal-minded, and prosperous people in the center of the Roman provinces of Asia Minor. Young Dr. Luke may have had some hand, under the spirit of the Lord, in leading Paul and Barnabas to that decision. On the second missionary journey, again, the Apostle had his eyes on Ephesus; but the Spirit of the Lord Jesus was sent more directly to his servants Paul, Silas and Timothy and they were guided into Europe, where they found the Macedonians better prepared for the reception of the gospel than the Asiatics of the great metropolis of Ephesus would have been. It would have seemed that Paul, now, with his world-vision more clarified than ever by his work in Macedonia and Achaia, would have wanted to press on to Rome, about which he was already thinking and dreaming. But the statesmanship of the man had learned, ere this, the greater wisdom of God, and recognized that the "hiatus" of Western Asia Minor must be filled in before going farther afield.[9] So, it was on this region that he hastened to descend on the third journey.

Here in Ephesus, the more difficult conditions he would have to meet, would require a ministry of longer duration, and he would spend there two and a half to three years. But he would not go away before the gospel was firmly established, sending the rays of its beacon light out over the vast regions of darkness of the Asian and other adjoining provinces and across the waters of the Aegean and wider Mediterranean to many a distant shore.

Ephesus was a city of great importance as a political metropolis, the commercial emporium of a vast region, and an idolatrous religious center of incomparable heathen darkness and superstitious influence, with its temple of Diana (Artemis), one of the seven wonders of the world.

It possessed a fine harbor, through which flowed back and forth the trade of Greece and Europe, of the West, with the vast regions of the Orient. It had access, by various long rivers, to the extensive plains of Western Asia Minor with its inland trade. Situated on the great thoroughfare which passed through Antioch and Iconium, it was the highway to the Euphrates and the wider stretches of the East. It thus became the greatest commercial center and chief emporium for all western Asia Minor. At the time of Paul, it was at the climax of its greatness as the capital of the greatest and most prosperous Asian Roman province. Under the administration of Rome it became the most important political center of all Asia Minor.

The city was well-located on the banks of the Cayster River, a short distance from the splendid harbor. It was a free city, with its own assembly and council like those of Athens before the time of Paul, but its popular government declined under the Romans and passed into the hands of Roman officials, chief

8. Cf. Section of Introduction and W. M. Ramsay's Testimony etc.
9. Cf. James Stalker: *The Life of St. Paul*, p. 86.

of whom was the Town-clerk. It still retained however its senate and magistrates and much of its autonomy of previous years. The size and magnificence of the city are evidenced by the extensive ruins which yet identify the more interesting sites, scattered partly over the long ridge of the Coressus, partly on the circular eminence of Mount Prion and partly on the lower level of the plain near the windings of the Cayster and about the edge of the harbor. Looking from the summit of Prion, with its marble quarries which furnished the building materials for the city and on the edge of which was the stadium well known to Paul, and from the games of which he derived many of the beautiful similes of the Christian life, one may identify the sites of the vast theater, the outline of which is still distinct, where the mob incited by Demetrius shouted for two hours in honor of Diana. Below also is the Agora or market-place from which the mob gathered to its meeting place in the stadium, on that occasion.

In a straight line from the theater to the harbor ran the main street, beautifully colonaded on both sides. Along this street were the lecture halls among which that of Tyrannus figured, libraries, and idol temples. The market place was at the juncture of this main street with another, cutting it just in front of the theater at right angles. In this theater, prisoners fought with wild beasts in the arena. Paul says he was compelled to fight with the beasts at Ephesus but probably he meant with the beastly men who were enemies of the gospel and its promoter (I Cor. 15:32). On a spur of the hill Coressus stands an ancient tower, called the prison of Paul. Between Prion and Coressus are the ruins of one of the gymnasia where the athletes were trained for the games.

At the head of the harbor and separated from the business center of the city, stood the far-famed temple of Artemis or Diana, glittering in its beauty, reckoned as one of the seven wonders of the world, because of its extraordinary structure; built by Grecian architects of highest distinction, from the marble quarries of Mount Prion. The original temple, at least five centuries before Paul's time, which occupied in its building many years, was burned down by a fanatic on the night that Alexander the Great was born. It was afterwards rebuilt with yet more sumptuous magnificence, the ladies of Ephesus contributing their jewelry to the expense of its restoration. It was embellished with the pictures of its most famous artists, among them Parrahassius and Apelles. Its greatest piece of art was Apelles' painting of Alexander the Great.

This was the temple which was the center of heathen worship in the time of Paul and later of John and Polycarp. It was built in the graceful Ionic style, the feminine beauty of which was adapted to the Asiatic temperament, was 425 feet long and 220 broad, and its 127 columns which towered sixty feet high above the platform were each contributed by a different King. The folding doors were of cyprus-wood, the partial roof was cedar and the staircase was made of the wood of a single vine from Cyprus. It was the treasury or safety deposit of a vast part of the wealth of Western Asia. No other building in the world perhaps ever concentrated a greater admiration, enthusiasm, and superstition. It became an asylum for fugitives from justice. Here doubtless Onesimus, the runaway slave, found a refuge during some time.

The image enshrined was rude, and oriental in character like the idols of India, representing the life of all animated beings, as fed by the breasts of nature. The material was wood and a box of metal was in each hand. The idol was covered with mystic devices and was concealed by a curtain in front. It was believed to have fallen from the sky (Acts 19:35). Portable images or shrines were made of it, out of terra cotta, wood, silver, or gold, and sold to the vast throngs of pilgrims, worshippers and tourists who came from far and near, even from the whole world, as amulets, household gods and souvenirs. This developed into a trade which greatly influenced the business of the city. Demetrius was the silver-smith who headed the mob against Paul because of the devastating influence of the gospel on this business. The worship of the goddess was conducted by a twofold hierarchy: one head, the highpriest, ranking high among the officials of the city. The priests were eunuchs from the interior. There was a swarm of priestesses named melissae who served the deity, and a great number of slaves (neocoroi) or temple-sweepers (Acts 19:35). The whole month of May was dedicated to do honor to the goddess of the "temple of Asia," with games, revelry and contests. Politics were merged with the religion of Diana and customs were subservient to her superstitious worship. Copies of the mystic characters engraven on the ancient image were sold as charms. The city itself swarmed with wizards, fortunetellers, interpreters of dreams, who hum-bugged the mariners, merchants, pilgrims who had come for worship, and tourists and travelers who flowed in a constant stream along this thoroughfare linking the West and the East. The words of Kipling could not be true of Ephesus:

The East is East, and the West is West
And never the twain shall meet.

On the contrary the amalgamation process of the melting pot was already in full operation in Ephesus when Paul arrived with the universalism of the Gospel, which could make real the brotherhood of man. But the reign of darkness, oriental and occidental, held sway in the temple of Diana. Superstition preyed on the minds and hearts of the vast populace of this great heathen city set at the confluence of the East and West. This is why this benighted metropolis had so great a challenge and appeal for Paul. Here he would preach in the market-place to Jewish sorcerers, oriental mystics and magicians, vendors of superstitious objects, writers of the books on magic, and teachers of the black art of exorcism. Here Paul's profoundest theology and highest philosophy would find its greatest challenge, which should result in the Ephesian epistle, containing the deepest thinking and sublimest expression of the Christian world-view which humanity has ever received.[10] This was to be the arena where he would meet and defeat the darkest superstitions of the Orient and

10. James Stalker: *The Life of St. Paul*, p. 87f.

Occident and gather from the midst of the darkness of the heathen population a great mother church, around which would grow up seven churches, which like the seven-pronged candlestick of the Temple would shed their beneficent light over the great province of Asia and the world, in years of primitive Christianity and of all time. Here Paul was to lay the real foundation of the great Divine Commonwealth[11] of the Nations and the City of God.

a. Paul arrived in Ephesus after Apollos had gone. He came from Phrygia by the safe *upper mountainous road, through the highlands,* thus avoiding, for his health, the lowlands of the valley of the Maeander River to the south, through which the main thoroughfare passed. On his arrival, he soon found the home of Priscilla and Aquilla and again joined in their craft of tent-making. He knew from them doubtless of a small group of about twelve disciples who believed in Jesus, but were not well instructed as to His resurrection and the advent of the Holy Spirit, on the day of Pentecost, which followed later after that vital event. He looked them up and *said unto them, "Did ye receive the Holy Spirit when ye believed?" And they said unto him, Nay, we did not so much as hear whether the Holy Spirit was given.* (v. 3) *And he said, Into what then were ye baptized? And they said, Into John's baptism.* (v. 4) *And Paul said, John baptized with the baptism of repentance, saying unto the people that they should believe on him, who should come after him, that is, on Jesus.* (v. 5) *And when they heard this, they were baptized into the name of the Lord Jesus.* (v. 6) *And when Paul had laid his hands upon them, the Holy Spirit came on them; and they spake with tongues, and prophesied.* (v.7) *And they were in all about twelve men.*

The difference between Apollos, and the couple Priscilla and Aquilla, religiously, when he first met them, was, that Apollos had not had an experience of the grace of the Lord in regeneration. After he received more accurate instruction at the hands of those sincere and humble Christians he was ready to receive the Holy Spirit as he did, and doubtless he was reimmersed also, as all the twelve believing disciples, who had not followed out the complete teaching of John about Jesus, as the Messiah, after He appeared and was immersed by John in the Jordan. Apollos could not continue to teach in the synagogue after receiving the complete truth and Priscilla and her husband led the church in placing Apollos in the way of a helpful ministry in Corinth. *He helped them in Corinth much who had believed through grace.* This is the plan of salvation "by grace through faith" in the risen Christ. Neither the zeal of Apollos nor the sincerity and earnestness of the twelve was sufficient to secure their entrance within the spiritual society of the Kingdom. Pentecost showed that even those who had crucified the Lord, could through repentance and faith in Jesus be saved. The reception of the Holy Spirit in conversion was accorded to the Samaritans when they accepted Jesus. Cornelius, a Gentile, entered the open door of Christianity by believing in Christ, and he received the Holy Spirit. And now these twelve disciples had, through negligence, failed to follow out instructions of their Master and carry through the whole program.

---

11. Harrold Dodd: *The Meaning of Paul for Today,* Ch. IV.

They had believed in Jesus, but not as the living and reigning Messiah, whose resurrection from the dead gave a new and fuller meaning to baptism. So they were reimmersed by Paul. This was a relevant example for those who, through believers in the efficacious atonement of Jesus and in the death to sin and resurrection to a new life symbolized in baptism (Rom. 6:4), have never observed this kind of baptism. After completing this part of the program they were prepared to receive the infilling of the Holy Spirit for service, which was accorded to them along with the symbolic laying on of hands. They were rewarded by the evident coming of the Spirit upon them, manifested in their speaking in tongues and in prophecy.

One cannot well see why Ramsay should fail to understand the "strange episode" which is presented by Luke in the very beginning of the narrative about Paul's work in Ephesus. Paul was confronting a polemical battle with the subtle oriental magic and superstition, which called for clear discriminations between the real and the unreal. The whole narrative about Apollos as also about the small group possibly, of disciples won by Apollos, before he was "taught the way of the Lord more perfectly," has a direct bearing on the character of the work Paul must do in Ephesus. These two exceptional cases were one by nature. There was no vital connection in either case of a living faith in Christ but only an intellectual assent to the Messiahship. Paul explained to the small group (Acts 19:4) that John had preached, that his own disciples must believe on Jesus as the Messiah who was the fulfillment of prophecy. Some of them did believe and followed Jesus and were rebaptized or immersed by the apostles of Jesus, and here was a group of those who were yet calling themselves disciples of John, having received his baptism only, while professing at the same time to believe in Jesus but without carrying out the program of being reimmersed in the Christian baptism. There is a reality in Christian baptism as a symbol, setting forth the previous internal operation of the Holy Spirit in regeneration. Outward profession must follow the inward experience of the grace of regeneration. This group had neglected the identification of themselves with the Christian church through the act of obedience to Christ in immersion. There is no statement that Apollos was not rebaptized. Paul required rebaptism of the group of twelve, as being right in all cases. The importance of the principle justified the emphasis Luke gave it by being set in an obtrusive position seemingly out of order, to make it emphatic. There is no authority in the Ancient MSS or Versions "for omitting the episode."[12] John's baptism was not the real baptism; its intent was not the same as that of Christian baptism (cf. Romans 6:4 et al). This is not a matter of attaching too much significance to baptism.

(1) Three months of ministry in the synagogue and two years in the Schoolhouse of Tyrannus (19:8-10). The Jews were more friendly in Ephesus (v. 8) and *Paul entered the Synagogue and for three months spoke boldly, reasoning and persuading as to the things concerning the Kingdom of God.* This was

---

12. Cf. W. M. Ramsay, *St. Paul the Traveler and Roman Citizen*, p. 270.

the usual procedure of Paul in beginning work in a new place. Priscilla and Aquilla had doubtless frequented the synagogue regularly, carrying on their craft in the hours of trade and doing the work of personal evangelism quietly as occasion presented itself. They thus prepared the way for the coming of Paul, sowing the seed of the gospel through personal contact and conversation (v. 9). *But when certain persons were hardening*[13] *their hearts and obstinately and actively disbelieving,* were *speaking evil of the way in the presence of the congregation; withdrawing from them, Paul separated also the disciples and went on* with his work *daily reasoning in the school* or lecture-hall *of Tyrannus* a friendly rhetorician. *And this continued for two years; with the result*[14] *that all the inhabitants of* the Roman province of *Asia came to hear the Word of the Lord, both Jews and Greeks.* Here we note the usual disbelief, stubbornness, and antagonism of the Jews, of such a nature that Paul had to stand off from them and separate also the Christian disciples from the Synagogue circle. The Jews, far from being neutral, were hindering the work by slandering or speaking evil things of the Christian way of life. This they did even in the open meetings in the synagogue. So Paul led his group of disciples out from the synagogue and hired the lecture-hall, of a certain well-disposed teacher Tyrannus, conveniently located on the principal street of the city. The use of this school-house Paul could obtain only for certain hours of the day, from 11 a. m. to 5:00 p. m. He would thus employ his morning hours in the craft of tent-making. There were daily public meetings in which Paul reasoned, argued, taught and persuasively preached. Along with this was mingled his pastoral visitations, personal evangelism, and systematic indoctrination. His ministry in the school-house of Tyrannus continued two years and with the three months in the synagogue and other time, covered about three years in all.[15] The result of his work thus carried on intensely was that all the residents of the province of Asia, of all nationalities, heard the Word of the Lord. The region evangelized was about the same area as that of the New England states in the United States of America. The influence of Paul's work was widely extended and a number of churches were founded as a consequence. Many of those who came in from the interior of Asia and the other surrounding provinces heard Paul preach and the many mission churches widely founded were the direct result of the dissemination of the gospel by those who heard Paul in Ephesus. Most of these churches according to a late word of Paul had never been visited by the Apostle personally, doubtless because of his intensive activities in the large capital city, Ephesus. Philemon, Epaphras and others, who were converts under his ministry in Ephesus, went out as evangelists to the interior places.

Paul left for us, in his speech to the elders of the Ephesian church, who were, at his request, in Miletus, on the occasion of his stopping there on his final trip to Jerusalem some months later, a brief but illuminating word about the

---

13. Imperfect Indicative Middle of *Sklēroō.*
14. *Hōste,* result.
15. Cf. I Cor. 16:8, 19; 15:32; II Cor. 1:8-10.

intensity of his ministry in this great strategic center. He went from house to house in his pastoral ministry, ceasing not to admonish every one night and day with tears (Acts 20:17-35). This work was done in the midst of persecution from the Jews. He labored with his own hands for his support during the morning hours, while Tyrannus was using his lecture-hall, and from eleven a. m. until five p. m.[16] this great servant made use of the school-house in his preaching and teaching ministry, receiving his students from everywhere in the city and also many visiting students and friends from far and near in the towns, cities and country places of the interior of the Asian and other provinces.

The preacher became known as "one who comforted the bereaved," and to those afflicted with disease he ministered physical cure for the body and spiritual enlightenment and regeneration from God for the soul, through faith in the Lord Jesus. He did not work for personal gain, but "gave from his own to those who were in need."

(2) Many notable miracles featured in Paul's work (vv. 11, 12). God endowed his servant-apostle with great powers, setting his seal upon his work, by *doing many extraordinary miracles through Paul's hands.* We must remember that Ephesus was the home of Eastern Magic and the miracles performed by Paul were adapted to the needs of people in a local situation. Medical science also had not reached an advanced stage of development there. Weak and superstitious faith was honored by the Lord himself, on occasion, in His ministry, to lead into a true and enlightened belief on Him, such as the cure of the poor Gentile woman who touched the hem of the Lord's garment in the thronged street of Capernaum. (Matt. 9:20) So here, as in the case of Peter's shadow,[17] *handkerchiefs or aprons were carried away from his* (Paul's) *body to the sick and diseases left them and the evil spirits came out of them.*[18] The faith of the needy was helped here by physical contact and symbols and all these "extraordinary" powers or miracles cited by Luke were used for beneficial helpfulness in an age when medical healing was little developed.[19] "The humble channel of an apron need not of itself debar belief." (Robertson)

(3) Opposition of the soothsayers, and the victorious bonfire (Acts 19:13-20).

The antagonism of the Jewish exorcists, who were mere charlatans, who professed to repel diseases by the use of charms and incantations and to cast out the demons to which the physical and mental maladies were attributed, was overcome by the reality of the cures by Paul in the name and by the power of Jesus. Paul's miracles brought him in conflict with those quacks but also were the occasion of a comparison of his work with theirs, with the inevitable result of a great success for the cause of the gospel. (v. 13) *Then some of*

---

16. Codex Beza (D) Acts 19:9. "from the fifth to the tenth hour."
17. Acts 5:15.
18. The Revised Standard Version is used here and consulted constantly alongside the Revised Version and Nestle's or Westcott's Texts.
19. W. O. Carver: Commentary on Acts p. 192.

the itincrant exorcists undertook to pronounce the name of the Lord Jesus over those who had evil spirits, saying, "I adjure you by the Jesus whom Paul preaches." (vv. 14, 15) *Seven sons of a Jewish highpriest named Sceva were doing this. But the evil spirit answered them, "Jesus I know*[20] *and Paul I know but who are you?"* (v. 16) *And the man in whom the evil spirit was leaped on them, mastered both of them, and overpowered them, so that they fled out of that house naked and wounded.* (v. 17) *And this became known to all the residents of Ephesus, both Jews and Greeks; and fear fell upon them all and the name of the Lord Jesus was extolled.* (v.18) *Many also of those who were now believers came, confessing and divulging their practices.* (v. 19) *And a number of those who practiced magical arts brought their books together and burned them in the sight of all; and they counted the value of them and found it came to fifty thousand pieces of silver.* (v. 20) *So the Word of the Lord grew and prevailed mightily.*[21]

The wide influence and prevalence of the black art are evidenced by this illustration from the collapse of magic in the onward sweep of the gospel in the city of Ephesus. The onset of the demon-possessed man in violence against the two sons of Sceva, in the incident cited, inspired fear in many who had been practicing magic. Other magicians were converted and confessed to their former wrong-doings and hypocrisy in the practice. There was a great bonfire. This was different from the Bible-burning bonfire, incited by priests in Recife, Brazil, in 1905. But the Bible gained a great victory there, as the Gospel did in Paul's work in Ephesus. The value of the parchments burned was calculated at about 50,000 drachmae, approximately 2,000 pounds or 10,000 dollars. A big bonfire, like the Holocaust of Vanities in the Florence of Savanarola![22]

(4) Plans and delays (vv. 21, 22).

All of Paul's plans at this stage of his work were set down by him in the sphere of the influence and direction of the Holy Spirit, not just in his own (human) spirit. He thus made his plan to pass through Macedonia and Achaia on a flying visit to the churches, winding up in Corinth. From there he would sail for Palestine with the purpose of visiting Jerusalem. "*After I have been there I must also see Rome.*" Perhaps he did not fully realize how necessary it would be that he should go to Rome nor did he foresee how he would go. But there was an inner urge that he must also see Rome. "He had the vision of a world-mission in his soul." To prepare the way for his visit in Greece he sent ahead of him two faithful workers, Timothy and Erastus. Thus, he himself "*got some time for Ephesus*" and Asia. "A great door and effectual was opened to him but there were many adversaries," closing with their net of plots and traps about him. Great and peculiar perils were about him. Twice, as he revealed in his letters to the Corinthians, his life was especially imperiled. A Roman citizen could not be sentenced to death by a provincial

---

20. Ginōskō, I recognize.
21. The Standard version is quoted verbatim in this incident.
22. David Smith: *Life and Letters of St. Paul*, p. 233.

governor nor cast to the wild beasts in the arena (II Cor. 11:23-27). Once he despaired of his life (II Cor. 1:8), whether from a plot of the Jews or Gentiles he did not say (Acts 20:19), but he stood in jeopardy every hour and died daily (I Cor. 15:30, 31), "His sufferings there were commensurate with his successes."[23] The great victory already evidenced by the collapse of the magic arts in Ephesus foretold the greater struggle just ahead for Paul in Ephesus but it also caused him to lift his eyes and look away to greater fields of conquest, even to Rome. In Ephesus idolatry was trembling for its fall but it would not go down without a final struggle.

(5) A great riot promoted by the idol-trafficers under the leadership of Demetrius (Acts 19:23-20:1). The close of Paul's work in Ephesus was to come in through a clash with the economic interests of the idol-manufacturers.

(a) But this was covered up under the pretext of a defense of the worship of Diana (vv. 23-27). The real motive was in the progress of the gospel or Way, which had undermined to a large extent the idolatry of the heathen worship of the goddess Diana (Latin) or Artemis (Greek). The god-factories of Demetrius were rapidly losing their trade and vast gains, through the sales of diminutive shrines and idols made of wood, terra cotta, and silver. Demetrius, a silver smith, led in an indignation meeting of the craftsmen. He made a speech in which he confessed to the real motive of the meeting, which was the loss of their trade through the influence and progress of the gospel in the capital and throughout the province of Asia. Primitive Christianity was here in mortal conflict with "big business" and small business too as it was being wrongly conducted. The gospel had turned away many people from being humbugged by the vanities and delusions of their idol-worship. Demetrius commanded the working force of his guild. His impassioned appeal was to the sordid interests of gain. A great mob of people rushed to the theater and nobody knew much about the purpose of the meeting. Finally the religious motive was used as a pretext to cover up the real aim of Demetrius. (v. 25) "*Men you know that from this business we have our wealth,*" he said, addressing the mob-meeting of workmen of like occupation.

(v. 26) *And you see and hear that, not only at Ephesus but throughout all Asia, this Paul has persuaded and turned away a considerable company of people, saying, that the gods made with hands are not gods.* (v. 27) *And there is danger not only that this trade of ours may come into dispute; but also that the temple of the great goddess Artemis may count for nothing and that she may even be deposed from her magnificence, she whom all Asia and the world worship.*"

(b) Then followed a great mob-riot for two hours (vv. 28-34). Demetrius was a demagogue and was not mistaken about the current of the mob-spirit. An uproar followed. He had first played upon the motive of economic interests and now appealed to their superstitious religious fear about their goddess Diana. So the cry was started, "*Great is Diana* (or Artemis) *of the Ephesians!*" It soon became an enraged howl *and the city was filled with confusion;*

23 G. H. Gilbert: *The Students Life of Paul*, p. 153.

and they rushed together into the theater, dragging with them Gaius and Aristarchus, Macedonians, who were *Paul's companions in travel.*

(v. 30) *Paul wished to go in among the crowd but the disciples would not let him;* (v. 31) *Some of the Asiarchs* or rules in the province of Asia, *who were friends of his, sent to him and begged him not to venture into the theater.* (v. 32) *Now some cried one thing, some another, for the assembly was in confusion, and most of them did not know why they had come together. Some of the crowd prompted Alexander, whom the Jews had put forward* to ward off the current of antagoism from the Jews and turn it upon the Christians; (or he might have been a Christian (Jew) whom the unbelieving Jews wanted to expose as the real antagonist against the idol-traffic). So, *Alexander,* prompted by them, *motioned with his hand wishing to make a defense to the people.* (v. 34) *But when they recognized that he was a Jew,* (that was sufficient, for they did not discriminate clearly between Jews and Christians); *for about two hours they all with one voice cried out, "Great is Artemis of the Ephesians!"* It was a bedlam of enraged howls; the spirit of the mob was rampant! Imperial policy was not yet hostile to Christianity and the Asiarchs were friendly toward Paul. Jews hated idols and so the current of the rage of the mob included all Jews with Paul and his Christian disciples. The Jewish face of Alexander set the mob wild!

(c) The call to order by the Roman officer, the town-clerk, and the dispersion of the mob (vv. 35-40).

The mob spirit at the end of two hours was about spent and the town-clerk, who kept the archives and presided at public assemblies as the responsible and official representative of the Roman government, quieted the crowd and reminded them of the sobering fact; that everyone already knew that Ephesus was the sacred center of the worship of Artemis. The city was the very janitor or care-taker of the Temple of the goddess, 'who fell from Jupiter.' It was not necessary that the people should be so stirred up about their goddess. "*Gaius and Aristarchus*" whom they had dragged into the theater, "were not sacrilegious or blasphemers of their goddess," he said. Then he took Demetrius to task as the one who had caused this disturbance. "*If Demetrius and the craftsmen with him, have a complaint against anyone, the courts* of the imperial government *are open, and there are proconsuls.* Thus he set Demetrius and his party on the defense. As to the crowd of people he added, "If they desired to make any further inquiry they should seek it in the meeting of the regular assembly which convened three times every month." He reminded them further of the fact that Ephesus had been given a large and special autonomy by the Roman Imperial Government and such a riot as this was dangerous. *For we are in danger of being charged with rioting today, there being no cause that we can give to justify this commotion. And, when he had said this he dismissed the assembly.* It is plain from Acts 20:1 that Paul did not tarry long in Ephesus now. It was useless, and would precipitate more serious trouble, to remain. *After the uproar ceased, Paul sent for his disciples and having exhorted them took leave of them and departed for Macedonia.*

CHAPTER XIV

The Corinthian Epistles

First Corinthians

PAUL'S work at Corinth had been initiated under peculiarly difficult circumstances, being preceded immediately by his disappointing experience in Athens, where the philosophers treated him with a supercilious indifference and shallow ridicule. But from the beginning in Corinth his work was more successful, in spite of the fact that the apostle hoped to return and finish his interrupted work in Macedonia. When the hand of providence closed the door in Thessalonica and opened the way for an effectual work in this city of Corinth, notorious for its idolatrous darkness and proverbial for its multiform immorality and vice, Paul set his face toward the building up of a strong church out of the heterogenous racial elements from many sources in the melting pot of this busy commercial emporium. Here for two years he wrought as a master-builder in the founding of a church which proved to be a beacon light, that would shine out over the darkness of the heathen populations of the surrounding regions of Gentile Europe and send its beams down across the centuries to a war-beset world of our modern global days.

Paul was working in a Grecian environment, where there were many sophists, whose philosophy of life was superficial, like some of the modern types, which divorce knowledge from practical life. Paul would have to show them the difference between true and false *gnosis* and lead them to a deeper understanding which would transform their practice. Furthermore, the Greeks as a people failed, because of their tendency to a divisive spirit. They were a bright, intelligent people but could not unite, being much divided in factional strife in the church as they were in their environmental civic life.

It is in this Corinthian church that we have a picture of the inside working of the primitive gentile Christianity; and in Paul's dealing with its manifold problems, we have revealed to us many angles of the personality of the great apostle to the Gentiles. We have presented to us also how this master-builder dealt with each of many typical problems which arose. He carefully applied the Christian principles here and found them adequate, to every kind of situation arising in the life of any church. There were enough problems dealt with in this apostolic church, made up of a heterogenous composition of many types and classes not to say nationalities, to exemplify the power of Christian principles to meet every need and problem in all church life as well as in any type of civilization, of all times and places, wherever the Gospel may have thorough application.

Paul worked nearly two years in Corinth when he founded this church on his second missionary journey. Corinth located as it was on the isthmus, connecting northern and southern Greece, was in the most strategic point in the country. Vibrant with commercial activity and enterprise, it was at the same time proverbially corrupt, with its degenerate idolatrous and immoral people. The great temple of the pagan goddess Aphrodite put its stamp of approval on the nefarious traffic of a thousand courtesans of its cloisters. The intelligencia of Greece took a keen interest in the false Gnostic philosophy set forth in the superficial teachings of the sophists. In spite of these apparently unfavorable conditions, Paul's simple message of Jesus Christ and Him crucified (2:3) took firm hold in the city and a great church sprang up rapidly. But it was not without strong antagonism, which Paul met from the Judaist enemies here as in Thessalonica and other places in Asia Minor and Macedonia.

It was after Paul had returned to Ephesus on his third missionary journey that serious trouble arose in this church composed of elements converted from the contaminated populations of a vitiated city soon after his initiation of his ministry of three years in the large city of Ephesus, capital of the Roman province of Asia, just across the Aegean sea from Corinth, he got a whiff of the news about flagrant immoral abuses which had spread to some of the Christian disciples from the corrupt Corinthian environment. He undertook to extend a helping hand to the church by means of a letter which is referred to in the First Corinthian Epistle (I:5:9). This letter warned the members of the church not to tolerate fornication within the membership of the church and to excommunicate the outstanding man who was living in incestuous relations with his stepmother. The church misinterpreted the letter to mean that they should hold aloof from any fornicator, even among their heathen neighbors. In First Corinthians Paul corrected this misunderstanding of his previous letter. He meant that they should not harbor a member in the church who was living in fornication.

Soon "some of the household of Chloe," who seems to have been a business woman in Corinth, brought an alarming report about factional divisions and strife in their church and further news about the prevalence of fornication heading up in the outstanding case of incest. Worst of all, it was being countenanced and tolerated by the church, in spite of the letter from Paul counseling them to eliminate such a member. Apollos also had returned from Corinth confirming the evil reports.

Paul at that time began his First Corinthian letter dealing with these problems. He had hardly begun when a committee of three, Stephanas, Fortunatus and Achaicus (I:16:17f), appeared bearing a letter from the Corinthians, appealing to the Apostle for information and counsel concerning certain questions and problems in the church's life. Paul had sent Timothy over to reenforce his first brief letter, which was probably lost, but the content of which may be indicated by II Cor. 6:14-7:1. He went in order to deal with the questions of factional strife and fornication in the church but young Timothy's ministry was antagonized sharply (4:17, 16:10f), and he returned to Ephesus to give a negative report to Paul.

Meantime, the Apostle had written out his letter known as I Corinthians correcting their wrong interpretation of his first brief letter of counsel. First Corinthians dealt with many other subjects, such as partisan factions in the church (Chs. 1-4), the case of incest (5), law-suits among Christians (6) Marriage and divorce (7), meats offered to idols (8-10), veiling of women (11:1-16), the Lord's supper (11:17-34), spiritual gifts (12-14) the resurrection (15), and personal greetings and concluding exhortations (16).

I
Analysis and Exposition

I. Salutation and Introduction I:1-9.

Paul saluted the church as an authoritative apostle, over against the accusation of the judaizing enemies that he was not an apostle. He gave thanks to God for the spiritual gifts which had been given to this church. He was fully persuaded that the Lord Jesus would firmly establish these brethren until the day of His coming.

1. Salutation 1:1-3.

v. 1. *Paul, a called apostle* having the same authority as any one of the Twelve, (the Judaizers to the contrary), whose call came *from Jesus Christ,* Whose he was and Whom he served, *through* the agency of *the* divine *will of God* the Father, salutes them, along *with Sosthenes* who might have been an *amanuensis,* less probably the Sosthenes, successor of Crispus, ruler of the Synagogue in Corinth, if converted afterwards. v. 2 *To the church* or called out assembly *of God which is in Corinth* whose members have been *sanctified* or set apart from the service of Satan and consecrated permanently,[1] *in Christ Jesus,* for the service of God, *called saints* as surely and divinely as he himself is a called apostle. His salutation is addressed not only to the brethren in Corinth but along *with all who* call *upon the name of the Lord Jesus Christ, yours and ours,* as Savior, Messiah and authoritative Lord, *in* this and in *every place* in the province of Achaia and elsewhere. v. 3 May the *grace* or free and unmerited favor *and peace* which comes from reconciliation with Him, be granted *to you from God our Father and from the Lord Jesus Christ.* Here we have the three essentials of the salutation: the sender, the ones addressed and the greeting itself. In this salutation the Apostle skillfully defines his apostolic authority as from Jesus Christ, addresses the local church in Corinth as composed of brethren in Christ, permanently consecrated, and as genuine Christians of a veridic calling, to be saints, not only set apart but actually holy in their lives. His assumption that they are the recipients of the abundant grace and favor of God, unmerited by all in truth, and of the peace which should

1. Perfect participle *hagiosmenois* denoting permanence of status in the Christian life in those who were in the sphere of the redemption of Christ.

always flow out of a real and vital experience of regeneration and attendant reconciliation with God, is timely.

2. Thanksgiving for the spiritual gifts and mercies bestowed and hope that Christ will strengthen and establish them firmly to the end. 1:4-9.

v. 4 *I go on giving thanks continually, at every time, concerning you, for the grace of God,* which was definitely *given*[2] *to you in* the sphere of the redemptive work of *Christ Jesus* when you believed and were brought into union with Him. Paul assumed that they were real Christians.

v. 5 In view of the fact *that in everything ye were made rich*[3] *in him* in that transaction of regeneration, *in every kind of utterance and every form of knowledge* for giving and receiving instruction pertaining to the doctrine of Christ, (Paul knew that the members of this church were not lacking in intellectual gifts, delighting in eloquence and wisdom).

v. 6 *Just* in the proportion in which the *testimony of* my preaching *concerning Christ was firmly established in you* in your minds and hearts. Paul here makes real eloquence and wisdom to depend on having the real message of Christianity in their regenerated hearts.

v. 7 *So that* as a result (as we may hope) *you are not* behind or lacking *in any gracious gift waiting* with patience and hope *for the revelation of our Lord Jesus Christ* to you personally and individually in experience more and more until the day of His coming. This realization of Jesus Christ in their experience was the thing necessary and to be hoped for and worked for with patience.

v. 8 And this hour you need not dread, for *He is the One who will establish you* in security *until the end*, against any accusation or reproaches, so that you shall be *blameless in the day of our Lord Jesus Christ*, where He shall appear to judge the world. The apostle experiences confidence in the Lord's good will and ability toward them, while at the same time he declares by implication the reality of reproaches actually in some of them and expresses the hope that in Christ they shall be blameless in the end.

v. 9 *Faithful* and worthy to be believed and trusted *is God, through whose agency you were called* definitely *into the fellowship of*, (participation with) *his son Jesus Christ our Lord.* He reminds them again of the incomparable fellowship with Jesus Christ and with all "who call upon Him as Savior and Lord" (v. 3) as a basis for appeal for delivery from their present snares and reproaches and for security in the day of the final appearance and judgment by Jesus Christ.

II

Factional Division and Partisan Spirit in the Church (1:10-4:21)

After his tactful expressions of hopeful confidence and generous appreciation, the Apostle comes to the difficult and painful treatment of the deplorable conditions just reported to him by some of the household of Chloe and also

2. First aor. passive participle of *didomi*, a definite bestowal of God's unmerited favor.
3. First Aorist Passive, a definite transaction as above.

by Apollos who had just returned from Corinth. There were several serious things reported, chief among which were factional division, moral infection, and litigation. He deals first with the factional divisions and party-spirit as the chief cause of disorder in the church.

A. Paul exhorts to unity and reproves the partisan spirit. 1:10-17.

v. 10 *But I beg you, Brothers, through* the effective agency and power of *the name* and leadership *of our Lord Jesus Christ,* who is the chief bond of unity, *that you all may speak the same thing,*[4] being united in word, *and* that *there may not be among you*[5] *divisions,* of the character of internal disputes and dissensions, *but that you may be perfected together*[6] by being put into order, *in the same mind* or in your thinking *and in the same judgment,* flowing out of your thinking, and resulting in resolutions and decisions. The trouble makers were stirring up the partisan spirit in the Corinthian church and seeking to break it up into cliques and factional parties. Against such the apostle begs and exhorts to spiritual unity both in thought and action and hopes that the members of the church will come into the maturity of full-grownness in the Christian life.

(v. 11) *For it was reported* or made known plainly *to me, concerning you, my Brothers, by Chloe's people* (whom you know to be brethren of good repute) *that there are strifes among you,* resulting from divisions into factional groups in the church, in wranglings and quarrels.

(v. 12) *And what I am saying is this,* I mean, *that each one of you* has a party cry for himself and *is saying*: "*I belong to Paul*" the founder of our church; another says, "*but I belong to Apollos,*" whose style of eloquence and Grecian philosophic thought please me. Another, (especially of the Jewish members), influenced by the Judaizers says: well, "*I stand by Cephas*" (Peter), the great outstanding leader of our orthodox Jewish Christianity, whose apostleship, unlike that of Paul, is beyond question, and who respects and observes the ancient laws and rites of the religion of our forefathers. And others, who repudiated proudly the sectarian tendencies, raise the cry, "*but I am of Christ*" and I will stand by Him and no mere human leader.

(v. 13) To these various party cries and the spirit of division, Paul answers: *Does Christ stand permanently divided?*[7] Is Christ parcelled out or to be claimed as the exclusive possession of any group. Paul repels this parcelling out of Christ by an indignant question expecting an immediate and negative answer: "*Paul was not crucified for you was he?*"[8] *or were you baptized into the name of Paul?* Did Paul require you to pledge allegiance to him when you were baptized? Paul thus chooses the party or faction which held with himself in doctrine and addresses these words to them. He was not a preacher that built up the church around himself, but rather around Christ. Christ was not

---

4. Continuative *de*, but also adversative.
5. Locative, among you, in your midst.
6. Periphrastic Perf. Pass. Subjunctive, to be completed by being put in order permanently.
7. Perfect tense from *merizō*.
8. *Mē* with the imperative.

divided, nor was He the exclusive share of any party in the church, as one of the groups would claim. That group became as truly factional as the other three.

(v. 14) In view of this factional division, *I am thankful that I baptized no one of you with the* incidental *exception of Crispus* the ruler of the synagogue, *and* my old personal friend *Gaius*. Paul was not out for making Paulinists. He would not have his name attached to any factional (denominational) division of the Christian church, which should be one in doctrine and fellowship.

(v. 15) *In order that no one*[9] *of you might say that you were baptized in my name.* Paul was not a sacramentarian. He followed Jesus in this example, Who did not baptize anyone, relegating that function to His apostles, as Paul did to his helpers. This was a general practice in his ministry in Corinth and elsewhere.

(v. 16) *Now,* I remember on second thought, *I did baptize also the household of Stephanas,* my first converts in Achaia; *besides* these, *I do not know if* there was *any other* that *I baptized,* He did not consider baptism to be of equal consideration with the vital faith which saves the believer through bringing him into union with Christ.

(v. 17) *For Christ did not send me* as his apostle *to baptize, but to proclaim* his gospel of *glad tidings,* which is my almost exclusive task, which I perform *not with wisdom of speech* or studied rhetoric after the manner of the Greek sophists, in a philosophical exposition of the faith, but in plain words *in order that*[10] *the Cross of Christ might not be emptied,* but prevail by its own inherent power.

B. The character of his preaching, the Apostle next justified in an exposition of God's wisdom (1:18-25). He discusses the false wisdom and the true in the work of preaching, and shows that his use of the plain message of the cross is the true method.

(v. 18) *For the* plain *story-message*[11] *of the cross is foolishness to those who are perishing* in the road to destruction, whether to the sign-seeking Jew or to the wisdom-seeking Greek sophist *but to us who are* in the process of *being saved,* by having trusted in Christ and experienced the new birth, *it is* surely *the* supernatural *power of God,* which worked out the miracle of personal regeneration and is working out the gradual sanctification, which together constitute complete salvation or full-grownness in Christ Jesus in a ripe Christian maturity in holiness.

(v. 19) *For it stands written* in the Scriptures:[12] *"I will destroy*[13] *the wisdom of the wise, and will set at naught the intelligence of the* arrogantly *intelligent.*[14]

(v. 20) *Where is the wise* (Greek sophist or philosopher)? He is nowhere in God's sight! *Where is the* (Jewish) *scribe* learned in the letter of the law?

---

9. In order that not any man may say.
10. Hina, clause expressing purpose.
11. Word or doctrine.
12. Isa. 29:14.
13. Future active indicative of *apollumi, to destroy.*
14. The discernment of the discerning.

In God's sight he is nothing. *Where is the* skillful *disputer*[15] or debater *of this* evil *age* (Jew or Gentile)? *Has not*[16] *God made foolish,* by convicting it of folly, *the wisdom of this world?* as demonstrated in the example of the great philosophers, who never revealed to a soul how to be righteous before God? Not even Socrates or Plato did this!

(v. 21) *For since, in the wisdom of God,* in His sovereign providential government of the universe, *the world did not know God, through its wisdom,* in spite of all its boasted intelligence of both Jews and Gentiles, but failed to attain to a real knowledge of Him, *it pleased God* (was His good pleasure) *through the foolishness* or "silliness" *of preaching* (as the intellectuals think of it), *to save those who believe,* (by their exercising a vital faith in Jesus Christ).

(v. 22) *Seeing that the Jews are demanding signs* (miracles) *and the Greeks go on seeking for wisdom,*

(v. 23) *on the other hand, we will continue preaching Christ the crucified,*[17] *to the Jews indeed a stumbling-block* or mere idea *and to the Greeks foolishness* or absurd silliness,

(v. 24) *But* on the other hand *to those who are really called of God,* the evidence of which call is in their acceptance of Jesus, *Jews indeed and Greeks,* (we proclaim) *Christ* crucified, *the* manifest *power of God and wisdom of* God. Christ sums up in himself both the power of God in redemption through the cross and the wisdom of God exhibited in both the method and conduct of preaching.

(v. 25) *Because* that which seems to the intellectuals among the Jews and Greeks to be *the foolishness of God* in a plan of salvation through a crucified Messiah *is wiser than men and* this apparent *weakness of God* as judged by the world, *is stronger than men.*

Thus Paul defends the simplicity of preaching in words that can be understood by all, of the message of the cross as being the true wisdom. The simplicity of the gospel message is its glory and it is shorn of its power when it is apparelled in the vestures of a showy and studied rhetoric.

C. The wisdom of this method was verified in the experience of the Corinthian Christian 1:26-31. The character of the first converts to Christianity in Corinth exemplified and reenforced the truth of Paul's declaration about simple, positive preaching of the gospel.

(v. 26) *For consider*[18] *your own calling,* by God, *Brothers,* unto the circumstances of your present rank in life, *that not many* of you *are wise according to the flesh* as men count wisdom, *not many are mighty* (powerful, influential), *not many,* of you are *noble* (well or high-born, of high rank according to the flesh).

---

15. Joint investigator or debater.
16. Emphatic negative *ouchi* in beginning of sentence.
17. Perfect participle *estauromenon,* permanent result and status implied.
18. Imperative of *blepō* behold, look at, consider.

(v. 27) *But the foolish things* including persons *of the world did God choose out for himself*[19] *in order that he might put to shame the wise* philosophers, by showing them the vanity of their wisdom; *and God chose*[20] *the weak things,* including people, *of the* world *in order that he might put to shame the strong* or mighty, triumphing where that worldly strength failed.

(v. 28) *And* it was *the low-born of the world and the things counted as nothing,* which *God selected for himself, the things that* have no existence, and *are not, in order that he might make completely useless the things that are.*

(v. 29) *So that all flesh* together, *might not* be able to *boast* before the face of God. No human being can boast in God's presence.

(v. 30) *But from him* who is the bounteous source of grace, *you are* adopted *in Christ Jesus, who became for us* the *true wisdom* manifested *from God,* which embraces the initial imputed *righteousness* as well as the closely connected and consequential *sanctification* (consecration and actual holiness) *and redemption,* setting us free from the bondage of sin through the price of His blood which bought us.

(v. 31) *In order that* it may come to pass as a purpose realized, *just as it stands written* in Scripture: *'The one glorying* (for himself[21]) *let him glory in the Lord!*[22]

Thus in the lowly born members of the Corinthian church was exemplified the true nature of divine wisdom, in preaching, which is not a matter of human cleverness or intelligence, but of divine revelation set forth for the understanding of the humble. In the person of Christ and in His work of redemption through His atoning death is revealed the wisdom and expression of God's divine power and grace, meeting and satisfying the needs of man. Paul is here applying the great principle of the grace and love of God, set forth and demonstrated in the cross, to the practical, needs of the church in Corinth. One of the needs was salvation from the divisive and factional tendency, born of egotistic self-assertion and a partisan spirit, splitting the church up into four, three, or at least two distinct and antagonistic parties. This is a malady very common in church life. Its sources are always the same selfish egotism and a partisan spirit. It always works the same sad result, the destruction of spiritual unity among the brethren.

The Corinthians must make their boast in the Lord, in Whom God had placed them and given them true rank. God's wisdom is upsetting to human standards. The highest wisdom is not intellectual knowledge, but living in Christ. Some of the members of the Corinthian church were departing from the ways in which they had accepted the simple message of the church and were desiring to hear preaching of a philosophic type, savoring of vanity in the preacher: not remembering that through the simplicity of Paul's message God had chosen not many considered wise men, not many influential social

---

19. Aorist indicative middle, for himself, subject acting.
20. *Ibid.*
21. Middle voice.
22. Jeremiah (LXX) 9:23, 24.

leaders, not many from the higher social circles of the high-born and the rich.

D. The preaching of Paul was in view of this wisdom of God (2:1-5). After this word on the Wisdom of God in the story of the cross, which was the creative power to which the Corinthian church owed its existence, Paul recalls negatively (2:1-3) and positively (vv. 4, 5), how his message had been brought to Corinth. His preaching had not been eloquent but had revealed the wisdom of God in His purposes of grace, hidden from the intellectuals, but revealed to those who through acceptance of the Christ came to have the powers of spiritual perception, to be able to perceive the spiritual things of God's hidden wisdom.[23]

(v. 1) *And I, coming to you, brethren, came not with* (according to) *superiority of speech,* of eloquence, *or* in the manner *of wisdom but proclaiming to you the testimony*[24] *of* (in regard to) *God,* particularly about what He has done for the salvation of the race, though the cross of Christ.

(v. 2) *For I did not resolve* (judge it) *to know anything among you except Jesus Christ and him* (as) *crucified.* Paul did not have any thought or determination to know anything besides Christ and that too as crucified, though such a message might be offensive and even repugnant to their understanding. But the usual English rendering is warranted (Boise), "I determined not to know" etc.

(v. 3) Here the preacher is described, as in v. 2, as to his theme. (Bengel). *And I came became known to you in weakness and in fear and in much trembling.* Paul felt keenly the responsibility of the task before him, especially in view of his experience in Athens. It *became* apparent to them that he was weak physically, timid and painfully nervous, when he appeared in Corinth. His malarial malady may have come upon him in renewed attack at that time.

Paul denies that he had used any of the catchy methods employed by the sophists in Corinth, of a sensational type of subject and of method, so many times used yet in preaching. His message had become the unattractive theme of *the crucified Christ.* To the Greeks a Christ, at all, was new and did not appeal; but a crucified Christ was ridiculous. To the Jews a suffering and dying Messiah was unthinkable! But Paul's resolve was firm and his method was anything but acceptable from the standpoint of the world. The Saving purpose of God whether expressed by the term mystery (*mustarion*) or testimony (*marturion*) was his constant theme. His presentation was not that of glib self-assurance and in the confidence of a sophist lecturer, using eloquence and sophisms, to attract and hold his audience. The wisdom of his method was not his use of the cleverness of his native ability and wits *but was in the power and demonstration of the Holy Spirit,* which resulted in conviction for the mind and change of heart in his hearers. Paul felt his incapacity in dealing with so high a theme and a fear of proving unequal to the task. Such an attitude of dependence on the Holy Spirit instead of on one's own resources

---

23. Objective genitive, *sofias,* noun in the genitive the object of action (Vede Dana and Mantey, *Grammar of N. T. Greek* in loco.

24. *Marturion,* witness (cf. 1:6). West and Hort prefer reading mystery.

and wits, is the first and principal condition of successful preaching. So, Paul asserts positively about his preaching.

(vv. 4, 5) *And my word,* both argument and delivery, *and my preaching* which is the proclamation of a message of truth to be accepted), *were not in persuasive words of* philosophic *wisdom, but in demonstration* (pointing to) the presence *of the Spirit,*[25] and *of the power* of God, *in order that your faith might not be* anchored *in the wisdom of men or* dependence on human wisdom, *but in the power of God* and its effectual working in the salvation of men. It was the power of God, using Paul as a mouthpiece and instrument, that converted the Corinthians to Christianity.

E. Discussion of the nature of the true religious Wisdom of Christianity 2:6-16.

The gospel has a wisdom of its own which does not belong to the present world-order but is revealed by God and is understandable only to these initiated into the revelation in Christ. True wisdom is hidden to the worldling. The man who is not initiated into the Kingdom cannot comprehend it. The simple message of the cross carries with it a philosophy of the world-order, past, present and future,[26] embracing the saving purpose of God. To mature Christians, Paul and the apostles speak this true Wisdom of God revealed to them by His Spirit.

1. A true wisdom described (vv. 6-13).

(v. 6) *And yet we* (Paul and the apostles) *speak a wisdom among the mature* or full-grown Christians, but *a wisdom not of this world nor of the rulers of this age who are coming to naught,* and are doomed to pass away.

(v. 7) *But* on the contrary *we speak* (impart) *God's wisdom in a mystery or secret, which has been hidden*[27] completely and not hitherto revealed — the divine plan and purpose of universal redemption — *which God predetermined* (ages ago) *before the ages for* (or with a view to) *our glory,* or glorification in eternal salvation.

(v. 8) *Which no one of the rulers of this age has known,*[28] *for if they had known*[29] *they had not crucified* in an ignominious or shameful death *the Lord of glory.* Annas, Caiaphas, Pilate and Herod did not understand the wisdom of God.

(v. 9) *But, just as it stands written* in the prophecy of Isaiah 64:4; and 65:17: "*Things which eye saw not, and ear heard not and which entered not into the heart of man, whatsoever things God prepared for them that love him.*" Here we have from Isaiah a reference to future glory with the glorious Lord of glory! Paul interprets from the insight of his present experience under the inspiration of the Holy Spirit what the future glory will be.

---

25. Objective genitive, pointing to the Holy Spirit's presence.
26. James Moffatt, *Com. on I Corinthians* p. 26.
27. Perfect participle of *apokrupto.*
28. Perfect, Act. Ind. of *ginoskō.*
29. Second class condition contrary to fact.

(v. 10) *For to us* Christians *God revealed them already* in history *through* the agency of *the Holy Spirit; for the Spirit searches, or explores all things, yea* (even) *the deep things of God.*

(v. 11) For, *who* of men has *known* (cognized) the *things of man* (the human being) *except the spirit of the man which is in him? So also the things of God no one has known* definitely *except the Spirit of God.*

(v. 12) *But we did not receive the spirit of the world but the spirit of God, in order that we may know the things,* graciously, *freely given to us by God.*

(v. 13) *Which things also we speak not in words* (arguments, discourses) *taught by human wisdom but in words taught by the Spirit, combining spiritual things with spiritual words* and so interpreting spiritual things to spiritual people who are able to understand them.

(v. 14) *But,* an unregenerate *or natural man does not receive* or understand *the things of the Spirit of God;* for *they are foolishness unto him; and he cannot know them, because they are spiritually judged* or discerned. The natural man (*psuchīkos*) is the human soul endowed with the power of thinking, feeling and willing but is not alive spiritually *pneumatikos.*[30]

(v. 15) *But the spiritual man* (*pneumatikos*) regenerated in the new birth through the work of the Holy Spirit, *judges all things, but himself is judged or examined* and properly *by no one,* who, whether spiritual or not, is not enlightened by the Holy Spirit. He is in character and real inner life immeasurably above the *psuchikos* or natural man. The motives of his life can not be understood by the unregenerate.

(v. 16) No unregenerate man understands the inner life of the regenerate man, because: *For who has known the mind of the Lord.* To understand the mind of the regenerate man one would have to understand the mind of the Lord (Christ) *so that he will instruct him* (*the Lord*)? *But we have the mind of Christ,* by the agency of the Holy Spirit through vital union with Christ in the Spirit. Through his discussion of the contrast between the spiritual and mere natural or animal character, Paul is led back to its application to the unspiritual dissensions and factional wranglings in the Corinthian church. The disputings were unspiritual and pointed to the low status of spirituality in the church, as is always the case where such conditions exist.

Paul distinguishes two classes of Christians: the mature, (*teleioi*) called later (2:13-3:1) spiritual (*pneumatikoi*) and on the other hand the babes (*napioi*) who are carnal in their retarded stage of development (cf. 3:3). Many Christians like some of those in Corinth have to be treated as babes and carnal and raised to the standard of maturity and of the full-grown spiritual persons (*teleioi*). He recognizes the gradation and graduated scale in the development toward maturity and ripeness of experience in the Christian life. His aim was to raise all such undeveloped Christians up to the normal standard as far as possible. This is a great task for the ministry in all times, since the great majority of Christians in all the churches never get much beyond the infantile stage of growth. There is no barrier between the initiated and the

30. Bishop Ellicott, *Com. Corinthians* in loco. v. 14.

average Christian, as (cf. Eus. *Eccl. Hist.* 5:11) the Gnostics taught. There can be no caste gradations in the true Christian brotherhood but there are many differences in kind and degree in the matter of development.

F. The preaching of Paul was too simple and unattractive for his 'Christian' critics because they had not reached maturity enough to understand it 3:1-4.

His preaching had to be plain and simple in accommodation to their spiritual incapacity and dullness. In his preceding argument the Apostle had shown that God and his message of a Christ crucified constitute the center of emphasis in Christian preaching, which was not, as the critics thought, foolishness, but in Christ was the real 'wisdom' of God. Judged from that point of view these Christian critics were sadly lacking. The fact that there were factional contentions among them was evidence that they were acting like mere humans (*psuchikoi*) and not mature Christians (*teleioi*). That was a keen thrust which is applicable to all Christians, who make their likes and dislikes about preachers and their form of preaching the main emphasis, over against Christ and his cause in the church and the world (3:1-4).

(v. 1) *And I, Brothers, was not able to speak to you as to mature spiritual Christians but* was obliged to adapt my message *as to babes in Christ,* who have been born into the Kingdom but who have not on account of selfish ambitions, partisan spirit and contentions among yourselves developed into real Christian maturity.

(v. 2) *I gave you milk to drink; not solid food, for not yet were you able to bear it.*

(v. 3) *But neither are you yet able to stand it, for you are yet* (sarkikoi) *carnaceous,* with the desires and the appetites of the flesh yet working in you.

(v. 4) *For where* (there is) *among you jealousy and strife, are you not carnaceous* (*sarkikoi*) *and are* you not thus *conducting yourselves according to the manner of man or a mere human being. For when anyone says, I am of Paul, and another, I am of Apollos, are you not mere sarkikoi?* Paul reproaches them for having left God out of account. Thus they had made no progress toward real maturity in the Christian life. Partisan contention among them was sure evidence of their having made no progress toward maturity of full-grownness in the Christian life.[31]

G. The relationships, functions, duties and responsibilities of the servants of God in the Christian pastorate. 3:5-4:21.

1. As illustrated in the examples of Apollos and Paul in their work of teachers and builders. 3:5-15.

Paul passes now to consider the teachers' activities and relationships, working together with God and with one another for God.

(v. 5) *What then is Apollos? And what is Paul?* The apostle answers his own question as to Apollos and himself. We are just his *servants through whose agency you* came to the knowledge of the word and *believed.* We are

---

31. David Smith: *Life and Letters of St. Paul,* in loco.

not leaders of parties or factions but occupy the function of servant for God's work *just as the Lord gave to each* of us in His God-assigned task.

(v. 6) So it was my work to plant, and *I planted* the seed in the first work of evangelization and founding of the church; *Apollos watered* the plant of your faith as it sprang up and nourished it in his subsequent ministry; *but it was God who gave*[32] *the increase* in growth and fruitage.

(v. 7) *So that neither the one planting* is *anything* by himself *nor the one watering but God who causes the growth* is everything.

(v. 8) *Now he who plants and he who waters are just one* and the same thing in heart and in service, and are not disunited. Paul and Apollos co-operated as successive pastors. Each had his own strong points and his weak ones, as all pastors. A church gets one-sided if it has the same pastor too long unless he is a many-sided man. *But* in any case *each one* of the workers *shall receive his own* reward or *wages according to his own toil* or the merits of his own work. *For we are fellow-workers belonging to God*, being united in His one glorious task and not divided in factional strife.

(v. 9) *Ye are God's* tilled *field* (husbandry), *Gods building.* The first of these metaphors Paul had developed (in verses 6-8) and the second, of the building, he follows through to the end of the paragraph (v. 15). God takes us into His partnership as fellow-workers. He is the major partner in the enterprise (Robertson, *W. Pictures*), but He lets us work with him: Ye are God's husbandry. He works through the sunshine and the rain and the tilled field, the earth contains the elements for the development of the plant. Christians are the building God erects as the Great Architect.

(v. 10) *According to the grace of God* who was the giver of the work *as* a *wise architect or* skilled master-builder, under whom others work, *I* placed or *laid the foundation and another who* succeeds in the pastorate *builds upon* (it). *Let each one give heed* and look well *how* (in what manner and of what material) *he builds* upon (it). Paul absolves Apollos from the blame of the factional strife but also himself. The judaizers were to blame. They should have appraised the work justly and not attacked him, involving him personally with his loyal friend Apollos.

(v. 11) *For other*[33] *foundation no one is able to lay than that which was laid,*[34] *which* (who) *is Jesus the Christ,* Who has appeared in person as the Messiah. Paul was not seeking the praise for all the work, but he claimed the authority of having laid the proper foundation which was Christ. Others must be careful to build of the right material and in the right way the superstructure. But the main thing is, that there is but one true foundation for true Christianity and that is Jesus as the Savior and the divinely sent Messiah and Son of God, which He claimed to be.

(v. 12) Paul had in mind, not only his fellow-workers who were loyal to him, but his enemies the Judaizers who claimed to be authorized teachers

32. Imperfect indicative active.
33. Masculine of Pronoun referring to Jesus.
34. Pres. Mid. Part. used often as perfect. (Robertson).

from Jerusalem, but who were sowing discord in the church in Corinth. They were also less obtrusively and slyly sowing the seeds of error, teaching salvation by faith plus the works of the law, instead of by faith alone. Paul warned those subtle enemies as well as his fellow-servants in the harvest field and the work of temple building that: *if any man ever builds upon the foundation,* (even though that were Christ), *gold, silver, precious stones, wood, hay, stubble.*

(v. 13) *The work of each will become manifest. For* the *day will make it plain* (Rev. 20:11-15), *because it is revealed by fire, and each man's work of whatever sort it is, the fire itself* will test or *prove.* The durable materials like gold, silver, precious stones (marble etc.) will remain, like the marble and gems of the temple of Artemis at Ephesus, and also from the burning of the city of Corinth by the Roman conqueror, the columns of marble which are seen to this day in the ruins. They must not build of perishable materials, such as those used in the building of the huts of the poor in some countries in ancient and modern times, which are constructed of wood, hay and stubble.

(v. 14) *If any man's work remains,*[35] which he built upon the true foundation, after the fiery test of time and the final day of judgment, to which the work of all workmen is inevitably to be submitted, *he will receive* (wages), *a* suitable *reward.*

(v. 15) *If the work of anyone shall be burned down, he will suffer loss, though he himself shall be saved but so as through the agency of fire.*[36] *There* is no reference here to an imaginary purgatory the like of which is not found in the New Testament or entire Bible. Paul is talking about the character of the work of Christian workers (servants). If the superstructure of a building, though it be on a good foundation, is destroyed by fire because it was built of perishable material, the workman suffers the loss of a reward; but he himself having built on Christ and being in Christ shall be saved. He shall bring no sheaves with him to the garner, no souls for his hire, no enrichment of character, no growth in grace. Of such a minister, his sermons were of windy words and had no edifying power. They left no eternal mark on the lives of hearers. Here is the tragedy of a fruitless life. A servant built of perishable materials and his life and work went up in smoke! (Robertson)

2. Warning against factional strife, which would destroy the 'temple for God's habitation,' in the church. 3:16-23.

Here there is a change of subject, reverting to the factional divisions which tend to the banishment of the Holy Spirit from habitation in the local church. *Naos* (temple) is from the verb *naein,* to dwell. All local Christians are one temple in the local church, but each individual Christian is himself a small temple, for God's indwelling; but here the reference is to the local church.

(v. 16) *Do ye not know that ye* (plural) *are a temple of God and the Spirit of God dwells in you?*

---

35. First class condition denoting that such will be true.
36. *Dia* with genitive, *through* the agency of *fire.*

(v. 17) *If any man destroys*[37] *the temple of God, him shall God destroy; for the temple of God is holy, which temple ye are* (in the local church).

Naos is the Sanctuary or most holy place in the *hieron,* temple. There God manifests Himself in His Shechinah (Glory) in the hearts of His people in the local church. It is a terrible sin to tear down a church of God. Some were doing that very thing in Corinth as Paul asserts here, through their partisan spirit and factional strife.

(vv. 18-20) is a stern warning particularly to the leaders and votaries of speculative 'wisdom.'

(v. 18) *Let no one go on deceiving himself,*[38] as an excited partisan in his pious frenzy. *If anyone seems* to himself or others *to be wise among you in this* passing *age, let him become a fool,* in the eyes of the world, by voluntary renunciation of all pretension to worldly wisdom, *in order that he may become* truly *wise in that wisdom which is divine.*[39]

(v. 19) *For the wisdom of this* present *world* order *is foolishness with God* as is verified by the statement of Holy Writ, *for* it is written (Job 5:13) "*He* (takes) *seizes the wise in their own craftiness,*" in unscrupulous conduct, a 'conceit of wisdom without reality.'

(v. 20) *And again* in the Psalmist (94:11)[40] "*The Lord* (Jehovah) *knows the reasonings* (of men) *of the wise, that* (such reasonings) *they are empty,* or vain, having nothing in them.

(vv. 21-23) is a recall of the Christians of the Corinthian Church to the right understanding of their privileges in having such teachers (servants), and preachers.

(v. 21), *Lets no man glory in men,* who are their favorite teachers or preachers. For such glorying in party or faction is self deceit which is inconsistent with glorying in the Lord.

(v. 22) *For all things are yours* as heirs, *whether Paul or Apollos or Cephas,* all of whom are personal ministers to your instruction; also all things of circumstance as *the world, or life or death;* or times: things *present* or things *to come* in the future. *All* these *are yours,* working together for the good of the Christian, who should therefore not wrangle about favorite teachers and preachers causing factional divisions in the church.

(v. 23) *But* with all your rich heritage *you* are *of* and belong to *Christ and* therefore should be subordinate and loyal to Him as He the *Christ is* (of) subordinate in category and belongs to *God,* as His Son.

Every teacher is an interpreter, and his interpretation is partial, as is the message of the prophet or preacher. One pastor supplements in work that of another, his predecessor. Each one has his peculiar abilities and also his weaknesses. Christians should make use of both and all, because each is their serv-

---

37. First class condition denoting reality. By factional strife these church members were destroying the local church.
38. Pres. Mid. Imperative.
39. Boise *Notes* on Paul's Epistles p. 162.
40. Vede LXX, substitution of sōfon in the place of anthrōpōn by Paul in accord with the context. (Robertson, *Word Pictures*).

ant. But all interpret Christ and belong to Him as His servants and are to be included in the blessed unity of Father, Son and Disciples.

3. Paul explains clearly the point of view from which to regard Christian teachers and preachers. 4:1-5

He refers to himself and Apollos as together, so as to defeat the Judaist who would drive a wedge between them, and thus Paul would divest the brethren of the church of any idea of antagonism between him and his loyal friend.

(Ch. 4 v. 1) *So let a man,* whoever he may be of our critics *consider us,* my friend Apollos and myself along with any of my other fellow-workers here in Corinth or elsewhere like Cephas in Jerusalem, let him think of us *as servants* (underrowers or attendants) *of Christ* (Who is our Superintendent),[41] *and as stewards of the mysteries of God,* which have been concealed from the world in past ages but are now made known through the apostles, who are God's stewards of the Gospel.

(v. 2) *Here, in the* office of *stewards, moreover, it is sought* or required *that anyone be found faithful* or trustworthy.

(v. 3) *But to me it is of the least* possible importance *that I should be* closely examined or *judged by you* to see if I am faithful, or not, or *by a human* court *day* or tribunal.[42] *But* as a matter of fact *I do not even judge myself* to ascertain whether I am faithful or not for I am not the right person to do so nor able to judge this.

(v. 4) *For I am not conscious of anything in myself* of delinquency in my relations to you, as founder of the church and as your father in the faith, *yet not in this am I declared justified* or righteous, because, in fact, my consciousness is not the ground on which I am pronounced righteous, *but the one judging me is the Lord* Jesus. His judgment is unerring where my judgment or that of anyone of you is not infallible.

(v. 5) *So, stop judging in respect to anything before time until the Lord shall have come, who will turn the light on the* now *hidden things of darkness and will make manifest*[43] *the counsels* and purposes *of* all *hearts; and then that*[44] *praise shall come to each one,* which is due Him *from God.*

The presumptious critics in the church in Corinth were usurping the divine prerogative of God's evaluating the work of his servant-stewards! They were assuming in their brazen complacence to sit in judgment on one whose superiority to any one of them was as the light over the darkness. Their *day* tribunal of human criticism was a mere matter of errant judgment based on intellectual opinions and not on the recognition of the manifest favor of God on the sacrificial life and ministry of the apostles, especially that of Paul. This was the only "preliminary examination" that Paul acknowledged. He protests both man's criticism and even his own estimate, and appeals to God's judgment already manifest in the divine approval of God on the character and work

41. Peter addressed Christ in the boat as Superintendent, Luke 5:5, *Eniotata.*
42. Reference to human critic-judges over against the divine tribunal or the judgment day.
43. Causative verb *Phanerōsei.*
44. Definite article sometimes has the force of the demonstrative pronoun.

of these apostles and workers before their critics' very eyes. In view of this they should stop judging their servant-preachers and teachers.

4. The practical aim of his references to Apollos and himself was intended to divest themselves of all connection with party spirit and pride. A picture of the actual present life of the apostles should convince the Christians of Asia of the character of these men. 4:6-13.

(v. 6) *Thus these things, brethren, I have in a figure transferred, unto myself and Apollos on your account, in order that you may learn, from this* object *lesson of our examples, "not to go beyond the things which stand written"*[45] in the Old Testament Scriptures, that all honor belongs to God and that glorying in men is wrong and foolish (Boise Notes). This the Apostle would have them do, *"in order that ye may not be puffed up one against the other,"* acting in a partisan spirit, one party against another, destroying unity in the church.

(v. 7) *For who distinguishes you,* as superior, brother? *What do you have that you did not receive? And if you received*[46] *it* as you certainly did, then *why go on glorying as if you* were *not receiving it?* This is a clear declaration of salvation by grace alone. Paul punctures the bag of self-conceit and egotism of the critic in the Corinthian church. There is no foundation for self-complacent assertion of personal superiority of one brother over another in the attitude of "I am better or holier than thou." The sole hope for such a critic would be the grace of God and predestination and a timely repentence and confession of his sins to God. Who gives you the right anyway to prefer one man to another and name Paul and Apollos as leaders of factions? And what ability or gift do you possess that was not given you by God? If you did receive your salvation and all from God why do you go on boasting as if you had gained it yourself and not received it?[47]

(v. 8) Ironically the Apostle adds: *Already ye have been filled* (satiated)! *already ye have become rich! apart from us ye have already become kings!*[48] *Intense irony and sarcasm!* These Christian (?) critics in the church assumed to have reached the highest heights in the attainments and graces of the Kingdom. With burning sarcasm the Apostle scorches them with his withering fulmination. He pictures them as basking in the thrones of kingly Messianic judgment, judging spiritual Israel! (Sarcasm!) In undiminished intensity he goes on: *And I would that you had in truth become kings*[49] (though you have not), *in order that we your teachers also might have become kings with you,* reaching the same stage in Christian progress! The irony here was a severe rebuke!

(v. 9) *For,* (it seems to me) *I think God set us, apostles forth, last, as if condemned to death,* as gladiators in the arena (*bestiarii*), *that we might*

---

45. Apparently a proverb or rule, one of Paul's ellipses.
46. First class condition indicating reality.
47. Robertson and Plummer, *I.C.C.* in loco.
48. Punctuation of Revised Standard Version.
49. *Ōphelon* used with second Aor. Ind. to express unfulfilled wish.

become a spectacle in the universe both to angels and to men. The (*bestiarii*) gladiators were condemned criminals or prisoners who in the fight with each other "to make a Roman holiday" rarely came out alive.

(v. 10) *We for Christ's sake are,* in the eyes of the world, *'fools' while you are* accounted *sensible in Christ! We are weak but you are strong! You are honored but we are in disrepute!*

(vv. 11-13) *Until the present hour we both hunger and thirst; we are lightly* (insufficiently) *clothed and knocked about, we are waifs* without any permanent homes, as transients; *we toil in hard labor, working with our hands; we put up with it* patiently; *being reproached* or railed at *we speak kindly* in return; *being persecuted, being defamed, we go on speaking words of encouragement* to one another and mutual exhortation, trying to conciliate and appease. *We become* (were made) *refuse* (filthy substance thrown away in cleansing) *of the world* (the very "scum of the earth"), *until now the offscouring of all things.* They were pictured as scapegoats before their own disciples! How different their plight by contrast with their self-complacent critics! What a picture of humiliations to strike shame and remorse in the hearts of these proud self-exalted judges of the persecuted and real founders of the church in Corinth! Would they humble themselves in contrite repentence for their sins of captious criticism, and vile calumniations against their pastors in the Lord? These severe rebukes and this scathing sarcasm were intended to puncture their immeasurable pride and boundless conceit of these shameless critics, the Judaists.

5. The Apostle closes with an affectionate remonstrance. 4:14-21 There was love in his severity and after all he was their father in the faith. He is writing in the terms of counsel and of discipline which a father administers. He is sending Timothy to them. He hopes for the best. He would have them put away factional strife and windy bragging. He will soon appear in their midst. He does not wish in any case to have to make use of the rod of discipline when he comes.

(v. 14) *I do not write these things to shame you but to admonish you as my beloved children.*

(v. 15) *If you may have ten thousand tutors in Christ yet you have not many fathers,* but only one. *For in Christ Jesus, through* the means of *the gospel I begat you.*

(v. 16) Wherefore (since I am your spiritual father) *I beseech you, become imitators of me.*

(v. 17) On this very account (that you, might become imitators of me) *I sent*[50] *you Timothy who is my child beloved and faithful* in the Lord, who will bring *to your remembrance my ways in Christ Jesus, just how everywhere in every church I* am accustomed to *teach.*

(v. 18) *But* acting *as if I were not coming to you some have been puffed up.*

---

50. Epistolary aorist.

(v. 19) *But I will come to you shortly, if the Lord will; and I will know not the word of them that are puffed up*[51] (for this I care nothing) *but the power.*
(v. 20) *For not in word* (is) *the Kingdom of God but in power.*
(v. 21) *What will ye* (do you wish)? *Shall I come to you with a rod* of discipline? *Or* shall it be *in love with a spirit of meekness* (gentleness?)

III

Immoral Practices in the Church (V:1-VI:20).

The church in Corinth was the child which had been begotten amid many sorrows (I Cor. 4:15), and which, most of all, the Apostle had nourished with the tenderest care and concern. In the city of Corinth the quest for pleasure and sensual enjoyment was mixed with vain intellectual culture and egotism. Naturally the church was composed of elements from all categories of the mixed racial population, including those converted from the midst of the impure and vicious, who had grown up in a corrupt environment, which for its vices had become notorious far and wide.

The gospel is the strongest purifying power known to human experience, but some of the members of the Corinthian church had been subjected to the strong temptations in their daily contacts with the universally prevalent contagion of immorality and had relapsed into the old practices. The apostle, having received some report months before, of this, had written a letter, not now extant, warning them against "associating with fornicators" (I Cor. 5:9), but his admonition had been lightly considered by the majority of the church. His Judaizing enemies, having arrived in Corinth in the meantime, had misinterpreted the counsel of Paul, saying that, "if the members of the church were to avoid association with fornicators," it would be necessary "to go out of the world" to do so. This argument would be employed easily by the disorderly members of the church to excuse their sins of immorality and assert their shameless libertine resentment against moral restraint. In this our First Corinthian Epistle, Paul deals with the question of immoral practices or sins which were being practiced flagrantly by certain disorderly members of the church, particularly one who was living in fornication with his stepmother. The apostle corrects the misinterpretation of his counsel in his previous letter that they should not tolerate the standing case of shameless fornication in a member of the church, which was proving to be an undermining of all moral standards in the church-community.

Another abuse closely allied to this was that of accusing one another and carrying their complaints before the heathen courts, instead of settling their difficulties in the church.

A. The apostle deals first with the fornicator and the lack of moral discipline in the church (5:1-13).

1. He stated the case and recommended what action the church should take. Paul was an authoritative apostle inspired by the Spirit and could rightly as-

51. Perfect tense denoting status of his critics, being puffed up permanently.

sume the attitude he did in dealing with the matter (vv. 1-8).

v. 1 It is *widely heard* (reported) *that there is fornication among you and such* a case of *fornication as* is *not found even among the pagans* (Gentiles); *that a certain man has his father's wife*, his own stepmother, as his concubine. This sin had been one of long standing, having been known far and wide as a notorious case of incest, not tolerated even by the Roman Court in society or by the Jewish law (Lev. 18:7, 8). But the church had passed the matter over lightly and had not dealt with the offender at all.

v. 2 *And you have continued to be puffed up;*[52] but *you did not rather mourn in order that the one who practiced this* evil *work* might *be taken away from your midst.*

v. 3 *For I indeed being absent in body, but present in spirit, have already judged* personally and individually *as if present* in body, *the one who has so practiced this (deed)* and given this perpetuated example for times.

vv. 4, 5 *In the name of the Lord Jesus, when you and my spirit were gathered together* in prayer, *with the power of our Lord Jesus* thus invoked, *to deliver over such an one to Satan*, who sifted Peter, *for the destruction of the flesh* (fleshly nature in the man), *in order that his spirit may be saved in the day of the Lord Jesus*, when He comes to judge all mankind.

v. 6 *Your glorying is not good. Do you not know that little leaven* of evil *goes on leavening*[53] *the whole mass?*

v. 7 *Purge out at once*[54] *the old leaven*, of Corinthian contagion *that you may be a new mass* of pure Christianity *even as you are* souls which were regenerated, *without the leaven* of such sin within you. *For truly our passover was sacrificed* (even) *Christ*, in order to remove the leaven of sin from His people.

v. 8 *Wherefore let us keep the feast* of Christians *not with old leaven*, in the state of life before you became Christians. *and not in the leaven of malice* (moral badness and vice) *and wickedness* (knavery) *but with the unleavened elements of sincerity and truth* which are characteristic of the true Christianity of the Christ.

The counsel of the Apostle about the case of incest had been disregarded by the church, and now he urges that drastic action be taken in the elimination of the guilty person (vv. 1, 2). He explains his own prayerful decision individually and desires that jointly in prayerful solidarity he and the church should come to the realization of his proposed action of elimination from the church, for the sake of the purification of the man himself, looking toward his final salvation and because of his example, subversive of moral standards (vv. 3-5). The existence of such an example of flagrant immoral life lived out in the midst of the church community was sure to act as an evil influence, leavening the whole mass of the membership of the church. Let them purge out the old leaven of evil that the church may become the true leaven of the Christianity of the

---

52. Perfect passive periphrastic indicative — a continued status of immoral living.
53. Present progressive tense.
54. Aor. imperative, indicating prompt action.

Christ, Who was sacrificed as the passover for His people for their protection and salvation. Such a salvation was symbolized in the blood sprinkled on the door posts that the destroying angel might leave unharmed every true son of Israel. "There was no place for leaven in a Jewish house at the time of the Passover (vv. 6, 7). The unleavened bread was to be discarded. The life of the Christian community must be a spiritual Passover (v. 8). Temporary elimination or religious and social boycott must be the penalty in order to bring the offender to repentance. This measure must be drastically enforced in such cases of flagrant and scandalous sin (vv. 9-13). Expulsion from the church did not carry with it the damnation of the willful offender, who was not to be regarded as an enemy but admonished as a brother (II Thess. 3:14f). Paul's aim was to use remedial punishment to bring the offender to repentance and reformation.

2. Correction of a misapprehension or possibly a willful misinterpretation respecting his former Apostolic admonition and command; with a more definite added statement (vv. 9-13).

v. 9 *I wrote to you formerly in the epistle* (the one now lost), *'not to associete with fornicators,'* who are members of the church and living in fornication brazenly. This would involve both religious and social boycott as a penalty imposed by the church but not necessarily a formal elimination from the church (Boises' *Notes* in loco).

v. 10. *Not at all* meaning that you were not to associate *with the fornications of this world or with the covetous or rapacious or with idolaters since you would be obliged in that case to go out of the world.* Society was largely made up of many such characters in a heathen civilization.

v. 11 *But now* my actual meaning was *when I wrote to you not to associate* with fornicators; *if anyone,*[55] *called a brother may be a fornicator* (immoral), *or a covetous* person (lustful) *or an idolater* (practicing idolatry) *or a reviler or a drunkard* by habit, *or a rapacious person* (extortioner), *with such* a person do *not even eat.*

v. 12 Paul further adduces the reason why he should have been understood to be writing about church members and not outsiders: *For what* business *is it* (of mine) *to me to judge those who are without* the church, who are not Christians at all. *Do not ye*[56] *judge those who are within the church?*

v. 13 *But those who are without,* on the outside of the church *will God judge.* We have nothing to do with judging them (Boise). *Remove at once*[57] *the wicked person from among yourselves!*

There were various types of sin current in the church in Corinth. The case of incest was outstanding, but along with the fornicators, of which there were more than one, were the lustful, who had a taste for gross sensuality and indulged habitually this carnal desire. Also with these were classed the Jewish idolaters, who, though Christians, indulged in the idol-feasts with their heathen

---

55 Third class condition, supposable cases. (Robertson, A. T.).
56 Negative *ouchi* expects an affirmative answer.
57. Aor. imperative, indicating prompt action.

friends. Habitual thieves who robbed the people by incorrect weights and false measures or by extortion, "selling above ceiling prices," were also of the tribe. Habitual drunkards, Paul also ranked along with the immoral sinners, and also the abusers, those of slanderous tongue, speaking freely about supposed defects of character in others, making use of "free speech" in order to undercut their brethren through motives of vengeance for supposed injuries inflicted or from motives of ambitions defeated. Hot tongued abuse and sly and tricky slander are fatal to the Christian spirit of love and brotherliness. Paul ranked these things along with immorality and idolatry. Jesus Himself had taught that a man is in danger of hell-fire who calls his brother "fool." Abusive rancour is one way to kill a brother under the pretense of ministering to his good discipline in brotherly love. Such a pretense sometimes covers up a heart of defeated ambitions, boiling over with vindictive hypocrisy.

B. Paul next passes to deal with the second abuse of taking their complaints before heathen courts. He shows the way to settle disputes in the Christian church. The saints shall judge the world. It is better to suffer wrong than to take your complaints before the tribunals of the unbelieving and iniquitous heathen (VI:1-11).

1. This evil and the occasion for it are first stated (vv. 1-8). This litigation grew out of covetousness (*pleonexia*), as the other practice of sensual indulgence had, out of sensual lust (*porneia*). Paul attributed to the Christian church the right to sit in judgment on their own disputes about property rights and Christian justice. He had disclaimed anv prerogative in judging the "outsiders:" he now asserts that the heathen outsiders were not qualified to judge aright the disputes among Christians. The Romans had given the Jews permission to judge and settle questions relating to their own religion, and breaches of their tombs, in the local Synagogue-tribunal. There were Roman "fellowships" (sodatilites) which arrogated to their organizations the right to settle their own disputes privately instead of taking them to the civil courts.[58] Such a practice, Paul argued for the local church, on the basis that Christianity must ultimately judge the world and control it.

Ch. VI, v. 1 *Does any one of you, having a matter* of dispute or complaint (law-suit) *against the other* (his brother or Christian neighbor) *dare to go to law*[59] *before the unrighteous* in pagan courts *instead of* laying the case *before the saints* or Christians of the local church. Such tribunals of arbitration were known to exist among the Jews, and it was justifiable that Christians assume the same manner of judicature.

v. 2. *Or do you not know that the saints will judge the world?* (Matt. 19:28; Luke 22:30) *And if the world is being judged*[60] (among you) *by you in*

---

58 Cf. James Moffatt, *Com. on I Corinthians*, p. 63.
59 Present Middle infinitive, to go to law by personal choice before the heathen in pagan courts.
60. The process is actually going on in local Christian church assemblies; progressive present passive (krinetei).

assembly and it is[61] *are you unworthy of judgments* which are the *least* in importance. Christians are to share with Christ in the final judgment also; much more should they be able to settle trivial questions and disputes among themselves.

v. 3 *Do you not know that we shall judge angels? How much more, things that pertain to this life?* This future exaltation of Christians and Christianity should humble the members of the church in their judgments and criticisms of one another. Christians are already exalted to the places of privilege with Christ in the heavenlies now.

v. 4 *If then you have* or may have *small tribunals for judging things pertaining to this life, why do you cause those, who are accounted as nothing in the church,*[62] *to sit as judges* of cases between Christians? Some of the Greek Christians may have been carrying their cases among themselves into heathen courts.

v. 5 *To your shame I say this to you. So then, does there not exist among you any wise man who shall be able to decide* (act as arbitrator) *between you, with respect to one's own brother,* who brings an accusation against him.

v. 6 *But a brother goes to law with a brother and this before unbelievers?*

v. 7 *Already indeed then, it is wholly a loss* (detriment) *to you that you have lawsuits with each other. Why do you not the rather suffer injustice? Why do you not suffer yourselves to be defrauded?*

v. 8 *But instead of this you do wrong and defraud and that even your brothers. They were unjust.* (*adikeite*)

2. Unrighteousness in all its forces in Christians is a survival of the habits of unregenerate days and the "old man" which should be "put off" at once (vv. 9-11).

vv. 9, 10 *Or do you not know that the unrighteous* (unjust) *shall not inherit the Kingdom of God?* All unjust or unrighteous persons, (*adikoi*), must divest themselves of their unrighteousness because such cannot dwell in the Kingdom. *Be not led astray* into error by false teachers. *Neither fornicators, nor idolaters, nor adulterers,* those untrue to marriage obligations, *nor effeminate* persons who live in excessive luxury, nor those who are victims of male lust or *sodomites, nor thieves* or those who live by theft; *nor covetous, nor drunkards, nor revilers* who have slanderous or dirty tongues, *nor exortioners shall inherit* or have any part in *the Kingdom of God.*

v. 11 *And such were some of you,* in preconversion days, and vestiges of the old nature and habits have reasserted themselves in you. *But ye washed yourselves,*[63] *but you were set apart* to a consecrated life, *but you were justified in the name of the Lord Jesus Christ* in the sphere of His atoning sacrifice *and by the* Holy *Spirit of our God* in your regeneration when you were born into the Kingdom.

---

61 Conditional sentence of the first class, according to fact.
62 Instrumental case with the preposition.
63 Middle voice indicating obedient baptism after regeneration through acceptance of the Savior.

IV

Questions in the letter from Corinth with referencec to marriage answered by Paul. Chapter VII:1-40.

A. The apostle lays down first a basic principle in marriage. Against sensualism he asserts that a single life is not wrong but good; but, over against rigorists, marriage was natural, and, being God-ordained for the propagation of the race, both useful and safe (7:1-7).

Paul has no one-sided view of marriage and is here applying the basic principle of marriage as a sacred contract. To remain unmarried may be good in certain cases and for practical ends, contingent to the work of the Kingdom; but for the majority it was a safeguard and its conjugal dues must be honored unless by mutual consent of husband and wife for a season.

v. 1 *Concerning* the questions which you church-members asked in the letter *which you wrote, it is good* and honorable *for* an unmarried *man not to touch a woman*[64] by union in marriage.

v. 2 *But on account of* the prevalent *fornications* in Corinth now and the world in general always, *let each man have his own wife* as the surest protection against temptations to immorality, *and each woman her* very *own husband,* over against the practices of pagan society of polygamy and polyandry.

vv. 3, 4 *And let the husband render to the wife her* conjugal *dues and* in like manner *the wife also to her husband,* thus making marriage complete. Husband and wife have mutual obligations in the propagation of the race, but marriage is not for the ends of mere sensualism. "In wedlock the separate ownership of the person ceases."[65] *The wife has not* exclusive *authority over her own body but the husband* shares this authority with her *and in like manner the husband has not* sole *authority over his own body but the wife* shares it with him.

v. 5 *Let them not withdraw from one another* and deprive each other of the normal right relationships sexually *except it may be by* common *consent for a season* for special and justifiable reasons religious or other, such as, *that you may have* leisure *for* or *may devote yourselves* to special *prayer* or other religious activities *and may* later *be together again.* All of this *is in order that Satan may not tempt you* to commit adultery *on account of your incontinency* or lack of self-control.

v. 6 *But this I say by way of allowance* to you, as a permission to you and *not as a command.* This does not involve doubt in Paul's mind or deny in any sense his inspiration.

v. 7 *Yet I would that all men* and women *might be even as I myself am,* having the power of self-control. *But each one has his own* gracious *gift from God, one in this manner and another in that.*

The question, then, which the Corinthian brethren proposed to Paul was whether a Christian should marry at all. Could not the life of a Christian be

---

64. *Gunaikos,* Genetive case with verbs of touching.
65. Robertson and Plummer, *I. C. C.* p. 134.

better without marrying? The ascetic rigorist said it could and even urged Christians who were married to desist, even so, from sexual relations. Paul answered, that for some abstinence from sex-relations, by remaining unmarried, was good. But he did not identify chastity with celibacy, which is the negative side merely of a positive devotion to Christ, which can be equally strong in the normally married. He counsels that married life should be normal in reproductive relationship, which is the obligation of each party to the marital contract, except for temporary religious or other purposes by mutual consent.[66] This counsel was given to those Christians who faced the constant and extraordinary temptations to fornications abundantly current in the heathen environment of Corinth and also prevalent elsewhere in the environing world.

B. Principles for the unmarried, and for the married, especially in reference to separation. Paul here applies the inward principle of Christianity in relation to the outward circumstances of life (7:8-24).

From the general principle of the marriage contract, of the two merged personalities into one, the Apostle proceeds to some more definite instructions.

vv. 8, 9 *But I say to the unmarried and to the widows,* it is *good* or honorable *for them if they may remain* unmarried *as I.* Paul may have been a bachelor or more probably a widower. He does not say it is better but simply good. *But if they are lacking in self-control* or have not continency, *let them marry. For it is better to be in the married state than to be inflamed with lust.*

vv. 10, 11 But to those members of the church who have been married[67] *I give charge, not I but the Lord* Jesus (Matt. 5:32; 19:9) *that a wife be not separated by* others or any circumstance or separate herself[68] *but if she might be separated* already *let her remain unmarried or be reconciled to her husband and I charge a husband not to put away his wife* except for the cause of fornication (Matt. 5:32). Desertion and expulsion equally are condemned.

1. The next paragraph deals with other members of the church who were married to non-Christians before they were converted. Paul makes plain that Christianity did not come to break up relationships in families already formed.

vv. 12, 13 *To the others* not included in the above classes, *I* say, *not* quoting *the Lord* who gave no commandment in this respect; *If any brother has an unbelieving wife and she is well-disposed* or content *to dwell with him let him not proceed to put her away* (v. 13) *and a wife if any one has an unbelieving husband and he is contented to dwell with her, let her not put away the husband,* by Roman law or by collaboration with the church assembly, if that might be possible.

vv. 14, 15 The reason for these precepts is that *the unbelieving husband is sanctified in the* believing *wife and the unbelieving wife in the* Christian brother-husband, *since* then *if* that is *not* true *your children are unclean but now they are consecrated* in the same sense as the unbelieving wife or husband by the believing (v. 15). *But if the unbelieving one separates himself let him*

66 Moffatt, *The New Testament Com.*, Corinthians p. 73f.
67 Perfect tense
68 Middle voice, subject of verb acting, either voice same form.

continue separated. The brother or the sister in the church *is not bound down in servitude* for life *in such* circumstances. The one who maliciously deserts another (v. 11) cannot remarry but in the case of the desertion of an unbeliever the one deserted may marry again. Wilful desertion on the part of the unbelieving partner to the contract leaves no Christian ground for appeal or for discipline. Marriage is not here considered to be a mere civil contract which can be dissolved at the pleasure of either contracting party but is a deeply religious institution having its origin as divine and its nature that of a divine safeguard against temptations incident to loneliness and to an immorally corrupt environment. *But in peace God has called us* and not to maintain a wrangle with an unbeliever who wilfully deserts and lacks all basis for a Christian reconciliation. Wilful and final desertion, resulting in the unfaithfulness and adultery of the unbeliever, in this case, should not enslave the believer who is deserted but leaves him free to marry again.[69] This interpretation is not against the teaching of Christ (Matt. 5:32; 19:9) but in accord. It is also in accord with the immediate content which calls for the dissolution of the marriage bond as a consequence of this kind of desertion over against the other above, which is prohibited.

v. 16 The reason stated in verse 15 that God "called us for peace" and a peaceful life is the following rendering of a further reasonable consideration. *For what dost thou know* (about this) *O wife whether thou wilt*, by refusing to permit the wilful deserter to separate himself, *save thy husband?* A peaceful separation is meant here instead of an impossible and abortive effort to retain the deserter. *Or how dost thou know O husband whether thou wilt save thy wife.*

2. v. 17 Only (nisi) *as the Lord* Jesus *has imparted* or given a part *to each one, as God has called each one, so let him walk* using discretion so as not to give occasion for unbeliever-desertion. *And so, in all the churches* in Europe or elsewhere, *I ordain. Paul lays* down here a general principle to be followed in all the churches (7:17-24).

The principle holds good in regard to circumcision.

vv. 18, 19 Was anyone circumcised when called? *Let him not* attempt to efface the sign of circumcision, *drawing upon himself* (a foreskin) by surgical operation to hide his identity as a Jew. *Or has anyone been called* or converted in *uncircumcision? Let him not be circumcised* (v. 19). *For circumcision is nothing but* what is important to the Christian is *keeping the moral commandments of God.*

vv. 20, 21 *Let each one remain in the calling* or status socially *in which he was* when he *was called* religiously, in the moment of his acceptance of Christ's call. "Conversion to Christianity makes a radical change in the moral and spiritual life but need not make a change in our external life" or social status. In the case of marriage the Christian partner must not do anything to bring about a dissolution of marriage any more than a Christian slave claim emanci-

---

69 Bishop Ellicott, *Com. on First Cor.* p. 181f.

pation.[70] If the heathen party insists on dissolution of the marriage bond and deserts, let him separate himself. If he grants emancipation to the slave then let the slave accept it (v. 21). *Wast thou a slave when thou wast called? Let not being a slave give you concern; but if thou art able also to become a freeman* and thou hast the choice between slavery and being a freeman, then make use of the opportunity to become free.

vv. 22-24 *For the one called in the Lord while a slave is the Lord's freeman* just the same. *Likewise* the contrary holds that *when one is called being a freeman he is* at the same time, *the slave of Christ* (v. 23). *You were bought with a price,* His blood, and to Him you belong. *Do not* voluntarily *become slaves of men,* selling your freedom, and do not consider yourselves the slaves of men (v. 24). The general rule: *Each one in the* occupation or social status *in which he is called. Brethren is that let him remain content, alongside of God* and counting on his protection and guidance.

C. The apostle lays down principles to aid unmarried virgin daughters and their fathers in decisions relative to marriage (7:25-40).

1. He does not claim any authoritative command from the Lord (Jesus) but gives his judgment.

v. 25 *Concerning the virgin-daughters* and their marriage (according to custom) by their fathers *I do not have any commandment* or order *from the Lord* (Jesus) *but I give my judgment* (or decided opinion) *as one having had mercy shown me by the Lord to be faithful* and worthy of trust.

2. *I think that on account of the present* necessity, *distress* on earth or constraint, *that it is good for a man* or woman *to continue in his present state* (vv. 26-31).

v. 26 *I think, then, that this is good by reason of the present constraint that it s well for a man to be thus* as he is.

v. 27 *Are you bound* by marriage *to a wife?* Do *not seek a separation* (loosing). *Have you been loosed from a wife* or never been married? *Do not seek a wife.*

v. 28 *But if you even shall marry, you committed no sin* in marrying. *And if a virgin* (maiden) *marries she has committed no sin* in so doing. *Yet, affliction in the flesh, such shall have. But I am seeking to spare you this* trouble or affliction.

vv. 29, 30, 31 *But this I affirm, brethren, the time* of trial and affliction *is shortened,*[71] *in order that, henceforth those having wives might be as though* not *having* them, *and those weeping as though not weeping, and those buying as not possessing, and* those *using the world as if not* eager to *use it fully; for transitory indeed is the outward fashion of this world.*[72]

3. Furthermore, this leaves one more free for God's service vv. 32-35.[73]

---

70 Robertson and Plummer, *I. C. C.*, First Cor. p. 144.
71 Periphrastic perfect.
72 Cf. Robertson and Plummer *I. C. C.*, I Cor. p. 150.
73 Outline cf. Moffatt *N. T. Com.* I Cor. p. 90.

v. 32 *I wish you to be free from worldly anxiety* in view of the present distress. *The unmarried man has care for the things of the Lord, how he may please the Lord* (v. 33) *but the married*[74] *for the things of the* material *world, how he may please his wife*, neglecting thus to care for the higher nature in the interest of the material life, *and there is a difference.*

v. 34 *Both, the unmarried woman and the* maid or *virgin has a care for the things of the Lord in order that she may be holy both in body and in spirit. But she who is married has a care for the things of the* material *world how she may please her husband.*

v. 35 *Now this I am saying for your own spiritual profit; not in order that I might cast a noose upon you, but for that which is becoming and* for *constant, waiting on the Lord without* distraction.

4. In the existing circumstances marriage is inexpedient in view of the distress, yet, better than the evils, current in the bad Corinthian environment (vv. 36-38).

v. 36 *But if any man thinks that he is acting in an unbecoming manner toward his unmarried daughter*, by withholding his consent to her marriage,[75] *if she may be of full age and if it ought to take place thus, let him do what he wishes* about giving his consent to her marriage, *he does not sin* by so doing. *Let them* (the daughter and her lover) *marry.*

v. 37 *But he who stands firm in his heart not having* misgivings as to the (distress or) *necessity but has* legal *authority* (vested in the father by Roman law) *concerning his own will and has decided this* matter *in his own heart, to keep his unmarried daughter, he will do well.*

v. 38 *So that,* the conclusion follows, *both the one who gives in marriage his own unmarried daughter does well* or honorably *and the one not giving in marriage will do better* in view of the bad environment.

5. About the remarriage of widows.

v. 39 *A wife is bound for so long a time as her husband lives. But if the husband dies, she is free* to be *married to whomsoever she wishes.*

v. 40 *But she is happier if she remain thus single, according to my opinion. And I also think that I have the spirit of God.*

V

Reply to the questions in the letter from the Corinthian church about eating food offered to idols, and to taking part in feasts made in honor to idols. VIII:1-XI:1.

The prejudice against food offered to idols was deep-seated in all strict Jews. But the common source of the meat-foods in Corinth was the general markets where such meats were commonly sold. Idol feasts were held in connection with the temple of Artemis in honor of this patron deity and also in other

74 Aorist points to the time when the change of interest took place. Cf. Robertson and Plummer in loco.

75 Boise's *Notes on the Epistles of Paul,* I Cor. p. 188 (v.36).

places in honor of other heathen gods. Many of the Greek Christians did not have the same attitude toward the use of such meats, knowing that the heathen deities whom they had honored before they became Christians were mere figments of the human imagination, as are for example, the idea of purgatory or the worship of saints. But this question was one of religious scruples within the Christian church and had to be handled by Paul with care. The apostle makes "generous allowance" for the weaker party with his over-conscientious misgivings while at the same time he "pleads with the enlightened to be tolerant and considerate."[76] His treatment lays down an eternal principle, though the concrete occasion giving rise to the question from the church was local and temporary. In the principle laid down for Christian conduct in questions of prejudicial scruples, and doubtful or border-line practices in the Christian life, we have a basis for the resolution of many problems in modern Christian churches. Paul formulated the basic principle and applied it to the problem of the Corinthian church first. Some members of that church were accustomed on occasion to sit down at the tables of feasts of their pagan friends which were in honor of certain heathen deities of which there were many. The meat used in these idol feasts was naturally from the markets where the *eidolothuta* or food offered to idols was sold. Other members of the church among whom the Jewish Christians would naturally often be numbered, seeing their fellow-Christians in this practice were made to stumble. It was a question of whether this should be done and naturally allowed or tolerated by the church.

A. General principles VIII:1-13.

1. For those who had the right view of idols the eating of meat which had been offered to idols was no sin.

vv. 1-6 An idol is but imaginary and had no real existence and in consequence the foods offered to idols differed in no respect from other food not offered.

v. 1 *Concerning the meats offered to idols, we know that all* Christians *have knowledge* that an idol is nothing. But ironically he points out the conceit of those who boasted uncharitably of their superior knowledge. *Knowledge puffs up but* Christian *love builds up.*

vv. 2, 3 *If anyone seems to have known something, not yet did he know as he ought to know.* (v. 3) *But if anyone loves God, this one has been known* permanently *by Him.* This was a reflection which would humble the brother who was puffed up with his "superior knowledge."

v. 4 *Concerning, therefore, the eating of things sacrificed to idols, we are assured that there is no idol in the world and that there is no true God, except one.*

vv. 5, 6 Then parenthetically the apostle adds, *For even if there are so-called gods in the heaven or upon earth, just as* in fact *there are many* heathen *gods and many* human *lords.* (v. 6) *But to us* Christians *there is* but *one God, the*

76 Moffatt, *New Testament Commentary,* I Cor. p. 103.

Father, from whom, as creation come *all things and we exist for Him, and one Lord Jesus Christ, through whose intermediate agency*[77] *all things came into being and exist and we also exist through Him.* Through this brief parenthetical statement Paul confirms their Christian rejection of all pagan beliefs in idols or their imaginative magical demonic powers over material things or people.

2. But for the sake of the brother, weak in the faith, who may stumble, it is the duty of the enlightened to refrain. vv. 7-13.

v. 7 *But not in all* men is there *the* definite *knowledge* about the non-entity of idols; *but certain ones* even among the Christians *by their acquaintance* until now *with the idol, are eating* the meat *as idol sacrifice, and their conscience being weak is defiled.* When one does something against his own conscience, however uninstructed that conscience may be, he sins, by breaking down his own will power to resist temptation to do other things which are really wrong.

v. 8 *But food* in itself *will not commend us to God or* otherwise affect our relation to him, *neither if we may not eat are we the worse nor if we may eat are we the better.*

v. 9 *But look out, lest your right* or authority *may itself become a stumbling block to the weak* brothers. This is an important consideration and principle which must underlie all Christian conduct.

v. 10 *For if any* Christian brother *may see you who have knowledge* about the unreality of an idol *reclining* at the table *in an idol feast, will not the conscience of him who is weak* in the faith and uninstructed *be built up* leading *into the* practice of *eating the idol sacrifices?* Thus you will give approval to the idol worship, by habitually partcipating with pagan friends and acquaintances at the idol tables.

v. 11 *For the one who is weak is destroyed by your* definite *knowledge, on account of whom Christ died* an atoning death on the cross.

v. 12 *And thus sinning against the weak brethren and smiting their conscience when it is weak, you sin against Christ.*

v. 13 So Paul lays down the fundamental principle in the conduct of the "enlightened brother" in his relationship to the brother less-informed and weak in the faith: *If anything eaten causes my brother to stumble, I* certainly *will not eat*[78] *meat ever again, that I may not cause my brother to stumble.*

B. Declaration of the apostle about the rights of the strong Christian and his liberties in conduct (9:1-22) and the reward in denying self and, foregoing his rights for the sake of others illustrated (9:24-27).

1. The broad principle of behavior in self-denial Paul illustrates from his own conduct as a freed-man in Christ, (vv. 1-3) in his own rights as to marriage and support from the church (vv. 4-18), and in his own personal conduct in every way (vv. 19-23).

---

77 Cf. John 7:3 f.

78 Double negative *ou mē* with the second aorist subjunctive.

a. He asserts his freedom (vv. 1-3) over against his declaration of self-denial (8:13) and defends his apostleship. The apostle was not understood by some because he did not accept support from the church and did not have a family like Peter and other apostles. His self-denying conduct about eating the meat offered to idols seemed contradictory to his declarations about the nothingness of an idol. He explains his adapted conduct in view of possible misinterpretations of his motives.

v. 1 *Am I not free? Am I not an apostle? Have I not seen Jesus our Lord?*[79] *Are not ye my work in the Lord* (Jesus)? All these questions expect an affirmative answer.

v. 2 *If to others I am not an apostle;*[80] *yet, at least, I am to you; for you are the seal of my apostleship in the Lord.* The emphasis is upon 'you' and the apostle thus appeals strongly for their backing in his defense of his apostleship. Their very existence as a Christian church authenticated his character as an apostle.

v. 3 *My defense*[81] *to them that examine me* critically to find fault *is this,* which I have said i. e. the Christian testimony of you who believed through my work in Christ.

b. Paul's right to marry and to have support from the churches (vv. 4-18).

v. 4 *Do we*[82] *not have the right to eat and to drink* that which our own conscience says is not hurtful?

v. 5 *Do we not have* authority or *right to take around* with us in our missionary journeys, *a wife* who is *a sister* in the church, *as also the rest of the apostles, and the* half-*brothers of the Lord,*[83] *and Cephas* (Peter).

v. 6 *Or is it only I and Barnabas who have not the right, not to work* for a living any longer? Those two apostles on the first missionary journey worked for their maintenance but had a right to refrain from working.

v. 7 *What soldier ever serves at his own expenses* or charges? *Who plants a vineyard and does not eat of the fruit of it? Or who shepherds a flock and does not eat of foods* made of *the milk of the flock,* or drink of the milk? Paul likens a pastor to a soldier, a vine-dresser and a shepherd all of whom live from the fruits of their work.

v. 8 *Do I speak these things,* (according to human judgment or) *as a man; or the law also, does it not speak these things?*

v. 9 *Yes, for in the law of Moses it stands written* (Perf) *"Thou shalt not muzzle the ox while treading out the corn"* (Deut. 25:4).[84] *It is not for the oxen only that God cares, is it?*[85]

---

79 Cf. Acts 9:17,27; 18:9; 22:14,17f; II Cor. 12:1f.
80 His apostleship had been questioned by a factional party especially of the judaizers in Corinth.
81 *Apologia,* in original sense of defense.
82 Editorial we referring to Paul's own conduct which he was here defending, perhaps referring to Barnabas also.
83 For example James.
84 Form of prohibition, *ouk* with fut. indicative.
85 Use of *mē* expecting negative answer to the question.

v. 10 *Is it not on our account altogether that he says this?* For, *on account of us certainly it was written,* "*the one plowing ought to plow in hope and he who threshes,* ought to thresh, *in hope of sharing* in the product of his labor.

v. 11 *If we sowed for you spiritual things, is it a great matter if we shall reap your carnal* or material *things?*

v. 12 *If others have a share in the authority over you,*[86] *do we not, still more? But we did not use this authority but we bear all things that we may not cause any hindrance to the gospel of Christ.*

v. 13 *Do ye not know that those who work at the sacred things,* as the priests in the Jewish temple, *eat* from *the things of the sacred place* or temple, and that *those who attend at the altar take a share with the altar?*

v. 14 *So also the Lord arranged for those who preach the gospel to live from the gospel.*

v. 15 *But I have not used any one of these things, and I did not write these things in order that it may become thus* (in my case) *in me.* For to me it is *good rather to die* than — that my glorying any man shall make void.[87] Paul had glorified in his self-support and did not wish to lose that ground of his glorying and rejoicing, since it avoided any criticism of his attitude toward using the ministry as a means for enriching himself financially.

v. 16 *For if I go on preaching the gospel, there is no ground for me for glorying* at all, *for a necessity is laid upon me, for woe is me if I preach not the glad tidings.*

v. 17 *For if I practice this* self-support *willingly,* of my own choice, *I have a reward; but if unwillingly,* not of my own will, *I have been entrusted permanently with a stewardship.* Paul could be faithful as a steward but that would not be any reason for self-glorying but for the approval of the Master, "Well done, good and faithful servant."

v. 18 *What then is my reward?* it is *in order that in preaching the gospel I might make the gospel without expense* to my hearers *so as not to use in full my right in the gospel,* which is that of maintenance, or financial support. Paul had denied himself this support and refused to accept money from the churches, except the Philippian church, to prove his disinterestedness and put the Kingdom first (Matt. 6:33).

c. Paul continues his digression, declaring his freedom in his own conduct (vv. 19-23).

v. 19 *For being free from all* (men) *I made myself a bond-servant*[88] *to all, in order that I might gain the greater number.*

v. 20 *I became to the Jews as a Jew, that I might gain Jews; to those* who are *under the law*[89] *as under the law, though not being myself under the law,* that I *might gain those who are under the law.*

---

86 Objective genitive, *humōn.*
87 Epistolary aorist.
88 Causative verb *douloo,* made myself a bond-servant.
89 The Mosaic law with all its ceremonies.

v. 21 *To those* who are *without the law as without the law,* not observing the Jewish ceremonies and feasts, *though not without the* moral and spiritual *law of God*[90] which is universal and eternal, *but in the law of Christ,*[91] in order that *I might gain those* who are *without law.*

v. 22 *I became weak to the weak in order that I might gain the infirm* Christians, who are weak in the faith and enlightened (cf. 8:13) with reference to the nothingness of idols with their imagined magical powers. Paul respected the scruples of the weak brother.

v. 23 *To all men* (generic) *I have become*[92] all things that are legitimate and right, in tactful adaptation without compromise of the right principles, *in order that I may go on saving*[93] *some. And I do all things* on this sound principle of right adaptation and expediency in conduct, *on account of the gospel* and for its sake, *in order that I may become* progressively *a fellow-sharer of it* with others who do not have it.

2. Duties of his readers to follow his example and illustrations of the reward in doing so. 9:24-27.

v. 24 *Do you not know that those who run in a stadium* (in a race course) — *all indeed run, but only one receives the prize. Thus,* like those who run in the race course, *do ye go on running*[94] *that ye may surely*[95] *take the prize.*

v. 25 Another illustration from the Olympic games is cited. *And every man who engages in an athletic contest is temperate in all things, those, indeed then, in order that they may receive a corruptible crown, but we,* in the Christian contest *an incorruptible* one.

vv. 26, 27 *I therefore so run* making use of abstemious self-denial *as not uncertainly. But I discipline* severely[96] *my body and bring it into bondage,* (condition of a bond-servant *doulos*) subjecting the physical appetites and passions to the control of reason and conscience with the help of Christ, *lest* by some means *having made proclamation* of the gospel to others, *I myself should be disapproved* or disqualified for the prize in the race.

The foregoing chapter is an integral part of the discussion of the subject of eating food offered to idols. It is not a mere defense of Paul's apostleship. In this part of his instruction on that subject the apostle makes plain: that Christians might use this food offered to idols, in their homes and elsewhere, without fear of the imagined polution by the supposed magical power of the idols. But in eating this food they might cause their weak brethren in the church to stumble. Where there was danger of harming a weak brother, they must by self-denial avoid the peril.[97]

---

90 Genitive of specification.
91 *Ibid.*
92 Perfect tense denoting complete action and a permanent continuing result.
93 Note change of tenses to the progressive present.
94 Present Imperative.
95 *Vede,* force of preposition kata in composition.
96 Boise's *Notes.*
97 Robertson and Plummer, *I. C. C.,* I Cor. p. 176.

C. The importance of the foregoing principles Paul illustrates from Jewish history (10:1-11:1) in warning and exhortation (vv. 12, 13) against the danger of mingling idolatrous ideas and practices with the Lord's Supper; (vv. 14-22), concluding with practical instructions, by way of application, about eating meats offered to idols (10:23-11:1).[98]

1. Take a warning, Paul admonishes, against the perils connected with idol feasts, from the sins of idolatry, murmuring against Moses, and fornication, committed by the Israelites in the wilderness journey. Distrust self and trust in God. 10:1-13.

The backsliding of Ancient Israel was real and furnished an apt and vivid example of the unfaithfulness of many of those who had come by miracle through the sea but did not in the end enter into Canaan.

vv. 1, 2 *For I do not wish you to continue ignorant*[99] of the fact *that our* Israelitish *fathers were all under the cloud* of God's protection *and all passed through the* Red *sea, and were all baptized into Moses in the cloud and in the sea,* thus recognizing Moses as their real leader and entering into covenant relation with the God of Israel, the God of Moses, by this signal experience. To compromise with the idolatrous practices of heathen peoples afterwards was not an imaginary but a real peril (Robertson, *Word Pictures*). They had marched under the wings of the pillar of cloud by day which protected them from the hot rays of the Syrian sun, fiercely beating on the desert plains, and were led by the pillar of fire by night, which had saved them from the pursuing Egyptians, when hemmed in by the sea before them and the mountains on either side, with Pharaoh's army coming in sight in the rear. Just then the pillar of fire had removed from the front of them to their rear, separating them from their enemies. They were buried, as it were, in the depths of the bed of the sea beneath the same cloud, with the protecting waters of the sea miraculously shielding them on either side. That was a complete immersion[1] under the cloud and in the midst of the sea.

v. 3 *And they all ate the same spiritual*[2] *food* (*broma*) *and all drank the same spiritual drink* (*poma*).

v. 4. *For they went on drinking continuously* (imperfect) in the journey, *of the spiritual rock which followed, and the rock was* the (Messiah) *Christ.* The events on the journey toward the Promised Land were miraculous and spiritual. The rock from which God miraculously provided for the two millions of Israel to drink was typical of Christ, the one who slakes the spiritual thirst of mankind, but it was more. It was Christ, the Messiah, Who was preexistent and Who was the source of the water at Rephidim, Kadesh and other places as He is our source of spiritual and living water today. The

98 Boise, *Notes on the Epistles of Paul* in loco.

99 Present Infinitive, progressive action.

1 BKLP read *ebaptisanto*, constative first aorist middle, while Aleph, ACD, have *ebaptithesan*, first aorist passive; the former, *they got themselves immersed* (*baptized*), the latter they *were baptized.*

2 **Manna** called spiritual because supernatural (Robertson) typical of Christ (Jo. 6:35).

rock was really a manifestation of the Messiah (Robertson and Plummer *I. C. C.* in loco).

v. 5 *But not with the greater number of them was God pleased, for they were strewed* or laid out, corpses *in the desert,*[3] as if by a cyclonic force.

v. 6 *And these things became types or* examples *for us, to the end that we may not be lustful of evil things as* they lusted.[4]

v. 7 *And stop becoming idolatrous just as some of them* became. *Even as it stands written: The people sat down to eat and drink and rose up to sport*[5] (play).

v. 8 *And let us not go on fornicating as some of them fornicated, and fell in one day twenty-three thousand.*[6]

v. 9 *And let us not continue to test* or strain exceedingly[7] *the Lord* (God) tempting Him, *just as some of them tempted Him and continued to be destroyed*[8] *by serpents.* They had committed voluntary sins against God and went on sinning with a high hand testing or tempting God beyond measure.

v. 10 *And do not continue to murmur,*[9] *but stop murmuring, just as some* kept *murmuring and perished by the destroyer* (Num. 16:41ff) *in a plague.*

v. 11 *And these things happened to them typically* or by way of example *and were written* or recorded *for our admonition* or warning *unto whom the ends of the ages have come,* "the last period of history from Christ's coming on," (Boise) (Heb. 9:26; I Pet. 4:7).

v. 12 *So that* as a conclusion, *let him that thinks that he stands look out constantly lest he may fall* into sin and loss of his Christian privileges and opportunities. Paul is not referring to any possibility of eternal damnation to a child of God who loses his life's usefulness by some grave sin. Israel lost her mission, as a nation, for a long period unended yet.

v. 13 *A temptation has not taken you except* such as is *human* and man can hear. *And God is faithful and will not permit you to be tempted* (tested) *above what you are able to bear, but will make with every trial the way of escape also, to the end that you may be able to bear up under it.*

2. The vital bearing of participation in idol feasts and eating meat offered to idols from the point of view of the Lord's supper, is here used as a basis for Paul's appeal to them to flee from idolatry. 10:14-22.

Those who participate in the worship-service of the Lord's supper and fellowship with God, in honor to Christ, should not participate in the idol feasts of demons, connected with the worship and honoring of idols. The two things are mutually exclusive.

---

3 Numbers 11:4, 34.
4 Ibid. (cf. Nestle's text).
5. Robertson and Plummer, *I. C. C.* in loco.
6 Numbers 25:1-9. Some MSS read 24,000.
7 *ekpeirazomen.*
8 Imperfect tense denoting continued progressive action.
9 Present tense.

v. 14 *Wherefore, my Beloved, flee* continually[10] *from idolatry,* the worship-service of idols.[11] This is Paul's conclusion from the foregoing arguments vv. 1-13. If they will separate themselves from idol feasts and participation with those honoring idols, they will escape and be saved to God.

v. 15 *I speak as to wise men; judge ye* once for all[12] *what I say.*

v. 16 *The cup*[13] *of blessing, which we bless* in the celebration of the Lord's Supper, with prayer and thanksgiving: *is it not a communion* with Christ in a fellowship or a participation *in the blood of Christ. The loaf which we break: is it not*[14] *the participation of the body of Christ?* These elements were employed as symbols of the blood and body of Christ and were not changed in character from that of any other wine or bread, as Romanists claim. The supper is not a mere fellowship with one another but with the Lord Who shed His blood and Whose body was broken for us. The Supper does not contain the "real presence of the body, blood and divinity" of Jesus in it. The elements are symbols only.

v. 17 *Because there is one loaf and we the many are one body,* the church. *For we all partake of the one loaf.* Here then is the explanation for the affirmation, and it supports the general assertion, that they were participating with Christ and so must not have fellowship with demons in the idol feasts.

v. 18 *Behold,* for example, *Israel according to the flesh* or lineal descendence. *Were not those, who were eating the* meat a part of which was offered in the temple as *sacrifices, sharers with the altar?* A portion of the sacrifice was burned on the altar in the Jewish temple worship and a part of the flesh was sold in the markets and eaten by the Jews. Those Christians therefore who were accustomed to share in the idol feasts and eat the meat offered to idols were in truth partakers with the idol-altar and sharers with demons.

v. 19 *What then am I saying: that meat offered to an idol is* in reality *anything* different from other meat? *or that an idol* made of wood, stone or other material *is anything?* A negative answer is expected to these questions.

v. 20 *But* (I do affirm) *that the things that they sacrifice, "they are sacrificing to demons and not to God." I do not wish you to become sharers with the demons.*

v. 21 *You are not able to* or cannot *drink the cup of the Lord and the cup of demons: You are not able to share the table of the Lord and the table of demons also.*

v. 22 *Or do we* by persistent practice of attending the idol feasts with pagans *provoke to jealousy the Lord* (Jesus)? Christ instituted the Supper and His cup used at the supper and His table where it is celebrated in His memory must not be desecrated also by drinking of the cup and eating at the table of

---

10 Present Imperative, progressive and continued action.
11 Eidolatreia, idolō-latreia, worship-service rendered to an idol.
12 Aorist Imperative, *krinate,* judge quickly.
13 *Potarion,* diminutive, little cup, which is blessed brings a blessed memory of Him who blesses.
14 *Ouxi* expects an affirmative answer.

idols wherever that might be, in the idol temple or in the pagan home. *We are not stronger than He, are we?*[15]

3. General principles governing the conduct of the Christians and instructions and warnings as to the idol feasts. 10:23-11:1.

v. 23 *All things are lawful; but not all things are expedient* or profitable. *All things are lawful, but not all things edify.*

v. 24 *Let no man seek his own, but* each *his neighbor's* good.

v. 25. *Whatsoever is sold in the* shambles or *market, eat, asking nothing on account of the conscience.*

v. 26 *for the earth is the Lord's, and the fullness of it.*

v. 27 *If anyone of the unbelievers biddeth you to a banquet in his home and you wish to go, eat whatever is placed before you, asking nothing for the sake of conscience.* This friendly courtesy in response to his kindly invitation will win him to the Savior.

v. 28 *If anyone at the banquet may say to you, 'This hath been offered to sacrifice,' do not eat, for his sake that showed it,* and for conscience sake.

v. 29 *Conscience, I say, not thine own, but that of the other. For why is my liberty judged by another conscience?* This is a self-limitation of the strong in favor of the weak brother.

v. 30 *If I by grace partake, why am I evil spoken of for that for which I give thanks?*

v. 31 *Whether then you eat or drink or whatever you do, do all to the glory of God.*

v. 32 *Give no occasion of stumbling, either to Jews or to Greeks or to the church of God.*

v. 33 *Even as I also please all men in all things, not seeking mine own profit, but the profit of many, that they may be saved.*

Ch. 11, v. 1 *Be ye imitators of me, even as I also am of Christ.*

VI

Paul reveals the divine disapproval on the disorders in connection with the public worship in the Corinthian church.

(1) Respecting the veiling of women (11:2-16) and (2) In connection with the Lord's Supper (11:17-34).

First he discusses the conduct and dress of the Christian women in the public assemblies of the church (11:2-16).

v. 2 *Now, I praise you* brethren of the Corinthian church *that you remember me in all things, and are holding fast the traditions* or teachings, v. 3 *just as I entrusted them to you. But I wish you to know that Christ is the head of every man and the man is head of woman and God is head of Christ.* This is a right order of creation, many times wrongly misunderstood. It in no wise contradicts the right relationships between man and woman in the Christian

---

15 *Reductio ad absurdum.* (Chrysostom)

social order. It is of divine appointment that woman is rightly subordinate but not wrongly enslaved to man.

v. 4 This order was being disregarded in the process of the emancipation of woman by Christianity from paganism. In the conduct of some of the 'enlightened' women in the Corinthian church, who misinterpreted the true work of social redemption, which Jesus instituted and Paul was carrying forward, there arose an abuse of arrogant independence in some. *Every man praying* in the public service *on prophesying, having* a veil hanging *down from his head,* like the tallith or four cornered shawl used by the Jews later,[16] *dishonors his head.* Some of the Christian women had fallen into the error of disregarding the Christian tradition Paul had given them, based on the Genesis record of creation, and were praying and prophesying or speaking in the public assemblies of the church without using the veil, which was the symbol of their correct subordination in the worship service. This was proving a scandal and obstruction to the progress of the cause, because among the Greeks, only the lewd women (heterae), who were very numerous in Corinth, went about the streets unveiled.

v. 5 *But every woman praying or prophesying with her head uncovered*[17] *dishonors her head: for it is one and the same as if her* head were *shaven* as the wanton's was. Paul would not have the Christian women, thus, by disregarding the custom of veiling, to place themselves in a class with the courtesans or lewd women.

v. 6 *For if a woman persists in being unveiled,*[18] *let her also cut her hair close. If it is a shame to woman to* be shorn or shaven, as it certainly is,[19] *let her veil* herself.[20] This was the Apostle's unqualified and uncompromising requirement, under God.

vv. 7-12. Paul gave as his reason for the veiling of women in public worship, that the creation-order of sexes should control life in Christianity. His interpretation of that order was rabbinic, but a correct one, as to God's permanent plan for the sexes.[21] The veil was the symbol of woman's subordination in the order of creation.

v. 7 *For indeed man ought not to cover his head, being* man (*anēr*) by constitution from the hand of the creator, created *in the image* or moral likeness in respect to the sovereignty of free will, reason and personality, *and glory of God,* as the crown of creation, with the priority in order.

v. 8 *But the woman is the glory,* representing the supremacy or sovereignty *of the man,* who was thus in the position of a certain superiority over her in order of creation. *For man did not originate from woman but woman from man.*

---

16 Robertson, A. T. *Word Pictures* (I Cor. 11:4). The Greeks and Romans both men and women, remained bareheaded in public prayer in their pagan worship.
17 Associative instrumental case *kefalēi.*
18 Present tense of continued persistent action.
19 Conditional clause of the first class, according to fact.
20 Middle voice.
21 Not merely his original plan as in Moffatt *Com. I Cor.* p. 150.

v. 9 *Furthermore man was not constituted* or made *on account of*[22] or for *woman but* on the contrary *woman* for or *on account of man*, being made from a rib taken from man and to be his helpmeet. The moral obligation therefore rests on woman to dress in the public services in a manner to show her subordination to man in the order of creation.

v. 10 A spirit of reverence in the worship, instead of a false attitude of independence and immodesty such as that exhibited in some of the Christian women in the church at Corinth, was to be expected. *For this cause the woman ought to have a symbol of authority* the veil *upon her head, on account of the* holy *angels who* demonstrate an attitude of great reverence in the worship as illustrated in their veiling their faces as well as their feet in the presence of Jehovah (Isa. 6:1-5).[23] and thus they would uphold the divine order of God's supremacy. This assumed independence of some of the women members in the Corinthian church was an abuse and did not show due reverence. Women should recognize the divine order of creation and render due subjection in the right sort of deference to their husbands (Eph. 5).

v. 11 Paul finds the correct unity, parity and mutuality in the relation between man and woman to be in the Lord. Each sex is incomplete without the other. *Howbeit, neither the woman is complete apart from man nor man (anēr) apart from woman, in the Lord.*

v. 12 *For just as* in the beginning *the woman came from the man* being created of one of his ribs *thus also the man through* the agency of *woman* is born into the world. So the dependence of woman is right but has its limits in the Lord. Neither sex has any exclusive privileges, *but all things are from God.*[24] Let us conclude this section with Tinddal (Exp. Gr. Test, I Cor. p. 875) "woman is subordinate, not inferior. . . if man is the fountain, woman is the channel of the race's life." Under the rule and in the sphere of Christ the Lord, woman's rights are realized. She has an equivalence in the divine order of nature. "Either sex alone is half itself. . . each fulfils defect in each and always thought in thought, purpose in purpose, will in will they grow, . . . the two-celled heart beating with one full stroke, life" — Tennyson.

vv. 13-15 Again, Paul appeals to the natural fitness of things.

v. 13 *Among you yourselves judge ye; is it seemly* or becoming *for a woman unveiled to be engaged in prayer to God* in the public assembly of the church?

v. 14 *For does not nature herself teach you that if man may let his hair grow long it is a dishonor to him but in contrast if a woman let her hair grow it is her glory? Because her long hair is her glory given to her* permanently[25] by God *for a covering.* By nature woman is endowed with a symbol of modesty; and the veil was merely the artificial continuation of her natural God-given

---

22. *Dia* with the accusative, on account of, because of or for.
23 According to Jewish traditions the holy angels are in the worship always I Cor. 4:9; Ps. 138:1. Cf. Robertson A. T. *Word Pictures* in loco.
24 Robertson and Plummer, *I. C. C.* I Cor. p. 227.
25 Perfect tense denoting a permanent gift of God.
26 Marcus Dods, *The Exp. Bible I Cor.* p. 253.

gift of hair.[26] In the sculptures of the catacombs the (Christian) women have a close-fitting head-dress while the men have short hair.[27]

v. 16 The apostle closes the argument citing the usage in the Christian churches and affirming the authority of apostolic teaching over against the contention of any disputatious man. Yet if anyone seems to be so contentious as to persist in objection, I here affirm that *we* the apostles universally *do not hold to such a custom, neither do the* Christian *churches of God.* This affirmation carried in itself divine appointment and was not a mere dogmatic opinion of Paul.

B. Second, the Apostle discusses the disorder connected with the Lord's Supper (11:17-34). He calls attention to and denounces another grave abuse in their public worship. He does not commend them but blames for dissensions and divisions in their 'love-feasts,' preceding the celebrations of the Lord's Supper (vv. 17-19). These abuses motivated by selfishness were desecrating and defeating the proper observance of the supper (vv. 20-22). The Apostle reminds them of the gospel tradition he had received through the apostles as to the origin of this ordinance of the Supper, at the Last Pascal Meal which Jesus ate with the Twelve. (vv. 23-25). He further explains the meaning and real purpose of Jesus in the ordinance and calls their attention to the grievous judgments coming upon them resulting from the profanation of the supper. (vv. 27-32). And concludes with a practical exhortation to avoid the penalty of these judgments by stopping the sin of their profanation.

vv. 17-19 *Now, with respect to this*[28] matter of disorder in the love-feasts and supper, about which *I am charging you, I do not commend you, because you do not come together* in your worship services *for the better but for the worse.*

v. 18 *For, indeed, first* of all, *when you come together, in the church* assembly, *I am* continually *hearing*[29] that partisan *divisions*[30] *are there* among you *and some part* of these recurrent reports *I believe.*

v. 19 *For it is necessary* and naturally inevitable that *there should be* divisions in the way of taking sides and which proceed from diverging theories. These things are the occasion of God's purpose being worked out *in order that*[31] the true and *tested* men *may become evident* or be revealed *among you.*

vv. 20-22 The result of this factional strife is that *when you come together to the same place it is impossible* because of this selfishness for you *to* partake of or *eat* the *Lord's* supper at all.

v. 21 *For each one takes, before* the others, *his own supper, in the eating,*[32] during the love-feast and that in a disorderly way. *This one*[33] *is hungry,* being

---

27 Vincent, *Word Studies*, in loco.
28 Adverbial accusative specifying in regard to the charges about the veiling and the other disorder to be referred to now.
29 Present tense, progressive and continued action.
30 Factional splits are manifest.
31 Hina clause of purpose.
32 Articular infinitive adverbial phrase.
33 Demonstratives hos men . . . hos de.

unable to get sufficient food while *another is drunken*, going to excess; what a disgusting picture of a Christian congregation.

v. 22 Paul expresses his horror at the sacrilege. *What! Have you not houses* to *eat and drink* in? *Or do you despise the church of God and treat with contempt those* brethren *who* are poor and *have nothing? What shall I say*[34] *to you? Shall I praise you?* In *this* thing *I* certainly *do not praise you.* Far from it!

vv. 23-26 Paul is led by divine inspiration to relate in plain words what he had learned about the origin and purpose of the Lord's supper.

v. 23 *For I received*[35] *from the Lord*, both the oral and written tradition, through the apostles and also apostolic men like Luke, confirmed also by personal inspiration of the Holy Spirit, *that which also I delivered*[36] *to you*: namely, *that the Lord Jesus on the night*[37] *on which He was betrayed*[38] *took a loaf of bread* and having given thanks,[39] He broke it and said. "*This is my body* in symbol now being broken[40] in prophecy of what did happen on the morrow in the crucifixion, *on behalf of you* in the act of atoning death. *This act of observance go on repeating habitually*[42] *in remembrance of me* to recall me to your minds vivdly and affectionately.

v. 25 *In the same manner also* in which He had taken the loaf and given thanks, *He took* the little *cup*, after *partaking of the supper* of the Pascal lamb, *saying*: *this cup is*, (contains the symbol of) *the new covenant in my blood. This go on doing*[41] *as often as you may drink of it, in remembrance of me.*[42]

v. 26 *For as often as you may eat*[43] *the loaf and drink of the cup you are announcing forth the death of the Lord* until He come again,[44] in the second coming.

vv. 27-32 *So that* as a consequence *whosoever may eat the bread or drink of the cup in an unworthy manner will be guilty* of profaning *the body and blood of the Lord* and committing a crime against His atoning death. Paul does not say that anyone must be worthy to partake of the Lord's Supper else no one could ever qualify. He does mean that those who were acting selfishly

34 Deliberative aorist subjunctive expressing bewilderment on the part of the Apostle.
35 Aorist of definite occurrence at a given time or period.
36 Imperfect indicative of continued past action including the period of his betrayal. Note also the force of the prepositions *para* in this verb as well as *pro* in the preceding verb, in the transmission of the message. Paul knew the Christian traditions and they were confirmed for him by inspiration from the Lord.
37 Locative case of point of time, *nukti.*
38 Note aorists tenses of definite occurrence in the narrative.
39 Aorist participle, having given thanks, *eucharistēsas.*
40 Broken, ekalesen, clearly Luke says given didomenon Perfect tense of permanent gift.
41 Present progressive, tense of habitual action.
42 In remembrance of me, emēn objective use of possessive pronoun (Robertson).
43 Aorist Sub. for future time. (Robertson's *Grammar*, p. 975).
44 This verse (26) should be included in the paragraph according to Nestle's text to complete the explanation of the design of the Lord's Supper to call to mind the atoning death.

and getting drunk at the feast or supper would be guilty and partake unworthily thus.

v. 28 Consequently *let a man put himself to the test,* examining his own motives and conduct in partaking of the Supper as to whether he is selfish toward his brethren and irreverent toward the Lord, being unmindful of the true meaning and symbolism of this ordinance, *and so let him* after this examination *eat of the bread and drink* of the cup.[45] No false piety or more false misinterpretation of the Scriptures like this of Paul should be given as a reason for refraining from the observance of it.

v. 29 *For anyone who eats and drinks without discerning* or discriminating *the body* and blood symbolized by the bread and wine, in atoning death *is eating and drinking judgment on himself* for he is as it were despising that death rather than benefiting by it.[46]

v. 30 *On account of this* very thing of failure to interpret correctly the symbols aright and of the consequent desecration of the Supper *there are among you many* who are *infirm and ill and a considerable number who are* already *sleeping in death* as a result. The selfish and immoral conduct in the 'love-feasts' leading to the profaning of the supper, was a sacrilege which produced physical enervation and sickliness resulting finally in their enfeebling physically to the point of death.

v. 31 *But if we had discriminated ourselves,*[47] judging of our motives, conduct and discerned the real meaning of the symbols and been governed in our actions thereby *we should not be judged* and condemned *by God.*

v. 32 *But being judged* (and our conduct being condemned) *by the Lord we are chastened* (by Him) *that we may not be condemned* (ultimately and wholly) *together with the world.* The Lord is gracious in making use of chastisement to burn out the sins and imperfections of those who are really His ering children. Afflictions are used to separate His saints from the doom of the wicked world.

vv. 33, 34 Paul concludes with a final exhortation: *So that, my brethren, when we come together to eat* in the love feasts and especially at the Lord's supper, *wait for one another* and on each other in Christian courtesy.

v. 34 *If anyone is hungry let him eat at home in order that we may not come together for judgment* and condemnation. *The rest of the things* of conduct and order not referred to now *when I shall have come* (Aorist subjunctive in temporal clause) *I will set in order.*

---

45 To make of the supper a mere banquet to satisfy ones appetite or to treat a brother with disrespect and thus violate the binding fellowship of the church is to profane the sacred supper of the Lord. James Moffatt. *Com. I Cor.* p. 161.

46 A. T. Robertson, *Word Pictures* in loco.

47 Condition of second class indicating that some had not so judged themselves.

VII

Paul responds to the questions about Spiritual gifts, especially those of prophesying and of speaking in tongues. Chs. 12-14.

There was much egotism, many rivalries and a rampant partisan spirit in this young church in Corinth, composed of converts from a pagan culture and of a vari-talented membership. It had grown up mainly from a Grecian ethnological environment and intellectual background. Paul knew many of its members to be richly endowed with natural gifts, which under the liberty of the gospel principle, had grown into earnest desires and strong personal enthusiasm and ambition for the highest achievements and experiences possible to the Christian life. It is not strange that the partisan spirit here ran riot into splits and taking sides in doctrinal and practical matters. Some earnest individuals followed the ideal of asceticism with religious fervor, and others sought achievement in the cultivation of various intellectual and spiritual gifts, where others were lost in the mazes of liberality and compromise. Such was the intensity of this intellectual and spiritual movement in the church that many questions and rivalries arose about spiritual gifts. In the letter sent by the church this seems to have been one of the main problems about which they asked Paul.[48]

It appears that the questions on this topic turned mainly on the mysterious gift of tongues and its relation especially to that of prophesying and also to other gifts.[49] In his reply to their questions, Paul discussed the nature and relations of the spiritual gifts (Ch. 12), and explained the principle upon which the value of all gifts depend for their right and useful exercise — the principle of Christian love (Ch. 13), and gave careful directions as to the right use of "speaking with tongues and prophesying," whch would help to correct the contentions in the church about the use of spiritual gifts (Ch. 14).

A. The nature and relations of spiritual gifts. Ch. 12.

To this Gentile church which sprang up under his ministry from a heathen background, Paul needed to point out first of all the acid test, showing what is the true origin of spiritual gifts (12:4-11), and finally he illustrates the relationship between those possessing spiritual gifts, using the analogy of such gifts with the members of the human body (12:12-31). The Corinthians, being recently converted from paganism, were ignorant and confused as to the nature and character of these gifts, and could not distinguish between the incantations and spells of the heathen and the *glossalia* and tongues of some professed Christians.

1. The test of spiritual gifts (vv. 1-3).

v 1 *Now concerning the spiritual gifts* and their manifestation, *Brethren, I do not wish that you should go on being ignorant*[50] or uninformed.

---

48 Robertson and Plummer *I. C. C. I Cor.* p. 257.
49 Ellicott *Com. I Cor.* p. 22.
50 Periphrastic imperfect of a continued and progressive action.

v. 2 *You know that when you were Gentile, you were being led away to the dumb* or speechless *idols as you were led*[51] in your ignorance.

v. 3 *Wherefore I give you to understand*[52] *that no one speaking by*[53] *the Spirit of God says* that *'Jesus is Anathema'* (devoted to God without being redeemed and therefore doomed to destruction.[54] Such a saying was of frequent occurrence among Jews. Sometimes also persecutors tried to force Christians to recant with these words (Acts 26:11). *And no one is able to say, if not by the Holy Spirit.* 'Jesus is Lord.' The term Lord (*kurios*) refers in the Septuagint to God. In Emperor worship it was used to attribute divinity to the Emperor. Polycarp therefore suffered martyrdom rather than obey when ordered to recant saying, 'kurios Caesar.' The confession of the deity of Jesus was thus made by Paul the acid test of genuine supernatural origin for spiritual gifts of those who claimed such in the Corinthian church. This confession had to be backed up by conduct and life, and not be merely one of words.

2. Some other things these converts from heathendom, now members of the Christian church, must understand about spiritual gifts, namely; their variety, unity and true purpose and use. (vv. 4-11).

vv. 4-7 *Now there are diversities of* these gracious gifts (*charismata*), but the same Spirit, Who assigns (accords) different gifts to different persons Paul enumerates some of the classes or categories of these gifts.

v. 5 *There are diversities of ministrations* (services cf, *diakonos*) *and the same Lord* (Jesus) Who is Master of all His servants. (*diakonoi*). These ministrations were therefore unified in Jesus.

v. 6 *And there are diversities of workings* (operations, effects wrought) *but it is the same God who works all things in all* persons, who! are energized or empowered by the Spirit sent by the Father and the Son.[55]

v. 7 The purpose of these diversities of gracious gifts (*charismata*) is set forth plainly by the Apostle. *But to each one is being given the manifestation of the Spirit*, showing forth his work and energy, the purpose of all of which is, *for that which is profitable* to the cause, not being for vain show, neither having the effect of producing disorder in the assemblies of the church as had happened.

vv. 8-11. In these verses Paul illustrates the distribution of the gracious gifts (*charismata*) to different individuals. Some of the gifts are of the nature of intellectual power working itself out in the 'word of wisdom,' in speaking or reasoning with wisdom, and in another the 'word of knowledge.'

v. 8. *To one is given through the* agency of the *Spirit the word of wisdom* about Christ and His global work on earth (sofia); *but to another the word of*

---

51 Robertson's *Grammar* p. 74.
52 Causative verb, *gnorizō*, cause to understand.
53 Instrumental or locative.
54 Robertson A. T., *Word Pictures*, in loco.
55 This principle of the workings or effects applies in the creative and sustaining powers of the Trinity in the material universe also. This is the true basis of science.

knowledge relating to all things of the Christian philosophy, or of the Christian system of thought about the universe, *according to the same Spirit.*

v. 9 A second class of gifts is that based on faith, and its workings in healings, miracles, prophesying and discerning of spirits.[56]

v. 9. *To another faith* in the sphere *of the same spirit.*[57] Faith itself is a gift which in higher measure enables its possessor to excell in life's great achievements (cf. Heb. 11) in works, sufferings and even martyrdoms. *To another the gift of healings in the one Spirit,* Who is the center of unity, as distributor of all these diverse gifts to different individuals. There was no room for boasting egotistically of their gifts, making an ambitious show of themselves.

v. 10 *To another workings of miracles* or powers,[58] through the supernatural supply of energy (*energēmata*). *To another the gift of prophecy* or preaching and foretelling; *to another* different *kinds of tongues,* whether languages as at Pentecost or ecstatic utterances; *to another the interpretation of tongues,* serving as interpreters, as foreign missionaries often do, as for example in preaching missions; or as scholars interpreting the original text of Scripture to their churches or in books to their constituencies.

v. 11 *But all these things the one and the same Spirit works, distributing separately to each one as He wills* or wishes. The Holy Spirit is a Person and is the center of spiritual unity in the church, being as He is the one who distributes all the different gifts, and works out in and through the individual members the wonderful works of the Christ of God.

3. The character of the working of the spiritual gifts in the church members illustrated by the unity in the working of the members of the physical body. (12:12-31).[59]

The analogy cited, showing that the members of the physical body symbolize the members of the church as being one organic whole vv. 12-14.

v. 12 *For*[60] *indeed just as*[61] *the physical body* of man *is one and has many members and all the members of that*[62] *body being many are one body, so also is* the body of *the Christ.*

v. 13 *For, also in* the sphere of *one Spirit, we were all baptized*[63] *into one body* of Christ, *whether Jews or Greeks; whether bond or free. And were all made to drink*[64] *of one Spirit,* partaking of the inword spiritual experiences in His regenerative action. Like the different members of the human body have various functions and offices in the activities of the body so the several members of the church have complementary functions which should in the operation be in unison and harmony. Christ is identified with His church. He is the head

---

56 Meyer *Com. I Cor.* in loco.
57 Locative case cf. *dia* and *kata* V 8.
58 Illustrated in the blindness of Elymus.
59 *Cambridge Bible for Schools and Colleges,* in loco.
60 *Gar* post positive, (confirmatory).
61 Kathaper, *kata* and particle per (emphasis).
62 Demonstrative force of the article.
63 Aorist (constative) the church membership considered as a whole.
64 First aor. pass. ind. of *potizō,* made to drink. Here Paul refers to the embibing of spiritual gifts. (Robertson).

of the Body, His church, pouring out His gifts into each and all of its members. Each member should be in vital sensitive nervous connection with Christ Who must govern and direct all the members, infusing into each His life. As members of His Body, these members should not be envious of the gifts of each other or neglectful of the use each of his own.[65]

v. 14 The reason for this is: *For the body is not one member but many.* This is the key to the whole problem of church life both local and general. This old fable of the body and its members was referred to by Socrates who pointed out how absurd it would be if the feet and hands should work against one another.[66] Menenius Agrippa (Liv. II:32) referred to the 'center of nourishment' but Paul's main point in the illustration was that of unity, harmony and unison in action. The church is a living organism not a mere organization. In the church there should be a oneness in mutual help and in devotion to the Body as a whole, as there is mutual dependence which calls for a full fraternity of feeling and action.

vv. 15-21. The absurdity of separate and conflicting interests in the relationship of the members of the Body of Christ is further explained in detail by Paul.

v. 15 *In case the foot should say "because I am not a hand I am not of the body,"* *but* am independent, *not on account of this*[67] is it therefore *not of the body.*[68]

v. 16 *And if the ear may say, Because I am not an eye I am not of the body, not because of this* mere assertion *is it not* therefore not *of the body.*

v. 17 *If the whole body were an eye* however good the eye might be, *where* would be the *hearing? if the whole* were *hearing, where* would be *the smelling?*

v. 18 *But now* in contrast to such an absurdity *God* Himself definitely *placed the members, each one* of them *in the body* for Himself[69] and His own purposes and *just as He willed* or wished.

v. 20 *If all* were (actually) *one member, where* would be *the body?* One outstanding member in a church has many times been the undoing of it.[70] *But now,* as a matter of fact, *there are indeed many members but just one body.*

As a consequence of application to the examples of the illustration in analogy to the church is apparent (v. 21ff)

vv. 21-26 The superior organs need and are dependent on the inferior ones, which are indispensable.

---

65 Dummelow, *Com.* in loco.
66 Xen. *Mem.* II:777; 18 ch. Seneca also referred to in Robertson's *Word Pictures* in loco.
67 *on para tonto* — not on account of this mere saying so is it true that it is not of the body. Cf. personification (fig. of speech). Robertson *Grammar* p. 616.
68 Cf. condition of third class, a supposed case, also note two negatives do not destroy each other.
69 Aorist middle subject acting for himself.
70. Cf. Robertson's *Word Pictures,* in loco.

v. 21 *And the eye cannot say to the hand, I have no need of thee,* or again *the head to the feet I have no need of* thee.

v. 22 *Nay, by much more*[71] *those members of the body which seem more feeble are necessary* or vital.

v. 23 *And those members of the body which seem* to us to be *less honorable we place around these more abundant honor, and our uncomely members have more abundant comeliness* or eternal beauty, *while our comely* members *have no need* or lack.

v. 24 *But God has united* or adjusted *the body together, to the* part *lacking giving more abundant honor.*

v. 25 *In order that there may not be any discord in the body but that the members may have the same care one for the other.*

v. 26 *And if one member suffers all the members suffer together with it* or if on the other hand *a member is made glorious* (adorned with lustre) *all the members rejoice with it.*

vv. 27-31 The application of these principles to the life of the church follows:

v. 27 *Now you are the body of Christ and* related *members* severally, each having his own place and function in it with the accompanying awards and honors, according to the responsible action of each.

v. 28. *And God set some in the church* (general) for His own service,[72] *first apostles,* including the Twelve, and also Paul himself and some apostolic men like Barnabas; *second prophets,* for speakers forth-tellers and fore-tellers of God and Christ; *third teachers* (*didaskaloi*) applied to apostles and prophets also, who are possessed of aptness in teaching, as it should be of all preachers many of whom degenerate into mere routine exhorters and nothing more.[73] Paul continues with his list of roles and functions: *then miracles* to describe more the objective results, as also *then gifts of healing,* helps or helpers in the functions probably the same as those of our deacons of today in the visitation of the sick for prayer, accompanied by medical ministration as described briefly in James (Ch. 4); the *ministration of alms* to the poor as illustrated in helping the "poor saints in Jerusalem" in Paul's great collection among the Gentiles, Christians, the like of which was handled practically by the deacons after the institution of the diaconate (cf Acts Ch. 6). Deacons can be great helpers in the multiform activity of the life of a church, leaving the pastor to his proper role, not too heavily encumbered with the financial side, and also by their entering into the activities of evangelism, as Stephen and Philip did, in the expansion of the aggressive evangelistic plans of the Body of Christ. Paul adds another role or function, as that of *governments* or pilotings[74] of the church affairs, probably in such organizations as the modern

---

71 *Argumentum a fortiori.* cf. instrumental case by much more.
72 Middle voice, aorist tense God acting for himself, definitely set apart some to act in specialized function. His church was not left without organization and definition of roles and functions of individual workers.
73 Robertson A. T., *Word Pictures* in loco.
74. Cf. Boise's *Notes* on the Epistles of Paul p. 227.

Bible School and Training activities for the preparation and enlistment of all the members of the church. The last thing mentioned in Paul's list is that of *all kinds of tongues*, which was that of different languages necessary to carry on the work in the racial melting-pot of commercial Corinth and as in the work of modern missions. Paul did not magnify the exploitation of the showy and egotistic use of tongues, on the side of the *glossalia*, because it did not minister to the edification of the church and gave such an opportunity and was so great a temptation to the exaltation of the ego (cf v. 10 above). Here are many roles and functions mentioned, the principal ones of which would be what we know today as bishops or elders, one and the same person, known to us as preacher (evangelist and teacher) or pastor,[75] leading and directing principally in the general activities of the church with the deacons. Neither of these offices in mentioned explicity until later in the history of primitive Christianity.

vv. 29-31 Paul adds to emphasize the idea of the great galaxy and diversity of gifts.

v. 29 *All these ar not apostles, are they?*[76] *Not all are prophets? Not all are teachers? Not all are workers of miracles?*

v. 30 *Not all have the gracious gifts of healings, do they? Not all are speaking in tongues?*[77] *Not all are serving as interpreters?* All of these questions expect negative answers, a very effective rhetorical use of the Greek language itself by the Apostle without any semblance of boasting about it. Then Paul concludes effectively with an exhortation.

v. 31 *But strive earnestly for the better gifts. These Christians might desire* and pray for the higher gifts, of greater usefulness, but not envy one another in their possession. *And further, I point out to you a more excellent way* according to which you may attain what you desire. which is not the way of envies and jealousies but of Christian love.

B. The Most Excellent Way — Christian Love (Ch. XIII). In the talented membership of the Corinthian church the possession of many and diversified spiritual gifts had become one of its greatest perils. Paul wisely turned the attention of these gifted individuals to the more excellent Sovereign Way of Christian love, in a paean of praise that sounds one of the deepest notes[78] of all his doctrinal teachings. This psalm to Love is a guiding star of the first magnitude, to lead in the way out of the desert wilderness of individual envies and jealousies and partisan struggles in any local church or general body of the churches of the living Christ. It did not curb ambition in the individual. to excel in attainment of the highest and most useful roles and functions of the Christian life and service, but presented the adequate and basic principle which makes possible the fraternal exercise of the best gifts that are in all individual members, in the most harmonious and effective promotion of the

---

75 The bishops and elders are identified in Philippians and other epistles of Paul as one of the same and their functions as those of the office of preacher or pastor of today.
76 *Mē* expecting a negative answer.
77 May be locative or instrumental, in or with.
78 The greatest, strongest, deepest thing Paul ever wrote (Harnack).

unified goal of the Christian cause. Without this most queenly of all the family of gifts, the others would become a chaos of contending elements within the church and a scandal to the cause of Him whose life was the only thing that made possible the writing of this lyric ode to divine Love.

This hymn in praise to Divine Love which characterized supremely Christ and God and should reign in the lives of Christians, flowed out from the brain of the great Apostle of Faith in the rhythmic cadences of a lyric ode. It is at the same time a supreme work of art, an unparalleled expression of the profound infallible truth shining forth from the throne of God in a complete philosophy of the Christian life, thru a gleam of inspiration. It falls clearly into a natural and logical arrangement in three distinct parts: (1) the necessity of Christian love (vv. 1-3); (2) its glorious characteristics, (vv. 4-7) and (3) its eternal and sovereign nature (vv. 8-13).

1. The indispensable character of Christian love.

vv. 1-3 The indispensable character[79] of Divine Love is that it makes valid all the other gracious spiritual gifts. Without it tongues, prophecy, knowledge, wonder-working faith and devoted works, avail nothing; without it the Christian reveals nothing, edifies no one, achieves nothing, is nothing. The lack of Christian love makes all other gifts without value. No gift of intellect or power is profitable to man without the true love (*agapē*) to God and man, but on the contrary may become to himself and to others a deadly peril and loss. Man may or may not have or hold this gift, summum bonum, of life.[80]

v. 1 *If I may speak with tongues of men and* with the rapturous sound like *angelic voices,* (the least profitable of the spiritual gifts, much emphasized by Corinthian Christians), *but have not divine love* (*agapē*), *I am become*[81] mere *resounding brass*[82] *or a clanging cymbal*[83] instruments used in pagan worship. Paul is here comparing the use of the hollow sound of unintelligible tongues in the Christian church to the din of gongs and cymbals used in pagan worship.

v. 2 *And if I have* the gift of *prophecy* (inspired preaching), *and may know all the mysteries* of God's counsels and will,[84] *and have all knowledge* about these things which comes only through revelation, *and* (having these things, yet have) *not love,* if such were possible. *And if I have all* and every kind of *faith,* even wonder-working Christian faith, *and* that in *so great* measure to be able *to remove mountains* of difficulty, impossible to mere human power, *but*

---

79 Cf. Robertson and Plummer, *I. C. C. I Cor.*; Dummelow Com., Boise's *Notes on Paul's Epistles* et alias.
80 Third class condition *ean* with the subjunctive, if the condition is fulfilled the consequence follows.
81 Second perfect active indicative. *gegona* in conclusion shows the permanent result in not having fulfilled the condition.
82 *Chalkos an echoing* bronze instrument, mere sound.
83 *Kumbalon alalazon* two hollow brass basins to clap together producing a clanging loud noise when struck thus.
84 *I. C. C.* (Robertson and Plummer) I Cor. p. 289.

have not love I am nothing, not even a nobody,[85] but a veritable spiritual zero and good for nothing.

v. 3 *And if I might dole out in charity all my* personal *possessions to feed* the poor; *and if I might surrender my body that it should be burned*[86] in honorable martyrdom *and have not love, it profiteth me nothing*, help me in no wise.

Here are three results growing out of three spiritual gifts, when not accompanied by love. vv. 1, 2, 3.

(1) One produces nothing of value for the world of humanity. (2) One is of no worth to himself. (3) One gains nothing of profit[87] for himself and God.

2. Paul next (vv. 4-7), in a marvelous rhapsody, declares the glorious character of personified Christian love in a lyrical rhythm which swings from the positive characteristics to the negative and then back to the positive in artistic poetic measure. He presents fourteen characteristics in pairs, the first pair being positive, the four pairs following negative save the last which is both positive and negative and finally two pairs of the positive.[88]

v. 4 *Love suffers long* with patience, *love is graciously kind.*

Love is not jealous or envious, vaunts not itself in brag, does not puff itself up[89] with pride (like a toad), v. 5 *does not behave itself indecently, seeks not her own* interests selfishly. *Nor is not easily provoked* or irritated becoming embittered. *Love does not go on counting up*[90] *wrongs* in a ledger of resentment, *she rejoices not in wrong doing,* hearing and telling the faults and follies of others, *but rejoices along with*[91] *the truth* in her triumphs; *beareth all*[92] *things* with patience forbearing, and kindly excusing and covering up the slip, *believeth all things* without suspicion, trusting to good intentions, *hopeth all things,* though evidence seems adverse, *endureth all things* with courage and patience even the bare ingratitude of friends and the bitter and subtle persecution of foes.

3. Having explained the inadequacy and worthlessness of other gifts apart from Love, and having set forth the glorious characteristics of the most queenly of the given virtues, Paul concludes his poem of praise to love declaring her supremacy because of her eternal nature and sovereign power. Other gracious gifts are for this world; only two like prophecy, knowledge, and tongues twin sister graces dependent on Love, are eternal. Love remains, the perfection of our humanity because she is sovereign.

v. 8 *Love never*[93] *fails* (or falls, *pipto*) in the face of adversities; but is

85 Neuter gender *outhen,* not *outheis.*
86 Future passive indicative of *kaiō,* the gift would be made once for all.
87 Robertson and Plummer *I. C. C. Com.* I Cor. p. 291.
88 Cf. Robertson and Plummer *I. C. C.* in loco.
89 Present middle indicative.
90 Notice the present progressive indicative of most of the verbs of these verses.
91 Hyperbole easily understood, not to be aboslute perfection.
92 Preposition *sun* in composition with *chairei.*
93 Never at any time comes to an end.

eternal. *But whether* there are *prophecies* (preaching and foretelling) *they will be done away;*[94] *whether* there are *tongues,* the miraculous gift of speaking in foreign languages,[95] *they will* automatically *cease to be,* of themselves. *Whether there is knowledge,* such as the gnostics profess, or other, all being human, *it will be superceded.*[96]

v. 9 *For* (*in part,* imperfectly) *we know and* incompletely *little by little we prophesy;* v. 10 *but whenever that which is perfect* (full grown or mature) *is come*[97] in the parousia *then that which is incomplete shall become useless.*

v. 11 *When I was a child* (babe), *I used to talk*[98] *as a child, I used to understand*[99] *as a child, I used to reason as a child. Since I have become*[1] *a man I have put away* once for all[2] *childish things.*

v. 12 *For now we are seeing* as it were *by means of a* metal-like *mirror* of human knowledge *darkly,* as in an obscure saying or *enigma; but then* we shall *see face to face. Now I know only partially but then I shall know accurately*[3] and definitely, *just as I was* completely *known* by God and not in a fragmentary way, from the beginning.

v. 13 *But now abide* eternally *faith, hope and love; these three* remain, while all other gifts shall be unnecessary longer. *But the greatest of these* three *is love,* "because it contains in quantity the root of the other two."

Christianity is supreme over all the ills and ails of humanity because Christian love, the kind of love of God expressed in Christ, is in Christians. It is more powerful than any force that science has revealed or will ever reveal. This love, if planted in the hearts of the world-rulers, will rule the world of men and bring universal peace when the kingdom of this world shall have become the kingdom of our Lord (God) and of His Christ (Rev. 11:15). The presence of this Love which is the 'Sovereign Way' out will finally banish all envy and jealousy, all selfishness and partisan-strife from mankind and there shall be a new "earth in which dwelleth righteousness."

C. Orientation or direction as to the choice and use of Spiritual gifts. Chapter XIV. In the first place spiritual gifts were not subject to the choice of man but were bestowed by the Holy Spirit, as gifts. God does not bestow worthless gifts and each one who has received a spiritual gift should seek to improve and develop it and employ it in the best manner possible. One may mar his gift by misusing it.[4]

---

94 First future passive.
95 As at Pentecost.
96 Future middle indicative (Cf. Robertson *Word Pictures*).
97 Second aorist subjective with *hotan,* indefinite future tense.
98 Imperfect expressing customary continued action.
99 *Ibid.*
1 Perfect active indicative.
2 Perfect active indicative permanent and complete action.
3 *Epignosis* — accurate or clear and complete knowledge in the future life, future middle indicative.
4 Robertson and Plummer. *I. C. C., Com.* I Cor. p. 301.

The Apostle here deals with the misuse or abuse of the gift of tongues. Those who possessed it often burst forth in worship in a rhapsody of unintelligible words, several members at the same time, producing an unedifying spectacle, calculated to scandalize unbelievers and embarrass believers as well. But this gift appealed to the pride of some and became a grievous abuse and stumbling block to many and a hindrance to the cause in the Corinthian church.

1. The gift of tongues subordinate to that of Prophecy. Ch. 14:1-25.

This gift at Pentecost was miraculous and followed the baptism of the Holy Spirit. The apostles there spoke in various dialects and were readily understood by the peoples who were present from various widely distributed countries, as they told of the wonderful works of God. But here in the Corinthian church the words spoken were unintelligible to the hearers and even to the speakers themelves, unless there should be an interpretation. Both were connected with the Holy Spirit whose supernatural power produced different effects in the two phenomena. What then does Paul teach about this difficult subject of speaking with tongues? First he states the superiority of the gift of prophecy over the gift of tongues in two respects.

(1) The gift of prophecy, he declares, is superior to the gift of tongues because it edifies believers (vv. 1-19).

v. 1 He urges the Corinthian Christians: *Pursue after Love; but strive zealousy for spiritual gifts, most of all that you may keep on prophesying.*[5] He thus discriminates between "inspired preaching" and "speaking with tongues," in that the former edifies the church while the latter was unintelligible to men apart from an interpreter. And yet speaking with tongues was a phase of and closely allied to the gift of prophecy.[6]

v. 2 *For one who talks with a tongue talks not to men but to God. For no one hears* and understands, *but* in the *Spirit he speaks mysteries* in an ectasy.

v. 3 *Whereas one who prophesies talks to men edification*, building them up spiritually, *and encouragment* or exhortation,[7] stimulating them to active service, *and comfort*[8] or consolation when in trouble, distress, or bereavement.

v. 4 *He who speaks in a tongue edifies* or builds up *himself* spiritually by communion with God; *whereas he who prophesies edifies the church.*[9] *I wish that all of you* had the gift *to speak with tongues but rather that you may go on prophesying; and greater is he who prophesies than he who speaks with tongues, except* (unless) *he interprets,*[10] *in order that the church may receive edification.*

(2) The reason why prophecy or inspired preaching is superior to tongues is that the latter are not intelligible and do not edify the congregation (14:6-19).

---

5 David Smith, *Life and Letters of St. Paul* p. 304ff.
6 David Smith, *Life and Letters of Paul* in loco.
7 Paraklēsi cheer (encouragement, exhortation).
8 Paramuthian, incentive (consolation).
9 James Moffatt *Translation.*
10 The speaker of tongues sometimes had the gift of interpretation and sometimes not.

v. 6 *But now brethren, if I come to you speaking with tongues, in what respect shall I benefit you, unless I speak to you either in revelation, or in knowledge or in prophecy or in teaching?* "Revelation and knowledge are the internal divine gifts and prophecy and teaching are the exterior manifestations of the twofold divine communication."[11] Inspired preaching is forth-telling in the sphere of the work of revelation, while the transmission of knowledge about the inner exclusive secrets of Christian experience is in the sphere or by the instrumentality of teaching.[12]

v. 7 Paul's second argument is in the form of an illustration. *Likewise inanimate* or lifeless *things giving a sound* (or voice), *whether pipe or harp, if they may not give*[13] *distinctness to the sounds how shall it be known what is piped or harped?* A mere monotony of sounds as in some 'Pentecostal' "talking in tongues," makes concrete this illustration. Music must be varied to guide and produce in people the different effects leading them to be elevated and inspired or to experience the different feelings of sorrow, distress and resolve and to decide issues.

v. 8 A further illustration is added. *For also unless a* military *trumpet should give an uncertain sound* (voice) or signal for attack *who will know to prepare himself*[14] *for battle?*[15]

v. 9 The application of the illustration is made clear. *So you also unless you give by the tongue distinct utterance* in articulate discourse *how will the* meaning of *that which is spoken be known* or understood: *for you will be* continually *speaking*[16] *into the empty air* in a useless gibberish.

v. 10 Paul seeks to correct the ultra-emotional tendency of those who are attracted to a self-assertive type of religion which makes confusion between subjective over-wrought feelings and the objectively real leadership of the Holy Spirit. This argument is based on the sounds of different human words or languages. The speaker of any language is not understood by hearers who know only other tongues. *There are, for example, so many kinds of languages* (voices) *in the world, and none without* its own *meaning* or distinct voice. *If therefore I do not know the force or meaning of the language, I shall be to the speaker* as *a* barbarian or *foreigner, and the one speaking to me* as *a foreigner, too.*

v. 12 *So also, you, since you are zealous for spiritual gifts, begin* now *and keep on seeking, in order that you may excell in edification* of the church.

v. 13 *Wherefore let the one speaking in an unknown tongue pray that*[17] *he may interpret* also his speech to the edification of the church.

---

11 Boise's *Notes on the Epistles of Paul* p. 233.
12 Aorist subjunctive with *ean,* third class condition.
13 Third class condition, cf. Grammars on N. Test. Greek (varias).
14 Direct middle future indicative.
15 Polemon in classical Greek means war but here battle, as frequently in Homer.
16 Future progressive linear action, vide Grammars on N. T. Greek (Dana, Robertson, Davis et al).
17 *Hina* with subjunctive in purpose clause.

v. 14 *For if I pray in an unknown tongue my spirit prays but my mind* or understanding *is fruitless,* in that it does no service for others in their edification.

(2) Having dwelt upon the superiority of the gift of prophecy for the edification of believers, the apostle climaxes his argument by showing it is better also for convincing unbelievers (vv. 20-25).

v. 20 *Brethren, stop being*[18] *little children in understanding* and do not set your hearts on the glittering gifts, *but be babes in malice,* or jealousy *and in understanding go on becoming full-grown and mature men,* desiring the more useful gifts.

v. 21 *For it stands written in the law of Moses with other* (alien) *tongues and by the lips of others* (aliens) *will I speak to this people but even so they will not obediently hear* (listen to) *me saith the Lord.*[19] The Jews had refused to hear the blessed tongues of the prophets and had to be chastised by being made to listen to the strange tongues of the foreign invaders, the Assyrians in this case.

v. 22 *So then the tongues are intended* to serve (those not having faith) *for a sign* of judgment *not for believers* (those having faith) *but for unbelievers*[20] *and prophecy* or preaching *not for unbelievers but for believers* who ought to be able to appreciate it.

v. 23 *If therefore the whole church may come together at the same place and all are talking with tongues* and any unbeliever or ignorant person enter, *will they not say you are mad?*

v. 24 *But if all are prophesying and any unbeliever or plain man enter, he is convicted by all* and tested out (v.25) *by all, the secrets of his heart become manifest and thus falling on his face he will worship God declaring, 'God is really among you.'* Thus talking in tongues produced on the unbelieving world when the Christians talked in a hubbub the opposite effect to edification. It led rather to confusion and to scorn and scoffing (vv. 20-23) but when various ones preached, each in turn, the unbelievers were convicted of sin and converted to Christ, making confession of their sins before God (vv. 24, 25). By the inspired preaching of the word the unbelievers are warned against sin and judgment to come and are brought to repentence, but by a jargon of pretentious "tongues" they go forth scoffing and are driven to confirmation in their sins. The unbecoming behavior of Christians in their assemblies, in any show of pride or selfishness, drives the godless to be more so, but by the conduct of true humility Christians win sinners for the kingdom. But the disobedient people of Israel had to suffer and learn the results of their disobedience, too, through the hateful sound of the language of the Assyrian invaders and Christians who are contentious in the church for preeminence, envying and manifesting jealousy toward one another, will suffer a like judgment of God for spoiling the work of the church.

---

18 Use of the present imperative. Cf Dana and Mautey, *Grammar in N. T. Greek.*

19 Isaiah 28:11 including idea of the entire O. Testament.

20 Tongues are meant to impress unbelievers as a sign of the existence of spiritual influences.

2. Regulations to secure decency and order in the church assemblies. 14:26-40.

(1) Paul rebuked the disorderly offenders for their much speaking (vv. 26-34).

v. 26 *What then* follows, *brethren,* in the church assemblies? *Whenever you come together,*[21] *each one*[22] has something he wants to do, to be seen in manifesting his gift: one has *a song to sing,* another *has a teaching* to present, *another has a revelation* or explanation of some truth, another has to speak in some unintelligible *tongue, another has an interpretation,* pretended or not. So, there was a Babel of disorder and confusion, reaching its climax in the "talking with unknown tongues," followed by the equally showy and imaginative "interpretation" by some other. So the apostle enjoins: *Let all things be done for edification.*

Paul authoritatively but tactfully in exhortation lays down here (vv. 27-28) a regulation obliging the one who might speak in a tongue to give or provide his interpretation at the same time, thus rationalizing the process and cutting out the egotistic show. At least one would have to present an intelligible utterance, the value of which would be weighed by its actual worth for the edification of the church. Thus Paul would rob the speaker of tongues, the most disorderly element of all, of the subterfuge and camouflage of mystery, and bring him into the traces of an orderly statement of his contribution toward the edification of the church — a clever way to eliminate the vainglory and self-assertive egotistic desire for popularity without smothering out or discouraging individual initiative of the right sort.

vv. 27, 28 *If anyone speaks in tongues,* let *two or at most three* speak at any one meeting *and that in turn,* and *let someone interpret. But if there may be no interpreter let the speaker in tongues keep silence in the church and let him speak to himself* and to God and thus indulge his private ecstacy.[23] *But let two or three prophets* (inspired preachers) *speak and the others* discern and *judge* what is said whether really it be of the Spirit. The Apostle thus declares that there is a possibility of preachers not speaking the mind of the Spirit always in their utterances. This should be a prayerful concern for the man who stands behind the pulpit in the church of the living God. Let him give God's message. This is an important regulation for prophecy.

v. 30 *Should a revelation come to one who is seated,* as in the meetings of the Quaker brethren, when the Spirit moves someone to speak, *let the first speaker be quiet* and give way courteously allowing the next speaker a chance to make his revelation and contribution.

v. 31. Thus *you may all prophesy, one by one,* in turn in order[24] *that all*[25] the members of the church *may learn and all be encouraged* or comforted.

---

21 Present middle subjunctive, at any time.
22 Imperative mood. ginestho, 3rd person, but hortatory.
23 A. T. Robertson, *Word Pictures.*
24 Hina with subjunctive in purpose clause.
25 Pantes emphasized all the members of the church.

v. 32 *And the spirits of the prophets are subject to the prophets.* Some of the preachers in Corinth had forgotten this principle. Courtesy and humility in the prophet of God are a great gain. In honor prefering one another is a good rule in the ministry or turbulence.

v. 33 *For* our[26] *God* is not (a God) *of disorder but of peace* or quietness, *in all the churches of the saints.* This last clause in parenthesis is included by the W. H. text and most of the leading scholars with what precedes rather than with what follows which seems to be more logical. Paul cited the general consensus fidelium for a norm of conduct for the Corinthian brethren who were disturbers of the worship. This construction would yet leave the women of the church to be governed by the same general standards, anyway.

(2) The public ministration of women in the church is forbidden (vv. 34-36). This order was occasioned by the disorderly conduct of some of the women in this church, in the first place, through their prejudicial irregularities in their dress and conduct in the public meetings of the church. They now added disturbing conversations while the meeting was in progress.

v. 34 *Let the women keep silence* in the public assemblies *in the churches.* It was a counseling order as some of the other foregoing ones had been to the disorderly "speakers of tongues"; but it was inspired and based on the same ground principles.

In the church meetings in Corinth it seems that there was a shameful disorder on the part of some of the women, so Paul observes: for it is not permitted to them to speak or talk idly prattling in a disorderly conversation, *but let them be in subjection even as the law* or teachings of the Old Testament say about woman.

vv. 35, 36 *And if they wish to learn anything*, by asking questions in public in the church meetings as they did in an unwomanly unbecoming fashion, about the doctrinal teachings *let them* rather, *at home, ask their own husbands* questions, *for it is disgraceful for a woman to be talking in the church*, in a disorderly way while the meeting is in progress. There is too much light disorderly conversation on the part of men as well as women while in the church especially in the instruction hours. Paul said "there can be no male and female for all are one in Christ Jesus" (Gal. 3:28 et al) but the differences in the natures of the two sexes makes always the relationship of women in general what God intended, subordinate but many times superior. Paul knew there would be objection to his disposition of the matter of sex and so protests and appeals to his role of a divinely inspired apostle: *Or from you did the word of God come forth or did it come into your midst alone.* The fundamental teaching of God about the sexes remains unchanged and unchangeable as Paul testified.

(3) The apostle concludes in a final exhortation to obedience and order (vv. 37-40).

---

26 Notice the use of the definite article, *ho* Theos.

v. 37 *If any man seems to be a prophet, or* endowed with *any spiritual gift let him know definitely*[27] *the things* that *I write to you, that they are the command of the Lord.*

v. 38 But if anyone ignores or disregards (fails to recognize the truth of what I have written) *he is ignored* of God (if passive voice) or he is ignorant for himself (if middle voice) and must take the consequences of his ignorance.

vv. 39, 40 *Wherefore my brethren, keep on seeking earnestly the gift of prophesying,* that which is more to be desired, *and do not hinder the speaking* in tongues. But let all things be done decently, in a becoming manner *and in order* (according to due or right arrangement).[28]

VIII

The Certainty and Nature of the Resurrection of the Body (ch. XV)

It seems from the best historical evidence that no question was asked the apostle by the Corinthians about the resurrection, though it might well have been. There were certain members of the church in Corinth who denied the doctrine of the resurrection of the body. It would be natural for the Greeks who constituted a large part of the membership of the church, from their traditional background, to discard the teaching about the resurrection of the body. Paul had doubtless learned that there were such (1:12).

Unbelief in the bodily resurrection and indifference to sin sprang from a common source of a false spiritualism and contempt for the physical human nature, found in the theosophy of Greek culture. Liberty for Greek Christians, from the restrictions of the Jewish ceremonial, had been construed into general license and a depreciation of moral standards.

Paul had to grapple with this problem, in dealing with the character of the bodily resurrection and the redemption of the body as an integral part of the process of salvation. He must show that salvation to be complete must include the recovery of the body. Salvation was not a deliverance of the Spirit from the body but a recovery of the body through redemption, so as to be the eternal habitation of the spirit.

The doctrine of the resurrection and future life was not clearly set forth in the Old Testament literature and history. Death was followed by the shadowy existence of Sheol (Ps. 6:5; 88:5, 12; Isa. 38:18). But God gradually led his people into a clearer understanding from the nature of their communion with Him, which they could not think that death could lead. (Ps. 73:24-26). Furthermore God's justice could only be vindicated on the basis of a future life. Job and other Old Testament saints had a conviction that their Redeemer lived and they would see Him with their own eyes. His feeling about that was shared by some other Old Testament saints. The hope of the future

---

27 *Epiginōsko* know accurately or definitely.
28 Cf. Boises' *Notes on the Epistles of Paul* p. 239.

life gradually unfolded to them, until, in the times of Jesus, the Pharisees held to it firmly, though the Sadducee rationalists denied it.

Since the Corinthian Christians did not deny the resurrection of Jesus, they accepted it as a unique symbolical occurrence, being thus His means of bringing about for believers a complete spiritual redemption from the flesh and the material body.[29]

A. The certainty of the resurrection of the bodies of believers in Christ. Ch. 15:1-34.

This was the crux of the problem of belief for the Gentile Christians. Greek philosophy, current in all the Gentile world, considered matter to be essentially evil and consequently impurity to be an essential part of our human nature. The immortal spirit could only escape corruption when disembodied from the mortal body. This philosophy was basic in monastic mortification. While in the body, impurity was a necessity and therefore philosophers were morally indifferent. To meet this false philosophy and solve the problem of believers in Jesus, securing them against Antinomian libertinism was Paul's difficult undertaking. To do this he cites first the certainty of the facts of the Evangelical tradition of the death and resurrection of Jesus in which the Christians professed to believe. With this introductory word we have to consider Paul's first point in the argument.

1. The resurrection of Jesus Christ which is the firm foundation of the resurrection of the bodies of believers is the most fundamental article of the Gospel.[30] (vv. 1-11). This section of the argument is divided into three subdivisions (a) The most important evangelical oral tradition cited by Paul in his preaching to them had been that of the Passion and Resurrection (vv. 14). (b) The original witnesses of the resurrection of Jesus cited, only partially as sufficient (vv. 5-8). (c) Paul's personal testimony to the resurrection of Jesus was in harmony with that of the apostles (vv. 9-11).

(a) Paul cites his preaching when he first entered Corinth (1-4).

v. 1 *Now I continue to make known*[31] *to you, Brethren, the gospel* or glad tidings *which I preached*[32] *to you* when I was with you during eighteen months, *which* gospel *you received*[33] definitely in personal acceptance, at that time, of Jesus Christ, *and in which you have stood*[34] *in* permanent conviction of truth, *and by means of which you are continuing to experience salvation.*[35]

---

29 Cf. *Expos, Gr. Testament I Cor.* (Findlay G. G.) p. 917.
30 Robertson and Plummer *I. C. C.*, p. 330.
31 Present progressive tense with continuative *de.*
32 Aorist middle indicative, Paul did this for himself with a personal interest.
33 Second aorist active indicative, a historic occurrence.
34 Perfect active indicative indicating their permanent acceptance and experience of the gospel.
35 Present passive indicative in the progress of the gospel through a period.

v. 2 *If you are continuing to hold firmly*[36] *the word with which I preached* it (the gospel) *to you, if you did not* make *a vain profession of belief*[37] at that time.

v. 3 *For I delivered to you* as the *first* things in importance *of all that* tradition which I received in direct revelation on the Damascus road and elsewhere, *that Christ died*[38] *on behalf of*[39] *our sins according to the* Old Testament *Scriptures.*

v. 4 *And that He was buried*[40] *and that He* hath been raised on the third day[41] according to the Scriptures.

(b) Citation of the testimony of well-known eyewitnesses. (vv. 5-8).

v. 5. *And that He actually appeared to Cephas* (Peter) not in a mere vision (Cf. Luke 24:34), then to the Twelve (official names not all given).

v. 6 *Then He appeared to above five hundred brethren at once,* presumably on the Mount of Beatitudes in Galilee, *most of whom* remain until now still living, *though some have fallen asleep* in death.

v. 7 *Then He appeared to James,* His half-brother *and then to all the apostles* — perhaps the reference is to the occasion of the Ascension.

v. 8 *And last of all* those mentioned, (representing others to whom He appeared in the ten distinct appearances recorded in the gospels) *just as if to an abortion or* one born out of due time, *He appeared to me also,* after His Ascension, when Paul went on the way to Damascus to persecute His followers.

(c) Paul adds his personal testimony which is in harmony with that of the other eye witnesses (vv. 9-11).

v. 9 *For I am the least of the apostles, who am not fit to be called an apostle, because I persecuted the church of God* (cf. I Tim. 1:12-14).

v. 10 *But by the grace of God I am what I am,* an apostle to the Gentiles. *And His grace which entered into me did not become* in *vain* and fruitless, *but more abundantly than they all,*[42] *I toiled yet not I.*

v. 11 *but the grace of God is with me.* Well it is of no importance *whether I or they* laboured *more effectually*: what does matter is this, that *we all continue to preach and* that *you believed.*

2. The certainty of the resurrection of the bodies of the believers in Jesus. (vv. 12-34).

The major premise of the apostle: "If Christ is risen," had been shown to the satisfaction of the Corinthian Christians to be sure, the minor premise of his syllogism Paul goes about to establish, citing:

---

36 First class condition Paul affirms his belief in their genuine conversion and are holding fast.
37 Conditional sentence of first class.
38 Second aorist active indicative, historical fact and crucial event. Cf. Robertson *Word Pictures.*
39 *Huper ton hamartiōn huper* like *peri* here but elsewhere on behalf of instead of (Gal. 3:13).
40 Perfect passive indicative denoting the permanence of the resurrection (not like that of Lazarus).
41 Locative of point of time.
42 Than any of them, of The Revised Standard Version.

(a) The denial of the resurrection of the dead would lead to the denial of the resurrection of Jesus (vv. 12-19).

v. 12 *If Christ is being preached*[43] by the apostles *that He has been permanently raised* from the dead[44] as He certainly is how are *certain ones among you saying that there is not a resurrection of the dead,* which is contrary to your professed belief in the resurrection of Jesus.

v. 13 *But if a resurrection of the dead is not possible, neither has Christ* Who was human as well as divine *been raised,* which is against the strong evidence already cited.

v. 14 *And if Christ has not been raised then* as a logical conclusion *our preaching is vain* (empty) and was void of truth *and your faith* in Christ and His offered salvation *is* also *vain* and of no real value, which is contrary to the facts of our Christian experience of conversion.

v. 15 Another consequence of such unbelief in the resurrection is that *we are found false witnesses of God*[45] *because we testified of God that He raised up the Christ, Whom He did not raise up, if as a matter of fact the dead are not raised.*

v. 16 *If the dead are not raised, neither has Christ been raised* (v 17) *and if Christ has not been raised your faith is vain;* (devoid of truth), *you are yet in your sins* and lost.

v. 18 *Then also those who fell asleep in Christ* in death *perished.*

v. 19 *If in this life only we are having hope*[46] *in Christ we are more to be pitied than all other men* even than the Epicureans who live for mere worldly pleasures.

(b) The reality of the resurrection of Christ makes complete His age-long work of redemption (vv. 20-28).

v. 20 *But, now* as a matter of fact *Christ has been raised from the dead, the first fruits of those who have fallen* asleep.[47] All the negative, foregoing suppositions were not true.

v. 21 *For since through man* (came) *death, also through man* (came) *the resurrection of the dead.*

v. 22 *For just as in Adam all die* spiritually as Adam died when he ate of the forbidden fruit *so also in Christ* the last[48] Adam *all shall be made alive.* He who is in Christ is made alive.

v 23 *But each in his own order*: the first fruits Christ, then those of Christ, who have anchored their trust in Him, at His appearance (second coming). The great resurrection of believers will be when He comes again to the earth at the end of time.

---

43 First class condition present active indicative, confirming the preaching of the resurrection as a fact.
44 Perfect passive indicative resurrection of permanent character not that of Lazarus.
45 Objective genitive.
46 Periphrastic perfect, denoting continuation of the hope.
47 Boise's *Notes* on the Epistles of Paul p. 244.
48 Eschaton.

v. 24 *Then cometh the end* of time *when He shall* deliver *up the kingdom to His God and Father, when He shall have rendered powerless every government and every authority and power.* Jesus is reigning already and must increase in His effective reign until His shall be the sole kingdom on earth.

v. 25 *For it is necessary for Him to* continue to *rule till He shall place all His enemies under His feet.*

v. 26 *Death is the last enemy that shall be abolished* or destroyed.

v. 27. *For He* (God) *put all things under His feet. But whenever He shall say that all things have been subjected, it is evident that except the one who subjected all things to Him.*

v. 28 *Whenever He shall subject all things to Himself then also Himself the Son will be subjected to the one who subjected all things to Himself in order that God may be all in all.*

(c) The practical effects of the hope of the resurrection upon Christian life and practice. (vv. 29-34).

This is an argument based on the lives and Christian experience of the believers in Corinth.

v.29 *Since,* if the resurrection is not certain, *what* shall they do (what is the meaning of action of those) *who* are being baptized *for* or in relation to *the dead.* Thirty explanations have been given by different expositors of this difficult passage. Interpreted in the light of the circumstantial background and the parallel examples in the context, some hold that living Christians were, after a custom which existed in the Corinthian Church, later baptized in the place of those believers who died before realizing their intended baptism. Paul cites the illustration not to approve the custom but to illustrate his point in relation to the necessity of the resurrection, which would seem hardly justifiable. Another explanation more congenial perhaps to the context is that some had been led, by their love for relatives or friends who had died, having failed to repent of their sins and accept Christ and His baptism, borne on by the hope of continued fellowship with loved ones in the future life. For if the dead wholly fail to be raised why are they even being baptized for them?[49]

Another illustration Paul cites from the experience of himself and others (vv. 30-34).

v. 30 *Why* also *are we* in peril *every hour?*

v. 31 *I die daily, by the glorying respecting you, Brethren, which I have in Christ Jesus our Lord.* Paul had great pride in and concern about the believers in Corinth.

v. 32 *If, after the manner of men, I fought with the wild beasts in Ephesus,* as a *bestiary* [50] what is the profit to me? *If the dead are not raised,* [51] let us,

49 It was against Roman law for a Roman citizen to be such. Paul might have waived his rights of protection as at Philippi.

50 Paul does not mention elsewhere such an incident as being cast to the lions in the arena in Ephesus, cf. II Corinthians written shortly afterwards. He might have been imprisoned; there are in Ephesus today ruins of a "prison of St. Paul." Robertson *Word Pictures* p. 193.

51 The negative mē with the first class conditional frequently used. Paul means, "but the dead are raised certainly."

as the Epecureans, "eat and drink for tommorrow we die." But such a relaxation in morals is not in accord with belief in the resurrection life.

v. 33 *Be not led astray; be not led into error.* [52] *Evil communications* of such companions about you *corrupt* (destroy) *good* manners (morals). *Become sober and stop sinning*: *for some have no knowledge of God*, as your Epicurean neighbors. There are many such people even in our times.

v. 34 *I speak to you to move you to shame.*

B. The manner of the resurrection and the nature of the resurrection body and the triumph of the resurrection (15:35-58).

(a) The manner of the resurrection and character of the resurrection body. (vv. 35-49).

v. 35 *But some one will* surely *say, How are the dead to be raised?* [53] *With what sort of body do they come?* The cold corpse has always presented a problem to humanity. The body disintegrates and returns to the dust. Some primitive Christians were solicitous to preserve the "mortal remains" intact in view of the resurrection and paganized persecutors scattered the ashes of many of the primitive Christian martyrs that bore them far away, to mock and jeer at this hope. Paul answered their question from the analogy of nature. He meets the keen sceptical objector with a sharp rebuke of the egotistical v. 36 claim to intelligence. *Thou foolish one* or senseless man, seeing nothing, hearing nothing, understanding nothing, like an idol image. Daily experience, if you would reflect, will answer your questions. *You! that which thou sowest is not quickened* or made alive, *except it die* [54] first. The seed must decay and the new life takes in many new elements into the plant which springs up. The plant is not composed of identical atoms of the dust of the decomposed corpse from the soil.

v 37 *And* that which thou *sowest,* thou sowest *not the body that shall be resurrected but a bare grain,* it *may chance of wheat or of some* other *of the rest* of the vegetable species.

v. 38 *But God gives to it* (the naked kernel or seed) *a body just* of the kind that *He wished or willed*[55] and to *each of the seed a body of its own*[56] species adapted to the nature. No man can explain the transformation of the seed into the plant any more than he can the death and resurrection of the body and the change from the natural (*psuchikon*) body to the (*pneumatikon*) spiritual body. Neither can he explain the origin of species apart from the original touch of the fingers of God in original and originating creation.

---

52 The false Platonic philosophy denied the resurrection of the dead while teaching immortality. This was a very subversive teaching and Epicureanism was purely atheistic and grossly materialistic. The Christians needed to be on the alert against errors.
53 Cf. the expression of Matthew Arnold. "Miracles do not happen." Scientifically we know the how of few things. Robertson, A. T. *Word Pictures*, Pauls Epistles p. 194.
54 Aor. Subjunctive, third class condition.
55 Aorist of definite action and decision at a definite time or period of time.
56 Each kind of seed or kernel God gave a body of its very own, *idion soma.* Thus the species came to exist each afterwards producing after its own kind. God works through natural law.

v. 39-41 There is a great diversity of seeds and of bodies terrestrial and celestial, all unified in having the same creator God. The same is true also of the diversity of species in the animal world. *Not all flesh is in the same. But there is one flesh of men, and another flesh of beasts* (cattle) *and another of fish.* They are all animal but there is diversity in the kinds of flesh.

v. 40 *And there are heavenly bodies* the sun, moon and stars, *and earthly bodies* of men and animals. *But the glory of the heavenly is one,* being superior, *and the glory of the earthly is another*, being inferior to the heavenly.

v. 41 *There is one* degree of *glory of the sun, another* less brilliant *glory of the moon, and* still other grades of *glory of the stars. For one star* even *differs from another star in* the *glory* of magnitude and brilliancy. So there is diversity even within any class of bodies, as the stars.

Paul illustrates from nature the possibility and character of the resurrection change. The seed sown in the ground decays and the germ within it gives origin to a new plant. Thus in the resurrection the natural body laid as a corpse in the grave will be followed by a better and spiritual body adapted to the immortal's spirit in the man. This is altogether possible and reasonable, although we may not understand the processes which take place in either case as we do not, except that the Spirit indwells the Christians.

(b) The change in the body of man explained from Scripture, history, and nature. This is the crux of the whole problem (vv. 42-53).

(1) There will be diversity and change in the resurrection bodies (vv. 42-44). Paul goes on to apply his illustrations in his argument setting forth the kind of body we shall have in the resurrection. It is transformed from the material or natural (*psuchikon*) body to the spiritual (*pneumatikon*) body like the seed to the plant.

v. 42 *So also is the resurrection of the dead* body: *It is sown in corruption;* [57] *it is raised in incorruption* [58].

v. 43 *It is sown in dishonor;* [59] *it is raised in glory* [60].

v. 44 *It is sown in weakness;* [61] *it is raised in power* [62]. *It is sown a natural body;* [63] *it is raised a spiritual body.* [64] *If there is a natural* [65] *body; there is also a spiritual body.*

(2) This change from the natural to the spiritual will be effected through Christ the life-giving spirit.

v. 45 This is the meaning of the Scripture: *Thus it stands written;* [66] *The first man Adam became a living* [67] *soul. The last man Adam became a*

57 In a state of decay or decomposition.
58 Imperishable.
59 Disability as a corpse having lost all rights of citizenship and humanity.
60 In a glorious form and glorious new life.
61 Infirmity.
62 Dunamis, power, spiritual power and might beyond our knowledge.
63 Psuchikon, an animal body adapted to the soul (psuchē).
64 *Pneumatikon* a spiritual body adapted to the life of the spirit.
65 Animal body suited to the soul.
66 Gen. 2:7.
67 Zōsan, life-having, living.

life-giving spirit. The first Adam received temporal life (psuchē). The second and last Adam imparts eternal life (pneuma).

(3) The priority of the natural or animal to the spiritual (vv. 46-49).

v. 46 *But not first* in order the spiritual but the natural (animal), then the spiritual.

v. 47 *The first man was made from*[68] *dust of earth. The second man* was *from*[69] *heaven.*

v. 48 *As is the earthy such also are they that are earthy. As is the heavenly such also are they that are heavenly.*

v. 49 *So, just as we bore*[70] *the image*[71] *of the earthy let us*[72] *also bear the image of the heavenly.*

(4) The change from the animal (*psuchikon*) to the (*pneumatikon*) spiritual body is necessary in order to inherit the kingdom of God. The change consists in the translation of corruption into incorruption (vv 50-53).

v. 50 *Now, this I say* in assurance to you *Brethren* that human *flesh and blood is not able to inherit the kingdom of God, nor does corruption inherit incorruption.* There must be a change, in the process of death, from the natural (*psuchikon*) to the spiritual (*pneumatikon*) body. Jesus said He was in a transition state before the Ascension to the Father.

v 51 *Behold I tell you* now *a mystery* or truth not revealed hitherto about our future state. *Not all* of us *shall fall asleep* [73] in death, *but we all shall be changed* [74] or translated. Not all Christians will be dead when Christ returns but all will be transformed and their bodies translated.

v. 52 *In a moment,*[75] *in the twinkling of an eye, at the last trump. For the trumpet shall sound, and the dead* (Christians) *shall be raised incorruptible and we shall be changed.* (I Thess. 4:13-1, 8).

v. 53 *For this corruptible must put on*[76] as a garment *incorruption and this mortal must put on immortality.*[77]

(C) The final triumph of the resurrection is in victory over death and sin. (vv. 54-58). When the resurrection body is received it will be the end of death and the grave. Sin will have disappeared and the need of law will be eliminated. The victory will be given through Christ the Savior and Lord.

---

68 Source and substance.
69 Christ was the crown of humanity and has the power to give us the new body. Paul saw him in heaven.
70 Likeness.
71 Aorist tense, constative, covering unregenerate period of life.
72 Subjunctive of exhortation so common in Paul's appeals.
73 Future passive indicative of *koimaomai.*
74 Second future passive indicative of *allassō.*
75 *atomo* from *temnō* to cut and *a* privative. The atom was considered indivisible before the day of protons and electrons (Robertson *Word Pictures*).
76 Aorist middle infinitive the subject acting.
77 Cf. I Tim. 6:16 only other place in New Test. where athanasian is used and latter of God.
78 First aor. mid. subj.

v. 54 *But when this corruptible* nature *shall have* put *on*[78] *incorruption and this mortal shall have put on immortality, then shall come to pass the saying, that stands written: Death is swallowed up* [79] *in victory.*

v. 55 *O death! where is thy victory? O death! where is thy sting?* [80]

v. 56 *The sting of death is sin, and the power of sin is the law.*

v. 57 *But thanks be to God who is giving us the victory. Through our Lord Jesus Christ.*

v. 58 *So that, Brethren my beloved. Become stedfast* [81] *and unmovable. Always abounding in the work*[82] *of the Lord. Knowing that your labour*[83] *is not vain in the Lord.*

"She is not dead but sleepeth," said Jesus. The true view of the Christian's death-asleep in Jesus.

"Safe in the arms of Jesus; Safe on His gentle breast; There by His love o'ershaded; Sweetly my soul shall rest."[84]

IX

Concluding Exhortations and Salutation Ch. XVI

A. In concluding his first epistle to the Corinthians Paul made provision that the Corinthian church should deal with the matter of the collection for the Jerusalem saints before his intended visit. (vv. 1-4). A special arrangement that the collection should be sent in the care of a committee appointed by them was also requested. The enemies of the apostle had scattered a calumny in other places where this general collection was being raised in the Gentile churches for helping the poor Christians in Jerusalem, saying, that Paul had a dishonest and personal interest in the collection. Such an odious insinuation would be defeated so far as the Corinthian church was concerned by this wise plan of Paul. Incidentally the Apostle recommended the systematic plan for raising this special fund for missionary charity. He thus, led by the Spirit, initiated the method of proportional giving weekly on the Lord's Day, the first day of the week, according to how God had prospered each one.

v. 1 *Now concerning the collection* which is already being raised in the Gentile churches in Asia on behalf of the poor among the members of the Jewish church in Jerusalem, *just as I arranged for in the churches of Galatia*

---

79 First Aorist passive timeless aorist of *katapino.*
80 The scorpion of *death* has lost his sting.
81 Present imperative "Begin to become stedfast if you have not, and go on becoming stedfast, unmovable."
82 *Ergein* means the expenditure of energy.
83 *Kopos* is the labor resulting in fatigue. For they rest from their labours (of fatigue) and their works (of the resurrection body in heaven which will not fatigue) do follow them (there). There will be work in heaven. "The best answer to doubt is work" (Robertson).
84 Sung by request of father at the funeral of sister Agnes, whose years were few but beautiful.

so also do ye. He not only invites them into this fellowship of giving but lays down eternal principles basic in the maintenance and expansion of Christian charities.

v. 2 *On the first day of the week, let each one of you have the habit of laying by himself, treasuring it, whereinsoever he may be prospered, in order that when I come then there may not be any collections*: He wished to avoid the very appearance of financial calumnies already being put out subversively against him by his enemies.

v. 3 *When I shall have come, those whom you shall approve by letters I will send by* special approval *to bear your bounty to Jerusalem.* The committee was to be indicated by them to be approved by him on his arrival and sent through the means of letters which they would bear to Jerusalem.

v. 4 *And if it be meet for me to go also they will go with me.* He would have nothing to do actually with handling the money, a very wise provision for any preacher or secretary in charge of raising funds for the expansion of the cause locally or otherwise. Incidentally he hints that they should raise a worthy collection and if they did he would think it worth while to accompany the committee as a worthy representative of the church in connection with this important work of missionary charity and brotherly fellowship. As a matter of fact Paul did make this, his fifth journey to Jerusalem. Nor was it the first time he had borne alms to the poorer brethren (mais pobres irmaos) in the Jerusalem church from their fellow Christians among the Gentiles, in a real tie of fellowship.[85]

(B.) The approaching visit of the apostle (vv. 5-9). Paul was yet in Ephesus when he wrote this epistle. He had made a brief visit into the church in Corinth some time earlier during his three years of ministry in Ephesus now nearing its close, but his visit had not been accepted as it should have been.

The Judaists had passed through Macedonia recently and upset the churches which had been convulsed with the eschatological question some time before. It was necessary that Paul should send Timothy as his representative to Macedonia to help straighten out matters there, after the subversive work of these emissaries of Judaism from Jerusalem which had left things in a bad way. Timothy was to go by the overland route from Macedonia to Corinth and would likely arrive more or less at the time of their reception of this letter which he was sending them by Titus, after its greater and necessary elaboration, when he had received their communication by the hand of Stephanas and his associates of the Committee. It was in this letter that they requested his discussion of a number of vexatious problems which had arisen in the Corinthian church. He himself would follow up the work of Timothy in Macedonia and come on to them for an extended visit soon to cover the winter season probably.

---

85 Campbell Morgan I Corinthians makes Christian fellowship a basic idea in this last chapter and the whole epistle.

The apostle expected to remain on in Ephesus until Pentecost because there was a great and effectual door of opportunity open to him in Ephesus but also many adversaries who were determined to defeat his purposes there. As a matter of history the mob riot promoted by Demetrius the Silversmith brought the ministry of Paul in Ephesus to a rather sudden and violent close soon after this.

v. 5, 6 *But I will come to you when*[86] *I have gone through Macedonia; for I am going through Macedonia, and having come to you, perhaps,*[87] *I will remain* (a while) *or even pass the* Winter, *in order that you may send me forward wherever I may go.*

v. 7 *For I do not wish to see you now,* just *in passing, for I hope to remain with you some time, if the Lord permit.* Paul assumed and presumed a great deal on their friendly disposition, an attitude both justifiable and necessary in dealing with the Christian work on a fraternal basis, always to be assumed as present.

vv. 8, 9 *But I shall remain in Ephesus till Pentecost*[88] (cerca May 15). Paul assigns as a reason for his remaining in Ephesus longer: *For a door* of opportunity is standing *open to me, great and effectual, and* there *are many adversaries* — a "reason for all the more effort."[89]

C. Commendation for his fellow-workers Timothy and Apollos (vv. 10-12). Paul commends young Timothy, his representative in Macedonia now, his beloved child in the faith being converted probably at the time when the brutal mob in Lystra had stoned Paul and dragged him out of their city leaving him for dead, cast upon a heap of refuse.

v. 10. *Now, if Timothy shall arrive* in Corinth, as he has planned to do soon (4:17), by the overland route from Macedonia with Erastus, *see* to it *that he becomes without* fear *in your presence.* The reason for such deserved treatment is, *because he is doing the work of the Lord as I also am.* Paul was in doubt about what kind of reception Timothy might receive at the hands of the Corinthian church.[90]

v. 11. He adds further *Let not any one therefore set him at naught,*[91] *but send him forward* promptly[92] in peace, by your kind reception, *that he may come to me; for I am expecting him with the brethren,* Erastus and the others.

v. 12. *But concerning Apollos, our good brother, I besought him much that he might come to you with the brethren* of the Committee which is bearing this letter to you, *and certainly it was not his will that he should come now, but he will come when he may have a favorable opportunity.* Paul's request was sincere and urgent, but Apollos thought it inexpedient and untimely that

---

86 Indefinite temporal conjunction hotan with second aorist active subjunction of diōrchomar.
87 Neuter accusitive of second aorist active participle of tugehano, used as an adverb.
88 The riot promoted by Demetrius hurried Paul away (Robertson) cf. Acts 20:1.
89 Cf. Boise's *Notes* in oco; Acts 19:23.
90 Cf. I Cor. 4:17-21.
91 Exoutheneo stronger than katafroneito. Cf. Boise p. 255.
92 Aorist active imperative of propempem, to send forward quickly.

he should visit them at this time, doubtless in view of the recent factional movement in the church. He was loyal to Paul, the founder of the work, and his presence would perhaps not be salutory and conducive to the spirit of unity that should prevail. Paul was eager to send him, trusting wholly to his discretion in handling the situation, but the loyalty of this brother dictated another way in accord with the will of the Lord.

D. Exhortations.

In these five final exhortations the apostle gathers together five duties, inculcating earnestness and love. They are vigilance, stedfastness in the faith manliness, spiritual strength and finally Christian love, in the sphere of which all these traits are to be exercised. There are five present imperatives indicating continued action habitual and customary in the life of the Christian soldier.

vv. 13, 14 Four of these imperatives are directed against spiritual foes and perils.[93] 1. Vigilence, watch *ye* (wake up and stay awake). 2. Stedfastness, take your *stand fast in the faith.* 3. Courage, *quit you like men*[94] and be courageous. 4. Strength, *be strong* progressively. 5. Love; *let all things on your part* ever *be done in Christian love.* This last sums up the duties of Christian soldiers to one another.

E. The Corinthian leaders.

Paul exhorts the Christian church to follow worthy leaders (vv. 15-18). He calls attention first to the household of Stephanas as that of a worthy and mature leader.

v. 15 *Now I beseech you brethren; ye know the house of* Stephanas *that it is the first fruits of* the province of *Achaia* and that they (the members of his household) *arranged themselves for service to the saints,* the impoverished brethren in Jerusalem.

v. 16 *That you also set yourselves in order, under* the lead of *such* devoted *persons and to every one who works together with* (them) *and toils.*

v. 17. *I rejoice in the coming,* (of the committee) of *Stephanas, Fortunatus and Achaicus; because that which was lacking on your part these supplied.*

v. 18 *For they refreshed my spirit and yours.* Recognize *therefore thoroughly such persons.* Paul thus reenforces the leadership of these men who had come with the letter from the church and commends their example in good charitable works. He also quietly rebukes the neglect of the Corinthians of himself.

F. Salutations (vv. 19-21).

The Corinthian committee had protracted its visit, creating as a consequence a widespread interest among the churches of the Asian province as well as among the various congregations in the city of Ephesus. These churches sent their greeting to their brethren in Corinth along with those of Aquilla and Priscilla who had come to occupy so important a place in the life of the lovely apostle. This fine couple sent special salutations to their numerous friends in

---

93 Robertson and Plummer, *I. C. C.* p. 393.

94 Andrizesthe, middle voice, show yourselves men.

Corinth, where they had lived for many months during the time of Paul's ministry there. They were joined by the associate members of the church which functioned in their home in Ephesus. All the brethren in the church in Ephesus joined in expressions of interest in the work in Corinth and good wishes to the brethren in the Lord, Paul bids the brethren in the Corinthian church to *salute one another with a holy kiss*, men saluting men and women, women — thus affirming their affection as members of the divine family for one another. This would help them to forget their unhappy partisan divisions and miserable jealousies: and overcome their clique-spirit.

v. 19 *The churches of* the province of *Asia*, including the seven churches of the Apocalypse (Rev. II and III) *salute you.* Aquilla and Priscilla *with the church in their house salute you* earnestly and *much in the Lord* with true Christian salutations. *The brethren all salute you. Salute one another with a holy kiss*, a frequently used form of salutation.

G. Signature authentication and benediction (vv. 21-24).

v. 21 *The salutation with my own hand*[95] *of Paul.* A solemn warning follows this certification of the letter in the apostle's own handwriting. *If anyone* does not love the Lord let him be anathema or accursed. The refusal of the Christian to sincerely love Christ is deserving of the curse which will be his lot.

v. 23 Maran and Atha are two aramaic words, not one word only, and the expression was probably a sort of watchword expressing a lively hope that the Lord will come (Robertson, *Word Pictures* p. 204). The King James transliterates the two words as one. However Maran means *the Lord* and Atha signifies *comes*, has come or will come.

v. 24 *The grace of the Lord Jesus be with you. My love is with you all in Christ Jesus.*

---

95 Instrumental case, cheiri.

CHAPTER XV

Second Corinthians

THERE is abundant proof of the circulation and genuineness of this epistle previous to 120 A. D. Polycarp and Irenaeus are among those who testify to this fact through citation and otherwise. The evidence is yet more copious for early circulation dating from 175 A. D.; the Murantonian Fragment, Marcions Canon, and the citations from Clement of Alexandria and others being witnesses. Clement of Rome quotes the First Epistle (96 A. D.) regarding the *factional spirit* but not the Second about the *rebellion,* showing that this epistle was not known in Rome until after that date. The internal evidence of Pauline authorship is so clear in the matter of style, vocabulary, and character of its general teachings as to render its authenticity unmistakable. So strong is both the external and internal evidence that only a small group of "eccentric critics" any longer call in question its genuineness. The Pauline authorship is now admitted by the consensus of the outstanding scholars, though there is doubt by some as to the unity of the Epistle. But, in "spite of three distinct subjects treated in it, the epistle is still a unity" (Robertson).

2. Place, Date, Occasion and Purpose. Second Corinthians was written, therefore, in Macedonia in 54 or 55 A. D., probably a year or more after I Corinthians and before the writing of Romans (Acts 20:1-3; Rom. 16:1). Timothy had been sent on an errand through Macedonia to Corinth and joined Paul sometime later, being with him when he wrote II Corinthians (1:1). His report had been the occasion of Paul's sending Titus with a "severe letter" to reprove the stubborn minority under the leadership of Judaistic opponents recently come to Corinth from Jerusalem, who had been unyielding and who in open rebellion denied the apostolic authority of Paul. Paul's threefold purpose in writing this third or fourth letter, if there were so many, was: (1) to defend his apostolic authority, yet denied by a small group of Judaistic-led brethren in Corinth; (2) to promote the collection for the poor saints in Jerusalem; and (3) to reprimand the obstinate remnants of the "Cephas" and "Christ" factions for their persistent opposition.

3. Character and Contents. This, more than any of Paul's letters, reveals his personal character. He was deeply stirred by the happenings in the Greek Church in Corinth and frankly expressed his alternate feelings of joy and sorrow, hope and discouragement. He condemns the fornicator severely and later pleads before the church for his forgiveness when repentant. The integrity of this epistle is maintained in spite of arguments by some critics for its dissection (Bernard). The result of the epistle was to reconcile the majority

in the church, since Paul later followed and had a peaceful visit of three months with the church. The obstinate minority then disappeared. In the First Epistle there is doctrinal instruction and personal matter, with the former predominating; in this Second Epistle the personal element is emphasized, especially in the first and third divisions. The Apostle's conduct and authority are to the front throughout.

PERIPHRASTIC EXPOSITION — HISTORICO-GRAMMATICAL

According to the theory of the historical and grammatical character of exposition, it is necessary that we should have a clear understanding of the historical background of the epistle. The question of the unity of II Corinthians is a vital element in its historical setting and necessarily bears on the correct interpretation of the three different sections of the letter. We cannot disregard certain questions that relate to the disunity of this epistle if we are to have a clear exegesis. One part (II Cor., chapters 10-13) is identified by many scholars with the severe or stern letter, written to quell the rebellion in the church several months before II Cor., chapters 1-9 was written. The fact that the three sections of the epistle might have been written at different times does not mean that they could not at the same time be each a part of a single plan and purpose in the mind of the Spirit, fulfilling the conditions of unity in one epistle. In our treatment we shall look upon the epistle as a composite whole, possessed of all the true character of a unit in the plan and purpose of God.[96]

INTRODUCTION I:1-11

I. Apostolic salutation, vv. 1, 2.

v. 1 *Paul an apostle* from[97] *Christ Jesus, through the will of God,*[98] *and Timothy* now with him in Macedonia, having been sent ahead on a special mission, *our*[99] *brother,*[1] *to the church of God*, including the congregation being *in Corinth along with all the saints,* not churches but individuals, *in the whole* province *of Achaia,* (which covered half of Greece from Athens southward). It is not known if there was an organized church in Athens at this time, but there was one in Cenchreae, the eastern part of Corinth.[2] Paul is writing to the great city church, with all the problems of such a church in one of the most corrupt cities of all times. These saints, *hagioi,* in all Achaia were closely associated with the Corinthian church.

---

96. Discussion elaborated in the Introduction.
97. Ablative of source, he came from Christ and possessed His authority. The same form of expression might be the genitive of possession.
98. Paul was a slave of Jesus through the means of the will of God, genitive with preposition *dia.* This is the final and highest authority.
99. Definite article *ho* used as possessive pronoun.
1. Timothy was not co-author anymore, then Sosthenes (Robertson), but might have served as Paul's secretary (*amanuensis*).
2. Preposition *sun* with the associative instrumental.

v. 2 The salutation which follows is similar to that in the first Corinthian epistle, *Grace to you and peace from God our Father and from our Lord Jesus Christ.* This salutation bore within it all the graciousness of the free grace of God in all his gracious purposes in relation to mankind, but also the gracious good-will of Paul, against whom the church was now in rebellion. Paul loved most when he was least loved, as God loved us when we were his enemies.[3] Paul wishes them peace, such peace as can come from God alone through our Lord Jesus Christ. There is a direct reference here in the phrase "*from* our Lord Jesus Christ" to the deity of Jesus Christ, who, as the Divine Savior, is classed with the Father as a person of the Trinity.

2. Thanks to the compassionate God of mercies for his comfort in affliction and sufferings and for his deliverance from recent peril. 1:3-11. The key word *comfort* appears in Paul's thanksgiving ten times. He had passed through a great affliction (trial) and had received comfort and strength. (A) He was under a great burden of anxiety about the rebellion in the church in Corinth, and when he met Titus in Macedonia (Philippi), the burden wass lightened by the mercy of God through Titus' report.

(vv. 3-7). (B) He was also under bitter persecution at Ephesus (Acts 19:23-41), and possibly was sentenced (v. 9) or at least was in peril of being cast to the wild beasts in the arena vv. 8-11.

(A) vv. 3-4 *Blessed*[4] *be the God and Father of our Lord Jesus Christ, the Father of Mercies and God of all Comfort.* Paul finds his basis for gratitude in God, not in an ungrateful church or in misunderstanding and critical brethren. He is the Compassionate Father, characterized by his bounteous and freely bestowed mercies to those who need and ask for them.

v. 4 *The one comforting*[5] *us in all the pressure of our affliction,*[6] to the end and purpose ***that we may be able***[7] ***to comfort them that are in any affliction,*** *through the comfort wherewith we ourselves are being comforted of God.* The purpose of God's comfort, ministered through the Holy Spirit in the heart of Paul, helping him to be strong to suffer and endure in the midst of affliction. was that Paul might be able to comfort, stimulate, and strengthen others.

v. 5 *For just as the sufferings of Christ*[8] *abound and* overflow *unto us, even so our comfort also abounds* (overflows) *through Christ*[9] *unto others.* Personal experience prepares one for administering comfort to others in like experiences.

---

3. Rom. 5:8.
4. Perfect passive participle.
5. *Ho Parakalon,* Pres. participle, the one comforting, and *paraklēsis,* the substantive, are from the same root, meaning to call alongside of one's self. The Holy Spirit becomes a companion in our afflictions, to be strong and bear up the burden along with us, as our English word "comfort" denotes.
6. Affliction, verb *thlibo* — to press, (latin tribulum, a roller).
7. Purpose clause, prep. *eis* with articular infinitive used with accusative of general reference.
8. Subjective genitive, Christ's own sufferings overflow to us so that we suffer vicariously like sufferings.
9. Genitive of agency with preposition *dia.* It is through fellowship in Christ-like sufferings that we come to have fellowship with one another, being partners in suffering.

The sufferings of Christ flow over into us, making it possible that our comfort may flow over, through the working of Christ in us, unto others.

v. 6 *And whether*[10] *we are afflicted*, it is for *your comfort and salvation or whether we are comforted* it is *for your comfort, which works out in patience of the same kind of vicarious sufferings which also we suffer.* v. 7 *And our hope is firm* (stable) *on behalf of you, knowing that as you are sharer's or partners*[11] *of the sufferings, so also you shall be of the comfort.*

3. Thanks also for his deliverance from recent peril (vv. 8-11). Paul's thanks are addressed to God, not to the church. This is by tactful implication but sincere and frank expression.

The peril from which Paul was delivered in vv. 9, 10 was probably the persecution by Demetrius in Ephesus, coupled, perhaps, with an almost fatal illness, though we do not know for certain. The Corinthians would understand what the apostle referred to in each case, but the underlying principle and purpose of vicarious suffering and its natural result in comfort are the same, whatever might be the affliction and distress or the comfort and encouragement growing out of such trials.

vv. 8-11 *For we* (editorial) *do not wish you to be ignorant* (uninformed), *Brethren, concerning*[12] *our affliction which befell us* (happened to us) *in Asia*,[13] probably Ephesus, *that* (because) *we were weighed down*[14] *exceedingly* according to an overflowing measure *beyond our power to endure it alone, insomuch that*[15] *we*[16] utterly *despaired* even of life (living).[17] There seemed to Paul no way out from death.

v. 9 *Yea, we have had*[18] *the sentence* or judgment *rendered in* v. 10 *answer* to prayer *of death within ourselves, that*[19] *we should not trust in*[20] *ourselves but in*[20] *God, who raises the dead, who* actually *delivered*[21] *us*[22] *out of so great a death and will deliver us* (again and again), *In whom we have*[23] permanently *set our hope that he will also still deliver*[24] us in the future.

v. 11 *Ye also helping together*[25] *(on our behalf) by your supplication, in order that for the gift* of comfort *bestowed on us from many (upturned) faces* in prayer for us, *thanks may be given* by many (persons) *on our* behalf for the mercy which has been shown to us.

---

10. The alternatives *eite* — *eite*, whether — or.
11. Robertson *Word Pictures.*
12. *Huper*, on behalf of, some MSS read peri, concerning, he wanted them to have an interest in his recent experience of suffering.
13. Probably in Ephesus the capital.
14. Aorist active indicative, an actual and definite experience.
15. *Hōste* with the Aorist passive infinite *exaporēthēnai* — perfective use of *ex*.
16. Editorial we (I).
17. Abl. of articular infinitive.
18. Perfect act. indicative, the impression of the vivid experience yet remained.
19. Purpose of God in Paul's experience, *hina* with perfect periphrastic subjunctive.
20. *Epi* — upon.
21. Aorist middle, it was God's active interest at work.
22. Editorial use of pronoun again.
23. Perfect active indicative, permanence in a firm faith.
24. Future linear action, continued indefinitely and progressively.
25. Genitive absolute.

I. A conciliatory review of his apostolic conduct, character, and authority. 1:12-VII:16.

A. Apologetic defense of his conduct in relation to the Corinthians and especially in view of the accusation of lightness in dealing with his promised visit, and also how to treat the "great offender" in Corinth 1:12-2:11.

1. In his change of plan to visit them he was not 'fickle' but sincere. He explains the reason for his change of plan. 1:12-2:11.

a. The testimony of his conscience (vv 12-14).

v. 12 *For our act*[26] of *glorying is this, the testimony of our conscience, that in holiness and sincerity of God* (the God-kind),[27] *not in fleshly wisdom* such as the Greek sophists and gnostic philosophers boasted of,[28] *but in the grace of God, we have behaved ourselves*[29] *in the world, and more abundantly* in relation *to you.* Paul was very scrupulous, and they had abundant opportunity to verify his conscientiousness.

v. 13 *For we write none other things unto you than what ye read*[30] *or even acknowledge,* those things that you know well and accurately, *and I hope ye will* continue to *acknowledge* them, because you know them as clearly verified, *unto the end.* Titus reported that the majority of the church now understood Paul, and the apostle hopes that they shall continue to do so.

v. 14 *As also ye did acknowledge*[31] *us in part* in the Pauline party in the church, *that we*[32] *are your object of glorying, even as ye also are ours and shall be in the day* of the return *of our Lord Jesus Christ* to receive us unto himself.[33]

b. He changed his plan to accord with God's plan. (vv 15-22) Paul continues his reference to an accusation of "fickleness", defending his integrity. He asserts that his motives have been correct.

v. 15 *And in this confidence,* such as I have just expressed, *I was minded* (wishing[34]) *to come to you before, in order that*[35] *you might have a second benefit* (blessing, grace, joy).

v. 16 *And by you*[36] *to be set forward on our way into Macedonia. And again from Macedonia to come* back *to you* (for a second beneficial visit), *and by you to be sent forward into Judea.* He thus opened opportunity for them to help him later and so demonstrate their loyalty to him. He spoke of his visits as "benefits" of God's grace to them, as they really were.

---

26. *Kauchasis,* an act of glorying, not the thing gloried about, which would be *Kauchēma.*
27. Cf. Rom. 1:17, the God-kind of righteousness, the kind that characterizes God.
28. Cf. I Cor. 1:17, 2:4, 13f.
29. Aor. Pass. Ind. used as middle, to behave, walk, conduct oneself.
30. *Anaginōskō,* recognize.
31. Second Aor. Act. Md., occurred in the party divisions, some stuck by him. I cor. 1:12, 3:4.
32. Editorial we frequently used in this very personal narrative.
33. Boise's *Notes on the Epistles of Paul,* p. 263.
34. Imperfect indicative, had the desire and purpose in mind.
35. Purpose clause with *hina* and Aorist subjunctive.
36. *dia* with genitive, means they were to help him on his way. Cf. Amer. Standard version.

Paul's antagonists had led the anti-Pauline party to criticise him, accusing him of vacillation, of not keeping his promises. The apostle wisely explained his conduct as a responsible worker in the vineyard.

v. 17 *Wherefore while wishing this* and planning it, *I did not show fickleness* (a spirit of levity) *did I?*[37] *Or the things which I am purposing, do I purpose* them *according to the flesh,* as an unconverted man might do, *that with me there should be the yea, yea and nay, nay,* of lightness and fickleness? I am not the kind of man who proposes one thing today and does the contrary tomorrow without a good and valid reason for doing so.

v. 18 *But God is faithful* (trustworthy) *in that our word that we preach to you is not yea and nay,* saying yea and meaning nay.

v. 19 *For the Son of God, Christ Jesus, the One who was preached in your midst by us, by me and Sylvanus and Timotheus, did not become yes and no, but in Him it has become yes,* and has proven true in your experience of salvation.

v. 20 *For how many soever be the promises of God, in Him is the yea. Wherefore through Him is the Amen,* used in the worship, *unto the glory to God through us.*

v. 21 *Now the one who establishes*[38] *us with you in Christ, and anointed us,* for the work of the ministry *is God.*

v. 22 *Who also sealed*[39] *us and gave us the earnest* or pledge *of the Spirit in our hearts.*

C. He next explains his action and the motive in his change of plan. (1:23-2:4).

v. 23 *But I call upon God for a witness upon my soul that, seeking to spare*[40] you from disciplinary reproof *I came* (no longer) *not again into Corinth,* according as was my earlier plan.

v. 24 *Not that we have lordship, as the Judaizers say we claim, over your faith* or inner life in which you are accountable to God alone, *but we are fellow-workers* or helpers *of your joy. For in your vital faith you stand firm* Ch. 2:1 *But I determined this for myself:*[41] *not to come again to you with sorrow.*[42] It was consideration for them that had kept Paul away. A second distressful visit would have meant stern rebuke and so he had stayed away. He had written them a "severe" letter from Ephesus, inspired by love, but had not desired to repeat the distressful visit, painful to him and to them also, as it would have to be if he should come.

v. 2 *For if I make you sorry, who then is the one making me glad but he that is made sorry by me?*

---

37. This use of negative *mē* called for an indignant negative answer.
38. Present active participle, in current action.
39. Aorist participle actual occurrence at a definite time of God's choice of Paul. Also Aorist participle.
40. Perfect tense denoting permanence.
41. Dative of advantage, reflexive pronoun.
42. Instrumental case.

v. 3 *And I wrote*[43] *this very thing, in order that coming I might not have sorrow from them of whom I ought to rejoice, having confidence in you all that my joy is the joy of you all.*

v. 4 *For out of much affliction and anguish of heart I wrote you through many tears, not in order that you might sorrow, but that you might know the love which I have more abundantly for you.*

2. The grievous offender, sufficiently punished, should be forgiven. 2:5-11.

The brief, painful visit of Paul to Corinth is best placed between I and II Corinthians. In I Cor. 4:21 Paul contemplates the possibility that his next visit to Corinth might be of a "painful" nature. "Shall I come to you with a rod?" It proved to be a painful one to Paul when he was outrageously insulted by the effrontery of the "offender."[44] It seems that the apostle also suffered from an attack of his malarial malady, rendering him unable to deal effectively with the rebellion in the church. Luke's whole account of two years is condensed into one verse (Acts 19:10), and he did not mention this brief visit. Several things had happened after 1 Corinthians was written which affected the status of the Corinthian church. (1) The Judaists had arrived and begun their work of seduction, (2) Paul had made the brief visit (3) and written the "severe" letter, the effect of which was radical and salutary.[45] The Corinthians were stung by the reproaches of conscience and the offender was disciplined by the majority of the church for his attack on the apostle. (II Cor. 2:6). The church had also acknowledged its founder once more (II Cor. 7:11). Titus helped to bring about this happy change (II Cor. 7:6,7).[46]

v. 5 *But if one hath caused sorrow he* (the offender) *hath caused sorrow not to me but in part, that I press not too heavily* upon him to you all. Paul would not press the matter as personal. The offender had caused sorrow to Paul, but also to the whole church.

v. 6 *Sufficient to such a one is this* (punishment of rebuke which was inflicted by the greater number, the majority of the members of the church).

v. 7 *So that contrariwise ye should rather forgive him and comfort him, lest by any means such a one should be swallowed up with his overmuch sorrow.* Instead of inflicting additional punishment, they should now in view of his repentance show forgiveness or favor and comfort.

v. 8 *Wherefore I beseech you to comfirm your love toward him*, by a public expression of the church, as they had shown their disapproval by a public expression.

---

43. This is not an epistolary aorist referring to the letter he is writing but refers to some letter written before. The language vv. 3, 4, 9, 12 and 7:8-12 can hardly refer to I Corinthians, the last letter. Paul must have sent a later severe letter.

44. Cf. II Cor. 2:1; 2:2-10 and 7:12.

45. Cf. F. H. Chase *Com. II Cor.* pp. 18, 19.

46. J. R. Dummelow, *Com.* pp. 922, 923.

v. 9 *For to this end did I write, that I might know*[47] *the test or proof*[48] *of you, whether ye are obedient in all things.*

v. 10 *But to whom ye forgive anything, I forgive also: for what I have forgiven, if I have forgiven anything,* I have done this *on your account,* as an example to you with a view to peace and harmony in the church *in the presence of Christ, in order that*[49] *we may not be overreached by Satan. For we are not ignorant of his devices.*[50] This final appeal for the forgiveness of the now repentant (incestuous) offender was effective and, as the subsequent visit of Paul confirms, the object and result of the severe letter attained. The offender whom Paul admonishes that they forgive seems to be a personal enemy of Paul, but some identify him with the incestuous person of the First Corinthian epistle.[51] Others deny the identity; either view is possible (Robertson in *Word Pictures*). The apostle urges that they restore the repentant man, who had given evidences of God's forgiveness and approval. Satan had gained one victory over the man through his lust[52]; Paul would urge that the brethren of the church should not allow Satan to gain a second victory through undue severity in the disciplinary measures, by showing Christian love toward him. God forgives sin wherever there is true repentance shown by the life after God's forgiveness has taken place.

We come to the conclusion, after weighing the evidence as best we can, that the matter of immorality in the church, particularly in the example of the incestuous person, which had not been dealt with as Paul had admonished in the First Epistle (I Corinthians), was the occasion of his brief, distressful visit to Corinth near the close of his period of ministry in Ephesus, and of a "severe letter," a part of which may have been embodied in II Cor. 10:13:10.

B. Paul, defining his attitude toward his apostolic office, passes to discuss the grandeur and dignity of the evangelical ministry. Chs. 2:12-5:21.

1. The right attitude of the minister toward his ministry one of confidence and humility. 2:12-17.

a. Transition[53] from the narrative beginning at 1:8 f and continuing at 1:15 f, to the new subject of his independent and divinely granted apostolic authority (2:12, 13). Ch. 2: vv 12, 13. *And having come*[54] *into Troas* on the way

---

47. Ingressive second aorist active subjunctive, come to know.

48. *dokimōn,* a proof as a result of testing as to the readiness of the church to obey, *hupakouō.*

49. Purpose clause, hina with the subjunctive.

50. *Noēmata,* evil plans and purposes, the products of an evil mind (nous).

51. Campbell Morgan *Com. II Cor.* pp. 232, 233.

52. His carnal lust, either of the incestuous man or of the ambitious ringleader of Paul's jealous enemies. A. T. Robertson seems to lean toward the idea that the incestuous person was the one in mind who had repented. He gave sorrow, not the godly kind, not merely to Paul personally but to the church. It would seem that Paul would have mentioned the fact that it was the incestuous person if such was the case, yet on the other hand he uses the indefinite relative *tis,* and *toioutos,* and *Satanaz* as in the narrative of I Cor. 5:1 and since all would know the identity, for delicacy and since the offender was repentant, he does not use names.

53. Surely a new paragraph should begin here (A. T. Robertson). Cf. Nestle's text versus R. Version and West and Hart text.

54. Second Aor. Act. Participle.

from Ephesus to Macedonia *for the preaching of the gospel of Christ*[55] (concerning Christ), *and a door having been opened to me in the Lord,* the sphere within which the providential opening and opportunity was effected, *I had no rest*[56] *for my spirit.*[57] He could not enter this open door adequately, but it was not selfishness that prevented him because *I found not*[58] *Titus my brother,* but *taking my leave of them*[59] *I went forth into Macedonia.* Paul's anxiety for the future of the church at Corinth was the trouble. But the rebound of his faith follows. Paul considered himself Christ's captive in His triumphal train and His priestly minister in the glorious gospel.

b. His attitude toward his own ministry is one of humility and courageous faith in its successful outcome.

vv. 14-17.

v. 14 *But thanks be to God who always leadeth us in triumph,* in his triumphal train in *Christ, and makes plain through us* ministers of His the sweet smelling incense or *the savour* of the *knowledge of Him* (Christ) *in every place.* In God's victory over us as ministers he gives us the victory. We partake of His victory through being captive to his will.

vv. 15, 16 *For we are a sweet perfume* or sour redolent *of Christ,* ascending as the incense before the victor's chariot, *unto God, in them that are being saved and in them that are perishing, to these indeed as a savour* (or odor) *from death unto eternal death and to the others a savour from life into eternal life.* The sweetness and winsome attraction of the gospel attracts some who accept it and live and attracts others who reject it and die. The incense was burned before the Imperial victor's chariot by the priest who bore the censer. The priests' own clothing became redolent of the perfume of the incense. The preaching of the gospel produces life in those who accept it, but it is the occasion of death unto those who reject it. The perfume of the knowledge of Christ's gospel is redolent in the life of His ministers.

v. 17 *And for these things who is sufficient?* This was Paul's feeling about the ministry as he viewed its responsibilities. But by what he says in the following words he dares to affirm that he is sufficient (Robertson). His reason for his affirmation follows. *For we who are ministers truly are not as many Judaizing teachers, corrupting the word of God* by its adulteration, after the tricky and dishonest manner of the hucksters who sell fruit in the streets. *But we speak as* those who speak *from sincerity,* with pure motives and no thought of dishonestly making money by the ministry, as some in Corinth are accusing us of doing, but *as from* God, *in the sight of* God and being conscious of his presence, we speak in Christ. The false preacher, like the false fruit-vender who puts the best fruit in the top layer in the basket, puts his best doctrines to the front and covers up the bad ones until they finally appear later.

---

55. Objective genitive, concerning Christ *ton Christon.*
56. Perfect act. indicative denoting a complete and continuing state of anxiety and unrest.
57. Dative of interest.
58. Dative of interest.
59. Instrumental case of articular infinitive with negative *mē.*

The efficacy of Paul's ministry was in the truth of his message, which was honestly presented. He did not preach false doctrines but was faithful to the Word of God. So his preaching cut both ways "It was life-exhaled and life-exhaling or death-exhaled and death-exhaling,[60] according to the attitude of the hearers of the message.

2. The superiority of the ministry of the New over that of the Old Covenant (3:1-11).

a. Paul was not commending himself to them as self-sufficient. He had been forced to defend and commend himself before. He had been accused by the Judaists of not having letters of commendation from Jerusalem, as they professed to have. Paul did not need letters of commendation from the Jerusalem church. His work was his letter of commendation (3:1-3).

Ch. 3 v. 1 *Are we beginning again to commend ourselves? Or do we need, as do some,* — the false Judaists who claim to have letters from the leaders in Jerusalem, — *letters* of commendation *to you* from others *or from you* to others? Such letters of commendation[61] were used sometimes, as in the case of Apollos, Timothy, Phoebe, Mark, Titus and his companions, but Paul obviously needed no such letter to them.

v. 2 *Ye are* in yourselves *our epistle, written in our hearts, yours* and *ours, known and read by all men.* The lives of the members of the Corinthian Church were engraved on the heart of the apostle, and all the world could read what was written there in the kind of lives they were living. The proof of Paul's ministry was in their lives. This was his letter of commendation from them to the rest of the world, and also all they needed of commendation to themselves.

v. 3 Paul turns the metaphor around (Robertson), *being made manifest that ye are an epistle from Christ,*[62] authorized by Christ, *ministered by us* (Paul and Timothy as *amanuenses*), *written not with ink, but with the Spirit*[63] *of the living God, not in tables of stone but in tables which are hearts of flesh.* "In so far the Corinthians, in their Christian character are as it were a letter which Christ, through Paul and Timothy, by means of he Holy Spirit, has caused to be written in their hearts."[64] So Paul's letter of commendation was from Christ, written by Paul under the inspiration of the Holy Spirit, on the hearts, personalities, intellects, emotional natures, wills, the whole conduct and character of the Corinthian Christians, directed to all men who wished to read it. He needed no better credentials nor does any true minister of His. But they should remember that in Paul's heart were chronicled their shortcomings, along with their good which bound them to the apostle with hooks of steel.[65] It was a ministry of life (vv 4-6).

---

60. David Smith, *Life and Letters of St. Paul*, p. 354.
61. Acts 15:25; I Cor. 16:10f; Rom. 16:1; Col. 4:10; II Cor. 8:22f.
62. Ablative.
63. Associative instrumental, the Spirit inspiring Paul.
64. Heinrich August Wilhelm Meyer *II Cor.* in loco.
65. A. T. Robertson, *Glory of the Ministry,* p. 49.

v. 4 *And such is the confidence which we have through Christ toward God.* Even in the presence of God, Paul felt confident of the value of his work, wrought out in the lives of the Corinthians with the help of the Lord.

v. 5 *Not that from ourselves* or any ability we have *we are sufficient of ourselves to account anything as* proceeding *from ourselves, but our sufficiency is from God*:

v. 6 *Who also made us sufficient as ministers of a New Covenant; not of the letter, but of the Spirit; for the letter killeth but the Spirit giveth life.* The power and glory of the ministry of Paul was in the fact that he was a minister of the New Covenant and not of the Old, which was embodied in the Law. That was negative, stern, and impossible for the attainment of man, because of the weakness of the flesh.[66] The superior power of the evangelical ministry is that it is based on a New Covenant of grace, not a written code but a Spirit;[67] for the written code kills, but the Spirit gives life. The superiority of the New Covenant is in the fact that it is not negative and obsolete like the Jewish Law, but positive and new; not an eternal legal instrument but an indwelling power of the Spirit; not a judicial enactment, putting to death the one who transgresses it while conferring no power to keep the enactment but the indwelling Spirit who makes the recipient not only able but willing to obey.[68] "The Law finds a man gathering sticks on the Sabbath and stones him; grace finds robbers and murderers and illuminates them, and gives them life. The one turns a living man into a dead one; the other out of dead men makes living ones." (Chrysostom). The Law is incomparably inferior to the Gospel because man is unable to keep it, while the gospel of grace gives disposition to be saved and confers on the recipient the power to experience it.

c. The superiority of the evangelical ministry is in its dealing with the permanent and not the transient (vv. 7-11).

v. 7 *But if the ministration* which wrought *death, written and engraven on stones, came with glory, as it in fact did,*[69] *so that the sons of Israel were not able to look steadfastly on the face of Moses on account of the glory of his face; which glory was passing away*, being merely transient, to be superseded by the Gospel of Christ;

v. 8 *How shall not rather the* Christian *ministry of the Spirit which brings life be with glory?*

v. 9 *For if the ministration of condemnation* which is that of the Law *hath glory, much rather doth the ministry of righteousness* in the gospel *abound in glory.*

v. 10 *For verily that* Law of Moses, *which hath been made glorious* in its origin and mission, *hath not been made glorious* relatively, *in this respect, by reason of the glory* of the Christian dispensation *that surpasseth* it.

---

66. Cf. Rom. 8:3.
67. Cf. Jeremiah 31:31-34; Heb. 8:13.
68. A Plummer *Com. II Cor.* p. 59.
69. Condition of the first class, *ei* with indicative.

v. 11 *For if that which* is transient and *passeth away* before the Gospel was *with glory, much more that which remaineth* transcendent is invested (*within*) *glory*.

Paul cuts the ground from under the Jewish point of view (Chrysostom). The inferiority of the law to the gospel is cited in three aspects (1) that it is a ministration of death, (2) and of condemnation, (3) it is of transient character.

3. The great boldness of the ministers of the New Covenant. (3:12-4:6).

Paul was dealing with full revelation, not one in which something was covered up with a veil. Moses covered up his face when he came down from the mount because the "sons of Israel" could not fix their eyes upon his face because of the brightness. That they might not perceive the gradual vanishing of the brightness, implying the gradual diminishing of the glory of the Law, Moses put the veil on his face until he was ready to return to God's presence on the mountain top. In the very promulgation of the law its transience was portrayed.

v. 12 *Having therefore such a hope* as that in the Gospel, *we make use of such boldness*,[70] telling all without reserve of the gospel message. Paul did not put any veil on his face.

v. 13 *And are not as Moses, who was putting*[71] time after time *a veil upon his face, that the sons of Israel might not look*[72] *steadfastly upon the end of that which was vanishing*, which was the law, destined to disappear before the gospel. This was not dissembling. Moses was afraid to let Israel see the vanishing glory of the Law, afraid for them.

v. 14 *But their minds* (thoughts) *were hardened*,[73] being made callous as by a thick covering as of tough skin, *until this very day*, and even now in modern times, *at the occasion of the reading of the old* (ancient) *covenant*,[74] *the same veil remains* as unlifted, covering up from their hearts the gospel, which veil in reality is *that which is being done away in Christ*, who is the key to the understanding of the ancient covenant, the Old Testament entire.

v. 15 *But until today wheresoever the writings of Moses* (the Pentateuch as an illustration from the Old Testament) *may be read, a veil lies upon their heart*, because they do not accept the antitype Christ who is the fulfillment of the Old Testament types.

v. 16 But *whensoever it* (their heart) *shall turn to the Lord* (Jesus), *the veil is taken away*[75] from around it, and they are able to understand the weakness of the Law, which is in the weakness of the flesh, and the inability of man to keep [76] the Law perfectly.

---

70. Instrumental case, with *chrometha*.
71. Imperfect indicative of periodically repeated action, time after time on occasion.
72. Purpose clause with *pros* and negative *mē*.
73. Aorist passive indicative, constative aorist covering a period of time, *epōrōthē*.
74. The (Old Testament) covenant.
75. Futuristic present to express certainty, and the beginning of the future fact. (Boise). p. 271.
76. Cf. Rom. 8:3.

v. 17 *And the Lord* (Christ) *is the* life-giving *Spirit,* over against the dead letter of the Law which makes restrictions on external conduct, while Christ gives life and transforms the inner life, implanting his love in the heart of man. The work of the Holy Spirit is tied up intimately with that of the spiritual Christ.[77] The distinct personality of the Holy Spirit is unmistakably and clearly taught in many parts of the Scripture.[78] *And where the Spirit of the Lord* (Christ) *is,* there *is* true *liberty* from the bondage of sin, found in the acceptance of the new ties of spiritual union with Christ.[79] Christian liberty does not mean the casting away of all ties in a license of libertinism as some have thought most wrongly.

v. 18 *But we all* who have been introduced into the kingdom of Christ *with unveiled face*[80] in perfectly unveiled communion with God and reflecting perfectly his revelation of his will and message, who keep on *beholding* and reflecting *as in a mirror the glory of the Lord* (Christ), *are being* gradually *transformed*[81] *ourselves.* By the process of assimilation of that which we contemplate *into the same image, from his glory into* Christ-like *glory* in our personal lives *even as from the Lord, the* life-giving *Spirit,* who is the source of the spiritual power, effective through the Holy Spirit in us, making us more like Him.[82] The transforming power is in Christ and His redemptive work, but it is applied through the work of the Holy Spirit in our hearts.

Ch. 4:1-6. The apostle continues to magnify the glory of the evangelical ministry and the gospel.

v. 1 Therefore, on account of this superiority of the ministry of the new covenant, *seeing we have* this ministry (or service) *just as we obtained mercy,*[83]

v. 2 *we faint not,* losing our courage, *but have renounced* definitely *the many hidden things of shame, not walking in craftiness* or cunning *nor handling with deceit the word of God,* corrupting it with error as in the adulterating of milk or wine, *but by the manifestation of the truth, commending ourselves* by this evident integrity to every man's conscience, before the face of God.

v. 3 *But if our gospel stands veiled*[85] or covered up completely, it is covered up *in them that are*[86] in a condition of *perishing* by being consigned through their own actions progressively to eternal misery.

---

77. Cf. I Cor. 15:45.
78. Cf. P. Gardner, *The Religious Experiences of St. Paul* p. 176f. This passage should be interpreted with care in the light of the context. Christ works through the Holy Spirit.
79. Cf. Romans Ch. 7:1-6.
80. Instrumental case of manner.
81. Present indicative progressive passive of *metamorphēs.*
82. Cf. A Plummer *Comm. Gr. Test., II Cor.* on whole section Ch. 3:12-18.
83. Aorist passive tense (definite experience in Paul's life and applicable in the life of every true minister.
84. Indirect middle second tuneless aorist of aperpon.
85. First class condition affirming the fact, with perfect periphrastic passive indicative of *Kaluptō* indicating permanent status.
86. Present middle participle, being consigned by their own action determining their own destiny.

v. 4 *In whom* Satan, *the god of this world*-age, *hath blinded the thoughts*[87] *of the unbelieving,* to the end *that the light*[88] *of the gospel of the glory of the* risen *Christ, who is the image* likeness or manifestation *of God, should not dawn*[89] *upon them* or they should not see clearly the illumination.

v. 5 *For we preach not ourselves,* in which there would be no illumination of divine glory, *but* on the contrary we do preach *Christ* (the Messiah) *Jesus the* Savior as *Lord* (God) *and ourselves* as your bond-*servants for Jesus' sake,* the sufficient reason for all our sacrificial effort in heralding the word.

v. 6 *Because* it is *God that said, "Light shall shine out of darkness"* (Gen. 1:3) (*"and this is fulfilled in our case"*),[90] *who shined in our hearts,* for an *illumination*[91] to others or *to* give *the light of the knowledge of the glory of God in the face*[92] *of Jesus Christ.*

vv. 1-6 The apostle perseveres with his vindication of the apostolic office, with special reference to the charges of insincerity and self-seeking.

So the messengers of the gospel ministry have confidence courageously to preach Christ, who revealed the glory of God completely. They do not seek to cover up, as it were, with a veil any part of their message, as the Judaistic enemies of Paul did as "tricksters." They did this in order that they might if possible defeat the work of Paul. They made "unscrupulous hints and disgraceful insinuations," seeking to adulterate the milk or wine of the gospel of grace in Christ and make the acceptance of Judaism the door to Christianity. They were legalists; Paul preached the simple message of Christ and him crucified. If his gospel were not understood, it was only among those who were by their own actions consigning themselves to eternal misery and loss. Paul did not preach himself, his desires and his ambitions. To do so would have been to do as his enemies were doing. He preached Christ the Messiah, Savior and divine Son of God. In the beginning God who created physical light was also the author of spiritual light which Paul saw shining in the lovely and loving face of Jesus Christ on the Damascus road. That was the light that kindles a flame in every Christian heart which is not veiled by sin or traditional false beliefs but unveiled to catch the glory from His face and reflect it to humanity lost in a world of darkness. 4. The sufferings and supports of this ministry. Chs. 4:7-5:10. Here, there is another turn in the defense of his apostolic office, another aspect of his life as a minister of the new covenant. He had defended himself against the accusation of levity and pardoned the great offender (1:12-2:15). He had dwelt on the glory of the evangelical ministry and eternal glory of the gospel message (2:16-4:6). He now reveals some of the sufferings he had experienced in this ministry, along with the supports and hopes which gave him comfort and courage in the midst of the work and struggles.

---

87. *Noēmata,* thoughts.
88. Illumination.
89. Transitive of *angadzō.*
90. Boise Notes p. 272.
91. *Pros photismon,* for an illumination.
92. Locative.

a. From the study of the power of his ministry he turns to consider its tribulations and its hope. The gospel is entrusted to frail messengers like him, that its glory may be seen to be of God. His afflictions enable him to help his converts. (4:7-12).

v. 7 *But,* in contrast,[93] *we have this treasure* of the limitless power, to pass on this "illumination of the knowledge of the glory of God," stored *in frail earthen vessels,* made out of baked clay, as it were,[94] in order *that*[95] *the exceeding greatness of the power may be from God,*[96] *and not from ourselves.*

v. 8 We are *pressed on every side* by tribulations as grapes in the vintage, *yet not straitened* (kept in a tight place and reduced to straits); *perplexed, yet*
v. 9 *not unto despair;* (*lost* but not lost out);[97] *pursued* (persecuted), *yet not forsaken* or left in the lurch; *smitten down* as if overtaken by those pursuing, *yet not destroyed* (even as seen by the experience at Lystra).

v. 10 Always *bearing about*[98] *in the body* (as Ignatius, the martyr, called the God-bearer) *the dying of Jesus,* in the peril of which death I constantly live, in order *that*[99] *the life also of Jesus,* the kind of life He lived, *may* or might *be manifested in our body* as an example to the Christian converts everywhere and in all times (as it has proved to be).

v. 11 ***For we who are living thus are always being delivered unto death, in*** our perils, *for Jesus, sake,* in order *that*[1] *the* kind of imperishable *life also of Jesus,* as he lived it, *might be manifested* and exemplified *in our mortal body.*

v. 12 *So that*[2] as a result, physical *death,* in our expendable lives, goes on working, *worketh in us,* who suffer the tribulations and perils *but* the new elevated spiritual *life* is begotten and gendered *in you* through God's use of our ministry.

The light of the knowledge of the glory of God is entrusted in the hands of frail and suffering ministers to reflect to others, that it may be manifest that the super abounding power which is seen to be effective in their ministry, in spite of all their physical frailty and imperfections of personality, is not from the preachers themselves but from God. Paul suffered many things for Christ's sake. The taunts of his enemies were keen-edged. Their sarcastic criticism uncovered his all too apparent physical defects and other personal weaknesses.

It is a signally important fact that when his enemies could not defeat Paul's type of Christianity of salvation by grace for all men, Jew and Gentile, they attacked the Apostle's personal character, which is always the weak side of the ministry's defenses. To the charge of being a false apostle who "did not keep his promise to visit them," he replies that he did not keep that plan to visit them because God had the management of his plans. Paul had changed

93. *De* has the force of contrast with the exultation of v. 6 (Robertson, *Word Pictures*).
94. *Ostrakinois skeuesin,* loc. case.
95. Purpose of God in this purpose clause with *hina.*
96. Ablative of source, from God parallel to 'from ourselves.'
97. Robertson, *Word Pictures* in loco.
98. *Peri,* around or about.
99. Purpose clause, God's purpose in Paul's life.
1. *Hina,* expressing purpose.
2. Present middle indicative, *energeitai.*

his plan exactly because they were not acting loyally toward the apostle and were not worthy of such a visit.

b. Faith producing testimony, and hope based on the resurrection, comfort and strengthen Paul in the midst of his trials (Ch 4:13-18).

v. 13 *Having therefore this same spirit of faith according to that which stands written*[3] in the Psalms 95:1. *"I believed, therefore I spoke," we also are believing, therefore we also are speaking* and giving our testimony.

v. 14 *Knowing that the one who raised the Lord Jesus shall raise up us also with Jesus, and shall present* us with *you* at his appearance. Paul was not sure that he would be alive when Jesus should come again (Robertson). But he was sure of his presentation after his resurrection along with the Corinthian Christians.

v. 15 *For all things are* (done and suffered by us) *for your sakes* and benefit in order *that the grace being multiplied through the many* (greater number) *may cause the thanksgiving to abound unto the glory of God.*

v. 16 *Wherefore* in view of this assurance (vv 13-15), *we do not faint* or lose courage; *but though our outward man* or physical body *is decaying* or wasting away through the natural processes of advancing age and over-intensity of work, struggle and anxieties, *yet our inward man* of the spiritual nature *is being renewed*[4] *day by day.*[5] Here the decay of the bodily organism, the lower nature of the flesh, is set over against the renewed or the higher nature of the Spirit (Bernard).[6]

v. 17 *For our for-the-moment*[7] *lightness of affliction goes on working out* for us *far more exceedingly* (from exceeding to exceeding) *an eternal weight of glory.* Note here the wonderful contrast in the words: momentary with eternal, lightness with weight, and affliction with glory. Preachers who do not suffer vicariously cannot come to the full measure of power and ability to minister to others.

v. 18 *While we are not looking at*[8] or contemplating *the things* which are *seen* by the natural eye, *but at the things* which are *not* thus *seen; for the things* which are *seen* are temporal (for the time or season);[9] *but the things* which are *not* thus *seen are eternal.* This is the reason[10] why we do not continue to contemplate the things seen by the natural eye. Paul kept his eyes fixed on the glorious invisible goal of life, with the motto, Look to the end! *Respice finem!*

c. The hope of eternal glory in an invisible but real resurrection life gives Paul consolation and strength to endeavor to seek to please Christ always (5:1-10). Hope is made up of desire and expectation. There is a relation

3. This is the formula in legal documents in the *papyrii.*
4. Present active indicative, progressive action.
5. A hebraism, Cf. Boise's *Notes* in loco.
6. Cf. A. T. Robertson, *Word Pictures* in loco.
7. Adverb. *parautika* momentary.
8. Present participle denoting progressive action used with genitive of *hemōn*, Gen. Absolute.
9. Proskaira adverb.
10. Gar. adduces the reason.

of the outward condition and present experience to the realities corresponding to the aspirations of the believer. The spiritual instincts implanted in the soul of man are prophetic. Jesus spoke of this longing hope for immortality as revealing the reality of dwelling places of the heavenly home. Paul passes in 2 Cor. 5:1-10 from the consideration of the outlook on the future, presented in general terms (4:18) as the "unseen things which are eternal" into the definition of some details in the glorious prospect of the replacement of the earthly material body by an eternal heavenly one. He has no fear that, if his physical body should fall on the sleep of death before Christ's return, his spirit would be left in a disembodied state in Sheol, so abhorrent to the Hebrew mind. He will be given a spiritual body in which he will be presented to the Lord.

vv. 1-5 The old mortal tent exchanged for a new spiritual house.

v. 1 *For we know,* by revelation (not philosophy or science), the Spirit working through man's[11] intuitive powers, *that if our earthly tent-house* of the mortal physical body *might be dissolved,*[12] destroyed or taken down as the booths after the feast of tabernacles, *we have*[13] of a certainty *a building from God, a house not made with hands* (immaterial and spiritual), *eternal, in the heavens.*

v. 2 *For verily, in view of this, we groan, longing to be clothed upon with our habitation*[14] or spiritual body *which is from heaven.*

v. 3 *If, at least, also, having put on this* heavenly habitation, being thus sheltered by it, *we shall not be found naked*[15] or destitute of covering and shelter (according to the traditional ideas of the Jews).

v. 4 *For indeed we who are in the tabernacle* of the physical body, *groan, being burdened, for that we do not wish to put off* the clothing *but to put it on in order that what is mortal*[16] *may be swallowed up by the life* eternal.

v. 5 *Now the one who wrought* or fashioned *us for this very thing,* the transition from the earthly tent of the physical body to the heavenly mansion, is *God,* the one *who gave to us the earnest* or down payment *of the Spirit,* who indwells every true believer in Christ, the Holy Spirit.[17]

vv. 6-10 Paul is sure he will be with Jesus and makes it his chief aim to be pleasing therefore to the Lord and meet Him well pleased.

v. 6 Being *therefore* always *of good courage, and knowing that while we are at home in the* mortal *body we are* in a sense *absent from the Lord.* (Phil. 1:26,27).

v. 7 (*For through faith we walk* and *not through* the means of *sight*).

---

11. Appositive genitive.
12. Third class condition with preposition *ean* and aorist passive subjunctive.
13. Present indicative, expressing absolute certainty.
14. *Oikētērion* (not diminutive), spiritual body, the abode of the spirit of man. Here a mixed metaphor, a putting on as a garment the dwelling place (Robertson).
15. *Gumnoi.* naked as disembodied spirits in Sheol, after the manner of the conception of the Hebrews.
16. Only what is mortal (the physical body) perishes, the personality consisting of soul and body. A. Plummer *I CC. II Cor.* p. 149.
17. Genitive of opposition, *Pneumatos* — the earnest, (Boise).

v. 8 *We are of good courage, I say and are well pleased*[18] *rather to be absent from the body, and to be at home with the Lord.*

v. 9 *Wherefore also we make it our* ambitious *aim*[19] (striving) *whether at home* in the body *or absent* from home out of the body *to be well-pleasing unto Him.* This was the chief ambition of Paul and that of a correct ministry. The principal motive of the preacher should be to please Christ. It was a question of honor to Paul to put Christ first.

v. 10 *For we must all be made manifest before the judgment-seat of Christ; that each one may receive* as his due as wages, the *things done* through *the body according to what he hath done,*[20] *whether* it be *good or bad.*

Paul had seen Jesus in His resurrection body and knew also from the teachings of Jesus that there would be "dwelling places" in heaven. He could wish for himself that Jesus might return before his death and then the transformation of the physical into the spiritual body would be made in an instant and he would not have to pass through the Jordan of death to get to the heavenly Canaan. The Hebrews had a dread of passing into Sheol "where the spirit would be left disembodied." But Paul leads us to hope that we shall be clothed with the spiritual body and not be left naked spirits, as it were, in Hades. It was for this very purpose that God "wrought in us" and he had given us also the Holy Spirit as a down payment or pledge of the full inheritance, when we reach the Canaan-land. But Paul did not fold his hands. He kept working in all sorts of aggressive undertakings against sin and evil in the world. He strove earnestly and was willing to trust Christ and do all he could, whether he might receive his resurrection body immediately, after the dreaded experience of death, or not. At least he was assured of being with Jesus, as the thief on the cross, who believed and was saved immediately, on the passage through physical death into the heavens to be with Jesus, to sit at His feet and be in His presence, *pros*, forever more.

There is no disharmony between Paul's views about the resurrection as expressed in I Corinthians Ch. 15 and those found here. Paul was fully aware that Christ died and was raised, that his followers are not separated from Him in life or death, and that they are all to be judged by Him before His *bema* or judgment seat, which is not to be identified with "the great white throne." They will be rewarded according to their works, whether good or evil. Paul was willing to die for the truth of his hope in the future life with Christ in the heavenly home. His hope overleaps all that might be between death and resurrection and hurries on to its goal in reunion with Jesus.[21]

5. The life of the faithful apostolic minister of Jesus Christ. Chs. 5:11-6:10.

Every true minister of Christ in his role of preacher is an ambassador-apostle, one sent on a glorious mission.

---

18. *Endokoumen*, "we are well pleased, we prefer if left to ourselves" to decide (Robertson) to be at home with the Lord.
19. *Filotimoumetha*, Present Middle, to be ambitious from love of honor, ambitious in the good sense (Robertson, *Word Pictures*, p. 229).
20. Aorist Indicative Active, recording an occurrence.
21. H. A. A. Kennedy, *St. Paul's Conception of the Last Things*, p. 272.

a. He must be motivated by the reverential love for Christ, begotten by the love of Christ for him, which love will determine his method of dealing with God and man vv. 11-19.

v. 11 *Knowing therefore*, from the fact of the judgment, the reverential *fear* we should have *toward the Lord* Jesus, *we* seek to *persuade men*,[22] of our true character of integrity and also to be reconciled to God and so be ready for that day. *But to God we have* already *been made manifest* and we are at peace with him;[23] *but I hope that we are made manifest also in your consciences* and that your misapprehensions have been removed permanently.

v. 12 *We are not again commending* (recommending) *ourselves to you but* we say these things *giving you occasion for glorying on our behalf, in order* that *ye may have* such *ground of glorying against those who are* making their boast *in outward appearance and not in heart*, as the Judaizers, who were braggarts about their orthodox. Judaism (Robertson) and descent from Abraham. Paul appeals to his friends to defend him by pointing out the fact that he devoted himself (myself) to God.

v. 13 *For whether*[24] *we* (I am)[25] *were beside ourselves* (insane), as indeed I was to many, speaking in tongues and having visions,[26] *it was for God;*[27] *or whether we are of sound mind, it is for you* for your advantage and because of our personal interest in you to serve you. This being the case they should have ground for glorying in him.

v. 14 *For the love of Christ* which he has for us *constrains us*, producing love in us for Him and leading us into *judging this, that one died*[28] *for*[29] *all*, an important conclusion definitely reached, out of which another grew that, *therefore all died*.[30] This is the fundamental doctrine in Paul's Christology. Those who believe in Christ will not have to die, but are immortal and beyond the power of spiritual death;

v. 15 *And he died on behalf of all in order that those living might no longer live unto themselves but for him who died on their behalf and was raised from the dead*. "We should live His life for Him who died our death for us." This is the precious fact, that He died to atone for our sins.[31] Paul was motivated by reverent fear, lest he might not please the Lord Jesus, being trustful and submissive to the sovereign will of God. He had passion for Christ, born of the knowledge that Christ loved him and died for him. Life now for him was life in Christ.[32] The new eternal life through

---

22. Conative present indicative — attempt to persuade.
23. Perfect tense carries the idea of completion, permanence of the status, *peanerōmetha.*
24. Condition of the first class in affirmative declaration.
25. Editorial use of pronoun.
26. Acts 26:24; I Cor. 14:18; II Cor. 12:1-6.
27. Dative of interest.
28. Aorist active indicative, a definite event fulfilled in His death on Calvary.
29. *Huper pantōn*, on behalf of all doctrine of substitution in the atoning death of Jesus.
30. Second constative aorist act. indicative, embracing all men in the history of humanity.
31. Boise's (Of Robertson) Notes pp. 277, 278.
32. David Smith, *Life and Letters of St. Paul* p. 361.

the atoning death calls for corresponding high obligation on the part of those who live because of him.[33]

b. The ideal of the minister a new humanity and a new social order. vv 16-19.

v. 16 *Wherefore we* (Paul and his fellow ministers) *henceforth from the now time* since we came to know that Christ died for the sins of all men and we all potentially died to sin in Him, *know no man according to the flesh,* or mere human way of considering the outward circumstances and position rather than the inward state of character and personality:[34] *If we (I) have known* even *Christ after the flesh,* considering him as a mere historic person Jesus, at best a prophet who made higher claims than he could sustain,[35] *now we know him* in this manner *no longer.* When Paul saw Jesus on the Damascus road, his conception of Messiah was changed to that of a risen and glorified Savior, not a mere man but God.

v. 17 *Wherefore* (so that as a result) *if anyone is in Christ,* as the sphere in which he lives, *he is a new creature;* he looks at all things from a different standpoint, judging them on the basis of a different standard. All such men use their time and talent to glorify Christ. There is a new motive and purpose in life, *the old things* having *passed away;*[36] *behold they become new* (new in character and use for the new man). A new world, a new social order, a new evaluation of things and people, open up to the new man. A new humanity will grow out of the new man. This was Paul's revolutionary ideal, the ideal of a new humanity in a new world-order. The risen Christ is the cause and basis for this new humanity and new world-order.

v. 18 *But all things* of permanent change in man and the world of people and things about him with a new standard for evaluations *are from God,*[37] the one *who reconciled*[38] *us to himself through Christ*[39] *and gave*[40] *to us the ministry of reconciliation.* God provided the means and basis for man's "change of mind" toward himself, against whom man had sinned, by giving his Son as a propitiation for the sins of mankind.[41] He did not need to be reconciled himself because he had always loved man. The winning of unreconciled individuals among men to become reconciled to God is by persuading them to accept in the work of Christ the basis and means of their at-one-ment with God.

---

33. Robertson's *Word Pictures* in loco.
34. Dummelow, *Com. on II Corinthians,* in loco.
35. Paul doubtless knew of Jesus as renegade Jew and revolutionary rabbi and had thought he was rightly put to death. So evidently he had persecuted the followers of Jesus before his conversion.
36. Second aorist indicative active, a definite transaction in the life in its character and point of view.
37. Abl. of source or origin.
38. Aorist middle participle, God did it for his own ends, purposes and interest.
39. Prep. *dia* with genetive denoting means or agency.
40. Aorist active participle, a definite act.
41. Rom. 3:25; Col. 1:20; I John 2:2; 4:10.

v. 19 *To wit* (how), *that God was*[42] *in Christ reconciling the world of* sinful men *to himself, not reckoning*[43] *to them* (the sinners who accept Christ) *their trespasses* when they stepped over the boundary line between right and wrong many times and afterwards repented, *and has committed*[44] (or deposited) *into* (*or in*) *us the word* (or message) *of reconciliation.*

c. The minister's conduct in the role of ambassador vv. 20, 21.

v 20 *On behalf of Christ, therefore, we are serving as ambassadors,*[45] as *of God beseeching through us.*[46] *We entreat* (beg) *on behalf of Christ, be ye reconciled*[47] *to God.* This message the minister bears from God to men. God needs not to be reconciled to man but man to God, having become estranged toward him through his own sins. The minister wins people to Christ. He must remain loyal to God in winning the world of sinners to him.

v. 21 *He* (Christ) *who knew*[48] *no sin,* in his own life and experience, because there was none, *him* (God) *made to be sin,*[49] *for us* or on our behalf. *in order that* (or to the end that) *we might become the righteousness*[50] *of God in Him* (Christ). In the sphere of Christ the Christian must come to possess the God-kind of righteousness in his life through the redemptive work of Christ. The minister who bears such a message becomes thus an ambassador from God on behalf of Christ to men, entreating them to become reconciled to God.

c. Paul in lyrical strain pictures the conduct and character of the herald of salvation. Here is how the ambassadorial minister does his work and what he has to endure. Paul soars to the empyrean heights in this climactic outburst of sacred eloquence as he describes the apostolic ministry that shall take the world for Christ. (Ch. 6:1 - 7:4.)

1. The minister, as ambassador to whom God commits the word of reconciliation (5:20, 21), is God's fellow-worker, carrying forward the work of Christ. Ch. 6:1-10.

v. 1 *But working together with him* (God), *we also entreat you not to receive*[51] *the grace of God* in salvation in *vain,* as some did when it was preached in Corinth. Some fell back into their old sinful acts and lost their lives of service, bringing reproach to the cause.

v. 2 *for it* (the Scripture) *says:*

---

42. Periphrastic imperfect in the progressive work of reconciliation in the incarnate Christ who was God in the person of the Son.
43. Present middle participle, progressive action.
44. Aorist middle participle, definite occurrence.
45. An ambassador is a dignified representative of one nation to another, and must be acceptable to both. This appellation dignifies the ministers and the ministry. (cf. Robertson).
46. Prep. dia with genetive of agent.
47. Second aorist passive imperative. *Katallagētē* from *Katallassa.* "Get reconciled to God" now, quickly.
48. Second aorist participle from *quiēsko* meaning to know by experience.
49. Accounted or reckoned Him to be in effect a sinnner.
50. Reckoned so at first but really possessing the God-kind of righteousness in the end.
51. Timeless aorist infinitive.

In an acceptable time I listened to you,
And in a day of salvation I brought help to you.
Behold now is the day of salvation![52]

v. 3 Hence the minister, *giving no occasion of stumbling in anything,* must conduct himself most carefully in order *that our ministry be not reproached.* Paul is addressing these words to a church in which there were some weak believers, signifying what manner of moral conduct should be that of the preachers, as well as of all the members of the church.

vv. 4-10 In the following paragraph the apostle describes the conditions and the characteristics of the faithful apostolic ministry in a burst of poetic eloquence in cadences and balanced antitheses comparable to those recorded in Rom. 8:31 - 39 and those in I Cor. Ch. 13.

1. Referring indirectly to the accusation of his enemies "that he was continually commending himself," the apostle

v. 4 says, *but in everything, as God's ministers* commending themselves by their rectitude of life (Bernard, *ICC.*) not by unfaithful, tricky and false ways as servants of men in the world but in the habit of much patience. This endurance under strain was one of the most commendable features of Paul's conduct as a minister of Christ. It was exercised in the midst of manifold experiences described in three triplets of terms, veritable "snow-showers constituting a blizzard of troubles."[53] These triplets of terms are introduced by the same Greek preposition *en* (in) (vv 3 - 7) which occurs altogether eighteen times; then the preposition *dia* (through) avoids monotony and in describing three other aspects of the ministry advances with aggressive measures in a beautiful summary of the characteristics of the "dignity and glory of the ministry" (vv 7b, 8); and finally a series of seven contrasts each introduced by the preposition hōs (as), bringing to a glorious climax the highly literary and artistic picture of the apostolic minister (vv 9 - 10).

Each well chosen word of this long list echoes a story of a different type of experience in the ministry of Paul, and is reechoed in the ministry of the faithful successors of the apostle in this glorious calling down through the ages. Those of the first three triplets hang together like brilliants of a necklace strung on the thread of patience.

(a) v. 4b *in afflictions*, which crush like a heavy weight but which might sometimes be avoided; *in necessities*, which are more inevitable; and *in distresses*, narrow passages or tight places in life from which there is no escape, which one must endure (Stanley). These troubles are largely uncaused by human agents.

(b) v. 5 A second triplet, more particular, makes concrete the character of these outword hardships, all of which were illustrated in Paul's ministry:

52. Isa. 49:8.
53. John Chrysostom.

in *stripes,* humiliated under the Roman flagel at Philippi and on two other occasions, besides being beaten at least five other times; *in imprisonments,* in Philippi, Cesarea, and Rome, perhaps worse for Paul because they curtailed his activities in the work of preaching; and *in tumults,* as in Thessalonica and at Ephesus, where the riot terminated suddenly his ministry in that city. There was progression in the seriousness of these three types of experiences because they increasingly impeded his work, closing the doors of opportunity for him in the work of the gospel in certain areas, just as it was in the three years' ministry of Jesus in Palestine.

(c) A third triplet of experience, taken on voluntarily by the apostolic minister in the prosecution of his work: *in toils,* of strenuous effort and anxious prosecution of difficult plans all the days bringing weariness and fatigue; *in vigils,* often of sleeplessness caused by anxiety for his work; *in fastings,* which were due to over-intensity and to voluntary abstentiousness to save time for his religious activities and avoid also being "a burden to others." Paul often suffered the pangs of hunger and sacrificed in order to give himself as expendable. He had business ability but did not care always to "make ends meet."

(d) In verses 6,7 we have other virtues of the ministry mentioned, which are coordinated with the patience recurring through all the string of outward hardships in the above triplets.

v. 6 *in purity* of life, both in chastity and in integrity of purpose; *in knowledge,* exhibited in practical wisdom in dealing with men and in understanding of the comprehensive principles of Christianity, giving him a keener perception of spiritual realities; *in long-suffering* or forbearance, also a divine attribute, which endures injuries and evil deeds without being provoked to retaliation; *in kindness* or sweetness of temper, another divine attribute which does all to avoid offense to others; *in the Holy Spirit,* who indwells the spirit of the true disciples and who is the root and principle of all these virtues; *in love unfeigned,* not hypocritical, appearing to be sincere when it is not.

v. 7 *in the word* or teaching which is *of truth,* a ministry of preaching the truth or true doctrine, the Word of God. Paul preached God's Word, not his own, as some ministers who take a topic and speak some things "just from their own heads," *in the power of God* which comes from God, given by the minister for empowering his ministry.

(2) Paul passes next to the aspects of a more active and aggressive character of the ministry, using the preposition *dia* (through) versus that of passive endurance of hardships in patience: *by the armour of Christ's righteousness* and his own (Paul's) too, both the offensive weapon *on the right hand,* as the sword of truth[54] *and* the defensive *on the left,* as the shield of faith.[55] Let the minister put on the shield of faith when he is attacked but also bravely take up the sword of the Spirit,[56] that the church be not a mere respectable

54. Ephesians ch. 6.
55. *Ibid.*
56. Cf. the temptations of Jesus, Matt. Ch. 4 et *alias.*

nonentity.[57] The preacher must fight evil with positive truth, with apologetic armor,[58] aggressive activities at the same time *through* (attended with) *glory* sometimes *and dishonor* of calumnious criticism and false insinuations as to conduct and even character at others; *by* (accompanied by) *evil report and* also *good report,* today praise and flattery, tomorrow imputations of motive and slanderous rumor. Paul learned how to "take life as it is" (Robertson) with outward complacence and with a message, a program and God-given personality to face courageously the issues as they come, with the armor (*hoplōn*) of a heavy-armed soldier (*hoplitōs*).

(3) In a final flight the apostle soars to the highest heaven and reveals his inmost heart (vv. 8-10) *as deceivers and yet true,* in conflicting reports. Paul was called a deceiver[59] of the people, and so was Jesus.[60] Paul and Jesus let time give the final answer to the calumnies of their enemies. The apostle was (to his enemies) a wandering vagabond leading others astray in a trackless universe,[61] but on the contrary, truly was the very soul of integrity. *Unknown and yet well known* was another antithesis of the life of Paul. His enemies said he had no credentials. But the apostle was well-known in his own and much more in subsequent times, the best known man of the Roman Empire.

As dying and behold we live. He lived much of his life in prisons where he might expect the executioner's sword any hour as John the Baptist, but the hand of death was stayed. His enemies would have been glad to see his death at any time and thought they had secured it many times, (but) he would soon suddenly reappear again. He lived strenuously and "dangerously" too when it was necessary, but he did not neglect his body; he buffeted it and did not abuse it. His body, he knew, was the temple of the Holy Spirit; *as chastened and not killed* his enemies judged him a sinner, afflicted by God. But Paul accepted the chastening rod of wholesome discipline and profited thereby.

As sorrowful yet always rejoicing. Paul knew sorrows but kept happy. He could not be downed by sorrow, but gave thanks to God for all things, even for sorrows, in all his letters to the churches. He rebounded often when stricken down by griefs. Paul was cheerful even in the midst of sorrow. He did not wear his troubles on his sleeve.

As poor yet making many rich. Though his enemies accused him of being in the ministry to make money, he refused to receive money from the many congregations that he might not be a burden to anyone. He worked by night with his hands in tent making. Like his Master, he often had not where to lay his head. The home churches in Palestine and even in Antioch did not support his missionary plans. A small mission church in Philippi gave him limited help, which was more than all the rest had done. But Paul opened the treasure house of God's wealth for multitudes of his own time and to the generations unborn.

---

57. Robertson, A. T, *The Glory of the Ministry.* p. 232.
58. Nehemiah in the rebuilding of Jerusalem.
59. Clement *Hom. II,* 17, 18.
60. John 7:12.
61. *Planos* (a wandering planet).

As having nothing, yet possessing all things: He was almost penniless but the richest man in all the world when he wrote these words, because he possessed the enduring wealth of the eternities, "They that turn many to righteousness shall shine as the brightness of the firmament and the stars forever and ever." Such are the faithful ministers of an apostolic ministry.

D. Affectionate appeal of the apostle to the Corinthians for a complete reconciliation with him, excluding familiar association and intimate relationships with their heathen neighbors and claiming their sympathy for himself (6:11-7:4). He is glad for the message from Titus and assumes their desire for completed reconciliation toward himself. (7:5,6).

1. The appeal begun (6:11-13).

v. 11 *O men of Corinth, our* (my) *mouth is opened*[62] *toward you,* to tell you everything about myself (our) heart is enlarged,[63] to take you all into my confidences.

v. 12 *You are not straitened in us,* there being no restraint in my feelings toward you, *but you are straitened in your own* hearts' *affections* toward me.

v. 13 *But now* let there be a *recompense* to me *in the same kind* and character on your part as that of mine to you, of open-mouthed confidence out of an expanded heart, *I speak* to you *as to* (my own) *children* still young in the faith, *be ye also enlarged* in your hearts toward me.

2. Digression (6:14-7:1).

The theory that 6:14-7:1 is an interpolation, while apparently plausible, is not a necessary and evident conclusion. On the other hand, it would be natural for Paul in the midst of his argument and warm appeal to go out in a brief digression as was his custom and style at times (Eph. 3:2), to show here that the Corinthians did lack in "the same kind of warmth of affections" which he had just expressed for them. He also assigned the cause for such lack. In VII:2, having relieved his mind by frankly warning them about some kind of dangerous intimacy with the heathen neighbors, which he knew to exist on the part of some of them, the apostle returns to his appeal.

v. 14 *Stop becoming*[64] *unequally*[65] *yoked together with unbelievers,* who are antagonistic and not converted heathen; do not have fellowship with them in marriage and much less in other intimate and immoral ways. *For what fellowship* has *righteousness and lawlessness or what communion has light*[66] *with*[67] *darkness?*

v. 15 *And what concord* (agreement) *is there* between *Christ* the head of the heavenly kingdom *and Belial,*[68] the Satanic head of the infernal kingdom and on earth the incarnate Antichrist?

---

62. Second perfect active indicative of *anoigō*, permanent status.
63. Perfect passive indicative of *platunō*.
64. Present imperative, some had been guilty alreadv of this prohibited relationship.
65. Lev. 19:19; Deut. 22:10. It was prohibited to plow together an ass and an ox, two different species.
66. *Pros,* facing.
67. Dative, *fōti* — dative, of interest.
68. Hebrew signifies worthlessness.

v. 16 *Or what portion* has *a believer with a disbeliever,* who is not a mere unbeliever who does not approve of Christ, but antagonizes Him?

v. 16 *Or what agreement* has *the temple of God with idols? For we are the temple of the living* (real) *God. Just as God said,*[69] *"I will dwell in them and walk in them And I will be their God and they shall be my people."*[70]

v. 17 *Wherefore, come out from the midst of them and be ye separated saith the Lord and touch*[71] *not any unclean thing and I will receive you*

v. 18 *And will be to you a Father and you shall be to me sons and daughters, Saith the Lord Almighty."*[72]

Ch. VII:1 *Wherefore having these promises, Beloved, let us cleanse*[73] *ourselves from all pollution, of the flesh and the spirit,* such as filthiness: moral, mental or ceremonial; *perfecting holiness,* both aggressively and progressively[74] *in the fear*[75] *of God,* by a continued process of self-consecration.

v. 2 *Make room for us* (me) in your hearts. *We* (I) *wrong*[76] *no man,* we (I) *corrupted no one* in money, morals or doctrine, we (I) *took advantage of no one.*[77] Paul here disclaims having done anything against any one of them.

v. 3 *For* your *condemnation I do not say* this. In defending himself he was not blaming anyone. *For I have said* before: *you are in our (my) hearts to die together and live together.* No change in my condition can change my affection for you; you are in our hearts to share death and life.

v. 4 *Great is my boldness* of speech *toward you* in speaking thus; *great is my glorying* to others *on your behalf* (in praising you). *I am filled*[78] *with comfort* and encouragement, *I overflow*[79] *with joy* in the midst of *all my afflictions.*

D. Reconciliation completed by further explanation of his confidence in them 7:5-16.

v. 5 *For even when we*[80] (I) *had come into Macedonia,* our flesh *had no real relief,* but in everything *we were afflicted,* being hard pressed; *without* were *fightings;* conflicts with enemies; *within* were *fears,* forebodings about you.

v. 6 *But God, who comforts and encourages*[81] *the lowly* (those bowed down

---

69. *Hoti,* which follows in the text, is not translated, being used to introduce the quotation.

70. Lev. 26:11ff.

71. Present imperative, indicating that they had done so previously.

72. Cited freely ideas apparently from memory, according to the LXX, from various passages Cf. Isa. 52:11; Ezek. 20:34; 2 Sam. 7:14.

73. Volative aorist subjunctive from *Katharizō,* Paul including himself in the reflexive pronoun.

74. *Epiteleō* — present tense denoting a continuous process in the attainment of a hagiōsunēn full-grown holiness.

75. Location of "sphere within which."

76. Aorist, not a single case actually occurred.

77. A. V. Defrauded, but too definite in referring to financial dishonesty.

78. Perfect middle indicative.

79. Vulgate, superabundo.

80. Editorial "we."

81. *Parakaleō* signifies to comfort (and encourage).

in trouble and depression), *comforted* and encouraged *us* (me) *by the coming of Titus.*

v. 7 *But not only by his* (appearance) *coming* was I comforted, *but also by the encouragement* you gave him *by which he was encouraged respecting you, announcing to us* (me) *your longing* for you to see me again, *your mourning* in regret because you had grieved me, *your zeal for me* (on my behalf and my defense), *so that I rejoiced the more,* on receipt of such good tidings, than I had rejoiced at first on account of the arrival of Titus.[82]

v. 8 *Because, though I made you sorrowful* (grieved you) *by the* "severe" *letter, I do not repent* having written it. *Even if I did regret it* before the arrival of Titus, *for I see that the letter made you sorrowful, though but for a season* (an hour),

v. 9 *I now rejoice, not that you were made sorrowful, but that you were made sorry unto repentance: you were made sorry after a godly sort, that you might suffer loss by us in nothing.*

v. 10 *For godly sorrow worketh repentance unto salvation,* a kind of repentance which bringeth no regret; but *the sorrow of the world worketh* eternal *death.*

v. 11 *For behold* and consider *this very thing, that you were made sorrowful according to* the will of *God, how much earnestness it wrought in you, yea what clearing of yourselves* to me through Titus; *yea what indignation* because of the scandal in the church, *yea what fear* lest I should come with a rod, *yea what zeal* to punish the great offender, *yea what avenging* by some kind of punishment (administered to the offender). *In every respect* you *commended yourselves as pure in* regard to *the thing* which had been done.

v. 12 *Wherefore, even if I did write to you,* making you sorrowful, *it was not on account of the one who did the wrong* (injustice) *nor on account of the one who suffered injustice;*[83] *but on this account, that your earnest regard on behalf of us might be made manifest to yourselves in the sight of God.*

v. 13 *On this account,* since this has been accomplished *I have been comforted* and encouraged.

On the occasion of a brief visit in Corinth Paul had possibly been attacked and denounced in the public assembly by some leader of the rebellion against him. Another explanation is that it might have been Timothy who had been sent by Paul who suffered this effrontery and ridicule. In a severe letter afterwards Paul had insisted on the imposition of punishment on this offender. This was done later and Paul now writes to let them know how he feels now about the offender and his forgiving attitude toward him.

And in our comfort we (I) *joyed the more exceeding at* seeing *the joy of Titus, because his spirit has been refreshed by you all.*

v. 14 *Because if in anything I have gloried to him on your behalf* and in your praise, *I was not put to shame, but as we* (I) *spoke all things to you in*

82. Cf. Boise's *Notes on Paul's Epistles* in loco.
83. Possibly Timothy or else Paul himself, which is more probable.

truth and sincerity, *so our glorying also* which I made *to Titus,* was verified to be *the truth.*

v. 15 *And his inward affections are turned the more abundantly toward you, while he remembers the obedience of you all, how with fear and trembling ye received him.*

v. 16 *I rejoice that in everything* (every respect) *I am of good courage concerning you.* Paul thus closes the discussion in this part of the epistle of his personal relations with the Corinthians with a very frank and hearty expression of hopeful courage with reference to them.

II The Collection for the poor saints (Christians) in Jerusalem. 8:1-9:15.

The subject of this relief fund for the poorer members of the Jerusalem church is referred to in four places in the New Testament: I Cor. 16:1-3; II Cor. Chs. 8,9; Rom. 15:26,27 and Acts 24:17. The purpose of this collection was first to render charitable aid to a large number of the members of the Jerusalem church who were poverty-stricken, and for a number of reasons, wholly justifiable, were in the emergency of sorely needing such help. Paul not only desired greatly to help meet this real need of his Jewish brethren in the church in Jerusalem, the center from which Christianity went forth originally, and especially in the first church of Christ founded by the Apostles who had walked with the Master during his earthly ministry. The statesmanship of Paul as the founder of Christianity in the Gentile world was never more clearly demonstrated than in his plan to unite the Jewish and Gentile Christians in the bonds of fraternity of a common Christian cause.

Apparently the Corinthian church, which had been much divided by factional strife within, had not been over-enthusiastic or shown any deep and special interest in the raising of this fund, up to this time. Their collection never was very large, since it seems there was no need of a special representative from that church in constituting the Committee to bear the gift to Jerusalem. (Acts 20:4). The Judaists had gotten in their work and for a while this church had been in open rebellion against Paul. He had been deeply grieved and was compelled to write them a painful letter. But now the church was reconciled to him as its founder and Paul seeks in a tactful but firm and tender way to deepen their interest and stimulate their activity on behalf of this commendable enterprise. He was anxious that this great church, so full of talented individuals, should take a leading part in the collection and urged his confidence that it would.

These two chapters which present his splendid effort to get them to do so have ever been one of Paul's greatest contributions to the teaching about stewardship in the New Testament. Their rich content may for convenience of treatment be divided into five sections (1) The worthy example of the Macedonian churches and congregations in liberality. (8:1-7); (2) The example of Christ in its spontaneity and finality (8:8-15); (3) The definite and complete plan for the collection, using Titus and two other brethren. (8:16-24):

(4) Exhortation to have all in readiness when he comes (9:1-5); (5) Exhortation to them to be liberal for the benefit both of themselves and of the church (9:6-15).

A. The worthy example of liberality set by the Macedonian churches (8:1-7).

1. The apostle makes known to the Corinthian brethren the progress of the collections for the Palestine relief fund, particularly among the Macedonian churches, who had given very liberally in spite of their deep poverty due to the fact that the Romans had seized the mines and at the same time imposed heavy taxation. (vv. 1, 2).

v. 1 *Moreover* (1) *we make known to you, brethren,* the important matter[84] *with respect to the grace*[85] *of God, given in the midst of the churches of Macedonia,* exhibited in their liberality in spite of their difficult circumstances, occasioned by civil wars, bringing the impoverishment of many in that Roman province.

v. 2 *That in much testing of affliction* which has proved the genuineness of their Christianity *the* overflowing *abundance of their joy and their down-to-depth poverty* together *abounded in* the production of *the* spiritual *wealth of their* single-minded *liberality.*

Three circumstances are enumerated in these two verses relative to the giving of the Macedonian Christians. Their affliction tested out their Christianity and proved its ability to give joy in time of trial; their down-to-depth poverty did not keep them from giving liberally; and their liberal giving was marked by single-minded simplicity and joyfulness.

2. The reasons for this statement of the Apostle is further explained in vv. 3-5 following:

v. 3 *For according to* their *power* or ability *I bear witness,* even *beyond their power,* and *of their own accord,*

v. 4 without being asked or urged; also *with much entreaty, begging of us the favor* of being allowed to contribute *and* to enjoy *the fellowship of ministering* along with others *unto the saints* or fellow Christians

v. 5 in Judea, who were in dire need; *Not just as we had hoped* or expected of these poor members of the church, *but they gave their own selves first* of all *to the Lord* and *also to us through* the agency of *the will of God.*[86]

We note here four particulars in their giving: the extent, up to and beyond their means; their willingness, for they were not asked to give but requested the privilege for themselves of giving; their excelling the expectation of the apostle; and they gave themselves first of all, to Jesus Christ who is the rightful owner of every Christian. Their liberality was preceded by complete consecration to Christ and to His apostle. The result of this surprising readiness and consecration (v 6) was that Paul was encouraged by it *to exhort*[87] *Titus in order*

84. Cf. Paul's use of the verb *gnorizō.*
85. Adverbial accusative, Cf. classical acc. of specification.
86. *Dia* with genitive expresses agency.
87. *Eis* with articular infinitive with accusative, expressing result.

that just as he had before begun the raising of the relief fund in Corinth, on a former visit, *so now he should* go and *finish*[88] *for you this* work of *grace.*

v. 7 *But just as in everything you abound; in faith and eloquence and knowledge and in all earnestness and love from us*[89] *in you,*[90] see to it *that you may abound also this grace* of liberality. Paul gently reminds them that they have fallen behind in the gift of Christian giving.

B. Paul gives no orders, but merely mentions the all-sufficient example of Christ and leaves them to faithful, voluntary, and spontaneous, liberal giving in completing the collection according to their ability.[91] Ch. 8:8-15.

v. 8 *Not by way of command, do I speak* (8:8-15) *but through* the example of the *earnestness of others,* making use of the example of the Macedonian churches, also, thus testing and *proving the genuineness of your love.*

v. 9 *For ye know* the act and example of *the grace of our Lord Jesus Christ, that,* though *being*[92] *rich, on your account he* definitely by the act of his incarnation, voluntarily *became poor,*[93] *in order that*[94] *you* (by means of) *through his poverty*[95] *might become rich.*

v. 10 *I give,* not a command, as I said before, but *my* opinion of conviction and *judgment in this* matter of the relief fund *for this* giving of an opinion merely *is expedient for you, who began a year ago before* (others), *not only to do but also to will,* having the mind and intention to act, from last year. Thus I am not doing those, who voluntarily began, any injustice in merely giving a counsel or opinion and not a command relative to completing the collection.

v. 11 *But now do complete the doing also; that just as there was the readiness to will,*[96] *so there may be the completion* of the collection *also, from what you have,* in proportion to your means. "Those who had been foremost in willing should not be hindmost in performing." (Plummer).

v. 12 *For if the readiness of* mind *is there,*[97] *it is acceptable according as* one *may have and not according* to what (*as*) *he hath not.*

v. 13 *For,* the object of this relief fund is *not in order that to others* (the Judean brethren) there should be *relief,* while *to you* there is *pressure.*

v. 14 *But from* the consideration of *equality; at the present time, your abundance for* meeting *the want of those* brethren, *in order that,* at some

88. First Aorist (effective) active subjunctive of *epitileo* and perfective use of epi in composition.
89. Abl. of source.
90. Location or sphere within which.
91. Cf. J. H. Bernard, *The Expos. Gr. Testament,* Vol. III, p. 86.
92. Concissive present participle *ōn* from *eimi,* to be.
93. Ingressive aorist active indicative pointing to the definite act.
94. *Hina* with aorist active subjunctive in purpose clause.
95. Instrumental of means.
96. Expressed in voluntary pledges perhaps.
97. *Prokeitai,* lies before us.

other time, *their abundance also may come* to meet *your lack, so there may be equality; as it.*

v. 15 *stands written,* about the Israelites gathering manna in the desert, ("*He who* gathered *much had not too much and he* who gathered *little* had *not too little*") (Ex. 16:18). The equality, forced upon the Israelites, should be joyfully and voluntarily accepted in the fraternal reciprocity of mutual and helpful exchange of material and spiritual things. This principle put into practice among Christians universally would relieve them from the peril of atheistic communism.

C. Paul commends Titus and two approved companions, who, bearing the letter of commendation with them, will help the Corinthians to gather the collection at Corinth for the relief fund. 8:16-24. The apostle was very careful in planning for this collection that it might be successful and that there should be no underhand dealing in the raising of the fund.

v. 16 *But thanks be to God, who gives the same earnest care an your behalf in the heart of Titus,* which I myself always entertain.[98]

v. 17 *because,* to begin with, *he received* gladly *our appeal,* and *being* characteristically *more earnest, of his own accord* is going (went) *forth*[99] *to you.*

v. 18 *And we are sending*[1] *along with him the*[2] *brother, whose praise in* proclaiming *the gospel* rings *through all the churches.* This was probably Luke.

v. 19 *And not only this,* but he (this brother) *was appointed by the churches* to be *our fellow-traveler in this work of grace, which is being administered by us for the glory of the Lord* Jesus *himself*[3] *and* to show *our readiness.*

v. 20 *Taking precautions about this,*[4] *lest anyone should criticise or suspect our conduct in the matter* of *this* charity fund which is being *administered by us.*

v. 21 *For we aim at* doing *the beautiful things, not only in the sight of the Lord* Jesus *but also before the face of men.*

v. 22 *And with them, we are sending* another *brother of ours whom we have tested* and proved *in many things, frequently, to be earnest, but now much more earnest,* (than ever before) *because of much confidence which he has in you.* The names of these two companions of Titus are not mentioned.

v. 23 *If indeed* there is conjecture *about Titus, he is a partner of mine and* (in relation to) *for you a fellow worker, or if* inquiry is made relative to *our* two *brethren* whose names are unrevealed they are *apostles from the churches, the glory of Christ.*

---

98. A Plummer *I. C. C. Cf.* paraphrase.
99. Epistolary aorist translated as present.
1. *Idem.*
2. A definite brother.
3. *Auton,* used for *heanton* the reflexive pronoun, many times in the New Testament *Koinē* Greek.
4. *Touto,* accusative of specification in classic Greek but adverbial accusative of reference. Cf. Dana and Mantey, *Grammar* in loco.

v. 24 *Show therefore to them before the churches, the proof of your love and of our glorying respecting you.*

IX:1-5 Having assumed all the while that the plans for the collection in the Corinthian church would be put through, Paul suggests reasons for a liberal contribution and all to be in readiness before he should arrive in Corinth soon. He was uncertain as to the result of the collection at Corinth, hence some apparent repetition of instructions about details of the plans. The genuineness of Chapters 8 and 9 is not to be discredited by this apparent tautology. These chapters always belong to II Corinthians, for the dismemberment or detachment of which there is no reason.

v. 1 *For concerning the service* of raising the fund *for the saints* in Jerusalem, *it is superfluous for me to write to you* more at length.

v. 2 *For I know your readiness, of which, in your behalf, I am* in the habit of *glorying*[5] and praising you *to the Macedonians, 'that Achaia has been prepared* to make and send the collections *from a year ago'; and your zeal stirred up* by its influence, *the greater number* (majority) of them. Paul did not give them praise which they did not deserve in order to lead them to be liberal. But he did praise their intention, expressed a year before this, and earnestly assumed that they had not relinquished such a desire and purpose.

v. 3 *But I sent*[6] *the three brethren in order that our* (my) *glorying, on your behalf, might not be in vain in this particular* (part), *in order that just as I repeatedly said,*[7] to the Macedonians, *'you may* really *be prepared'.*[8]

v. 4 *Lest* by any means *if* any *Macedonians might come*[9] *with me,* which is very probable, *and* they shall *find you unprepared, we might be* put to *shame, not to say* anything of *you, in this confidence* respecting you.

v. 5 *Therefore I thought*[10] it *necessary to exhort the* three *brethren to go to you and previously prepare your promised bounty* (blessing) so *that* the same might *be*[11] *ready thus as a* (blessing) *bounty and not as* a matter of extortion.[12] These five verses (9:1-5) are closely connected up with 8:16-24. The chapter divisions as the verse divisions of the authorized version are artificial and not always closely connected logically.[13]

D. Exhortation to the church to give liberally and cheerfully. (Ch. 9:6-15). The Corinthians must remember that the blessings they will receive will be in proportion to their giving. The interchange of sympathy and circulation between them and the Macedonians will result in spiritual benefit to both.

---

5. Present progressive indicative of habitual action.
6. Epistotary aorist active indicative of *pempō.*
7. Imperfect active indicative, repeated action in past time of *legō.*
8. Perfect periphrastic passive subjunctive from *paraskeuazō.*
9. Third class condition, undetermined but highly probable.
10. Epistolory aorist active indicative.
11. Infinitive used to express purpose.
12. Cf. Plunmer *I. C. C.* in loco for 'covetousness' instead of extortion.
13. *Idem ICC* for logical connection.

v. 6 *And* remember *this* principle: *He who sows sparingly*[14] *will reap also sparingly and he who sows bountifully will reap also bountifully.*

v. 7 Let *each one* give *just as he has purposed*[15] *in his heart, not* (out of sorrow or regret) *grudgingly or out of necessity* (out of constraint as if forced to contribute); *for God loves a cheerful* (hilarious or propitious) *giver.*[16]

v. 8 *And God is able to make all grace abound in you; that in everything, always, with every sufficiency, ye may abound unto every good work. As it stands written,*

v. 9 in Psa. 112:9 (LXX).[17] "He (the man) that fears the Lord *hath scattered abroad; He hath given to the poor; His righteousness abideth forever."* Here is a picture of the beneficent man (cf. Ps. 92:3, 9). He scatters abroad (like the sowing of seed), to the poor and hungry. His righteousness is set forth and exemplified in his beneficence.

v. 10, 11 *And he who supplies seed to the one sowing 'and bread for eating,' will supply and multiply your seed for sowing and will increase 'the fruits* (products) *of your righteousness'; while in everything you are being enriched unto all liberality, which works through us* (who are bearing the bounty) *thanksgiving to God,* by those who receive it.

v. 12 *Because the ministry of this worship service is not only supplying the wants of the* poor *saints* in Jerusalem *but is also abounding through many thanksgivings to God.* There is a spiritual outcome in such giving always.

v. 13 *Since they through the proof of this service glorify God for the obedience of your confession* (subjection) *unto the gospel of Christ and for the liberality* (openness of heart or sincerity) *of your contribution for them and for all.*

v. 14 *and themselves with supplication* to God *for you, long for you, on account of the exceeding grace of God* (bestowed) *upon you.*

v. 15 *Thanks be unto God for his* (indescribable) *unspeakable gift* of the Christ, who draws all other divine gifts after him. Paul views from afar the complete unification of the race through Christ (Cf. Eph. Ch. 2). In the collection from Gentile churches for the poverty-striken among the saints at Jerusalem this great blessing was being realized.

III Paul's Vindication of his apostolic authority to the church, the majority of whose members were repentant, in a great invective directed against a small but stubborn minority of the church led by his Judaizing enemies. This assault on his enemies was to clear out the bad leaven in the church before his last visit to them. Chs. 10:1; 13:10.

This third and last main division of the epistle, consisting of four chapters, has been considered by a number of critical but able students, as part of an

---

14. Adverb derived from present middle participle, *pheidomenos.*
15. Perfect tense, giving from conviction, not from mere impulse.
16. Cf. Ex. 25:2.
17. Cf. Boise, *Notes on Paul's Epistles* in loco.

earlier 'severe letter' referred to in Chs. 2:4; 7:8. It is argued that the tone in these chapters XI-XII, is so radically different from that which immediately precedes in Chapter I-IX, which were conciliatory, that only a considerable separation in time and circumstances would be sufficient to explain such an alteration of attitude of Paul.

The natural order might seem the invective part first and then the conciliatory when the majority of the church had become repentant. However, there were probably many factors in the development of the Corinthian church which are unknown to us, such as, for example, the constant and increasing influx of Judaizing enemies of Paul, who had begun their work in Corinth after the apostle's ministry in other parts had so engrossed his attention as to leave little time to tend to the inroads of these enemies in Corinth. Such a laborious ministry as that in Ephesus, in an effort to fill in the *hiatus* between the work already done in Asia and his wider campaign in Europe, even to Spain and other parts later, would be an example.

A. The Apostle's authority and the extent and area of his mission Ch. 10:1-18.

Paul is writing to the whole Corinthian church in these four chapters 10-13, just as in the rest of the epistle. The majority of the church, now repentant of their incorrect treatment of their apostolic-founder during the period of their rebellion against him, would derive great benefit from the apostle's frank denunciation of the remaining stubborn minority, which was determined to carry on their subverting activities to the end. The main intent of these chapters was to unmask the subtle work of the Judaists and expose injustice and disloyalty of both method and character of their ambitious schemes. The now loyal members would be brought to see the difference in character and work of Paul as a true apostle over against the false assumptions of the Judaists, who were self-constituted and self-commended teachers. So Paul discusses:

1. The apostle's authority and the extent of his province or territory (10:1-18).

2. The apostle's 'foolish' glorying (11:1-12:10).

It is to be remembered that Paul had to literally beg the half-repentant church, proferring his confidences and assuring them of his entire committal to them with a heart 'broadened' to receive them all into his warmest affections. On top of this full and frank expression going out from him is his accompanying plea that they reciprocate with the same kind of good will and take him back into their confidences as he has offered to take them into his, and more important still, to take him into their hearts' affections as he had declared himself as doing for them for dying (death) or living (life).

1. The apostle's authority and extent of province on field of labor Ch. 10:1-18.

v. 1 *Now, I Paul myself beg you by the meekness and gentleness* exhibited always in the example *of Christ,* which was that of one who was humble and submissive to the will of God in his treatment of Him and that of acceptance of the treatment of men, with a "sweet reasonableness", as being in accordance with God's will.[18] *Who in* personal *appearance indeed am lowly* among you. They had accused him of cowardice and 'weakness in appearance'; he responds in terms of the 'meekness and gentleness' of Christ, who was his great example, *but 'being absent am courageous toward you.'* This was almost the repetition of the exact words of the statement of the accusation.

v. 2 Yea *I entreat* (you) *that I may not when present,* (when I come soon) *be courageous with the confidence with which I account* (calculate) *to be bold against some* persons *who take account of us, as if we were walking according to the flesh.*

v. 3 Paul presents his work as an apostle as in contrast to that of his antagonists. *For* while *in the flesh* or mortally weak physical body *we walk around,* yet *we do not carry on our* Christian *warfare according to the fleshly principles* or carnal nature, which would be wholly unsuccessful in God's sight.

v. 4 *For the weapons of our warfare are not of the flesh* or carnal nature *but* are *mighty for God* (as judged and evaluated by him), *to the casting down of* the *strongholds* of evil, even though they be wielded by one whose mortal body is frail and beset by physical weakness and limitations.

v. 5 *Casting down I* say *reasonings* or vain imaginations *and every high thing* of human pride *that is exalted against the* true *knowledge of God,* even *bringing into captivity every thought, unto the obedience unto Christ,*

v. 6 *having in readiness* (always being ready) *to avenge* (punish) *every disobedience, when your obedience shall have been fulfilled,* and the disobedient (members of church not yet repentant) shall have had ample time to come over and join the obedient. This was exactly the situation in Corinth. The majority of the brethren were already turning and some had entirely turned to obedience. Paul wished to push the matter opportunely to get the whole church lined out together for Christ.[19]

v. 7 *You are looking*[20] *on the things before your face,* you claim, as in your ridicule of me as 'weak' or feeble. Well then take the human standpoint of looking on my outward appearance[21] which you say is weak. *If any man of you has trusted*[22] *to himself that he belongs to Christ*[23] and has a special nearness to Him, *let him reason* or consider *this again* by himself humanly in the same human way of judging by the outward appearance, *that even as he himself belongs to Christ,* as judged by his outward conduct and demeanor, *so we* (I) *also* belong to Him, judged by the same standard. He challenges his critics to judge of his genuine claims to apostleship even by a just human standard, applied with fairness by comparison with their own life and conduct.

---

18. Plummer, A., *Camb. Gr. Test for Schools and Colleges* in loco.
19. Cf. Alford cited by Boise's Notes in loco.
20. Form *blepete* either imperative or indicative but latter more in accord with context.
21. "Man looks on the outward appearance but God on the heart."
22. Perfect tense
23. Genitive of possession

v. 8 *For if,*[24] *indeed, I boast somewhat more abundantly concerning our* (my) apostolic *authority, which the Lord gave* me for your building (edification) *and not for your down tearing* (or demolition), *I shall not be put to shame,* by being declared to be a pretentious imposter.The work of Paul's opponents was one of tearing down and this to an unbiased judge was perfectly evident.[25]

v. 9 *That I may not seem as if I would terrify you by my letters.* Paul's opponents had said that his letters were weighty and strong but his 'bodily presence was weak.' But the Lord would take care of his apostle who was but asserting what was just in claiming his apostolic authority which was being declaimed by his antagonists. So in vv. 9-11 Paul is repelling the accusation that his letters are 'weighty and strong' (meaning severe and violent), which was very uncomplimentary. The same words might mean in other context "impressive and vigorous."[26] The opponents did not mean to be complimentary as is evident in the next phrase about the 'appearance or presence of his body as being weak and his speech contemptible.'

v. 10 They say *that the* (his) *letters are weighty and strong,* calculated to terrify the members of the Corinthian Church, *but* his *appearance* (or presence) *of his body is weak and his* manner of *speech* of *no account,* (utterly despised). These enemies sneered at Paul's personal appearance. In Lystra the natives thought Barnabas to be the god Zeus, but Paul's meager size and facilities in speech and activity Hermes almost brought him to premature martyrdom. His bodily appearance was pictured in the second century as "small, short, bow-legged, with eyebrows knit together and an aquiline nose.[27]" The Corinthians liked the rhetorical manner of speech of Apollos rather than the plain presentation of 'Christ and him crucified' in the preaching of Paul. There was much biting criticism by his enemies about his looks and speech (Robertson). But the traditions as to Paul's looks and manner of speech cited above are of little significance, since they certainly did not depreciate the efficiency of his work.

v. 11 *Let any such a person reckon this, that, what sort we are in word, by letters, when absent, such are we also in deed when we are present.*

v. 12 It was a keen rebuke that Paul measured out to those enemies of his gospel work among the Corinthians when he said: *For we* (I) *were not bold to pair or compare ourselves with some of those that commend themselves,* using a standard of orthodoxy as well as conduct of their own fixing. *But they*[28] *themselves, measuring by themselves and judging themselves with themselves, are without understanding.*[29] They do not put things together properly in correct interpretation and understanding.

---

24. Concessive conditional clause of third class with ean, with future indicative Kanchasomai, which indicates confidence, a fine point in exegesis (Tischendorf).
25. Cf. A Plummer I. C. C. II Cor. in loco.
26. Cf. A. T. Robertson, *Word Pictures* on Paul's Epistles in loco.
27. Acts of Paul and Thekla.
28. *Autoi,* — his opponents and critics.
29. Cf. A Plummer *Com. II Cor. Camb. Series,* for playing on words in this interesting example of Paul's use of sarcasm.

v. 13 *But we* (in contrast) *will not glory* (entering) *into the things without measure of the province* (or territory) *which God apportioned to us as a measure, to reach even into you.* Paul did not accept the standard of his enemies or critics but only the standard which God gave him.[30] He had been allowed by God to go to Corinth and his work there though difficult was evidently blessed of the Lord and successful. This approval of God on his work then was the claim in which Paul gloried and the basis for his persistent and tenafious hold of the province of Achaia and its great capital city of Corinth. His enemies had no claim. His was a chain of priority.

v. 14 *For we are not over-stretching ourselves as if not having reached into the midst of you; for* until (unto) *you also we came before* (anyone else) *in the gospel of Christ.*

v. 15 *Not into the things without measure* (going beyond the bounds of the province God assigned me), *glorying in the labors* (toils) *of others; but having a hope* (that) *when your faith increases* (to be) *magnified among you, according to our measuring line* or province assigned by God entering *into an abundance* (a wide

v. 16 field), *into the regions beyond you to preach the gospel; not into the things* or fields of labor *which are ready, to glory in another man's province.*

v. 17 *'But he who glories let him glory in the Lord.'*

v. 18 *For not the one who commends himself,* (not) that *man is approved; but he whom the Lord commends he is approved.* This will be the final verdict for each one, whatever men say now.

B. The apostle's glorying is a folly which was forced upon him. 11:1-12:18.

Paul had not intruded on the 'province' or territory of any Christian worker ("the rights of his enemies"), if they might be said to have any; but they on his. He defends his apostleship by resorting, for a moment, to the folly of self-glorying or self-praise which folly was a habit with the Judaists. He thus "answers them according to their folly." He would not enter into this comparison of himself with them, except in order to save the Corinthians, who had been deceived by the self-commendation of these Judaizing teachers. But he must resort to their method and make a fool of himself, for a moment, in order to unmask their hypocrisy and defend his apostleship.

1. Paul first states the reasons for his assumed folly. (11:1-6).

v. 1 *Would that you could bear with* me in *a little foolishness; but you* are indeed[31] *bearing with me.*

v. 2 *For I am jealous about you*[32] *with a godly* jealousy, a jealousy such as God has for his people; *for I betrothed*[33] *you to one husband* (Christ) *to present you* (that I might present you) *a pure virgin to Christ;* the Bridegroom of his church — bride.

---

30. A Plummer *Com. II Cor., Camb. Series,* p. 154.
31. *Ophelon* second aor. act. ind. of *opheilō,* expressing a wish (*Koinē*).
32. Adverbial accusative of reference (Grammar of Dana and Mantey).
33. Middle voice indicating Paul's personal interest and action in the transaction.

v. 3 *But I fear, lest* (how) *by some means, as the serpent in his craftiness beguiled Eve, your minds* (thoughts) *might have been corrupted*[34] *from your simplicity* (single-mindedness) *and the purity which is* (into) *in Christ.*

v. 4 *For*, let me explain that *if he who comes shall proclaim another Jesus*[35] *whom we have not proclaimed, or you are receiving another spirit which you did not receive* in our preaching *on another* and different gospel *which you* did *not receive, you bear* with them *beautifully*. Paul by the context is sarcastic here.[36] He is charging these Corinthians with disloyalty toward Christ in receiving these false teachers with such show of broadness and boasted 'open-mindedness.' He warns them that they were acting very unworthily in receiving these Judaistic teachers in Corinth, whom he had withstood before in their efforts to split the Galatian churches.

v. 5 *For I consider myself in nothing* to be *inferior to those* (over much) *arrogant* deceivers, who called *themselves apostles* or even to the 'chief apostles' to whom they proclaim their exclusive loyalty.

v. 6 *But if I am even 'rude* or unskilled *in speech,'* as my enemies declare, *yet I am not such in knowledge; but in everything we have made* that (fact) *plain among* all men *for you* in my relations to you as a teacher of the gospel. Paul's mastery of the things of Christ was plain and evident among all men. He knew his subject. (Robertson).

2. Paul had refused maintenance and so was not inferior to his adversaries. He gloried in the fact that he was not a burden to the Corinthians. (11:7-15).

v. 7 *Or did I* commit a *sin in humbling myself*, by making tents for a living while preaching in Corinth, *in order that you might be exalted,* by being lifted from the degradation of heathendom to the high plane of moral life and privileges of Christianity.

Because I preached the gospel of God to you freely, without any charge. His enemies cast reproach on him for this and criticized him saying that he had done this to subvert people and not from any other motive.

v. 8 *Other churches I robbed, taking wages* (the means of subsistance) from them *for your service,*[37] *and my presence with you* in Corinth, *and fell behind* in my resources, even then, *I did not burden*[38] *any man.*[39]

v. 9 *For the brethren having come from Macedonia* opportunely *supplied my deficiency*. The church at Philippi sent several times to help the Apostle. *And in everything I kept myself from being a burden to you and will keep myself* carefully so as not to be a burden to anyone anywhere in the future. This

34. Second aorist passive subj. of *phtheirō* with *mē* post.
35. Jesus here instead of Christ. The Judaists would not use Christ as a proper name. Cf. A Plummer I. C. C., p. 296.
36. Cf. Idem, *II Cor.* p. 296 for irony. Cf. A. Robertson also *Word Pictures* in loco.
37. The Macedonian church at Philippi had contributed to his maintenance while he was working at Corinth.
38. Kata-narkaō, weigh down upon, heavily.
39. Oudenos from audeis, Cf. texts W. H. and Nestle pronounciation Aorist. Cf. Thayer noone, two negatives in Greek make a positive.

was Paul's policy, in order that he might 'become all things to all men' and thus if possible 'save some.'

v. 10 *The truth of Christ is in me that this glorying* about my not being a burden to anyone *shall not be stopped* by my enemies by thrusting a hedge into me, 'to fence me in,' *within the regions of Achaia.* Paul claimed this region as his field of work by God's manifest approval on his ministry when there, in important policy!

v. 11 *Why?*[40] *Is it because I do not love you? God knows I do.* Paul wishes to anticipate any idea that might creep in that he did not love them.

v. 12 *But what I am doing, I will* continue to *do,*[41] *that I may cut off the occasion of those who wish*[42] *an occasion* for slander, to thus undercut me and aggrandize themselves, *in order that wherein they are glorying they may be found even as we.* His refusal of maintenance might drive them to refusal also thus freeing the Corinthians from the burden of supporting these false teachers. Thus they would be found on the same plan as Paul and his fellow-workers.

v. 13 *For such* men fairly viewed *are false apostles, deceitful workers,* who are active in their deceit *fashioning themselves,*[43] or 'cutting themselves out *into* the fashion of *apostles' of Christ* by putting on the habiliments and posing as ministers of Church, 'gentlemen of the cloth,' and as Robertson said 'such are nothing but cloth.' Those men who pestered Paul at every turn made 'occasion' to slander the man who had founded the church in Corinth. There are heresy hunters but worse still there are those who magnify the faults of their fellow Christians but especially of the preacher if they have some private-axe ambition to grind some selfish interest at stake.

v. 14 *And not a strange thing,* to be wondered at; *for Satan himself*[44] *transforms himself*[45] *into an angel of light.*

v. 15 It is *not a great* and unexpected *thing, therefore, if his servants transform themselves* and masquerade *as servants of righteousness* to deceive the saints. Thus by implication Paul was unmasking the Judaistic teachers who were working desperately to divide the church in Corinth because of their own ambitions to make the church adopt their false theory and saddle Jewish ceremonialism on all the members of the church. They could do this by classifying the members into two qualities of Christians, the good (Gentile) and the better (Jewish) members, and so split the church permanently. About the final result of the career of such teachers, Paul says: *the end of whom shall be according to their works.*

3. His labors, sufferings and trials for them are evidences of his true apostleship (11:16-33). If he has to resort to boasting, he certainly has more to boast

40. On account of what?
41. Boise's Notes on Paul's Epistles in loco.
42. Ablative of origin, there are always some who are waiting to get occasion to originate something against a Christian worker or minister.
43. Present middle participle of metaschematizō, to fashion one's-self into the likeness of another.
44. Reflexive pronoun *autos* in Koinē Greek Cf. *heautos.*
45. Present middle indicative, subject of verb acting.

about than these false teachers. He too is of the chosen race; in labors and sufferings for the gospel he had excelled them. He had been beaten, scourged, stoned and shipwrecked. He had run many risks in his travels, through dangerous and perilous ways, to carry the gospel; had endured much of privation and suffering, anxieties about the churches and ministries of sympathy and consolation to the weak brethren. His Corinthian brethren should indulge him while answering the accusations and criticisms of his enemies, "according to their folly." They had been wise in receiving and harbouring these false teachers, had they? Well, they had been deluded, cheated and insulted by them, just the same. Paul admitted that it was foolishness in himself to even compare himself to any such as these Judaizing teachers were.

v. 16 *Again I say let not anyone* think[46] *me to be foolish* or lacking in reflection and intelligence because of this folly of glorying.

But even *indeed if* you do receive me, *as foolish,* yet *receive me* at least, *that I also* (as well as they) *may glory somewhat.*

v. 17 *What I am speaking, I do not speak according* to the example or explicit instruction of *the Lord* (Jesus), *but as* it were in a state *without reflection, in this confidence of glorying.*

v. 18 *Since many are glorying after the flesh,* in a spirit of having regard for their national or racial extraction and their achievements, *I also will glory.*

v. 19 *For ye being wise cheerfully* bear *with those who are deficient in intelligence.*

v. 20 *For you bear up under it, if anyone enslaves you* abjectly, *if anyone devours you* stripping you of your possessions, *if anyone seizes you,* by force or craft, *if anyone is proud* or arrogant exalting himself against you, *if anyone smites you in the face,* as indeed it sometimes happens. These Corinthians were submitting to tyranny, extortion, craftiness, arrogance, violence and insult from others; they might have patience with Paul's glorying a little[47] especially when he apologizes for doing it and acknowledges that it is contrary to the teaching and example of Jesus, but that he is doing it to show them up.

v. 21 *I speak by way of disparagement* of myself *as if* it were a fact *that we have been weak. But* (in what) *wherein anyone may be bold, in foolishness I say it, I also am bold.*

v. 22 *Are they Hebrews? I also* am a Hebrew of the Hebrews; *are they Israelites? I also* am of pertain to the chosen race; are they *of the seed of Abraham? I also* am a descendant from the same.

v. 23 *Are they servants of Christ? being beside myself I speak, I am* that *above* and preeminently: *in toils* (hard labors) *more abundantly* than they; *in prisons more abundant* (at least five times); *in stripes* (blows) *above measure; in* peril of imminent *death* frequently.

---

46. Aorist subjunctive *doxēr* with *mē* in a negative prohibition. Cf. A .T. Robertson *Word Pictures* in loco.

47.Cf. A Plummer, *I. C. C., Com. II Cor.* in loco.

v. 24 *From the Jews five times I received forty strips* (blows of the scourge, forty being the legal limit by Roman law) *less one,* to make sure they had not passed the limit;

v. 25 *thrice I was beaten with rods* by the Roman magistrates, a punishment not to be administered to Roman citizens by express prohibition of the Lex Porcia. Paul voluntarily suffered this in Philippi, the only time mentioned in the narrative of Acts (Cf. 16:23,37); *once I was stoned* (at Lystra); (Acts 14:19), *thrice I was shipwrecked* (one time mentioned in Acts 28); *a night and day I passed*[48] *in the deep.* (on the voyage to Rome, Cf. Acts Ch. 28);

v. 26 *in journeyings often,* (in three or more missionary campaigns); *in dangers of rivers* (on these journeys); *in dangers of robbers* (also on trips through mountain fastnesses); *in dangers from my* (Jewish) *kindred* (everywhere); *in dangers from the* Gentile *peoples* (in the persecutions as in Lystra); *in dangers in the city* (as for example in Damascus, Jerusalem, Ephesus and others); *in dangers in the desert* wilderness; *in dangers in the sea* (voyages); *in dangers* among false brethren (who persecuted him persistently) which was the worst of all, as viewed in the lurid light of II Corinthians Chs. X, XI and many experiences with the Judaists.

v. 27 *by labors* (toil) *and travail* (giving birth to churches); *by vigils* (watchings) *often* in the watches of night when sleepless by over-strain and nervous anxiety about the churches; *by hunger and thirst* (often suffered in many privations); *by fastings,* involuntary and voluntary, because of sacrifices and the intensity of his work; *by cold and nakedness.* (Paul lacked sufficient clothing at times; he sent to ask Timothy to bring his mackintosh). This catalogue of the sufferings of the apostle covers a wide range and vast variety in a crowded and intense life of devotion to the Lord.

v. 28 *Besides* this list and *the* (many) *things omitted, I have the pressure day by day, the care and anxiety about all the churches.* Paul had a pastor heart and took his work seriously.

v. 29 *Who is weak* (infirm) *and I am not* sympathizingly *weak* with him? *Who is made to stumble* and sin *and I do not burn* with grief because of it? Here is comfort for those who, like Paul, have passed through the trials and temptations in the midst of periods of depression and misunderstanding brought on by false brethren.

v. 30 *If it is necessary to glory, I will glory in the things pertaining to my weaknesses,* frailties of body, perhaps thorns in the flesh, of maladies caused by excessive work and distressing trials and testing times.

v. 31 *The God and Father of our Lord Jesus, he who is blessed forever, knows that I do not speak falsely.* The list of experiences recited by Paul was inclusive of so many trials and difficulties that it was almost unbelievable to most men even to the more experienced Christians; hence Paul's solemn declaration he sets as a seal of his entire sincerity in its recital.

---

48. Perfect tense, (a permanent and lasting memory).

v. 32 *In Damascus the ethnarch under*[49] *Aretas was guarding the city of the Damascenes to take me, and in a basket*

v. 33 *I was let down* (lowered) *through the wall* (of the city) *through a window* (a small door or opening)[50] *in a basket* (made of rope) *and escaped* (fled out from) *his hands.* The recital of this experience, more in detail, stood out vividly in the memory of the apostle as he reviewed his earlier experiences in the beginning of his long ministry for Christ. It happened soon after his return from the three parts of years of sojourn in Arabia, naturally after his conversion.[51]

Paul boasted of his weaknesses because thus he could show how Christ had used such a feeble servant. So in Damascus he had suffered ignominy, being pursued like a criminal by the governor. It was exceedingly humiliating to have to escape from the city as he did, being spirited away, even if it were by the help of devoted students of his theological class. Any boasting or glorying by the minister of God, such as Paul was, seemed utterly out of place and foolish, even madness. But it was for the sake of saving the Corinthians and he was willing to make a fool of himself in order to save them.

4. Glorying about the revelations granted to him along with a reference to the accompanying demonic thorn in the flesh. (12:1-10). Paul unwillingly resumes his boasting (glorying) and tells of the very intimate, sacred and privileged experiences of his (supernatural) revelations from God and some (thorn) physical or other infirmity, through which the grace of Christ was manifested in him (Dummelow). The purpose of the infirmity which was the sequel of the revelation was, as he confesses, to keep him from vanity respecting this divine favor. This was by the permission of God and served a good purpose.[52] First, he refers to his supernatural revelations (vv 1-6).

v. 1 *It is necessary for me to glory.* It was forced upon me. The circumstances demanded that Paul go on, foolish as it seemed, *though it was not indeed expedient* or profitable to him or the church for him or for any minister to boast. *And*[53] *so I will come into* another worthier matter, that of *visions and revelations* granted me *from the Lord* Jesus. These were not delusions or illusions but solid fact.[54]

v. 2 *I know a man* who was in ecstacy *in Christ fourteen years* ago,[55] (*whether* he was *in the body, I do not know; or whether out of the body I*

49. A. Plummer, *Camb. Gr. Test. for Schools and Colleges*, p. 189f.

50. Cf. Smith's *Bib. Dict.* et al. Art. Damascus.

51. Cf. Acts 19:9; Gal. 1:17. Aretas ruled Arabia Petraea from 9 B. C. to 40 A. D. Damascus was taken by the Romans in 65 B. C. and seems to have been restored to Aretes in 40 A. D. from motives of policy. Cf. Dummelow *Bib. Com. II Cor.* in loco.

52. Cf. Book of Job concerning his sufferings.

53. *De* — and illative.

54. A. Plummer *I. C. C.* in loco.

55. The date would indicate that it was while Paul was at Tarsus after fleeing from Jerusalem Cf. Acts 9:30 — 11:25. We have no details of that period of his ministry (Robertson *Word Pictures*).

do not know, *God knows, caught up*[56] *such a one* (was) *into* (until) *the third* (highest) *heaven* where God is.[57]

v. 3 *And I know such a man,* (*whether in the body or apart from the body, I know not, God knows*),

v. 4 *Such a one, caught up into Paradise, heard unspeakable words, which it is not lawful for a man to utter.*

v. 5 *Respecting such a person* in this exalted state, *I will glory; but respecting myself* in my earthly condition *I will not glory except in my infirmities* (weaknesses).

v. 6 *For if I should wish to glory* respecting myself *I shall not be foolish* in this case *for I shall speak the truth* and there will be reasons in what I say[58] *But I forbear* from boasting or glorying respecting myself *lest any man* regarding me (looking into me) *should estimate me beyond* (above) *what he sees me* to be *or hears from me.*[59] Paul did not wish to say anything that would lead the Corinthian brethren to overestimate him but wished that they should form their estimate from their own personal observation. Secondly, he dwells on his infirmities especially his 'thorn in the flesh' and its purpose. (vv. 7-10).

v. 7 *And by* reason of *the exceeding greatness* (excess) of the revelations, *wherefore, in order that I should not be exalted overmuch, there was given me a thorn in the flesh*, a physical malady, *a messenger of Satan,* as in the case of Job *in order that he* (Satan) *might buffet me* giving me blows as with a fist *in order that I should not be overmuch exalted* "This messenger of Satan kept slapping (striking) Paul in the face and Paul sees that it was God's will for it to be so."[60]

v. 8 *Concerning this* thing (messenger of Satan) *I besought the Lord* Jesus *three times that* he *might stand off*[61] (make it depart) *from me,* once for all.

v. 9 *And he* (the Lord) *has said*[62] *to me: 'My grace is sufficient for you'*, to ward off all danger permanently. *For my power is made perfect*[63] *in weakness.* The human weakness in his devoted servant furnished the occasion for the greater demonstration of the effectiveness of Christ's power and grace. *Most gladly, rather*, than ask more times than the three, *will I glory in my weaknesses in order that the power* (strength) *of Christ may rest upon me,* as a Shechinah tent of the Lord overshadowing me.[64]

v. 10 *Wherefore I take pleasure in infirmities* (weaknesses), *in insults* (injuries), *in necessities* (forced situations), *in persecutions and in straits* (dis-

---

56. Second aor. pass. part of harpazō.
57. A. Plummer *I. C .C. II Cor.* in loco. Cf. also A. T. Robertson, *Word Pictures.*
58. Boises Notes on the Epistles of Paul in loco.
59 For punctuation and consequent division of verses 6 and 7. Cf. A. Plummer in loco and texts of Nestle and W. H. The logical connection of the argument seems to favor the order we follow, with Plummer and others.
60. Robertson's *Word Pictures.* Vol. Paul's Epistles p. 265.
61. Second aorist active subjunctive from *aplustēmi.*
62. Perfect active indicative, a final and permanent answer 'once for all,' to Paul's prayer.
63. Present passive indicative.
64. First aor. subj., *episkānosū,* rest as a tent upon him. A bold figure and a lesson hard to be borne but learned at last by Paul permanently Rom. 5:2; II Tim. 4:6-8.

tresses or narrow places), *for the sake of Christ; for whenever I am weak then am I strong* (powerful) through the assurance Christ gives me. Paul's enemies could not make Paul unhappy even though they should persecute him to the death.

Paul was glorying about the sublime revelations he had received from the day of his conversion on the Damascus road through his months of meditation in Arabia, his second brief ministry in Damascus, his brief ministry in Jerusalem where he had a supernatural vision, and on through his ministry in Tarsus and Cilicia, where he might have had the experience in Paradise about which he speaks (vv. 1-10). These visions were not merely psychological and internal but real and sober facts. Paul's infirmity was of a kind to humiliate him.[65] But the apostle had been graciously saved and sent into the work of his apostleship to the Gentiles, than which blessing man never received a greater. He was therefore willing to suffer "wanton injuries, dire hardships," persecutions unmitigated, necessities inescapable, narrow places of unendurable pressure but all of which things he suffered for Christ's sake. These experiences were pressed upon him from without and his suffering was vicarious making evident his patience, forbearance, devotion to Christ and good will to all men, whether to persecuting worldlings or to devil-inspired false brethren who sought to defeat the apostle in order to defeat his Lord's doctrines. This kind of suffering could do God's apostle no harm but would greatly serve and glorify the Lord and his work.

5. The genuine credentials of an apostle Paul possessed: mighty and disinterested works and exceeding love for those for whom he worked. (12:11-18. Miracles were a part of Paul's work and served as the signs of God's approval on his apostle. The love of Paul was an exceptional and disinterested love, making him disclaim all maintenance that his love might appear more evident to them.

v. 11 *I am become*[66] *foolish*, by writing in this boastful fashion. *You compelled me* by commending my opponents. *I ought*[67] now *to be commended by you*, instead of having to glorify myself. *For in no respect was I inferior to the superextra apostles*, the Judaizers, even if 'I am nothing.'

v. 12 *Indeed the signs of the*[68] *apostle were wrought out in your midst in all patience, by sign-miracles, and mighty works* demonstrating supernatural power: all three of the principal types of miracles performed by Jesus, in his ministry.

v. 13 *For what is there wherein you were made inferior to the rest of the churches, except that I myself was not a burden to you? Forgive me for this* wrong, of depriving you of the profit of being fellow-helpers to the truth in contributing to my maintenance. I did you an injustice in depriving you.

---

65. A Plummer I. C. C.
66. Imperfect active indicative of *ginomai.*
67. Imp. indicative expressing an unfulfilled obligation about the present (Robertson).
68. Force of the definite article here evident as demonstrative.

v. 14 *Behold, this is the third*[69] time *I am ready to come to you, and I will not* you may be assured, *burden* or "sponge on you." *For I seek not yours but you.* This expression describes the true attitude and motto a minister should have toward his people. *For the children ought not to* have to *lay up for the parents but the parents for the children.* He thus expresses indirectly and forcefully his claim to be the spiritual father of most of the members of this great church, and its founder.

v. 15 *And I most gladly will spend* everything I possess *and will be spent.* myself *completely for the sake of your souls. If I love you the more abundantly am I loved the less?*

v. 16 *But let it be* established as a fact that *I did not burden you,* but someone of my enemies has said that *being crafty I caught you with guile.*[70] Paul uses these words as if they were his own, in playful irony. The following question makes plain this interpretation. He took nothing from them directly but robbed them indirectly through the collection for the poor saints in Jerusalem. Paul's enemies were accusing.

v. 17 *In respect to any one of* those *whom* I have sent to you, *I did not take advantage of you through him* to overreach you financially *did I?*[71]

v. 18 *I exhorted Titus* to visit you *and I sent with him the brother.*[72] *Titus did not take advantage of you, did he?*[73] *Did we not* (conduct ourselves) *walk in the same Spirit? Did we not walk in the same steps?*

On the eve of this third visit to the city of Corinth, counting his first appearance there as one, Paul was determined not to accept any financial support from them, as he did not formerly. The same motive actuated him is this purpose, that of making it evident that he wanted them disinterestedly by and not their money. They were his spiritual children and he wanted to provide for them, not they for him. He was dispendable in the service for them and sought with a yearning heart their love for himself. His Judaizing (brethren) enemies were whispering around that Paul was a keen rogue, refusing with great show any help for his maintenance, while secretly appropriating for his own use the money raised in the collection for the poor saints of Jerusalem. They said he was a crafty rogue making use at deceit to catch them. Paul makes a direct thrust of this vile accusation spread secretly in a smearing campaign, by his direct questions in the appeal of vv. 17, 18, positively asserting his innocence.

C. Final warnings before his approaching visit (12:19-13:10).

1. The purpose of his glorying was their edification (12:19-21). They must not mistake his glorying for personal apology unto repentance for his conduct.

---

69. Paul had changed his plans once after promising them a visit. He assigned the reason why he had not gone later, because of their rebellious conditions.

70. Moffatt puts this clause in quotation marks.

71. This is idiomatic enough but clearly the question expects a negative answer. Cf. negative *mē*.

72. Brother of Titus probably.

73. Negative *mēti*. Cf. above.

v. 19 *For a long time you have been thinking*[74] *that we*[75] (1) *are defending ourselves to you.* Paul's own reputation was not the thing he had in mind. *Before God in Christ we speak. But all things, Beloved, are for your edification.* "Think not that I am on my defense before you." It is before God and in Christ, to whom I am responsible, that I speak. And it is for your edification that I speak, for it is you that have to be judged by me[76] as your spiritual father and Christ's undershepherd.

v. 20 *For I fear lest in some way* (possibly) *I may, when* I come (literally having come) *find you not such as I wish, and I may be found in relation to you*[75] *such as you do not wish,*[76] *lest by any means*, there may be *strife, jealousy, angry passions, factions,* intriguing for office, *backbitings,* talking-down in deformation, *whisperings,* secret slanderings, swellings, puffed up with vanity and egotism, *tumults.*

v. 21 *Lest when I come again* (in the contemplated visit) *my God should humble*[77] *me before you, and I should mourn for many of them who having sinned heretofore and not repented for their uncleanness, and fornication and lasciviousness* (wantonness) *which they practiced.*

2. The apostle announces another visit, exhorts them to repentance and warns them that he may not spare. Ch. 13:1, 2.

v. 1 *This is the third time I am coming to you.* The second visit was probably brief and, due to some unknown cause, was not recorded in Acts. It might not have been attended with any special results. *At the mouth* (verbal testimony) *of two witnesses, certainly three,* (emphatic) *every word shall be established.* Quoting thus Deut. 19:5 he warns that he will proceed to deal with justice according to the legal mode of procedure, allegorically symbolized now by the number of his visits in establishing a cause.

v. 2 *I have said beforehand and I do say beforehand, as when I was present* with you on the second visit *and now being absent, to them that have sinned before and to the rest* of the members of the church who need warning, *that if I come*[78] *again* and find them unrepentant and still sinning *I will not spare.*

3. Christ is his strength, let them see to it that He is theirs also. Ch. 13:3-10.

Paul was severe because they demanded proof of his apostolic authority from Christ. That proof they should find in their own religious experience with Christ, who was crucified but yet lives. Paul had used forbearance and they had mistaken it for weakness. He would exhibit his strength in the power of God when he came.

v. 3 *Since you are seeking a proof of the fact that Christ speaks in me,* (Christ would give that proof in his manifest approval on Paul), *who to you-*

---

74. Second aorist participle of *erchomai.*
75. Dative of personal interest in relationship.
76. Present tense of linear action. (Robertson, *Greek N. T. Gr.*).
77. It is probable that Paul had suffered a severe humiliation in a brief visit, being insulted in the public assembly of the church by one of the brazen leaders of the rebellion in the church against Paul.
78. Condition of the third class.

ward is not weak though he was crucified, *but is powerful in you,* working in your salvation.

v. 4 *for he was crucified through* apparent *weakness* as the world sees it, *yet he rose from the dead and liveth, through the* resurrection *power of God. For we also are weak in him* in the same manner as he was weak *but we shall live with him from the power of God toward* or for *you,* when we are there in your midst.

v. 5 *Try yourselves* to see *whether you are* actually *in the faith, prove yourselves* that you are approved by God, *or do you not know definitely* (accurately) *your own selves that Christ Jesus is in you or else that you are not approved.*

v. 6 *I hope that you will know* (definitely) *that we are not without approval,* not mere pretenders, but we are entitled to our claim of apostolic authority.

v. 7 *But we pray to God that you may not do any evil, not in order that we*[79] *may appear* to be *approved, but that you may do* and go on doing habitually that which is *good and* that *we may be as if* (in the judgment of men) *without approval.* Paul was willing even to sacrifice his own reputation among men if he can thus secure the spiritual welfare of his brethren.

v. 8 *For we are not able to do anything against the truth* as his apostles *but on behalf of the truth* we work.

v. 9 *For we rejoice whenever we may be weak or* infirm *and you may be strong* and healthy, *this also we pray for* even *your perfecting,* which is the most desirable result.[80]

v. 10 *On this account, since we pray thus for you success I write these things, being absent, in order that when present, I may not use severity* in my treatment of you, *according to the authority which the Lord gave to me* for building up (for edification) *and not for casting down.* Paul thus affirms with decision positively his apostolic authority in the side of discipline and practice as well as in instruction and edification.

Concluding exhortation (v 11) salutation and benediction (vv 12, 13).

Finally (as to the rest) *brethren, rejoice* and keep on rejoicing, *be perfected* in a progressive growth, *be comforted* and exhorted and encouraged in an ever increasing measure, *keep on thinking the same thing* in spiritual unity, *be at peace,*[81] (v. 11) *and the God of love and of peace will be with you* continually.

v. 12 *Salute one another*[82] *with the holy kiss. All the saints* those in the place where Paul was writing the letter somewhere in Macedonia) *salute*

---

79. Editorial we turning attention away from himself to his group of fellow-workers, so as to fight away from apparent egotism.

80. Ending *sin,* indicating result.

81. Note the present progressive imperative tenses indicating that they should go on progressively and habitually doing the things commanded.

82. Here the aorist tense indicates that this act as a significant occurrence used then but not necessary perpetuated as a Christian habit or custom. At that time it was a form of salutation frequently used among the brethren.

you. The men also saluted one another in the same way, kissing each other on the cheek.

v. 13 *The grace of the Lord Jesus Christ and the love of God, and the communion* (fellowship) *of the Holy Spirit be with you all.* This benediction, presenting all the persons of the Trinity, is the most complete of all the forms of benediction used by Paul in any of his epistles and naturally as a consequence the most usually employed in public worship. This letter was written probably by Paul with his own hand at least in part, Timothy aiding as *amanuensis.* But this sentence at least would be his seal of holy apostolic love, his handwriting serving for identification and expressing his blessing upon the Corinthians. Paul passed through Illyricum en route to Corinth, sending the letter direct by the hand of Titus. It must have stirred the church deeply as it had the desired effect, and Paul soon arrived in Corinth to remain with them for three months, writing the epistle to the Roman church while there.[83]

83 The Galatian Epistle may have been written earlier.

CHAPTER XVI

Paul's Second Visit to Europe

THE APOSTLE'S Ministry in Ephesus was terminated suddenly by the riot promoted by Demetrius. Hostility continued unabated against him, and Paul escaped providentially through the intervention of the brethren and the Asiarchs. Ch. 20:1.

v. 1 *After the riot ceased, Paul having sent for the disciples and exhorted them bade them farewell and departed, to make his way into Macedonia.*

v. 2 *And having made a progress through those parts and exhorted them with many a word, he came into Greece,*

v. 3 *and when he had passed three months and a plot was laid against him by the Jews, as he was about to set sail for Syria, he determined to return through Macedonia.* This brief account is all that Luke recorded (Acts 20: 1-3) of the extensive activities of the apostle during ten of the most strenuous months of his life as a missionary evangelist. This period covers also the writing of three of his most important epistles: II Corinthians, Galatians and Romans. For the filling in of the details of the record, we must have recourse to these epistles, which reveal many incidents of the greatest import and interest relative to the great and rapidly growing movement of Christianity. They also present a vivid picture of the dynamic personality of the man who was the major human factor in it all.

Paul departed from Ephesus by the less perilous route by sea, in company with Trophimus and Tychicus who were Ephesians and faithful brethren who accompanied him all the way to Corinth (Acts 24:4) and also appear later with him in the journey to Jerusalem.

Timothy and Erastus a valiant pastor in the province of Asia, had been sent forward to Macedonia to work in the interest of the collection for the poor saints in Jerusalem, which was one of the major interests of the Apostle at this time. Titus, probably a brother of Luke,[1] had not been with Paul on his second missionary journey from the motive of expediency, but rather Timothy went along who, beng circumcised, would be *persona grata* with the Jews.[2] For the contrary reason, Titus was taken along on the Third Missionary journey. Paul had refused to let him be circumcised in Jerusalem when Gentile liberty was the issue in the Conference and so among Gentile Christians he would now be held in high esteem.[3] Paul had been obliged to have

---

1. Alexander Souter, *Expository Times* 1907.
2. Ramsay, *St. Paul the Traveler* p. 285.
3. Ramsay, *St. Paul the Traveler*, pp. 284-85.

recourse to His policy of expediency, in this choice of workers, in the first and second missionary journeys, in spite of the fact that Titus was greatly useful and prominent in the Apostle's ministry later, in connectión especially with the church in Corinth. There he accomplished with great ability the most difficult tasks assigned to him. He was put in charge of the great work in Crete at a later date, being one of the most efficient workers on the third missionary journey, in the second tour of Paul through Europe. He and one other brother, whose name is not mentioned, were Paul's representatives in charge of the work of raising the collection in Corinth and elsewhere in Greece, in which they succeeded admirably.[4]

'In the fulness of time' Paul had come in his second missionary journey, Spirit-led to Alexandria Troas and in obedience to the divine messenger in the vision, had crossed over the Hellespont, into Europe, attended by three fellow workers as Alexander of Macedonia had over years before crossed with his army of thirty-five thousand men to conquer the hordes of Darius, in Asia. Which was the mightier, Paul or Alexander, history would soon record. Now, he comes back to that city of Troas again, where he could not on the first visit pause for evangelistic activities and finds now in this town of such strategic importance an 'open door' for the preaching of the Word. Titus, whom he had expected to meet here, not having arrived with news from Corinth, Paul, in spite of his ill health and his disappointment because of the non-arrival of Titus, turned his attention for a brief period to evangelistic activities. Some weeks passed and "his spirit had no rest" as he awaited anxiously the coming of Titus with tidings from the Corinthian church. But it was thus that Paul in spite of all untoward circumstances succeeded in laying the foundation for a church in Troas (II Cor. 2:12).

Nevertheless the Apostle was compelled to leave the new church in Troas to go to meet Titus in Macedonia and so he immediately set sail from Troas for Neapolis and Philippi, where he would be embraced in the arms of affection by the church, which had always been eager to show its devotion to him in loyal cooperation. Contributing many times to his material support, this church thus released his energies, to be concentrated on the activities of the ministry of the Word. This was a church commended for its liberality, 'contributing from its poverty and in the' midst of perscutions, arising not only from hostile Jews but also especially from the Roman government which accounted Christianity as a "religio nova et illicita." Unto this church it was given on behalf of Christ, "not only to believe on him but also to suffer for his sake." Paul needed the consolation of such a befriending brotherhood at this time when he was sorely depressed and declared, "my flesh had no rest; without were fightings and within were fears." The "care of all the churches" also was upon him. Would Christianity in Corinth be smothered down by her enemies into a mere sect of the Jews?

4. Cf. II Cor. 2:13; 7:6f., 13f, 8:6f, 16, 24, 12:18.

In Philippi, at last, the long expected Titus arrived with good news that the Corinthian church or the majority at least of its members, now repentant, had dealt with the 'incestuous person' and no longer followed the Judaizing enemies of Paul, who with increasing bitterness falsely charged the Apostle with having mercenary motives and vanity coupled with boldness in threats, but weakness in 'bodily presence.' This stubborn minority in the church would hear from Paul later.

The apostle now moves forward from Philippi after dispatching Titus on a further difficult mission to Corinth, to encourage the Corinthians to go forward with the raising of the collection for the Jerusalem 'poorer brethren.' He planned to spend the summer and autumn of 56 A. D. in Macedonia.[5] Timothy was in Thessalonica or Beroea. Here in the company of this beloved 'son in the faith' the Apostle wrote the Second Epistle to the Corinthians, which in its threefold character was adapted to the needs of a factionally divided and corrupted church, which must become unified around a common Lord and his great common cause.

When Paul had finished writing and dispatching this remarkable letter, his missionary *wanderlust* would not let him rest and he went forward in company with his beloved Timothy on whom he leaned heavily now as the responsible burdens of the cause grew heavier and the antagonisms he must meet became ever fiercer. Titus, older than Timothy and a veteran of much experience, also became a strong protagonist of the aging Apostle, in the carrying out of his plans with the Corinthian church and in the raising of the fund for the Jerusalem 'poorer saints.' He returned from Macedonia with the II Corinthian letter, accompanied by two brethren chosen by the Macedonian churches to take charge of their collection and accompany Paul and others who would bear the fund to Jerusalem.

Paul had given instructions as to how the collection should be raised by systematic giving, in an intelligent and thorough-going stewardship (Chs. 8, 9). He had designed this plan on the basis of Scripture and also with a view to healing the division in the Christian churches, which the Judaizers had striven to create. He spared no pains in carrying out the work of this collection in such a way that the workers would be without reproach. He placed no restraint on anyone in the churches. It was to be a spontaneous offering and he also laid down the basic principles in it, of liberty and liberality. The example of Christ was the final appeal. Each Christian was enjoined to 'lay by him in store on the first day of the week in proportion to the blessing of the Lord upon him (I Cor 16:2). The churches in Macedonia gave a fine example in liberality and in Paul's letter to the Corinthians and churches of the province of Achaia in general (II Corinthians) the Apostle made a clear exposition of the principles of stewardship in giving, as applied to the concrete collection they were raising for the poor. This

5. Sir William Ramsay, *Paul the Traveler* p. 286.

was a test case of the Christian love of Gentile Christians for their Jewish brethren.

Paul had not been able in his second missionary journey to evangelize the whole of Macedonia or Greece. So, after dispatching Titus and his companions with the second Corinthian letter, he took Timothy and set forth to preach the gospel in regions where he had never preached before, north of Greece, penetrating into the mountains of the interior, and possibly beyond, to the shores of the Adriatic.[6] He now fully 'preached the Gospel of Christ round about unto Illyricum.[7] *And when he had gone through those parts, and had given them much exhortation, he came to Greece.* The Illyricum mentioned in the Roman Epistle was probably a "definite district, ruled as a province, by a governor from Rome." It was the Apostle's policy and ambition to preach Christ where He had not yet been proclaimed, so as not to build on another's foundation.[8] Nor do we have any record, for that matter, of his work in Arabia, Judea, Cilicia, Crete, Spain, if to this last place he went as it had been his purpose to do.[9]

Several months must have elapsed to give time for an extensive work in Illyricum, not to say anything of the "much exhortation to the churches in Macedonia," before Paul could enter Greece. He had covered a wide territory and yet had given time enough in the churches in and around Philippi, Thessalonica, Beroæ, and other places evangelized by these churches, during an interval of several years during which Paul labored some time in Athens and also at least eighteen months in Corinth and three years in Ephesus. It was necessary that some months should pass before the final effect of II Corinthians should work out in the turning of the rebellious minority in the church in Corinth, away from the Judaistic leaders to loyalty to the founder of the church.

It would seem that Paul should have received information of the situation in Galatia during the three years in Ephesus. Possibly the inroad of these emissaries might have come as a sudden attack, at the same time that Paul was engrossed most with the trouble in Corinth on the one hand and with the tremendous crisis which came in his work in Ephesus when the riot was precipitated, on the other.

The Lord graciously spared Paul, while under the crushing burden of the apparent disruption of his great work in Ephesus and the distressing trouble caused from the corruption in the morals of the Corinthian church resulting in the final complete rebellion against his apostolic authority, in spite of his earnest endeavors to hold them to the true course. He did not allow the news of the wholesale defection in the Galatian churches to come to him before he arrived in Corinth and found the church there reconciled to him, almost wholly. He could settle down there in the home of Gaius his hospitable friend,

---

6. Conybeare and Howson, *Life and Letters of St. Paul* p. 467
7. Rom. 15:19.
8. Rom. 15:20.
9. A. T. Robertson, *Epochs in the Life of Jesus* p. 200.

who received him with open arms of brotherly affection and filial reverence, to spend the Winter with him before going forward to Jerusalem.

But there was no rest for this veteran servant of the Lord, it seemed, for the news came about the Galatians and it fired him with surprise and consternation but stirred him to the depths and stimulated him to rise to the heights of renewed energy, to deal the final and terrific blow, to crush Judaizers with what proved to be his greatest apologetic of the Christian Faith. This thunderbolt, of more than atomic power, was smelted in the burning crucible of the love of the great heart of the Apostle for the Gentiles. It proved to be the more than sufficient agent of the almost complete obliteration of Judaistic proselytism in the Gentile churches of primitive Christianity!

It was a great blessing that the Apostle found a reconciled church in Corinth. He had written the Second Corinthian epistle in Macedonia, after receiving the report of the success of his First Corinthian letter, reenforced perhaps by the severe arraignment of his Judaistic enemies in a brief severe epistle sent when he received the negative report of Timothy on his return from Corinth. His glad letter (II Cor. Chs. 1-7) and his exhortation to the church (II Cor. Chs. 8, 9) to united activity in the raising of the charity fund for helping the poorer brethren in the church in Jerusalem, had left his enemies in a hopeless minority in the church in Corinth, which dwindled yet more under the withering invective of Paul, to almost complete obliteration, before he arrived from Illyricum, refreshed by the evangelistic experiences of new territory conquered for Christ.

The Apostle addressed himself now to the masterful statement of the doctrine of justification by faith in Christ alone, as he rested from the great activities of ministering to the people of a large area in Europe, whom he had not reached in his second missionary journey. Timothy had been with him in that trip through the interior regions and was his strong young helper when he received the news of the Galatian defection. Paul had previously exposed the Judaistic minority in Corinth with an invective in which he employed irony, ridicule, sarcasm, denunciation and a threat to use the rod if necessary when he should come. It was a time, when he must lift up his voice and spare not.[10]

From the gigantic task of producing this great polemic, which uprooted the work of the Judaists, held yet as he was in the loving embrace of the Christian hospitality of the home of his loyal friend Gaius, this great missionary statesman addressed himself during the remaining part of the winter spent in Corinth, in laying foundations for his long cherished visit to the church in Rome in the interests of his larger plans of evangelization in other countries and nationalities yet unevangelized. He would soon conclude the extensive plan of the collection in the Gentile churches for the much needed help of the "poor saints" in the Jerusalem church. He understood that there would be bitter antagonism in a reaction from his personal enemies against

---

10. II Cor. 12:12; 13:2, 10.

him in Jerusalem. For him life would henceforth have many perils wherever he should go. He also recognized that he must personally administer the funds for the poor members in the Jerusalem church. But he would do it through loyal fellow-laborers, who must needs go with him to Jerusalem before he could carry out his fond hope of at last reaching Rome, the capital of the Roman Empire. That was the greatest strategic center from which he must operate henceforth in his evangelism in Spain and other countries, in the strategic centers of which he hoped to plant the gospel.

During the rest of his stay in Corinth, his personal presence would be sufficient to iron out any remaining difficulties in the Corinthian church. Thus he was able to turn all his attention to writing a letter to the Roman church, preparing the way for his visit to them and enlisting them in his plan of Empire-wide evangelization. He had never visited this important church and he magnified his authorial office, in the composition of an epistle which would become the instrument in their indoctrination in the fundamental and complete statement of the plan of salvation and the planting in their minds of the great missionary ideal and supreme mission of Christianity. This letter was personal to them but would become Paul's greatest work in the use of his pen to forward the interests of the gospel in the world. He had serious forebodings about his necessary visit in Jerusalem, as to what might be the outcome for him. If his life should be terminated as his enemies might devise, he would have left a complete statement of the plan of salvation which would serve as a basis for those who should follow him in the work of world-wide evangelization. This fondest hope the apostle must have had in his mind as the threatening storm clouds hovered over his immediate future as he "set his face" like his Master had done shortly before his crucifixion, under similar conditions, "to go to Jerusalem." That he must go there and face his enemies was clear to him.[11] And even now a plot of his enemies was disclosed to fall upon him in Cenchrea, the port where he was to embark for Jerusalem. If they should fail to kill him there, it would yet be easy for them to carry out their murderous plan aboard the ship, and if not there, surely in Jerusalem, where the nest of his most rancorous antagonists were awaiting his next appearance in their midst.

---

11. David Smith, *Life and Letters of St. Paul* in loco.

CHAPTER XVII

Galatians

Introduction

THE VALUE of the Epistle to the Galatians for Historical Christianity. It is one of the earliest authentic basic documents. In it are set forth the fundamental principles of Paul's theology, further elaborated mainly in Romans and also in his other epistles. His interpretation of the Christianity of the Risen Lord in this treatise declares for its universality and its independence of the traditional Judaism. He "takes up the iconoclastic cudgel and hammers his way through the idols of a superceremonial and legalistic religion to spiritual emancipation and freedom for all mankind."[1]

2. Authorship, date and location of writing.

The authorship of this brief letter has never been seriously questioned, but about the date and locality of its writing there is a wide range of opinion. Matter and style alike point to the authorship of the great Apostle to the Gentiles. None of his Epistles are more certainly genuine or reflect more clearly Paul's intense spirituality and absolute devotion to the Lord. Some would make this the earliest of the epistles, but the predominance of scholarship today places it within the group of great epistles following the Thessalonian letters (A.D. 50-51) and the two canonical letters to the Corinthians (A.D. 55-57), and before Romans (A.D. 57-58). Thus it would be after the Conference in Jerusalem (A.D. 49) over Gentile Liberty, referred to in Acts 15 and Galatians 2:1-10. When Paul reached Corinth in late autumn or early spring (A.D. 55 or 56) (Acts 20:1) he received news of the damage done in Galatia by the Judaizers. The struggle with the false Judaistic teachers had grown during this period. It is possible to note from the teaching of the two Corinthian Epistles and Galatians an increase in the suffering of the Apostle. At this time there is an evolution also in the defense of his apostolic authority from Second Corinthians to Galatians and of the doctrine of justification, merely mentioned in the second Corinthian Epistle but pungently argued in Galatians and elaborated in Romans. Paul had already won in his fight against the Judaizers in Corinth and now, hurls the Galatian epistle like a thunderbolt at the Judaists in Galatia. Luther used the epistle in the same way against corrupted historic Christianity in the sixteenth century, bringing on thus the great Reformation. It has served as a bulwark against a hostile and wild criticism which recently sought in vain "to remove the Paul-

1. *The Expositors Greek Test.* Vol. Galatians, Introduction in loco.

ine Epistles from the realm of historical study" (Robertson). The contention that the place of writing the Epistle was Philippi, Ephesus or Syrian Antioch is not so well founded.

3. The Galatian Churches and the Destination of the Epistle.

The location of the Galatian Churches to which the Epistle was directed has been much discussed over a long period. The so-called Northern Galatian theory, advocated ably by Lightfoot, held that Ancyra, Pessino and Tavium were evangelized by Paul on his second missionary journey and visited later as he went to Ephesus on his third journey. This hypothesis does not accord well with a number of facts of the historic development of Christianity in Asia Minor. Paul's break with the Judaizers came in Antioch of Syria between the first and second journeys. The first attack by the Judaists in Antioch of Syria in which the church was seriously stirred, was defeated in the subsequent Conference in Jerusalem (Acts 15). An obstinate minority from Jerusalem carried the fight to Antioch again later in an intrigue but there Paul successfully stemmed the tide and "withstood Peter," who was yielding to the influence of the Judaists. Following this, Paul and Silas visited the churches founded in the first Missionary Journey by Paul and Barnabas in South Galatia and fully established the independence of Greek Christianity. For a while the Judaists were not able to make much headway, but after Paul's second visit to these churches on his way to Ephesus they followed the missionary party and were successful in seriously undermining the Galatian brethren whom Paul had left "running well."

These churches had been established on the principal highway through the center of Asia Minor from West to East, the most strategic part of the country, both from the character of the population and of the strategic towns and cities and from the nature of the civilization which would lend itself to founding an aggressive and self-propagating Christianity. Paul here found a suitable enviroment for working out a Christianity free from and independent of the ceremonial bondage of a narrow, traditional Judaism. Here he could show that Christianity was not a mere sect of the ancient national church of the Jews but a new interpretation of the promises to Abraham and of Mosaism, and was a spiritual religion. It was to these churches of Southern Galatia that Paul directed the Epistle. This conclusion is confirmed, by the leading part assigned to the Galatian Churches in the collection for the poor saints in Jerusalem.[2]

4. Background History of the Judaistic Opposition and of the Founding of the Galatian Churches.

Seventy-five years before the writing of this Epistle Galatia had been formed into a single province of the Roman Empire. It included the regions known in this discussion as Northern and Southern Galatia, the latter including Southern Phrygia, and parts of Lycaonia and Pisidia. It was in southern Galatia that Paul and Barnabas wrought out their successful ministry, found-

---

2. Cf. Rendall, F., *The Expositor's Greek Testament*. Com. Galatians, Introduction.

ing the churches in Antioch of Pisidia, Iconium, Lystra and Derbe. In these churches the Greek members constituted an overwhelming majority and the Jews were a decided minority. The conditions in Asia Minor, at the place of confluence of Eastern Oriental thought and religion with western or Greek and Roman Religions and philosophies and the Jewish religion as a third factor, were favorable to the entrance of Christianity. The new and large influx of Gentiles into the ranks of Christianity in Asia Minor and their hearty reception of the new universal salvation in Jesus Christ, offered by the preaching of Paul and Barnabas, aroused in the Jews intense jealousy and brought on bitter opposition. This antagonism culminated at Antioch of Syria, where the Jews first heard the impotence of their law announced in their own synagogue and the new way of salvation set forth through repentance and faith alone in Christ Jesus. To them henceforth Paul became the most formidable opponent of Judaism.

It is likely that Paul's original plan was to go first to Ephesus, the great strategic city near the western extremity of Asia Minor, a veritable gateway between Asia and Europe. But his plan was changed by the Holy Spirit, and the conversion of the Galatians became the first step in the evangelization of Asia Minor.

On his second missionary journey Paul revisited, this time with Silas, the Galatian Churches, leaving them in a progressive and prosperous condition before he initiated the work in Europe. Three years later he came on a third missionary journey and visited again these favorite churches. After he left them this time the Judaizers revived their work of undermining and succeeded in seriously demoralizing these churches in Southern Galatia, causing widespread defection. This was the occasion of Paul's writing this Epistle, when the news of the instability and defection of the Galatian Christians reached him.

5. General Character and Content of the Epistle.

After Paul passed through southern Galatia on his third missionary journey, visiting churches which he and Barnabas had founded years before, the Judaizers came, and, during a period covering two or three years, sowed the seed of their false doctrines. They carefully inculcated the teaching that the Law of Moses was of divine origin and the promises antedating the Law had been given to Abraham and thus pertained to the Jews. Jesus, the Christian Messiah, was a Jew and had scrupulously "observed all righteousness" by keeping and honoring the Mosaic Law. He had been circumcised on the eighth day and had followed out consistently all the ritual of the system of Moses. These false teachers thus insisted that the example of Jesus should be followed by Gentile Christians and they should therefore be circumcised. (Galatians 5:2, 11; 6:12,13). They should also rigorously observe, as He did, all the law (Galatians 3:2; 4:21; 5:4,18) including the observance of days and months (Galatians 4:10).

In order to undermine Paul's work and get for themselves the leadership in these Greek Churches, they attacked insidiously the personal character and conduct of the Apostle in order to destroy his apostolic influence and authority. They said, first, that Paul was not one of the Apostles, as Peter, James and John, the great "pillars of the Church." They themselves had come from Jerusalem and falsely claimed to have the teaching and backing of those Apostles. These Galatian brethren should give heed to those Apostles in Jerusalem and not to Paul. They reinforced this counsel by pointing out the inconsistency of Paul in having Timothy, one of his adepts and ministers, circumcised, after refusing, in Jerusalem, to allow Titus to be forced to submit to that rite. (Galatians 5:11; Acts 16:3). This repudiation of the rite in Paul's teaching they said was to please and thus gain the favor of the Gentiles (Galatians 1:1; 2:3; 5:2,11). This was, they declared, a bald inconsistency. They also attacked the character and conduct of Paul in many other points, seeking to tear down the Apostle's reputation and influence so that they might undermine thus his doctrinal teaching and defeat altogether his work in the spreading of the Gospel.

Paul recognized that their contention for circumcision and the observance of the whole law as a part of the plan of salvation was subversive of the very spirit of Christianity itself and destructive of the true faith. If Christ was not sufficient in Himself to save men but circumcision and the law must be added for the Christian to be saved, then Christ had died in vain.

Paul began his refutation of their heresy by an indignant denunciation of it in which he declared it to be a perversion of the true Gospel which he had preached to the Galatians. These brethren should not listen, he urged, to any other Gospel than that which he had preached, even though an angel should come and announce a different Gospel to them.

Paul perceived the necessity of vindicating his apostolic authority before stating to them plainly the principles of the Gospel, which was the main purpose of the Epistle. He had been the champion of Gentile liberty and his antagonists must not be allowed to discredit his authority as a teacher if he was to win out in this conflict. The circumstances of his strenuous life presented some favorable opportunities for their insidious and slanderous attack on his character and his claim to be an apostle.

In the first two chapters of the Epistle Paul repelled the attack against his apostolic authority and character. He affirmed first his apostolic authority (Gal. 1:1) as derived from Jesus Christ and God the Father by whom he was called. He next states that he did not receive his Gospel from the apostles but from the Risen Christ (1:12). He had departed for Arabia immediately after his conversion and spent there many months in rethinking his Jewish theology learned at the feet of Gamaliel, converting it into a Christo-centric system around the Risen Lord, whom he saw and from whom he received his commission to the Gentiles (Acts IX and XXVI). The Pillar-Apostles had added nothing to this revelation he had from the Risen Christ, but gave their approval on his work among the Galatians and other Gentiles when he met them in the Jerusalem Conference (Galatians 2:6,9). Another evidence of his independence was that he "withstood Peter," who, after opening the door to the

Gentile converts in the house of Cornelius in Caesarea, had later withdrawn his table-fellowship from Gentile Christians in Syrian Antioch. On that occasion Peter and Barnabas had been won back by Paul after their temporary defection, and Gentile liberty was maintained. Paul did not feel it needful to defend himself against the charge of inconsistency (1:10). His whole character was that of one whose motive was to win men to Christ, and, in a right sense, he "became all things to all men" in order to do this.

The more important part of the Epistle bears the clear statement as to the character of the true Gospel, which offers salvation through faith without the works of the Law. In the third and fourth Chapters of the Epistle Paul presents his incomparable statement of the fundamental principle of the Christian faith. He first called attention to the fact that these Christians in Galatia had received as they well knew, the Holy Spirit in regeneration through faith and not through the works of the Law (3:1-5). He next cited the example of Abraham, who was justified by faith and not by the works of the Law, which came centuries later (3:6-9). Then he pointed to the negative character of the work of the Law which becomes a curse when depended upon for salvation (3:10-14). Again he reminds them that the Law did not annul the promises that were made to Abraham, which antedated the Law by four hundred years.

What then was the value of the Law? Paul showed that the Law did a great work of preparation for the coming of the Gospel. It served as the pedagogue (servant) to lead the "children" to the school of Christ (3:24). In his masterful use of the allegory (Ch. 4) he showed the transience of legalistic bondage and the permanence of Christian liberty of the spiritual Israel. Responding to the accusation of his enemies "that his gentile liberty had degenerated into the moral abandon of libertines," he vindicated the doctrine of Christian liberty and exhorted the Greek Christians to stand firm in their Christian liberty (5:1-12) and not to submit themselves to the slavery of Jewish ritual. At the same time he warned them against using their liberty to "give occasion to the flesh" (5:13-6:10).

In his autograph written in large letters at the end of the Epistle (6:11-18), Paul contrasted his unselfish interest in them with the selfish interest of the Judaists who wished to glory in their flesh, while he gloried rather in the Cross of Christ. The proof of his sincerity was to be found in the scars received in the persecution in Lystra and elsewhere. They would remember, when he was stoned and left for dead on the rubbish heap outside the city, where he was rescued by friends of the house of Eunice, the mother of young Timothy, and by others.

Analysis and Exegesis

The epistle is divided naturally into three sections of two chapters each. In the first two chapters the Apostle Paul vindicates his apostolic authority; in the second, which is apologetic and of the nature of refutation, he sets forth the plan of salvation, presenting the doctrine of justification by faith alone and refuting the error of his enemies; and in the third, he exhorts the Galatian Christians to firmness in the faith, and against the abuse of their liberty in Christ. This is an application of the true gospel in human conduct.[3]

I Personal vindication of defense of his apostolic authority. Chapters I, II. The apostle was addressing all the professing Christians in Galatia, especially the Gentile converts. The Judaizers were insidiously seeking to divide the churches, by insisting, against the decision of the Jerusalem Conference, that a Jewish Christian who kept the law was better than a Gentile Christian who did not observe the ceremonial law, because the Jew, they said, had the Gospel plus the Law. This classification of the members of the church into the good and better Christians would naturally split all the churches along the line of racial cleavage, which has ever been a most subversive and divisive element in Christianity everywhere since.

Introduction. Ch. I: 1-10

A. Salutation and praise, with the introductory word about his apostolic authority. Ch. 1:1-5.

v. 1 *Paul an apostle,* though not of the Twelve,[4] *not from men,* man or humanity as a source, nor through[5] the agency of *man* (or mankind) *but through* the agency of *Jesus Christ,* both the divine Savior and Messiah, classed here as on equality with God in the transaction of Paul's call to apostleship; *and God, the Father;*[6] *who raised Him from the dead.* The claim of his independent apostleship, not dependent on the Twelve for its origin or projected through man or mankind as its agent, is stated in the very opening sentence of the epistle to assert Paul's apostolic authority to found churches in Galatia or anywhere, independently of any authorization of the Twelve or the church in Jerusalem, or even that in Antioch. His enemies were denying bitterly his apostleship because he had not been ordained by the church in Jerusalem, which they claimed as the mother church. The Father and Jesus his Son whom the Father raised from the dead, the Risen Messiah, had called him into apostleship.

v. 2 *Also all the brethren with me* are included as participants, being my fellow-workers, and the Christian churches of western Asia and Europe, in representation at least,[7] together address our salutation *to the churches* of the Roman province *of Galatia,* which churches are located in Southern Galatia, in the sphere of the missionary operation of Paul and Barnabas, on the first missionary journey, and the churches in Northern Galatia if there were such at the time, which is not probable.

---

3. Cf. Dana. H. E. *The Life and Literature of Paul,* in loco.
4. Paul bluntly denies the charge of the Judaists "that he is not a genuine apostle because not of the Twelve."
5. *Dia* with the genitive case denotes intermediate agency.
6. He was an apostle commissioned by Christ but also by the will or wish of God.
7. Paul did not mention the names of the brethren desiring to take personally all the responsibility.

v. 3 *Grace,* the unmerited favor of God, we wish *to you and peace* based on faith in Christ and coming *from God* our Father *and the* divine *Lord Jesus Christ,* who is the true Messiah,

v. 4 *who gave himself,* as the only Savior, in atonement *on behalf of our sins,* vicariously, *that*[8] *he might lead us out* in deliverance from the bondage of sin[9] *from the present evil age,* as symbolized in the work of Moses, who led Israel out from the physical bondage of Egypt, and that, *according to the will of God our Father,* who wishes the salvation of all men, and not the destruction of any,

v. 5 *to whom* let there be ascribed *the glory* and honor in praise (forever and ever), *unto the ages of the ages* of time and eternity. *Amen,* so let it be.

B. Rebuke of the Galatian Christians for their inconstancy (v. 6,7); denunciation of the false teachers who pervert the gospel, at whom he hurls an anathema; and a clear declaration of the true character of the gospel he had preached to the Galatians. He had not sought to please men, as they accused, but God. 1:6-10. Alarming news had reached Paul of the rapid defection of the Galatians and that in only a suprisingly brief period after his last visit to them when they were running well. The intrigue of the Judaistic emissaries from Jerusalem was a plot to defeat Paul's work and revive Pharisaic Judaism with its plan of making proselytes among the Gentiles, by first subverting the Apostle's influence and undermining his apostolic authority. They accused him of an inordinate desire to please men, which he here refuted.[10] He had set faith as his principle of action, tactful efficiency and expediency but not compromise when he said, "he became all things to all men in order that he might save some." They had misinterpreted him, as adopting the way of compromise, in order to be popular. But his motive was to win souls to Christ, and not by compromise.

v. 6 With surprise and indignation the Apostle says: *I marvel* (am wondering), *that you are so quickly,* after my recent visit and so easily, after the coming of the Judaizers, *removing*[11] (*transferring*) *yourselves over from him* (God the Father) *who called you in* the sphere of *the grace*[12] *of Christ into* another and *a different gospel;*

v. 7 *Which is not* in reality *another*[13] gospel: *only* (except in the sense that) *there are some* (certain ones) *troubling you and would* (are wishing to) *pervert the* true and only *gospel of Christ.*[14]

v. 8 *But though* (even if) *we*[15] (I) should turn renegade to Christianity, *or* even *an angel from heaven should* appear and *preach*[16] *unto you any gospel*

---

8. *Hopōs* with aroist middle subjunctive in a final clause expressing purpose or plan.
9. The gospel is a rescue or emancipation by Christ from the bondage of sin.
10. Cf. v. 10.
11. Present Indicative active of continued action of *metatithēmi.*
12. Locative case preferable but instrumental case 'by the grace of Christ,' possible here also. Cf. Ep. 2:8, 10.
13. No gospel or good news at all but a yoke of bondage to the law.
14. Present active participle continued action in process at the time.
15. Literary plural of the pronoun used for emphasis.
16. *Ean* with aorist subjunctive middle *enangellizētai,* general third class condition unfulfilled.

other than (not in accord with) *that which we preached unto you, let him be anathema* (accursed).

v. 9 *As we have said before,*[17] *so* (I) *say now again, If any* man *is preaching unto you*[18] *any gospel, other than* (not in accordance with) *that which you received* from me,[19] *let him be anathema* (accursed).

v. 10 *For, am I now persuading men or (of) God? Or am I striving to please men? If I were still pleasing men* [20] as I am not, *I should not be a servant of Christ.* Paul felt there was condemnation outside his gospel and was not seeking popular favor but to please God.

C. Personal apologetic defense of his apostolic independence of all human authority by receiving the gospel directly from the risen Christ. The purpose of Paul's vindication of himself against the charge of the Judaizers, that the Apostle had received his gospel from human sources. 1:11-2:21.

1. Paul did not receive his authority for preaching or his gospel from men, but immediately from God through the intermediate agent of revelation, Christ Jesus. 1:11, 12. Answering the charge of his Judaizing enemies 'that he had not received his commission from the Jerusalem church and the Twelve', Paul states here his claim to apostolic authority from Jesus Christ Himself whom he saw in person after his resurrection.

v. 11 *For, I make known to you, brethren* of the Christian faith, *as touching the* character of the *gospel, which was preached by me, that it is not according to man,* merely human in its character or mediated by an apostle of mere human commission having its origin in the Twelve.

v. 12 *For neither did I receive it from man,* the Twelve Apostles in Jerusalem or human source, *nor was I taught it by* mere *human* teachers (as Gamaliel) *but* it came to me *through the revelation,*[21] by God *of Jesus Christ,*[22] when Jesus appeared as the resurrected Messiah and when God the Father revealed, in Paul's experience, Jesus Christ, as the content of the Gospel.

2. The evidences proving his independence of all human authority, cited from his experience of conversion. His former zeal in persecuting the church showed his independance. 1:13-14.

v. 13 Paul first cites his experiences before his conversion. *For you have heard*[23] *of my manner of life in time past,* before my conversion, *when I* was yet *in Judaism,* the traditional religion of my Jewish fathers, *That beyond measure I was continually persecuting*[24] *the church of God,* the Christian church, *and made havoc of it,* destroying it persistently.[25]

---

17. Perfect tense indicating conviction and reflective thought.
18. Present tense of progressive action in process currently.
19. Aorist indicative active, actual occurrence at a given time.
20. Second class condition ei with imperfect indicative *ēreskon*, contrary to fact.
21. *Apokalupseōs*, revelation, the taking off of the covering.
22. Cf. Acts 9. This was not an hallucination but a real vision. Cf. James S. Stewart, *A Man in Christ* pp. 124ff.
23. Constative aorist covering a period of time when they had heard it various times.
24. Imperfect tense here denoting continued action, *edikon*, was persecuting.
25. Imperfect of continued action, *eporthoun.*

v. 14 *And I advanced*[26] *in* the knowledge of this traditional *Judaism*,[27] *beyond many of my own age, in my own race, being more exceedingly zealous* than they *for the religious traditions of my fathers*. In the midst of such persecuting activities against the gospel of Christ, it is evident that Paul was not in any condition to receive, from the apostles of the Christianity which he was harrowing, any teaching about the gospel. His zeal for the Judaistic religion, with all the traditional accretions of humanly devised ceremonialism and legalism, was unbounded, and he was indeed "as touching the Law, a Pharisee." Paul's conversion was but the beginning of the apocalypse or revelation of the resurrected, living Jesus Christ, in many other subsequent visions and an interminable string of vital experiences, in which Christ became more known to him.

3. He did not receive his gospel through the Apostles of the circumcision. 1:15-17. Paul's independent apostleship was witnessed to in the circumstances of his conversion and call to be the apostle to the Gentiles, followed by his immediate withdrawal into Arabia for reflection and the rethinking of his Jewish theology. He did not go to Jerusalem to consult with the apostles of the circumcision, in the work of recasting his theology, in which Christ was to be the center. (vv 15-17):

v. 15 *And*[28] *when it was the good pleasure* of God, the one *who set me apart* for this work even *from my mother's womb*, (at the time of my birth,) *and called me, through* the means and disposition of *his grace*,

v. 16 *to reveal his Son* Jesus Christ *in me*, as at the time of my conversion, visibly bringing me for the first time to know him as the risen Jesus and the living divine Messiah, and who since that time is constantly revealed more and more in my experience, *that I* might *go on preaching him among the Gentiles, immediately I conferred not with flesh and blood;*

v. 17 *Neither went I up to Jerusalem to them* that were *apostles before me*, (in order of time but not in rank), *but I went away into Arabia* (probably near Sinai); *and again*, after some time, (parts of three years probably as the Jews counted time), *I returned again*[29] *unto Damascus.*

These facts, narrated simply, of his movements immediately after his conversion, show conclusively that the apostle did not derive his commission of apostleship from the twelve apostles, who were with Jesus through his ministry, nor from the Jerusalem church. He had his gospel directly from the resurrected Lord Jesus Christ whom he saw on the Damascus Way and who later revealed to him through Ananias his servant in Damascus, that he (Paul) was commissioned by Him to go forth as the apostle to the Gentiles. Every minister of the gospel should have recourse primarily to his divine call to the ministry

---

26. Was cutting my way forward *proekopton.*
27. Tradional Judaism was not much like Mosaism of the Jewish religion in its pristine purity.
28. *De* illative, and, instead of but.
29. Paul had preached in Damascus immediately after his conversion and so *palin.*

by God through Jesus Christ and not recognize finality in any human order or even in the church, which should only approve the call, when it is duly recognized in the character and vocation of the called.

4. Furthermore, on his first visit in Jerusalem after his conversion, there was no sufficient opportunity for him to receive the gospel system of thought, for lack of time, since the visit was limited to fifteen days. 1:18-20. The apostle had received in the vision of the resurrected Christ, on the Damascus road, a new center for his theology, which thus must of necessity suffer a revolutionary revision, being as it was the Jewish theological system of thought, which he had learned at the feet of Gamaliel. Paul went to Arabia not to carry on a campaign of evangelization, as someone peculiarly surmised,[29a] but to rethink his theology, based on the Old Testament Scriptures, in the light of the "apocalypse" or revelation through and in Jesus Christ. He must have remained there parts of three years, and his ministry in Damascus, before and after his residence in Arabia, would make approximately three full years after his conversion and first entrance into Damascus.

v. 18 *Then, after three years*[30] (during which Paul had not even seen any one of the Twelve) *I went up to Jerusalem* for the first time after my conversion *to* visit and *get acquainted*[31] *with Cephas* (Peter) *and I remained with him* exactly *fifteen days,* which was not enough time to receive the kind of reflected gospel I preach.

v. 19 So Peter did not start Paul on this apostleship[32] (Robertson). *And no other of the apostles did I see at* all *except James,*[33] (an apostolic man but not of the Twelve), *the* (half) *brother of the Lord* Jesus. Paul visited Peter and James as equals and did not receive any commission from them. James and Barnabas were called apostles. They were apostolic men.

v. 20 *Now* as respects *the things which I write to you, behold,* and solemnly take notice, *before God, I am not lying.* His enemies had accused Paul of being a slick talker. He asserts his genuineness by a solemn affirmation, made as in the very presence of God. His Word was as good as his oath, as Christ had taught in his Sermon on the Mount every Christian's word should be, thus making the oath unnecessary in Christian dealing. But Paul was dealing with professed and not real Christians.

The apostle had been preaching the gospel in Damascus for a while before going to Arabia and for a longer time after returning from Arabia, before he went up to Jerusalem for his personal and friendly visit with Peter and other apostles. The disciples in Jerusalem were afraid of him and it was necessary that Barnabas should present him to the church. He preached for a brief

---

29a. Zahu, *Neue Kirche Zeitschr.* 1904 pp. 34-41.

30. Cf. Acts 20:31 and 19:8, 10, 22.

31. First Aor. infinitive of *historeō*, to gain knowledge by visiting.

32. Cf. Robertsons *Word Pictures*, Vol. on Paul's Epistles p. 220.

33. There were four half-brothers of Jesus.

time in Jerusalem but had to leave because of persecutors and was spirited out of the city by his brethren and went to Tarsus, Silicia and Syria.[34]

5. Moreover, Paul's extensive and lengthy ministry in the regions of Syria and Cilicia was an evidence of his independent commission and apostleship. Ch. 1:21-24. This ministry covered a number of years, during which the Apostle tested out his rethought theology and his new Christo-centric gospel.[35] 1:21-24.

v. 21 *Then, I went into the regions of Syria and Cilicia,* which I certainly would not have done under the direction of the apostles of the circumcision, because these were provinces of the Roman Empire, composed of Gentile peoples mainly.

v. 22 *And, I* have *continued to remain unknown,*[36] *by face, to the churches of Judea,* Samaria and Galilee, *which were in Christ.* It would have been in in these parts that Paul, had he been an apostle, commissioned by the Twelve, would have worked. He was known in Jerusalem by face, because he scattered that church in the persecution he waged against them, putting them to flight and even pursuing them and dragging them when found to prison and to death also in certain cases.

v. 23 *But they,* members of those churches *kept on hearing* from time to time, *only that he who was persecutor then* (in times past) is *now* (announcing) *preaching the* (Christian) *faith of which he was then* (formerly) *making havoc* (ravaging),

v. 24 *and they were glorifying God,* seeing his grace demonstrated *in me,* especially in my conversion, from a persecutor to a preacher of the gospel of Christ.

6. Again, the decisive independence of Paul's apostleship was clearly evidenced on the occasion of the Conference in Jerusalem Ch. 2:1-10. In the Conference at Jerusalem the fourteenth year after Paul's conversion, the Judaists were defeated in their defense of the 'permanence of the ceremonial law', against the impact of the aggressive work of Paul and Barnabas in the first missionary journey.

Ch. II, v. 1. *Then,* (following chronologically), *after fourteen years I again*[37] *went up to Jerusalem with Barnabas, taking along with me also Titus,* A Greek convert to Christianity. This was after the ministry of Paul in Cilicia and when

---

34. Cf. Acts 9:26-30. Pauls ministry in Tarsus and Cilicia following this covered from seven to nine years. Cf. also David Smith's *Life and Letters of St. Paul,* (Chronology).

35. Some estimate the length of this ministry covering that in Antioch of Syria to be from eleven to fourteen years cf. E. Burton *ICC.* David Smith's estimate is nine years, vide *Life and Letters of St. Paul.*

36. *Emen de ognoumenos,* periphrastic imperfect passive of agnotō; not to know. So he continued to be unknown by face or personal acquaintance to the churches in Palestine (i. e. Galilee, Samaria and Judea).

37. Paul skips over a second appearance in Jerusalem with Barnabas, bearing alms for the poor saints, Acts 11:30. Peter was not in Jerusalem at the time (Acts 12:17) and the other apostles were not mentioned either.

he had been summoned by Barnabas to help in the evangelistic campaign in Antioch of Syria.

v. 2 *And I went up in accordance with* (in obedience to) *a* special *revelation,* and after their first missionary journey and return to Antioch. Paul was acting under the direction and guidance of the Holy Spirit. *And I laid before them,* the Christians in Jerusalem in public assembly of the Jerusalem church, *the Gospel which I preach*[38]*among the Gentiles; but privately* also *before them of repute,* who were the apostolic leaders of the church, *lest perchance I should be running or had run in vain.* Paul recognized that the disapproval of the apostles and Jerusalem church or some of the members of it might undo what he and his fellow-workers had already done on the first missionary journey. He wanted to maintain unity and fellowship with the brethren in Jerusalem thus avoiding a split in Christianity.

v. 3 *But not even Titus,* [39] *who was with me, being a Greek* convert, admitted into the church without circumcision, *was compelled*[40] *to be circumcised,* in spite of the counsel of the apostles, under the influence of the Judaists. In this test case, since Paul's view prevailed, the authority of Paul was demonstrated beyond question, to be independent. He and Barnabas had not been preaching Gentile liberty in vain, but on the contrary had won now the full approval of the leaders in Jerusalem, especially of the apostles, Peter, James, and John.

v. 4 *And on account of the false brethren* privately brought in slyly into the membership of the Jerusalem church, *who came in* (slipped in unexpectedly, surreptitiously) *privily, to spy out,* making a treacherous investigation *of our* spiritual *liberty, which we have in Christ Jesus, that they might* (shall certainly) *bring us into bondage*[41] to the ceremonial law, which they wished to accomplish by pressure on the apostles. So Peter, James and John at first were counseling Paul and Barnabas to compromise the individual matter of Titus' circumcision and thus preserve the unity between the Jewish church in Jerusalem and the Gentile church in Antioch, a matter so very important for the unity of the fast spreading Christianity. Paul's keen perception of the issues of this 'test case' of Titus, led him to stand firmly for the fundamental principle and win thus the victory for Gentile liberty. These false brethren were native to Jerusalem.[42] The pressure was brought to bear by them in the private meeting of the apostles, with Paul and Barnabas, after the first public assembly of the church to hear Paul, and Barnabas, which ended in a question being raised by the false brethren.

---

38. Paul was still preaching, when he wrote this epistle the same gospel he had preached at the time of the Conference. Vede Present indicative active of *kērussō.*

39. A brother of Luke who wrote the third gospel and the Acts.

40. Aor. Pass. Indicative of *anagkazo,* be compelled. Paul withstood the force successfully.

41. A *Katadoulōsousin,* future indicative active after hina, never in classical Greek, definite expectation of success.

42 Cf. E. Burton *ICC.* Gal. p. 78f.

v. 5 *to whom, we gave place* (yielded) *in* the way of *subjection*,[44] *no, not for an hour; in order that the truth of the gospel might continue* (remain) *with you.* The whole future of Gentile Christianity was bound up in the test case of the circumcision of Titus. The way the decision went here would determine whether Christianity would be a modified legalistic type of Judaism or a religion of the spiritual Israel, the true sons of Abraham.[44] Paul contended for the principle of spirituality in religion and won the fight. The truth of the good tidings of the Gospel is. "that man is justified for the sake of the merits of Jesus Christ by faith in Him, and not for man's own works or deservings."[45]

v. 6 *But from those who were reputed to be somewhat* (who had a high reputation) — (*whatever they* once *were, makes no difference to me; God accepts no man's person*), *for to me, they of* reputation (eminent men) *imparted nothing* new of doctrinal or experiencial understanding of the gospel,

v. 7 *but on the contrary, seeing that I had been intrusted*[46] *with the gospel of the uncircumcision, just as Peter with that of the circumcision,* —

v. 8 (For he who *wrought*[47] *in Peter for the apostleship of the circumcision wrought in me also for* the apostleship unto *the Gentiles*);

v. 9 *And when,* I say, *they perceived*[48] *the grace which was given unto me, James and Cephas and John, who were reputed to be pillars* of the church, *gave to me and Barnabas* the right hands *of fellowship, that we should go unto the Gentiles and they unto the circumcison,* (unto the Jews).

v. 10 *Only* they wished *that we should remember the* poor saints in Jerusalem; *which very thing I was also zealous* (made haste) *to do.*

Paul recognized Peter's apostleship to the Jews in the work of the gospel, and here says that Peter and James and John recognized his apostleship to the Gentiles. This was a complete answer to the Judaists who had been undermining his apostolic authority in Galatia. The signs and wonders of God's approval were manifest in the work of Paul and Barnabas in their missionary campaign and the apostles in Jerusalem saw this manifestation of the "grace of God" which was the cause of their success. They "gave to them the right hands of fellowship," in token of their approval, and as a pledge of fidelity to the agreement to work together in their respective spheres. This was in general a division of territory into 'spheres of influence'; but the work of alms, of brotherly love and charity, had no distinct spheres of labor or influence. Paul was glad of this more complete Gospel unity of labors, working together in giving and receiving in fraternal mutuality.

7. Again, Paul's independence of all human authority, in his apostleship, is witnessed by his rebuking Peter in Antioch for his inconstancy in his relation to Gentile Christians Ch. 2:11-21.

---

43. Locative of sphere within which, *hupotagei.*
44. Cf. A. T. Robertson, *Word Pictures,* Gal. p. 284.
45. *Perowne,* E. H. Camb. *Bible.* Gal. p. 17.
46. Perfect tense, denoting completed action and present status, *pepisteumai.*
47. Constative aorist active indicative, occurrences in a period, miracles and signs.
48. Second aorist participle of *ginoskō,* perceive.

In this incident of the rebuke of Peter, the chief apostle among the Jews, by Paul, the argument of the independence of Paul's apostleship reaches a climax. How could Paul then receive his gospel from Peter or any other man,[49] after rebuking this chief of the apostles?

v. 11 *And when Cephas came to Antioch* soon after the Jerusalem Conference, and, under the influence of Judaists, retracted from his initial stand on arrival for Gentile and Jewish social equality in the fellowship of the Antiochian church, and separated himself from the Gentile Christians; *I withstood him,* as an apostle *face to face* with an apostle, *because he* (Peter) *stood self-condemned*[50] and guilty of being hypocritical. At first, on coming to Antioch, Peter had shown himself a true New Testament Christian,[51] recognizing the Gentile brethren as his social equals, by eating with them at their tables, as a Gentile was accustomed to eat, disregarding the Jewish ceremonial law as to foods. He had been instructed, in the vision on the housetop of Simon the tanner in Joppa, not to consider any man common or unclean. Now, when the Judaists were there, he did not have the courage to maintain this stand which at first he had taken. This intrigue of the Judaists at Antioch, to affix the stigma of 'unclean' on the Gentile Christians who were not circumcised, was countenanced by Peter and Barnabas, but unsparingly denounced by Paul in his rebuke of Peter (vv. 11-21).

v. 12 *For before, the coming of certain ones from James*[52] *he* (Peter) *was eating with the Gentiles* at their tables, *but when they came he began to draw back* gradually[53] and separated himself[54] socially from them. *fearing those* brethren *from the* pharisaic *circumcision* party of the church in Jerusalem.

v. 13 *And the rest of the Jews* of the Antiochian church *dissembled likewise with him; so that* as a result *even Barnabas was carried along* with them *by their dissimulation* (hypocrisy).[55]

v. 14 *But when I saw 'that they are not walking uprightly* (straightforward) *in relation to the truth*[56] *of the gospel' I said to Cephas in the presence of all: If you being a Jew, live as the Gentiles,* disregarding the statutes relating to foods *and not as the Jews,* observing them, (for this was just what Peter had been doing on his arrival in Antioch) *how are you* now *obliging the Gentiles to Judaize* or become Jews by observing the Jewish statutes.

In this incident Peter did not preach false doctrine but was guilty of inconsistent conduct, not in keeping with the truth of the gospel. Boldness at first, in eating with the Gentiles, and timidity later, when the Judaists appeared, was just the character of Simon which had led to his denial of Jesus when on

49. *The Lutheran Commentary on Galatians* by H. E. Jacobs (Trans.) p. 360.
50. Periphrastic past perfect passive of *kataginoskō*, to know against.
51. *The Luhteran Com.* p. 361.
52. The Judaists professed to have come from James with authorization to act on his behalf, which seems contradictory to the action of James in the Conference (Robertson).
53. Imperfect inchoative action, *hupestellen* from *hupostellō.*
54. Imperfect act. ind. inchoative. Action Cf. Acts 20:20, 27.
55. *Hupokrisei,* instrumental.
56. *Pros* with accusative toward or to.

trial, cropping out here again in cowardice before the Judaists. Peter was bold in Gethsemane when Jesus was arrested and would have given his life for the Master, whom he truly loved.[57] Paul's unsparing rebuke of Peter now revealed his apostolic independence of all merely human authority especially that of Peter who took an inferior role. That was the only reason why his friend Peter's conduct should be cited and in such a way yet to retain the friendship of one who should hold him later as "our beloved brother Paul"[58] (II Pet. 3:15, 16).

Finally, Paul's address in Antioch 'before all' the brethren when he rebuked Peter is here expanded and continued in application to the Galatians and the gospel which he preached to them. Ch. 2:15-21. He explains that both he and Peter had followed the same course that all Christians must follow in securing justification in Christ and not by works of the law. He, through the law, died to the law, in order to live to God. In his death to law he became a sharer in the new life, through the redemption in Christ. By this method he says, Christ lives in him, becoming the motive power in his will, his desires and choices and in his conduct. To make the law the means of justification makes the death of Christ become superfluous.

v. 15 *We, being Jews by nature, and not* outcast *sinners* derived *from Gentile origin,* as the Jews think of all Gentiles, calling them (heathen) "sinners."

v. 16 Yet *knowing* as we did (aorist) *that a man is not justified*[59] *from works of the law, except through faith on Jesus Christ,*[60] *and we* definitely *believed*[61] (into) *in Christ Jesus, in order that we might be justified*[62] *from our faith on Christ*[63] as a source of our justification *and not from works of the law, because, from the works of the law,"shall no flesh be justified,"* (all flesh shall fail to be justified).

v. 17 *But if* through *seeking to be justified in Christ, we were found ourselves also to be sinners* (learning this fact by coming close to Christ, as every man will who comes to Christ), *is Christ therefore the minister of sin? God forbid!* (by no means or *may it not be*, far be it). Possibly this is a rebuttal to an argument of the Judaists that salvation in Christ is incomplete.

v. 18 *For if I am* (now) *building up again these things which I* (then) *pulled down*[64] i. e. Judaism or salvation by the works of the law, *I prove* (establish) *myself* the beggarly element of *a transgressor,* (in so) leaving sal-

---

57. Cf. John 21.
58 Paul's rebuke was in tactful terms: I withstood him saying that he had condemned himself cf. *hōti* declarative, being used with that periphrastic past perfect passive (Robertson, *Word Pictures* p. 286 (vol. Paul's epistles).
59. Pres. Ind. Pass of *dikaiō* to be justified (passive).
60. Objective genitive, Christon *Iēsoun.*
61. Aor indicative active, a definite occurrence.
62. *Hina* with the aorist subjunctive in purpose clause.
63. Objective genitive, Christ's atoning death is the accomplished work of Christ for our sins.
64. Aorist Act. Indicative *hase* things of salvation by works Paul destroyed by teaching salvation by faith in Christ's atonement.

vation in Christ to return to salvation by works of the law, a plan that has failed in our experience.

v. 19 *For I* personally, *through the* agency of the *law, died* in my relation *to the law, in order that I might* (shall)[65] *live* in my relation *to God.* To die to a thing is to cease to have any relation to it so that it has no further claim upon or control over one (Burton *I. C. C.*)[66]

v. 20 *I have been crucified*[67] *with Christ; and it is no longer I that live but Christ lives in me,*[68] his will rules in my will, his spirit possesses and controls my spirit, in my character and conduct. My personality is merged in his, *and the life that I now live* (what (*hō*) I now live) *in the flesh,* (the natural life), *I live by faith which is in the son*[69] *of God, who loved me and gave himself for me,* in his death on Calvary when he surrendered himself[70] on my behalf.

v. 21 *I do not make void the grace of God*: *For, if* imputed *righteousness*[71] is *through* the agency of *the law, then Christ died for naught,* (in vain), a conclusion both logical and real. But such a supposition is wholly alien to the purpose of God's grace.

How then is the Jew to be saved? The plan of salvation here set forth is a foretoken of the more elaborated form in the Epistle to the Roman church, which was written a short time later. We have the above question raised and answered in vv. 15-21. Is the Jew, who faithfully observes the law and ritual of Judaism, saved by his works? Paul in mental dialogue with Peter says: "We were Jews by birth and not Gentiles whom the Jews consider 'sinners', outside the covenant of Abraham. We were convinced that man cannot be accounted righteous before God by his mere obedience to the Law, which is as ineffectual as trying to climb the precipitous cliffs of Sinai with a weak and short step-ladder. It is through the merits of Christ's atoning death that man may receive by trustful and obedient faith, the effectual work of grace in his heart, resulting in his new birth unto the kingdom. If the imposition of the ceremonial and ritual should be added to the plan of the gospel of salvation by faith alone in Jesus Christ, then those who impose this two-fold plan of "the Gospel plus circumcision" on themselves thereby make the death of Christ ineffectual, since salvation had been found to be complete for the Gentiles, by faith alone without circumcision, in the home of Cornelius and elsewhere.

---

65. *Hina* followed by the future indicative *zēsō* a rare construction, denoting the purpose and with certainty of the result. The fut. ind. and aor. subj. are closely akin in such purpose clauses.
66. Paul was not subject to the legalistic statutes, such as circumcision, any longer (Burton *I. C. C.*).
67. Perf. Ind. passive, *sunestauromai*, compound verb with prep. sun., action completed, state continues.
68. Locative of sphere within which the Holy Spirit of Christ dwells within the Christian controlling mind and heart.
69. Objective genitive, Christ the object of faith.
70. *Paradomtos* — surrendering.
71. *Dikaisosunē* — cf. Rom. 1:17.

II *Doctrinal and Refutory Part of the Epistle.* Chapters III, IV.

Paul's doctrine of the plan of salvation is here clearly stated and illustrated, and the attacks on it, by his enemies are refuted by adequate positive affirmations of the truth in contrast with their errors. He had already affirmed his divine commission given by Jesus through Ananias in Damascus. He now refutes the objections to it, citing first (Ch. 3:1-5) the initial experience of grace in the conversion of the Galatian Christians and, after expressing his surprise at their ready apostasy, making an appeal to them on the basis of what they had received and felt in their conversion. Further on he discusses the call of Abraham, who was justified long before he was circumcised, and his heirs in the succession also were exactly those who experienced justification by faith as he did and not by the works of the law (Chs. 3:6-4:31).

A. The experence of the Galation Christians in the reception of the Holy Spirit, when they believed, proves that justification is by faith and not by works (Ch. 3:1-5). The Judaizers said that to be saved one must be an heir physically of Abraham or a proselyte who had submitted to the ceremonial system of traditional Judaism, illustrated by the rite of circumcision. Paul here proves from the Christian experience of these Gentile Christians of Galatia that justification worked in the heart of each of them: peace, access to God, joy and hope in the midst of their tribulations (Cf. Rom. 5:1-3). Those were certain evidences of their justification before God. But they knew nothing of the circumcision system and therefore were not saved by the ceremonies and rites of Judaism. They had received the Spirit and regeneration by faith in Christ alone. This first argument Paul sets forth in the following manner (vv 1-5).

v. 1. *O foolish* senseless *Galatians,*[72] *who did bewitch you, before whose eyes Jesus Christ was openly set forth,* portrayed, as it were placarded, (on a sign board for public proclamation), as having been *crucified.* This event thus dramatically preached one could never forget. Paul's graphic preaching was summed up (I Cor. 2:2) in the expression "Jesus Christ and him crucified."[73]

v. 2. *This only*[74] *would I learn* (I wish to learn) *from you, Received* ye *the* (Holy) *Spirit by* (on the ground of) *the works of the Law* (as a source) *or by the hearing of Faith?*

v. 3. *Are you so foolish? having begun with the Spirit,* whom you received in your initial religious experience, as Christians, *are you now* attempting to make yourselves *perfected*[75] *in the flesh,* by the use of the ceremonies of Ju-

---

72. First aor. act. indicative of *baskaino,* to bring evil on one by feigned praise or the 'evil eye' (hoodoo) (Robertson).

73. Perfect passive participle, *estauromenos,* a complete and permanent sacrifice.

74. The answer to this one question would be a decisive argument (Burton *I. C. C.* in loco p. 167). Was their religious experience by some sacramental process or through an effective hearing of the Words? Their answer could only be 'through the hearing of faith.'

75. Middle voice, finishing yourselves. Cf. I Pet. 5:29.

daism? In the contrast of 'Spirit' and 'flesh' are to be found the opposite poles of religion, the spiritual in contrast over against the ceremonial.

v. 4. *Did you suffer so many* things *in vain? if it* really is to *be indeed in vain.*[76] They had suffered, because of their acceptance of Christianity, at the hands of an evil world, when they received Christ in conversion. In south Galatia Paul was stoned, and we may be sure that others among the converts suffered persecution also. This is one fact in favor the south Galatian theory, so much debated among the scholars.

v. 5. *He* (God) therefore *who is supplying* habitually *to you the* (Holy) *Spirit and is working miracles in you* and among you, *doeth he it by the works of the law or by the hearing of faith?* The contrast of verse 2 is continued here. Evidently it was when they exercised faith in Christ that they began to experience the spiritual results in their own lives, evidenced by outward expressions of the supernatural and miraculous in their work.

B. Abraham was justified by faith alone (looking forward to the Christ), as also we are as his spiritual sons, looking back to Him. (Ch. 3:6-9). Thus Paul refutes the argument of his opponents, the Judaists that 'only through circumcision and conformity to the law men could become sons of Abraham.' The thread of this argument runs through to the end of the doctrinal refutation (Chs. 3:6-4:31). The statement of the fundamental thesis to be proved, hinges on to the experience of the Galatian Christians as follows:

v. 6. *Just as,* for example, *Abraham believed* in the word of *God* when he promised that the progeny of this chosen servant should be as the stars of heaven or the sands of the seashore innumerable, at the time of his call,[77] *and it was reckoned*[78] (accounted) *unto him for righteousness,*

v. 7. *Know then that they who are* sons *from faith* as a source, *these* and these only *are* true *sons of Abraham.* The promise of a Messiah was contained or included in the covenant of God with Abraham. The sons of Abraham, therefore, are all who exercise faith in the Christ, whether Jews or Gentiles. Spiritual Israel embraces all those who believe; the elect race with a universal mission.[79] Abraham was accounted righteous and acceptable to God without circumcision, which rite the Judaists on the contrary made an absolute condition of acceptance with God.

v. 8. *And the Scripture*[80] *forseeing that God would* (does)[81] *justify the Gentiles by faith* (on the grounds of faith), *announced*[82] *the gospel to Abraham beforehand, saying, 'In thee* as their spiritual progenitor *shall all the nations of the earth be blessed.*[83] The Judaists said that all the nations would be blessed

---

76. Translation of Burton, *I. C. C.*, in loco.
77. Gen. 12:1-3.
78. First aorist passive, an actual occurrence at the time when Abraham exercised faith in the promise of God, in Ur of the Chaldees.
79. Cf. I Peter 2:9, 10.
80. Scripture here personified.
81. Present indicative active of *dikaioō.*
82. First aorist middle of compound verb pro — *euaggelizomai.*
83. Future passive of *eneulogeō.*

in Abraham therefore they must get into Abraham by being circumcised. Paul, citing the fact that Abraham was justified by faith and not by circumcision, refuted the argument of his opponents by citing their major premise as true, but showing that Abraham was justified before he was circumcised and therefor that their minor premise was faulty and therefore their conclusion wrong.

v. 9. *So that*[84] *those who are justified from faith,* as a source *are blessed* along *with faithful* (believing) *Abraham.*

C. The Law, instead of saving, becomes a curse when depended upon for justification. Ch. 3:10-14. Those whose standing is fixed by works of the Law must admit that the sentence of the Law is one of condemnation, since no man ever succeeded in keeping the Law perfectly. But the Old Testament prophecy teaches that man shall live by faith.[85] The Law demands perfect "obedience as antecedent to the gift of life,"[86] but life by the prophet is dependent upon faith,[87] which is 'the heartfelt trust in God which prompts the convert to embrace Christ. This is justifying faith, in the pitying love of God, which assures the repentant of forgiveness in spite of a guilty past.'[88]

v. 10. *For as many as are of the law,* counting on justification by the keeping the Law, *are under a curse.*[89] *For it* (stands) *is written,*[90] *"Cursed is every one that continueth not in all the things that are written in the book of the law to do them."*[91] The principle of legalism is not the basis of God's judgment on men. All men, by that principle, are under a curse, because the breaking of the law entails a curse of sentence on guilt. All men are included under this sentence in the curse of guilt. The legal statutes (law) demand a perfect obedience in all things and a continual obedience. So all men are under the condemnation and curse of the Law.[92]

v. 11. *And that man is justified by the law* as an instrument in the sphere of the Law,[93] *in the sight of God* (alongside of God) *is evident.* This is because no mere man ever kept all the Law perfectly, as Jesus Christ, the God-man did. So far as the legal system is concerned, it may have a perfect standard, but as far as humanity is concerned, it has never measured up to the standard of the law, much less that of Christ. Christ alone fulfilled all righteousness of the Mosaic Law. *Because, the righteous man shall live by faith.*[94] Paul cites this passage elsewhere[95] in proof of his doctrine of justification by faith, using the term in the forensic sense to mean the man approved by God through the im-

---

84. *Hoste,* so that, adducing the result in conclusion of this argument.
85. Habakkuk 2:4.
86. Frederic Rendall, *Expos. Gr. Test.* Galatians p. 169, Cf. Rom. 10:5.
87. Cf. Rom. 1:17; Heb. 10:38.
88. Ibidem Rendall, *Expos. Gr. Test* in loco.
89. *Hupo katōran* under a curse hanging over them.
90. Perfect tense, completed action and continued result.
91. Infinitive expressing purpose (Boise) Cf. Deut. 27:26.
92. Cf. Rom. Ch. 3:9-20. Cf. Deut. 27:36 the curse at Mt. Ebal.
93. Locative of sphere or instrumental case either.
94. Hab. 2:4.
95. Rom. 1:17.

puted righteousness of Jesus Christ. It is by faith that he who is approved by God is approved and saved by faith. The meaning of faith in Habakkuk is a faith resulting in faithfulness, integrity and steadfastness.[96] God pointed to the only way to justification in the Old Testament or Covenant (Hab. 2:4). It is faith not law that gives righteousness and life.

v. 12. *But the law is not from faith* as a source, for the two principles of legalism and faith are mutually exclusive as bases for justification, *but* on the contrary the principle of legalism is expressed in the Old Testament as follows: "*The one doing these things shall live by them.*"[97] The law requires everything and can give nothing to save a man. It condemns him but cannot make him righteous. Man cannot because of the 'infirmity of the flesh' render a perfect obedience and so remains under the bondage and curse of the law until redeemed or freed from that bondage and curse by Christ's redemption.

v. 13. *Christ redeemed*[98] *us,* (bought us out) *from the* state of condemnation or *curse of the* violated *law, having become*[99] *a curse for us,*[99a] *as it is* (stands) *written*[1] "Cursed is every one that hangeth[2] on a tree."[3]

v. 14. *That upon the Gentiles might come* (become a reality) *the blessing of Abraham* realized *in Jesus Christ; in order that we* (both Jew and Gentile) *might receive the promise of the Spirit* made to Abraham, *through faith* in Jesus (not through the works of the law).

The argument of Paul's polemic advances from step to step in this setting forth of 'his gospel.'[4] In the first step (3:1-5) Christian "experience" attests faith in Christ as the only pathway to righteousness and eternal life. The Galatians were drifting from the gospel of faith back to the futile method of ceremonial observance. They were forgetting the quickening effect in them of the Christ placarded on the cross in the preaching of Paul and the blessing of peace with God, the assurance of access, the joy and hope in their hearts when they believed, and the wonderful experiences in the reception of the Holy Spirit with the works he had operated in themselves and others among them. All this had come into their experience when they heard and accepted the gospel and exercised faith in Jesus Christ.

In the second step the argument turns on the faith of Abraham at the time of his call by God four hundred and thirty years before the time of Moses and the

96. To say that Paul was using the LXX translation and did not understand that 'faithfulness' in the full sense depended on a vital faith is beyond the mark.

97. Cf. Lev. 18:5; Hab. 2:4; Heb. 10:38; Rom. 8:1-3, the weakness of the flesh is the link in the chain that always breaks inevitably. Hence the necessity of Christian help.

98. First aorist active of *exagorazō* — to buy up out of the agora or market place, as in the purchase of slaves (Deissmann, *Light from the Ancient East*) p. 324.

99. Adverbial clause of manner, by having become.

99a. *Huper hemōn,* we were *hupo* under the curse and Christ became *huper* over us and the curse fell on him our substitute.

1. Perfect middle participle he became our substitute because he wished to do so.
2. Present middle part from *krenammin,* to hang.
3. Cf. Deut. 21:23, *Zulon,* wood, used of crosses.
4. Cf. Chapters III and IV.

law. Faith was the condition of the blessing bestowed on Father Abraham and he was pronounced and considered righteous. The blessing included great material possession and innumerable progeny. All the nations of the earth would come to share in the blessing by faith becoming spiritual sons of faith-filled Abraham, both Jews and Gentiles. This is the gospel-way and there is no other to righteousness and life. The law of statutes brings a curse, because of man's failure and inability to keep the law through the weakness of the flesh. Christ enables man to finish by faith the perfection of his life, by redeeming him from the bondage and penalty of the law, taking on himself the curse.

D. The promise of the gospel was made to Abraham more than four centuries before the law was given by Moses and was not made null by the coming of the law. Salvation is free and not merited through works of the law (Ch. 3:15-18). The experience of salvation from sin is a fulfillment of God's promise to Abraham. It was to be shared by all nations, not on the condition of observance of the law of the Jews but by faith alone in the Christ of the promise which God made to Abraham. Christ was the fulfillment of that promise and in him all the nations shall be blessed.[5] The initial condition of the Covenant with Abraham was that of faith. Even a human covenant is inviolate, once it is confirmed. The terms of the Covenant of God with Abraham could not be altered by the Law, which came four hundred and thirty-years later by substituting the 'works of the Law in the place of the principle of faith. What is earned by works is not a free gift of grace, such as was life eternal through faith in Christ.[6]

v. 15. *Brethren, I speak after the manner of man,* taking an illustration from human affairs. *Though it be but of man, a covenant when it hath been confirmed no one maketh void or addeth thereto.* A contract can be annulled only when both parties agree to annul it. How much more must a contract which was not merely human but was between God and his servant Abraham, be inviolate. The law coming into existence more than four centuries later being the product of God's work through Moses, would not annul but rather reenforce the Abrahamic Covenant and Gospel contact based on faith and faithfulness.

v. 16. *Now to Abraham the promises were spoken* being frequently repeated.[7] *and to his seed,*[8] of the Messianic people, summed up after the manner of rabbinical interpretation, in Christ.[9] *He saith not, and to seeds as of many; but as of one, And to thy seed, which* (who) *is Christ.* The word seed applies to spiritual Israel composed of both Jews and Gentiles.[10]

v. 17. *Now, this I say,* meaning that: *A covenant confirmed beforehand*[11] by

---

5. H. E. Dana, *The Life and Literature of Paul* p. 74.
6. David Smith, *Life and Letters of St. Paul* p. 204.
7. Cf. Gen. 12:3; 13:15; 17:8; 18:18; 22:18.
8. *Sperma* is used here as a collective noun.
9. *Hos* relative agrees with Christos, emphasis and attraction of relative.
10. Robertson, A. T. *Word Studies,* Vol. Pauline p. 295.
11. Compound verb, *prokekuromenēn,* perfect passive participle, completion and permanence involved.

God, the law having[12] *four hundred and thirty years later,*[13] *does not annul, so as to make the promise* (void) *of none effect.*[14] The point of the argument is in the precedence of the blessing (*pro*) and the fact that the Abrahamic Covenant was made by God, whose law came later (*meta*). The precedence of the promise was also validated in its fulfillment in Christ, the Savior of the world of humanity.

v. 18. *For, if the inheritance,* of the messianic blessing of the kingdom *is of* (from) *the law*[15] as a source, *it is no longer of* (from) *the promise; but*[16] (on the contrary) *God has granted it* as a free gift *to Abraham through* the means or method of *the promise.* The Covenant with Abraham is still in force and the method or means of obtaining the inheritance by faith was not superseded by that of the works of the law. Paul is classical in his logic. A new law may replace an old law or previous legislation but it cannot replace a Covenant. The law of Moses in its legalistic interpretation was emphasized by the Judaists. "*If the inheritance is by law it is not by promise; but* (the inheritance) *it is by promise therefore it is not by law.*"[17] Legalism has ever been a curse when emphasized to the prejudice of the gospel of grace.

E. What was the purpose of God in the Law? 3:19-4:31. *What then* is the use of *the law?* 'It had, if the foregoing conclusion is true, no reason to exist,' says the Judaist objector. Paul here answers this objection by showing the real purpose of God in the law (Ch. 3:19-23). He explains the function of the law in revealing sin, denies its power to give life, and ascribes to it the temporary role of leading man up to Christ, the Savior.[18] This is the purpose and use of the law in relation to the justification of the sinner and there is no other.[19]

1. The law testified against sin and thus prepared for the advent of Christ and his gospel grace (Ch. 3:19-23).

v 19. *What then* is the purpose and function of *the law? It was added because*[20] *of transgressions,* "to make transgressions palpable." (Ellicott), "thereby pronouncing them to be from that time forward transgressions of the law." (Rendall) As Paul said later "when the law came, sin revived and I died."[21] Sin is a willful disregarding of known regulations and prohibitions of law; *till the seed* (Christ) *should come,*[22] *to whom the promise hath been made*[23]; and

12. Perfect participle, *gegōnos*, having become (come).
13. This chronology includes the time of the patriarchs in Canaan.
14. *A Kuroi* (Cf. *kuroō*, contract verb) with a privitive, without authority, invalidate.
15. Ablative of source, *nomou.*
16. *De*, adversative.
17. Ernest De Witt Burton, *I. C. C.* Gal. p. 186.
18. Burton, E. DeW, *I. C. C.* p. 187.
19. E H. Perowne, *Camb. Bible,* Outline of Galatians Introd. p. 24.
20. *Charin* adv. acc. of *charis* used as a prep. also *telic* (Robertson).
21. Romans Ch. 7:9; cf. also Rom. 2:23.
22. *Achris,* marks the period until this function should be causal but superseded.
23. Perfect passive, impersonal use of verb, *epangellomai.*

it was ordained[24] *through angels*[25] *by the hand of a mediator* Moses.[26] The period of the Covenant goes on by its fulfillment in Christ but the law in this function of making palpable sin was temporary in part and now modified by the coming of Christ. The law is still useful in defining and revealing sin but is wholly subservient to Christ, whose teachings reveal sin much more clearly. It is entirely supplementary to Christ who 'filled it up to the full.'[27]

v. 20. *Now a mediator is not of one; but God is one.* A mediator is a middleman between two. There was no middleman between God and Abraham. The law came from God, not directly but through a mediator, to Israel the second party to the agreement, and is therefore not on a par with the promise in which God dealt directly with Abraham.

v. 21. *Is the law then against* (contrary to) *the promises of God? God forbid* (may it not be). The law had its own functions which were different and supplementary to those of the promises but not contradictory. The Judiasts said that man is justified by the law, which is impossible from man's failure to keep it perfectly. The sentence of the law is always one of condemnation, the revelation of man's legal standing always the same. The promises justify man on the basis of faith which identify man with Christ. Man is justified on the basis of Christ's imputed righteousness, when his heart turns in repentence and love to the Savior. *For if a law had been given* that was *able to make alive* spiritually, which there was not,[28] *verily righteousness*[29] *would have been from the law* as a source.[30]

v. 22. *But the scripture shut up all things under* the condemnation of *sin*, and the Old Testament law[31] is the Scripture referred to evidently, the verdict of this law is condemnation to the sinner always *in order that the promise*, (on the grounds of) and from the source *of faith in Jesus Christ, might be given to those who believe.* The purpose of the 'shutting up' is achieved in the gospel of God. The law was given by God to prepare for the coming of Christ and his gospel. It shows that man does not attain justification and spiritual life by his own merits. So Paul rejects the legalism in the law as it was applied by the Judaists, while recognizing the divine origin of the law at the same time.

2. The function of the law is illustrated in the pedagogue-servant. By the law we were tutored until the coming of Christ, the real Master, who liberates us (Ch. 3:23-29).

---

24. Second aor. passive participle of *diatossō*.

25. Cf. 33:2 (LXX); Acts 7:38, 52; Heb. 2:2; Joaplues Act XV 5, 3.

26. Moses was the mediator in this case but Christ also later. Cf. I Tim. 2:5; Heb. 8:6; 9:15; 12:24 (Robertson).

27. Cf. Matt. 5:17.

28. Condition and conclusion an *ēn*, second class contrary to fact determined as unfulfilled.

29. *Dikaiosunē* generally used of imputed righteousness in N. T.

30. Ablative of source, *nomou*, from the law as a source.

31. Cf. Deut. 27:26.

v. 23. *Before faith* in Christ[32] *came,* when Jesus Christ came historically, *we were being kept guarded*[33] (in ward) under the wardenship and tutorship of *the law, shut up unto the faith* which was *about*[34] *to be revealed.*

v. 24. *So that the law is become our tutor*[35] (pedagogue-servant) to bring us *unto Christ* (our school Master) in order *that*[36] *we might be justified by* (from) *faith.* This was the ultimate purpose of the law, as a pedagogue-servant, illustrated here by the Greek slave-tutor who conducted the child to school.

v. 25. *But now that faith* in Christ *is come* historically in the advent of Jesus Christ in the incarnation *we are no longer under a tutor.* We are in the school of the Master (Robertson).

v. 26. *For you are all,* both Jews and Gentiles who are Christians, *sons of God through*[37] *faith in Christ Jesus* and spiritual sons of Abraham to whom the promise of an innumerable progeny was made.

v. 27. *For as many of you as were baptized*[38] *into Christ did put on Christ,* being thus clothed metaphorically in Christ, with a uniform of identity with him and his cause. Baptism in water does not save but merely symbolizes the immersion into the spirit and character of Christ. It is an oath of fealty to Christ. We are justified by faith in Christ not by baptism, nor by circumcision or any works of the law.

v. 28. *There is neither*[39] *Jew nor Greek,* racial and national distinctions do not exist, *neither bond-*(servant) *nor free,* class differences vanish, *neither male nor female,* sex rivalry in privileges are done away in equality (Cf. Robertson *Word Pictures,* Gal. p. 299.) Reasoning from the problem of spiritual versus ceremonial religion in Galatia, Paul generalizes the picture of one universal religion and God as a condition to one united and peaceful world, a blissful hope. *For you are* all *one in Christ Jesus.* The spiritual unity of humanity can only be attained along the way of faith in Christ, life in Christ, inspiration and control in Christ.

v. 29. *And*[40] *if you are Christ's,* as you surely are assumed to be *then are you Abraham's seed* and *heirs according to the promise.* Believers in Christ share the promises made to Abraham of such possessions as Christ offers to

32. Cf. v. 22.
33. Imperfect tense, passive denoting a continued condition and treatment, of tutorship which was strict.
34. *Mello* with first aor. pass. infinitive *apokaluphthēnai.*
35. The tutor *pedagogos,* attended the boy from six to sixteen in the Greek home, watching his morals and manners.
36. *Hina,* in purpose clause, in order that, with Aor. subjunctive.
37. *Dia* with genitive, the means through which is faith in Christ Jesus.
38. The reference is to Christian baptism when they had believed and experienced the death to sin and resurrection to a new life by faith in Christ. This change was symbolized in the baptism which took place after the exercise of faith and regeneration occurred. This baptism was by immersion. (Burton *I. C. C.*) which is the uniform meaning of the verb in Paul.
39. *Ouk eni* means there is not (a fact), 'not there cannot be' Cf. Rev. 11:15.
40. *De* is continuative and the clause with *ei* and the primary tenses in the conditional sentence which follows is of the first class, condition, according to fact.

his people, and also of God's love and paternal care. The inheritance promised to Abraham belongs to them in virtue of their relationship to Christ.

3. Under the law we were uninstructed children, needing a tutor; but through faith and redemption in Christ we became sons of God and free (Ch. 4:1-7). As long as the heir is a minor (*napios*) he is kept under strict authority, surveillance, and restraint, through guardians and stewards. But since the promise of Abraham was fulfilled in Christ, the heirs of the promise, who are in Christ, have received the inheritance, having attained their majority. They now have free access to the benefits of the inheritance without restraints. The Galatians had been freed by the gospel from the bondage of heathen rites and customs, but were now lapsing back into another form of bondage, in the rites and customs of traditional and ceremonial Judaism.[41] Paul here contrasts the conditions under the law, when the heir is placed under a guardian with no freedom of action, with (over against) the conditions under grace in Christ, when the heirs, as sons of God, live in his joyous fellowship[42] of spiritual liberty and freedom (Ch. 4:1-7).

v. 1. *But I say that so long time as the heir is a child* (babe) he differs nothing from a slave (bond-servant), *while* at the same time *he is* really *Lord of all* the inheritance.

v. 2. *but is under guardians*[43] *and stewards*[44] *until the time set by the father.* Paul illustrates from the human custom of guardianship the condition of the heir when under the law, and characterizes it as being practical bondage.

v. 3. *So we also, when we were children* (babes) under the law, we *were held in bondage*[45] *under the rudiments of the world.* The conditions under the pre-Christian life were those of enslavement which was a permanent and continued state of existence. All people were in this elementary status before Christ came, whether Jews or Gentiles.

v. 4. *But when the fulness of the time came, God sent forth* from himself *his* preexistent *son, born of woman*[43] and therefore truly human, *born under law* as every human being is, whether Jew or Gentile, if Jew under the Mosaic law, if Gentile under the natural law of conscience, inherent in all men in virtue of their creation by God in his image.

v. 5. In order *that he might redeem*[47] *those under the law,* in order *that they might receive the adoption* of sons, from God into his family.

v. 6. *Because you are sons,* in God's elective grace, *God sent forth the* (Holy) *Spirit of his son*[48] *into our hearts, crying Abba Father.* This was the expression

41. Cf. H. E. Dana, *The Life and Literature of Paul* p. 75.
42. Burton *I. C. C.* in loco.
43. *Epitropous,* overseers (Matt. 20:8) or those in charge of children, *nēpioi.*
44. *Oikonomous,* stewards were managers of estates.
45. Perfect periphrastic tense of *douloō* contract verb, to enslave in the rudiments of the law as it applies to all alike whether Jew or Gentile, to the Jew as the law of Moses, to the Gentile the law of conscience.
46. "The language here agrees with the virgin birth and the virgin birth with the language." Cf. Robertson, *Word Pictures* in loco.
47. *Hina* with the aorist subjunctive in purpose clause, in two successive clauses.
48. The Holy Spirit is called the Spirit of Christ Cf. Rom. 8:9f; Phil. 1:19; John 15:26.

which Jesus used in the Garden of Gethsemane, knowing both Aramaic and Greek, and in his agony using both in repetition, in that tragic hour of extreme testing and temptation.

v. 7. *So that, no longer are you a slave but a son. And if*[49] you are *a son* as indeed you certainly are, *then also an heir through God,* by his means of grace through a living faith in Christ, the resurrected and living Lord and Savior.

4. The peril of turning back from Christ to seek salvation (justification) through the law. (Ch. 4:8-11).

In their former condition the (Gentile) Galatians were in bondage to heathen gods who were but imaginary and not real beings. Paul warns them against the apostasy of turning to Judaism and appeals to them not to leave the fellowship of Christ and God the Father to go over to the weak and beggarly rudimentary teachings of the Judaists, which are no better than the heathen religion. He fears that his labors on their behalf have been in vain.

v. 8. *But, then* (at that time) *indeed, not knowing* the true *God, you served* as slaves *those who by nature* being only idols, *are not gods* in verity. They have no real existence, being only figments of the human imagination.

v. 9. *But now having come to know God* through my preaching *or rather to be known by God* in religious experience through faith in Christ, *how are you turning back again to the weak and beggarly elements, whereunto thus again,* anew *you wish to be enslaved?* The Galatian Christians were tempted to find satisfaction in the superficial philosophies and religious quests of heathen religions of the Graeco-Roman World.[50] But worse still the fickle Celts were easily led by the Pharisaic legalists (who pursued Paul everywhere he went. seeking to destroy him and his work), to abandon their new religion and embrace Judaism which was still a bondage to a lifeless ceremonialism not better than the heathen cults about them.

v. 10. *You (are) observing*, with interest and scrupulous care the meticulous requirements of the Pharisees' *days*, fast-days and feast-days, *and months. and seasons* of passover, pentecost, tabernacles *and* sabbatical *years* especially the year of jubilee, as the Judaists instruct you.[51]. Gentile freedom had been won for them in the Jerusalem Conference and they did not need to observe these things of Judaism.

v. 11. *I fear (for you) lest by any means I* have *spent*[52] my *labor on you in vain.* Paul feared for the worst, having a conviction that all his labor for them had been lost.

5. Personal affection of the apostle for the Galatian Christians, based on his former relationship with them. The expression of this affection involved a

49. Condition of the first class *ei* with the indicative mood of the verb to be here understood, according to fact or reality.

50. Cf. Ramsey, W. M., *The Religious Quests of the Graeco-Roman World.*

51. Present Middle Indicative, *paratēreisthe,* to stand beside and watch carefully (Robertson *Word Pictures*).

52. Perfect active indicative instead of subjunctive. The indicative expressed a conviction that he had lost his work on these unstable, fickle people. How foolish they were and others are who turn back to the beggarly elements and flesh-pots garlic of Egypt.

revelation of his disappointment in their changed feelings when he recalled his past fellowship with them. He begged them to return to that fellowship while protesting against their estrangement toward him. Ch. 4:12-20.

v. 12. Having expressed his feeling of fear lest his 'toil' of love for them had been spent in vain leaving the door open for a hopeful doubt that he might be mistaken,[53] he pleads: *I beg you brethren* (keep on becoming) *become as I am,* free from Judaism, *for*[54] *I* forsaking Judaism, *became as you are,* (as a Gentile), independent of the Mosaic law. *You did me no wrong.* In respect to nothing did you wrong me.[55]

v. 13. *But, you know that on account of the infirmity of my flesh,* being detained by my malady (sickness) *I preached the gospel unto you the first*[56] time, on the first of the visits[57] in Galatia, (the first was when the work was founded). Paul was suffering from some malady when he arrived in Antioch from Pamplylia.[58] He was treated with great kindness by the Galatians at that time. He reminisces opportunely, now, on their care of him then.

v. 14. *And that which was a trial*[59] *to you in my flesh,* because my malady was offensive to behold and to treat, *you did not despise nor* literally *spit upon me but,* on the contrary, *received me as an angel* or messenger *of God,* even *as Christ Jesus,* my Lord.

v. 15. *When then is that gratulation*[60] (congratulation) *of yourselves? for I bear you witness, that, if possible, you would have plucked out your* own *eyes*[61] *and given them to me.* The Galatians evidently sympathized greatly with Paul when he was there, and he reminds them of his gratitude to them. which was undying. They no longer congratulated themselves now at having Paul with them. How changed was their attitude toward him. This change he laments, and protests his faithful love for them with a heart-felt plea.

v. 16. *So have I become your* personal *enemy by telling you the truth?* He chides them for their fickle disloyalty but with a strong love in his heart for them.

v. 17. *They zealously seek you not well in* no good way, *but wish to shut you out* from the influence of other teachers (such as Paul) with the purpose *that you may zealously seek them.* They went to monopolize your affections selfishly, and be the popular teachers themselves, and for their ulterior motives of promoting Judaism in you.

v. 18. *Now, it is good to be zealously sought in a good matter always, and not only* (or just when) *I am present with you.* He was the teacher of their

53. *Hina* is usually employed with the subjunctive but here with the indicative.
54. Because, *hoti.*
55. Use of the adverbial accusative, *ouden,* acc. of specification in classical Greek, Cf. Dana H. E. *Grammar, N. T. Gr.*
56. The former — *to proteron,* the former visit, the first visit.
57. Acts 16:6, 18:23.
58. Cf. Ramsay, W. M. *Paul the Traveler,* in loco.
59. Trial to bear.
60. Cf. *Makarizō.*
61. The inference naturally is that Paul suffered from opthalmia, an offensive eye trouble which was a trial to behold even.

first love but in his absence these proselytizers had come in and sought to steal their hearts away from him. He protests with true jealousy his love for them. He tenderly pleads with these spiritual children of his ministry.

v. 19. *My little children, about whom I am again in travail, until Christ be formed in you.* These babes in Christ had not developed. Paul had been in the travail of prayer for them when they were first won to belief in Christ; now again he is in the same kind of birth pangs on their behalf, that they may have the indwelling Christ formed in them into maturity.

v. 20. Yea *I could with to be present with you now and to change my voice* to tones more pleasant to hear, *for I am perplexed about you,* "I am at a loss to know what to do." (Robertson).

In this section the apostle appeals to his readers to return to their former allegiance to the gospel. He was fearful lest the labor which he had bestowed upon them might have been in vain, but he refuses to believe it was and appeals tenderly to their chivalry as Gentiles for whom he had abandoned Judaism. He being a Jew had identified himself with them, incurring thus persecution, obloquy, and the determined opposition of the Judaists. He remembered the great kindness of the Galatians to him when he began his ministry in Antioch of Pisidia and also in other places where he and Barnabas had labored. He wondered at the great change in their attitude, from great personal sympathy for him to enmity and distress. He had loved them always. He does not even now charge them with any wrong. His enemies had been to blame, using as they did great zeal in their jealousy against him, especially in their self-interest, seeking to come between him and the churches by the use of calumny. He did not object to other teachers visiting them if they did so in the good work of the gospel. But the Judaizers had sought to shut them off from any teachers besides themselves, especially from Paul. What these Judaists were seeking was to undo his good work of securing Gentile liberty and equality in the church, which he had done in the Jerusalem Conference, and to get them to seek circumcision and the other requirements of the Judaists, who had in view their becoming Jews by proselytism. That was the true situation. He tenderly remonstrates with his dearly loved children in the faith and frankly professes his deep concern that they should grow into full manhood in Christ.

6. The relation of the two covenants, illustrated by the allegory of Sarah and Hagar, pointing to real liberty in Christ alone. Ch. 4:21-31. Abraham's relation to his heirs is primarily spiritual rather than physical, as illustrated in the allegory. Hagar (meaning Rock) represents the Sinai covenant, being a bondwoman; and Sarah the covenant of promise, being free. The offspring of the bondwoman are in bondage from birth and the children of the freewoman are free. Those who are free in the grace of Christ are the true heirs of Abraham.

This passage is an example of Paul's use of the rabbinical allegorical method of interpretation, which found a hidden sense embodied and supposed to be intended in many parts of the Scripture. In this case a historical narrative is aken as revealing the truth that those who adhere to the law are in bondage ınd those living by faith in Christ are free. Philo, who was a past-master in he use of the allegorical method, defines the allegory as "speaking something lse than what the language means, revealing a deeper spiritual sense." Paul ısed it not to teach something which he merely wanted to teach without regard o the reality and truth related to the language, presented in the allegorical llustration. He used the historical event as an illustration to present his argunent to the fluctuating Galatians, going over to the bondage of Judaism. This abbinical method of interpreting Scripture was much abused by Philo and ater by Augustine, and especially by Origen, who used it more extensively han any other. Paul's skillful use of this allegory is the climatic point of his ırgument about Abraham and his seed.

v. 21. *Tell me, you that wish to be under the law, do you not hear the law?* This apparently abrupt turn of the argument seemed to indicate that the apostle hought this might be a way to prevent his readers from taking the final step of decision to accept Judaism. They had not made their decision yet at least and he would forestall their doing so, as they drifted nearer the brink of the peril.

v. 22. *For it is written*[62] *that Abraham had two sons, one by the maidservant*[63] *and one by the freewoman.*[64] The Gentiles had come recently out of the bondage of idolatry and idolatrous sins. Paul would save them from leaving their newly found spiritual liberty, which he had purchased for them in Jerusalem, by suffering severe persecution.

v. 23. *But the* (*one*) *son of the maid-servant was born*[64a] *according to the flesh,* by natural generation in the ordinary course of nature; *but the* (other) *son of the freewoman through the* definite *promise* made to Abraham (Gen. 17:16); in the atmosphere of an environment of freedom and faith.

v. 24. *Which things* (this scripture speaks allegorically), *contains an allegory*: *for these women are* an illustration *of two covenants*: one *from Mount Sinai,* and so connected with the covenant of the law, *bearing children* as a bondwoman *into bondage,* as a consequence of her status, under the covenant of the law, *which is Hagar*, an Egyptian whose name meant Rock (Sinai).

v. 25. *Now, this Hagar is in* the allegory, *Mount Sinai in Arabia,* connected with the Covenant of the law as the place where it was given, which was sometimes called Hagar, (a Rock), *and answereth* (corresponds) *to the Jerusalem*[65] *that now is*: *for she* (Jerusalem) *is in* bondage with her children,[66] to the law.

v. 26. *But the Jerusalem which is above,* (the heavenly Jerusalem) *is free which is our mother* (the Mother of spiritual Israel, which is Christianity).

---

62. Perfect passive indicative, it stands written.
63. *Paidiskē,* a female slave, Hagar.
64. Cf. Gen. Chs. 16, 17.
64a. Perf. pass. ind., referring especially to the existing result of the fact (Cf. Burton *I.C.C. Romans,* p. 253).
65. Use of Metonymy for the Judaism which had its chief source there.
66. A severe condemnation of the emissaries who came from Jerusalem and were seeking to seduce Galatian Christianity.

v. 27. *For it is* (stands) *written: Rejoice thou barren that bearest not Break forth and cry thou that travailest not: For many are the children of the desolate more Than of her that hath the husband* — Isa. 54:1, LXX.

Jerusalem after the return from exile would have more children than she had before the exile. Sarah was barren and Hagar had the husband. Spiritual Jerusalem has a multitude of sons but old Jerusalem (Judaism) yet wails at the place of ruins and her sons are slaughtered by the sons of Ishmael.

v. 28. *And you brethren, like Isaac, are children of promise,* not born just in the course of nature, but when Sarah was beyond age to bear. So the standing of spiritual sons of Abraham, is not one of mere physical descent. The Judaists wished to enforce this upon the Galatian Christians and bring them into bondage to circumcision and the whole ceremonial law, as proselyted Gentiles in the Jewish national fold.

v. 29. *But as then,* in the case of Ishmael and his sons, *he that was born after the* manner of the *flesh* by natural or mere physical generation, *persecuted him who was born according to the spirit* or through the promise and intervention of God, *even so it is now* in the case of the Judaists, who are seeking to destroy the true Gentile spiritual sons of Abraham, the Christians.

v. 30. *Howbeit, what saith the Scripture?*[67] *Cast out the handmaid and her son, for the son of the handmaid* (slave woman) *shall not inherit* (share the inheritance) *with the son of the freewoman.*

v. 31. *Wherefore, brethren, we are not the children of a handmaid, but of the freewoman.* He had made thus a complete exposure of the Judaists and their nefarious persecution of the free spiritual sons of Abraham. It completed the argument of refutation of Judaism with a climactic allegorical illustration. The first verse of the fifth chapter is tied up more closely with this argument, the climax of which was expressed in the allegory. The heritage of the Christian is freedom in Christ. The chapter division, which is arbitrary, and the original MSS would justify the closer connection of this verse with the foregoing argument, as the Revised Version shows by its paragraphing.[68]

III. Hortatory Part of the Epistle. Chs. V-VI.

Having vindicated his independent apostolic authority (1:11-2:21) and having answered the arguments of the legalists who were seeking to induce the Galatians to accept the bondage of the law, the Apostle passes to the application of the doctrine of Christian liberty in Christ to the needs of the Galatian churches.

A. Practical exhortations growing out of the doctrines of the letter of the law versus the Spirit, to stand[69] fast in the liberty of Christ (5:1-12).

---

67. Gen. 21:10.

68. It maintains the chapter divisions because Nestle disagrees with Westcott and Hort in the paragraphing and the R. V. follows the A. V. in chapter division at this point which is not of supreme importance in the exegesis. In Frederick Rendall's exegetical outline he separates 4:31 also with 5:1-12. Exegetes like Grammarians differ in the mechanical disposition of the text in certain passages.

69. Perfect imperative, make a complete stand and keep on standing. Cf. *New Test. Greek Grammar*, Dana and Mantey.

1. Submission to the rite of circumcision, Paul warns the Galatian Christians, is yielding themselves again to the bondage of Law-plan of salvation. This he declares is wholly and altogether incompatible with the plan of salvation by grace through faith in Christ, in every way. vv. 1-5.

v. 1. *For this* (exactly) *freedom,*[70] which belongs to the children of the freewoman the son of Abraham by faith, *Christ set us free. Stand fast therefore,* and keep on standing[71] and stop being held in *by a yoke of bondage and do not be so entangled again.*[72]

v. 2. *Behold I, Paul,* with full apostolic authority *say unto you, that if you should receive*[73] *circumcision,* as the Judaists desire, *Christ will profit you nothing* and cannot longer help you. Christ obtained freedom for us not only from the bondage of sin, idolatry, death and the devil; and to turn back and embrace Judaism (or its modern equivalent, Catholicism) would be to exchange the bondage of heathen idolatry for that of ceremonial Judaism, which with its legalistic restraints and restrictions was no better for the one seeking true justification in salvation than heathen idolatry. Furthermore, they would thus barter away their liberty in Christ and they could not combine Judaism and Christianity in one plan of salvation because that plan was one of faith in Christ alone.

v. 3. *Yea, I testify again,* emphatically, *to every man that receiveth circumcision, that he is a debtor to do the whole law* to keep it in every detail. One would assume anew in circumcision the badge of the law-system of salvation.

v. 4. *You were severed thus from Christ* definitely,[74] *you, who are being justified* as you think *by the law;*[75] *you have fallen*[76] away *from grace* once for all, by leaving the sphere of grace in Christ and taking your stand in the sphere of the law as your hope of salvation.

v. 5. *For we* Christians, *by the Spirit, from faith, wait for the hope of* the realization of *righteousness.* One does not fall from grace by some occasional sin but by substituting once for all the law,[77] in the place of Christ as the agent of salvation.

2. Paul warns against false teachers, and expresses his confidence in true believers. Ch. 5:7-12.

v. 6. *For, in Christ Jesus,* the true sphere of salvation, *neither circumcision nor uncircumcision availeth anything* (is strong to effect anything) *but faith* of the believer, in Christ, *working through* the means and agency of *love.* This

---

70. Dative case of *eleutheria.*
71. First perfect imperative active, *stēkete* indicating a permanent standing.
72. They had been in bondage to sins of Gentile idolatry formerly; they are now on the verge of turning themselves over to another bondage, Judaism.
73. Third class condition, not determined as fulfilled but possible of fulfillment and, as it seemed, probable.
74. First aorist passive, *katērgēthēte.*
75. Present passive constative indicative, you who are trying to be justified in the law.
76. Second aorist active indicative of *expiptō* with a variable vowel of the first aorist cf. koine Greek Grammars.
77. H. E. Dana, *The Life and Literature of Paul* p. 76.

is the 'Moral dynamic' of Paul's conception of freedom from Law.[78] Faith identifies the believer with Christ in the sphere of grace and love.

v. 7. *You were running well,* in the beginning, like successful runners in the games of the stadium.[79] *Who*[80] *did hinder you,* by throwing obstacles in your race-course, or by cutting in on you, as it were, in the race, intercepting your free course of action, to turn you from Christ, *so that you should not obey the truth?*[81]

v. 8. *This*[82] art of *persuasion,* used by the Judaizers, comes *not from the one calling you,* which is the Father in heaven. Paul warns them that the source of this influence is not from heaven but from the Devil, working in those false and hypocritical leaders.

v. 9. The pervasive power of *a little leaven* of error once admitted or of a person of evil influence *goes on leavening,*[83] by its unperceived presence and continued working, *the whole lump* of the churches which harbor it. It would be so with the Galatian churches who receive these false teachers, Paul earnestly warns them.

v. 10. *I have confidence in you in the sphere of the Lord* Jesus, *that you will be none otherwise minded,* through influence of these former false-teachers, the Judaizers. *The one troubling you shall* surely *bear his judgment* in the end, *whoever he may be.* God's judgment will be upon him at the last.

v. 11. *But, I brethren, if I still preach circumcision,* as my enemies accuse in slander, *why am I still persecuted* (by those who are the perpetrators of this slander)? They had misconstrued Paul's act of having Timothy circumcised when he was returning on his visit to the Galatian churches on the second missionary journey, *then,* (if circumcision be maintained), *hath the stumbling-block of the cross been done away.* The cross cuts the way of salvation by human merit up by the roots. There is no compromise in true Christianity. Justification is by faith alone. The offensiveness of the cross to the Jews is that salvation is obtained without circumcision and obedience to the ancestral statutes of Moses (Chrysostom, cited by Burton, *ICC* p. 287).

v. 12. *I* (was wishing)[84] *could wish, that they which unsettle you* disturbing your minds shall, even going beyond circumcision, cut themselves, making of themselves eunuchs[85] as the priests of Cybele, glorying in their flesh as they do. The Galatian Christians knew of this custom in heathenism. Paul did wish that they would "cut themselves off," withdrawing wholly from the nefarious work they were doing; it would be well, but this may not be the concept in

---

78. Burton, *I. C. C.* Galatians in loco.
79. Cf. I Cor. 9:24, 27 in *Word Pictures* by Robertson.
80. It is likely that it was some ringleader of the Judaists.
81. Dative case, *alētheia,* to the personal interest to the cause of the truth. It was also to the interest of their own personal welfare if they would but recognize it.
82. Demonstrative force of the definite article.
83. Present indicative progressive tense, goes on leavening, imperceptibly though it be.
84. Cf. *Word Pictures,* Robertson on I Cor. 4:2; II Cor. 11:1.
85. Future middle of apokoptō, to cut off or mutilate one's self, Cf. Acts 27:32 in *Word Pictures* by Robertson.

his passage i. e. the mutilation of emasculation which would, as a matter of fact, exclude them from the congregation of the Lord.[86] If this is the true interpretation it reminds one of the imprecatory Psalms. Paul might mean rather that they cut themselves off from any contact with the Galatian Gentile Christians.

B. Exhortation against the abuse of Christian liberty in their personal conduct (Ch. 5:13-26). Paul's enemies lost no opportunity to attack his personal character; and one of their criticisms was that his teaching of salvation by faith alone let down the gap to immorality by removing the restraints of the law. So Paul urges that the Christian standard must and is to be the highest of all moral standards, and if they live up to it they will fulfill the true requirement of the law of Christian love. He presents meaningful lists of the works of the flesh which must be avoided and eliminated and others of the Spirit which must be cultivated. The doctrine of Christian freedom by no means allows the Christian to yield to the gratification of fleshly desires. It is, on the contrary, a freedom from such passions and lusts of the flesh through the help of Christ, through the Holy Spirit, in living a clean, spiritual, victorious life in Him.[87]

1. Paul explains what the right use of Christian liberty is and warns against its abuse. Ch. 5:13-25. Christian liberty is freedom from the bondage of lust, and also power given to live a victorious life for Christ. The Apostle exhorts the Galatians against falling into error. In Christian love they should serve one another and thus fulfil the requirement of the law, the bondage of which they had discarded for the liberty in Christ.

v. 13. *For* over against the mere formal practice of circumcision *you brethren were called*,[88] at your conversion definitely, *for liberty* (freedom) and not for bondage; *only do not use your*[89] *liberty for an occasion* or 'spring board' of opportunity *for the flesh*, by turning liberty into license, *but* on the contrary *be* continually *serving*[90] *one another through* Christian *love*, the motive power in a true conduct. The Christian must crucify not only sensual indulgences but selfishness of all forms and sin in general.

v. 14. *For the whole moral law* relative to our relationships to others *has been* and is *fulfilled in this one word* (expression): "*Thou shalt love thy neighbor as thyself.*" Love is the fulfilling of the law, as a result, in the life in the Spirit. Christian love is a strict and successful master.[91]

v. 15. *But if you go on biting and devouring*[92] *one another, take heed*, (watch out) *lest you be consumed by one another*. These expressions picture a condition of church strifes which is terrible, and leads men to act like beasts of the

---

86. Cf. Burton, *I. C. C.* Galatians pp. 288f. Cf. Deut. 23:1,2.
87. Cf. Burton *I. C. C.*, Dana *Life and Letters of Paul* and *The Lutheran Com.* Galatians in loco.
88. First aorist passive of *kaleō*.
89. Use of article for pronoun of possession.
90. Present active imperative, begin and continue serving.
91. Lutheran Commentary p. 394.
92. Two present progressive tenses indicating a continued process.

forests and not as brethren. The biting of slander, criticism, and abuse lea on to mutual destruction. "If the spirit of Christian love does not preven brethren from 'preying' on one another, they are in danger of utter destruc tion."[93]

2. Christians who regulate their lives by the Spirit will not carry out th lusts of the flesh because God has placed these two forces in antagonism withi Christian hearts. The Spirit masters unlawful lusts before they issue in action No law can condemn the one who bears the fruits of the spirit, (vv. 16-26).

v. 16 *But I say*, and this is what I mean, *Walk by the Spirit*[94] *and you shal not fulfil*[95] *the lust of the flesh.*

v. 17 *For the flesh lusteth against the* (Holy) *Spirit and the Spirit against the flesh; for these are contrary the one to the other*, in your hearts, *that you may not keep on doing*[96] *these things, whatsoever you may wish.*

v. 18 *But, if you are being led by the Spirit,*[97] then it follows that, *you are not any longer under the law.*)

v. 19 But *the works of the flesh are manifest* (evident) *which are these*: *fornication* (prostitution or harlotry), *uncleanness* (or moral impurity), *lasciviousness* (wantonness),

v. 20 *Idolatry, eidolatreia* (worship of idols), *sorcery* (or witchcraft) (*pharmakeia*) with the ministry of drugs; sins of personal relations follow, as: *enmities* (*echthrai*) or personal animosities. *strife* (*eris*) of rivalry or discord, *jeolousy* (*zēlos*), *wraths* (*thumoi*) stirring up the emotions of temper resulting in explosions; *factions* (*eritheiai*) manifest in party spirit or partisanship; *divisions,* (*dichostasiai*), in splits; *factions* (*haireseis*), or choices based on preferences; *envyings,* (*phthonoi*), feelings of ill-will, (*methai*) *drunkenness;*

V. 21 revellings (*komoi*) as in drunken parties for Bacchus; *and such like*: *of which I forewarn you even as I said before, that they who practice such things shall not inherit the kingdom of God.* The habit of practicing these things shows that such a one is not in the kingdom of God and will not inherit it.[98] There are four distinct groups of these words covering sensual sins, idolatry, sins of personal and social relations, sins of drunken excesses and revellings in drunken parties.

vv. 22ff bring a list of the fruits of the Spirit which must characterize the Christian life:

v. 22 *But the fruit of the Spirit is* like a tree bearing nine representative types of good fruit which are *love,* (*agapē*), different from (*philia*), friendship, and sensual love (*eros*); *joy,* (*chara*); *peace,* (*eirēnē*); *long-suffering* (*makrothumia*); *kindness* (*chrestotēs*); *goodness* (*agathosunē*); *faithfulness* (*pistis*), *trustfulness; meekness* (*prautēs*) active meekness; *temperance* (*egkrateia*), self-

93. Rendall, Frederic, *Expositor's Greek Test.* p. 186.
94. Instrumental case, (walk) by the Spirit.
95. Double negative with aor. act. subj.
96. Present subjunctive *poiēte* with negative *mē*.
97. Robertson, A. T. *Word Pictures* p. 312f; Boises' *Notes.*
98. Robertson, A. T. *Word Pictures* p. 312f; Boises' *Notes.*

control. Paul's list of the virtues is better than that of the Stoics: temperance, prudence, fortitude, and justice (Robertson).

v. 23 *Against those* who possess and practice such virtues *there is no law.*

v. 24 *But they that are of Christ Jesus* by having surrendered themselves into his hands, *have crucified the flesh,* the force in men which makes for evil (Burton) along *with its passions and* its dispositions toward evil or *lusts.*

So Paul concludes with an exhortation (vv. 25, 26).

v. 25 *If we live by the Spirit,* as it is evident[99] we do, having exercised faith in Christ, then *let us also walk* in our daily conduct *by* making use of the help and guidance of *the Spirit,* being guided by Him who was sent to be our guide.

v. 26 *Let us not become vainglorious, provoking one another, envying one another.* When Christians compete for earthly glory, the result is that they are soon provoking one another and are filled with envyings as the fickle Galatians came to be.

C. Finally, Paul exhorts to fraternal love, bearing one another's burdens; to fruitful liberality and to persistent activity in Christian fellowship. Ch. 6:1-10.

1. Exhortation to mutual burden-bearing love. (6:1-5).

v. 1. *Brethren, even if a man* (brother) *be overtaken in* any trespass or fault, *you that are spiritual,* being led by the Holy Spirit, *restore such a one* to wholeness, dealing with him *in the spirit of meekness* or gentleness and forbearance, and not in the attitude of 'I-am-holier-than thou,' but *considering thyself* and looking well to the possibility of your being tempted yourself, *lest indeed thou also be tempted* and fall into the same or some other sin.

v. 2. *Bear ye,* (begin to bear and keep on bearing[99a]) *one another's* heavy *burdens* of diverse kinds, carrying them with endurance, when the load is about to press your brother down, *and so fulfill*[1] (or you will fulfill) *the law of Christ.* which is that of self-sacrificing love. This was the new commandment Christ gave.[2]

v. 3. *For if*[3] *anyone thinks* himself *to be something* 'a big number,' *when he is nothing,* 'a zero,' (as men do), *he deceives himself,* leading his own mind astray, for he deceives no one else. (Robertson).

v. 4. *But let each one put to the test his own work* habitually[4] so as to avoid self-deception *and then he will have* ground for *glorying* or boasting *in respect to himself alone and not in regard to the other*[5] (his brother neighbor). Boasting is often born of measuring the cloth of a brother's character and conduct by the yardstick of one's own conceited opinion of himself. Let him therefore examine his own work rigidly that he may humbly help in bearing any too

---

99. Condition of the first class, *ei* with the indicative, according to fact.
99a. Pres. Imv. progressive action of *bastazō.*
1. Imperative, (or future indicative) in some MSS.
2. Cf. John 19: 34; I John 4:21.
3. Condition of the first class, according to reality.
4. Present imperative of 3rd per. of *dokimazō* pronounced dokima (d) *zō.*
5. Cf. Rom. 13:8.

heavy burden of a brother's fault when such there may be.

v. 5. *For each one shall bear his own private load* of weakness and sin, and being conscious of his own load he will sympathize and help to bear the burdens of others.

2. Exhortation to Christian liberality in the support of the cause and in fellowship with the saints (6:6-10).

v. 6. *And* let *the one who is being taught or instructed in the word of God*, by the teachers in the churches *communicate*,[6] contributing systematically and habitually *in* respect to *all good things* of temporal material support and also spiritual things, *to the one teaching* him. Paul did believe in the liberal financial support of the ministers as well as their spiritual backing by the churches.

v. 7. He warns the Galatian brethren as well as all Christians of the consequences of not giving this support. *Do not be deceived*,[7] if you have not been, and if you have, stop being deceived, *God is not mocked*, if you have been deceiving yourself by negligence as to this duty and privilege of contributing. God does not allow a believer to 'turn up his nose'[8] in mockery by withholding of his material support from the due and just contribution to the cause of Christ, however small his contribution may be in comparison with that of others. This is the common view of the right interpretation of this verse of Scripture but it is not generally preached or practised by the great mass of Christians. God will not be mocked and the Christian would best not attempt with impunity to neglect this solemn requirement of Him, to whom we owe all we have and are, much more our financial support of His cause.

v. 8. The reason is adduced: *for whatsoever a man may sow this* very thing *shall he also reap*, in the same proportion and kind. *Because the one sowing unto his own flesh*, as in the case of circumcision as a means to salvation or in the case of sowing to material wealth and a selfish, carnal life, the principle of the law of life, material or spiritual is, that like produces like and sowing to the material carnal life, one *shall from the flesh reap corruption; but the one* sowing *to the Holy Spirit*, the embodiment of all things spiritual, shall from *the Spirit reap life eternal* and all the blessings it embraces.

v. 9. *And while doing*[9] *the good* (beautiful), *let us not keep on giving in to the evil, for in* its own *proper*[10] time or *season we shall be reaping*,[11] *if we faint not*.

v. 10. *So then, as we may have opportunity, let us be working*[12] the good to all men whether believers or not *but* especially *to the householders of the faith*, who are the true spiritual Israel or real Christians who serve sincerely the Christ of God.

---

6. Present passive participle of *koinōneō* to contribute (Burton).
7. Present passive imperative, *planāsthe* with *mē*, stop being led astray.
8. *Mukterizein*, to sneer or turn up the nose in mockery.
9. Present progressive participle *poiountes*, doing.
10. *Idiōi*, locative of point of time.
11. Future tense, progressive action in the future.
12. Volative present middle subjunctive of *ergazō*.

Conclusion

1. Final warning against the Judaizers and summary of the letter in conclusion. Ch. 6:11-16.

For identification of his letters Paul usually wrote a few lines in the conclusion of each, in his own hand, in larger characters (or capital letters), than were those in script used by the amanuensis who had taken the rest of the epistle from dictation. Here Paul repeats his warning against the Judaistic teachers and affirms again the spirituality of his teachings. Salvation was by faith alone in Jesus Christ and neither being a son of Abraham nor having been circumcised according to the ceremonial law, availed anything; but a new creation in Christ. He pronounces a benediction upon all who follow this rule and prays for the mercy of God to be upon the Israel of God, such as had exercised a faith like that of Abraham.[13]

v. 11. Paul takes the pen from the amanuensis and writes the conclusion of the letter (vv. 11-16) with large capital letters and calls the attention of his readers to the identity of the style and teachings with his other letters.

See[14] (behold!) *with what*[15] *large letters* (characters) *I have written*[16] *you with my*[17] own *hand.*

v. 12. *So many as wish to make a fair shou* (carnally) *in the flesh,* boasting of how many proselytes they have made to the Law of Moses and to Israel, *these are trying to compel you to be circumcised, only in order that they may not be persecuted for* (on account of) *the cross of Christ.* They wanted to escape persecution.

v. 13. *For neither are those who* from time to time *are* submitting to be *circumcised keep* truly and consistently *the law, but they wish you to be circumcised, in order that they may glory* (or boast) *in your flesh;* in reporting how many converts to Judaism they have made. This reminds one of the emphasis some pastors and other leaders put on statistics instead of on really effective work.

v. 14. *But to me, may it not happen* (God forbid!) *that I should glory, except in the cross of our Lord Jesus Christ,* symbol of His sufferings and death, *through whom the world has been crucified*[18] *to me and I unto the world.* Paul gloried in the cross as the ground of his hope of salvation. Paul's life-interest was no longer in the things of sense or in external religion of rites and ceremonies as circumcision and traditional Judaism.

v. 15. *For neither circumcision is anything* worth while *nor uncircumcision* in the matter of eternal salvation, *but* what is important is *a new creature* (creation) in Christ Jesus. This is what distinguishes Christianity

---

13. Cf. Gal. 3:7-9, 14, 29; Rom 4:11, 12.
14. Imperative, a command to look at his letters well.
15. Writing in characteristic style.
16. Epistolary aorist active indicative.
17. Personal pronoun, *emēi* instrumental.
18. Perfect tense completed action and permanent result abiding.

from traditional Judaism — the new birth which is the first and most important ear-mark of the Christian.

v. 16. *As many as shall walk,*[20] hereafter, straight forward, *by this* directing line maxim or principle[19] *rule,* may[21] *peace be upon them, and mercy, and* also *upon the Israel of our God.* Paul includes his hope that Israel, his people also may embrace this exclusive, spiritual salvation of Christianity.

Some commentators would hope that some believers among the sons of Jacob might have such a faith as Abraham looking forward to the Messiah, but Paul's whole argument favors the view that only spiritual Israel, composed exclusively of believers in Jesus as the Christ, can have the real peace and mercy of God.[22]

2. An appeal in conclusion, reenforced by reference to his struggle and sufferings. The final bendiction (vv. 17, 18).

v. 17. *From henceforth* (as for the rest) *let no man trouble me* (with the toils of a persecuting antagonistic controversy), *for I bear in my body the marks*[23] *of Jesus,* scars made by many scourgings and beatings received in persecutions.[24] Slaves of those times had the names of their owners branded upon their bodies. Paul gloried in having these credentials of his bond-service to Christ.

v. 18. *The grace of our Lord Jesus Christ be with your spirit, brethren. Amen.* The letter began with rebuke but closed with benediction and a prayer that they might have grace, the grace of the Lord Jesus Christ, which is the *sine qua non* of the Christian religion. But for His *Grace,* there would be no election, adoption in the Beloved, redemption through His atoning blood resulting in regeneration through faith in Him, no sealing of the Spirit in the new birth, against the day of final completed redemption in a sinless sanctification, "without spot or wrinkle or any such thing." This was the concluding benediction of the aging Apostle upon his beloved children in the faith in Galatia. It was a fit conclusion to the most pungent reproof ever administered by an apostolic founder to Christian churches, out of the love of a tender fatherly heart; *and the greatest apologetic of Christian history against the ever-abiding tendency of traditional humanistic* thought leading *Christian churches to drift back to the rudiments of a man-made paralyzing ecclesiastical ceremonialism and deadening sacramentalism of mere churchanity.*

This epistle it was that Luther used to attack the apostasy of his times in so-called historic Christianity by bringing on the Reformation! It is the concise, plain statement of the plan of salvation which should be used in the much needed indoctrination of all really evangelical denominations of Christianity in the fundamental preparation for world evangelization.

---

19. Cf. Meyer, in loco, also Boises' *Notes.*
20. Future, some MSS present indicative.
21. Optative of wish or prayerful benediction.
22. Cf. I Peter 1:9, 10.
23. Cf. II Cor. 6:4-6; 11:23ff.
24. The author recalls a deep scar on the forehead of Dr. W. B. Bagby, missionary founder of Baptist mission in Brazil S. A., received by a stone thrown by a persecutor instigated by a Catholic priest while the missionary was baptizing a candidate in a pool.

XVIII

Romans

Introduction

Paul's eyes had long been fixed on Rome, the great capital of the world civilization, as the strategic center from which to propagate the Gospel in other countries yet unentered. It was no sudden impulse, but his long-growing desire,[1] which crystallized into a conviction in his heart under the power of the Spirit, that 'he must see Rome.'[2] The church already founded in Rome was located in a place of great strategy and might become a mighty power in the evangelization of the western half of the empire. Almost all the previous years of his arduous ministry had been spent in the eastern part of the empire.

Paul was a Roman citizen and had great respect for the law and order which the Roman government had carried to the world on the plan of autonomy. He had been blessed personally in his ministry of the Gospel by the protection of the Roman authorities as he traveled long distances in his missionary work. This universal empire had indirectly influenced Paul's thought in his planning for the conquest of the universal Gospel.[3] The laws of Rome were good. The organization one of genius and the administration, though severe and sometimes cruel, was yet blessed by the benign influence of Seneca and some other philosophers. Withal pagan worship and immorality were widely prevalent and extreme, as the black portrayal which Paul gives of his times, was doubtless characteristic not only of Corinth, where he wrote the letter, but of Rome also.[4]

There was a considerable colony of Jews in Rome, dating from the taking of Jerusalem by Pompey in 63 B. C. Many of the Jewish slaves were manumitted and constituted a considerable colony beyond the Tiber. The colony had a varying fortune in its relationship with the Roman authorities, illustrated in the edict of expulsion of the Jews by the Emperor Claudius in 52 A. D., "because of tumults in the Jewish quarter, at the instigation of one Chrestus,"[5] which may probably refer to the effects of the preaching of early Christians there, about Christ, as the Messiah, in which activity Priscilla and Aquilla may have participated. They and many others did have to leave Rome tem-

---

1. Rom. 15:23; 1:13
2. Acts 19:21
3. Rom. 1:8-15
4. Rom. 1:18-32
5. Acts 18:2

porarily. But the policy of the government on the whole was liberal toward the Jews and some persons, even "of the household of Caesar" were affected by the Gospel and some Jews attained rank and position in Rome. In other parts of the Empire this liberal policy permitted the Jews in Palestine, as it did other peoples in various parts, to have their own judicial and administrative bodies.

The character of the church in Rome would naturally have much to do with his understanding interpretation of the epistle, as many of Paul's friends were in Rome and some of them had long been there. We do not know the origin of the church. Ambrosiaster, of the fourth century, held that it arose among the Jews in the Jewish colony across the Tiber. There were some 'visitors' from Rome in Jerusalem on the day of Pentecost, who may have returned and begun the preaching of the Gospel among the Jews in that city. There is nothing in the epistle to indicate that Paul knew of any apostolic founder of the church. That it was composed of both Jews and Gentiles seems clear but with a predominance of the Gentile element. There were as many as nine Jewish synogogues in the Jewish colony. The preaching of the Gospel might have been initiated by the visitors to Jerusalem at Pentecost, but if so the probability is that the Christian preaching of Jesus as Messiah had brought a separation from the synogogue, as in the preaching of Paul in various cities later in history. But there is no evidence, that Christianity of the distinct type of the Pauline Gospel was existent there when Paul wrote his letter. They evidently did not have a clear understanding of Pauline freedom from the Law in every way. Paul had it in mind to complete their limited understanding of the Gospel when he should arrive there on his visit. This would be true if they were Jews or Gentile proselytes. That the church was composed mainly of Gentiles being clear, the probability is that the majority of the members were Gentile proselytes. Paul addresses them as Gentiles in various places in the letter.[6] Most of the passages which are interpreted by some as referring to Jews can be understood as referring to the principle of law and not necessarily to the Mosaic law. The best conclusion as to the predominant composition is that, while the church was mostly Gentile, there was a minority in the church, of Jewish origin.

The date, place, and occasion of the letter are set forth in the introduction (1:1-15), and the epilogue and conclusion of the epistle (15:14-16:27), assuming (as I do) that chapter 16 was a part of the original manuscript of Paul. He was on his last visit in Corinth in the winter of 57-58 A. D. or possibly in the spring of 58 A. D. when he wrote this greatest of his epistles, though some think it might have been a year later.[7] The apostle was guest in the house of his friend Gaius, a wealthy Christian living in Corinth, and so freed from all necessity, for a brief period, of supporting himself while writing.

---

6. Rom. 1:5; 1:13; 11:25-28; 15:15f.
7. James Denney, Expos. Gr. Test, Introd. to Romans.

Analysis and Exposition

To the Romans (Pros Romaious)[8]

The Epistle of Paul[9]

Introduction 1:1-15

1. The apostolic salutation presenting the writer and his message. 1:1-7.

v. 1. *Paul*[10] presents himself as a bond-slave, possessed by and sent from,[11] *Jesus Christ,* divinely *called* to be *an apostle,* sent under and carrying the authority of the Master, *separated* permanently[12] for[13] the delivering of the *Gospel of God,* the glad tidings of salvation, and isolated from any other purpose or aim in his life. The best evidence of a divine call is complete separation, in devotion to the ministry in the glad tidings of countless treasures of abiding and unchangeable blessings, which the Gospel of God brings.[14] It is thus a gospel to cheer the heart from the outstart.

v. 7. His salutation was "*to all those* Christians *that are in Rome,*" a city of flagrant wickedness and the capital of the pagan world. Yet there were some people in Rome who were *beloved of God, called* out from the midst of an evil generation, to be *saints,* to become holy, by living lives of consecration to Christ. He addresses those Christians with his usual though none the less pregnant words of salutation: *Grace,* the free unmerited favor of God, *and peace,* that holy repose within and so around the Christian, which comes of the acceptance of God in Christ, and his abiding presence ever, both of which blessings are *from God our* heavenly *Father and*[15] equally from our sovereign, divine *Lord Jesus*[15], who is our Saviour and prophetically predicted *Christ* or Messiah of spiritual Israel. "Grace and peace are inseparable, the flower of peace growing from the root of grace, which is in God."

v. 2. The Gospel message, *which* Paul preached *was before announced*[16] *through*[17] the intermediate agency of *his* inspired *prophets in the*[18] *Holy Scriptures.* Paul definitely found God's Gospel rooted in the Holy Scriptures,[19] of the Old Testament.

v. 3. The subject and center of that Gospel was *concerning* (God's) *his*

---

8. Title as given in oldest Greek MSS. Aleph A. B. C.
9. These other words were added in later MSS up to the Textus Receptus.
10. Paulos, the Roman name of Saul of Tarsus.
11. Genitive or ablative possible under complete possession and direction, "Paradise in the concrete." (Moule)
12. Perfect passive participle of *aphorizō*, permanent status.
13. Eis with the accusitive expressing the end for which.
14. John Chrysostom.
15. Paul's theology sets before us at once the deity of Jesus in the coordination of the conjunction *kai.*
16. First aorist middle of *proeuaggelō.*
17. Prep. *dia* with the genitive.
18. No article expressed in Gr. text but yet definite (Robertson).
19. Robertson, A. T. *Word Pictures,* Romans in loco.

divine *Son, who was a* real human, *born from the seed of David, according to the flesh* or lineal descent, and *who was declared*[20]

v. 4. to be *the Son of God*, as a person of the Trinity in his preincarnate state, because declared in his incarnate state to be divine, *with power*,[21] *according to His* human *spirit of holiness*, being sinless *as it was and* by His own claim, which itself was sealed *by* his miraculous and supernatural *resurrection* from the dead, being raised *from the dead*, himself, three days, as He testified He would be, after his death on the cross. In virtue of this supernatural seal He is *Jesus the Messiah, our* resurrected *Lord*, forevermore.

v. 5. *through whom we received*[22] the *grace* of salvation *and of apostleship for*[23] *obedience to the faith*, once delivered to the saints, exercised in Christ, leading into a ministry *among all the nations*, including

v. 6. the Jews, *on behalf of His name, among whom you also are the called of Jesus Christ.*

In his unusually long salutation (1:1-7) Paul presents three things which characterize him as one who is writing a letter to this church in a field unknown to him personally: (1) He describes himself as a bond-slave of Jesus Christ; (2) he claims to be a divinely chosen apostle, and (3) he is set apart for the propagation of the Gospel of God, all of which traits would be of vital interest to the Christian church which he was to visit soon and to which he now addresses the letter with his expressed desire that they should be blessed with the grace and peace of God and of Christ.

About his message he cites (vv. 2-6) the reasons he has faith in the Gospel of God which he is to preach to them: (1) because it came through the Hebrew prophets of the Old Testament Scriptures, as its source and agents, (2) because it was about the divine Son of God, who by his birth into the regal line of David 'broke into human history,' as a sinless man, who verified his claim to sinlessness and to be the Savior of humanity by raising men from the dead and himself rising from the grave after His death. He is thus constituted the sovereign Lord over human life and final authority in all matters of religion for mankind. Paul claims to be commissioned, having received the grace of God in salvation and the gift for apostleship among the nations both Gentiles and also Jews, and so to this church and the people in Rome also.

2. Paul reveals to them his long deferred desire to see this famed church in Rome, for which he thanks God, and to deliver to them his own Gospel message of salvation, as he has to many other people of the

a. Gentile world 1:8-15. He records first, his thanks to God for all of the members of this noble church whose faith and faithfulness had gained for it a reputation in the whole known world. 1:8,9.

---

20. First aorist passive of *horizō*, to set forth or declare, to affirm.
21. Instrumental case with prep. *en*.
22. Second aorist act. of *lambanō*, to receive, here editorial *we*.
23. *Eis* with the accusative, unto, for etc.

v. 8. *First indeed, I constantly give thanks*[24] *to my*[25] *God* with a personal interest, praying through Jesus the risen Christ and in his name *about you all* and every one, *because your* strong and loyal *faith is being proclaimed,* as tidings from the imperial capital *over the whole* known *world.*

v. 9. *For God is my witness* and knows how much you are in my prayers, he *whom I serve* with adoration and obedience *in my spirit in the* propagation of the *Gospel,* praying for the mission churches, *of his Son.* He is aware *how unceasingly,* without leaving you out a single time, *I make mention of you.*

b. He tells them of his desire, long hindered, to visit them. vv. 10-13.

v. 10. *On every occasion at my prayer times, making* earnest and repeated *request,*[26] *if by any means now at length,*[27] *I may be prospered,*[28] *in the will of God, to come to you.* Paul made all his plans subject to the will of God.

v. 11. *For I long*[29] *to see you,* (in order) *that I may impart*[30] *to you some spiritual gift* of grace, *to the end that you may be established*[31] in the full knowledge of the Gospel of Christ.

v. 12. *that is, indeed,* I should explain, *that I may be comforted in you, along with you, through* mutual *faith in one another, both yours and mine* in a strengthening fellowship *together.*

v. 13. *I would not have you ignorant, brethren, that oftentimes I purposed to come unto you,* (and I was hindered hitherto), *that I might have some fruit in you also even as among the rest of the Gentiles.*

c. Paul recognized his universal obligation of the messenger in regard to his message. vv. 14, 15.

v. 14. *To the Greeks, indeed,* he had gone with the Gospel, spending more than two years on his second missionary journey among them and visiting them afterwards,[32] *also to* all other peoples classified by the Greeks as the *Barbarians,* including the Jews in Asia Minor and Syria for several years on his first and third missionary journeys. He had not limited his ministry to any class: *both to the wise* — the intellectuals — *and to the* ignorant or *foolish, I am debtor,* to deliver sympathetically the message of the glad tidings.

v. 14. *So, as far as it is* possible *to me,* and when the door of opportunity opens, *I am* eager and *ready to preach the gospel to you also that are in Rome.*

In many of Paul's epistles his salutation is followed by an expression of thanksgiving for the church and its accomplishments. In this epistle both his

---

24. Present indicative active, progressive and habitual action.
25. Dative of personal interest of intimate character using the possessive pronoun for intimacy of interest.
26. *Deomenos,* present participle, begging.
27. Four particles bunched together to express the apostle's emotion.
28. Future passive indicative of *enudoō, enudōthēsomai* expressing contingency in a condition of the first class in the form of an indirect question.
29. *Epipothō* — am homesick.
30. *Hina* with 2nd aor. active *metadō* subj. in a purpose clause.
31. *Eis* with first aor passive inf. of *sterizō* in a final clause. Paul wished to share with them some interpretation of the word, some spiritual experiences perhaps.
32. He went from Ephesus to Macedonia and also to Corinth for a period later.

usual salutation and thanksgiving are expanded because of the extraordinary importance of the church located in Rome, the greatest capital of world civilization at that time. It was exceedingly important that this church should become embued with the extraordinary missionary impulse which surcharged the intense activity of the apostle in his campaign to plant Christianity in all the most strategic centers of the Roman Empire.

Paul deftly turns his expression of thanksgiving into an expression of appreciation of the great church he is soon to visit. He refers to his deep sense of gratitude for their marvelous progress in the faith of the gospel and expresses his earnest desire to have a share in the further enlargement and strengthening of the church which was so strategically located in this logical center for the world campaign of the universal Christianity, the final religion for all humankind. With keen perception for the position of the Jews in the enlargement campaign of the Christian cause, in his discussion of the import of his message in this introduction, he makes plain the fact that the message of the Gospel was not inconsistent with the fulfilment of God's promises to Israel.

Theme

The theme of the Roman epistle, Paul's *magnum opus,* must needs be his most complete single expression of the missionary message of Christianity. It is a clear statement of the plan of salvation for all mankind, being condensed in the masterly ingenious thought of the Apostle to the Gentiles within the incredibly short space of the two verses (Rom 1:16,17). Every word in the two verses plays a vital role: there is naught included which is superfluous nor ought excluded which naturally pertains. It is the highest example of Christian thinking, being the sublimest peak of Paul's logical dialectic expression, capped by the light of intuitive religious inspiration. This light was kindled in the soul of Paul when he saw the Risen Christ on the Damascus road. Paul ascends here with a leap to the supreme idea of the reality of the righteousness which is the God-kind of righteousness, of justice on one side and grace on the obverse. In eight chapters with a matchless dialectic he unfolds the negative and positive views of righteousness, the self-righteousness by works and the God kind of imputed *faith* righteousness by faith in Christ, showing the development of each to its logical results. By a clear analysis of these two verses we derive a bird's eye view of the content of the theme which is to be more fully revealed by the paraphrastic interpretation of the epistle.

Exposition

I, Paul, known to you as a converted Jew from the remote province of Palestine, considered a renegade by most of my fellow-countrymen, but being also a Roman citizen by birth in Tarsus, a free city of the Empire, *am not ashamed,* feeling a sense of humiliation in my proposal to be a herald *of the Gospel* message *of* good tidings even in Rome, about the Jewish Rabbi *Christ* who died years ago, a felon's death on a cross near Jerusalem.. The reason for this is summed up as follows: *for, in it,* this story about the Nazarene prophet who was born in the little town of Bethlehem, *is* found to exist *the power of God,* in its experienced manifestation, leading *unto salvation to everyone who believes* and accepts its message, freeing him from sin and its destructive effects commonly experienced by sinful mankind universally. The secret of its dynamic effect on the heart of every man who experiences it is found in (v. 17): *For in it is being revealed,*[33] progressively and so certainly, *the God-kind of righteousness,* which by revelation in the ancient covenant and record of the historic manifestations of God's nature and being to his people Israel, is known historically and experientially. It is not of the nature of self-righteousness on which (we) Jews have thought to hang our hope of salvation from sin. This kind of righteousness has proven unavailing, not freeing us from the power of sin as does this God-kind of righteousness revealed in the life of the Nazarene prophet, before our eyes, and repeated though imperfectly now in the lives of his disciples. This God-kind of righteousness begins and takes its source *from faith,* in the experience of every man who puts his trust in Jesus Christ. It is substantiated by the experience of every believer in the immedate sense of pardon, peace, joy, hope, a new and direct access to God in Communion (Rom. 5:1-3), and a new impulse to activities in a life of righteousness or right action toward others and of reverence toward God. (Rom. 1:18f). It leads *into* a life of *faith,* such as that illustrated in the Old Testament forefathers like Abraham and others, yea like the pious Israelite, who, in the midst of the perils of invasion of the hordes of Chaldeans was saved by his peaceful and harmless tranquillity growing out of a faith and trust in Jehovah's keeping. The righteousness, which he knew to be in God's nature, was security enough for him who trusted God in the midst of the perils. But the God-kind of righteousness which makes man eligible for God's daily and constant fellowship must become, through faith in Christ, a characteristic thus planted in man's nature also. The cultivation of this faith in Christ reveals its results in the growth of the Christ-like nature and character in the believer. Salvation is the result of this new nature and disposition imparted by God to the man who accepts Christ into his life through repentence toward God and faith in the Lord Jesus. *The just man* according to the promise recorded in Habakkuk *shall live* in the midst of the eventualities of the Chaldean invasion *by* his tranquil *faith* or confidence in Jehovah the God of Israel.

I. *The Doctrinal Part of the Epistle. Chs.* 1:18-11:36.

A. The Universal necessity of the God-kind of Righteousness for man's salvation. Ch. 1:18-3:20.

1. The necessity for this kind of righteousness is manifested in the case of the Gentiles, who through their irreverence and rejection of God, Who was

33. Present indicative passive of the verb *apokaluptō* — to reveal.

revealed to them in the light of nature and their own reason or consciences, came to experience the results of the wrath of God against sin, in being left by God to work out wilfully their own destruction. 1:18-32.

v. 18. *For*[34] *the wrath of God is being revealed* in an unwritten but true revelation *from heaven* as truly as God's righteousness of love is revealed in the written word. It is not a wrath which boils up in temper but one of reason embodied in natural laws. The revelation of God's propitiatory righteousness embodied in Christ and the divinely inspired Gospel record was necessary for the Gentiles because they had failed and the heathen nations continue to fail to attain to the God-kind of righteousness without the Gospel. The wrath of God rests upon those persons who do not attain the righteousness of God whether they are Gentiles who do not have the revealed Word of the Bible or Jews who have had the oracles of God. The reason for this is that it is revealed *against* the lack of reverence toward God, *ungodliness* or irreligion *and unrighteousness* or lack of right conduct toward men. The basis of right conduct rests on the right attitude of men toward a righteous God and not on the unethical variable basis of the law of the jungle. Such a moral standard is exemplified in the conduct of men *who suppress the truth in their own hearts and hold down the truth* by their evil ways and deeds *in unrighteousness* or injustice.

There are three steps in the degeneration of the heathen nations: a. They begin with natural religion revealed in nature and reason. Every man has the knowledge of God put within his reach in nature and all created beings including himself. vv. 19,20.

v. 19. *Because that which may be known of God is manifest in them*[35] in their hearts and reason or conscience. For God manifested[36] it to them[37] in his marvelous works in the material universe (macrocosm) and in their inner nature of reason or conscience (microcosm). Every man, even the heathen, has the knowledge of God revealed to him in created things.[38]

v. 20. *For the invisible things of him*, his attributes namely, *his everlasting power and* his *divinity embracing* all attributes, *from* the time of *the creation of the* material *world* (universe) *are clearly seen, being perceived by* means of *the things that are made, "so that they* (heathen peoples) *are without excuse."*[39] Not even the rendering, "that they may be without excuse"[40] is strong enough to portray the situation of the heathen. The knowledge of God all might have, from his character imprinted upon creation, is the statement of the highest scholarship about the status of the heathen, covering Paul's inspired word (vv. 19,20).[41] Missionary experience had taught Paul and has been verified

---

34. Gar both explanatory and argumentative.
35. Locative of sphere within which, *en antois*, among or in them.
36. Aorist active indicative, an actual occurrence in the case of each.
37. Dative of personal interest, advantage, *antois*.
38. Cf. Robertson, A. T. *Word Pictures* p. 328,9 Vol. Paul's Epistles.
39. *Eis to* with pres. inf. *einai* and acc. of reference (Robertson *Word Pictures*) adverbial acc. for result.
40. Cf. Robertson A. T. *Word Pictures* p. 329; Moulton, *Prologonena* p. 219.
41. Sanday and Headlam *Com. I C. C.* Romans p. 39.

in the experience of missionaries universally, down through the centuries, that, without the Gospel, heathen peoples are hopeless. One chance in a thousand of such attaining to the "righteousness of God," which is in Christ alone, is too much to expect. If men are hard to get saved with the Gospel how much more without the preached word.

b. The second stage in man's universal degeneration vv. 21-23. The Gentile (heathen) nations, instead of adoring God whom they know in his works of creation, put him out of their minds and turn to vain speculation and idolatry; knowing God as portrayed in his created universe of humanity and things, they have not glorified him as God, but have always turned to vain philosophy and man-made theories about creation and man-made religions and beliefs, with the result that their mental powers and understanding have been darkened and lost in delusion. Thinking themselves to be wise they have become foolish and proudly exalted the creature (man or other animals lower still) above the Creator, God. Here is history of the past and present. Their only hope is wrapped up in the revealed word of God. The message of the revealed Gospel is the one beam of light looking toward a redeemed world[42] "in which will dwell righteousness."

v. 21. *Because that* (dioti) *knowing God,*[43] by actual experience, as evidenced among even savage tribes who erect altars to seek fearfully to appease offended deities[44] *they did not glorify*[45] him *as God,* in worship as they should, *neither gave thanks,* showing thus their ingratitude. Here we find the reason for the condemnation of heathen peoples: they know the better and do the worse. *But,* on the contrary to what they should do, *they become vain in their* humanism, speculative *reasonings, and their foolish*[46] *heart,*[47] involving intellect, feeling and will *was darkened.*

v. 22, 23. *Professing themselves to be wise* in their empty reasonings *they became fools,*[48] *and changed* or exchanged *the glory of the incorruptable* eternal *God* (for) *in the likeness of an image of corruptible man,* (as among the Greeks and Romans, gods and goddesses) *and of birds and fourfooted beasts and creeping things* or reptiles (as among the Egyptians and many other peoples) as in Africa and the islands of the seas, who worship the images of of animals.

C. The third step therefore in their degeneration was, that God had to abandon them for judgment to every kind of degredation through following their own unworthy desires, contaminating their bodies and minds (vv. 24-32). Refusing to recognize God, they turned themselves over to every kind of

42. Cf. Sanday and Headlam. *I. C. C.* Romans p. 39.
43. Second aor, active part. of *ginoskō,* to know by experience.
44. Cf. The altar to the unknown God in Athens (Acts 17:29) and altars in every even most degraded people of history and present experience. The Japanese had made a God of their mikado.
45. Aorist act. indicative, covering all historical fact.
46. *Asunetos,* unintelligent.
47. *Kardia,* includes intellect (Rom. 10:6); feeling (Rom. 9:2); and will (I Cor. 4:5) Cf. Robertson *Word Pictures* in loco.
48. Ingressive first aor. passive, *morainō,* to be a fool.

perverse sentiment, resulting in the practice of unworthy acts and disgraceful sins. In vv. 29-32 the Apostle presents a list of some of the sins which forced God to give them up to self-destruction. (a) The identification of the sinners with their sins was complete.

v. 24. *Wherefore, God gave them up,* because he could not do otherwise, leaving their wills free to act, *in the lusts of their hearts,*[49] *into uncleanness,* in the cesspool of their immoral practices, with the result *that their bodies should be dishonored*[50] *among themselves,*

v. 25. *who changed the truth of God into a lie* about the character and purpose in man's creation by their fabricated mythologies about the immoral gods (of the Greeks and Romans and of other heathen peoples) *and paid their reverence* in superstitious idolatrous and immoral worship *and their worship to the creature, service* to worshiping the idols, representing men and animals, who are creatures, *rather than the true Creator ,Who is blessed forever. Amen.*[51]

v. 26. *On account of this, God gave them over unto vile passions of dishonor. For their* (females) *women, indeed, changed their natural use into that which is against nature,* prostituting their sex uses to the sensual indulgence of the vile passions and also sexual lusts.

v. 27. *And likewise the men* (males) *abandoning the natural* procreative *use* or function *of the woman* (female) in legitimate marital relations for the propagation of the race, *burned out in their lust one toward another, men with men working* (indecent) *unseemingliness* in immoral lustful practices *and receiving* paid back to them *in themselves,* physically and spiritually, *the recompense of their* sinful *error which was due.* Sinful lusts bring their own judgment.

v. 28. *And even as they refused* stubbornly in the face of God's manifest testing and disapproval *to have God in their knowledge, God gave them up to a* disapproved, *reprobate mind,* after testing them, *to do those things which are not fitting,* like the doings of night clubs in modern cities and in the dives of the underworld, without God and in the darkness of unrestrained animal appetities (Robertson).

In verses 29-32 the Apostle presents a list of sins the practice of which forced God to withdraw his restraints and abandon them to their own wilfullness and in a total depravity. This list shows the complete identification of the sinners with their sin; that they had utterly corrupted their natures, body and soul; that their sins were habitual and ingrained; that knowing the righteousness of God by experience they continued to be workers of injustices toward their fellowmen; that they had become active sources of evils and deliberately approved sin in others, teaching others their own vile sins by precept and example.

---

49. Locative of sphere of their activities.

50. Contemplated result, articular infinitive in genitive, *tou atimazesthai,* to be dishonored by their immoral practices.

51. Paul inserts a doxology when he is deeply moved.

v. 29. Being completely[52] "*filled* to the brim with" four vices:[53] *with every kind of unrighteousness* and injustice, and *active wickedness, covetousness, maliciousness; full of* [54] *envy,* (*fthonou*) *murder* (*fonou*), *strife* (*eridos*), *deceit* (*dolou*), *malignity,* (a disposition to put a bad construction on things).

v. 30. Paul next gives twelve adjectives and substantives which are strokes of his pen to fill out the picture of the God-abandoned man: *whisperers* in the ear, (psithuristas); *backbiters, who talk back,* (*katalalous*); *hateful to God* (*theostugeis*); *insolent,* (*hubristas*); *haughty* (*huperēphanous*); *boastful* braggarts, (*alazonas*); *inventors of evil,* (*epheuretas kakōn*); *disobedient to parents,* (*goneusin apeitheis*) (a failing both ancient and modern) (Robertson);

v. 31. *without understanding* (*asunetous*); *covenant breakers,* (*asunthetous* false to their engagements), *without natural affection* or love to kindred (*astorgous*); *unmerciful,* (*aneleēmonas*).

v. 32. *Who knowing* well, accurately[55] by experience, *the ordinances* of the justice *of God,* which condemn such evil practices, *that they who practice such things are worthy of death, not only go on doing the same but also consent with* or give their approval or consent upon *them that practice them.*

The artist who painted this dark picture of human depravity was one who knew well the pagan, Graeco-Roman civilization. The heathen peoples of today, as then, know that God condemns such evil practices as these mentioned in Paul's list. Paul knew that idolatry, such as that in the temple of Aphrodite in Corinth, was accompanied by the licence of lust always. The heathen myths of Greece ascribed immoralities to their gods and goddesses, and the idolatry of Egypt put no moral constraint on its adepts. Paganism was and is unequal to the task of reforming and regenerating mankind.

That this picture was not overdrawn is evidenced by the testimony of many pagan writers, who were contemporaries of Paul. The pagans knew then as the heathen know even better in the present era, that there is a God of infinite power and wisdom. There is no other explanation for creation in all its myriad forms and infinite expansion in the material universe. The pagans did not have in most cases the Jewish Scriptures; but few of them had any direct or indirect contact with Christ, the Jewish Messiah; but they yet had the power of reason and the innate sense of conscience pointing away from the wrong to the right.

2. Following this he next presents the failure of the Jews and explains why they failed, even counting on the Law of Moses and writings of the Prophets to help them. The Jews need the Gospel as much as the Gentiles (2:1-3:8).

a. He states clearly, first that the Jewish critic is no better than the Gentile whom he criticizes before the tribunal of God's righteous judgment. Paul here appeals to the general principle of righteousness and condemns the critic whoever he may be (Ch. 2:1-16).

---

52. Perfect passive participle of *pleroō,* state of completion (Robertson).

53. Associate instrumental case of *adikkai* (unrighteousness), *poneriai* (active wickedness); *pleonexiai* (covetousness I Thess. 2:5) *kakiai* maliciousness or inward viciousness of disposition and character.

54. *Mestous,* adjective from *mestoō* to fill full.

55. *Epignontes* from epi-ginoskō to know accurately.

(1) God judges all men alike according to the actual moral facts. He is not partial in his judgment to any person or people (2:1-5).

v. 1. Paul states plainly first the situation of the *critic* whoever he may be. *Wherefore thou are without excuse, O man, whosoever thou are, that judgest;*[56] *for wherein thou judgest the other,* (in this case, the Gentile), *thou condemnest*[57] *thyself, for thou that judgest are practicing the same things,* for which thou condemnest the other. Paul has tactfully omitted to call the Jew by name here, but it is evident to whom he has reference.[58] The chief point of the picture he paints is the condemnation of the Jewish critic. He lines out proof of the Jew's condemnation and failure to attain the 'imputed righteousness' of God. The Jew's conduct may not be as vile as that of the pagans, but it is one of impenitence and rejection of the imputed Righteousness and of the judgment of God (vv. 2-11). Their sins were the same in kind, but not equal in vileness, as those of the pagan Gentiles (Cf. 1:18-32).[59]

v. 2. *And*[60] *we know that the judgment of God is according to truth against them that practice such things,* whether they be Gentiles or Jews. God is not partial in his judgments but judges according to truth or the actual facts in the conduct of whomsoever it may be.

v. 3. *And do you reckon, O man, who judgest them that practice such things, and doest*[61] *the same that thou*[62] *shalt escape the judgment of God?* Every wrong act is judged but a life of habitual sin is worse than one of occasional lapse with quick recovery through repentence.

v. 4. Or dost thou look down upon,[63] *or despisest thou the riches of his goodness and forbearance and longsuffering, not knowing that the goodness of God leadeth thee to repentence?*

v. 5. *But according to thy hardness and impenitent heart thou art treasuring up for thyself wrath in the day of wrath and of the revelation of the righteous judgment of God.*

(2) God judges all men by the same moral standard, according to their works. 2:6-11.

v. 6. *Who will render to each man according, to his works*—the facts in the case. The works of the Christian life are the fruit of faith, but are essential.

v. 7. *On the one hand, to those who according to* the standard of *patience, in* a life of *good work*[64] evidencing faith, *strive for glory and honor and in-*

---

56. Present participle, *krinōn* from *krinō* meaning to judge, leaving the context to indicate whether it is wrong judgment.

57. *Kata — Krino,* condemnest literally *seauton* itself to agree with *heterou,* neuter gender.

58. Dana H. E. *The Life and Literature of Paul.* p. 122.

59. Denney, James, *Expos. Greek New Test,* in loco.

60. *De* continuative cf RV in loco.

61. Present participle, denoting continued action which results in habitual practice.

62. *Su* emphatic, implying that being a Jew will not excuse him.

63. The Jew that looks down upon the goodness of God in sending Jesus Christ to be his messiah is inexcusable and must not be excused. The Jew who does it shows his inferiority and haughty pride. He is rebellious against the Father and the Son.

64. Collective use of the word. It is a life of faithful work and work of faithfulness growing out of a vital faith in Christ.

corruption of the Messianic Kingdom of Christ and not for self and the glory and honor of self but of Christ *he will give eternal life.* The life based on faith and which is the outgrowth of faith never perishes. It is eternal.

v. 8. *But on the other hand unto them that are factious* and of a partisan and contentious spirit, seeking for the glory and honor of self, which glory is corruptible, *and are disobedient to the truth but obedient to unrighteousness,* shall be[65] the reward anger, fury,[66] with other things worse.

v. 9. *Affliction and* the pressure of *anguish: upon every soul of man* or human being, who goes on working evil in a continuous life of selfishness *whether indeed he be Jew,* first in privilege, or *Greek.*

v. 10. *But, glory and honor and peace to every man working the good, to the Jew first* in line of precedence *and* also *to the Greek.*

v. 11. *For there is no distinction* of race with God: his judgment is impartial. The Jew being first in privilege of precedence in receiving the Gospel will suffer the more through his disobedience to its claims upon him.

(3) In the final tribunal before Christ, the Jew is judged by the standard of the Law of Moses, the Gentile by the law of his conscience and the light of nature. 2:12-16. The Jew regarded the Law of Moses a special benefit and help, but Paul makes it also an obligation; and if it is not kept but violated it becomes the condemnation of him who has it. The Law has a real and great benefit, but only if used to get to Christ through faith.

v. 12. *For so many as sinned*[67] *without the Law* of Moses and *shall go on perishing* through their own responsible free moral choices and actions, *without law* because they sin against the light of conscience which all have. They know the better and do the worse.

v. 13. *For not the* mere superficial *hearers of the law but the doers of the law shall be justified.*[68] The law was read in the Synagogues currently but the mere hearing of a sermon saves no one. The Jew is held responsible for the use he makes of the Law and other Scriptures of the Old Testament. He must employ them to get to Christ, the Messiah, who was the "prophet like Moses."

v. 14. *For whenever the nations* (Gentiles), *not having the Law* of Moses *do by nature the things of the Law, these not having the law are a law unto themselves.*

v. 15. *In that they themselves show the work of the law written in their hearts, their conscience*[69] *bearing witness therewith, and their thoughts one with another either accusing or else excusing* them;

v. 16. *in the day when God shall judge the secrets of men, according to* the *Gospel by Jesus Christ.* Paul's gospel was one which sprang out of the initial act of faith in Christ leading into a life of faith (1:17). It is a gospel of justification by faith and not one of reliance on the merits of one's own works.

---

65. Cf. Robertson, *Word Pictures* in loco.
66. Cf. Sanday and Headlam, *I. C. C.* Romans p. 54 better than R. V.
67. Constative timeless aorist covering all time. There is no time with God's judgment.
68. Future middle indicative, the subject of the verb being active.
69. *Simeidesōs,* means conscience here in genitive of present active participle *sunmarturouses.*

The conscience acts according to the light it has and the educative process through which it has passed, enlightening it more or less. In no case does a human being ever follow perfectly his conscience all the time, as man's reason sometimes approves and sometimes disapproves his actions. These hidden workings of the conscience God can judge, and he will judge Gentile and Jew impartially. No man, either Jew or Gentile, ever reached the standard of a perfect and sinless life. Otherwise, Christ died in vain (Gal. 2:21).

b. Paul shows that the Jews failed in spite of their having special revelation and the written law and ceremonial system. Their practice was no better than that of the Gentiles (2:17-29).

(1) The Jews had the special revelation in the Oracles of God in the Law of Moses and instruction in the Prophets, but even so had continued in their sins (2:17-24).

v. 17. *But if*[70] *thou bearest the name of a Jew,* with pride for your nation, as thou dost *and restest* leaning back upon the law, relying securely upon it, *and gloriest in God* as a national asset and private prerogative of the Jews,

v. 18 and knowest his will *and approvest the things that are excellent.*[71] *being instructed*[72] *out of the law,*

v. 19. *and art confident that thou thyself art a guide*[73] *of the blind, a light of them are in darkness?* This was God's intention and purpose, that the (Jews should be guides for the Gentiles, since salvation was from the Jews (Robertson). But he suffered disappointment when the high privileges consigned to them as a sacred trust were corrupted into conceited arrogance to their own condemnation.

v. 20. The Jew posed as *'a corrector or instructor' of the foolish* Gentiles who were termed 'dogs,' *a teacher of these babies* who were in instruction very undeveloped being novitiate proselytes to Judaism (from the Gentiles). It was the pride of the Jew that he was able to be a teacher, *"having in the law the form of knowledge and of the truth."*

vv. 21-24 How about the conduct of the Jew, so full of his pride about his religious superiority, his knowledge of God's will and his high ideal of conduct based on the Law of Moses? His conduct is shamefully contrary to his profession bringing dishonor upon the name of God before the heathen.

v. 21. *Thou, therefore, that teachest another, teachest thou not thyself? Thou that preachest a man should not steal, dost thou steal?*

v. 22. *Thou that sayest a man should not commit adultery, dost thou commit adultery? Thou that abhorrest idols, dost thou rob temples?*

v. 23. *Thou that gloriest in the Law, through transgression of the law dishonourest thou God?*

v. 24. *For the name of God on account of you* Jews *is blasphemed among the* (Gentile) *nations,* as it stands written. The vain boast of having the Law,

---

70. Condition of first class according to fact prevails in all the questions in verses 17-20.
71. Robertson, A. T., *Word Pictures* in loco.
72. The 'things that differ.'
73. *Hodēgon,* from *hodos,* road and *hegeomai,* to lead, a road-guide.

but by being the custodians and interpreters and at the same time the transgressors of the Law, made their condemnation all the deeper.

(2) They had the law of circumcision which was a sign of the promise, but external circumcision without circumcision of the heart avails nothing. 2:25-29. Circumcision among the Hebrews was a seal of the Covenant between God and Abraham, a symbol of separation from defilement to consecration to God. To confuse the symbol with the reality is to vitiate the symbol and make it a delusion, leading into error and confusion worse confounded.

v. 25. *For circumcision* indeed *profiteth, if*[74] *thou be a doer* or practiser *of the law. But if thou be a transgressor of the law thy circumcision has become*[75] completely changed into *uncircumcision.*

v. 26. *If*[76] *therefore the uncircumcision* or a man not circumcised *keep on* keeping *the ordinances of the law, shall not his uncircumcision be reckoned for*[77] *circumcision to him?*

v. 27. *And shall not the uncircumcision which is by nature, if it fulfil*[78] *the law, judge thee who with the letter and circumcision art a transgressor of the law?*

v. 28. *For he is not a Jew who is one outwardly; neither is that circumcision which is outward in the flesh.*

v. 29. *But he is a Jew who is one inwardly; and circumcision is that of the heart in the spirit, not in the letter; whose praise is not of men but of God.*

Another boast of the Jews which condemned and condemns them is that of the circumcision rite. The Jews of the dispersion were much addicted to robberies of heathen temples which was a flat negation of their boast of having the Law of Moses. So in that and other infractions of the Law they had laid themselves under a deeper condemnation than that which rested upon the heathen Gentiles, who were ignorant of the Law. The Jews ascribed magical efficacy to the rite of circumcision, which was a good symbol of purification if the reality should correspond in the life practice with the profession in the symbol.

c. The apostle finishes his argument for the equal necessity the Jews had for the God-kind of righteousness, pointing out the true advantages of being a Jew and the true function of the Law and Circumcision. 3:1-8. In answering these casuistical objections the apostle reveals his rabbinistic training.

First objection: If justification is by faith apart from the works of the law and the rite of circumcision is worthless, what about Israel's preeminence?

---

74. Condition of the third class and present tense continued active of *prasso,* to practice as a habit.

75. Perfect tense signifying a complete alteration in character and also the permanence of the result.

76. Present subjunctive of *phullasso,* to keep, with the preposition ean in third class condition, mere supposition.

77. *Eis* with the accusative, for.

78. *Telousa,* present active participle, conditional use, continuous action, continually fulfilling to the end 'as would be necessary' (Robertson). This of course never was known to occur.

Answer: Israel's greatest glory is that she has been the repository of revelation.

v. 1. *What then is the advantage of the Jew* if the requirements of God are inward and spiritual merely? Or what is the profit or gain of circumcision? Paul is here presenting more probably the dialectical process which might have come to him through actual experience of his own or in dealing with other Jews.

v. 2. *Much in every way,* he answers. *Because, indeed, the oracles* or words *of God,* all the Old Testament Scriptures *were entrusted*[79] definitely to the Jews.

Second objection: If the Jews rejected the promised Mesianic blessings, does that not cancel the promises?

Answer: nothing of man's unfaithfulness can make God unfaithful. They failed to make use of these messianic promises made to them as a nation in Abraham. This they did by their lack of faith, but this did not annul the faithfulness of God to the individual Jew who believed vv. 3, 4.

v. 3. *For what; if some* Jews *were without faith* especially concerning the Messianic promises, shall *their want of faith make of none effect the faithfulness of God?*

v. 4. God forbids: (*may it not be*) *Yea, let God* continue to *be found*[80] *true but* let *every man* be found *a liar; just as it stands written;* (Psalm 51:4): *"That thou mightest be justified in thy words, And mightest prevail when thou comest into judgment."*

Third objection: If our unrighteousness commends the rightousness of God, why should he punish us?

Answer: This is preposterous because it would do away with the moral government of the world. (vv. 5-8.)

v. 5. *But if our unfaithfulness commendeth the righteousness of God, what shall we say? Is God unrighteous who visiteth with wrath? (I speak after the manner of man).*

v. 6. *God forbid: for then how shall God judge the world?* But we know he will judge the world. The government of the universe must be maintained by God, who is the righteous judge. Shall not the judge of all the earth do right?

Fourth objection: If my sinning brings glory to God, why not sin the more? This was the slanderous accusation of antinomianists which was brought against Paul's teaching of justification by faith. Paul would answer this accusation at length later. At present he passes it over with assurance of sure condemnation for the accusers.

v. 7. *If the truth of God abounded by my lie unto His glory, why am I yet even being judged* as a sinner like other offenders? So the last objection runs.

v. 8. *And why not (as we are slanderously reported, and as some affirm that we say), "Let us do evil that good may come?" whose condemnation is just.* Such an unjust accusation against him Paul is sure will be condemned by God in due time and quickly enough.

---

79. Aorist passive indicative, an actual fact and occurrence.
80. Present imperative middle.

3. The apostle winds up his argument about the Jews, by concluding that the Jews and the Gentiles have both failed to attain the God-kind of righteousness and so stand condemned before God. They have failed for the same reason and in a similar manner. He appeals to the Scriptures of the Jews which pronounce all men under guilt and condemnation, both Jews and Gentiles. 3:9-20.

v. 9. *What then* is the conclusion we are to draw? *Are we surpassed*[81] by the Gentiles? *Not at all, For we before laid to the charge*[82] *of both Jews and Greeks*[83] *that they are all under sin,*

a. vv. 10-12 describe the sinful state of men as universal.[84] *Just as it stands written*[85] (Cf. Boise's *Notes* and Sanday *I. C. C.*).

There is none righteous, no, not even *one* (Cf. Ps. 14:1-3);

v. 11. *There is none that understandeth*[86] (Cf. Ps. 53:1-3), *There is none that seeketh*[87] *after God.*

v. 12. *They are all turned aside; they are together become unprofitable* (useless, of no account); *There is none that doeth good, no, not so much as one.*[88]

b. The sinful conduct of men in word (vv. 13, 14) and in action (vv. 15-17). This is the universal witness of the Testimonia.

v. 13. *Their throat is an open sepulchre,*[89] (Cf. Pss. 5 and 9); *With their tongues they have used deceit*[90] (Jer. 5:16); *The poison of asps*[91] *is under their lips*[92] (Ps. 140:3);

v. 14. *Whose mouth is full of cursing and bitterness;* (Ps. 10:7).

v. 15. *Their feet are swift*[93] *to shed blood* (Prov. 1:16);

v. 16. *Destruction and misery are in their ways;* (Is. 59:7, 8);

v. 17. *And the way of peace have they not known.*

c. The sinful source of all this (Cf. Boise) is in their lack of reverent fear toward God (v. 18).

v. 18. *There is no fear of God before their eyes.* (Ps. 36:1).

d. So the Jews are not better than the Gentiles (v. 19), the Scriptures refer to the universal guilt of humanity (vv. 10-18),[94] the Law which embraces (here

---

81. Passive voice.
82. First aorist middle *proeitiasametha*, editorial first person.
83. Cf. Rom. 2:17-24 and 1:18-32 Cf. Sanday and Headlam.
84. Cf. Ps. 14:1-3, "There is not a righteous man, no not even one." Cf. Robertson's *Word Picures* in loco. Cf. Boise's *Notes* in loco, also LXX Psa. 14.
85. Perfect tense denoting complete and permanent character of the Scriptures. The citations are from the *LXX* with slight changes and the order of thought is seen in the outline to follow.
86. Present active participle of *suniēmi.*
87. Ibid *ekzetōn.*
88. *Ouk estin heōs henos.*
89. An opened grave; perf. pass, part of *anoizō.* Some Greek and Roman literature stinks like an unopened grave Shedd. Cf. Robertson, *Word Pictures.*
90. Imperfect, continued action, *edoliousan* (Cf. Robertson). "They smoothed their tongues," (in the Hebrew).
91. Egyptian cobra (asp) a deadly serpent also Portuguese cobra.
92. Striking metaphor picturing character of a backbiter (Boise) of smooth and flattering lips.
93. *Oxeis* — sharp, swift.
94. Ps. 14:1-3, 5; 140:10; et al. Cf. *Testimonia* Ps. 14, LXX.

the entire Scriptures of the Jews), condemns them that are under the law and this law covers all humanity (v. 19), and the law does not justify any flesh because its purpose is to bring the knowledge of sin (v. 20).

v. 19. *Now we know, that what things soever the law saith, it speaketh to them that are under the law; that every mouth may be stopped, and all the world may be brought under the judgment of God*:

v. 20. *Because by the works of the law shall no flesh be justified in his sight*: *for through the law cometh the knowledge of sin.*

The final conclusion is that all are sealed up under sin and the only hope for man is in the intervention of God and the character and method of this intervention Paul reveals in the next step of his argument of the epistle (3:21-5:21).

Hackett calls Rom. 3:10-18 a Geography of Wickedness. Paul here ascribes sin to every part of us, body and soul. There is none that understandeth — our reason is ignorant; none seeketh after God — our will is disobedient; our tongues have used deceit; our feet are swift to shed blood; our eyes want the veil of reverence — there is no fear of God before our eyes. Plato speaks of his soul, "that it was scribbled all over with evil characters."

B. The Nature of this God-kind of Righteousness and the Method of its Attainment. 3:21-5:21.

1. By faith in Jesus Christ we receive, reckoned or imputed to us, the God-kind of Righteousness. 3:21-31.

a. Faith in Jesus Christ is the only and sole means by which we can receive as a free gift from God, this kind of righteousness. 3:21-26.

(1) This righteousness is independent of the Law but has the Law and the Prophets as its witnesses (v. 21).

v. 21. *But, now apart* (or independent) *from the law*, (whether of Moses or any other) *a righteousness of the God* kind, possessed by God and an attribute of his very nature, *has been manifested*[95] or revealed completely and permanently. It is *being witnessed* to at the same time *by the Law* of Moses *and the Prophets* (the two taken to cover the entire Scriptures of the Old Testament), *but this is a righteousness from God*[96] being *through faith* in *Jesus Christ*, an imputed Righteousness,[97] which is put to our account as a free objective gift by God.

(2) The law of Moses allowed no mercy but inflicted death on the offender were he ever so penitent; but the law of the spirit of liberty in Christ sets the offender, who is penitent, free, allowing pardon and remission of sins. Indeed, now we are passing into the "citadel[98] of the Christian faith" (Rom. 3:21-22). A free paraphrase of these two verses might express the meaning succinctly: now under the Gospel a method of justification is revealed of which God is

95. Perfect passive indicative tense denoting completion and permanence.

96. Ablative of source.

97. "The supreme manifestation of God's love is in redemption and from one point of view God's righteousness is his love seen in the aspect of moral holiness, as the expresson of his moral character with its demands for a life (in man) corresponding to Himself" (Moffatt, *Romans*).

98. *Olshausen* (vv. 21, 22).

the author, and to which all the Scriptures bear testimony,[99] that method which, rejecting man's obedience to the Law as the ground of justification, makes faith in Christ and His merits the only cause, and which extends its benefits to all belivers without discrimination, Gentiles as well as Jews.[1]

v. 22. *Even the righteousness of God through* the intermediate agency of *faith in Jesus Christ.*[2] *For there is no distinction* (diastole). While the faith is in Christ as its object, it is also in the sphere of Christ and his redemptive work that this vital 'faith lives, moves, grows and operates.' It is in Christ that God gives us this faith, in the sphere of His redemptive work, making possible God's initiative in stimulating within the man, dead in trespasses and sins, the very faith itself. Faith is a part of the gift of salvation because God gave the Gospel to illuminate the mind and also the very mind itself to be illuminated. All of salvation is God's gracious initiative.[3]

(2). We find in Jesus Christ satisfaction for all our needs, through faith in Him in whom we have salvation. This principle of imputed righteousness is not based on our works but on our faith and loyal love toward Jesus our Savior. It could not be limited to the Jews or any other nationality, but is for all men who believe on Him. The capacity for faith is common to all men, and it was never intended that there should be discrimination. (vv. 22-23.)

v. 23. *For all* men of the race from the beginning *sinned*[4] *and are still falling short*[5] as they have ever done *of the glory* or bright effulgence which irradiates to all who are in the favourable opinion and fellowship of the majestic goodness *of God.*

(3) The reception of this righteousness of God is possible only through the propitiatory sacrifice of Christ. This righteousness of God was partially hidden in the past ages in God, but is now revealed fully in the sacrificial atoning death of his Son Jesus Christ. 3:24-26.

v. 24. *Being justified*[6] *freely* (as a free gift) without any equivalent in return, reckoned to men who believe, as righteous for no merit of their own, but by the instrumentality of *his grace,*[7] *through the* intermediate agency of the *redemption,* or release by ransom, *which is* operative *in* the sphere of the life and work, all embraced in the person of *Jesus Christ.* This great deliverance was wrought at the price (*timē*) of the shedding of the life (blood) of Christ in his atoning death. This was a costly redemption or deliverance of men from the universal serfdom of sin. It was a historical transaction in which Jesus

99. Cf. foregoing citations as exemplary (Rom. 3:10-18).
1. Cf. Bloomfield cited by Moffatt, *Romans* p. 48.
2. Objective genitive, Christ as the object of faith, (Cf. Robertson). Not subjective genitive Cf. Robertson. Cf. Gal. 2:16. But this faith is exercised in the sphere of Christ cf. *en pistei en Christ ou Iesou,* Loc.
3. Cf. James Stewart, *A Man in Christ,* pp. 182, 183 also pp. 173 ff.
4. Constative second aorist active of *hamartanein,* to sin gathering up the whole race into one statement (Robertson).
5. Present middle indicative of *hustereō,* continued action in which the subject acts for himself in each case.
6. Present passive participle of *dikaiō,* to set right, repeated action in each indvidual case.
7. Instrumental case (chariti).

paid the price. This how and why or this ultimate necessity for this redemption is beyond the limited horizon of our understanding of the moral demands of the nature of God and his universe.

v. 25. *Whom* (God) publicly *set forth*[8] for himself in his incarnation, death, resurrection and exaltation, before the whole world, a propitiation[9] 'a votive offering for the salvation of men,'[10] *through faith in his blood*[11] (to the end) *for showing his* (God's) *righteousness*,[12] *on account of the passing over of the sins done*[13] *beforetime, in the forbearance*[14] *of God.* In previous ages the sins of mankind had been passed over without adequate punishment, hence the necessity of a vindication of God's righteousness in the time when Christ died for a demonstration (endeixin) of God's righteousness. With God there is no allowance for sin, but there is remission.[15]

v. 26. *For the showing* I say *of his righteousness*, in this signal exhibition, in the crucifixion of Jesus, of his justice and of his love, *at this present season*, in the fullness of time. The purpose was *unto* the end of manifesting *his being just* in his requirement and demand for righteousness in man *and* at the same time his being *the one justifying the ungodly* man or sinner *through his faith in Jesus.* Thus God revealed himself as just and at the same time demonstrated his righteousness in pronouncing righteous the loyal believer in the Christ. Faith identifies the repentant sinner with Christ, who first took the initiative in identifying himself with us.

The reformers, headed by Luther, gave this passage (vv. 24-26) the very central place in the Epistle and in the whole Bible. God the Father, in his great love, presented Christ as the willing voluntary sacrifice, through His own choice. He, the Son, made it possible for the Father to be propitious in his pardoning grace and loving acceptance of men.

b. This method of attaining the God-kind of righteousness is in perfect accord with the true meaning and nature of the Law and all the Old Testament teachings 3:27-31.

---

8. Second aorist middle indicative, God set Him before Himself as 'a propitiatory gift.'
9. Adjective *hilastērion* but used as a noun as elsewhere.
10. Deissman, *Bible Studies*, pp. 124-135.
11. The blood was sprinkled on the mercy seat on the day of the Atonement in the Jewish sacrificial system. Thus the death of Christ is appropriately connected with the symbolism of that chief sacrifice in the Holy of Holies.
12. God would not let sin go as if there were a mere slip but demanded and provided an atonement on account of the passing over of the sins done before the time when Christ came.
13. Second perfect active participle in genitive case, verb *proginomai*, paresin, the passing over of sin by not exacting the penalty due is distinct from *aphesin*, remission (Robertson).
14. *Anochēi*, holding back of God. Cf. Acts Ch. 17. "In times of ignorance, God winked at."
15. It was God who set Christ forth before the whole world as a 'propitiation,' a votive offering. Here is a clear statement of Paul that God the Father took the initiatve in the whole transaction of redemption. God's grace was the beginning of the plan of salvation. It is not therefore God who needs to be reconciled but he was in Christ reconciling men to himself.

(1) The conclusion is that human merit and boasting have no place in the Gospel-system or plan of salvation, for there is no merit in faith (vv. 27, 28). Human merit is a profitable result of a vital faith in the Christian's life but cannot purchase salvation.

v. 27. *Where then is the glorying* or boasting? *It was* definitely *excluded*[16] and is shut out once for all. *By what manner or kind of law* principle? By the principle *of works? Nay, but by a law* or principle *of faith*[17] which is in harmony with God's love and grace.

v. 28. *We reckon*[18] *therefore*[19] that *a man is*[20] *justified* or deemed just, *by faith, apart from the works of the law.* If God so reckons a man to be justified thus we surely should also thus consider him to be deemed just.

(2) There is only one God, therefore the Jews and the Gentiles are equal before the righteousness of God and the sole means of attaining this God-kind of righteousness is through faith in Christ (vv. 29, 30).

v. 29. *Or is God* the God of the *Jews* only? *Is he not also* the God of the Gentiles? *Yea,* of *the Gentiles also,* as Christians believe.

v. 30. If indeed God is one as he[21] certainly is, he *shall justify the circumcision by faith and the uncircumcision through faith.* He is ready as a righteous God who is impartial and just to treat alike the circumcised and the uncircumcised: the circumcised, with whom faith is the moving cause, and the uncircumcised, with whom the same faith is both the moving cause and the sole condition of his acceptance.[22]

(3) Says the objector, imagined or real, what then is the utility of the Law? Do we then annul the Law thus? By no means, answers the Apostle. We establish the law by the principle of faith, and the promise of Christianity is the fulfillment of this principle (v. 31).

v. 31. *Do we then annul the law through* the intermediate agency of *faith? God forbid,* by no means; *but we* on the contrary *establish the* principle of *law.* Justification therefore is based on the principle of faith which is the common possession of both Jew and Gentile. The other principle is that of the promise, and both of these principles are fulfilled in Christianity, in which both Jew and Gentile have one and the same God.

As Christians we do say that the Law does not justify man, because it is found universally that mankind violates the law through the weakness of the corrupted nature of man. But we do not discard the principle of law as of no use at all, for it does serve to show us what is the right, and though we cannot be saved by it, we use it by subordinating it to the principle of grace and of love, which establishes it by enabling us to fulfill it.

---

16. First aorist passive, definite occurrence or event.
17. Faith is a law or principle stronger and more binding than law in the sense of a legal system.
18. Present middle indicative.
19. Westcott and Hort read *gar* instead of *oun.*
20. The infinitive with the accusative occurs after *logizometha* (so certain verbs).
21. Condition of the first class according to fact.
22. Sanday and Headlam. *I. C. C.* Romans, in loco.

2. Against his Jewish objectors, Paul states that the Gospel plan of salvation by faith is not contrary to but in agreement with the Old Testament teachings. He chooses the outstanding illustration, in the case of the Covenant of God with Abraham, the founder of the Jewish race. Ch. 4:1-25.

a. Paul avers first that Abraham was justified not by works but by faith alone. He also refers to the statement of David, thus using both the Old Testament history and the Hagiographa[23] in substantiating his argument. Ch. 4:1-8.

(1) Abraham's case (vv. 1-5) was preeminent in the old dispensation. He was received into the special favor of God and great honor was bestowed upon him. God made with him a special Covenant which was sealed later with the rite of circumcision. There must therefore be a relationship between him and all the race of the redeemed.[24] The historic record makes evident the fact that Abraham was received into the favor and fellowship of God before he was circumcised. Circumcision was but an external sign or symbol of his standing with God already attained through faith. It followed the act of justification a good many years.

v. 1. *What then shall we say that Abraham, our forefather, found according to the flesh?* The question here arises as to why God chose Abraham to become the progenitor of the Jewish race as well as of spiritual Israel. Paul answers that question on the basis of the record of Abraham's call (Gen. 12:1ff). Abraham was not elected or chosen by God on the basis of his good works for then he would have had grounds for boasting. The record makes it clear that it was on the basis of the quality or principle of faith in Abraham, as illustrated in his response to the call, that God had elected him as our spiritual progenitor.[25] (Cf. Gen. 12:1-3).

v. 2. *For if Abraham was justified by works*, 'a supposition we make as true, for arguments sake,' then, *he has* ground for boasting or *whereof to glory;* which was shown already to be excluded (3:31). *But*, as is evident, Abraham, though doubtless a good man and highly to be praised, judged by the best human standards, could *not* have such grounds for boasting *before God.*

v. 3. *For what saith the Scripture?* The record of the call (Gen. 15:6) clearly states that *'Abraham believed God and it was reckoned unto him for righteousness.'* Abraham was not received into God's favour by the merit of his works but by his intuitive faith which was reckoned unto him for righteousness. It was still a free gift, for Abraham was not a perfect man but a human being with faults of his own.

v. 4. *Now to him that worketh* to attain his righteousness (justification) before God, *the reward in that case is not reckoned* on the basis *of grace but of debt* or dues for service;

---

23. Cf. Ps. 32.
24. Cf. Dana, H. E., *Life and Literature of Paul*, p. 126.
25. Gen. 12:1-3; 15:5,6.

v. 5. Whereas to him who does not work to gain his salvation by his own merits *but believes in him who accounts righteous the ungodly, his faith is reckoned for righteousness.* The record of Abraham's life show him not to have been perfect in all his ways. The Jews accounted Abraham the most righteous man of his generation and for this reason they believed he was chosen to be ancestor of the holy people. He was, according to their belief, the first of seven righteous men whose merit brought back the Shekinah, which had retired into the seventh heaven, so that in the days of Moses it could take up its abode in the Tabernacle.[26] If any one, Jew or Gentile, could boast, Abraham would be that one according to Jewish tradition. But Paul clearly shows by the record that it was on the basis of his faith that God accounted him righteous.

(2) Nor was his case unique but the Psalmist David long afterward testified to the same condition of attaining righteousness by faith alone (vv. 6-8).

v. 6. *Thus David also speaks of the blessedness of the man to whom God reckons righteousness apart from works:*

v. 7. *Blessed are they whose* (lawlessness) *iniquities are forgiven, And whose sins are covered.*

v. 8. *Blessed is the man to whom the Lord will not reckon sin.*

b. The same Scriptures show in the Law, by a true interpretation, that circumcision is not necessary to salvation, as the Jews believed it to be.[27] 4:9-12. Abraham's example in the record further on illustrates this fact also, seeing he was justified before he was circumcised. The moment he exercised faith he was accepted by God into his eternal fellowship. He was then accounted righteous immediately and henceforth. Abraham had long years to grow in grace, but the transaction of his salvation was made at the time of his call (Gen.12:1-3) once for all. Circumcision only served as a symbol or seal of that transaction. The Jews made circumcision the condition of justification just as some sects wrongly consider baptism to precede and be the cause of salvation. But repentence and faith are the cause and are inseparably linked with inward regeneration in the new spiritual birth. No inward renewal is to be attributed to circumcision any more than to baptism the symbolic ordinance of a renewal already attained through faith in Christ.

v. 9. *Is this blessing* (blessedness) *then pronounced upon* or reckoned *upon the circumcision* (circumcised) only *or upon the uncircumcision* (uncircumcised) *also? for we say: "To Abraham his faith was reckoned for* righteousness.[28]

---

26. Weber, *Altayn Palast Theologie*, p. 255f. cited Sanday p. 100.
27. Cf. Book of Jubilees 15:25ff. The law of circumcision was observed with the strictest exaction. One who did not receive the rite of circumcision was considered an alien to the Covenant and was destined to be destroyed and slain from the earth . . . there will be no pardon or forgiveness for them. According to the Jew's belief it was Abraham's circumcision and anticipatory fulfilment of the Law which qualified him to be the 'father of many nations.' (Bk. of Jubilees p. 256). It was at the root of this error that Paul struck by showing that Abraham's faith was prior to his circumcision. Cf. Sanday and Headlam in loco.
28. Cf. Genesis 15:5; Rom. 4:3.

v. 10. How then was it reckoned? when he was in circumcision, or in uncircumcision? *Not* while he was *in circumcision but in uncircumcision;*

v. 11. *and he received the sign of circumcision, a seal or symbol of the righteousness of the faith*[29] *which he had while he was in uncircumcision, that he might be the* spiritual *father of all them that believe though they be in uncircumcision, that righteousness might be reckoned unto them.* Thus the Gentiles could be saved without circumcision, since faith was the only condition to justification and they could be an integral part of spiritual Israel without circumcision

v. 12. *and* that Abraham might be the spiritual father of the circumcision kind to them not only of the circumcision having been circumcised, *but also* to those who *walk in the steps of that kind of faith*[30] which Abraham in the days of *his uncircumcision* even before the institution of that rite. Thus spiritual Israel is composed of Jew and Gentile of the circumcised and the uncircumcised.[31]

c. The promise made to Abraham of inheritance of the world-wide Messianic rule was based on faith and not on Circumcision or the Law. 4:13-16. The Jews had hoped to extend their temporal Messianic Kingdom through proselytism, which involved circumcision, but that was demonstrated to be ineffectual and not successful enough to give hope. The real Messianic Kingdom has been spread over the world extensively, but not through the instrumentality, to any great extent, of the Jews. The basis for the fulfillment of the promise was faith in Jesus Christ, which was the great and only means for the creation and extension of spiritual Israel. Christianity of the truly Messianic type is to rule and already is ruling, in some measure, the world today.

v. 13. *For not through the* intermediate agency of the *Law was the promise to Abraham or to his seed, that he should be heir of the world* rule and ownership but *through the* means of the *righteousness of* (produced by) *faith.* The promise embraced not only a son; but also descendants like the stars of the heavens for number; and the Messiah; with all the Messianic blessings through Him.[32]

The very character of the promise was contrary to the idea of a domain of Law. The spiritual Israel would be a creature of grace and not of Law. Under law, merit would be the measure of value, but the righteousness of faith is the

---

29. The circumcision did not convey the righteousness, but only gave outward confirmation of it.

30. There were many circumcised Jews who were Christians, some who were circumcised before they were converted to Christianity and others who had been circumcised even after they were Christians in certain cases, as that of Timothy, for the sake of expediency, and yet others not because they attributed to circumcision any saving power but because it was a useful tradition of the fathers and might possess certain hygenic and even moral advantages. They did not have faith in its spiritual power to save as many Jews did.

31. 'The in-the-state-of-uncircumcision faith' the whole hyphenated phrase being a modifier of the substantive, faith. It was that kind of faith which existed in Abraham before the rite of circumcsion was ever instituted.

32. Cf. Sanday and Headlam *I. C. C.* Romans in loco also Denney, James, *I. C. C.* Romans, in loco.

true measure of value and power in a realm of grace and merit, in sinful man can have no place.

v. 14. *For if they that are of the Law be heirs, faith is made void and the promise is made of none effect.* This Messianic promise is on the contrary, only to be received through faith and belongs to the domain of grace. Abraham's seed were to have world wide dominion, but they could not be vassals of a legal system. The inheritance of universal dominion must depend on the righteousness proceeding from a gracious God, appropriated by faith of men, who are members of the spiritual Israel. Without counting on this God-kind of righteousness in men there can be no material out of which to build a temple of humanity such as Paul envisioned in his epistle to the Ephesians.[33]

v. 15. *For the law* of Moses *worketh wrath;* being contrary in its action to grace, entailing as it does punishment and increasing guilt; but in the domain of grace the positive force of faith in and love for Christ produces the opposite effect in life, peace and joy. Where there is law and man is depending on it for salvation, failure is the result, but where there is no law principle binding man down, as there is not in God's gracious plan of faith in Christ, neither is there transgression to hinder the rescue of man by God's grace. By its very nature the Law would render void the promise of redemption, for it brings condemnation. "Faith on the contrary was the preemiment characteristic of Abraham, being the means of access to salvation in Christ."[34]

v. 16. *For this cause it* (the promised heritage) *is* of faith (by faith) *in order that it might be* acording *to grace,* a free gift to believing sinners. Even if the heritage could have been earned by keeping the written law (of Moses), none but the Jews would have been heirs, and even they could not have succeeded in keeping the law. So, God promised it on the basis of faith, which is possible to all men of all the races and so can be realized by God's grace through the gradual but effective growth of spiritual Israel in the world. This is Paul's conception of the kingdom of Christ.

v. 16. *to the end that the promise may be sure to all the seed; not to that only which is of the Law* the Jews, *but to that also which is of the* kind of initial *faith of Abraham,* while he was in uncircumcision, *who is the father of us all,* who pertain to spiritual Israel. These last include the Gentiles, who are saved without the rite of circumcision.

d. Furthermore, Abraham received his posterity by faith and, as it were, from the dead. His strong faith having a definite object must be the example and pattern for the Christian's faith which also received Christ, his Messiah, from the dead. Ch. 4:17-22; 23-25.

v. 17. (*Just as it stands written, A father of many nations have I made thee*). Such was the view Abraham had as he stood *before him whom he believed,* even *God who quickeneth the dead* as he was to rejuvenate the bodies of Abraham and Sarah,[35] *and calleth the things that are not* existing *as though they were*

---

33. Eph. 2:22f.
34. Dana, H. E. *The Life and Literature of Paul,* p. 27.
35. Cf. Hebrews 11:19

existing, issuing his summons to generations yet unborn, in number as the stars in the heavens or the sands of the sea. It was thus that Abraham considered God and God considered Abraham.

v. 18. *Who in hope believed against hope to the end that*[36] *he might become the father of many nations, according to that which had been spoken: So shall thy seed be.* What a pair, and what a yoke of friendship!

v. 19. *And without geing weakened in faith,* (not becoming weak in faith) through many things impossible to mere human resolution, *he considered his own body now as good as dead already*[37] *(he being about a hundred years old)*,[38] *and the deadness of Sarah's womb*:

v. 20. *Yea, indeed looking unto the promise of God, he* was not divided in his mind[39] in indecision, and *wavered not through unbelief,*[40] *but waxed strong*[41] *through faith, giving glory to God,* in praise and thanksgiving as if the promise were already realized;

v. 21. *And being fully assured that, what he* (God) *had promised he was able also to perform,* such a faith as was pleasing to God as is seen in the outcome.

v. 22. *Wherefore also it* (his faith) *was reckoned unto him for righteousness.* Here was the triumph of a true faith exercised by faithful Abraham, and the glorious response of the infinite God of Abraham, who is also our miracle-working God, when there is faith and faithfulness in us!

v. 23. *Now it was not written for his* (Abraham's) *sake alone, that it* (his faith) *was reckoned unto him for righteousness.*

v. 24. *But for our sake also, unto whom it shall be reckoned, who believe on him that raised Jesus our Lord from the dead.*

v. 25. *Who was delivered up for our trespasses, and was raised for our justification.*

His resurrection put the seal of God on his atoning death and lays open the way for faith in man, which closes the arc and makes effectual the atonement the experience of the individual who exercises faith in the Redeemer. This conclusion of the argument based on Abraham's faith in God is almost like one of Paul's doxologies, which burst forth in many places as he soars to some higher peak!

3. In making an exposition of his thesis on justification Paul next presents the marvelous consequences of justification, both immediate and remote, as evidences of the reality of imputed righteousness. 5:1-11.

---

36. Purpose clause with *eis to* and the infinitive as in verses 11 and 16 (Robertson, *Word Pictures* in loco).

37. Perfect passive participle of *nekroō* now already dead because he knew he was too old to become a father (Robertson, *Word Pictures*).

38. Gen. 17:17.

39. First aorist passive of *diakrinō,* to be divided in one's own mind.

40. Instrumental case, by unbelief, a privitive with *pistis,* lack of faith.

41. First aorist passive of *endunamoō,* definitely empowered, *tei pistei,* instrumental of means.

After making his exposition on Righteousness by Faith: its necessity (1:18-3:20), a profound statement of its glorious nature (3:21-30) a discussion of its character in relation to the Law and to all the Old Testament Scriptures, including the Prophets and the Hagiographs (3:31-4:25) the Apostle next, in a 'devotional interlude,' pauses to contemplate the immediate transcendant experiences[42] and blissful outlook of salvation to those who have faith in Christ (5:1-11), and to enter into an explanation of the deep meaning of the work of Christ historically for the race, as seen in analogy and contrast with the ruin wrought by Adam through the Fall (5:12-21).

a. In the discussion of the marvelous consequences of justification Paul logically considers first the immediate and remote results experienced by the believer upon his acceptance of Christ by faith (vv. 1-4).

Ch. V. v. 1. *Having been therefore*[43] *justified*[44] *by faith*, at the moment we exercised that faith in Christ, *let us have* to enjoy and keep on retaining and enjoying *peace* in fellowship *with God.* A Christian may never err so grievously as to lose all feeling of the certainty of his regeneration through the new birth into the kingdom and yet pass periods of lack of perfect peace. Hence Paul's exhortation to have and to hold on to the peace we should always enjoy in Christ. We have a right to claim this peace in Christ.

v. 2. *through whom also we have had,*[45] by acceptance of Him, *our access* (or introduction) freely, *into*[46] *this* sphere of grace, wherein we have stood and stand,[47] firmly and permanently grounded instead of cast on insufficient foundations, *and let us rejoice*[48] (exult but not boast) and keep on exulting *in*[49] hope in the desire and expectation *of the glory*, the effulgence of the favour *of* our glorious justifier, *God.*

v. 3. Carrying his exhortation to higher ground still Paul adds: *And not only* so, *but let us rejoice* (exult) *also in* our *tribulations,* finding wherein to rejoice rather than complain when we have to suffer. *Knowing that tribulation works out patience* and persistence through God's use of tests to produce in us reliance, *and patience* works out probation or developed *experience* through proof of trials, *and* probation or *experience* results in *hope,* both the desire and expectation of continued blessing in this present life and glory in that which is to come. The reality of the justification is evidenced by the peace, access, and

42. David Smith, *Life and Letters of Paul.*

43. *Oun* refers to conclusive arguments Chs. 1-4 extablishing the conclusion that justification was by faith.

44. First aorist passive of *dikaioō,* (to reckon or deem righteous), setting down the act of justification as a definite occurrence in the experience of each of those who believed.

45. Perfect active indicative, *eschēkamen,* from *echō have,* perfect tense complete action and continued result. A real Christian never loses his privilege of access through Jesus Christ his great High Priest.

46. *Eis* with the accusative *charin,* grace indicating end.

47. Perfect active indicative, *estekamen,* from *histēmi,* which indicates the permanence of the status of the believer in God's favour, though unmerited, as it always is.

48. Present middle subjunctive (volative) keep on rejoicing in blissful exultation based on the Christian hope. Cf. R. contrary to preponderant readings.

49. *Epi-on* upon with locative *elpidi.*

hope which attend our commitment to Him who paid the price of our redemption, by his atoning blood shed on Calvary.

b. The objective guarantee of all these blessed experiences and this unfailing hope is the love of God for us, which is shed abroad by the Holy Spirit in our hearts, assuring us that he will through Christ give us all things in complete salvation. Ch. 5:5-11.

v. 5. *And the*[50] *hope,* this Christian hope, *does not make ashamed* or disappointed ever, *because the love of God,*[51] *has been poured out*[52] *in our hearts by* the blessed intermediate agent, *the Holy Spirit,* definitely *given*[53] *to us,* when we were born of the Spirit in regeneration.

v. 6. *For Christ, while we were yet weak,*[54] *in due* (yet) *season,* came in the fulness of time in the incarnation *and died for the ungodly,* irreverent and rebelious human race, including impious sinners against God of every category. Ultimately all sin is against God (Cf. Ps. 5. 'Against thee and thee only'). The love of God transcends all human love as Paul next explains:

v. 7. *For scarcely,* in a rare instance, *for a just man*[55] coldly righteous but without sympathy *will one die.* For *on behalf of a good man,* kindly and beneficent, *perchance*[56] *someone would even* have the courage and *dare to die.*

v. 8. *But,* God commends *his own love toward us in that, while we were yet* plain common *sinners, Christ died for us.* A few may face death for a good generous lovable man, fewer for a man who is just and exemplary in character and conduct, but Christ died and God permitted his Son to die for the very sinful and hateful enemies of his beloved son Jesus Christ.

v. 9. The argument a *fortori* follows according to Paul's logical acumen: *By much more being already now* definitely *justified* and reckoned righteous, *by his blood*[57] efficacious in the atonement to be righteous, *we shall be saved*[58] *through him* in the end *from the wrath* of the judgment.

v. 10. The argument still continues logically: *For if, while we were* hateful *enemies we were reconciled*[59] *to God through the* agency of *the death of his Son, much more having been reconciled,*[60] *we shall be saved in the sphere of his risen life* as our High Priest[61] and eternal sacrifice.

---

50. Definite article having demonstrative force.
51. Subjective genitive, God's own personal love for us.
52. Perfect passive indicative, has been poured out completely and permanently.
53. Aorist passive participle, *dothentos.*
54. *Asthenon* weak, infirm, utterly impotent before the demands of the Law of God, utterly unable to help one's self.
55. *Dikaios,* a man who is coldly righteous but 'without sympathy' over against *agathos,* a good man — beneficent and kind.
56. *Tacha* — perhaps.
57. May be taken as locative, in the sphere of his atoning blood, but perhaps here better used as the instrumental of means.
58. Future passive indicative, *sothēsometha.*
59. Aorists *Katēlagēmen,* definite occurrence.
60. Aorist passive participle.
61. Hebrews 7:25ff.

v. 11. *And not only* so *but even* we shall go on *glorying* and exulting *in our God through our Lord Jesus Christ, through* the agency of *whom now we have received this*[62] *reconciliation.* The Christian shall meet his Judge at the bar as his best friend, his priestly Redeemer and Saviour.

4. Passing from the discussion of the practical consequences, of the imputed Righteousness of God in Christ, both immediate and remote, in the experience of the individual believer in Christ, Paul widens out his view to cover the whole history of the human race and presents a solution to the very difficult sin-death problem around which theological controversy has raged through the centuries. 5:12-21. Analogy and contrast of the effects of the God-kind of righteousness or the justification by faith through Christ alongside and over against the effects of the fall of Adam, are presented as an explanation of 'the way out' for humanity historically. He deals with the difficult problem of the sin of Adam in relation to heredity and in the light of the atonement of Christ, and compares and contrasts the character of Adam and Christ in their federal headship of the race. Here we have some of the most profound thought of Paul on the philosophy of history and the theological understanding of human life, its origin, character and destiny, including the origin, nature, and consequences of sin and death. This is at least one of the most difficult passages in all of Paul's writings to explain.

a. The comparison of the effects of Adam's transgression with the results of Christ's atoning work is the first point of this part of the argument. 5:12-14. Paul begins the comparison in verse twelve but at the end of the verse begins an *anacoluthon* covering verses 13, 14. In Paul's expression here, we understand, that from Adam until Moses there was no revealed Law and therefore no transgression after the kind that Adam committed when he violated the expressed command of God, not to eat of the forbidden tree in the garden of Eden. But there was yet sin after the kind which the Gentiles committed and the heathen, some of whom never have yet received the knowledge of the Gospel, commit against the light of nature and conscience. The Apostle attributes death physical and spiritual to sin of a vitiated nature received, bequeathed by Adam to his posterity by heredity, both physical and social because hereditary weakness and tendencies are universally adopted by all, when free choice comes into play. The status of infants is cared for by the atoning blood of Jesus Christ during the period of infancy until the child comes to understand right from wrong, which is variable in different individuals due to varying individual gifts and to differing social environments.

v. 12. *Therefore,*[63] on account of our justification and the peace, access and joy resulting from our reconciliation by the atoning death of Christ and because of the certainty of salvation by His eternal life, *just as through the* agency of *one man, sin*[64] *came into the* whole world to every individual of the

62. Definite article with force of the demonstrative.

63. Includes argument (vv. 1-10)

64. There are those who deny the fact of sin and say it is a mere notion, "an error of mortal mind." Here is a personification of sin, which came into the world of humanity at the fall of Adam, from whence Paul does not say.

human race, *and through* the intermediate agency of *sin personified, death, and thus to all men,* individually, *death*[65] *came,*[66] *in that all sinned.*

v. 13 *For, until* the Mosaic *law* came later in history the *sin* principle *was in the world but sin is not reckoned* where there is *no* revealed *law*[69].

v. 14. *But, death*[70] *ruled* as a tyrant *from* the time of Adam[71] *until* the coming of *Moses over those who did not sin* (after) *the likeness* or pattern *of Adam's transgression,* in disobeying the command of God expressed to him, about not eating of the fruit of the tree 'in the midst of the Garden,' *who* (Adam) *is a type of the One to come,* the great Antitype Jesus Christ, called the second Adam. The Fall of Adam (*paraptoma*) gave a tendency or predisposition to sin and linked up sin and death. The effects of the sin principle which started with Adam are universal and perpetual, but Adam's transgression and falling to one side can account for the universality of sin and death.

Sanday and Headlam point out three effects of Adam's Transgression and Fall which came down as a heritage to his descendants by the testimony of Jewish theology, (1) Death to himself and his descendants (2) Sin by physical and social heredity and the tendency to sin (3) The responsibility of the individual for his sin was not changed but perpetuated. The conclusion of the above cited authorities (Sanday and Headlam) is that Paul clearly states that man inherits his sinful nature but is not able to change his responsibility because he is free to choose and adopt sin or reject it and upon that power of free choice he must stand and overcome with the help of Christ.

b. The contrast between Adam's transgression which resulted in sin and death for the entire human race, with the atoning death of Christ, in the potential redemption of all mankind, to be tapped like a reservoir by the faith-line of 'whosoever will' vv. 15-21.

(1) The contrast in quality between the act of the transgression and fall of Adam which produced death in all men and the act of free grace in the

---

65. Death, physical but also spiritual which is more fundamental, still became universal on the basis of hereditary sin tendencies universally adopted, thus entailing both physical and spiritual death.

66. *Dielthen,* second aor. act. ind, idea of to each member of the race, distribution, *dia* in composition with *erchomai* to come. The inheritance from Adam included physical death and also the tendencies to sin which cause death both physical and spiritual. Cited by Cf. Robertson *Word Pictures.*

67. Because (in N. T.) in that, *epi hō,* (Robertson p. 930).

68. Constative second aorist, indicative active, pantes *hēmarton* definite spiritual death followed by physical death later and conditions of physical death at once. *Hēmarton,* (constative aor.) embraces all committed sin of the history of mankind.

69. The Jews were like the Gentiles before the coming of the Mosaic law, having the law of conscience and reason (2:12-16), but the coming of the law increased their responsibility. Before the coming of the law their sin was 'not taken into account,' set down on the ledger for penalty, on the same basis of responsibility. Cf. status of infants and idiots at all times. The sinful nature which they inherit from Adam is taken care of by the atoning death of Christ.

70. But physical death comes and that is a part of the heritage from Adam which has come to all at all times. Sin was in the world.

71. The federal headship of the race in Adam in respect to sin and death is contrasted with that in respect to righteousness and life in Christ.

vicarious death of Christ, which brought life for all who would accept it (v. 15).

v. 15. *But not as* (or like) *the trespass*[72] (*paratoma*, slip, fall to one side) *also is the act of grace* (charisma), the vicarious death of Jesus Christ. *For if by the trespass of the one* (Adam) *the many died,*[73] *by much more*[74] *the grace of God and the free gift by the grace, which is of one man, Jesus Christ, abounded into the many.* God's love delights much more in gracious pardon of sin than in inflicting a just punishment on the sinner. (Lightfoot). By the act of Adam all died; by the act of Christ, through faith in Him, many live, but not all believe and hence not all come to live eternally. (2) Contrast in results. By the fall of Adam came many offenses and because of the many offenses the free gift in Jesus Christ brought justification to many or all who accepted it by faith. v. 16.

v. 16. *And not as through* the agency of *one having sinned,* (Adam) is *the free gift* of life in Christ: *for on the one hand, the judgment* came *from one* sinning, as a source, *leading into condemnation; but on the other hand* the free gift came *from many transgressions,* which gave the occasion, *for justification.*

(3) Contrast between the whole character and consequences of the sin of Adam and Christ's work of grace. The act of Adam brought the reign of death; that of Christ the reign of life to all those who believe. v. 17.

v. 17. *For if*[75] *by the transgression of* the *one* (Adam) *the death came to reign* through the one, just as God said it would, and as it did in fact, *through the one* (Adam) *by much more*[76] *those receiving the abundance of the grace and of the gift of* imputed *righteousness shall reign in life through* the intermediate agency of *the one, Jesus Christ.*

(4) The conclusion of the argument: the fall of Adam introduced sin and death, and the law served to reveal sin, the limit of its proper function; but grace superabounded in Jesus Christ, cancelling the effects of sin and giving life eternal to those who believe (vv. 18-21).

v. 18. *So then as through one trespass* the judgment came *unto all men unto condemnation, even so through one act of righteousness,* the free gift came *unto all men unto justification of life.*

v. 19. *For just as through the disobedience of the one man,* Adam, *the many were made sinners; even so through the obedience of the one* man, Jesus Christ, *shall the many be made righteous.*

v. 20. *And the law came in alongside*[77] *in order that the transgression might abound*[78] in God's ultimate purpose and plan. *But where sin abounded, grace superabounded,*

---

72. Here is a contrast between the transgression of Adam and the vicarious act of grace of Christ.
73. Second aorist act of *apothnēskw.*
74. *Argumentum a fortiori* again.
75. First class condition, according to fact.
76. Another *a fortiori* argument.
77. *Para-eisēlthen,* to come in beside or alongside.
78. Cf. Robertson's *Word Pictures* in loco. aor. act. subjunctive with *hina* in clause of purpose.

v. 21. *In order that just as sin reigned in* (the) *death, so also grace might reign through righteousness into life eternal through Jesus Christ our Lord.*

C. The result of this God-kind of Righteousness in the life of the believer is sanctification and holiness. Chapters 6-8. Says the objector: "Is not justification by faith alone a dangerous doctrine?" If the works of man have no value for his salvation and if "where sin abounds grace superabounds" let us continue in sin after we are justified that grace may come. A modern statement might be as we have heard it: "If a man is saved when he is converted or when he gets religion, by exercising faith in Christ, what value do works have in his salvation? Can he not continue to live in sin as he has been living and get to heaven?" Paul replies to such an objector by a clear argunemt in three chapters 6-8:

1. That the mystic union with Christ by faith prohibits the continuation in a life of sin after regeneration. This mystic union is symbolized, first, by the ordinance of the baptism of the believer, which is a picture of death to sin and resurrection to newness of life. Ch. 6:1-14.

a. By his baptism the believer in Christ sets forth to the World his union with the Lord Jesus. (Ch. 6:1-11). To continue to live in sin would be wholly contradictory to this union of the believer with Christ as symbolized in baptism by immersion, according to the mode practiced in the primitive church.

v. 1 Continuance in sin is contradictory to the idea of fellowship with Christ. We are dead to sin. *What then shall we say* in answer to our Judaistic objectors? Paul was exultant in his understanding of the sure victory of grace over sin; but Satanic influence might introduce error into his doctrine and subvert the faith of some in the church. He therefore raised the point for discussion and clarification: *Shall we continue* or remain in sin, a sinful habit in life,[79] *that*[80] *grace may abound?* The sale of indulgences was an illustration of just such a teaching and practice. It encouraged sin as many practice yet in some (so-called) Christian churches. *May it not be,* that such a horrible thought, as that God's free pardon and grace should give such liberty to sin.

v. 2. *We* the very ones *who died*[81] in relation *to sin how shall we* (yet) *longer live* (therein) in it?

v. 3. *Or, are you ignorant that so many of us as were baptized*[82] or immersed *into*[83] *Christ Jesus were baptized* into his death? Our baptism is a symbol of Christ's death, burial and resurrection as it is also of the inward change in the believer. So the act of immersion is a symbol in relation to Christ's death.

---

79. Present active deliberative subjunctive the question of sin as a habit is here raised (Robertson).

80. Final clause with ingressive aor. subjunctive (*Ibid*).

81. Second aor. act. indicative, *actual* occurrence.

82. First aor. pass. ind. of *baptizo,* to dip or immerse.

83. Baptism is the public proclamation of the inward relation to Christ. Cf. Hist. of *Eis* and *en,* the same fundamentally.

v. 4. *We were buried*[84] *therefore with him through baptism into* (unto) *death: that like as Christ was raised from the dead, through the glory of the Father, so we also might walk in newness of life.*

v. 5. *For if*[85] *we have become united*[86] with him *by the likeness of his death,*[87] as we certainly have, *we shall be* united *also by the likeness of his resurrection,* a logical and real conclusion abundantly verified in experience.

v. 6. *Knowing this, that our old man was crucified* with him in order *that the body* of which *sin* had taken possession[88] *might be done away,* to the end *that*[89] *we should no longer* continue to *be in bondage to sin.*

v. 7. *For he that died*[90] *has been justified*[91] or set free *from sin.*

v. 8. *But if*[92] *we died with Christ,* as we certainly did, *we believe that we shall also live* and go on living,[93] *with him,*

v. 9. *Knowing that Christ was raised*[94] *from the dead, dieth no more*;[95] *death hath no longer dominion* or rule *over him.*

v. 10. *For in that he died, he died* in his contact with sin in this world *once* for all; *but* in *that he liveth*[96] *he lives* in relation *unto God.* The sacrifice of the mass is ruled out completely by the fact that Christ's sacrifice was eternal, once for all, not needing repetition, as is said, which would be sacrilegious.

v. 11. *Just so, ye also reckon yourselves*[97] *to be dead, indeed, to sin, but alive to God in Christ Jesus.*[98]

b. The believer must conduct himself in conformity to this union with Christ in all holiness vv. 12-14. He must dedicate his body in the service of God. Before his regeneration his body served the desires and lusts of the fleshly nature, but now the members of his body must become instruments of Christ in righteousness vv. 12-14.

v. 12. *Let not sin, therefore,* continue *to reign*[99] (or be king over) *in your mortal body that ye should* continue to *obey*[1] *the lusts thereof* (of it). This is direction and instruction at one and the same time.

---

84. Second aor. pass. ind. of *sunthaptō* to bury together with associative instrumental.
85. Condition of first class, according to fact and reality.
86. *Sumfrutoi* from verb sumpluro to grow together, unite by growth used with perfect tense *gegonen.*
87. Baptism symbolizes our likeness to his death in our death to sin. All personal communication with him physically here, ceased when he died.
88. Sanday and Headlam *I. C. C.* in loco.
89. Purpose clause followed by the present act. infinitive, *douleuein,* continue serving.
90. Second aor. part., of verb *apothnēskō.*
91. Perf. Pass indic. *dedikaiōtai,* stands justified, set free, complete and permanently.
92. Condition of first class according to facts.
93. Future active indicative, progressive and continued action.
94. Aor. pass. participle, *egertheis,* was raised.
95. Present tense.
96. Present act. indicative, continued action.
97. Direct middle imperative of *logizomai* denoting the imperative nature of the directive counsel of Paul. Believers are not sinless — dead to sin, hence the Imperative.
98. The operation in the sphere of Christ Jesus is spiritual.
99. Present active imperative 'Let not sin continue to reign.'
1. *Eis* with articular (neuter) infinite (with a view to obeying).

v. 13. *Neither present*[2] *your members* of your body, eyes, hands, feet, any, *unto sin,* as a ruler. Stop doing it if you have done it at all and do not go on in the habit of doing it, *as instruments hopla, weapons, of unrighteousness,* in the struggle between Satan and God; *but present yourselves* wholly, *unto God as alive from the dead and your members as instruments of righteousness unto God.*

v. 14. *For sin shall not* continue *to rule*[3] *over you. For you are not under* the dominion of Law *but under* that of *Grace.*

2. This God-kind of righteousness must produce holiness in the life because the justified one has been emancipated from the bondage of sin and has come under the reign of righteousness in Christ. Chs. 6:15-7:6.

a. The figure is that of bondage or slavery, and the transition of the believer is from the yoke of the Law to the liberty and service of righteousness through Christ. No longer does the believer have liberty to sin because he has changed masters or rulers. To whom one gives his service in obedience, to him he is servant. While in the service of sin he received the wages of sin which was death, but now in the service of righteousness in Christ he receives the free gift of God, which is eternal life (6:15-23).

v. 15. Here we reach another step in the argument.[4] *What then? Shall we continue to sin,*[5] *because we are not under the law but under grace?* Not a few professed Christians take liberties with their religion, not infrequently to engage in some questionable practices, of 'border-line' character. *God forbid!* We were emancipated from the service of Sin; but we are now privileged to enjoy another service, that of Rightousness. We were not as some say freed to sin, but rather freed from sin, to serve Christ.

v. 16. *Know ye not, that to whom ye present yourselves* occasionally in forays of sin as *servants* (slaves), leading *into the* formation of habitual *obedience, his* (Sin's) *slaves ye are,*[6] *to whom ye obey,*[7] *whether* it be *of sin* leading *into death or of obedience* to God leading *into righteousness* and life.[8] The new life in Christ does not admit of occasional deliberate indulgences in sinful or doubtful practices. In the Christian's release from sin there is a new service awaiting him to which all his energies may and should be devoted.

---

2. Present act.. imv. in prohibition, Stop!

3. Fut. act. indicative, 'shall not lord it over you,' even if you are not wholly dead to sin. Cf. II Cor. 1:24.

4. Robertson, A. T. *Word Pictures* in loco.

5. First aor. act, deliberative subjunctive. Occasional acts of sin versus epimenōmen tēi hamartiāi v. a. (Robertson), the continued action of the present progressive tense of habit.

6. Present tense denotes continued action.

7. *Ibid.* Present tense of continued action.

8. Aor. pass. indicative, obeyed, hupēkousate.

v. 17. *But thanks be to God, ye were*[9] once *servants* (slaves) *of sin* for a season; *but ye* became obedient, *from the heart,* sincerely and clearly *to that form of doctrine* (teaching) *whereunto*[10] *ye were delivered.*[11] Emancipation from sin was the prelude to the new service of Righteousness (Sanday). They had been delivered from sin in order to enter into the service of Christ.

v. 18. And being made free[12] *from sin ye became*[13] *servants to righteousness.* They had changed from one service to another. The breaking up of the old ties with sin gave way to the forming of new ties in the life of righteousness, serving the new Master, Christ.

V. 19. *I speak after the manner of man, because of the infirmity of your flesh,* and 'the lack of spiritual insight in you due largely to your moral defects, also' (Robertson). *For,* indeed *as you presented your members as servants* (slaves)[14] *to uncleanness*[15] *and to* (iniquity), *lawlessness* leading *unto* iniquity, *lawlessness;*[16] *so now* hasten to *present*[17] *your members* of your body and soul in like manner as servants (slaves) *to righteousness*[18] (unto) leading *into sanctification,* which is the result and proper goal and resulting consummation of the process of consecration in a life of service, which should be free from any occasional lapse into sin. It is a fact that such lapses do occur, bringing great devastation and evil consequences to the Christian but not loss of eternal life because true repentance follows. This is no risk which a true Christian should ever dare to take.

v. 20. *For when you were servants* (slaves) *of sin,* belonging to sin,[19] *you were* then *free* in respect to *righteousness.*[20] You were not in the service of righteousness.

v. 21. What fruit *had*[21] *ye then* (you used to have), *at that time,* at the memory *of which ye are now ashamed? For the* (full grown) *end of those* things is eternal *death.*

---

9. Imperfect, tense continued action in past time, during a period.

10. Attraction and incorporation of the antecedent.

11. The form or essential content of the gospel which Paul had been preaching over Asia Minor and Europe. Primitive Christianity made use of a form of instruction for new converts as the first part of the didache. This can be most effective in the indoctrination of young Christians in the practical side as well as in inculcating the deeper doctrines.

12. Aorist pass. participle, a definite occurrence when they believed and received Christ.

13. Aorist pass. indicative of *douloō* to be a slave.

14. *Doula* neuter to agree with *melē*.

15. Dative of personal interest in this case disadvantage. *Akatharsia,* uncleanness and *anomia* lawlessness fitly describe the characteristic features of Pagan life.

16. This is the case in sexual sins, drunkenness and narcotic habits, one leads into another frequently and persisted in, inevitably.

17. Aor. active imperative implying prompt action.

18. Dative case of personal relation, *dikaiosunēi,* this time personal advantage Cf. Hadley, *Gr. Gram.* in loco, also Goodwin *Greek Grammar.*

19. Genitive of possession, sin takes over and possesses the sinner.

20. Dative of personal relationship advantage (Classical Grammar).

21. Imperfect active, used to have.

v. 22. *But now* having been free[22] *from* the bondage of *the sin and having become servants to God, ye have your fruit* leading *unto sanctification and the* (full-grown) *end eternal life.*

v. 23. *For the wages*[23] of the tyrant sin, paid always in full, *is* eternal *death; but the gift* springing from the grace *of God* is *life eternal in Jesus Christ our Lord.* Only in the sphere of his life and its work of redemption, is eternal life given to the believer, and it is never given as wages but as a gift of God's special but unmerited favor to us.

b. The figure of marriage. Ch. 7:1-6.

The argument sweeps on majestically from one figure to another, using illustrations which are taken from the fundamental phases of human experience. The next figure of speech is that of the institution of the family in the sacred tie of matrimony. The believer in Christ was formerly wedded to sin and the Law but has passed into the sacred union with Christ and Righteousness. In the step, preceding the present one in the argument, the believer was emancipated from the slavery of sin and entered into the service of Grace and Righteousness. In the analogy of Marriage, the believer in Christ is freed from any obligation of the former union with Sin. Woman is subject to the law of the husband until he dies. Before justification, the believer was united to Sin and the Law, but sin dies in the life of the believer when Christ comes into the mystical union with him. There is no further relationship with the old life of sin. There is no obligation to sin after entering the sacred relationship with Christ.

In Paul's use of the analogy of wedlock to illustrate the change and exchange of ties of the believer, he assumes the well known principle that death dissolves all legal ties in a marriage. So the believer's participation in the sacrificial death of Christ, symbolized in his baptism, severs all ties with the old life of Sin. It also opened the way for a new life — union with the risen Christ, which may and should and must result in fruit unto God.

v. 1 *Or are ye ignorant, brethren, for I speak to men* that *know*[24] the nature of *law, how that the* marriage *law hath dominion* or force *over a man so long time as he liveth* (i. e. during his lifetime).

v. 2. *For the woman that hath a husband*[25] *has been and is bound by the* marriage *law*[26] *to her living husband while he lives; but if the husband dies,*[27]

---

22. Aor. pass participle, an occurrence in the pasttime Cf. rendering of aor. part. in R. V.
23. *Opsōnia*, plu. to denote different kinds of pay but only and always pay in kind and multiplied infinitely in eternal death. The devil has many kinds or types of pay for his servants.
24. Present participle, dative masc. plural, *ginoskousin* to those men knowing the principle of law.
25. *Hupandros* from*hupo* and*aner*, genitive case, *hupandros,* the under-a-husband woman.
26. Instrumental case.
27. Present subj. act., die, or might die. Condition of third class, ean with second aor, expressing a supposable case.

she is (stands) *discharged,*[28] no longer affected *by the law of the husband* which relates to their matrimony and life as husband and wife.

v. 3 *So then, if,*[29] *while the husband liveth,*[30] *she be joined to another man,* contrary to the law of monogamy *she shall be called*[31] *an adulteress; but, if the husband die,*[32] *she is free*[33] *from the* (that) *law, so that she is no adulteress,*[34] *though she be joined to another man.* By death to the old self the legal ties of the believer were severed and the believer is set free from the dominion of the Law.

v. 4. So that (my) brethren, *ye also were made dead to the mosaic law,* not the law dead to you[35] *through the* intermediate agency of *the body of Christ,* with which body your old self was crucified, (Cf. 6:6), *that you should be joined to another, even to him that was raised from the dead, in order that we might bear fruit unto God.* The Law had its hold on man through sin, but in discarding his sins man discards also the penalties exacted by the Law. He is under no obligation to anyone save Christ. Moral death of the Christian to his sins also does away with his relationship to the Law.[36]

v. 5. *For when we were in the flesh,*[37] and slaves to its lusts *the sinful passions, which were* revealed *through* the agency of the law, wrought[38] in our members, causing us *to bring forth fruit*[39] *for Death* as our Master. Sinful passions are antagonized and thus stimulate hostile passions connected with sin, as in the case of drunkenness and lust.

v. 6 *But now* in the new life *we have been discharged from the* (dominion of the) *law, having* ourselves *died to that* life of legal penalties *wherein we were holden*[40] *so that*[41] we are enabled to serve in newness of spirit in a life of devotion to Christ and not in oldness of the letter of the law, being governed by an elaborate code of commands and prohibitions.

In various references in this epistle Paul had spoken of the inadequacy of the Law.[42] In the foregoing verses (7:1-6) the statement that believers are not under the law (6:14) is explained more completely. The Christian believer, by the death of his old self, passed, as a consequence, from under the

28. Perf. Pass indicative from *katargeō* to make void or of no effect.
29. Third class condition *ean* with the subjunctive.
30. Genitive absolute with present act. part.
31. Future active ind from *chrēmatizō,* to be called from chrema, business. (Robertson in loco).
32. Third class condition, a supposable case. (Robertson, *Word Pictures* in loco).
33. Perfect active indicative, permanent and complete state.
34. Tou and infinitive, are used to express conceived result.
35. Paul would not say 'the law dead to you,' as the analogy would indicate.
36. Sanday and Headlam, *I.C.C.* Romans (p. 173)
37. The flesh is not inherently sinful but is subject to sin and the law (of physical death).
38. Imperfect middle indicative of *energeō,* were active, continued action is past time.
39. Purpose clause, *eis* with articular infinitive of the compound verb *karpo-phorēsai.*
40. Imperfect indicative passive of *echō,* with *kata, kateichometha,* incomplete continued action in the past.
41. Hōste with the infinite *donleuein* to express contemplated result which in the natural course ought to follow. (Sanday p. 175).
42. Cf. Ch. 3:20,21; 4:15; 5:20.

law into the state of grace, where he is free from the law. In the following step in the argument (vv. 7-25) Paul will show that the law is 'just' and 'good' in its character and work, but inadequate and unequal to the work of bringing man to the attainment of the God-kind of righteousness. This does not mean that the law is evil in itself. The Law reveals the hatefulness of sin.

3. The Law has no power to sanctify; only Christ brings deliverance in the struggle against sin. What therefore is the utility of the Law? Ch. 7:7-25.

a. Paul defines the role of the Law and its limitations (7:7-13). Is the law identical with sin? Such might seem to be the conclusion of the foregoing argument (Ch. 7:1-6). 'By no means' replies the Apostle. "The Law is holy and the commandment is holy and just and good." The Law plays the role of revealing the sinfulness of sin, reviving the conscience by stirring up the dormant sin to action and exposing it, while aggravating the guilt. The law thus intended for the life of man, becomes, through the sin of the sinner, the instrument of his death. It was necessary that we be set free from the law. (vv. 1-6) but the law is not evil. It works for the good by detecting the dormant sin in the nature of man and exposing its true character (vv. 7-13).

v. 7 *What then shall we say? Is the law* synonomous with *sin?* Such a question might have been asked by a Jewish objector or rhetorically by Paul himself. It was pertinent at least. The Apostle denies and repels the inference that the law was to be identified with sin. Away with such a thought: *May it not be,*[43] he exclaimed. On the contrary, *I had not known sin,*[44] *if I had not through* the intermediate agency of the *law,*[45] been able to form a judgment about it. For instance, I[46] was not perceiving the sinfulness of covetousness or illicit desire, if the law had not said: 'Thou shalt not covet.'[47]

v. 8. *But Sin* (generic, *hamartia*, personified) which was lurking within me, *taking occasion*[48] or a starting point *through the commandment*, which came into my consciousness at a certain age of my youth or boyhood days *worked in me intensively*[49] *every kind of coveting* or illicit desire, *for apart from the law sin is dead.*

Paul continues with his autobiographical confession. His early youth in his Jewish home was unvexed in its innocency. He was not conscious of any

---

43. This passage is autobiographical, a personal confession representing not Jews or the human race but universal experience of all men and human life regenerate and unregenerate. Cf. David Smith. *Life and Letters of Paul* p. 32 f: p: 414 Note.

44. Second class condition determined as unfulfilled with an in apodosis.

45. The Mosaic law, but here, by the absence of the article, the general principle of law more widely applicable to all men.

46. Paul is narrating his entire personal religious experience, as a Pharisee before his conversion (vv. 7-13) and the continuous internal conflict between the old man and the new man after conversion. Cf. Scotch Expositors, and Delitzsch, Alford, Hodge, Shedd, Robertson A. T., Dana, H. E., et al.

47. The tenth commandment of the Mosaic Code.

48. First aor. mid participle, effective aorist indicating intensive activity. Sin was dormant but sprang into consciousness when the commandment was known. That the 18th amendment provoked some to drink more is no argument against prohibition.

49. *Kala*, perfective use.

alienation from God until the occasion came in the study of the Law in the Synagogue school and the growing boy was overcome by some definite sinful act of covetousness and encountered the accusing finger of the law pointed at him. The commandment came into his knowledge and brought to his heart the feeling of guilt; for apart from law sin is dead. So the Law is used by the Spirit to stimulate guilt for sin wherever it exists.

v. 9. *And I was alive apart from* the knowledge of law *once* in early childhood; *but when the commandment came* into my knowledge and I understood it clearly for the first time *sin sprang into life and I died,* spiritually being separated from God by my sin. Conscience and reason quickened the consciousness of sin and guilt, and young Saul found himself in the grip of the law which separated between his rebellious heart and God. He found out that evil effect of sin for himself was spiritual death.

v. 10. *And the commandment, which was found* (meant) *for life for me the same was* found to be *for death* for me and for every sinner. It brought spiritual death in him.

v. 11. For Sin,[50] *taking occasion, through the commandment* like the serpent in the garden of Eden, *beguiled*[51] *me* making me lose my way *and through it, slew*[52] *me,* 'killing me off.'

v. 12. *So that*[53] *the law* not to be identified with sin but served as the discoverer of sin. It *is holy and the commandment* in its prohibition of covetousness, illicit desire and lust as well as other sins *is holy and just* (righteous) *and good* (beneficent). Its purpose is to prevent sin. When violated it becomes a harsh judge and remorseless enemy, inflicting guilt and penalty, and thus the feeling of rebellion stimulated in the heart of the sinner by the commandment drives him away from God further in spiritual separation and death.

v. 13. *Did then what is good become death unto me?* Away with such a thought![54] *God forbid! But* it was sin instead of the law that brought this evil, *that it might be shown* manifest or revealed to be *sin, by working spiritual death to me through that* (commandment) which is *good* — *yes, that*[55] *through the commandment sin might be shown,* and become revealed to be *exceeding sinful.* Paul repels the idea that the law of God was evil and asserts that it was holy and the commandment righteous, holy, and good, and that sin and not the Law had become the cause of death to him, thus revealing the character of its work in Paul, as it does in all sinners. The law revealed sin in its awfulness and pointed the way to spiritual life, but had no power to help or strength to lend to man to get him to life. The Commandment, intended

---

50. Sin, personified as in all this section.
51. First aor. act indicative, from *exapataō*, 'made me lose my way,' graphic enough!
52. First aor. act. indic. of *apekleinō*, 'killed me off,' also a graphic description of the action of sin.
53. *Hoste,* so that the conclusion of v. 7.
54. A liberal rendering expressing what might be the feeling of the Apostle as also *mē genoito* optative expressing a wish.
55. Purpose clause following *hina with the aorist.*

by God for the good of man, only awakens the spirit of rebellion and resentment the more, in the sinner, stirring him to resistence of the commandment. Civil law against crime produces this effect in the criminals, on account of their sins. The chain of thought is unbroken at verse 14. Paul acknowledges and asserts that the law is of a spiritual nature coming from God and that the value of the law remains for the Christian also to reveal sin.

b. In the life of the Christian believer, the struggle goes on between the good and the evil. The Christian must overcome the evil with the aid of Christ Ch. 7:14-25.

(1) The apostle recognized this struggle in his own personal life. The 'law of his mind was to serve Christ,' but there was a constant conflict between his mind, or inward man which reasons, having reverence for God's Law, and his lower animal nature in the flesh. Paul desired to restrain himself from the evil, while the principle of sin in his fleshly nature constrained him to do evil (vv. 14-17). The body of man is of flesh and blood. It is the half-wrecked body of death, doomed to pass away and be succeeded by a spiritual body. It is full of weakness and the seat of the temptations to evil. Paul would be free of that in the process of time.

v. 14. *For we know* as Christians *that the* Mosaic *law is spiritual,* framed through inspiration of the Holy Spirit, *but I, Paul, am carnal*[56] and my body and mental constitution tainted with self-will of the old man *sold*[57] *under sin* as it was before regeneration. The new self even now housed in the body of flesh and blood which is even yet vitiated by physical heredity and tendencies to evil, subject to temptations, which are met but not always successfully overcome. We have also a record in this section of Paul's personal testimony to his struggle against sin as a Christian. He would gain the victory through Christ but he was conscious of his imperfections and faults and made confession of them here. This is essentially only biographical.

v. 15. *For what I am working out I do not recognize,* because my spiritual perceptions are dulled and partially blinded by sin (II Cor. 4:4). "The dual life pictured here by Paul finds an echo in us all."[58] Man still has his human body of this death,[59] which is the seat of sin (Cf. 6:6) which in turn 'works out death:'[60] *for not what I would* (wish), *this do I practice; but what I hate* (as a Christian) *this I do.* This is the actual real experience of every Christian in the varying degrees and stages of spiritual growth.

v. 16. Just as the mortal body of the Christian is imperfect and serves as a basis for temptation and sinfulness, so the law continues its role of revealing the sin to the believer in his faults and failures, to attain to the standard of

---

56. *Sarkinos* does not refer to carnal mindedness so much as the flesh and blood of his body which was the weakest point in his human nature.

57. *Pepramenos,* perf. pass. part. from *piprasko* expressing the complete unregenerate status the vitiated Adamic nature, some of the results of which remain in the 'body of this death.'

58. Robertson, A. T., *Word Pictures.* p. 369.

59. Ch. 7:24.

60. *Ibid* v. 13.

the law and much more to that of Christ. *But if what I would not, this I do, I consent unto the law that it is good,* in spite of my failures which are evident, as in all men, even Christians, but in a different attitude in the regenerate by the new birth from that in the unregenerate.

v. 17 *But now,* since my wishing to do the opposite of what I do proves my acceptance of God's law as good (Robertson), *it is no longer I that am working it out but* (on the contrary) *the sin dwelling in me.* It is not my true self, my second-born personality, but my lower human nature of 'the old man' cropping out and having to be continuously curbed and suppressed. This does not in any sense free the Christian from full responsibility for every act of sin. The fundamental function of the law is to produce sin-consciousness, whether the sin be of a non-Christian or a Christian who is a sinner saved by grace. The struggle of human nature to satisfy the demands of the law single-handed is always hopeless, when he depends on the law alone and is not attended by the strength of Christ working through the Holy Spirit. Even in spite of the Christian having the law to reveal his sin and the Holy Spirit to lead him, many times through neglect of both he falls far short of the first by not making use of the strength and guidance of the second. As Denney well said: "To be saved from sin, a man must at the same time own it (that he is guilty of sin) and disown it (as having any right or place in the Christian life).

(2) And when Paul wished to do good evil was present with him even before his conversion but yet in a modified way after also. vv. 18-21.

v. 18. *For I know that in me, that is in my flesh,* the old man, which is the lower self, dwelleth *no good* thing, (which is absolutely good); *for to will* (wish) *is present with me,*[61] this wishing being of the better self *but* (the doing working out) *to do that which is good* (beautiful) *is not* present with me always.

v. 19. *For the good which I* (would) *wish* (to do), *I do not: but the evil which I would not,* that *I practice.* Through these verses Paul pictures the struggle in human experience between the good and the evil throughout man's unformed life. This struggle in the unregenerate ends in defeat but the struggle with the old-man, the lower nature yet present and not yet conquered in the Christian experience, presents a dualistic and a duelistic character. The Christian's reason, reenforced by the prompting, enlightenment, and strengthening of the Holy Spirit, should always come out victorious, but often does not because of the weakness of the flesh. That is not because of any defect in the law or Holy Spirit but in the human weakness of the flesh.

v. 20. *But if what I would* (wish) *not to do this I do,* in spite of my willing mind to do the good, *it is no longer*[62] (no more) *I* (my true self) *that* (am working it out) *do it, but the Sin* principle (personified) *which dwelleth in me.* Paul was surely speaking of his personal experience in these words.

---

61. Present middle indicative of the verb *parakeimai,* to lie beside (with dative) *moi. me,* Sin personified as a lion crouching at the door.

62. Cf. Robertson's A. T. *Word Pictures* in loco.

v. 21. *I find them, the law,* or principle already set forth in verses 18 and 19 works out in this way; *that to me who would* (wishes to) *do good, evil is present* and antagonizes the good, sometimes gaining the upper hand.

(3) What was the hope in such a struggle? Without divine aid he could not be victorious. He gives thanks to God that the victory is through Jesus Christ (vv. 22-25).

v. 22. *For I delight in the law of after the inward man*: (a thing which the non-Christian cannot be said to do, in most cases far from it, and always essentially in rebellion against it).

v. 23. *But I see a different law* (principle) *in my members* of the carnaceous body of flesh and blood, which principle is *warring against the law of my mind* or reason, prompted by the Holy Spirit, *and* which principle of the lower nature *is* bringing *me,* when possible into the power and *into captivity,* in striving instances temporarily *under the law of Sin, which is in my members* of my lower fleshly nature. The ancient pagan writers (Plato Ovid, Seneca, Epictetus) pictured this same kind of dualistic duel between the good and evil, between a man's conscience and his deeds. It is a reality there, but in a modified form in the Christian's life, where the Christian has the advantage of having the instruction of the law and the indwelling Spirit to help him. The outcome of the struggle in the pagan was relative but always final defeat; the outcome in the Christian's life is failure at times but always victory in the end.[63] This is because of the help of Christ operating with the Christian in his struggle.

v. 24. *O wretched man that I am! who shall deliver me out of the body of this death?* Death finds a lodgment in the body (Lightfoot). Paul did not exaggerate his own condition or that of anyone who is a Christian, hard-pressed in the struggle to overcome the 'old man' and 'put him off' and out. He had to overcome much of the Pharisaical pride and many other frailties in his human nature. But in this ejaculation he dealt honestly and turns to find his only and final hope and that of all Christians, in this struggle, to be through Jesus Christ.

v. 25. *Thanks to God, through our Lord Jesus Christ.*[64] It is through him that victory was in sight. But the struggle was not over yet. The duel yet continued. *Wherefore, then, I of myself,* the true self, *with the mind or* higher nature, *indeed serve the law of God,* through the help of the Holy Spirit, *but in my flesh* or lower human nature *the law principle of sin.* This is not an untrue representation of the varied experience of the Christian on the way of his pilgrimage. He has not reached perfection. He is not yet free from the imperfection and faults. He must struggle on in the process of the 'renewal of his mind' and the 'sacrifice of his body' in consecration to God. In the chapter 8 to follow the Apostle will point out the certainty of the outcome of the struggle up from this self-imposed, modified slavery in

63. Cf. Rom. 8:31-39.
64. Cf. Rom. 12:1-3.

which Christians go on appropriating in increasing measure the perfection of development, and development of perfection, in the Christian life.

4. The believer can be sanctified in Christ by the Holy Spirit. His sanctification ending in perfect holiness is certain and is complete with the new body Ch. 8:1-39.

a. The justification or righteousness through faith in Christ (3:21-5:21) is the basis for the sanctification through the Holy Spirit. The method of sanctification is here set forth. Through his incarnation death and resurrection, Jesus Christ dethroned sin and installed the Holy Spirit in man's life. (8:1-17).

b. Where the law of Moses failed Christ through his incarnation succeeded. The weakness of the law was in the fleshly nature and consequent death of man; the strength of divine love in Christ overcame sin in His flesh and also death, through his death and resurrection (vv. 1-4).

v. 1. We are ushered out of Chapter seven, an almost starless night of dualistic struggle, into the early dawn and hope of a perfect day in Chapter eight. *Therefore, now, no condemnation* is there *for those in Christ Jesus.* This sounds like a great announcement of an Angel on the judgment morn. As a result of this union in Christ Jesus, between the believer and the Savior, the Holy Spirit comes to reside in the soul of the believer and suppresses the inclinations of the fleshly or carnal nature which has its seat in the blood and flesh, physical body of man. In the ideal Christian life the indwelling Spirit gives victory over every sin. That there is no perfect Christian life is still a stubborn fact in Christian history and experience. But the new life in Christ is the basis of holiness and of the progressive increase in sanctification.

v. 2. *For the law* principle, *of the Spirit of life* (life-giving), operating *in* the sphere of the redemptive work of *Christ Jesus,* in his incarnation, atoning death and glorious resurrection, *made me* (you)[65] *free*[66] *definitely from the law* (principle or authority) *of sin and of death.* The Spirit dethrones sin which causes physical death of all men whether Christians or not. We are able by the help of the Holy Spirit to live the new life[67] but we fail many times. We are debtors to Christ, not to fail but to succeed.

v. 3. *For what the law could not do* (the thing impossible for the law)[68] *in that*[69] *it was* continually *weak,*[70] *through* the intermediate agency of *the flesh,* the carnal nature in the body of flesh and blood, *God sending his own Son in the likeness of sinful flesh* (not in sinful flesh himself) *and* also (concerning) *for sin condemned*[71] the *sin* of men, *in the flesh* of Jesus,[72] which paid the penalty

65. Mss. Aleph B. have *se* instead of *me* but the doctrine is the same with either.
66. First aor. act indicative, definite occurrence.
67. Robertson A. T., *Word Pictures,* Vol. Paul's Epistles.
68. (Cf. 7:7-24) Either nominative absolute or acc. of general reference.
69. In what or that in which.
70. Imperfect act, indicative, continued action in past time.
71. First aor. act. indicative, definite occurrence in his incarnation, death and resurrection.
72. Robertson A. T., *Grammar* p. 748.

of death and broke thus the sin-death connection. The Death of Christ showed that human nature might be sinless. He broke the power of sin upon him[73] and through the mystical union the sin power was taken away from death for the believer also. By his death Christ severed all possibility of contact for himself with sin. He resisted sin which had invaded humanity and thus expelled it, breaking its power over humanity.

v. 4 *In order that the ordinance* or requirement *of the law might be fulfilled*[74] *in us who are not walking* habitually *according to the flesh but according to the* renewed spirit (spiritually) or else the Holy *Spirit.*[75] Christ showed in his incarnation that man can through faith in him overcome sin.

(2) The believer can be sanctified through the Holy Spirit Who dwells in and aids him (vv. 5-13).

(a) The life according to the flesh and the life according to the Spirit are contrary to each other. One leads to transgression of the law of God, to rebellion and death; the other to reconciliation and life (vv. 5-8).

v. 5 *For those who are*[76] following after the bent of *the flesh are putting their minds on*[77] *the things of the flesh* or lower nature *but those* who follow habitually *according to the spirit,* put their minds on *the things of the spirit.*

v. 6. *For the* bent of the *mind* (thinking) and being toward the flesh is leading on to *death* and is death-dealing to body, soul and spirit; *but* on the contrary the bent of *the mind of the Spirit* produces and *is life,* present and eternal, *and* also *peace* with God, through reconciliation resulting in tranquillity and harmony in the experience of the believer. A Christian does not have the mind bent on sinning but he is a sinner in that he strays from right thinking many times and is not perfect in his conduct.

v. 7. *Because the mind of the flesh* leading habitually to gratification of the lower nature, *is enmity* or hostility *toward God: for it is not in subjection*[78] to the law of God, for it is 'not even able to be otherwise.' The state of unsubordination to God of a man who is thus apart from Christ, is hopeless (Robertson) unless he repents and turns to Christ.

v. 8. *For those beings who are dwelling in the flesh are not able to please God* because of the handicap of the lower nature which continues in bondage to sin. The only recourse is in repentence and faith in the Lord Jesus Christ, Who can rescue him from bondage. But it must be by a change of heart through the power of the Holy Spirit. A Christian is not perfect but he does not dwell deliberately in known sin.

---

73. Cf. Sanday and Headlam. Com. Rom. p. 193. The condemnation of sin took place in his death because he broke all relations or possibility of contact with sin by his sinless life and vicarious death.

74. First aor. passive subj. with hina, in purpose class, purpose of Christ's death (3:21-26).

75. The two laws of life kata sarka (7:7-24) and kata pneuma (8:1-10) in contrast.

76. Present participle indicates progressive or continued action habitually.

77. Fronousin — present tense, continued action.

78. Present indicative passive of hupotassō, in a state of continued insubordination.

(b) The believer in whom the Spirit dwells lives according to the Spirit. (vv. 9, 10).

v. 9. *But ye are not in the sphere* of the *flesh but in the sphere* of the *Spirit, if*[80] *indeed the Spirit of God is dwelling*[79] *in you,* as he is in every true son of God, born of the Spirit. The Christian may at times grieve or quench the Spirit by wrong conduct but he repents of it and seeks pardon, but *if anyone does not have the Spirit of Christ dwelling in him he* (this one) *is none of His.*

v. 10. *But if Christ is in you,* as he is,[81] *the body is dead* because of the seeds of *sin* in it, *but the* redeemed human spirit is God-begotten life, because of the God kind of *righteousness,* which comes through faith in Christ, if Christ is in you, in the person of the Spirit.

(c) The body is condemned to death, but the Spirit who dwells in believers will revive the body and transform it in the resurrection. Sanctification will be complete after the redemption of the body. The conflict with sin in the believer continues to the end of life. Without the indwelling of the Spirit, who suppresses sin there would be no hope of the complete sanctification of the spirit of the believer. The indwelling Spirit is the earner[82] of the believer's resurrection and reception of a new spiritual body (v. 11).

v. 11 *But if the* (Holy) *Spirit of* (God) *the one who raised Jesus from the dead is dwelling in you, the one who raised from the dead, Christ Jesus, will make alive also your mortal bodies through the intermediate agency of his indwelling Spirit in you.*

(d) Thus we believers have the obligation or debt to Christ not to live according to the flesh but according to the Spirit (vv. 12, 13).

v. 12 *Wherefore, then, brethren, we are debtors, not to the flesh* or lower nature with its sinful tendencies, *to live*[83] *according to the flesh,* following its tendencies toward sin. The fight, a real one, is on!

v. 13 *For if ye* (should) *go on living*[84] *after the flesh,* as ye are not, ye are about to *die; but if, by the Spirit,*[85] *ye are putting to death*[86] *the deeds* (practices) *of the body* (of flesh and blood, with its sinful tendencies) *as you are* in fact, *ye shall live.* Here there is a sharp contrast between the clauses showing clearly what the whole bent of the Christian's habit of life is in spite of his weaknesses and occasional failures which should be confessed always and not to be condoned by himself ever.

---

79. Present ind. act, denoting continued action.
80. Condition of first class according to facts — the Spirit was dwelling in them.
81. God begotten and sustained life zōē.
82. The pledge or down payment.
83. Articular infinitive does not have the article.
84. Second class condition ei with subjunctive followed by indicative primary tense, *contrary to fact.*
85. Instrumental case pneumati used with first class condition, according to fact in contrast to the other clause.
86. Present act. ind. in first class condition, according to fact.

(3) The believer can be sanctified, for another potent reason, because of his sonship in the family of God 8:14-17. The Holy Spirit, dwelling in the believer, testifies constantly to the reality of that sonship. Thus participating in the divine nature, the believer becomes an heir of God and joint-heir with Christ. With this vital relationship as a basis the certainty of complete sanctification is rendered absolute.

v. 14. *For so many as are being led*[87] habitually and progressively *by the Spirit of God*, the Holy Spirit, *these are the sons*[88] *of God* at least by adoption and even more here[89] (Ch. 8 v. 16) by being the real sons by birth into the family of God.

v. 15 *For ye received*[90] *not the spirit of bondage*, when the Holy Spirit was imparted, leading you back *again into* the bondage *of fear; but ye received the spirit of adoption* (of sonship) *in which spirit we cry, Abba*,[91] *Father*,[92] as in primitive Christian prayers.

v. 16. *The Spirit, himself*,[93] *bears witness along with our spirit that we are the own* ('flesh of flesh and bone of bone') *children*[94] *of God* being thus 'partakers of the divine nature' by birth into the kingdom.

v. 17. *And if we are*[95] *children, as we actually are, we are also heirs, heirs indeed of God and co-heirs* of (with) *Christ, if, indeed, we are suffering*[96] *together with him, in order that we might also be glorified* with him. The use of the conditional clauses here enabled Paul directed by the Holy Spirit to make perfectly clear the reality of divine sonship of the believers.

b. The certainty of the sanctification of the believer further elaborated. Ch. 8:18-39.

(1) We will be sanctified as believers in Christ in spite of the corruption and sufferings through which we pass. The way to perfectness is through suffering. vv. 18-25.

(a) All material creation was subjected to corruption through the fall of man and will participate also in his redemption. Its pangs are those of a new birth (vv. 18-22).

v. 18 *For I reckon* (calculate) *that the sufferings*, which we have to pass through and which are *of this present time, are not worthy* to be compared

---

87. Present passive indicative, are being led, continued action in present time.
88. huios term used generally for sons in New Testament, may express adoption or a more intimate relationship as that of Christ's sonship in the Trinity.
89. Cf. v. 16 to follow.
90. Second aorist active from tanibouō.
91. The Aramaic word adopted by Jesus and his disciples as sacred and dear use of the word. Father Abba, lieber vater (Luther, Abba dear Father) used in Christian prayers.
92. Nom. as vocative, often in N. Test. (Robertson).
93. Auto to agree with pneuma but cf. masculine pronoun used currently to refer to the Holy Spirit in Gospel of John et al.
94. Tekna is the more intimate and vital word expressing real natural relationship between father and son. Cf. Boise's *Notes*, Romans in loco.
95. Condition of first class, according to actual facts.
96. Condition of first class, followed in this case by purpose clause, hina with aor. subjunctive passive.

with the dazzling *glory*, which is *about to be revealed* entering *into us* with its transforming power.

v. 19 *For the earnest expectation of the* whole irrational *creation*, animate and inanimate, awaits with eager longing as it were *with outstreched* (neck) *head* as the rummering the Olympian races, *the revelation* of the *sons*, who are born into the family *of God.*

v. 20. *For the creation*[97] ages ago[98] *was subjected*[99] to vanity, to be in a useless state, not *willingly* of its own choice *but on account of him who subjected it* (God) Who did so to carry out his own purpose.

v. 21. *Because in* the sphere of *hope*, it is, *that the* irrational *creation itself also shall be delivered from* the bondage of the *corruption, into the liberty of the glory of the* own *children* (tekna) of the kingdom of *God.*

v. 22 *For we know that the* same *whole creation groaneth and travaileth in pain*, as it were, of child-birth, *together until now.*

(b) Christians also being subjected to corruption and decay of the body must pass through the experience of physical death but they have the earnest of the indwelling Spirit, the first downpayment, which is the guarantee of the full redemption or deliverance in a complete redemption, when the physical body is transformed or substituted by a spiritual body in the resurrection (vv. 23-25).

v. 23 *And not only* does the whole irrational creation groan together *but ourselves also* (while we have) *having*[1] *the first fruit of the* indwelling *Spirit,*[2] *we even ourselves*[3] *groan within ourselves, while expecting to the full* payment, namely the full *adoption as sons*, which is *the redemption of our body*,[4] the last step in our complete sanctification or sinless perfection.

v. 24. *For in* the sphere of *hope we were saved.*[5] *But hope*, which is *being seen is not hope* in the true sense, *for what anyone sees, why does he also go on hoping* for it.

v. 25. *But, if we are hoping for what we do not see, through* the means of *patience* we earnestly *go on waiting* for it.

(2) A second encouragement and additional reason for the certainty of our complete sanctification being realized finally, is, that the indwelling Spirit aids us in our infirmity. We do not have to struggle alone. If it were thus, we do not even know what to pray for or how to pray. The Holy Spirit comes in at

97. The creation personified ooks for the renovation Rev. 21. Cf. Acts 3:21, II Pet. 3:12, 13.
98. Gen. 3:17, 18.
99. First aor. Pass. Ind., an occurrence in history.
1. Echontes pres. past in temporal clause.
2. Partitive genitive, the first fruits of the Spirit (indwelling now) the full harvest to come later (Boise) in all the spiritual manifestations of Pentecost etc. but especially in resurrection of the body.
3. Repeated for emphasis.
4. Apposition, adoption carried out fully in the new spiritual body of the resurrection.
5. First aor. pass. indic. when we were accepted by Christ through faith we were reckoned righteous.

the time of need and intercedes in our hearts with groanings unexpressed and unutterable. (vv. 26, 27).

v. 26. *And in like manner,* while we are waiting with patience, *the Holy Spirit takes hold for himself*[6] *along with us at the point of our infirmity. For what*[7] *we may pray for, as it is necessary* (to pray) *we do not know, but the* Holy *Spirit himself*[8] (itself) *maketh intercession* (for us) *on our behalf with groanings*[9] *which cannot be uttered* (unutterable).

v. 27. *And he who searches the hearts* of men, that is God,[10] *knows what is the mind* (result of the thinking or the thoughts) *of the Spirit, because according to* the will of God he (the Spirit) *makes intercession* for the saints in their hearts. The Spirit interprets our prayers, straightens out our prayers, so that they become in accord with the will of God, by enlightening us.

(3) Our sanctification is certain also because all things work together for good, in the Father's providence,[11] to those who love God. This is a third encouragement (vv. 28-30).

v. 28. *All things*[12] *work together for good to those who love God,* since they are *the called according to his purpose.*

v. 29. *Because, whom he foreknew*[13] in eternity before the world was, *he also foreordained*[14] in eternity, to be *conformed*[15] *to the image of his Son,* by gradual change into the likeness of Christ, thus sharing in the glorified celestial being of the Incarnate Son, (Sanday) *to the end that he should be the first born* "from the dead,"[16] through the resurrection, *among many brothers.*

v. 30. *And whom he foreordained,* in eternity, *these he also called*[17] in time, *and whom he called,* by the preaching of his gospel, *these he also justified,* through their acceptance by faith of the call of the gospel, reckoning them as righteous; *and whom he justified, these he also glorified* through the process of sanctification until they received after death their glorious resurrection bodies. With God the whole process of many steps is considered as complete from the beginning since there is no time with God.[18]

---

6. Pres. mid. ind. of sunantilambonomai to take hold alongside with us, (assoc. inst.) at the difficult time and point of our infirmity (locative astheneiai Cf. Luke 10:40).
7. Use of *to* cf. Winer *Gram.* p. 109, also *Katho* p. 299.
8. Neuter agreeing with pneuma, but translated logically in masc. gender.
9. Instrumental case, with sign that baffle words (Denny) cited from Robertson's *Word Pictures* in loco.
10. Cf. I Sam. 16:7; Jer. 17:9 ff.
11. A and B have ho theos as the subject of sunergei. Cf. I Cor. 16:16, II Cor. 6:1. Anyway it is God who makes "all things work together," in our lives for ultimate good, Robertson *Word Pictures* Vol. Romans p. 377
12. The all things include their experiences and fortunes, trials, failures, successes.
13. Second aor. act. of verb proginosko ind. an occurrence in eternity.
14. First aor. act verb proōrisen, also occurrence in eternity.
15. An inward and not merely superficial conformity. Cf. Robertson *Word Pictures.*
16. Cf. Col. 1:18.
17. The aor. act. ind. recurring in all these phrases, here ekalesen.
18. The timeless constative aorists are used indicating the absolute certainity of the complete salvation of the believer from the beginning.

(4) Our sanctification is certain because God the Father is for us. He gave his Son for us, through love, that we might have our redemption in Him. Jesus Christ at the right hand of God intercedes for us as our Advocate. Divine love is the fulfillment of the Law. vv. 31-39.

(a) The believer, aided by the Holy Spirit has also God the Father, Judge of all, and Jesus Christ, on his side (vv. 31-34). Nothing can take us out of the hands of the all-powerful God. No one can accuse when Jesus Christ our Advocate is for us. If God gave his Son much more will he give all things necessary for our salvation.

v. 31. *What, then,*[19] *shall we say* (in view of) *to these things.* He speaks of the argument (from v. 12) as to the certainty of final sanctification of the sons of God. Paul now gives the objectors a chance as always. *If God* is *for us,* as he surely is,[20] *who is* (can be) *against us?*

v. 32. The reason for believing God follows. *Who,* indeed,[21] *spared not his own Son, but delivered him up for us all, how shall he not also with him freely give us* the *all things.*[22] Here redemption is provided for all believers. 'All things' that belong to salvation are included.

v. 33. *Who shall lay anything to the charge of God's elect,* as an accuser? Satan is a great accuser of the brethren (Robertson), but he cannot impeach, for, *It* is God *that justifieth.* He reckons the believer as righteous and he is the judge. The accuser must free the judge with his charges.

v. 34. *Who is he that condemneth?* Further assurance yet is at hand, for *It is Christ that died, yea rather that was raised from the dead and who is sitting at the right hand of God in the place of authority, as the judge of* mankind, *who also is* continually *making intercession*[23] *on our behalf.* This is double assurance. The Father is for us, and a living Christ of ever-active sympathy is constantly interceding for his people.

(b) The divine love of God in Christ is the final guarantee and certainty of our complete sanctification and redemption. Nothing can separate us from this love through which we are conquerors of all. Our complete sanctification is certain (vv. 35-39).

v. 35. *Who*[24] *shall separate us from the love of Christ?* It is his love for us and our love for him.[25] *Shall tribulation or anguish or persecution or famine, or nakedness, or peril or sword?*

v. 36. Just as it stands written;[26] (*on thine account*) *we are killed all the day long;*[27] *We are reckoned as sheep for the slaughter.*

---

19. Oun introduces a commentary on v. 28, 'all things' (Boise).
20. Condition of the first class ei with indicative, according to fact.
21. Ge, particle for emphasis.
22. The all things referred to already which God makes to work together for good of those who love him and are the called ones.
23. Present ind. act. continued and progressive action.
24. Tis is masculine or feminine agreeing thus with all the nouns which follow.
25. Both subjective and objective genitive should be used here for both are truly meant.
26. Psa. 44:23, LXX.
27. Holēn tēn hemeran — accus. of extent of time.

v. 37. *But in all these things we are more than conquerors through the one who loved us.* The love of Christ which had brought him through conflicts of past years would never fail him but attend him to the end of his days and reach out into eternity. We need this assurance every day. ....

v. 38. *I stand convinced* Paul declares *that neither death nor life, nor angels, nor principalities* (any of spirits) *nor present nor things to come* (no dimension of time) *nor powers* (supernatural) or (forces of whatever description).

v. 39. *neither height nor depth* (no dimension of space) *nor any other kind of creation* (invisible to us now), *shall be able to separate us from the love of God, which is in Christ Jesus our Lord.* An amazing issue indeed! The emotions of the Apostle overflow as he catches the rapturous vision of the highest peak of the epistle! God's love in Christ is victorious over all the believer's foes!

D. A "luminous example" (Sanday) of the rejection of this Godkind of righteousness through faith in Jesus Christ and the terrible result of the rejection. Chapters 9-11.

1. God's rejection of Israel as a nation in consequence of their rejection of Jesus their Messiah is an inexorable fact. 9:1-5. Paul here expresses his deep sorrow and grief because of their rejection of the place of high privilege they had occupied once but forfeited as a nation, thus losing their mission as a people for an indefinite time, which, alas, was to be for centuries yet unfinished in our day.

v. 1. To clear away the suspicion of some that in preaching to the Gentiles he was indifferent and hostile toward his people Israel, he makes a declaration solemn and emphatic, saying: *I speak the truth in Christ, I do not lie, my conscience bearing me witness in the Holy Spirit,* in order that you may have double

v. 2. assurance stronger than any oath, *that there is a sorrow,* a personal sorrow *to me, a great* one, *and an unceasing* grievous *pain*[28] which I cannot shake off but abides as an agony *in my heart.*[29]

v. 3. *For*[30] *I was* on the point of *wishing,*[31] *myself to be* accursed (anathema),[32] separated from Christ,[33] if it were possible, *on behalf of my brethren*[34] *my kinsmen according to the flesh,* in natural descent. Paul, like Moses (Ex. 32:32), would have been willing to make the sacrifice of his own salvation for the Israelitish nation if in that way he might save them.

v. 4. *Who are,* as a matter of fact, *the Israelites* the privileged and chosen people of God: *whose is the adoption,* in distinction from all other nations

---

28. Like the grief of a Jew writing after the fall of Jerusalem (Sanday and Headlam).
29. Adducing the reason.
30. Like angina pectoris.
31. Idiomatic imperfect in a second class condition (Robertson *Grammar* p. 886.)
32. Dialectical variation from anathenia, Cf. Ex. 32.
33. Apō with abl; pregnant use of preposition.
34. His fellow Israelites as in contrast to his Christian brethren.

(Cf. Ex. 4:22 et al), *and the glory* of the visible (Shekina) presence of God (Cf. Ex. 16:10), *and the* four *covenant* of God (Cf. Schiirer Geschichte, II p. 388) renewed from time to time (Gen. 6:18-Ex. 2:24), *and the giving of the law* in so much splendor on Sinai, *and the temple service* of God, *and the promises,* made in the Old Testament with reference especially to the coming of the Messiah.

v. 5. *Whose are the fathers,* the patriarchs, *from whom is Christ* come by natural descendence *according to the flesh, who is* the one being *over all,* God[35] blessed forever in his unending reign upon the throne of the universe.

In this introduction to the argument which follows (Chs. 9-11) the Apostle discloses the pain in his heart as he reflects on the wonderful privileges, and mission of Israel (vv. 1-3) and recounts some of those prerogatives in detail. vv. 4, 5.

2. The divine sovereignty and purpose of God in the rejection of Israel as a nation is vindicated and justified. 9:6-29 The claim of Israel to a title to salvation because of being the chosen people is inconsistent with the teachings of Scripture and the history of Israel also. Neither could they base their claim on their being merely creatures of God the Creator.

a. The rejection of Israel as a nation is not inconsistent with the promises of the Word of the Old Testament. Not all were rejected of God, but individual Israelites who believed in the Gospel were acceptable to him. vv. 6-13.

v. 6. *But it* (is) *not as though the word of God has come to naught:*[36]

v. 7. *for they are not all* (spiritual) *Israel* in reality *who are sons of Israel* by natural descent, *nor, because they are Abraham's seed are they all children,* of spiritual Israel *but "In Isaac shall thy seed be called."* The Sons of Israel are not included in Spiritual Israel as a nation though they were of the seed of Abraham. But they were the fruit of polygamy by the concubine Hagar.[37] Isaac was the son of faith because he was given in response to Abraham's faith in the promise, that he being beyond age and also Sarah, yet she would conceive and bear a child. The promise was given before the child was born or even conceived. He was the fruit of faith.

v. 8. *That is, it is not the children of the flesh that are the children of God* in the full sense. The privileges of the Jews were not due to their physical descent from Abraham, just as Jesus had taught,[38] but were the inheritance received through the faith of their forbears as the heritage of true democracy came down from men who learned it "from Christianity."

v. 9. *For this word* is one *of promise*: (According to) *about this season* of the year *will I come and Sarah shall have a son.*[39] The child was thus born according to promise and naturally after the promise had been given. Ishmael

35. God, in opposition to the substantival participle with the article, (ho ōn) adopted by the overwhelming majority of scholars identifying the deity of Christ. This punctuation is in accord with the best grammatical, logical conclusions, Pauline usage. (Cf. Sanday and Headlam, Robertson, Boise et al).

36. Ekpeptoken — Perf. Act. Ind., hoth failed or come to naught.

37. Cf. Gen. 21:12 when Abram cast forth Hagar and Ishmael.

38. Cf. Luke 3:8.

39. Combination of Gen. 18:10 and 14 from the LXX.

was born of a female slave girl, Hagar, according to physical or natural descent, which was not sufficient. Faith in the promise came before the birth of Isaac.

v. 10. *And not only* this but another illustration is adduced to show the liberty of God in election, *Rebecca also, having conceived*[40] *by one, our father Isaac.*

v. 11. For the twins not yet having been born,[41] *neither having done anything good or bad, in order that purpose of God according to election might stand* and remain apparent, as *not* being *from works, but*

v. 12. *from the one calling* (even God), *it was said unto* her (Rebecca) (that)[42], "The elder (greater in age)[43] *shall serve* as a bond servant *the younger.*"[44] This proved true in their descendants (Boise). The choice of God referred not only to the founder or father but to the children or descendants also (Sanday nd Headlam) *I. C. C. Romans* pp. 246 ff.

v. 13. *Even as it stands written*: *Jacob I loved and Esau I hated, before* their birth.[45] The inheritance of the promise is not dependent on natural descent or human merit. The Jews prided themselves on being the chosen race while the Ishmaelites had been rejected. Paul simply applies the same principle on which the Ishmaelites who were the illegitimate sons of Hagar and Abraham had been rejected, while Isaac and the Israelites were elected to be the chosen race.

b. The rejection of Israel by God was not inconsistent with divine justice. 9:14-29.

(1) A second objection Paul understood would be raised as to whether God is not unjust and arbitrary in conferring his favors without regard to privilege by birth or human merit in the recipients (vv. 14-18).

v. 14. *What shall we say then* to this objection? With (beside) (alongside) *God, there is no injustice* is there[46] *God forbid!* (May it not be!) Paul was only laying down the just character of Divine sovereignty as fundamental in all true theology. All of God's action as set forth in Scripture is just and for Paul Scriptural authority was inspired and final.

v. 15. He cites an Old Testament illustration from Moses' writing (Ex. 33:19). *For he says to Moses I will have mercy on whom I have mercy*[48] *and I will have compassion on whomsoever I have compassion.* God is absolute sovereign and has the inherent right of absolute choice which, he being God, is absolutely just and right. Mercy is the right thing in reality wherever God

---

40. Having a marriage bed. from one father, by his lawful wife.
41. First Aor. Pass. Participle, the event of birth had not taken place.
42. Ibid, First aor. Act participle in this case.
43. Hoti used in citation and so not translated.
44. Meīzōn greater in the sense of age, born first in order cited from the LXX. 6 The less or **smaller.**
45. Aorist active of both verbs agapaō and misseō used and contrasted as in Matt. 6:24 and Luke 14:26. For word 'hate' Cf. Robertson *Word Pictures.*
46. Me expects a negative answer.
47. Cf. Ex. 33:19.
48. Indefinite relative hon with present active subjunctive in both clauses.

has mercy and compassion, Pharaoh rejected God's mercy offered him ten times, each time before the plague came.

v. 16. *So then,* it (mercy) *is not of* (the one) *him that that willeth, nor of him that runneth*[49] *but of God* (the one) *having mercy.* He is the source of mercy and Israel has no claim on his grace, which when bestowed is an act of 'unmerited favor' freely given to man his creature as a free gift. All men sin and reject God's mercy and usually many times before God rejects them. He has the right to give every man a chance before man finally rejects and forces God to leave him alone in judgement.

v. 17. God's grace does not depend on anything which is according to his nature as just[50] but God's will. Paul here deals with individual election, giving an example well-known to the Israelites of one who hardened his heart against God's mercy and was as a consequence hardened more by God's continued mercy. *For to Pharaoh, that Scripture saith*[51] which God spoke through Moses, *"For this very purpose did I raise thee up that I might show in thee my power, and that my name might be published*[52] *abroad in all the earth."*[53] In the overthrow of Pharaoh in the Red Sea, the name of Jehovah has been published in all the earth through the centuries. Pharaoh had God's mercy shown him in offer after offer and warning after warning in the ten plagues.

v. 18. *So then* the fact and general principle stands: "On *whom he wishes,* (on him) *he has mercy and whom he wishes* (to harden), (him) *he hardens.* Pharaoh hardened his own heart first.[54] God's mercy to be the hard-hearted Pharaoh was the cause or occasion at least of the continuation of the hardening process in his heart. The Gospel hardens, negatively speaking, those who reject it. It is the occasion of their hardening. When man rejects God's merciful offer of salvation in Christ it leaves his heart less impressionable and more encrusted.

(2) The essential relation between creator and creature is next examined as it is always an ultimate defense of the server. The creature must not complain against the creator or presume on his mercy. This is where the retreating sinner seeks a subterfuge. vv. 19-21. A third objection, which Paul understood would certainly be raised by the objector was: If man's destiny is a matter of God's sovereign will why does God find fault. This is the 'hard-shell' inner's excuse. The image of the potter and the clay is adduced to illustrate the relationship between the Creator, God, and his creature, man. This familiar figure teaches that we as creatures have no right to question the wisdom of the provisions of this will of the Creator.[55]

---

49. Cf. II Pet. 1:20 a familiar figure indicating strenuous effort to gain a goal.
50. Cf. Sanday and Headlam in loco.
51. Ex. 9:13.
52. Result expressed by hopōs with second aor. subj. diaggeleī.
53. The citation from LXX partly changed, mostly verbatim. Cf. Ex. 9:16.
54. Cf. Ex. 8:15, 32; 9:34.
55. Cf. H. E. Dana, *The Life and Literature of Paul,* p. 134.

v. 19. *Thou will say then unto me, "Why doth he still find fault?" For who withstandeth his will,*[56] that is his deliberate plan and purpose (which is unchangeable)?[57]This is the blue print of God, the creator-constructor of the universe. It was known of God in detail before one item of the creation was ever effected or done. It is defiance in man when he says: 'For who withstandeth his will'? and Paul replies to puny man who would assume equality with God.

v. 20. *Nay, but O man, indeed, now, at least who art thou: that repliest*[58] *against God? Shall the thing formed* (the creature) *say unto him that formed it* (the Creator), *"Why didst thou make thus?"* The negative answer expected by the Greek particle *mē*[59] is that the creature will surely not be presumptuous to complain to the Creator or against him either and question the character of his creation. Man is fearfully and wonderfully made,[60] by God the Eternal, All-wise, and All-powerful. This is the hard doctrine for the humanist and the rationalist to admit. He knows as well as Paul that God is God and that man his creature cannot compass 'his thoughts and his ways.' If man could, there would be no need of revelation and inspiration of the Scriptures. But revelation is a fact.

v. 21. The illustration of the potter follows: *Or hath not the potter a right over the clay, from the same lump* (of clay) *to make one part* into *a vessel*[61] *unto honor*, for an honorable use *and another* (part) into a vessel *unto dishonor*, or dishonorable purpose. (Isa. 29:16; 45:9; Jer. 18.) God had a right to choose from the Israelitish race (lump) some to be an honor in his kingdom and to reject others on moral and religious grounds which he knew to be sufficient. God is not man that man should assume to raise a complaint just because he does not understand fully. If God could be understood fully and be rationalized wholly by man he would be no longer God. He does not act arbitrarily but in a freedom controlled by his own moral nature. But his ways are higher and his thoughts deeper than ours. In the next chapter (Ch. 10) Paul deals with the moral side and responsibility of Israel and of nations and individuals in relation to the sovereign God. Human presumption in the form of humanistic rationalism cannot plead its rights before God. To put man's judgment on a par with God's would be to reduce the universe to anarchy.[62] God's will is the basis of moral government in the cosmos. From v. 22 on, Paul explains that God has not acted arbitrarily but in a freedom controlled by moral law. In chapter ten man's moral freedom and consequent

---

56. Boulema, deliberate purpose, as against thelēma (Matt. 6:10) God's wish for his creatures which not like the boulēma, God's unchangeable plan of the cosmos, but which the creature can oppose or withstand.
57. Boulēma, Thayer's Lexicon. Unusual and emphatic order of the Greek words.
58. Present middle articular participle of double compound verb anta pokrisiomai.
59. *Me* in the beginning of the question expects a negative answer.
60. Cf. Psalm.
61. Skeuos, apposition with pronoun ho men with men particle, (part).
62. Cf. James Denney. *The Expositor's Greek Test.* p. 662f.

responsibility are explained so fully that a wayfaring man though a fool need not err therein.

(3) God's long-suffering and beneficent purpose revealed in the Old Testament show that the rejection of Israel as a nation was not inconsistent with divine justice vv. 22-29. Paul believed in the Old Testament Scriptures and rests the case of divine justice on the fact that those Scriptures describe the long suffering of God and his beneficient purpose and in dealing with the Jews throughout their history. That purpose and attitude was in God's action from the beginning of time and is revealed in the Old Testament writings fully with reference to the whole race.

v. 22. *What, if God,* through *willing*[63] *to show his wrath and make his power known endured*[64] *with much longsuffering*[65] *vessels of wrath*[66] *fitted* already for *destruction*: God restrained his wrath through kindness and beneficience when dealing with those who were fitted by their moral choices and actions for utter destruction. This is repeatedly shown in Israel's history.[67]

v. 23. *And in order that he might make known the riches of his glory upon the vessels of mercy,*[68] *which he before prepared*[69] *for glory.* On the other hand he poured out on those his glory, whom he had blessed and helped on to make vessels of mercy and honor through their proper response and cooperation with him.

v. 24. *even us whom he called, not only from* among *the Jews*[70] *but also from* among *the* (nations) *Gentiles?* By implication the rejection of Jews as a nation is told, while asserting the election of some Jews and some Gentiles. 2:23.

v. 25. As also in Hosea he says: *I will call that my people, which was not my people;*[71] *And her beloved, who was not beloved.* Paul cites Hosea in proof of the character of the new Spiritual Israel to be composed of Jews and Gentiles.

v. 26. *And it shall be, that in the place where it was said unto them, 'Ye are not my people, There shall they be called sons of the living God.*[72] There will be Christian Jews in the end when Spiritual Israel becomes a universal reality.

63. Concessive use of the participle.
64. Constative second aorist active indicative of pherō to bear.
65. Objective genitive of orgēs, objects of God's wrath.
66. Perfect passive participle, fitted completely, and permanently. They were responsible for this readiness (Cf. I Thess. 2:15f.) (Robertson) for endless perdition but not annihilation. (Matt. 7:13).
67. Purpose clause, hina with aorist active subjunctive of gnorizō.
68. Objective genitive, eleous, objector of God's mercy over against objects of his wrath preceding.
69. First aor. active indicative of proctoimazo, make ready. Cf. Rom. 8:28-30. (Robertson).
70. Ablative of Judaiōn, source or origins.
71. Ouk. used with substantives obliterates meaning of substantive (Cf. Robertson). Hosea refers to the ten tribes. He had a son named Lo-ammi, meaning (ou laos) not people and a daughter named Lo-ruhamah meaning not mercy.
72. Hosea 1:10 The gathering of the nations in Jerusalem seems to be foretold here.

v. 27. *And Isaiah crieth* on behalf of Israel, "*If the number of the children of Israel be as the sand of the sea,* It is *the remnant* that (will) *shall be saved.*[73] "Isaiah was in anguish about the outlook for Israel, but sees hope for the remnant" (Robertson). Along with the salvation of a remnant of Israel the other fact of national restoration seems to be.

v. 28. For the Lord will execute his word upon the earth, finishing it and cutting it short. "A sharp and decisive sentence the Lord would execute upon the earth."[74]

v. 29. *And just as Isaiah* hath said before: "*If the Lord of Sabaoth had not left us a seed*: *We had become as Sodom And had been made like unto Gommorrah.*[75] The final citation of Paul is from Isaiah setting forth the severity and also the goodness of God.

3. The real cause of the rejection of Israel as a nation by God. Chs. 9:30-10:21.

a. Because they sought justification through their own works and self-righteousness and not through faith alone. 9:30-10:4. When we consider God's sovereign grace, we must always keep in mind that we, finite beings we are, can never comprehend the infinite God. In his nature and in all his judgements He is a just God. The history of God's dealings with men like Pharaoh, a heathen ruler, and with Esan, an Israelite shows that God offered them mercy and compassion and when they rejected it they forced God to reject them, because he does not force men to choose the right: So Israel's rejection was due to their own wrong choice. God sent them the Messiah he had promised them through their prophets and they rejected him when he came. God had no alternative but to sign their sentence of rejection and doom which they themselves had written out clearly for themselves. God cannot do wrong.

b. A prevew of the arguments to follow vv. 30-33.

v. 30. *What then shall we say,* in conclusion of this argument (of Ch. 9)? Shall we say *that*[76] some *Gentiles,* though *not following after righteousness,* of a law-kind yet *obtained*[77] *righteousness, but* a God-kind of righteousness *of* the *faith kind?*

v. 31. *But Israel following* a *law*-kind *of righteousness did not come into a law of righteousness* or righteousness based on observance of law. They failed to live up to the standard of their law, because to do that would be to keep perfectly all the law (Robertson). This they no way ever did.

v. 32. *Why?* For what reason did Israel fail? *Because they followed after a righteousness not* resulting *from faith but as* if resulting *from works.* Such a pursuit was as a mirage in the desert. It was a vain delusion, followed by disillusionment for them in the end. *They stumbled* striking on the hidden

73. Isa. 10:22 (LXX) shortened quotation.
74. Sanday and Headlam, I. C. C. Rom. Paraphrase p. 252.
75. Cited verbatim LXX Isa. 1:9. The word Sabbaoth of host, is retained in the transliterated Hebrew in the LXX.
76. Hoti, that declarative.
77. Second constative aor. act. ind. definite occurrence covering period.

reef of *the stone of stumbling* just as foretold by the prophet Isaiah.[78] "*Behold I place in Sion a stone of stumbling And a rock of offense, And he who places his faith upon it*[79] *Shall not be put to shame.*" The stone of stumbling and rock of offense for the Jews was and is the Christ Jesus.[80] The lack of faith prevented them from recognizing and accepting him.

Paul sorrowfully states that Israel failed to see that Christ was the termination of the law as a principle or method of righteousness. Ch. 10:1-4.

v. 1. The Apostle addressing his Christian brethren expresses his personal grief because of this failure of the Jews. *Brothers, my heart's* craving, *good will* (desire) *and prayer to God on behalf of them* (Israel) is *for their salvation.* Paul did not believe they were reprobates (Bengel) else he would not have prayed for them. He understood that each individual Jew that would accept Christ would be saved.

v. 2. The Apostle assigns a reason for his grief on account of the failure of Israel. *For I bear them witness that a zeal for God*[81] and religion *they have but it is not according to* the more perfect or accurate, technical *knowledge*[82] of God and his religion.

v. 3. *For being ignorant of the God-kind of righteousness and seeking to establish their own,* (idian) kind of *righteousness, they did not submit*[83] *themselves to the righteousness of God.* God directed them to follow his way, that of faith, but they chose to follow their way and methods and so failed to reach the goal of the kind of righteousness necessary to eternal fellowship with God.

v. 4. *For Christ is the end* or termination *of the law, leading unto righteousness* (diaaiosune), that kind of imputed righteousness by faith in Jesus Christ, *to everyone* that is *believing.* There are two methods of righteousness contrasted here: one is by dependence on the law and is by the merit of obedience. That method Christ terminated or put an end to when he came and substituted in its place the method of faith in Christ as a personal Savior of everyone who believes in Him. The Old Testament Scriptures pointed to Christ but the Israelites did not have the accurate knowledge, epignōsis, to discern that fact. Everyone by believing may obtain the God-kind of righteousness, *dikaiosunē.* Through the Gospel in Christ, the moral law of Moses is fulfilled, being converted from external form into internal principle of life. The moral code of a Confuscius is external and does not avail because of the weakness of the

---

78. Is. 1:4; 28:16. Cf. I Pet. 2:6, 7.
79. Autō — locative case. personal of the Messiah, 'he that believeth on Him.'
80. Lithos seems to have been a name for the Messiah among the Jews Cf. Is. 8:14; 28:16, Sanhedrin 38.
81. Objective genitive. Theon.
82. The higher disciplined knowledge of the true moral discernment epignōsis. Cf. Col. 1:9. The Jews had knowledge of God in and so were superior to the Gentiles in having the Old Testament but sought righteousness in rules and rites and so missed real righteousness.
83. Second aor. pass. ind. of hupotassō, passive in sense of middle (Jos. 4:7).

flesh.[84] It can be salvaged for the good by being vitalized by the transformation of the heart by Christ.

b. Paul proceeds to contrast two methods: the old one by the law, difficult and impossible, versus the new, easy and in the reach of all. Ch. 10:5-10.

v. 5. *For Moses writes* about the righteousness which from the observance of the law *that the man who did it shall live thereby.*[85] The Jew's system was one of doing but God's was one of believing, one of grace.[86] The law and grace are mutually exclusive and antagonistic. When the Jew held to the law and insisted on saving himself by the futule effort to keep all the law, he was like one trying to climb the rugged and precepitous heights of Mount Sinai with a broken ladder. He thereby refused to accept God's method and so was not in subjection to the law of God.

v. 6. *But the righteousness, which is by faith* from[87] faith, says[88] thus: *Do not say in your heart,* 'Who shall ascend into the heaven', that is[89] *to bring Christ down.* Paul thus applies in interpretation, Moses' words to Christ. There is no need that one attempt the impossible, such as ascending to heaven to bring Christ down. He has already come down in the incarnation and manifested himself as deity. Faith is not a difficult but an easy thing since Christ came and dwelt in our midst.

v. 7. *Or 'who shall descend into the abyss,'* or more literally as Moses said 'go over to the further side of the sea for us, and receive it for us, and make it heard by us and we shall do it' that is,[90] *to bring Christ up from the dead,* from the abyss of Hades or Sheol,[91] the other world to which Christ went after death.[92] Christ had already risen from the dead when Paul wrote these words. Deuteronomy 30:10 had spoken of Israel turning to God with all their heart and with all their soul: Moses said that the 'commandment' (singular) he had commanded was not hidden from converted Israel. Paul was a true interpreter of the Old Testament and of Christianity. Man cannot save himself by trying to do the impossible. To the believer the 'impossible work' for man's salvation is already done by Christ.[93]

v. 8. *But what does the righteousness from* (or by) *faith* (personified) *say*: *Near to thee, the Word* to (rēma) *faith*[94] *is*: *in thy mouth and in thy heart*: *that is, the word concerning faith,*[94] *which we preach.* Paul seized hold of the Gospel message about faith and preached faith in the incarnation

84. Cf. Rom. 8:3, 4.
85. Cf. Lev. 18:5.
86. James F. Stifler, Romans p. 184.
87. Ek. pisteōs.
88. Faith righteousness personified. Cf. LXX Deut. 30:11-14 for verses 6-8. Paul selects certain words out of this passage to describe the characteristics of the *new righteousness* by faith, the kikasosunē.
89. Midrash, interpretation by Paul of Moses words Deut. 30:11-14.
90. Paul's midrash or application of Moses words to Christ.
91. Cf. Acts 2:27, 31.
92. Robertson, A. T. *Word Pictures* (Pauline) p. 388.
93. Cf. John 6:29.
94. Objective genitive, concerning faith in contrast to law.

and in the atoning death and glorious resurrection of the Christ. These are the fundamentals of the Christian faith or system of doctrine which sum up the conditions for salvation. It is ever the human tendency to want to do something to save one's self. God's way of salvation is 'by grace through faith' and 'it is not from works' to avoid completely any dependence on self and one's own works.[95]

v. 9. *That, if thou mayest confess*[96] sincerely *with thy mouth*[97] *Jesus as Lord*[98] and *mayest believe in thy heart,*[99] *that God raised him from the dead, thou shalt be saved*[1] or rescued from death and made a partaker of the salvation through Christ.[2]

v. 10. The reasons are lined out in (gar). *For with the heart*[3] not the head simply, (*man* one[4]) *believeth* (into or) *unto righteousness*[5] *and with the mouth confession is made unto salvation.* The *conversation* in Paul's usage stands for the whole character of man. Baptism may be an act of confession but it is not mentioned here.[6]

c. The new method by faith alone was clearly universal, for both Jews and Gentiles 10:11-13.

v. 11. *Everyone having faith resting upon Him shall not be put to shame.*[7] It is faith alone and everyone can exercise that faith, resting upon Him,

v. 12. *For there is no distinction* or discrimination (between) *of Jew* indeed *and Greek* in the acceptance by God of those who exercise faith in Christ; *for the same Lord* (belongs to) of *all,* is *being rich unto all those calling upon him.*

v. 13. *For every one, whosoever shall call* (have called)[8] *on the name of the Lord shall be saved.* The name of the Lord stands for his character of Savior, Redeemer, Justifier, Lord and final Judge (Hackett).[9]

Here then is the charter of universal salvation by faith in Christ alone offered to all men of every racial division alike, simply by calling on the magic name of Jesus,[10] or calling to Jesus the Savior.

---

95. Cf. Eph. 2:8-10.
96. Third class condition, ean with first aor. act. subj. general condition without asserting reality, thus making reality of the conclusion depend on carrying out the condition of the protasis.
97. Instrumental case with preposition eu.
98. B 71 read, the word in thy mouth that Jesus is Lord (Clement of Alex.). (Cf. I Cor. 12:3; Phil 2:11) kurios in LXX is used of God, hence confession of deity of Jesus.
99. Ibidem — note I.
1. Future passive of Sōzō.
2. Boise's Notes on Romans, in loco.
3. The heart in New Test. usage includes intellect, feeling and will.
4. Impersonal use of the verb, pistenetai, it is believed, one believes.
5. Eis, into, dikaiosunēn, righteousness, the imputed righteousness of the theme of the epistle Rom. 1:17.
6. Cf. Sanday and Headlam.
7. Cf. 28:16.
8. Aorist middle subjunctive of epikaleō. There is great similarity between aor. subj. and future indicative. Cf. Meyer in loco.
9. Cf. Joel 2:32 LXX verbatim; Acts 2:21.
10. Cf. David Smith, *Life and Letters of St. Paul* in loco.

d. They (the Israelites) had full opportunity to accept this beautiful Gospel but refused to accept it. They failed to discern the message of their prophets of the Old Testament and they did not accept Christ and his Gospel when preached in their hearing. Ch. 10:14-21.

v. 14. The question arises: had they the full opportunities for knowing the Gospel? *How then shall they call*[11] *upon* Him[12] *whom they* have *not believed? And how shall they believe,*[13] *in him, of whom they have not heard? And how shall they hear*[14] *without* (one preaching) *a preacher?*

v. 15. *And how shall they preach,*[15] *except they be sent.*[16] A powerful plea for missions here in these verses.

v. 15. *Just as it stands written: How beautiful are the feet of them that bring glad tidings of good things!*[17]

v. 16. *But not all* obediently *heard the Gospel*: And this was in conformity to the testimony of Isaiah about ancient Jesus. *For Isaiah says: Lord, who believed our report?*

v. 17. *Wherefore faith comes from hearing,* as a source, *and hearing through* the agency of preaching *the word* (message) *about Christ.*[18]

v. 18. *But I say, they did not*[19] *fail to hear did they?* Certainly not, *for into all the earth went out their sound, and their words unto the uttermost limits of the known world.*[20]

v. 19. *But I say Israel did not*[21] *fail to know did they? First Moses says: I will move you to jealousy with that which is not a nation; with a nation without discernment I will move you to anger.*

v. 20. *But Isaiah waxes bold and says: "I was found by those who did not seek me I became manifest to those who did not* ask for me."

v. 21. *And to Israel he saith, All the day through I spread out my hands unto a disobedient and contradicting people.*

4. God's beneficient plan in the rejection of Israel, which rejection was not total. Ch. 11:1-32.

While there is no evasion of the tragic fact that Israel could no longer claim to be the elect race, the royal priesthood, ministering the only true religion to the world, the consecrated and holy nation, the peculiar people for God's own possession,[22] still the merciful God extended and yet extends today his

---

11. Deliberative subjunctive first aor. middle.
12. Antecedent unexpressed, supplied.
13. Deliberative subj. aor. active.
14. Deliberative subjunctive again first aor. act.
15. Second aor. pass. deliberative subjunctive.
16. Negative condition of the third class.
17. Cf. Isa. 52:7 — like the Hebrew picturing the messengers of the restoration from Jewish captivity, the messengers of the Gospel in world wide deliverance.
18. Objective genitive.
19. Mē expects a negative reply.
20. Ps. 18:5 cited verbatim from LXX.
21. Again negative mē expecting negative answer.
22. Cf. I Peter 2:9, 10.

hands toward them as a nation and accepts individuals among them to be saved. Futhermore, the ultimate restoration of an elect remnant of Israel is assured.

a. God leaves open the door to individual Jews to be saved everywhere. Ch. 11:1-10.

(1) The fact that the rejection of Israel was not total is first illustrated in response to the question as to the rejection in vv. 1-4.

v. 1. *I say then, God did not cast away*[23] *his* chosen *people, did he?*[24] *God forbid!* By no means! The very idea of an irrevocable rejection of Israel to Paul was abhorrent. Personally, he is sure that such cannot be the case and reveals his reason. *For I also am an Israelites from the seed of Abraham of the tribe of Benjamin.* Paul was sure of his relationship with God, and there were not a few real Hebrew Christians. So he comes out with a firm and clear categorical conclusion:

v. 2. *God did not cast away his people, whom he foreknew.*[25] His illustration is taken from the well-known case of Elijah: *Or do ye not know what the Scripture saith about Elijah, how he pleadeth with God against Israel?*

v. 3. *'Lord they* (Israel) *killed*[26] *thy prophets and dug down thine altars* to the very foundations *and I only was left and they are even now seeking my life.*[27] Elijah thought that Israel had turned utterly reprobate under Ahab and Jezebel.[28] But the divine response corrected this idea that the prophet had.

v. 4. *But what saith the answer of God unto him? I have left for myself seven thousand men, who have not bowed the knee unto the* heathen god *Baal.*[29]

(2) So in this case there was a remnant left, divinely elected by the grace of God and not according to the works of man. vv. 5,6.

v. 5. *So then,* Paul concludes about Israel of his time, *even in the present time also, a remnant according to an election of grace has arisen,* permanently exists.[30]

v. 6. *But if it is by grace,* that it has come to exist, *it is no more of works,*[31] as a source, that it come to exist: *otherwise grace is no more grace.*

3. In this case then the rest of the Jews plainly rejected God's plan and were consequently hardened. The promise of God was fulfilled in the remnant. God's people are those whom, in his foreknowledge and omniscience he has chosen. They are not of the chosen ones, just because they were born Jews, but because they accepted Christ. vv. 7-10.

v. 7. *What then?* What must be our conclusion? *What Israel as* a nation *is seeking for*: (righteousness which will justify) *this it* (Israel) *did not obtain*

---

23. Aorist Ind. Mid. indicating the personal action of the subject of the verb.
24. Mē expects a negative answer.
25. Second aor, act indicative, clear statement of a historic occurrence.
26. Notice the *aor. act* indicative tenses indicating the actual happenings of the days just past.
27. These tenses are followed by the vivid present progressive tense.
28. Cf. I Kings 19:10-18.
29. Baal was the name for the androgynous heathen sure-God of Phoenicia.
30. Second Perfect act. ind. of ginomai.
31. Ablative case denoting source or origin.

as a nation, *but the election* (those who were elected) *obtained it, and the rest were hardened*[32] and proved no longer capable of religious impressions[33] because they hardened their own hearts more and more.

v. 8. *As it stands written:*[34] *God gave to them a spirit of stupor,*[35] *eyes that they should not see, and ears that they should not hear, until this very day.* This always happens to those who resist the waving of the Holy Spirit and the pleading of gospel messengers.

v. 9. *And David saith: "Let their table* (feast) *be made a snare and a trap And a stumbling block and a recompense unto them:*

v. 10. *Let their eyes be darkened that they may not see, And bow thou down their back alway.* This was a terrible imprecation not to be able to see. Another in that of captives, whose backs were bent[36] under burdens.

b. The rejection of Israel as a nation was accompanied by the choice of the Gentiles who were grafted onto the original stock of elect Israel. But the salvation of the Gentiles will prove a means of bringing Israel back as a nation because the course of elective grace has been widened to include individuals of all races in a spiritual Israel. Ch. 11:11-24.

(1) The rejection of Israel had a twofold aim: first to turn the stream of the gospel to the Gentiles and second to provoke Israel to jealous emulation. vv. 11-15.

v. 11. *I say then, they did not stumble*[37] *that they might fall,*[38] completely and for good, *did they?*[39] *'God forbid'* is his emphatic reply; *but by their fall*[40] aside, *salvation* is come *unto the Gentiles to provoke them to jealousy.*[41]

v. 12. *But if their falling* aside is *the wealth of the world and their loss* by their choice, *the wealth of the Gentiles,* as when Paul and his fellow missionaries turned to the Gentiles, when they were rejected by the Jew as missionaries of Christ, *how much more* shall *their fulness* become the plenitude of blessings to the world.

v. 13. *But I say to you Gentiles: in so far then as*[42] *I am an apostle to the Gentiles,*[43] *'I glorify my ministry,'* but at the same time having in my heart the conversion of my own nation, *if by any*

32. First aor. pass. indicative of pōroō to cover with a thick skin. Cf. II Cor. 3:14; Mark 3:5.
33. Boise's Notes on the Epistles of Paul in loco.
34. Perf. middle of graphō, the permanence of the Scripture.
35. Cf. Deut. 19:4; Isa. 29:10; 6:9f. katanuxis the torpor seems the result of too much sensation, dulled, by incitement, into apathy (Robertson *Word Pictures* in loco).
36. First aor. act. inv. of sunkamptō.
37. First aor. act. ind of verb ptaiō, to stumble.
38. Effective aor. act. Subjunctive.
39. Mē expects the negative answer.
40. Instrumental case, by their fall aside.
41. Eis with the articular infinitive.
42. Denoting quantity or degree.
43. Objective genitive.

v. 14. *means I may provoke to jealousy*[14] *them that are my flesh, and shall save some of them,* this is my desire.

v. 15. *For if the casting away of them is the reconciling of the world, what is the receiving of them, if not life from the dead?*

(2) The likelihood of Israel's restoration should move the Gentiles to humility and the maintenance of their faith. vv. 16-24.

v. 16. *And if the first fruit is holy, so is the lump,* from which the first fruit was taken: *and if the root is holy, so are the branches.* The patriarchs were the first fruit of Israel and Abraham perhaps 'the root' referred to here.

v. 17. *But if some of the branches of the* Israelitish *olive tree were broken off, and thou* (Gentile) *being a wild olive was grafted in among them, and didst become* a joint *partaker with* them *of the root of the fatness of the olive tree;*

v. 18. Stop *glorying* (boasting) *over the Jewish branches* which were broken out, if thou art accustomed to do so; *it is not thou that bearest the root, but the root thee.*

v. 19. *Thou wilt say then*: (a possible comment of a presumptuous Gentile) 'The branches were broken out in order that[45] I might be grafted in.'

v. 20. *Well*: *By their unbelief they were broken off, and thou standest by thy faith. Stop* thinking (haughty) thoughts, *but* rather *fear*:

v. 21. *For if*[46] *God spared not the natural branches,* as he did not, *neither will he spare you,* if you boast a faith which you have not.

v. 22. *Behold then the goodness and severity of God. Upon them that fell severity, but upon thee God's goodness if thou continue*[47] *in his goodness otherwise thou also shalt be cut off.*[48]

v. 23. *And they* (the Israelites) *also, if they continue not in their unbelief,*[49] *shall be grafted in*: *for God is able to graft them in again.* There is no falling from grace and second spiritual birth into the kingdom taught here since palin means back or 'again' into their original places of national privilege.

v. 24. *For if thou wast cut out from that which is by nature a wild olive tree, and wast grafted contrary to nature into a good olive tree: how much more shall these, which are the natural branches, be grafted into their own olive tree?*

Paul was addressing here mainly the Gentile believers in the Roman church. Some critics had accused Paul of being indifferent to the well-being of the Jews because he was an apostle to the Gentiles. He lets his Gentile brethren know that he is proud to be their apostle but warns them that the 'people of God's choice' had not been cast away irrevocably. He used the illustration of

---

44. Either future active indicative or first aor., act. subjunctive, here may be either in verb parazēlosō and sōzō.

45. Purpose clause, first aor., pass. subjunctive with hina.

46. Condition of the first class, prepositions ei with aor. mid. indicative, in protasis according to fact.

47. Third class condition, general condition can with pres. act. subjunctive in protasis.

48. Fut. pass of ekkoptō, to cut (off).

49. Locative of sphere, apistiai.

the process of grafting in horticulture in which he set forth the fact that it was unbelief manifested in barrenness that caused God to lop off the barren Jewish branches and graft in the Gentile believers who were coming into the kingdom. But the principle of unbelief might in the Gentiles prove equally fatal if they were found barren producing 'nothing but leaves.' Furthermore God would graft in again the unbelieving Jews if they would turn from their unbelief and come back and embrace the Messiah whom they had rejected. This is the promise yet open to all the Jews everywhere. What a missionary force they would become in the propagation of the Messianic kingdom, if only they would turn their faces to Him.[50]

c. Mercy to all humanity the ultimate purpose of God. (1) The apostle interprets the prophecies of Isaiah Chs. 59:20 and 27:9, and himself also predicts Israel's final restoration. Both the Jews and Gentiles shall finally embrace the Gospel. (2) Ascription of praise and honor to God in a *doxology* that sounds the very depths of eternity before and after time. Ch. 11:25-36. (1) Paul's prediction of the final restoration of Israel. vv. 25-32.

v. 25. *For I do not wish you to be ignorant* Christian (Gentiles) *brethren, with respect to this mystery* or revealed secret, *in order that you may not be wise,* in your own conceits in 'your inner circle,' *among yourselves* as the custom of the gnostics is *because a temporary hardening has happened in part, to Israel, until* the time *when*[51] (where,) *the fulness* or complement *of the Gentiles shall have come in.* Paul wished to prevent conceit in the Gentiles. It was not through any merit of their own that they were blessed with the privilege of coming into the kingdom; but was the eternal purpose of God, his 'plan of the ages.'[52]

v. 26. *And so all Israel,* as a nation though not necessarily every individual Israelite, shall be saved,[53] the Jews being converted thus to Christianity by the (fulness, pleroma) 'complement' of the Gentiles, (the Gentile world considered as a whole) stirring up the Jews as a nation and rousing them to jealousy. The reason for Israel's salvation will not be because of its hardening. Paul is not speaking of spiritual Israel in this verse (Cf. Calvin), nor of the remnant by the election of grace but of Israel as a nation now rejected but in that time restored as a people to divine favor. The Apostle cites Isa. 59:20 and 27:9 about the Deliverer who came out of Zion and shall come to Zion and to them that turn from transgression in Jacob. Cf. Ps. 13:7, 52:7 (LXX). Who will give from Sion the Savior of Israel. 'There shall come out of Zion the deliverer[54] He shall turn away ungodliness[55] from Jacob[56]

---

50. Cf. David Smith *Life and Letters of St. Paul* in loco.
51. Temporal clause referring to a time in history in the working out of God's plan.
52. Cf. W. O. Carver's Exposition of Ephesians.
53. Future pass. indicative of sōzō, sothēsetei.
54. Present mid. articular participle, ho ruomenos. The Hebrew Goēl, the Avenger, Messiah (in Paul's use). Cf. Robertson *Word Pictures* in loco.
55. Impieties, ungodly deeds.
56. Jacob, for entire nation of the Jews.

v. 27. And this is my covenant unto them. When I shall take away[57] their sins.'

v. 28. *As* far as *relates to the 'gospel* order, the principles by which God sends the gospel into the world,' *the Jews are viewed as enemies, on your account* as Gentiles, *but as relates to the* principles of *election,* they are accounted *beloved for the father's* (Patriarch's) *sakes,* from whom the Israelites spring and who were well pleasing to God (Cf. Sanday and Headlam.)

v. 29. Thus Paul comes to the reason why God will not desert his chosen people. *For the divine gifts* which he had copiously showered upon them *and the calling* of that people (Cf. Gen. 12:1-3); *are unchangeable* and 'not to be repented of' because they were *from God,* who does not change in his omniscient resolves.

v. 30. Paul adds the fact that God has dealt with the Gentiles in the same manner. *For just as ye* Gentiles in time past *were disobedient* toward *God* (Cf. Rom. 1:18-32), *but now have obtained mercy* because a merciful God made occasion,[58] *by the disobedience of these* unbelieving Jews: to show mercy to the Gentiles.

v. 31. *so these also have now become disobedient, in order that they also may now by your mercy* (shown to you), *obtain mercy.*

v. 32. *For God shut up* [59] *all into disobedience, that he might have mercy*[60] *upon all,* who accept his mercy and turn to the Messiah that they may be saved.

(2) Paul concludes his argument with a doxology of praise and honor as he contemplates from spiritual heights the glorious vision of God's wisdom and mercy and reveals the secret of the divine purpose. vv. 33-36.

v. 33. *O the depth of the riches, both of the knowledge and of the wisdom of God,*[61] *how unsearchable*[62] *are his judgments and his ways past tracing out.*[63] It is the insufficiency of our knowledge, at fault, when we criticize Him. His judgments on the philosophy of life are unsearchable. As a vast virgin forest God's ways are untractable.[64] Scientists, philosophers and theologians may think some of God's thought after him but there is here a vast universe yet unexplored by name.

---

57. Second aor. mid. subjunctive of aphaireō, note similarity to future indicative in use.
58. Cf. The experience of Paul in many places in his ministry and that of his fellowhelpers — when the Jews rejected them and the gospel they 'turned to the Gentiles.'
59. First aor. act. ind. of sunkleiō, effective aorist because of the disobedience of both Gentile and Jew.
60. Anexeraunēta inscrutable, some of God's wisdom can be known (Rom. 1:20). Paul recognized that this human planet could not reach the depths of the abyss of God's thoughts.
61. First aor. act. ind. of sunkleiō, effective aorist because of the disobedience of both Gentile and Jew.
62. See footnote 60.
63. Some of God's tracks are left plain to us in the wide domain of theological lore but most of the thoughts of God are tracks beyond us.
64 Second aor. act. ind. of ginōskō, timeless aor., did know, does know, will know.

v. 34. *'For who hath known*[65] *the mind of the Lord?*[66] *Or who hath been his counselor?* Some egotistic humans think themselves able to tell God how!

v. 35. *Or who has first given to him, and it shall be paid back to him again* in full? The answer is none and the reason:

v. 36. *For from him* as the source, *through him* as the agent *and unto him* as the all embracing end, *are all things. To him be the glory forever. Amen.*

II. Practical Application of Doctrinal principles in the relations of Christian Life. The New life in the process of salvation.[67] Chs. 12-16.

A. In the more general relationships. Chs. 12, 13.

1. Religious obligation in loving and grateful relationship to God in the new life. 12:1,2. The spiritual relationship to God naturally takes precedence in the consideration of the duties and obligations or norm of the new life. Here is a call to consecration. The doctrine of justification must issue in holiness.

v. 1. I do not command you but *I beseech* you *therefore,*[68] Christian *brethren* by means of the mercies (compassionate dealings) of God, seen in the foregoing plan of your personal salvation by faith in Christ, *to present your bodies a living holy sacrifice* well-*pleasing to God, which is your reasonable*[69] *worship-service.*[70] The body must, like the ancient sacrifice, be pure and blameless. It must be holy and free from the stains of passion (Sanday and Headlam).

The Jewish sacrifice was dead, the Christian is a living and active body; that sacrifice on the temple altar had to be acceptable so the Christian sacrifice must be acceptable or well-pleasing to God.

v. 2. *Stop being fashioned by this* (age)[71] *world pattern,* if you have been: *but be* (in the habit of being) transformed by the renewing[72] of your mind. As the body is to be pure and holy without the blemish of sin, so must the mental system be renewed, rebuilt with new thoughts of the Christian mould. The mind occupied by thoughts of the flesh is enslaved and must be set free redirected and renewed by the Holy Spirit. This is to the end *that you may put to the test,*[73] try and prove,[74] *what is the* will[75] (thelēma) *of* God, *good and well-pleasing* to him, *and* complete (full grown) or *perfect*: Thus Paul makes the will of God, which every Christian can know by the method of

---

65. Citation from Isa. 40:13 Cf. LXX.
66. Objective genitive, a counselor to him, Some men consider themselves quite competent to criticize God and his inspired Word of Revelation, which penetrates beyond the most advanced science and philosophy of mankind of all its history.
67. F. Godet, *Romans*. Vol. II in loco.
68. Oun gathers up the great agument of Chs. 1-11.
69. Legikēn, logical, reasonable.
70. Latreia worship service.
71. Present pass. imperative with mē; stop being fashioned.
72. Instrumental (assreiative).
73. Eis with the infinitive, expressing purpose.
74. Ibidem by the (new-birth) renewing.
75. Thelēma — God wishes every man, that he should not be destroyed but on the contrary saved.

'tried and proved,'[76] by the saints who are the 'set-apart' ones (hagioi). When a man is a saint (hagios) his body must be set apart too. God will renew his mind through the Holy Spirit, when he has fully surrendered his whole personality including his body to Christ. This method of knowing the will of God has been tried and proved by thousands of his saints.

2. The right attitude of the Christian in the use of spiritual gifts, in his relationship, as a member of the church, is one of humility. Ch. 12:3-8.

v. 3. *For, I say* in all humility but also *through the grace given to me* in apostleship to you, in spiritual guidance to admonish you, and I am speaking *to every one who is among you,* every member of the church, *not to be high-minded,* thinking high things about himself *beyond what he ought to think; but so to think as to think soberly,* not of any merit he may have, but *according* and in proportion *as God dealt to each* one *a measure of faith.*[77] Self conceit is a species of insanity. Each Christian has his gift from God. There is no place for undue pride (Robertson). So let each member of the church be content with his place and function well and wisely in it, in true humility.

vv. 4,5 One of the questions which vexed the church in Corinth was that of the diversity of spiritual gifts, which Paul had just dealt with in a letter to the Corinthians.[78] It was natural that he should cite this question which was and is vital in the life of every church, calling attention to the unity of the church and the mutual relationship between its members, illustrated in the natural body of man. As the spiritual endowments of the Christians are from God and must be used faithfully and harmoniously in the church.

v. 4. *For just as indeed, in one's body we have many members, but all the members do not have the same function,*

v. 5. *So* we *the many are one body*[79] *in Christ, and as to each one* separately we are *members one* of *another.*

vv. 6, 7, 8. The apostle next presents four spiritual gifts as illustrative of the diversity of endowments among members of the church. The directions he gives are based on his experience and are in the form of general principles such as that of prudence, harmony, and in proportion to the gift of faith. These principles are useful in dealing with all kinds of problems and situations which may arise in any church of Christ.

v. 6. *And having gracious gifts differing according to the grace given to us, whether prophecy,* let us prophesy, *according to the proportion of faith;*

---

76. T. and P. was found marked in the margins of the page of the Bible of a great saint of God, B. H. Dement, after his death. It was found in many places opposite the great promises of God. It was known that he was accustomed to write those initials as a sign that he had definitely tried and proved the truth of those promises.

77. Cf. the use of (pitis faith in the New Test., illustrated in Rom. 1:17, from faith as a source of the Christian life to or leading 'into' a life of 'faith' as in the faith of Abraham.

78. I Cor. Chs. 12-14.

79. The church is compared to the body, is the body of Christ.

80. Tō neuter article with kath hēis is used as an accusative of general reference.

v. 7. *Whether* the gift of *ministering* in the administration of alms or other similar services, let us use our gifts effectively in *our ministry; if* there is *one teaching*, let him go on *in his teaching* intently, and if there is one *exhorting*, let

v. 8. him continue *in his exhortation*: *he that giveth* let him do it *with simplicity* or singleness of motive and not for ostentation; he that ruleth or has the leadership in any work of the kingdom *with diligence* and energy, *and he that showeth mercy* in deeds of charity let him do it cheerfully (with hilarity).

3. The social attitude of all believers in Christ toward all people should stem out from the principle of Christian love (agapē). 12:9-21. The sequence of thought led Paul from the reference to spiritual gifts (I Cor. 12) on to the conception of Christian love (I Cor. 13) as the one way of conduct for the new-born member of the church. Paul was not depreciating the power of the Holy Spirit to work out the new life and conduct of the believer but gave in a practical non-poetic form, a group of maxims which would serve the broader needs, of the Roman church and world, more effectively. The spiritual heritage of Christianity was thus enriched the more by the many-sided application of the shining central principle of love.

The practical precepts (vv. 9-13) relate more to the conduct and behavior to fellow-Christians while the maxims (vv. 14-21) refer to the Christian's attitude mainly to outsiders, particularly persecutors; but all alike based on the principle of Christian love.

v. 9. *Let love* to all, both Christians and outsiders *be without hypocrisy. Abhorring that which is evil* in men, *cleaving*[81] *to the good* man and the good in men, and at the same time detesting the evil that is in them. 'Feigned love is disguised hate.'

v. 10. *In love of the brethren*[82] *be tenderly affectioned*[83] *one to another*, like the members of the same family; *in honor*[84] (anticipating) *preferring one another*, getting ahead in showing respect and courtesy to one another;

v. 11. *In zeal*, in the performance of Christian duties, *not slatternly*, flagging or 'slow-poky,' 'the king's business reguires haste:' in *spirit*, the Christian if indwelt by the Holy Spirit, is to be *fervent*, to the boiling point in the work of *serving the Lord*, doing bond service to Him with energy and warmth;

v. 12. (1) *rejoicing* continually *in hope*, that grows out of love, which hopeth all things;[85] (2) being habitually patient[86] in tribulation or affliction, which always accompanies the life, of faith. Quiet endurance is a shield

---

81. Glueing yourself to the good in one and abhorring continually and habitually the evil.
82. From Fileō and adelphos, brotherly love, philadelphia.
83. Old compound adjective, from philos and storge, mutual love of parents and children.
84. Timē, preferment, honor of position, preeminence, attribution of praise.
85. I Cor. 13:7.
86. Hupomenontes, remaining under the load persistently without complaint, a distinctly Christian characteristic.

against fretful complaint. 'When hope reaches fruition, affliction vanishes away;' (3) *continuing stedfastly* (instant) *in prayer*, both as individuals and as a church. Persistence in prayer involves perseverance of faith. Hope, affliction and prayer make up a large part of the Christian life.

v. 13. Communicating, (contributing) or sharing their own possessions and income *to satisfy the* dire wants or *necessities of the saints* or poorer brethren in the Christian fold; given to hospitality, pursuing[87] it as if in a chase or hunt, as those who were desirous to give entertainment without cost to Christian workers and brethren. Hospitality was highly considered as a Christian virtue from the beginning and was always a real help to the progress of Christian missions.[88]

v. 14. *Bless* and make it a habit to bless continually, *those persecuting* you; *bless, and* stop cursing them, if you have ever yielded to such an impulse. Primitive Christians were bitterly persecuted in the early centuries and needed this injunction for their enlightenment and encouragement and also as a warning in negative form. In this exhortation Paul is dealing with their relations to non-Christian outsiders.

v. 15. *Weep*[89] *with those weeping, rejoice with those rejoicing.* It is easier to weep with those weeping than to rejoice with those who are in high esteem enjoying great favor.

v. 16. *Have the same mind*[90] *one toward another*, thinking the same thing in a common understanding; Set not your *minds on high things but 'be carried away' with the lowly things*, as the humbler tasks of the church. Do not have the habit of becoming wise in your own conceits. This always brings disharmony when one is too self-sufficient he fails to give due respect to the opinion of others (Boise).

v. 17. *Do not ever return to any man evil for evil*, whether he is a Christian or not; *taking thought beforehand* to provide *things beautiful* (honest) in *the sight of all men.* Let your conduct commend itself to them by a well ordered life of prudence.

18 *If it is possible, as to that which proceeds from you, be at peace with all men.* It is the Christian's duty to use every method of reconciliation possible. There would be no church quarrels if this mode of procedure were followed and few even between Christians and outsiders.

v. 19. Do not continue avenging yourselves,[91] if you have done so, taking vengeance into your own hands, beloved, (and loved by God), for you do

87. Present participle, diōkontes, continued action.
88. Sanday and Headlam *ICC Romans* p. 303.
89. The absolute infinitive used as an emphatic imperative. (Sanday and Headlam in loco.)
90. The absolute participle.
91. Independent participle employed as present active indicative as in numerous cases in verses 10-13 and 16-18.

not need to do it, *but* rather *give place* quickly[92] *to the wrath* of God and let that be your shield, for it stands written, *Vengeance is mine,* it belongs to me, *I will certainly repay,*[93] *says the Lord.* Over what others do, you have no control; but God does. Just remember that and leave it to him.

v. 20. *But, if thine enemy hunger feed him, if he thirst give him drink*: This course of conduct recommended for the wronged man is the opposite of that which the freshly nature would prompt. This is the only kind of vengeance for the Christian *for in so doing thou shalt heap live coals of fire on his head.* Such kindness will bring a sense of burning shame and possibly repentence for the wrong perpetrated with consequent reconciliation.

v. 21. Stop being conquered by *the evil* thing done you, *but keep on conquering the evil* spirit of your enemies *by the good* of your treatment of them. Vincit malos pertinax bonitas. (Seneca).

The consecration of the Christian's whole personality set forth in Rom. 12: 1,2 is realized in his life as a member of the kingdom church, composed solely of regenerated persons, twice-born men, new creatures by the spiritual birth which accompanies a vital faith in Jesus Christ. Paul's treatment of that process falls into two parts: (1) The spirit-inspired self-limitation of the believer's conduct in his relation with his fellow members of the church, *in humility,* according to the will of God (12:3-8). (2) The divinely motivated self-giving of himself *in Christian love,* exercised in beneficent activities toward those persons who compose his immediate and more sympathetic environment (vv 9:16) and also toward hostile elements within the church or without, which come within his wider environment (vv 17-21). The experiences of the new-life man and the ways of dealing with them in Christian humility and love a most masterful presentation of the impressions and expressions a regenerated personality, acting and reacting from the Christian motive in the midst of a world-environment of the good and bad. It is artistically organized in an almost poetic form and covers vast areas of the totality of the social experiences of the Christian's life.

4. The life of the believer in his relationship as a citizen member of the state, as a subject of the government and to his fellow-citizens (Ch. 13:1-14).

a. Willing and patient submission to the state is the wisest and best procedure for Christians. vv 1-7.

The primitive Christians were not turbulent but were loyal and serviceable citizens of the Roman empire.[94] They were exposed to the suspicion of the imperial government because they were frequently identified with the Jews as a people who were troublesome and were often in insurrection because of their wrong belief in a temporal Messiah. Paul had to guard his preaching about Jesus as the Messiah making it clear that he was not a temporal ruler. His teaching about loyal submission to the state was timely then and based as it was on eternal Christian principles, valuable for all times and especially for the

---

92. Second aor, act. imperative of didōmi, to give, immediate action.
93. Future active of compound verb antapodōsō, recompense.
94. Epst and Diogn V; Tert. Apol 37, 42.

present age. He taught that the state was of God's appointment and that order and authority were approved by God but not the wickedness of bad rulers. He did not criticize the rulers personally. Young Nero was on the throne. The strong arm of Roman law shielded Paul many times in his work for Christ and he was a grateful and loyal citizen. He prayed many times for the rulers that they might be good men and directed by God[95] in good and peaceful living.[96]

v. 1. *Let every soul* (psychic man) be in the habit of subjecting himself[97] to the higher civic authorities.[98] *For there is no* civic *authority* or power *except* that created *by God*[99] and the powers[1] that be are (stand) ordained[2] by God. Here is no argument for divine right of kings, or for any given form of government but for civic orders. Paul does not oppose change in government but rather lawlessness and disorder.[3] He does not counsel violent revolution unless divinely justified in order to secure a better rule.

v. 2. *So that,* as a result, *the one resisting*[4] or lining himself up against *the* orderly *authority* of the state, *has* thus *taken his stand against the ordinance*[5] *of God*: *And* hence *those who have so taken their stand shall* surely *receive to themselves a judgment,* which will be human, coming through human instruments, having no reference to eternal punishment. A revolt against evil rulers may be justified for the purpose of securing a change of government but the revolters, even so, will have to pay the price in punishment, if the revolution against the evil rulers shall fail. A Christian may judge wrongly and join a revolution which is not justified and if he does he may be punished by the state, but he does not lose salvation.

v. 3. *For the rulers*, as a class, have the general ideal of ruling for the good of their people and *are not a terror to the good work*[6] of the people *but to the evil* work of some. *Dost thou wish not to be afraid? Practice doing habitually the good and thou shalt have praise from* (it) *the same.* The Roman persecution of the Christians later in history arose from the mistaken notion that Christians were against the state because they refused to worship the emperor. That error arose from the wrong conception of the union of the state and religion, the state forcing some of the people to worship the emperor, a mere man, which was idolatry. Christians could not engage in that worship and please God. So they had to be burned as torches in the public park by Nero who had become a monstrous ruler later in life.

95. Cf. David Smith, *Life and Letters of St. Paul* p. 444f.
96. Cf. I Tim. and II Tim. in loco.
97. Present mid. inv., habitual action.
98. Cp. I Pet. 2:13.
99. Hupo theon by best MSS, constituted by God.
1. Exousia, authority, and power used interchangeably.
2. Periphrastic perf. pass. indicative of tassō.
3. Robertson, A. T., *Word Studies* in loco.
4. Present mid. articular participle of anti-tasso to arrange oneself against the ordinance or institution of God.
5. Future mid. of lainbanō.
6. Collective use of ergon, hence in the singular.

v. 4. There is no fear of a good ruler when one practices the good *for he* (such a ruler) *is the minister of God to thee for good. But if thou dost*[7] habitually that which is evil then fear, for God put the sword the symbol of power in the ruler's hands, *and he bears it not in vain, for he is a minister of God, an avenger for wrath, to the one practicing the evil,* and he will exact the penalty. When the ruler punishes, he is the minister or agent of God, if the punishment is just and necessary to maintain order and respect for human life, which God created. Government is an agent to carry out the policing of society, with the end to preserve order and peace. It has to use the sword which is the instrument as well as the symbol of power in executing the wrath of God.

v. 5. *Wherefore ye must needs*[8] *be in subjection not only on account of the wrath* or power of the state which inflicts punishment, sometimes unjust though it be, maintains order; *but* submission to the state is a duty *also for conscience sake* because the state in the abstract, apart from the consideration of evil rulers, is a moral institution of God. The Christian must render allegiance to the state because it is God's divine principle or way of life and civilization; he must uphold the state while he disclaims the abuses of evil rulers, and frankly declaims against them.

v. 6, 7. *For* it is *on account of this* fact that the state is morally grounded, as God's institution, that *ye are paying*[9] *tribute* or annual tax on lands and other taxable properties; for they (the magistrates or rulers) *are God's ministers*[10] in his divinely consecrated sacrificial service, *attending perseveringly upon this very thing,* of administering this sacred governmental office. It is their duty 'to make justice reign by checking evil and upholding good.'[11] The restraint of evil by political administration has the divine sanction. The frequent corrupt abuse of that power does not. The men who serve continually in this work must receive their support from it. Hence the necessity of taxes.

v. 7. So in the support of and loyalty to this divine order, Christians must: *Render therefore to all* in authority *their dues: tribute to whom tribute* is due, in personal taxes, *custom to whom custom* is due in export or import tax; *fear* or respect *to whom fear,* because he bears the sword, symbol of the power of the state, *honor to whom honor,* for the position he occupies, honor of his office.

Paul deals with the question of the believer's relation to the state, laying down, as is his custom in writing, broad general principles. There was a wide-spread feeling among the Jews that they should not pay tribute to the Roman government. Their idea of a temporal Messianic Kingdom stirred their imagination and incited them at times to revolt. The Roman Empire, at the

---

7. Third class general conditional sentence eau with the subjunctive.
8. Anagkē — it is necessary.
9. Present active indicative, not imperative (Robertson).
10. Leiturgoi, those who work for the people from laōs people and work but also in N. Test. a priestly worker in a religious service.
11. Cf. Godet, *Romans* in loco.

time Paul wrote this epistle, was in a status of peace in the period of the Quinquinium (of five years) in the very beginning of young Nero's rule. Paul had enjoyed the protection of Roman law and order, which was a 're-strain' on disorder, for years in his ministry in Asia Minor and Europe.

Jesus had set forth the principle, underlying the relation of Christianity to the civil power, when he declared 'that his kingdom was not of this world' and when he told the Herodian student in Jerusalem to 'render unto Caesar the things that are Caesar's and to God the things that are God's.'[12]

So Paul states that the principle which lies at the basis of Christian political doctrine, in that the State is divinely appointed by God and should be respected and supported loyally by Christianity, in all its right functions and ministries, in preserving order and peace. According to Paul's teaching in Romans XIII the state represents the natural man of the psychic order[13] and has a religious character but not by nature a Christian character.

b. From the subject of justice in the state and the duty of submission on the part of the Christian, Paul passes to discuss justice and civic duty in relation to one's fellow citizens, based on the principle of Christian love (agapē). vv 8-10. The apostle continues the same subject of justice.[14]

v. 8. *Owe no man* (nothing)[15] *anything* of dues *if not* (except) *to love one another*: 'This debt of love can never be paid off but, we should at least keep the interest paid up.'[16] As Christianity substituted faith in the place of law in our relationship to God, it places love in the place of law in all our legal relations to man;[17] *for the one loving the other has completely fulfilled all law,* whether the general principle of law between all men or the Jewish law cited later. In the very act of loving thus the Christian finds that he has fulfilled all the legal obligations belonging to the domain of justice, which the law could have imposed.[18] Love is the essence of law for a man does not love those whom he kills, robs, etc.

vv. 9, 10. Paul cites the commandments of the second table which refer to man's relation to man, in the civil code of the Jews.[19] Justice does not use the positive for doing good but the negative of not doing wrong to 'the other.' Paul cites first of all the commandment relating to the relation a man holds to his wife as anterior to his relation to his neighbor.

v. 9. *For this: thou shalt not commit adultery, thou shalt not steal, thou shalt not covet; and if there be any other commandment it is briefly comprehended in this saying, namely, Thou shalt love thy neighbor as thyself.*[20] No man who

---

12. Cf. Sanday and Headlam, *I. C. C. Romans* pp. 369ff.
13. Let every soul, psuchē.
14. Cf. Godel, *Com. on Romans* p. 315.
15. Two negatives make an affirmative but the Greeks used the negatives.
16. Robertson A. T. *Word Pictures,* Vol. Paul p. 409.
17. Cf. words of Jesus on this subject, Matt. 22:37-40.
18. Godet, *Epist. Romans* Vol. II p. 315f.
19. Cf. Exodus in loco The Ten Words. Ex. 20, Deut. 5.
20. Cf. Lev. 19:18 Pilate did not love Jesus as himself John 18:34. Cp. Matt. 5:43; 22:39; Mark 12:31; Luke 10:27; Gal. 5:14; James 2:8 the 'royal law of liberty.' Plēsion, neighbor, adverb, 'the one near thee.' (Robertson).

loves another will do him wrong by adultery, murder, theft, covetousness or anything else of like character. All of the commandments relating to man's relationships to his fellow-men are summed up in the expression here, as in the Old Testament, 'Thou shalt love thy neighbor as thyself' (Lev. 19:18) which is called by James 'the royal law of liberty.'[21]

v. 10. *The* Christian *love* (agapē) *does not work* ill (evil) to his neighbor ('the one near thee'). *Therefore, love is the fulness* (pleroma) or fulfilling to completion and permanency, *of the law.* All the duties and obligations of the Christian are thus fulfilled by love, the love described so beautifully in I Cor. 13 in a marvelous rhapsody by Paul. Agapē, the Christian's love, covers protects, forbears, believes, hopes, endures, perseveres, survives all and never fails. This is why it fulfills the law, which one could never keep without it. This is why Christ, the perfect embodiment and incarnation of the love, the God-kind of love, became our complete Savior. Paul thus states the Christian's duty to society in general and how he is able to fulfil it.

c. The brevity of life[22] and the imminence of His coming constitute a strong motive for complete consecration in our relationships with all men. vv. 11-14.

v. 11. *And this fact* in addition also, *knowing* the character of *the time* or season and existing conditions of the status quo, as we do, *that now* it is (high time) *'the hour' for you to be waked out of sleep,*[23] *for now our* final *salvation* or complete redemption *is nearer than when we believed* and entered into the career for the goal of complete sanctification, at the hour of death or His second coming.[24] This is true of all Christians (Robertson).

v. 12. *The night* of forgetfulness and lack of altertness of our short period of earthly existence *is far spent*[25] *and the day* of death or else of His coming is (at hand) *has drawn nigh,*[26] when there shall be complete redemption for believers. That day is frequently spoken of, in our present age by leading scientists and prophetic spirits, of our times, as very near. *Let us put off therefore* as we do our night clothes, when we arise in the morning, *the works of the darkness* of sin *and let us put on*[27] *the armour of the light,* the fit clothing for the Christian in the day of conflict and struggle.[28]

v. 13. *Let us walk* (decently) *honestly,*[29] *as in the day* time: not in the indulgence of appetite *in revellings and drunkennesses,*[30] *not in chambering*[31] *and wantonness* or licentious acts, *not in strife* (quarreling in personal disputes) *or jealousy* in envious partisan contention.

---

21. Basilikos nomos James 2:8.
22. Boise's *Notes* on Paul's Epistles in loco.
23. First aor. pass. infinitive of egeisō.
24. Robertson A. T. *Word Pictures* Vol. Paul's Epistles p. 410.
25. First aor. act. indic. of prokōpto, to cut forward.
26. Perfect act. indicative, eggiken, to draw near.
27. Cf. Eph. 6:11ff.
28. Aor. mid. sub., apothōmetha, (volative), Robertson *Word Pictures* in loco.
29. Portuguese (seriamente), seriously or honestly.
30. Note the use of the plural denoting the continuity and habitual repetition of such sensual practices.
31. "Beds" of sexual indulgence.

v. 14. *But put ye on the Lord Jesus Christ,* Who is your santtification,[32] by appropriating in habitual communion with Him all His thinking, His sentiments and His manner of acting *and do not make for yourselves*[33] *provision,*[34] by forethought *for the flesh,*[35] *for lusts* to later indulge in them.

B. Hortatory discussion of the basic principles which must govern the internal relationships between the weak and strong in all churches and also Jews and Gentiles in the church in Rome and elsewhere. Ch. 14:1-15:13.

The apostle was anxious that this great strategic church in Rome should be missionary and unified and not fritter away its energies in preoccupation with questions about matters relatively indifferent, which would thus destroy its peace and unified effort for the main missionary push. So he discusses the freedom of the Christian faith and the comprehensiveness of Christian love, and insists on Unity. One of the questions which has ever disturbed the harmony of the life of the church has been censorious criticism and partisan contention. Paul discusses the necessity of forbearance of the strong toward the extremely scrupulous on the one hand, and the avoiding of censoriousness by the weak against the strong on the other. The duty of unity he enjoins upon all alike.

1. The conduct of the Christians in the relations between the weak and the strong[36] in matters not binding on conscience and conduct. 14:1-12.

a. Paul states three principles which should govern in the matters of conscience and conduct. From dealing with those who were lax in the indulgence of appetites and passions (13:11-14) the apostle passes to consider dietary questions, which were disturbing the church in Rome, more than questions purely spiritual. As usual he lays down no rule but discusses broad fundamental principles which are applicable in all questions of 'border line practices' in the Christian's life.

v. 1. *Him that is* in a status of being weak *in* respect to *faith*, which falters at traces, because of conscientious scruples *receive*, ye, who are stronger, into a fellowship of tenderness, *but not into doubtful desputations*, intended for decisions on opinions and in judgments which shall be dogmatically repressive.

v. 2. *One hath faith* firm enough, to *eat* without scruples *all things* or kinds of food: *but the one being weak eats* the garden *herbs* or vegetables to the exclusion of meats, being conscientiously a vegetarian. Denney thinks it was a partisan group of vegetarians in the Roman church.[37] Be that as it may we have Paul's counsel to the stronger brother:

---

32. I Cor. 1:30.
33. Middle voice, make not for yourselves.
34. Latin provisio, forethought.
35. Objective genitive.
36. For outline on this section Cf. Dana, H. E.; Boise's *Notes* in loco and various comm. on Romans.
37. Cf. Robertson's *Word Pictures* citing Denney in the Greek Expositor's New Testament.

v. 3. *Let not have that eateth* without scruples not *set naught*[38] or treat with contempt *him that eateth not* meats but only vegetables; *and let not him that eateth not* from scruples *judge*[39] or criticize *him that eateth* all nourishing variation of food: *for God hath received him* who is a vegetarian, for his own fellowship. God made no difference in his reception of both vegetarians and meat eaters into his intimate fellowship: The strong brother is not called upon to settle all the scruples of the weak brother. But each one whether weak or strong should settle them for himself, seeking to know honestly and with an open mind, as also in settling doctrinal differences of interpretation, the will of God as revealed in his Word and in Christian history and experience.

b. Each individual is amenable primarily to the will of God and not solely or wholly to the conscience of his fellow Christian or neighbor 14:4-12.

Paul is straight-forward in his reprimand of any over-scrupulous Christian who assumes the role of dictating a pattern of his own egotistic devising, and presuming to cut the cloth for his brother Christian's suit by the size and shape of his own personal opinions, likes, and dislikes and critical judgment.

v. 4. *Thou,*[40] *who art thou that judgest the servant of another*, when that Other is God? *To his* very *own* personal *Lord he stands or falls* and you whoever you may be are out of your right to obtrude yourself. *And he shall stand* (shall be made to stand),[41] in spite of your obtrusion, *for the Lord*, his Lord *is able*[42] (powerful) *to make him stand* (stablish him), in spite of your criticism of him. This is a sharp rebuff directed at the over-scrupulous vegetarian who assumes to criticize and foretell the downfall of his stronger brother who eats meat without scruples. The church also has no right to decide what shall be the diet of its members.

v. 5. *One man esteemeth one day beyond*[43] *another* observing 'holy days,' the other esteemeth every day alike, all as holy and no separation between sacred and secular. Rome condemns private interpretation of the Scriptures[44] and judgment accordingly. Paul lays the responsibility of decision upon each individual mind which should be enlightened by intelligence and the illumination of the Holy Spirit in a discerning interpretation of the Word. Let each one be fully assured[45] in his own mind.[46] It is an honest and intelligent use of the mind in a decision based on the knowledge and understanding of what the Word of God says. Man's natural intelligence unguided by the Word may lead one astray.

---

38. Present imperative with mē, exoutheneō. Let him not go on setting at naught. Also present imperative of krinō with mē. Let him not go on judging.
39. Aorist middle, proselabeto, God received both vegetarians and meat eaters into His fellowship.
40. 'Proleptic position of su.' (Robertson).
41. Future passive of histēmi.
42. Dunatei, verb derived from verbal adjective dunatos.
43. Use of para, beyond in comparison.
44. Vide Decrees of Council of Trent in loco.
45. Nous mind, intelligence, but enlightened in the Scripture.
46. Pres. Pass. imv. of compound verb plērophoreō.

v. 6. *He that regardeth the day,* like the Jewish Christians in Rome who yet observed certain Sabbath practices or at least had religious sentiments tied up with long years of Sabbath observance which were yet dear to them, *regardeth it unto the Lord: and he that eateth,* whether herbs or meats, *eateth unto the Lord, for he giveth God thanks* for the day, whether the seventh or first day of the week or whether garden vegetables or meats of various kinds. Paul pleads for liberty and freedom in non-essentials. This is the doctrine of freedom of conscience pure and simple. It is a most important principle for the guidance of Christians in their mutual relations and in the relation particularly between church and state. The root of the matter is regard for the Lord in an honest and enlightened conviction based on the diligent and discerning study of thankfulness for the food of each day and the days for the service and glory of the Lord.

v. 7. *For none of us liveth to himself*[47] alone and no one dieth to himself personally. Life and death are not nearly private and of isolated concern but are tied up with the Lord[48] and must look to his advantage and thus the advantage of our fellowmen.

v. 8. *For whether*[49] *we may live, we live unto the Lord, whether we die, we die unto the Lord: whether we live therefore or die we are the Lord's* and belong to him[50] to do what is to his advantage.

v. 9. *For unto this* end *Christ died,* crucified on the cross of Calvary *and came to life*[51] *in order that he might become* Lord[52] of the dead and of the living, Christians who have fallen asleep and Christians who are yet living.

v. 10. *But thou, why dost thou judge*[53] *thy brother? Or thou, again, why dost thou set at naught*[54] *thy brother? for we shall all stand before the judgment seat*[55] *of God.*

v. 11. *For it stands written: As I live,*[56] *saith the Lord, to me every knee shall bow, and every tongue shall confess to God.*

v. 12. So then, *each one of us shall give account of himself to God.*

Thus Paul warns the scrupulous brother against censoriousness but also exhorts the strong brother against placing an obstacle in the way of his fellow-Christian. There was a tendency toward incipient asceticism in certain members of the church and Paul calls attention to the fact that meat is a secondary thing. Instead of judging and criticizing one another there should be Christian love, peace, and unity in the church toward each other.

With Augustine we see Paul here showing indirectly the error of the weak, while he condemns the strong and urges them to Christian love.

---

47. Heautoi — Dative of advantage or disadvantage.
48. Kurioi, dative of advantage.
49. Eau with subj. in third class condition, zōmen, not saying anything about the reality.
50. Predicate genitive, kuriou denoting possession.
51. First ingressive aor. active of zaō.
52. Ingressive aor. active subj. with hina in a purpose clause.
53. Referring to the conduct of the weak brother who was a vegetarian, v. 3.
54. Referring to the strong brother who had in contempt his weak brother.
55. *Bema,* judgment seat, Cf. David Smith, *Life and Letters of St. Paul* in loco.
56. *Zō ego,* I live.

2. The duty of Christian love on the part of the strong toward those who are scrupulous and weak in faith, 14:13-23. Having addressed the weak and strong simultaneously (vv. 1-12) the Apostle continues (vv. 13-23) with a warning and exhortation to the strong that they use not their rightful liberty except in accord with the law of love. The strong has liberty, but let him sacrifice his liberty, not wounding the heart and conscience of the weak by irritating him but fearing least he destroy God's work in the weaker brother leading him to sin against his conscience.

v. 13. Christian love, *agapē*, calls for consideration of the feelings and consciences of all. *Let us no longer therefore go on judging*[57] *one another*, getting into the habit of criticising one another, *but judge this rather* as a line of conduct *the not* going on *putting*[58] *a stumbling block*[59] *or an occasion of falling* trap or snare, *in the way of his brother.*[60] The block over which one stumbles is close to the trap or snare into which he is thus precipitated.

v. 14. *I know and am* completely persuaded[61] *in* virtue of being in the sphere of fellowship of *the Lord Jesus,* and not by mere rationalization, *that nothing* in the way of meats *is unclean through itself* (since God made all things for their own proper uses) *except to the one who accounts anything to be unclean* or impure, to that *one* (person) it is *unclean*, by corrupting the conscience and weakening the will of him that uses it and by his sinning against his own conscience.

v. 15. The doing violence willfully and knowingly to one's own conscience is wrong. *For*, the reason for such conduct is this: *if on account of meats* (food) *thy brother is grieved, thou art walking no longer according to* the law of Christian *love. Do not go on destroying by thy meat* (food) *that one on behalf of whom Christ died* on the cross. That is too great a price to pay for your personal liberty. (Robertson). Christ died to save the man from sin whom you are causing by the use of your freedom of action to incur guilt by following your example.

v. 16. *Do not, then, let your good* understanding of Christian liberty and consciousness of the inoffensiveness of the meat or whatever food of like character, *be evil spoken of*[62] and thus become a cause of reproach. All the many good things possessed by a Christian, in his special position above non-Christians, may become a reproach by the consequent wrangling and disunity in the church about matters not essential.

v. 17. Christians are to put spiritual unity above their personal opinions about things altogether secondary. So let the strong who are conscious of

57. Pres. subj. active (volative) *krinōmen but* followed by *krinate,* imperative aorist, command.

56. Articular infinitive in apposition with toutō. Present infinitive denoting continuation of action.

59. Proskomma, a stumbling block from proskoptō, cutting against, and (skandalon) a trap or snare, illustrated in Jews, who stumbled into trap of waiting a temporal Messiah.

60. Dative of disadvantage, tōi adelfōi, Cf. Matt. 18:6f.

61. Perfect pass. indicative of peithō, stand persuaded.

62. Pres. Pass. imv. of *blasphemeō*. Cf. Matt. 9:3.

spiritual freedom about eating meats and not just vegetables, or eating meat which has been offered to idols and then sold in the shambles, not lay stress upon their spiritual liberty, but bend to the demands of Christian love, and not offend where it is possible to gain the brother to a better way and understanding by your proper treatment of the weak brother in humility and love. *Because the kingdom of God*, which must be the Christian's first interest, *is not* a matter of one kind of *food* or another, or this or that kind of *drink*, such as is not hurtful in itself, for all of those things are secondary, *but* the kingdom is *righteousness* (*didaiosunē*) the God-kind which deals justly, *and peace* with God and among men, especially brethren in the church, *and joy*, from living *in* the sphere of the life and influence of *the Holy Spirit*. The Christians who are dwelling in and being indwelt by the Holy Spirit are eternally and inseparably bound together in the bonds of Christian love.

v. 18. *For he that, in this* principle and sphere *is serving Christ, is well-pleasing to God and approved* of (in his relations) *to men*.[63] So the strong brother, who sacrifices his liberty in order to show his love for the scrupulous and sometimes over-scrupulous brother will succeed in winning the weaker brother to a stronger and more intelligent faith and understanding.

v. 19. *Wherefore then,* in conclusion of the foregoing, *let us follow*[64] *after things which make for peace*[65] *and things whereby we may edify one another*, building one another up to greater perfection in Christ.

v. 20. *Let us not on account of food pull down the work of God* built up in our fellow-Christian. Thus Paul concludes one argument and then proceeds to another. (vv. 19b-23). Let us not pull down in our brother the work of God, by leading him to do something against his own conscience. *All things, indeed, are clean: howbeit it is evil*[66] *for the man who eateth* with (stumbling) *offense*. These words are addressed to the weak brother who, eating against his conscience, does wrong, but are applicable perhaps more to the strong who by eating offends, becoming a stumbling block by the way he eats and exercises his freedom.

v. 21. *It is good not to eat flesh,* of any kind, *nor to drink* light *wine* even, which is a common drink of the orientals by custom *nor* to do *anything whereby thy brother stumbleth.* This is the law of Christian love, to be universally applicable and applied by Christian's 'border line practice.'

v. 22. *The faith which thou hast* whether weak or strong *have thou to thyself before God* without criticizing others. *Happy is he that judgeth not himself,* passing an adverse judgment on himself, *in that which he approveth,* having tested it out to be according to the will of God. The strong in the faith must not be subject forever to the caprices and whims of the eccentric brother of over-scrupulous, uncompromising obstinacy.

---

63. Dative of advantage or possibly instrumental, by men.
64. Present act. subjunctive, *diokōmen.*
65. Genitive case.
66. Note the emphatic position of *su*, thou, in the Greek text, in the initiation of the sentence.

v. 23. *But he that doubteth,* hesitating to eat, *is condemned* and incurs guilt *if he* then *eats,*[67] against his conscience, *because* he eateth *not of faith; and whatsoever* act *is not from faith*, in Christ as a source, *is sin,* because it is against conscience whether enlightened or not.

The same subject continues in the following Ch. XV and the epistle does not conclude at this point as some critics surmise.

3. The third general principle Paul lays down to help the Roman and all other Christian churches is to follow the example of Christ in dealing with all the internal questions and problems of the Church. The apostle continues to enforce the great principle of Christian love and the unity of the Church as the main consideration. The example of Christ is set forth in the Scriptures for the enlightenment and encouragement of all, both weak and strong, and all races, both Jew and Gentile. 15:1-13.

a. Paul goes on further with the same subject, whether written immediately or added later as some critics hold (vv1-6) and passes further on (vv7-13) to concentrate attention on the broad principle of Christian unity, with special application to the relationship between Jewish and Gentile Christians in the church in Rome and of course elsewhere also.

Ch. 15:v. 1. *We who are strong ought,* we owe it as a duty, *to bear,* even if it may be burdensome and require patience, *the* (weaknesses) *infirmities of the weak and not to please ourselves.* It was pretty severe reflection on the 'weak' brethren for Paul to be frank in this manner, but it was right that the ascetic tendency in the church should be curbed. It has ever been the tendency of the eccentric to be censorious and require on the part of the healthy normal-minded Christian to 'go the second mile' always with him. Christ gave the example of not pleasing himself, and Paul, his servant, followed the example.[68]

v. 2. *Let each one of us,* who are Christians, *please* (and thus gratify) *our neighbor* (one who is near, always with us, like the poor) with a conduct looking *to* (toward) *that which is good* and for his welfare, tending *unto edification,* building up the faith of the weak brother. Paul gave a back-handed slap to the infirmity of the weak brother while he called in the help of the strong by asking him to make a sacrifice and do a thing which would keep him humble and make him yet stronger.

v. 3. *For Christ also did not please*[69] *himself but* as his example was foretold, what it should be, *it stands written*: (Ps. 69:9). *"The reproaches of them that reproached thee fell*[69] *upon me."* The Messiah fulfilled this prophecy and bore the reproaches of others.

v. 4. *For whatsoever things were written beforetime were written for our*[70] *learning* or instruction (didaskalian),[71] *that through patience,* remaining un-

---

67. Ean with aor. act. subjunctive in third class condition.
68. Cf. I Cor. 10:33-11:1.
69. Aorist act. ind. of *aresko,* an actual occurrence foretold by the Messianic Psalm 69:9.
70. Objective sense of the possessive pronoun.
71. A *didaskalos* is a teacher, and he has not taught truly unless someone has really learned or made profit of his teaching.

der[72] the load of effort without complaint *and through*[73] encouragement,[74] *comfort of the Scriptures, we may go on having hope.*

v. 5. *Now, the God of patience and of comfort grant*[75] *you, to be of the same mind,* with *one another* (among yourselves) *according* to the example and character of *Christ Jesus in order.*

v. 6. *that*[76] *you may with one accord, with one mouth,* in unity of expression of feeling and understanding, *glorify the God and* also the own *father of our* divine *Lord* and Jesus Christ, our Savior and Messiah.

b. Thus the unity of the church of Rome, including its whole constituency whether Jewish or Gentile, would be attained. (vv 7-13).

v. 7. *Wherefore, take ye each other to yourselves,*[77] both the strong and the weak taking active initiative in mutual confidence and love, *just as Christ received us* all to himself, *for the glory* (unto the end of the glory) *of God.*

v. 8. For *I say*[78] (mean) this, that Christ has become permanently[79] *a servant* to the circumcision[80] (the Jews), *on behalf of the truth of God,* that he might confirm (for the confirmation) of *the promise* made to the Jewish fathers.[81]

v. 9. *That the nations* (Gentiles) *might glorify the* true *God for his mercy, as it stands written: On account of this, I will praise thee among the nations and I will sing unto thy name.*[82]

v. 10. *And again it* (the Scripture) *says,*[83] *Rejoice ye* (nations) *Gentiles with his people.*

v. 11. *And again: All ye Gentiles praise the Lord and let all the peoples praise him.*[84]

v. 12. *And again Isaiah saith: There shall be the root of Jesse, And he that ariseth to rule over the Gentiles, On him shall the Gentiles hope.*[85]

v. 13. *Now, the God of hope, fill you*[86] *with all joy and peace in believing,*[87] *that ye may abound*[88] *in hope, in the power* or might *of the Holy Spirit.*

---

72. *Hupomonē, Hupo, menō,* to remain under.
73. Prep. *dia* with genitive, signifies intermediate agency or means.
74. Exhortation, comfort, encouragement.
75. Second aor. act. optative expressing Paul's wish for them.
76. Final clause, *hina* with present active subjunctive of *doxazō.*
77. The middle voice here calls for activity in us including both strong and weak, both Jew and Gentile.
78. *Legō gar,* an expression of Paul's style for emphasis in setting forth something of special importance.
79. Perfect passive infinitive of *ginomai,* conveying the idea of a permanent ministry.
80. Objective genitive of *peritomē.*
81. Objective genitive, *paterōn.*
82. Psalm 18:49; II Sam. 22:50.
83. Deut. 32:43.
84. Psa. 117:1. slightly different from text of LXX.
85. Isa. 11:10.
86. First aor. act. optative of pleroō expressing a wish for the future.
87. Articular infinitive in locative with prep. *en.*
88. Articular infiinite in acc. case with prep *eis* expressing purpose, pres. infinitive periseuein from verb perisseuo used with acc. of general reference, *humas.*

CONCLUSION

Paul's conclusion (15:14-16:27) of Romans is longer than that of any other of his epistles for the same reasons assigned for the length of his salutation.[89]

1 His reason for writing was twofold: (a) That he might fulfill his mission to this great church so strategically located. (15:14-21).

(b) He desired to secure their cooperation in his missionary campaign in Spain and other countries where he would seek to carry the gospel (15:22-33).

In the first of these two sections (15:14-33) the Apostle (1) justifies his writing to them (vv. 14-16):

v. 14. *But I am fully persuaded* in the Lord, *my brethren,* although I have accused and rebuked you, yet *I, myself, am aware concerning you, that ye are full of goodness, filled up*[90] permanently and completely *with all our Christian knowledge* in its entirety,[91] *being able* thus *to admonish* one *another also.* This gifted church would be able to aid the apostle in his missionary campaign.

v. 15. *But I wrote*[92] *the more boldly, in part,* in certain places in the epistle, as if in some measure *reminding* you or calling to your remembrance the principles and commands of the gospel *on account of the grace given to me from God,* to the Gentiles.

v. 16. *to the end that I should be a priestly minister* of Jesus Christ *to the Gentiles, ministering the Gospel of God that the offering up of the Gentiles might be acceptable being sanctified by the Holy Spirit.*[93] Paul was the priest standing by the altar, offering up the Gentile churches to God.[94] The offering had been perfectly sanctified.[95]

(2) In the next place Paul would fulfill his duty as apostle to the Gentiles to this church (vv. 17-21).

v. 17. *I have therefore my glorying* (boasting) in the sphere of *Christ Jesus,* in respect to *the things pertaining to God,* while ministering as a priest in the gospel of God. My boast is not in myself or my work but in Christ and his gospel. Paul made plain that he was not boasting in referring to himself as the officiating servant in so great an act as that of presenting the gospel to the Gentile churches so as to make them an acceptable offering on God's altar. A church which was not thoroughly evangelical could not be acceptable as an offering without blemish on the altar of sacrifice and service.

89. Vide Salutation 1:1-7.

90. Perfect passive participle of *pteroō.*

91. Cf. Sanday and Headlam in loco.

92. Epistolary aorist.

93. Either the instrumental case *pneumati hagiō,* as I take it, or the locative of sphere within which the sanctifying process took place.

94. Cf. Sanday and Headlam in loco, but Paul did not attach a "sacerdotal" character to his ministry. He was not an Old Testament kind of priest but ministered metaphorically as a priest.

95. Perfect passive participle, *hēgiasmene of hagiazō.*

v. 18. *For I shall not dare to speak about any* of those things[96] *which Christ* and he alone *did not work through me, by* means of *word*[97] (preaching) *and work* in all the activities of life, with a view unto *the obedience of the* (nations) *Gentiles.* Paul made no false pretenses as to his work.

v. 19. But the ground of his boldness he states clearly. *In the* miraculous *power of signs and wonders,* covering both the miracles which evidenced the divine character of his mission and those which produced the profound effect of wonder in the people, evidently wrought *in the power of the Holy Spirit;*[98] *so that*[99] *I have made full the preaching of the gospel of Christ,* founding the work in the strategic centers, starting *from Jerusalem and* extending *in a circle round about even unto* Illyricum (Dalmatia), west of Macedonia. This was the extreme limit of Paul's evangelistic ministry up to this time (Robertson). This was work the character of which could not be denied; it was evidently of God, and when Paul related the fact of having done it, he was not boasting a fault grave enough in some religious workers. A real missionary does well to modestly narrate the experiences of his work. It was necessary that the true record of Paul's work be known, that such information might kindle the flame of missions in the hearts of the Christians in Rome and other places Making it known with the right motive was not boasting but fulfilling his mission.

v. 20. *And so,*[1] *making it my aim* (a noble ambition in a missionary) *to preach the gospel, where Christ had not been named* in the work of preaching *that I* might *not build upon another* (man's) *foundation.* Paul was a missionary pioneer with a high and dignified mission.

v. 21. But as it stands written;[2] *"They shall see to whom no tidings of him* came, *And they who have not heard shall understand."*[3] Paul cites this illustration from Isaiah, to describe the character of his pioneer work as apostle to the Gentiles.

(3) The apostle reveals his plans in coming to them. He desired to secure the cooperation of the Roman church for his campaign in Spain and other countries. (vv. 22-33).

v. 22. *Wherefore, also, I was hindered*[4] (in respect to) *many times* and by many activities of the current work[5] where I am laboring *from coming*[6] *to you.*

---

96. Toutōn the antecedent of hōu (by attraction of the relative) is omitted here.
97. Instrumental case, logōi kai ergōi.
98. Cf. II Cor. 12:12; II Thess. 2:9; Thess 1:5; I Cor. 2:4 cited instances of the work of the Holy Spirit in the work of Paul.
99. Hoste me peplērokenai used with euangellion, the act of announcing the gospel. He had fulfilled his evangelistic task, when he had preached in the strategic centers and started the work.
1. Closely connected with the preceding statement, not with W & H.
2. Perfect middle *gegraptai.*
3. Isa. 52:15 The genuineness of verses 19-21 is beyond question (Cf. Robertson *Word Pictures* Vol. Pauline Epistles p. 421).
4. Imperfect pass of *enkoptō,* to cut in, cut off, to hinder.
5. 'As to many things, other tasks at different and many times, Cf. Rom. 1:13.
6. Ablative of separation, art inf. *tou elthein,* after verb of hindering *enkoptō.*

v. 23. *But now no longer* as I judge *having place* or opportunity, *in these regions* (or climes), having established churches in the strategic centers, *and also having a longing for many years* to *come*[7] *to you*,

v. 24. *whensoever I may go*[8] *into Spain For I hope to see you when passing through* (in my journey) *and to be sent forward by you there if I first in part might get my fill of you* in gracious hospitality. A tactful hint of his wish to be received by them and helped as he should go on his way to other fields of labor. The great church in Rome would not require or need his ministrations but could help in his ministry of missions. He delicately invites them to this cooperative effort.

v. 25. *But now* another reason for my delay in coming, *I am going* unto *Jerusalem*, ministering[9] by this journey and other services *unto the saints*, in the church, who are the poorer members. Many were poor when they accepted Christianity and others became deprived of work through persecution, as occurs today in pagan countries and among people of antievangelical faiths.

v. 26. *For* the Christians of *Macedonia and Achaia took pleasure to make* (in making) *a certain contribution for the poor among the saints*[10] *that were at Jerusalem.*

v. 27. *Yea, for it hath been their* (the Gentiles) *good pleasure; and their* (the Jews) *debtors they are, For if*[11] *in their spiritual things*, the Jewish Christians *shared* with the Gentiles, as is evidently true,[11] *these ought also to minister to them* in turn *with their material things*, which belong to the natural life, not to the sinful practical aspects of the flesh. The Gentile Christians were collecting money and sending it on to the poorer Jewish brethren in Jerusalem. This plan of the collection worked strongly for unity.

v. 28. *Therefore, having accomplished this* service for the poor saints in Jerusalem, *and having sealed* securely *for them this fruit*, by placing in their hands the funds collected for them, *I shall go on*[12] by means of *you unto Spain.* Paul thus tactfully impresses them for the task in Spain and tactfully enlists their cooperation.

v. 29. *And I know that coming to you I will come in the fullness of the blessing of Christ.* The fact that Paul came to the church in Rome as a prisoner is no contradiction of this statement, as his prison experiences in Rome became a real spiritual blessing to that Church.[13]

v. 30. *Now, I beseech you, brethren, through our Lord Jesus Christ*, (an appeal of great force in view of the recent death and resurrection of Christ), *and through the* Christian *love* (agapē) which the Holy *Spirit* sheds abroad in the heart, *to strive* along *with me in your prayers to God in my behalf.*

---

7. Art. infinite in genitive case, with adjective of desire.
8. Indefinite temporal clause with hos an and the present mid. subjunctive, *porenōmai.*
9. Present participle, current action.
10. Partitive genitive, *tōn hagiōn.*
11. Condition of the first class, according to fact, first aor. act ind. with associative instrumental case, but no 'sacerdotal' function indicated.
12. Future mid. of *aperchomai,* to go on.
13. Cf. Phil. 1:12-19.

v. 31. *that I may be delivered*[14] *from those who are disobedient* or unbelieving, the Judaists who had long dogged his steps, who had their headquarters, *in Judea and that my service* or financial assistance, which is to be conveyed *into Jerusalem may become acceptable to the saints.*

v. 32. *in order that with joy coming to you through the will of God I may find rest with you.* He did not know that it would be more than two years and that all the eventualities of his arrest and two years of imprisonment in Cesarea lay between him and his arrival in Rome with a chain. *Amen.*

v. 33. *Now the God of peace be with you all.* The apostle closes his ingenious and moving appeal to the great church, for their loving hospitable reception, on his brief anticipated visit to them 'as he shall pass on his urgent way to Spain,' the next hope for field of activities in the ever-widening circle of his missionary conquests. He wishes them, over a solemn 'Amen,' the peace of God. He must have been thinking as his mind reached back toward Jerusalem, the goal of his imminent trip to bear the collection to the poor saints, of how he would need that same peace of the God of peace for the eventualities of that difficult task.

2. Personal matters of epistolary character clustered round and illustrative of Christian love. Ch. 16. This final personal message of the epistle was not a mere addition tacked on to the epistle by the amenuensis or some other. Despite the 'amen' closing the revelation of the apostle's motives in writing the epistle to the Roman church, this is not a separate brief epistle to the Ephesians, as some critics would make it. The evidence of the best MSS. are against such a conclusion and the whole character of the internal evidence of the epistle makes this series of personal salutations the most natural way to end it. Paul had many personal friends who had during many years drifted to this great metropolis, center of the civilization of the world. Thirty five names of these friends are mentioned in this final word of the epistle.

a. Commendation of Phoebe (vv. 1, 2).

v. 1. *I commend to you Pheobe, our sister* in Christ, who is *a deaconess*[15] *of the church which is in Cenchrae.*[16]

v. 2. *that you may receive her,* as being a Christian, *in the Lord,* in a manner becoming or *worthily of the saints, and that you may assist her* (stand by her) *in whatever business she may have need of you*[17] *for she also hath been a succorer of many, and of mine own self.*[18] In this port-town ten miles from Corinth, Paul had founded a church and Phoebe was a servant in special employment of the church. She was moving to Rome at this time and bore the letter to the Roman church. Paul commends her as a worthy worker who may be useful in the service of the Roman church.

---

14. Purpose clause with hina and the first aor. pass. subjunctive of ruomai after words of beseeching or praying.
15. Diakonon, deaconess, common gender, here feminine. Cf. I Tim. 3:8-13.
16. The harbor of Corinth on the eastern side of the isthmus.
17. Indefinite relative clause with *an* and pres. subj. of *chreizō.*
18. Of me myself, *emoū autoū.*

b. Various salutations or greetings to the many personal friends of the apostle in Rome (vv. 3-16).

vv. 3, 4. *Greet Prisca* (Priscilla) *and Aquilla,* her husband, *my fellow-workers in Christ Jesus,*[19] *who for my life* (psuchē) *laid down their own necks,* with unwavering devotion through many perils, *to whom, not I alone give thanks, but also all the churches of the Gentiles,* for they served in the founding of many churches among the Gentiles. Priscilla was the more aggressive and able of these two great mission workers. They had probably run the risk of their lives for Paul in the tumult at Ephesus and possibly left that city then to return to Rome.

v. 5. but, *also* (salute) *the church in their house.*[20] *Salute Epaenetus, my beloved, who is the first-fruit* of the province of Asia, of conversion *unto Christ.* Nothing is known of him except that he was one of the first converts made in the Roman province of Asia.

v. 6. *Salute Mary who bestowed*[21] *much labor on you.*

v. 7. *Salute Andronicus and Junias my kinsmen and my fellow-prisoners* (where is not known), who are of note and distinguished among the apostolic men, *who also have been born in Christ before me* or converted to Christianity before the date of my conversion and are yet among faithful members in the church.

v. 8. *Salute Ampliatus* or Amplias *my beloved in the Lord,* probably a Christian slave through whom Christianity had penetrated into a second great Roman household.[22]

v. 9. *Salute Urbanus a fellow-worker in Christ,* probably a slave *and Stachys, my beloved,* whose name indicates that he was a converted Greek and a member of the imperial household.

v. 10. *Salute Apelles,* a Jewish brother, *in Christ,* who had been put to the test and had shown himself an approved Christian. (Sanday and Headlam). *Salute those of the household of Aristobulus,* slaves but Christians. Aristobulus probably already deceased was according to Josephus a grandson of Herod the Great. The slaves, who were probably Jews, were considered a part of the household.

v. 11. *Salute Herodion my* countryman or else *kinsman,* worthy of mention in the list of Paul's Christian friends. *Salute them of the household of Narcissus who are believers in the Lord.* Narcissus, a freedman of the Emperor Claudias, had been executed by Agrippana four years before the composition of this letter, but his household seems to have still existed in Rome.

---

19. Cf. Acts 18:2; I Cor. 16:19. Priscilla was probably a noble Roman lady and her husband a Jew of Pontus, a tent-maker by trade. They were fellow-workers of Paul in tent making and Christian service. They had been expelled with other Jews from Rome once and went to Corinth, Ephesus and finally back to Rome where they were when Paul wrote the letter.

20. Many of the primitive churches worshipped in the private houses of their members.

21. Constative aorist, the labors covered a period of time.

22. Cf. Sanday and Headlam. *ICC. Romans* p. 424.

v. 12. *Salute Tryphaena and Tryphosa, who laboured in the Lord.* These who were probably sisters, possibly twins, bearing names signifying luxury, but quite to the contrary they had been 'toilers' in the work of the Lord, leaving a good record. *Salute Persis,* a Persian woman, *the beloved* worker of the church *who laboured much in the Lord.* She was probably now aged.[23]

v. 13. *Salute Rufus, chosen in the Lord and his mother and mine.* He was the son of Simon formerly from Cyrene, who bore the cross of Jesus to Calvary. Rufus was a distinguished evangelist, even when Paul was a student in Gamaliel's school in Jerusalem and Paul lived in that home and enjoyed the motherly care of Simon's wife and Rufus' mother, hence "his mother and mine." (Godet).

v. 14. *Salut Asyncritus, Phlegon, Hermes, Patrobas, Hermas and the brethren which are with them.* Here is a list of leaders in the evangelistic activities of the Roman church whose names are honorably mentioned as directors of the work.

v. 15. *Salute Philologus and Julia,* probably husband and wife, both of whom bear the names of slaves in the imperial household but bond-slaves also of Christ, *Nereus and his sister* whose name for some reason was not mentioned, *and Olympas* or Olympiadorus *and all the saints that are with them.*

v. 16. *Salute one another with a holy kiss.* This is yet the near-east mode of salutation. In the Roman church men kissed men and women kissed women.[24] Paul felt the need of expressing his affection for all the members of the church and asked that they do so for him making use of this customary salutation in the assembly of the church when his letter should be read to the church. Paul had journeyed among the other Christian churches of Europe and Asia and they were aware of his letter being sent now to the Roman church. The apostle bore their salutations to this sister church in the Imperial Capital and he would thus make concrete and impressive the expression of their salutations. It must have been a very impressive act in the church assembly, long to be remembered as each one turned to his nearest brother and saluted him in the name of Paul and the world of Christians — a real expression of the universal Christian feeling of fraternity, with the words of Paul: *All the churches of Christ salute you.*

This list of persons to whom Paul bade the church salute for him has been the occasion for regarding the sixteenth chapter as the ending of another epistle, which for some unknown reason attached to this letter to the Romans. There is no sufficient reason for such an hypothesis. Paul had many personal friends among believers who had moved to Rome, the great capital, for one reason or another. To these he sent greetings as one deeply interested in all the brethren individually as well as collectively.

c. Warnings against false teachers (vv. 17-20).

v. 17. *Now, I beseech you, brethren, to mark them that are causing the divisions and occasions of stumblings, contrary to the* (teaching) *doctrine,*

---

23. Use of the aorist tense.
24. Cf. I Thess. 5:26; I Cor. 16:20; II Cor. 13:12.

which you learned: *and turn away* always[25] *from them.* Sometimes a postscript bears the most important practical application of a letter. Here Paul puts the Roman church on guard against Judaists and other false teachers who were at work in other places and might be expected here in Rome. The Judaists had caused many divisions elsewhere, as in Corinth and Galatia and, would attempt the same here.

v. 18. *For they that are such serve not,* our Lord Christ *but their own belly; and by fair speech and* flattery *deceive the hearts of the* (simple) *innocent.* Paul warned the church in Philippi later against such sensual and hypocritical false teachers (Phil. 3:19). The gospel ministry served such deceivers as a means of gain and for satisfying their gross passions.

v. 19. *For your obedience has come abroad into all men. I rejoice therefore over you, but I would have you wise unto that which is good, but simple* (unmixed or unadulterated) *unto the evil.*

v. 20. *The God of peace shall trample Satan under your feet shortly.* Meanwhile patient loyalty is necessary. *The grace of our Lord Jesus be with you.*

d. Salutations from the companions of Paul (vv. 21-23). Another postscript adds the names of Paul's fellow-workers and conveys their joint greetings to the church.

v. 21. *Timothy my fellow worker saluteth you*: *and Lucius and Jason and Sosipater my kinsmen.*

v. 22. *I, Tertius,* (the amanuensis), who write the epistle, *salute you in the Lord.* Paul delicately indicated that Tertius wrote his own salutation.

v. 23. *Gaius my host and the host of the whole church saluteth you. Erastus, the treasurer of the city saluteth you, and Quartus, the brother.*

v. 24. is a repetition of v. 20. and hence omitted in nearly all the critical editions.

The Concluding Doxology

The sublime doxology which concludes this epistle sums up in a most unusual manner all its great thought. It constitutes a genuine conclusion of Paul's *magnum opus.* (vv. 25-27).

v. 25. *Now, to Him who is able to establish you according to my gospel and the preaching* (*kērugma*) *of Jesus Christ, according to the revelation of the mystery which hath been kept in silence through the times eternal.*

Paul's purpose in preaching his gospel about faith in Christ as the only way of salvation, for the world of lost men was to reveal God's love secret of universal salvation which had been hidden, which explained God's purpose in the world.

v. 26. *but now is manifested, and through the Scriptures of the prophets, according to the commandment of the eternal God, is made known unto all the nations unto obedience of faith;*

---

25. Present progressive imperative of habitual action, *ekklinete, ap' autōn.*

The purpose of God in man and the world is now made known through the interpretation of the Old Testament Scriptures summed up in the phrase 'through the prophets,' in the new method of salvation apart from the law but witnessed by the Law and Prophets. This unified message of the Old and New Testament, of salvation by faith, is to be preached to the nations by the apostolic messengers.

v. 27. *to the only wise God, through Jesus Christ to whom be glory forever. Amen.* Glory is ascribed to the only God of both Jews and Greeks. God is infinitely wise and his wisdom is demonstrated through the intermediate agency of Jesus Christ. *Glory be to God through Jesus Christ.* Amen!

So the doxology sums up (1) The power of the Gospel Paul preached, (2) 'the eternal purpose of God revealed in it (3) the method of it's faith in Christ (4) the author of it — the one wise God (5) the agent of it — Jesus Christ (6) the scope of it — the nations of the earth, both Jew and Gentile. This epistle has four benedictions within the last two chapters (Chs. 15:13,33; 16:20, 25-27). But the last states fully the fundamental proposition of the whole epistle: that salvation through Jesus Christ is unto all, regardless of race, upon the single condition of faith. This is the theme of missions and this constitutes Romans the greatest missionary document of all literature.

Part III

PAUL'S PRISON EXPERIENCES AND LETTERS

CHAPTER XIX

Paul's Last Journey to Jerusalem

The contribution from the four provinces would be borne by a committee of seven brethren chosen by the contributing churches represented, including *Sopater from Beroea, Aristarchus and Secundus from Thessalonica, Gaius of Derbe* and *Timothy* (Lystra) *and two from* the province of *Asia Tychicus and Trophimus* who went to Troas to meet the rest of the party. Learning of the plot of his enemies in Cenchrae, Paul had changed his plan, and taking Luke with him[1] made his way overland to Macedonia. He would be safer in Philippi with Luke than anywhere else until the hour arrived for his Committee to meet him in Troas.

That time soon came (Acts XX:6). *We sailed away from Philippi after the days of unleavened bread, and came unto them* (the seven committee-men mentioned already) *to Troas in five days; and there we tarried seven days.*[2] *And on the first day of the week* (Sunday) *when we were gathered together to break bread,* (celebrate the Lord's Supper, after the Agape, according to the custom in the primitive churches), *Paul discoursed* with the congregation of the church in Troas and the Committee on Charity, *being about to depart on the morrow;* Luke and Paul seem to have represented the churches in Corinth and Achaia. Paul had volunteered to do so but he did not handle the money personally. Luke had several duties as general evangelist and could well collaborate in representing such churches as did not have an official representative. Luke could also serve along with Paul in the work of administration of the fund. Paul's discussion was elaborate in the evening hours and *his speech was prolonged until midnight.* It was in an apartment in a tenament house on the third floor, the topmost.[3] The room was crowded, and stuffy being lighted with many grease lamps and so over-warm.

v. 8. *And there were many lights in the upper chamber, where we were gathered together.*

v. 9. *And there sat in* (on the ledge of) *the window a certain young man named Entychus, who was gradually oppressed by sleep as Paul extended his*

1. II Cor. 8:19 Luke was one of the administrators of the fund although he does not mention his name.
2. Luke who was along followed the method of stating the time of the stop and giving briefly the details of the activity in the period of time spent there.
3. Cf. Juv. III 199 cited by David Smith *Life and Letters* p. 461.

discourse further,[4] *and being borne down by his sleep he fell from the third story to the ground and was lifted up dead.*[5]

v. 10. *And Paul went down and fell on him and embracing him said, "Make ye no ado; for his life is in him."* Why did Paul, Elisha-like, fall upon the corpse (nekros) and embrace it? Life was restored to the young man miraculously but Paul did not want a commotion about it. He had things more important to transact now with the congregation and *He went up and broke bread and ate,* celebrating the Lord's Supper and afterward *talked with them a long while, even till* the *break of day; and he departed.* Paul had arranged to go alone to Assos while Luke and the seven men of the Committee with the sailors set sail and rounded the cape Lectum, arriving about the time Paul did after his walk across the Troad to Assos.

v. 12 After Paul had gone, the young man was *brought* in *alive and they* (the friends) *were not a little comforted.* Paul needed to be alone after such a day and night at Troas. He had stamina enough, this man of iron, to take a thirty mile walk through a short cut in order to be alone with the Lord for a season in close communion. Great events were out ahead for Paul and he needed these hours alone with the Master. He was nearly sixty years of age and for twenty years had been engaged in superhuman labors of unceasing evangelistic activities over wide areas while bearing on his heart crushing cares. But he could preach all night and then walk thirty miles through a verdure-covered country-side in communion with beautiful nature and God.

There was no delay at Assos. Paul passed, by the Sacred Way, down to the shore and without delay went on board, joining his companions, as the ship righted itself for the voyage along the shore of Lesbos to Mitylene, the capital of the island, home of the infamous Greek poetess Sappho. Due to the contrary breeze and a moonless night the ship lay at anchor sheltered from the north-westerly winds in the small harbor on the southeastern side of the island.

v. 13. *But we, going before to the ship,* (a craft apparently hired by the party to take them to Miletus, not far away), *set sail for Assos, intending to take Paul on board from thence; for so he had arranged, intending himself to go by land* as far as that place. Luke stated in his narrative that Entychus was dead, a corpse, when he was lifted up. He was not dead, as Paul was thought to be dead, by his enemies at Lystra.

v. 14. *And when he met us at Assos, we took him on board, and came to Mitylene.*

v. 15. *And sailing from thence on the following day, we reached* a point on the mainland opposite *Chios; and on the morrow we struck across to Samos and* (after a stay at Trogyllia) *on the next* day *we came to Miletus.* Here Paul sent to Ephesus for the Elders to come to him there as the ship was to spend some time in this port. The presbyters arrived back with Paul's

4. Bengel observes, commenting on this incident: Spiritual teachers ought not to be too strictly bound by the clock, especially on a solemn and rare occasion.'

5. Erthe *nekros,* was lifted up dead, not hōs *nekros,* as dead.

messenger on the second day and the Apostle had a whole day with them before he had to go on to Cos. Rhodes, Patara, Myra and Tyre.

v. 16 Paul had *sailed past Ephesus to avoid spending time in Asia; for he was hastening, if it were possible for him to be at Jerusalem the day of Pentecost.* So he sent a messenger to Ephesus and summoned the elders of the church.

v. 18. *And when they were come to him he said unto them,* in his farewell address: many things of permanent value recorded by Luke, the great historian.

I. He first reviewed his three years ministry in Ephesus. vv. 18-21.

(1) The spirit of his ministry had been one of humility; he had dealt with them with the tenderness of a mother; and with patience he had suffered under the plots of the Jews against him. vv. 18, 19.

(2) He had been diligent, making known to them all that was profitable; teaching them in public and in their homes, preaching to them repentence and faith toward God and the Lord Jesus. vv. 20, 21.

(II) He next revealed to them the present status of his ministry (vv. 22-27). (1) His present purpose and plan was to go to Jerusalem, although, bonds and afflictions awaited him. He had been warned by friends of the embittered hatred and hostility of his enemies and the perils and tribulations which he might expect. (2) In spite of all the warnings and predictions against his going to Jerusalem, he felt that he must complete his great work of the collection, administering it personallv at every risk. He would meet his enemies face to face. (3) He frankly reveals to these reponsible heads of the great work in Ephesus that they may not hope to see his face again. He reminds them that he fulfilled his obligation to the Ephesian churches and to those in Asia, in declaring to them the whole body of Christian truth (v. 27).

(III) Finally, he lays the responsibility for the carrying forward of the cause upon them vv. 28-35. (1) They had received their office from the Holy Spirit; and the flock for which they must care was puchased by the blood of Christ. (2) Perils were ahead of them, for heretics like wolves would invade the flock and even some of these elders themselves would prove false (v. 30). (3) For three years he had watched over them night and day with tears and prayers. (v. 31) (4) He commends them to God and to his Word. (v. 32) (5) They must be unselfish in their service. He had given them an example, working with his own hands to support himself and fellow-laborers too (vv. 33, 34) just as Jesus' own words said (v. 35).

The pathos and persuasion of this address wrought an impression in the souls of those men which was imperishable and those words have strengthened and stimulated the hearts of elders, teachers and preachers down through the centuries, to give full value to their responsibility for the progress of the gospel committed to them. Above all they must remember the words of the Lord how He said Himself: "It is more blessed to give than to receive."[6]

Having finished the discourse, Paul knelt with them on the sands by the beach, at the early morning hour, just before the ship was to sail, and prayed. It was a most impressive moment. "They would" he had said, "never see his face again." They crowded around him when his prayer was concluded to give him the customary farewell token, the holy kiss. They clung to him and wept and would hardly let him go. Paul and his companions of travel had to literally tear themselves away to resume their voyage on that beautiful Sunday morning (vv. 36-38). The total scene was a picture which would never fade from the memory of anyone who beheld it; and the impact of its influence has come down across the centuries and beats upon our shores like the wavelets of an Eternal Sea.

Paul had to trans-ship at Troas, as we observed, remaining in that city for a week before suitable passage to Myra could be arranged. Our supposition that his party chartered a small vessel to take them to Myra where they could trans-ship to a vessel bound for Tyre is entirely in keeping with the peculiar circumstances of the needs, for Paul would not want to stop at Ephesus for reasons already cited. He could easily effect his purpose of ministering to the Ephesian and Asian churches, by the plan he actually followed, of having the elders of the Ephesian churches meet him at Miletus. Instead of going on to Myra, the usual place to trans-ship they found a large vessel at Patara bound for Phoenicia and exchanged ships there. This vessel passing to the west of Cyprus brought them soon to Tyre where it delayed a week, for unloading cargo before sailing for Ptolemais, its destination. Paul and his companions had several days to spare before the Feast of Pentecost and so availed themselves of these days to visit the local church in Tyre, where the Christian work was yet little developed. The visit of the party of missionary founders of the work in Asia and Europe was an event in the life of the small Christian community in Tyre, where the small group of disciples was lost in the midst of so large a city. If this church like many others had its origin, at the time of the persecution, beginning with the martyrdom of Stephen some family of believers or small group of disciples found their way to the populous city of Tyre and secured themselves in the midst of the Gentile population. In time their small light grew in intensity and now there were prophets, whether inspired or not, who discerned the perils of Paul's proposed visit to Jerusalem and tried to dissuade him from his plan. But Paul was assured that the Lord who had put it in his heart to go to Jerusalem was abundantly able to deliver him out of the hands of his enemies. This storm-cloud, apparently so black for the time, would pass. The ship delayed a full week and Paul 'broke bread' with these disciples and preached to the congregation, composed of both Jews and Gentiles. Thus he sought, wherever he went, to strengthen and build up

---

6. These words were taken by Paul from the oral traditions and is the only one preserved in the Gospels which Paul quotes. Cf. David Smith *In the Days of His Flesh* p. XIX.

the faith of the weak and the strong alike. The same prayerful scene of the weak before at Miletus was duplicated at the embarkation in Tyre, all the disciples with their families and friends accompanying the Apostle and his fellow-laborers to the ship and watching the ship until it was borne on its way southward toward Ptolemais, its destination. Another opportunity was afforded there for saluting a similar small disciple-band, but the time was short as they must press on to Caesarea.[7]

Paul's party here changed from their ship to a smaller coasting vessel which would take them to Caesarea in a day. Philip, the deacon-evangelist had stationed himself in Caesarea several years after he baptized the Eunuch on the road to Gaza. He had been caught away by the Spirit to Agotus. He was in Caesarea now and in his family there were four daughters who were prophetesses. There the missionary party found a hospitable reception and remained for several days awaiting the proper time to arrive in Jerusalem just before the feast of Pentecost, which would be a fine occasion to present the fund to the proper authorities of the church. The gospel had claimed many trophies here since the conversion of Cornelius and his household, especially among the Gentiles. It was a divinely directed and blessed visit in the home of Philip in this important sea port, now the center built up by Herod as the seat of the Roman provincial government, for all of Syria including also Palestine. In a few days Paul was to be imprisoned in Caesarea, and his acquaintance with the local church under the oversight of evangelist Philip and his family, of such fine preparation, as was rare in that or any time. The four daughter propetesses with divine insight and sympathy foresaw the impending peril of Paul's situation and warned him, begging him not to commit himself into the hands of his enemies in Jerusalem. The news of Paul's presence in Caesarea soon reached Jerusalem and a prophet named Agabus who was well acquainted with the situation in that city hastened down to Caesarea and communicated to Paul and his friends the impending danger ahead in Jerusalem should he carry out his plan to appear there as he had made known to Philip and the church.[8]

The prophecy of Agabus assumed a dogmatic and picturesque form such as the ancient prophets were wont to employ at times.[9] Coming into a group of Paul's Christian friends he took Paul's girdle and bound himself hand and foot and said: (v. 11.) *'Thus saith the Holy Spirit, 'So shall the Jews at Jerusalem bind the man that owneth this girdle, and shall deliver him into the hands of the Gentiles.'*

v. 12. It was then that Luke and the other companions joined the friends of Caesarea in begging Paul not to go up to Jerusalem.

v. 13. But *Paul answered, 'What do ye weeping and breaking my heart? for I am ready not to be bound only, but also to die at Jerusalem for the name of the Lord Jesus.'*

---

7. Cf. Conybeare and Howson, *Life and Epistles of the Apostle Paul*, pp. 515-539.
8. Conybeare and Howson, *Life and Epistles*, p. 536f.
9. Cf. I Kings 22:11; Isa. 20:2; Jer. 13:1-11 etc.

v. 14. *And when he would not be persuaded, we ceased, saying, 'The will of the Lord be done.'*

So the preparations for the trip across country went forward. Special provision was made that Paul should have conveyance. He must not be allowed to arrive in the capital jaded and weary from the journey. The time was set so that it would be possible to divide the distance by staying overnight in the home of Mnason whose residence was in a village not far from Jerusalem. Luke was careful that his great hero Paul should not take a long journey of sixty-four miles on foot just before he entered upon an experience which would call for all his physical strength and intellectual acumen as well. Some of the brethren from Caesarea accompanied the missionary party to the home of Mnason and then returned with the animals[10] leaving Paul and his party of eight companions, including Luke to go on alone the next day unobtrusively and enter the city quietly in the midst of many others going up to the Feast. Paul would not enter with any pomp or ceremony but naturally humble and without fear. And so this missionary apostle after four years of absence, is again in Jerusalem, on his mission of turning over in order, the great collection he had superintended in the churches of the Gentiles during several years, to the proper authorities, for its use in the support of the poorer Jewish brethren in the Jerusalem church. But he was to face his old enemies in their lair and also extract if possible from the Jewish leaders a renewal of their expressions of approval on the vast work he had been doing and was yet to do among the Gentiles.[11]

10. Sir William Ramsey, *Paul, the Traveler and Roman Citizen*, pp. 301ff.
11. James Stalker, *Life of St Paul* p. 126f.

CHAPTER XX

Paul's Arrest in Jerusalem and Imprisonment in Caesarea

The real climax of the book of Acts and of the life and work of Paul falls within the historical scope of this chapter. The narrative of Luke here becomes much more detailed, concentrating on certain selected experiences without trying to cover all the details of the intervals between the chosen incidents. Thus Acts Chs. 21:17-24:23 details the incidents of twelve days; Ch. 24:24-27 of two years; Chs. 25:1-28:7 of five months; and Ch. 28:8-11 of three months.[1] The fate of Paul and of Christianity is in crisis and the element of suspense is reenforced and intense.

I Paul's Arrest in Jerusalem Acts 21:17-23:35.

To renew fellowship with the chief apostles and the majority of the members of the Jerusalem church, was one of Paul's chief objectives now. Misunderstandings might have arisen during the eight year interval and he was agreeably impressed when James called the elders together, for him and his companions to present the collection raised in the Gentile churches, to help the poorer Jewish Christians, of which there were many in Jerusalem. (v. 17) *And when we were come to Jerusalem, the brethren* (chief apostles and elders) *received us gladly*: *On the* second *day following*, Luke adds, *Paul went in with us unto James; and all the elders were present.* Luke was probably taking the initiative in presenting the collection which ought to establish an atmosphere of good will and fellowship. Paul assumed that such was the case though there was no mention made of the result in the narrative of Luke, the omission of which was significant. The fellowship was none too warm, if we are to interpret Luke's silence. Paul made the best of the situation and with his unusual ability and tact he *saluted them* (v. 19), *and rehearsed*, with concise account, *one by one the* great campaigns, victories and achievements of eight crowded years of intense and strenuous activities, *the things which God had wrought among the Gentiles by his ministry.* He did not brag about what the Lord had done through him but gave God the credit for all. So the result of his wonderful report was that (v. 20) *when they heard it they glorified God.* But they did not give Paul too much credit for all his strenuous and devoted work, but *said unto him, Thou seest, brother, how many thousands there are among the Jews of them that have believed.* They on their part could give a report of many thousands, a statistical report, which in numbers indicated great progress of the gospel among the Jews. Especially did they emphasize the fact that their converts were all "*zealous for the law.*" So

---

1. Cf. B. W. Robinson, *The Life of Paul* Ch. XI.

beneath the apparent harmony and fellowship of the Jewish brethren there was instead of spontaneous gratitude and thanksgiving to God and a true fellowship for his servant Paul, an element of reserve on the part of the leaders though they did glorify God formally.

There were in fact many Judaists in the church who had gone all lengths to defeat Paul's work among the Gentiles, because they had never from the first accepted Gentile liberty in their hearts.

James and the elders now revealed to Paul the fact that these brethren, (v. 21) *have been informed concerning thee, that thou teachest all the Jews who are among the Gentiles,* having become Christians of Gentile churches, *to forsake Moses, telling them not to circumcise their children, neither to walk after the customs* of the Jews. (v. 22) *What is it, therefore? they will certainly hear that thou art come.* Even some of these elders if not all of them condemned such a conduct, if Paul should be found to be guilty. It would seem to them that he had not followed out the policy of comity faithfully. Pressure was brought to bear on Paul, by their informing him as to the strength of the Judaistic party in their Jewish churches. They let him know that his Judaist enemies had been zealous in informing all the Jewish Christians in Jerusalem about him, reporting these things. As a matter of fact all of these elders had known of the fight Paul made against the Judaists in Corinth and possibly also of his Galatian epistles which clearly set forth the plan of salvation by faith alone in Jesus Christ. They now proposed a plan for the reconciliation of the situation, but a plan which would lead Paul to accept personally the obligation to keep the law himself or at least to give a visible demonstration of his loyalty to the law, so that observers seeing this manner of procedure would be convinced that Paul had not been guilty of leading Jews to abandon the law of Moses, the worship of the temple and the traditions of the Jews. The plan was that he should take the responsibility for the financing of the process of four Jewish Christians who had taken the Nazarite vow. He would thus exhibit his loyalty to the Mosaic ceremonies.

(v. 23) *Do this, therefore, which we say to thee. We have four men who have a vow on them:* (v. 24.) *these take and purify thyself with them, and be at charges for them, that they may shave their heads: and all shall know that there is no truth in the things whereof they have been informed concerning thee; but that thou also walkest orderly, keeping the law.* Paul had refused to allow these elders to impose on Titus the obligation of being circumcised, eight years before, while in the Jerusalem Conference, because it was a test case, of Gentile liberty from the bondage of circumcision and the law; and when he firmly refused, the elders complied, because the Holy Spirit had approved the conversion of Gentiles in the house of Cornelius, without circumcision or obedience to the law. The logical conclusion of this concession on their part was that, if a Gentile could be saved without the law-system, a Jew could also, since faith in Christ alone was sufficient to save. The compromise of the elders on that occasion was on the basis of a policy of comity by which Peter and the other Jewish apostles would evangelize the Jews and Paul and his co-laborers would evangelize the Gentiles. But this compromise was based on the scruples of legalists in the church and had, as its purpose and end, appeasement of these Judaists. Now, James and the Elders propose another measure of appeasement and Paul must in this case sign up and make the concession in order to bring about the reconciliation between the Jewish legalists and the Gentile Christians. They had in mind doubtless to hold on to the Jewish members of all the Gentile churches Paul had founded, and thus conserve the elements of Jewry throughout the world. They also had in mind the conservation of the Jewish nation and its traditions. To throw overboard all the heritage of Mosaism would mean to discard their most precious national heritage. They thought to conserve that and to do so meant they must oblige Jewish Christians to keep the law of Moses.

James and the Elders knew of the immoral conditions in the Corinthian church. They did not fail to inform Paul that they had been told about the case of incest and they remind him pointedly about the admonition they had sent to the Gentile Christians. (v. 25.) *But as touching the Gentiles who have believed, we wrote, giving judgment that they should keep themselves from things sacrificed to idols, and from blood, and from what is strangled, and from fornication.* It is to be noted that most of these items were regulations about foods. Paul's Judaistic enemies had accused him falsely of forbidding the Jews to circumcise their children.[2] Paul was willing to be a Jew to the Jews and so he carried out the plan suggested by the Elders since it was not contrary to the freedom of the Gospel. This had the effect of reconciling many Jewish Christians but exasperated his enemies the more.

On the next day was the great feast of Pentecost and Paul went to the temple with the four Jewish brethren who were to complete the Nazirite vow that he might defray the expense. (v. 26.) He was *to purify himself with them declaring the fulfilment of the days of purification, until the offering was offered for every one of them.* By this act, which was not one of compromise, Paul had saved the day with James and the Christian church as such, though there might be a group of Judaists in the church who were not satisfied.

But there was another dangerous factor in the situation, particularly in view of the fact that in the Feast of Pentecost there were thousands of Jews present from all the countries where Paul had been working for these eight years. Among these, many knew of Paul's activities, which they accounted as the work of a renegade Jew, proselyting his countrymen and particularly the "God-fearers" who frequented the synagogue services, leading them to accept Christianity through faith in Jesus, whom he proclaimed as the Messiah. Some of these Jews were from the province of Asia and had participated in the work of the mob in Ephesus which had made it necessary for Paul to withdraw from his large church and great work in that city.

2. Paul's experience with the howling mob. Acts 21:27-22:29. Some of these Jewish enemies of Paul, catching sight of him in the temple, cried out that "here was the heretic who had blasphened the Jewish nation, law and

2. Conybeare and Howson, *Life and Epistles of the Apostle Paul* p. 545f.

temple."[3] Instantly they "brought about him a raging sea of fanaticism." What they were unable to do with him in Ephesus, Corinth and other places they thought they could do here in fanatical Jerusalem. They merely supposed that he had brought Trophimus a Greek into the temple with him and into the holy place where no Gentile dared to enter.[4] They had seen him with this Ephesian Gentile the day before in the streets of the city. The excitement spread rapidly because his enemies stirred up all the multitude. They laid hands upon Paul accusing him of "teaching all men everywhere against the (Jewish) people and the law and this place and brought Greeks (plural) into the temple and had thus defiled the holy place" (the Jewish court into which a Gentile might not enter). Of course both of their accusations were false (vv. 27-29). But the riot spread all over the city and the people came running to the temple. The mob dragged Paul out of the temple and the Levites shut the big brass doors, so that the intended murder if carried through by the enfuriated mob would not defile the Temple. The plan of James had failed and Paul was in the hands of the howling mob and being dragged as Stephen had been to the outside where they might stone him. They were too religious to kill him in the Temple (v. 30).

But while they were dragging Paul and beating him as they went, the notice reacted the chief captain of the Roman cohort stationed in the castle of Antonia on the northwest corner of the Temple enclosure, that the whole city was in confusion. Gathering the soldiers and centurions at hand he rushed down the stairs leading to the court and came upon the tumult already active in the violence which would soon result in the intended murder. He promptly pushed his way into the midst of the mob and laid hold of Paul, commanding his soldiers to bind him with two chains to two of the guards. He made inquiry of the mob as to what the offender had done, but a mob has no mind to reason. Some shouted one thing and some another. There was only confusion. So the Roman captain could get no satisfactory answer and ordered that his prisoner be carried into the castle. There with the flagel he could find out from the prisoner himself what crime he had done. The mob, now a multitude, followed and pressed upon the band of soldiers, so that they had to carry Paul, literally lifting him above the crowd as they ascended the stairway leading to the castle. The howling mob cried out "Away with him." "Away with him!" The same angry shout which had been heard around the praetorium of Pilate when that officer brought the bleeding scourged Nazarene out to the people that they might take pity upon him and agree to his release. Paul may have witnessed that scene. He certainly was present when another mob had dragged Stephen out of the temple to the place where they stoned him, and he remembered now how he "gave his own consent" to the murder.

---

3. Cf. James Stalker, *Life of St. Paul* p. 127.

4. A warning to foreigners, engraved on a stone two feet high, three long and one thick, excavated by Haskell, is to be seen today in the Museum in Constantinople. Cf. B. W. Robinson, *The Life of Paul* p. 191.

At this moment the Roman guard had reached the landing of the stairway and Paul turning to the Captain, addressed him in Greek: *"May I say something to thee?"* The surprised Roman asked *"Do you know Greek?" Are you not the Egyptian, who before these days stirred up to sedition and led out to the wilderness four thousand men of the assassins.* Paul replied, *I am a Jew, of Tarsus in Cilicia, a citizen of no mean city: and I beseech thee, give me leave to speak unto the people.* Tarsus was a city of culture, a free city. The officer was impressed and at once gave his assent.

Taking his stand on the stairway, far above the multitude below, Paul raised his hand in his characteristic gesture and using the (Aramaic) Hebrew tongue, addressed the angry but now surprised and calming crowd. When they heard him speak in their own tongue there was "a great silence." Claudius Lysias could not understand the Aramaic but he watched the effect of Paul's speech on the crowd. Paul had informed him that he was not the Egyptian who had escaped with his life when most of his followers were slain.

Paul's speech was an apologetic narrative or story of his personal religious experience. Acts 22:1-21. He addressed them as "brethren and fathers" in a deferential way and appealed for a patient hearing of his simple defense.[5] He used their dialect to please and inform them. He declared first that he was a Jew and though born in Tarsus had been educated at the feet of Gamaliel, their great teacher in Jerusalem, being instructed in all the details of the laws and traditions of the Jews. He was only reciting to them facts which they might verify in the records of the school and also with the high priest.[6] His blood, training and religion had been the same as theirs and this was the basis of his appeal to them.

Furthermore, he was zealous against the Nazarenes as the Sanhedrin could testify, since he had once appealed to them for letters authorizing him to arrest and imprison the Christians who had fled to Damascus from Jerusalem to excape his persecution against them. (v. 5) This he did to suppress this new sect and maintain Judaism. Some members of the Sanhedrin were in the midst of them even now.

He next passes to narrate there the story of his conversion (Acts 22:6-16). This he said was due to the direct intervention of God. No one could charge him with being a renegade. He could not be so different now from what he had been before if he had not been changed by divine intervention. He was then the persecuting zealot; he is now suffering for the cause he then persecuted. On the way to Damascus he had in a vision seen with his own eyes Jesus and had spoken to him. By this experience he came to know Jesus as the Messiah. He had surrendered to him and been told by him to go into Damascus where a devout Jew Ananias would come to him and reveal to him what he should do. Ananias did come to him in Damascus three days later and restored to him his sight, impaired by the brightness of the vision, and confirmed him in his decision of surrender to Jesus as the Christ. Furthermore Ananias

5. Cf. W. O. Carver, *Com. on Acts* p. 277f.
6. Cf. Conybeare and Howson p. 555f.

baptized him (v. 16) with the Christian baptism, a pledge and symbol of his new and changed life by faith in Jesus. He also said to Saul, *The God of our fathers hath appointed thee to know his will, and see the Righteous One and to hear a voice from his mouth. For thou shalt be a witness for him unto all men of what thou hast seen and heard.* Paul was witnessing to them for Jesus even at that very moment, declaring his Messiahship.

Paul went still further with the story, omitting his experiences in Damascus and Arabia and coming directly to the short visit he made in Jerusalem with the purpose of preaching the gospel there to his former acquaintances of the school of Gamaliel and to the city. (vv. 17-21) He was in this very Temple praying about his plan when the Lord Jesus appeared to him, while in a trance, and said, "*Make haste and get thee quickly out of Jerusalem; because they will not receive of thee testimony concerning me.*" And I said, "*Lord, they themselves know that I imprisoned and beat in every synagogue them that believe on thee; and when the blood of Stephen thy witness was shed, I also was standing by, and consenting, and keeping the garments of them that slew him.*" *And he said to me,* "*Depart: for I will send thee forth, far hence to the Gentiles.*"

The apostle would have continued his address but the word *Gentiles,* so hated by the Jews, set the mob in a frenzy. They filled the air with their yells, with dust and with everything, even their garments, anything to cut short the words of the speaker, who was a despised 'Gentile-lover.' He would obliterate all race discrimination if he could!

Claudius Lysias, observing the angry sea of the mob and not understanding the Aramaic dialect, concluded that next move was to extort from this prisoner a confession of what he had done and what he said in his speech to bring on another demonstration of the bitter hatred of the people against him. He had given his prisoner a fair chance and it had failed. He conducted Paul into the place where the cruel flagel was used and had him bound with the thongs in preparation for scourging.

Then it was that Paul resorted to his only resource which would restrain the Captain of the Cohort. In the hearing of the centurion who stood by he said, '*Is it lawful for you to scourge a man that is a Roman and uncondemned?*' And the centurion hastened to Claudius Lysias and asked, *What art thou about to do? for this man is a Roman.* Immediately the chief Captain Lysias came to Paul and said, *Tell me, art thou a Roman?* As Paul replied in the affirmative, Lysias explained that he had bought his citizenship at a great price; but Paul replied, "I am a Roman born." Immediately he was loosed and the colonel was in fear because he had bound a Roman citizen. But Paul with dignity treated him with kindness and not in the spirit of pride or revenge and thus enlisted the officer's good will.

3. Before the Sanhedrin, Paul uses strategy (Acts 22:30-23:10). The only recourse now for the resolution of the case was to take the prisoner before the Sanhedrin, which was autonomous in dealing with all questions relating to the Jews, with the sole exception that they had not the power of life and death.

So the colonel on the next day ordered the assembling of the chief priests and entire Sanhedrin and presented Paul to them for a statement of their accusation against him (v. 30).

Paul came into the presence of the body of which he had probably been a member when Stephen stood before them (Acts 22:30-23:10). Taking a steady look around at them before he said anything, he began by courteously addressing them: "*Gentlemen, brethren I at every dictate of a conscience that is good have lived as a citizen for God up to this day.*"[7] The haughty high priest Ananias, who was a Sadducee, commanded that he "be smitten on the mouth," so angry was he that this prisoner should make this statement which seemed to him to be audacious. The indignation of Paul provoked by so gross an insult of ruffianism, on the part of one who should deal justly, brought forth an expression of protest and of biting sarcasm from the Apostle. "*God will smite thee, thou whited wall. Thou sittest to judge me according to the law, and commandest me to be smitten contrary to the law.*" This pronouncement of judgment by Paul may have been hasty. It naturally brought an angry reaction from the Sanhedrin attendants, who were mere sycophants and already hostile toward Paul.

Jesus denounced the Pharisees in his speech of warning to his disciples and of sarcastic reproof to the Pharisaic leaders for their hypocrisy,[8] comparing them to "whited sepulchres," fair without but foul within. The high priest was a whited wall, a barrier to the gospel, and God did smite him down. He was deposed a year later and assassinated twelve years afterward when the Jewish war broke out against the Romans. Paul's reply to these sycophants of the Sanhedrin was that he did not recognize, in the one who was presiding, the conduct expected in a high priest. Nevertheless, he rendered apology to the office of high priest and though the man might be unworthy, as Ananias was, he did not mean to "speak evil of the ruler of his people." We must believe that Paul sought the guidance of the Holy Spirit in all that he said and did in this great crisis of his life and of his work for the gospel. He was led in what he did in following out the counsel of James and the elders, "being all things to all men," in conforming thus far to their recommended plan. The church group did not come to his aid when the nationalistic group of Jews attacked him. But he got a chance through the strong hand of the Roman guard to give his testimony to the Jews, the people whom he loved, about the Messiah, Jesus, whom they again rejected now when, with mob-violence led by the Asian Judaists, they would have murdered Paul as they had Stephen.

Paul knew well the character of the Sanhedrin and the city of Jerusalem. The picture of the stoning of Stephen was yet vivid and fresh in his memory. He knew full well that the Judaists would not spare him. The Sanhedrin would have torn him in pieces if the Roman guards had not been at hand. Would they succeed with Lysias? The hours of the setting sun and the closing in of the darkness of the night brought gloomy thoughts to the almost exhausted

7. Cf. W. O. Carver *Com. Acts* p. 222f.
8. Matt. Ch. 23.

Paul. But suddenly the Lord stood by him in a vision and said, *Be of good cheer: for as thou hast testified concerning me at Jerusalem so must thou bear witness also at Rome.* So he rested in the assurance of this word of Jesus.

Lysias did not love the insubordinate and rebellious Jews too much and he had been outwitted almost by them that same day. He would not risk again, the life of a Roman citizen, for which he was responsible, in their hands. He made ample arrangements so that no band of assassins would be able to snatch his prisoner from him. He prepared with the military escort of four hundred and seventy soldiers to remove Paul by night to Caesarea, the seat of the Roman government and garrison. Hundreds of infantrymen and seventy cavalrymen besides two hundred spearmen started at the third hour of the night (nine o'clock) with Paul and Luke, his physician, who were mounted on beasts to facilitate haste. With them Lysias sent a letter to Felix, the governor explaining the reasons and necessity of his turning over this prisoner to the Governor in order to remove him from Jerusalem, where a plot had been formed to take his life away. Lysias gave himself full credit for taking care, at every cost, of this prisoner, a Roman citizen. The large escort went as far as Antipatris where the greater part returned to Jerusalem when a smaller group of the cavalrymen could finish the mission and turn the prisoner with the letter over to Felix the governor.

The letter carried the impression that Lysias had rescued Paul but failed to mention his having ordered this Roman citizen to be scourged. It said that he had found Paul guilty of nothing worthy of death or of bonds. The reason he had sent him to Caesarea was that he found out about a plot of the Jerusalem Jews to kill the prisoner. There is record that he had previously told Paul's accusers that they would have to go to Caesarea and present their accusations before Felix. The accusations related merely to questions of the laws of the Jews. When Felix received the letter and read it he inquired from what province Paul came, that he might not encroach on any other Roman official of neighboring provinces. Hearing that he was from Cilicia he ordered that the prisoner be kept in the barracks of the Herodian palace.[9] He promised Paul a full and prompt investigation. But Paul was a prisoner two years in the confinement in Caesarea. His trial took place five days after he was brought by the military escort.[10]

II Paul's Imprisonment in Caesarea. Acts, Chs. 24-26.

Caesarea was built by Herod the Great and named for the Roman emperor. It was a large city and seat of the Roman power when Paul was brought there as a prisoner. The official residence of the procurators the Praetorium, was the building in the barracks of which Paul was now to pass two years of prison experiences. This palace in which the Roman governor Felix resided was so located as to overlook the Mediterranean. Here the Lord provided a place where Paul would be obliged to rest from his strenuous career of twenty years of intense missionary activities and have the leisure to think on the great

---

9. Cf. W. O. Carver, *Com., Acts* 228f.
10. Cf. A. T. Robertson, *Epochs in the Life of Paul* p. 239f.

things of God's revelation in the Scriptures and in his own experience. It was a strange providence, but these two years of reflection brought a great harvest in the epistles of the captivity written later in Rome.

There is little left today of this great port-city with its manificent buildings of Paul's time. There had been a great heathen temple there but the sands of the sea and of a desert country round about have swallowed up most of the vestiges of the ruins[11] except the spongy looking fragments of rocks scattered widely over a large area. The scanty remains of the Cathedral of St. Paul built in Caesarea in the time of Origen and Eusebius, the church historian, are pointed out to the tourists who are interested enough to visit the Arab village to be found there today.

1. Paul under Felix, Acts Ch. 24.

Felix, the governor of Judea, and his notorious brother Pallas were formerly slaves in the house of Claudius, the Roman Emperor.[12] Due to the influence of Pallas, who had become rich Felix was freed and appointed procurator in 52 A. D. His origin was base, and when he became governor of Judea, according to Tacitus, he "exercised the prerogative of a king with all cruelty and lust in the spirit of a slave." His murder of Jonathan, the high priest of the Jews, who had presumed to expostulate with the governor on some of his evil ways, was through the use of hired assassins who perpetrated the crime in the sanctuary. This is one illustration out of many of his cruel crimes which characterized his rule, which was one of bribery, graft, and selfish indifference toward the administration of justice. Paul's Roman citizenship was a security against Jewish violence but not against the itching palms of a corrupt ruler who was open to the Jews of Jerusalem who would resort to every means. Felix was bound to protect Paul and he was doubtless impressed with a fact revealed in Paul's defense in his trial that he had come to Jerusalem with alms collected in the Gentile churches and destined for the poorer members of the church in Jerusalem. Paul might use some of that money to purchase his release. So, it seems, thought this corrupt political ruler. Better risk getting a bribe from Paul and play safe in the question of Paul's citizenship than to involve himself in the intrigues of the Jews.[13]

Felix exhibited his character of 'lust' in his matrimonial relations. His second wife was a grand-daughter of Anthony and Cleopatra, the third was Drusilla, a beautiful Jewess princess whom Felix had induced to leave her husband Azizus, king of Emesa. The corrupt reign of Felix was ended by his recall in 59 A. D. Such was the character of the man who dismissed his prisoner to a cell in the barracks of the Praetorium when he had read the letter from Lysias.[14]

It took five days for Ananias the high priest to get the charges against Paul organized. He employed Tertulus, a Roman lawyer-orator, and brought

11. H. V. Horton, *In the Footsteps of Paul* p. 419ff.
12. Cf. Conybeare and Howson, *Life and Epistles of the Apostle Paul* pp. 566-577.
13. W. O. Carver, *Com. on Acts* Ch. 24.
14. David Smith, *Life and Letters of St. Paul* p. 430ff.

with him certain elders for the prosecution of the hated renegade Paul. (24:1). Tertulus was adept in flattery. He probably spoke in Greek, because the Jews were present and gave their assent (24:9). He praised the governor as a reformer with many smooth phrases of unmerited adulation. He damned Paul as "this insolent fellow," a pest, a common nuisance.[15] In his presentation of the case he accused Paul of three things: treason, heresy and sacrilege. Naturally the Roman lawyer would present, as the first of these accusations, that of sedition or treason against the Roman government. To this Paul in his defense replied that the time was too short (v. 11). Half the time he was in Jerusalem he spent in the temple as a Nazarite and the other half as a Roman prisoner in the castle. As to his being disorderly and disloyal to the Roman government anywhere there was no proof of such. The second accusation was that Paul was a ringleader of the sect of Nazarenes. Paul in his defense, after Tertulus finished his speech, stated that he believed in the Jews' Scriptures and possessed and lived by the same religious hope as the Jews. Christianity could not be classed as a "religio illicita."[16] Of less importance to Tertulus but of more to the Judaists of Jerusalem was the charge of trying to desecrate the temple. The charge of having taken Greeks into the holy place was no longer made. Paul stated that he was in the temple fulfilling the rite of purification, having brought also alms to the temple for his Jewish people (vv. 17, 18). The competent witnesses to testify on this point did not appear (v. 19). He challenged those who were present as to his conduct in the council meeting. (vv. 20, 21). Paul ignored the charge of being 'a pestilent fellow.' His personal presence and his able defense of himself demonstrated a character too dignified to deign to respond to so base a slur as that. And Paul was no fawning sychophant to seek his release through flattery, not to say insincere mendacity. The charge of insurrection was groundless, that of heresy fell to the ground because of the close relationship between Christianity and Judaism in doctrine and association. The Romans had never considered Christianity a separate religion. Finishing the defense, Felix decided to adjourn the case sine die or until he could confer with Lysias about certain points involved. The prisoner would be detained in custody being granted libera custodia which included superior fare and the privilege of the ministrations and society of his friends who might visit him. Paul's defense was masterly and not only disposed of the charge of profaning the temple but it put the Jews on the defensive in the first charge of sedition and annulled the charge of heresy because the Roman law allowed Judaism.[17] Felix would hear from Lysias about the recent facts on this point. Luke was probably in Caesarea and with Paul much of the time during the two years.[18] He was probably gathering up the Christian traditions from various Christian centers in Palestine and other places where the eyewitnesses could be found.

---

15. Cf. A. T. Robertson, *Epochs in the Life of Paul* p. 240-246.
16. Cf. An unlawful religion, not permitted in the Empire.
17. Cf. Robertson, A. T., *Epochs in the Life of Paul* p. 244.
18. Cf. Acts 27:1.

There were many compensations for God's servant as he walked up and down the barracks which looked out upon the Mediterranean, around which his activities had planted a circle of Gospel lighthouses the beams from which penetrated to far distant places of the known world.[19] Now and then his messengers would come and bring reports of the progress of the work and receive short written or verbal messages back from him with many a suggestion about problems which vexed them.

He was visited by Felix now and then and on one occasion Drusilla, his Jewess princess, whom he had taken unlawfully from Azizus, King of Emesa, expressed a desire to see this Jew who had created so much trouble and hear from him some of the new heretical doctrine he was accused of teaching. Accordingly the Apostle was summoned to appear in the audience chamber, which he did, facing fearlessly, this couple whose lives were so characterized by unrighteousness and self-indulgence, with his doctrine "concerning the faith in Christ Jesus."[20] Paul, forgetting that he was a prisoner, preached to them his gospel of faith in Christ Jesus[21] and drove home on their consciences the necessity of righteousness, self-control and the future judgment, with such spiritual fervor that the guilty procurator quailed and shuddered.[22] He was convicted of his sins and terrified but stifling the impulse of the Spirit "he answered, *Go thy way for this present time; and when I have a convenient*[23] *season, I will call unto thee.* Luke, who was present, observes that the procurator *hoped withal that money would be given him by Paul: wherefore also he* sent for *him the oftener and communed with him.* By no further record of his conviction for sin or his yielding to any impressions of the Spirit, through the continued conversations with the greatest of all missionary evangelist of all times, is left. He had hardened his heart and lost the opportune time, forever.

Paul was held by the governor as a prisoner, in hope of a bribe for two years, until Felix was recalled because of mal-administration. The Jews were bitter against him. He certainly received no money from Paul. Ramsay thinks that Paul had inherited money from his family in Tarsus[24] with which he was able now to meet any just expense incurred in his trials or otherwise but there is no record that he spent money on his trials though it might have cost something to appeal to Caesar; and we know he lived in his own hired house in Rome. Felix did not liberate Paul though he recognized his innocence, but left him to languish in prison. If he should liberate him, the Jews would be more bitter.

The call to his work as he looked out across the Mediterranean must have been a constant heartache to one so accustomed to activity in the great missionary vision and plan of his life.

---

19. Cf. A. T. Robertson, *Word Pictures,* Acts, in loco.
20. Cf. Acts 24:24.
21. Cf. A. T. Robertson, *Epochs in the Life of Paul.*
22. Cf. David Smith; *Life and Letters of St. Paul.*
23. Cf. *Kairon,* an opportune time or opportunity. p. 480ff.
24. Cf. W. M. Ramsay, *Paul the Traveler and Roman Citizen* in loco.

But we may be sure that Paul's hours were not spent in pining. He did not have the liberty in Caesarea which he afterwards enjoyed in Rome, to preach to the people, though bound with a chain to a soldier guard. But his instruction to his fellow-workers who visited him would be a perpetual training school of the greatest value. He was a vital factor thus in the building of the working force. Philip the evangelist must have availed himself of this fine opportunity frequently and led his fellow-workers in Caesarea to do the same. A great Christian church grew up later in history in that city, which gave to the world Origen one of the outstanding theologians of all times, and Eusebius the greatest of the ancient Church historians. One of the most famous cathedrals was built in the locality where the Apostle passed two years in prison and substantial vestiges of its ruins are to be seen yet by travelers who pass that way.[25]

Another boundless occupation in which this great missionary spent much of his time was that of delving into the profundities of the Old Testament Scriptures, especially the writings of the prophets. Doubtless he made good use of the results of Luke's research activities in collecting the Christian traditions. It is well nigh impossible to think that Luke would leave his great friend and hero longer than was necessary to sally forth into the various centers of Christian work in Palestine, seeking out every eyewitness yet living who was with Jesus during the years of his public ministry. Many witnesses of those who had seen Jesus were yet alive.[26] Paul would be deeply interested in these traditions and especially in Luke's superb collection of both the verbal traditions and written documents of all kinds embodying or quoting any of the teachings or giving any account of the works of the strenuous ministry of the Lord Jesus.[27]

The 'captivity epistles' were written later but materials which went to compose them, we may well conclude, were drawn largely from the profound meditations of Paul, during these two years of confinement in Caesarea when he did not have 'a hired house' as later in Rome where he could carry on his evangelistic activities during much of the time. There is no record of any letters he wrote to the churches nor is there any account of conversions through his efforts in Caesarea. He was within the territory of the 'circumcision' and the policy of comity was one of the galling bands which bound him against any effort in Palestine to win the Jews to Christ. There is no record of any visits from the brethren of Jerusalem nor even of Jewish brethren from any place, though doubtless there might have been some from the churches in Asia and Europe. It was not popular for Jewish Christians to come about Paul much. In Rome the Apostle invited the Jews to come and let him explain his work past and present to them for their enlightenment as to his character and intentions; and some of them came. Only Luke, who was a Gentile, was constant in his ministrations medically and otherwise to Paul's needs

25. Cf. H. V. Morton, *In the Steps of St. Paul* p. 405ff.
26. Cf. I Cor. Ch. 15:6.
27. Cf. Conybeare and Howson, *Life and Epistles of St. Paul* p. 576.

while in prison in Rome and as we must believe also here in Caesarea (Acts 27:1). But Paul went on faithfully in his service of the Master regardless of how his Jewish brethren might neglect him.

2. Paul before Festus. Acts Chs. 25, 26. Festus was a better man morally than Felix, but Paul and the gospel fared no better in his presence. He was anxious to please the Jews and went up to Jerusalem three days after his arrival in Caesarea.[28] There he met the Jewish leaders, who lost no time in asking him the favor of having Paul brought up to Jerusalem for trial. Their hidden intention was to have Paul assassinated on the way over. Festus did not fall for their plan but replied that he was returning to Caesarea shortly and the competent accusers should prepare to go to Caesarea and there present their accusations according to the routine order of the Roman court. During the next eight or ten days the Judaistic leaders availed themselves of every opportunity to prepare the mind of this new Roman governor to understand as they did the case of the trouble-maker Paul. They did not take the Roman lawyer Tertulus as before with them, but selected those of their number who were most bitter against the Apostle to represent the Sanhedrin against Paul. There was no delay when Festus returned to Caesarea, but the trial was called for the next day; and these Jews stood round the prisoner, bringing various heavy accusations against him, when he was brought into the audience chamber. But while the same charges were made which had been preferred in their previous trial before Felix they were unable to prove their charges and Paul's simple defense was a declaration: *Neither against the law of the Jews, nor against Caesar have I sinned at all.* Festus could see that Paul's offense, which so incensed the Jews, related to Paul's religious views which were not acceptable to them. Festus was perplexed not understanding their sectarian views, because he saw nothing worthy of death in Paul. The Jews were clamoring for this very thing. The new governor bethought him of a way out of the difficulty, since the problem involved, apparently in the main, the divergence of conflicting religious opinions. This excuse seemed plausible at least and so he proposed to Paul that the examination of these questions be made before the Jewish Sanhedrin in Jerusalem, but under his own supervision and assessment. This would please the Jews and the governor promised he would be there to safeguard the life of a Roman citizen. Paul knew very well that the assassins, backed secretly by the approval of the Jews in Jerusalem, would be waiting to carry out their plan before he should reach that city. Even if he should arrive there he could not be assured of much protection from this affable politician, who as governor was seeking to ingratiate himself with the Jewish provincials. Paul was divinely guided in his decision and surprised Festus by his calm but bold declaration in response to the proposal of a trial in Jerusalem; *I am standing before Caesar's tribunal* (in Caesarea); that is *where I ought to be judged. I have wronged the Jews in no respect as you know perfectly well. If then I am a wrongdoer and have done anything worthy of death I do not refuse to die; but if none of those things is true where-*

28. Conybeare and Howson, *Life and Epistles of St. Paul* pp. 578ff.

of these accuse me, then no one can give me up to them, Appelo Caesarem![29] *I appeal to Caesar!* Paul thus deliberately chose to avail himself of this privilege of Roman citizenship. He could not hope to secure justice before the Sanhedrin. His recent experience justified his decision. He well knew the fate of Stephen, to say nothing of Jesus the Christ, who, being what He was, went from the mock trials of the Sanhedrin to the cross of Calvary. Festus hastily conferred with his counsellors and came back with the announcement: *You appealed to Caesar; to Caesar you shall go!* (Ch. 25:1-12).[30] Not all cases of appeal were honored but about that of Paul there was no question. To make sure Festus had called a meeting of his counsellors and then announced his decision.

3. Paul speaks before Agrippa. Acts 26. Festus had been willing to dispose of the vexatious case of Paul by turning him over to the Sanhedrin, thus gaining the favor of the Jews. He offered to Paul, when he proposed this method of resolving his case, the protection of his personal presence as in the trial in Jerusalem a guarantee for his safety. When Paul appealed to the supreme court of Nero, Festus found himself under the necessity of presenting in legal form the charge against Paul and an explanation for why he had not liberated the prisoner when he was not found guilty of anything worthy of death.

It happened about this time that Agrippa II King of Chalcis, grandson of Herod the Great and son of Agrippa I, who had beheaded the apostle James (Acts 12:1-3), had come with his sister, the infamous Bernice, on a visit of courtesy to the new governor, Festus. King Agrippa II was well acquainted with the Jewish law and customs and was at this time superintendent of the temple, in Jerusalem, with the power of appointing the high priest. The visit was opportune for Festus, who took advantage of the opportunity to talk over the whole case with his distinguished visitor. Agrippa expressed an interest in seeing the prisoner and hearing him about 'one Jesus who had died and was alive again.' Festus appointed the next day for the interview. Agrippa came in great pomp, bringing Bernice with him.

The royal party was ushered into the audience chamber of the Praetorium with all the glitter of military and civic display and after the statement of the case by Festus the prisoner was conducted to their midst bound with a chain to a soldier. Festus with courtesy explained his perplexity as to what he should say in his legal statement of the case to the Emperor which did not furnish the governor with any clear charges to send to Rome,[31] and turned the presidency of the meeting over to King Agrippa who presiding, for courtesy to Festus, condescendingly granted Paul persmission to speak.

Beginning with his characteristic gesture, Paul raised his hand and addressed the distinguished but sinful visitors first with a complimentary but true word

---

29. Latin form of the appeal.
30. The imperial tribunal had become a kind of supreme court of appeals from all inferior courts in Rome or the Provinces.
31. Cf. G. H. Gilbert, *The Student's Life of Paul* pp. 199f.

of salutation to Agrippa who had for several years been king and was now on good terms with the Jewish leaders. He had lately shown a strong hand, deposing Ananias and appointing Ishmael as high priest in his stead. Paul felt free to speak to Agrippa. *"I think myself happy, King Agrippa, that I am to make my defense before thee this day touching all the things whereof I am accused by the Jews: especially because thou art expert in all customs and questions which are among the Jews: wherefore I beseech thee to hear me patiently."* (Acts 26:2, 3). Paul's defense was a personal narrative of his life from his youth on. Many of those who were present in this assembly, he declared, had known of his student life in the school of Gamaliel. After reference to this he rehearsed the grounds on which he was being accused. (vv. 4-7). The real cause of the hostility of the Jews against him was the hope of the Messianic promise which all the tribes of Israel longed to see realized. This promise had been realized already in the Messiah, Jesus, proof of which was that he had risen from the dead. His accusers had failed to recognize in Jesus the fulfillment of this promise. He had not of himself come into this belief, as his former life of a Pharisee who actively persecuted the 'Nazarene sect,' proved. He had gotten authority from the chief priests and led many of this sect to prison and to death. He had diligently "procured the adverse vote" leading to their condemnation, when they refused to recant and 'blaspheme' the name of Jesus.

The next and most vital argument of his discourse disclosed how he had come to this complete change in his attitude toward the Nazarene and his followers. He was on his way to Damascus with authority to arrest many who had fled to that city to escape from persecution which he was waging against them in Jerusalem, when he had a vision. *Whereupon as I journeyed to Damascus, O King, I saw on the way a light from heaven, above the brightness of the sun, shining round about me and them that journeyed with me; and when we were all fallen to the earth, I heard a voice saying unto me in the Hebrew language, "Saul Saul, why persecutest thou me? It is hard for thee to kick against the good." And I said, "Who art thou Lord"? And the Lord said, "I am Jesus whom thou persecutest. But arise, and stand upon thy feet: for to this end I have appeared unto thee, to appoint thee a minister and a witness both of the things wherein I will appear unto thee; delivering thee from the people (Gentiles), unto whom I send thee, to open their eyes, that they may turn from darkness to light and from the power of Satan unto God, that they may receive remission of sins and an inheritance among them that are sanctified by faith in me. Wherefore, O king Agrippa, I was not disobedient unto the heavenly vision.* (Acts 26:13-19).

Obedience to that 'heavenly vision' had been the sole cause of the Jewish opposition (vv. 19-22a). His teaching, he affirmed, was in accord with that of Moses and the prophets (vv. 22b, 23). Paul was a strict Pharisee, believing in Moses and the prophets; he believed in the Messianic promise made to the fathers; and his opponents believed the same. Paul, before his encounter with Jesus on the Damascus road, had not believed in His Messiahship. But now he was at the command of the risen Christ, who "should suffer according to the Scriptures and on the third day arise from the dead to be a light not only to the Jews but unto the whole world of humanity." (vv. 22b-23). He is under commission of the risen Messiah to go to both Jews and Gentiles and announce to them that *"they should repent and turn to God, doing works worthy of repentence."* It was for this cause they had seized him in the temple and tried to kill him. As for his present status he is depending upon the help from God and going forward with his work of testifying both to small and great. His message about Christ the Messiah is wholly in accord with what Moses and the prophets said would come to pass. If the Jews did not accept the universal message for Jews and Gentiles alike it was no fault of his. How did this sound to Agrippa? Paul was not concerned so much about that.

At this juncture Festus, not comprehending anything of the Hebrew Scriptures, came to the conclusion that Paul was a fanatical, half-crazed, religious enthusiast. He interrupted the speaker crying out: "You are mad Paul!" "Your great learning is turning you mad."[32] "No" answered Paul "I am not mad, Festus, your Excellency. These are words of sanity I am uttering."

Then Paul appealed to Agrippa. The narrative and impassioned address of Paul had evidently deeply impressed the King. He was a Jew and understood Jewish history and knew about their hope for a Messiah. Paul was indeed a masterly speaker and the Jewish King, though deeply immersed in voluptious criminal sin of the darkest dye, was profoundly moved. This argument of Paul was one of the masterpieces of spontaneous eloquence of all time. "King Agrippa, do you believe the Prophets?" he said and not waiting for an answer added "I know you do." Agrippa was in a place of great embarrassment. He could not commit himself before Festus the Procurator. With a non-committal complacency Agrippa said to Paul: *"With but a little* (effort or time) *you are trying to persuade*[33] *me to make me a Christian.* Whether these words were spoken by Agrippa partially in sarcasm or not, Paul took them as a sincere expression and said, *"I would to God that whether with little or with much* (effort), *not you only, but also all that hear me this day, might become such as I am,* (a believer in Christ) *except these bonds.*

Paul had finished his appeal. *The King rose up, and the governor, and Bernice and they that sat with them;* and when they had withdrawn from the audience chamber, *they spoke one to another, saying, This man is doing nothing worthy of death or of bonds. And Agrippa said unto Festus, "This man might have been set at liberty, if he had not appealed unto Caesar."* Thus Paul, though not guilty, was sent to Rome as a prisoner.

---

32. Cf. David Smith, *Life and Letters of St. Paul* p. 488.
33. Conative present active indicative of *peithō*.

CHAPTER XXI

Paul's Voyage to Rome and His Imprisonment

Acts 27:1-28:37

Paul had long desired to go Rome and had made his plan to plant Christianity in at least one strategic center of each of the Roman provinces. After finishing his work in Ephesus he was ready to turn his face toward Rome the great capital of the Empire and greatest of all strategic centers of the world for the gospel. He is at last ready to go though it must be to face Nero one of the worst Emperors who ever sat upon the throne of the Empire in a trial. He was sent in bonds, though innocent, along with some other prisoners who were destined to die in the great Coliseum arena, to make a 'Roman holiday' for the blood-thirsty populace. This part of the narrative of Luke in Acts was transcribed from his diary as an eyewitness and participant in most of the remarkable experiences recorded. It is a masterpiece of the historian who even in the preface to his Gospel[1] reminds one of Thucidydes the greatest of the Greek historians. Here Luke is at his best sketching the incomparable picture of his great hero,[2] the Apostle to the Gentiles, as Paul faced, what seemed to be the final and greatest test of his life, in the Roman capital. The Apostle is to 'testify' before the Roman imperial court for his life, while at the same time planning and personally launching a campaign for the evangelization of the 'inhabited world'[3] the influence of which campaign would solidify everywhere the work of the gospel already planted, and silence forever the cavil of his old Judaists enemies who had dogged his steps everywhere he went. He was to demonstrate also, in his personal example, the heroic character of the workers and the work, which would be required to carry through this aggressive campaign to a complete victory. In chains he preached and taught in Rome incessantly while awaiting the uncertain issues of a trial before the monstrous Nero. His letters written while in the period of his first imprisonment were to be the most profound of all his writings, coming as they did out of the heart of the 'prisoner of the Lord,' "a man in Christ."[4] He was to give to the world within these epistles, the greatest Christology, and the greatest 'world philosophy' ever penned by the hand of man.

---

1. Cf. Luke 1:1-4.
2. Cf. Sir William Ramsay, *Paul the Traveler*.
3. Cf. eikoumena
4. Cf. James Steward, *A Man in Christ* (the whole book).

It is no wonder then that Luke penned in the narrative of this long voyage of the Apostle an account which is "recognized as a classic for its literary skill, descriptive vividness, detailed accuracy even to the exact scientific use of terms, and for its skillful proportion, so that the great idea of the superintending presence of God dominates the whole story notwithstanding the entrance of so many secondary interests. The twenty-seventh chapter of Acts (also) has been a bulwark of defense against the radical assaults on Luke's reliability as a historian."[5]

1. The account of the first stages of the journey takes the voyagers from Caesarea around the coast by Sidon to a southern port of the island of Crete (Acts 27:1-13). Agrippa had announced the verdict of the council in Caesarea: "This man might have been set at liberty if he had not appealed into Caesar." But the appeal could not be denied and so Paul with other prisoners was entrusted to a centurion called Julius of the Augustan or imperial cohort. Paul's doctor and great friend Luke and another faithful brother Aristarchus of Thessalonica, who later suffered imprisonment with Paul, were allowed to accompany him in the voyage as his ministering friends. They may have been registered, as Ramsay thinks, under the classification of 'slaves' though this is hardly probable. Luke would have a good excuse to go along as Paul's physician.

The embarkation of Caesarea was in a ship of Adramyttium which was about to sail to places on the coast of Asia. The voyagers would have to trans-ship in Myra to a vessel going to Italy.

On the first day of the voyage they reached Sidon. Having sailed up the coast, this being a coastal vessel, they dropped anchor at Sidon where Julius, the kind centurion, allowed Paul to go ashore "to his friends and refresh himself." Paul had visited the little church in Tyre nearby about two years before. The centurion was impressed with the personal dignity and bearing of Paul and treated him, from the first, humanely and with the utmost deference.

The coasting voyage was accomplished rapidly as far as Sidon and somewhat less speedily on to Myra.[6] There *the centurion found a ship from Alexandria sailing for Italy.* Thus far they had avoided the contrary winds, sailing under the lee or shelter of the island of Cyprus, the first mission field of Barnabas and Saul. On the opposite side Paul could see the hills of Cilicia, his native province, in the distance and he could almost glimpse Tarsus, the city of his boyhood days. He would here remember the first nine years of his active ministry when he was testing out in the province of Cilicia the new gospel and theology of the risen Christ Jesus. Further on the ship passed the lowlands of Pamphylia recalling to the Apostle the experiences of the first missionary tour with Barnabas from Perga via Antioch to Iconium, Lystra and Derbe. Thus far their sailing had been without great difficulty and they reached Myra and Julius passed his convoy to the grain ship from

5. Cf. W. O. Carver, *Com. on Acts* p. 253, for this remarkable descriptive characterization.
6. Cf. Periodoi Barnabae (quoted by Ramsay) *Paul the Traveler*, p. 318, 320.

Egypt, one of the many that supplied the great capital Rome with food. From this port they must face a strong westerly wind and hug the coast in order to make but slow progress, but rounding cape Salome and sailing *under the lee of Crete, coasting along with difficulty, we came to Fair Havens, nigh to which was a city Lasea* (vv. 7, 8).

They must have arrived there some time late in September.[7] It had been a slow voyage from Myra, attended with great difficulty due to the adverse westerly wind so they decided to delay at Fair Havens waiting for better weather for they were in the shelter of the island from the N. W. wind.

The ancient Greeks liked the sea but these Romans disliked, even hated it and the Israelites loathed and feared[8] it. Some reason why most of the ancient peoples feared the sea was that their ships were small[9] and unsafe, their coasts unlighted, they had no compasses, and in the darkness of night and cloudiness of the day, when no land was in sight, they were utterly lost. The reefs also were unmarked and ships frequently struck them even in broad daylight and went down.[10]

A council was held after some days in which the Centurion presided to decide what they should do about the rest of the voyage. According to Ramsay the Centurion outranked the Captain of the ship and so had the final decision of the course to be followed. These two officers counselled with Paul whose long and varied experience in sailing as well as otherwise was valuable and so recognized by all. The question to be decided was whether they should winter at Fair Havens or go on to Phoenix, a better port of Crete about forty miles further west, (Modern Lutro).[11] The professional opinions of the Captain and the Centurion carried the majority of the voyagers and Paul's advice, though based on reasonable grounds and with warning against the perils was not followed, much to the regret of all later on. The time of the Fast of the Atonement, corresponding to the (equinox) was past and the period was one of great danger for sailing. Said Paul: (v. 10.) *Sirs, I perceive that the voyage is likely to be accompanied with hardship and much loss, not merely to the ship and cargo but also to our lives*: He knew well how to include in his appeal all the interests both material and other, but the nautical opinions of the sailing master and the captain, and the fact of the shortness of the distance to Phoenix[12] prevailed with the centurion, especially when the weather conditions seemed to have changed and a southerly wind had

7. Cf. Ramsay W. M., *Paul the Traveler*, Ch. Voyage to Rome.
8. Cf. Old Testament literature, Metaphors.
9. Cf. Conybeare and Howson p. 588f. Five hundred to a thousand tons was the limit of cargo for most ancient merchantmen, and seven knots or less than ten miles an hour the rate of sailing. These ships could sail in seven points of the wind. It was a westerly and north-westerly wind that was impeding their progress.
10. Cf. H. V. Morton, *In the Steps of St. Paul* pp. 428-29.
11. Cf. Gilbert, G. H., *The Students Life of Paul* p. 203f. The size of the ship to which Julius transferred his prisoners was probably about 500 tons' cargo and carried 276 passengers on this voyage.
12. The distance was about forty to fifty miles. Cf. H. V. Morton, *In the Footsteps of St. Paul.*

started up. Anyway, the port of Fair Havens was poorly suited in comparison with that of Phoenix and if they could get that much further without too much danger it would be some gain. The season for navigation ending about the middle of November might in this case yet give them a chance to get across to Sicily and even to Italy.

2. Two weeks of storm ending in a wreck was to be the penalty for this decision which seemed not to have been without fair reasons. (vv. 14-43). Soon after putting out to sea from Fair Havens there was a sudden change of the wind, at first, followed quickly by a hurricane from the Northeast from the mountains of Crete, seven thousand feet high. It "snatched hold of the ship," which could not weather the gale but only suffer itself to be borne helplessly before the storm. Happily they were driven after considerable time into a half sheltered area of a small island, Cauda, which gave them a momentary respite and opportunity to haul aboard the small life-boat and that with great difficulty.[13] They also hastened to brace the hull of the ship, frapping it by passing cables around it transversely, supplemented with timbers. Borne on at the mercy of the typhoon,[14] the blanching fear fell upon them lest they should drift into the quick sands of the Syrtis, off the coast of Africa, where many ships had been lost beyond recovery. The horror of such a death by sinking beneath the sand appalled them. In order to retard the progress of the ship which perhaps was being driven in that direction they lowered the gear, which was some device of the nature of an anchor, and which caused the ship to be whipped about much and belabored by the storm. On the next day they began throwing overboard some of the cargo and the day following all hands (including Luke) threw out the loose furnishings of the ship.

The tempest grew ever worse and without sun or stars there was no way of knowing where they were at any time. The storm now was so violent that "*all hope that we should be saved was gradually taken away. And when there had been long abstinence from food, then Paul stood forth in the midst, of them, and said: "the right course gentlemen, was to have hearkened to me and not to have set sail from Crete and thus incurred this trouble and loss* (v. 22.) *And my advice to you in the present is to take heart; for loss of life there shall be none among you, but of the ship. For there stood by me this night an angel of the God, whose I am, whom also I serve,* (v. 24) *saying: "Fear not, Paul; thou must stand before Caesar; and, lo! there have been granted thee by God all them that sail with thee.* (v. 25) *Wherefore take heart, gentlemen; for I believe God, that it shall be even so as it hath been spoken unto me. Howbeit we must be cast upon a certain island.*

This supreme emergency was Paul's opportunity to take the lead in the situation (vv. 21-26). After reminding them casilly of his advice which they had not taken, he now offers again in the hour of their greatest crisis his counsel, based on the solid ground of a vision he had experienced, of a special mes-

---

13. Cf. W. O. Carver *Com.* p. 256ff.
14. It was a Northeastern Euraquilo from the mountains of Crete.

senger, an angel from his God, with a message that concerned them all. He assured them there was to be no loss of any of their lives. Only the ship would be lost but all 276 of the passengers and crew would escape to an island. His God had answered his request for their deliverance and it had been granted. He was assured that it would be even so because he himself must give his testimony in Rome. This revived hope in the hopeless. They understood what his gospel testimony was.

Paul further took his place to prepare them for the trying experience ahead when the ship should near land. Two weeks of such a tempest, and that in so poor a vessel that they all were hopeless was enough to completely prostrate them, since there had been no regularity in the taking of food.

The sailors whose ears were accustomed to the sounds of the sea already sensed that the ship was approaching land. The sea became choppy. In fear they took soundings and sure enough the first test showed twenty and a second, taken, after a brief interval, registered fifteen fathoms. The breakers could be heard ahead in the black-out of a starless night. The sound indicated a rocky shore. The sailors, now alarmed, gave order to lower the anchors and four were dropped. To hear the roar of the breakers, at every slight lull in the storm, and not be able to see the coast struck terror into their hearts. The leak at the mast was rapidly increasing. The listing ship might go down at any time.

At this moment of greatest peril there was a selfish scheme conceived by the sailors, to lower the life boat and abandon the ship and its passengers to their fate. But Paul was alert and sensing the treachery informed the Centurion, who, with military despatch ordered the ropes cut that held the lifeboat, leaving it to drift away.

Paul was now virtually in command, and without any assumption of authority he stood forth in the midst of the passengers and exhorted them to partake of sufficient food. While he was calmly giving thanks to God and partaking heartily of the food himself, the example was followed by all. Their spirits and their bodies also were revived by the religious example and confident assurance, which Paul had imparted, that they would escape.

Day broke and the ship was hastily lightened by throwing overboard the cargo of wheat. Thus lightened, the vessel might be run aground. Having decided on the sandy beach near the inlet of a creek which seemed favorable for such a grounding of the ship, some of the sailors unlashed the lashings which secured the rudders and hoisted the foresail with which to aim the ship, while others cut the boat's hawser or cables attached to the anchors. The plan proved partly successful but the bow of the vessel stuck fast in a concealed shoal and the stern of the vessel was rapidly being shattered to pieces by the terrific force of the breakers. It was a terrible sight and they were not out of danger yet!

The soldiers, thinking that some of the prisoners might escape, asked the Centurion if they should kill them and thus avoid the penalty of paying with their own lives the loss. But, again, we see the great influence Paul had won over the Centurion, for this high-minded officer, through the admiration and respect he had for Paul, took the responsibility for the prisoners on himself and prevented this inhuman and useless cruelty. The Centurion desired to save Paul's life even if it might be at the risk of his own.

Counseled by Paul, this strong man next gave orders that all who knew how to swim should cast themselves into calmer waters of the more protected bay and make their way first to land so that they could help others who would follow on planks and other objects from the ship. This is a vivid picture of all the large group of passengers getting out from the stranded ship and struggling to get to the shore by various means.[15] Sure enough all succeeded, without the loss of one, as Paul had said they would. He was the master of the situation, under God. On this voyage he had won the confidence of the Roman Centurion Julius and of all the crew and passengers including the prisoners. Because of him, the God of Israel became the Lord of Providence ruling the seas and the lives of men. To his own friends he became the man and hero of the hour and God's great Apostle. His testimony to Jesus as the Messiah and Lord of History became valid in the experiences of all on board. This was but a token of the contagious influence he would soon exert in the great capital of the Roman world.

3. Three months with the Barbarians on the Island Melita.[16] Acts 28:1-10. The inhabitants of this island were civilized and spoke the Greek language (koinē). All of those living near the place where the ship was wrecked soon found out and came rushing down in spite of the rain and wind storm yet raging. They joined in helping many get to the shore and aided Paul and others in getting a fire started, as their homes were in a town, Melita, some distance away. They manifested an open-hearted kindness toward the wet, shivering, and exhausted passengers bringing to them food and seeking to aid them in every way. Paul was especially active in looking after his fellow passengers. He had experienced, now, himself his fourth shipwreck and knew well how to sympathize with those with whom he had been so greatly used in delivering from an untimely death. He was gathering fagots with others and placing them on the bonfire to warm and dry the clothing of the forlorn voyagers, when, a viper came out of the brush-wood he had brought and fastened itself upon his hand. The snake was considered poisonous by the natives who thought that this prisoner must have committed some grave crime and avenging Justice of some divinity had overtaken him, even though he had escaped the perils of the sea. They expected to see him fall dead and when he did not, like the Lystrans they concluded he must be a divine being. The serpent was "hanging from his hand." It is more in keeping with the whole situation to admit divine intervention in cure in this case than to try to explain it by saying that the serpent may not have injected poison into Paul's hand. He had evidently been bitten. The natives learned Paul better later on and accepted his friend-

---

15. Cf. Robertson, A. T., *Epochs in the Life of Paul* p. 264.
16. The same as the modern Malta. It was part of the Roman province of Sicily and the people classed, by the Greeks, were called Barbarians.

ship and ministries along with his fellow-voyagers. Paul's congregation was increasing rapidly and he was "growing in favor with God and man," in his great gospel program. Publius, the chief magistrate of Melita and the island took Paul and his attendants Luke and Aristarchus to be his guests until they should have time to find a lodging of their own, which they did after three days.

The liberal hospitality of Publius was richly rewarded, for his father having fallen ill with intermittent fever accompanied by dysentery, as diagnosed by Doctor Luke,[17] Paul prayed and laid his hands upon the sick man, after explaining that the cure was to be by the power of Jesus Christ, and he was cured. This brought on a general healing of many sick folk on the island who came to be cured. The gratitude of the people of the island was great and expressed itself in opportune generosity in the supply of the needs of Paul and his friends during the three months of their sojourn on the island and even for the time of their voyage on to Puteoli and the overland trip to Rome. This philanthropic interest on the part of the people was indicative of a real and deep interest on their part in the gospel.

4. The final stages of the journey. (Ch. 28:11-15). While Paul and his fellow voyagers were detained in Malta, another grain[18]-ship, the Castor and Pollur, (Twin-Brothers) named for the constellation in the list of Latin gods, especially the gods of the sailors, lay at anchor in the shelter of the harbour. It was arranged that it should take the centurion Julius and his convoy to Italy.[19] About the eighth of February, the ship set sail and making a stop of three days at Syracuse, and one day at Rhegium on the extreme southern tip of Italy and reached in another day Puteoli, (Italy), her port of destination located on the bay of Naples. This principal port of the south of Italy was a hundred miles distant from Rome, by the Appian Road and 365 miles from the island of Malta.

Paul was met in Puteoli by a group of friends from Rome and at their request he was allowed to remain seven days in this city with them, as there was a Christian church community there and Paul needed a rest after the hard test of his physical strength in the voyage and especially in view of the severe ordeal out ahead. Julius was glad to comply with Paul's desire, for he had to communicate his arrival to Rome and get instructions from the imperial authorities as to the disposition of his prisoners. This would take a short time but he was quite willing to allow Paul to follow at the end of seven days in company with his friends and the one soldier-guard. Paul looked up the Christians in Puteoli and was warmly received by them. Paul was reassured by the fact that the Roman brethren received the news of his arrival. Perhaps Julius, the centurion was the self-appointed bearer of the news, for a company of brethren from the Roman church came to meet him at the Appii Forum, forty miles out from Rome. The apostle's heart was gladdened, yet

17. Cf. Hobart *Medical Language of Luke* p. 52 cited by David Smith. *Life and Letters of St. Paul* p. 499, Plural puretoi.
18. A ship loaded with wheat (not indian corn).
19. Cf. David Smith, *Life and Letters of St. Paul* p. 500.

more when a second group met him ten miles further on. Such a demonstration of love confidence and sympathy stirred the heart of the Apostle deeply. These brethren had received the great epistle Paul had written them three years before and knew how to evaluate his great personality, though they had never seen his face. Paul thanked God and took courage. Even the great Apostle to the Gentiles, who had borne the burdens of many upon his great heart for years needed the sympathy and help of real loyal brethren who could strengthen the sinews of his soul as he came to face the supreme crisis of his incomparable career.

2. Paul's First Imprisonment in Rome (v. 16) *And when we entered into Rome* Julius, the centurion delivered his prisoners to the chief of Camp, (Stratopedarch or (Latin) Princeps Perigriorum.[20] *Paul* was near to the Praetorian[21] Camp but *was permitted* to live *in his own hired house* (Acts 28:30). He had been cheered much by the many brethren in the Roman church whom he knew personally and who had gone out eagerly to meet him. His living circumstances in Rome were much better than he had enjoyed in Caesarea. He had come to Rome as a prisoner, but he was a prisoner in triumph. He thought of himself as an ambassador in chains (Eph. 6:20). He was permitted freely to preach in his own hired house and he probably preached occasionally to the Praetorian Guard. He was guarded by a soldier being bound to one at a time each day by a chain (Acts 28:20; Philemon 1, 9, 10, 13; Col. 3:18; Eph. 3:1; 4:1). The friends of the Apostle, Aristarchus, Luke and others had unrestrained access to him and many of the churches[23] were in contact with him through friends who were coming and going. He appealed to them for their prayers on behalf of the work he was carrying on (Col. 4:3, 4). It was during this period, probably early in 61 A. D., that he wrote the epistles to the Philippians, Colossians, Philemon and the (circular) letter to the Ephesians with all the churches in the province of Asia.[24]

One of the first things Paul did after arriving in Rome and getting himself disposed in his own hired quarters was to get in contact with some of the leading Jews of their extensive colony in that great Metropolis. Pursuing his policy of 'first to the Jew and then to the Greek,' just three days after he arrived,[25] not being permitted to visit the synagogue, he invited the Rulers of the Synagogue and some others to visit him that he might tell them why he had been arrested and imprisoned and also why he had been obliged to appeal to the Emperor. He declared that he was innocent of having done any wrong to the Jewish people or their customs; but they had delivered him up to the Romans, who would have set him at liberty but for some of the Jews who were bitter against him. He declared also that he had not come to Rome to

20. Cf. Mommsen, Berlin Akad. Sitzungsber p. 501 (9895) cited by W. M. Ramsay in *St. Paul the Traveler and Roman Citizen* p. 347ff.
21. Cf. Phil. 1:13; 4:22.
22. Robertson, A. T., *Epochs in the Life of Paul*, pp. 266, 267.
23. Cf. Conybeare and Howson, in loco.
24. Cf. W. M. Ramsay, *Paul the Traveler*, p. 349.
25. Robertson A. T., *Epochs in the Life of Paul* p. 268ff (Cf. Acts 28:17).

accuse his people because he nurtured the same religious hope that they did relative to the resurrection from the dead.

They, in their turn, coolly ignored any knowledge of his case, not having received any letter from the Sanhedrin against him. They would hear him concerning his sect though they harbored no high opinion as to the Nazarenes, 'so spoken against everywhere.'

They were willing to hear and so Paul marked a day for them to come, which they did in considerable numbers. The Apostle preached to them, proving that Moses and the Prophets foretold the coming of a Messiah, and that he had appeared in the person of Jesus. His discourse ran through the entire day and the result was that some believed but others disbelieved. To the latter the Apostle cited the prophecy of Isaiah 6:9ff, tactfully warning them of the curse upon those who obstinately refuse to believe. Nevertheless they remained obstinate, but Paul knew the Gentiles would believe (Acts 28:28).

It was now after the *quinquennium* or first five years of the administration of the boy Emperor, Nero, had passed. The Prefect of the Praetorian Guard proved to be well disposed toward Paul and Seneca the brother of Gallio knew about the Apostle and his excellent work in Corinth, where he had been befriended by the Proconsul of Achaia, (Gallio), when attacked by his Judaistic enemies in 52 A. D. Seneca, the greatest philosopher of the Romans, wielded for a time a strong influence over Nero the handsome young emperor, who, at first, followed the example of his predecessor Augustus in "liberality, clemency and courtesy." For the period of five years his administration went well.

Luke, for some reason did not give many details about the circumstances[26] of the activities of Paul during this period of his imprisonment. To be sure we know from Paul's Prison Epistles most of the things necessary to be known. Luke may or may not have had the intention of writing a third book, filling out the record of Paul's life to the end.

We know that Paul's friends from near and from afar came to see him and some of them were with him almost constantly. He calls Aristarchus "his fellow-prisoner" because he seems to have dwelt with Paul in his rented dwelling for some time. The word of God "was not bound" in Paul though he was chained to a soldier always. He would thus have an opportunity to converse about the gospel, with each of these soldiers, who were exchanged frequently, and by this contact the word became known in all the Praetorian Guard.[27] Thus the way was opened, also, for this interesting prisoner to speak to groups of the soldiers of the Guard, on opportune occasions.

Paul became the center of a far-reaching, aggressive evangelism in Rome.[28] He was also in contact with all the work in Asia, through Epaphras from Ephesus; Luke also who was busy always coming and going, gathering

26. Cf. Robertson, A. T., *Epochs in the Life of Paul* p. 260f.
27. Cf. Phil. 1:12-18.
28. Caesar's household came to know about the gospel. Phil. 4:22.

materials for his gospel, but ever constant as Paul's physician and great friend. Tychicus, Mark, Timothy and Epaphras, the founder of many of the churches in the province of Asia were among Paul's helpers also and others visited him.

The trial of Paul was delayed, perhaps because the Roman officers Lysias, Felix, Festus, Agrippa, Julius and others had given favorable reports about Paul; also the Jerusalem Jews found it difficult to get at the matter in distant Rome. Furthermore, the Emperor was much preoccupied with his own affairs and there seemed to be no reason for hastening the trial. Anyway the prosecutors must appear and the distance to Rome was great, the circumstances unfavorable and they delayed.

While the trial was deferred, Paul did not pine but was alert to every opportunity and his testimony to Jesus as the Messiah reached far and wide not only in Rome but to distant parts, through his messengers and also through his converts, like the run-away slave Onesimus[29] who was converted out of the lowest slums of Rome and sent back to his Master Philemon a member of the church in Colossae. He bore a personal letter to Philemon, his Master, from Paul, in the brief lines of which, was a message about Christian brotherhood, which is the complete antidote to slavery. It would be also to atheistic communism that is so prevalent in our times, if the principle should be carried out in practice by the Christendom of today, including all who have really experienced genuine conversion. The experiences of a genuine conversion makes the master and the slave brethren and fellow-workers in the Lord and does away with all racial, class distinctions and all subordination in bonds too. Such was the type of aggressive evangelism carried on by the Apostle, who had to raise a manacled arm always when he began his sermon and when he pronounced the benediction. Paul's aggressive campaign soon became the talk of the city and many came to see him personally and hear his unceasing messages of teaching and preaching.

The Prison Epistles

The so called Prison Epistles, were, by almost universal opinion of the world's best Biblical scholarship, written during Paul's imprisonment in Rome.[30] During the imprisonment in Caesarea the Apostle's activity in evangelism was very limited, due to the policy of comity and to his confinement in the barracks of the Herodian praetorium. The Apostle, during these two years, carried his studies about the Christ, revealed to him on the way to Damascus as the one who dominates the history of the world on to greater depths. He presents Him here as the extra-mundane Christ, who is the intermediate agent in the creation of all things and the Lord of all created intelligences. He is the end of all things and all the procession of time moves on toward his second coming. He deals in these epistles with the relations between the believer, already

---

29. Cf. Paul's salutations to the Philippian church included also those "of Caesar's household." Cf. W. M. Ramsay, *Paul the Traveler* p. 352.

30. Cf. B. W. Robinson, *The Life of Paul* p. 206, et al.

justified, and his Lord the head of all creation and supreme ruler over all authorities and powers.[31] The union of the believer with Christ is the constant source of all his life and activity. The Christian becomes more and more like Christ by this union with him.[32]

Luke and Aristarchus left Paul in the midst of his devoted activities for a brief period and Timothy came and served as amanuensis while Paul was writing the 'captivity' epistles, the first of which was written to the Philippians. This letter was written when Epaphroditus came with a gift from the church in Philippi and remained to aid the apostle in his strenuous activities in the ministry of the gospel. Luke later informed the church in Philippi[33] of Paul's circumstances and they at once sent this beloved brother to bear their gift and he remained to render devoted service as the defender of the truth until he fell ill and almost despaired of his life. Paul was in need of the material help and the church in Philippi which had been so faithful in previous years now sent a liberal gift to sustain the aged founder of their church. They sent with the gift a letter expressing their loyalty and concern, and hoped for good tidings from him when Epaphroditus should return. The Judaistic enemies seem to have arrived in Rome[34] and Epaphroditus was the champion of defense of the truth of the gospel until he fell ill. Paul finally sent this beloved fellow-worker back to Philippi and he bore with him this beautiful letter to the Philippians, so full of the message of thankfulness, good-will, joy, and optimism, one of the best of all of Paul's letters preserved to us.

The epistles to the Colossians and Philemon were the next in order among the prison epistles, followed by Ephesians. It was toward the close of 60 A. D. when Epaphroditus left Rome with the epistle to the Philippians. Timothy was with him and Luke and Aristarchus came back to take up their ministry at the side of the aged apostle tired and worn with the long confinement, the strain of the work and of the anticipated trial. Tychicus also, who had been with Paul in Jerusalem when he was arrested, came later from Ephesus, bringing with him John Mark who sought reconciliation with Paul. Paul had known about Mark's loyal activities from others and received him graciously and gladly back into his complete confidence. One of the Jewish Christians of Rome is also found among Paul's fellow-workers at this time.

Epaphras had been with Paul for some time, serving the apostle in his home, during the temporary absence of Aristarchus. This worker had been very useful in the work of Paul in Ephesus and had been chiefly responsible for scattering the gospel from Ephesus throughout the province of Asia. He was the founder of several churches among which were numbered those in Colossae, Hierapolis and Laodicea, all three of which he had pastored, with the help of Philemon and other workers.[35] It was he who brought news of the new heresy

31. Cf. Eph. Ch. 6; Col. 1:18 et al.
32. Cf. James Stalker, *Life of St. Paul* p. 130f.
33. Cf. Phil. 4:3 Luke must have been the sunzugos gnasios.
34. Cf. Phil. 3:2.
35. Cf. David Smith, *Life and Letters of Paul* p. 520ff.

gnosticism in the Lycus valley where these churches were located.[36] Paul now sends Tychicus and Onesimus, the converted run-away slave to Colossae bearing the letters to the Colossians, to Philemon and the circular letter, (Ephesians), to be read in all the churches in Asia. This letter seems to have been read first in Laodicea and afterwards in Colossae and perhaps other churches and finally deposited in Ephesus the largest and most influential church in the province, thus coming to be called the letter to the Ephesians.

The Trial

Ramsay thinks that Luke must have had in mind the writing of a third book as the conclusion of a rationally conceived history. The first trial of Paul seems to have begun toward the end of 61 A. D. The earlier stages of the trial were over before he wrote the Prison Epistles.[1] The Praetorium was the Imperial Court, which represented the Emperor as the 'fountain of justice,' including the Prefects and high officers of the court. Paul's influence had spread among the members of this court. The issue of the trial had been so successful in its earlier stages as to embolden the timid brethren in Rome. Paul's defence had been personal and courageous as always. It had produced a good impression on the Court.[2]

It was probably soon after Epaphroditus, Paul's "brother and companion in labor, and fellow-soldier had departed with the letter to the Philippians that Epaphras came from Colossae and brought the news about the invasion of the heretics in Asia. Paul now applied himself for some time in writing the epistles to the Colossians, Philemon and the circular letter, Ephesians, to the churches in the province of Asia Minor. Luke says Paul had remained under military custody in Rome for two whole years (Acts 28:16, 30).

It is universally believed that Paul's appeal to Caesar terminated successfully and he was acquitted of the charges made against him, and spent some years in freedom before his second imprisonment in Rome and his final condemnation and execution. The evidence for this conclusion is limited but all the historic references point the same way. Clemente mentioned it in the Philippian epistle (4:3). He was afterwards one of the bishops in Rome, and his testimony was that Paul had preached the gospel in the East and in the West and "had instructed the whole world" (the Roman Empire) "in righteousness." He also added that "he had gone to the extremity of the West." This would mean in the current terminology nothing less than Spain. Paul had intended to go to Spain.[3] (Rom. 15:24-28). Muratori's Canon A. D. 170 says in the account of *the Acts of the Apostles* that Luke relates to Theophilus events of which he was an eyewitness, as also in a separate place (Luke 22:31-33), he evidently declares the martyrdom of Peter, but (omits) "the

---

36. Cf. Col. 1:7; 4:12, 13; Acts 19:10.
1. Cf. Phil. 1:12.
2. Ramsay, W. M., *Paul the Traveler* pp. 356, 357.
3. Cf. Conybeare and Howson, *Life and Epistles of St. Paul* pp.678, 679.

journey of Paul from Rome to Spain." Eusebius tells us: "After defending himself successfully, it is currently reported that the apostle again went forth to proclaim the gospel, and afterward came to Rome a second time and was martyred under Nero." John Chrysostom also states it as an undoubted historic fact that, "Paul after his residence in Rome departed to Spain." Jerome also says: "Paul was dismissed by Nero that he might preach Christ's gospel in the West." If we add to this array of testimony the stubborn fact of the Pastoral Epistles which bear unmistakably the imprint of Paul's style and content-character, we must come to the solid conclusion that Paul traveled and laboured widely after his liberation, visiting in various places where he had wrought before and evangelizing many new places where he had never preached.

The Period of Freedom

After visiting the East Paul went to Spain and was probably there when the burning of Rome took place July 19, A. D. 64. The terrible persecution of the Christians by Nero took place during the absence of Paul because he certainly would not have escaped had he been in the hands of Nero. Christianity was now a *religio illicita* and the persecution of Christians anywhere had the imperial sanction. Paul may have remained in Spain until A. D. 66. He was concerned for Timothy and probably wrote I Timothy late in A. D. 67. The Apostle wrote Titus from Corinth and manifested his confidence in the work of that valiant preacher in the difficult field of Crete.

The Second Imprisonment

The arrest of Paul took place probably late in A. D. 67. He was held in close confinement in the Mamertine Prison. In his second trial before Nero Paul had to stand almost alone. The Lord stood by him when all others had left him. He was lonely in the prison and sent for Timothy and Mark. He was condemned this time and was executed outside of the city on the Ostian way. He wrote II Timothy a short while before his death. So ended the career of the great Apostle, the greatest Christian of the ages.

CHAPTER XXII

Epistle to the Philippians

Historical Background

1. The author of the epistle to the Philippians, by strong external and internal evidence, was Paul. What he wrote in this epistle is a *self-revelation* of his character, as reflected in his experiences during the first period of his imprisonment in Rome about 61-63 A. D. His determination to go to Rome, evidently dated from early in his ministry in Asia Minor, since his deliberate choice of many strategic centers for planting the Gospel was that of the capitals of various Roman Provinces. He did not go to Rome, which he felt he must see, in the manner he had thought but as a prisoner. On the voyage thither he had won the confidence of the Roman officer in charge of the prisoners, and so was allowed to live in his own rented house in Rome when he arrived, though he must be chained to a soldier-guard day by day. This would have been a galling chain, he being thus humiliated, had he not assumed the attitude of making use of it for the advancement of the kingdom interests. The apostle to the Gentiles had clearly grasped the universal nature of the Gospel and recognized that he, as the champion of Gentile liberty, must rise to the heights above national and racial prejudice, in order to be an adequate representative of Christianity in this corrupted Roman center of the forces of heathen darkness. He did not therefore tactlessly precipitate any contest with these forces by reproving them, but won, where possible, the favor of the rulers by frank and courteous treatment with a just loyalty to their established powers (Rom. 13). He was equally tactful in handling the Jewish people, especially those Jews who were members of the Christian congregations in this great metropolis, the greatest center of trade and civilization of the whole world. He had written the longest and greatest of all his epistles to this Roman Church before coming there and in spite of a cold reception by his Jewish brethren on his arrival, he made a special opportunity at once to have them come together in order that he might sincerely lay his whole case before them. Thus they could not accuse him of neglect and he would get ahead of his Judaizing enemies who might arrive from Jerusalem at any time.

Paul made as good use of such liberty as his favorable prison conditions permitted, and the Gospel "cut its way forward" among Nero's Imperial guard and with other Romans also. He had "appealed to Caesar" and Nero did not hasten the trial, so the prisoners carried on diligently his work of personal evangelism and evangelization of the city, working in contact with the Roman Christians. Several fellow-workers who came from various places to be with him, helped in the work and served as messengers to and from the churches he had founded in various parts of the Empire, and thus greatly aided the aged apostle in this important activity. His ministry thus went on vigorously and converts were made and churches strengthened.

Among the workers who came to Rome at different times during the years of his imprisonment were Timothy, his young "son in the faith," and Luke, the beloved physician, both of whom had been with him when he founded the church of Philippi, also Epaphroditus, who brought the contribution from the Philippian Church. The last named remained for some time for a valuable but difficult work, until he fell ill and had to return. Aristarchus, an old companion in the work in Thessalonica, Tychicus, perhaps from Ephesus, and Epaphras from Colosse, reporting the sad news of heresy, were also among those who came. Changes in the leadership of the Praetorian Guard occurred through the death of the officer Burrhus, who had been friendly toward Paul, and the trial was delayed.

2. It was while Paul was in the midst of these activities in Rome that Epaphroditus came with a message and contribution from the Church at Philippi, the first church Paul had founded in Europe ten years earlier (Circa 52 A. D.). The interesting circumstances and incidents of its founding are recounted in another place above.

The character of a church is influenced in many ways by the environment in which it is founded. The constitution of the church embraced various classes and conditions of people, illustrated in Lydia, the prosperous and intelligent sales-woman, the Grecian slave-girl, and the hardened and cruel Roman jailer. The church was mostly of Gentiles with very few Jews. For this reason the Judaists did not find it easy to gain a foothold in this church.

The influence of the church on the social life of this city was great in the elevation of the slaves and the improvement of the social position of women. There were outstanding women workers in this church, and Macedonian inscriptions indicate that women had, in this city, a social position much more elevated than in other places. Paul mentioned the work of the women especially in this church, exhorting them to cultivate unity and harmony.

Of the subsequent history of the church in Philippi we know few details. The Apostle said in his letter to them that "it was given to them not only to believe in Christ but also to suffer for Him." A generation later, in the beginning of the second century, Ignatius passed through Philippi on his way to Rome where he later suffered martyrdom. He probably put Polycarp in communication with the church, to which that great leader directed many words of comfort and instruction when the church was passing through a crisis of persecution. He reproved the elder of the church in Philippi, Valens, and his wife, because of the ignominy which they brought upon the church through their avarice. This is the last notice that we have of the church in history. Thus we have seen that the church from its origin was perhaps the most loyal and devoted of all the churches to the great Apostle, its founder, and the most faithful in carrying out the great commandment.[1]

3. Date, occasion and content of the letter.

The four epistles of the captivity were written most probably during the years A. D. 61-63. Philippians fits in most naturally in the first place in order among these four epistles: Philippians, Philemon, Colossians and Ephesians, which deal progressively with Christological problems. The church in Philippi, being acquainted with the fact of the imprisonment of Paul in Caesarea and having watched the course of his trial in Caesarea until his final appeal to Caesar, would likely hasten to send their financial help to Rome so as to arrive in opporture time to help the beloved founder of their church in this critical experience. The character of the doctrinal content would also place this letter between the four great epistles dealing with the fundamental doctrine of justification by faith alone and those treating more elaborately the doctrine of the person of Christ in refutation of Incipient Gnosticism. The whole content of the epistle favors the period and circumstances of Paul's imprisonment in Rome as the place of writing. The Apostle had doubtless been there a year or more before writing it.

The occasion of the writing of this delightfully intimate and warm letter was Paul's reception of a letter with liberal financial help, characteristic of this most beloved of all the churches. (Philippians 4:18). Epaphroditus, one of Paul's fine fellow-workers, a member of the church in Philippi and the bearer of the gift, remained for some time in Rome, laboring with Paul in the Gospel with such strenuosity that he fell sick (Phil. 2:27). Knowing that the church was anxious about him, Paul sent Epaphroditus on the return journey with the epistle he had written to the church (Philippians 2:25).

One of the useful clues to the interpretation of the letter is to remember that it was a reply to a letter from the church inquiring about the Apostle's health and prospects (1:26). They had been anxious also about the condition of Epaphroditus (3:2). From Paul's reply to this letter it seems that the Judaists had either appeared there or were expected and Paul warns the Philippians, in spite of the fact that there were few Jews in the Philippian church and consequently less peril from these false teachers than in other churches, where the Jewish contingent was larger. The Philippians apologized for their failure to supply his needs adequately (4:14,15). Paul made plain to them that he was not displeased, but, on the contrary, most grateful and thankful for *them*, "his joy and his crown." This he did with exceeding great graciousness and in expressions of delicate courtesy and unfeigned love (4:10-19).

Paul tells us of the zeal and devotion of the Philippian Church. They sent twice to supply his needs while he was working in Thessalonica (Acts 17:1-9; Philippians 4:16). While he was in Corinth founding the church, they also supplemented what he could make by working at his trade (II Corinthians 11:9; Philippians 4:15). Probably the churches in Thessalonica and Berea

1. Matt. 28:19, 20.

joined the Philippian brethren in his support later, as Paul praised the "liberality of the Macedonia Churches" (I Thessalonians 1:7,8). But the Philippian church led the way in the missionary spirit not only in Paul's support but also in the collection for the poor saints in Jerusalem. (II Corinthians 9:2).

PARAPHRASTIC EXPOSITION

I. Introduction 1:1-11.

A. Salutation 1:1,2.

Paul (Roman name used instead of Saul, his Hebrew name) *slave-servant* and apostle *of Jesus Christ,* especially to the Gentiles, *and Timotheus,* one of his converts in Lystra, who afterwards became a beloved fellow-worker, being present with Paul when he initiated the work at Philippi, also a *bond-servant* of *Jesus, the Christ address all those who* from their conversion, *were set apart to a life, separated* from sin and *dedicated to be and become holy, in* the sphere of the redemptive grace in *Christ Jesus, living in Philippi* at the time of the writing of the epistle from the Roman imprisonment. The laymen of the church were put in the first place, in this already now well organized church, in the salutation of the apostle and Timothy his son in the faith, but the officers elected by the local church, *the bishops,* elders or presbyters, the lolcal preachers who superintended and watched over the growing missionary congregations in this important city, *and the deacons,* who shared in the services and ministries, spiritual and material, were included along with and not separate from the total membership of the church addressed. There was no discrimination between clergy and laity, the "bishops" or overseers being identical with the "elders or presbyters" so-called in other epistles (Lightfoot), and all the titles given the local pastor or preacher covered both the status (elder) and function (bishop) of the preacher or pastor, as it appears from the study of these titles in the various epistles of Paul and in the Christian literature of the New Testament times or in the early primitive churches. In the New Testament usage the Christian ministry appears to be in a more or less fluid stage (Robertson), as to the functions of different members, and we find in Ephesians 4:11f the mention of apostles, prophets, teachers as the spiritual guides of the church. Bishops and deacons are local officers. (*Teaching of the Twelve Apostles* 11:4-7; 13:3 and 15:1). There was probably a plurality of "elders" or "bishops" in Philippi as in the Ephesian and Roman churches, different preachers having different congregations in the city as in our work in large cities today.[2]

v. 2. Paul and Timothy salute the "saints" at Philippi wishing for them *grace* in the Christian-filled significance of that great word, all the free favors of acceptance and the divine presence (Moule) and lovingkindness of God the Father, in Christ (Vincent), covering the kindred meanings of "gift, gratitude, charm, good will and joy" (Robertson). The other word in the salutation is *peace* which pictures the harmony and health of that life which is rec-

2. Cf. The Didache'; also Robertson's, *Paul's Joy in Christ.*

onciled to God through Jesus Christ (Kennedy). Peace flows out of grace and is the repose it brings within you and around you when you are in a state of grace (Ephesians 4:7). Jesus bequeathed to his disciples his kind of peace which the world cannot provide and this kind of peace Paul wished for the saints in Philippi, so that they might have repose in the midst of their struggles. These blessings are to come *from "our Father-God* who is Father of all his creatures in a general sense but of his "saints" in a peculiar sense. They come also *from the divine Son who is Lord,* to whom Paul many times in a perfectly unconscious and natural way attributes Deity (I Cor. 12:2f; II Cor. 13:13; Titus 3:15). Paul here uses the title *Lord* consciously for attribution of deity and the name *Jesus* (Savior) and *Christ* (Messiah) to point out as elsewhere in his epistles the full character and mission of Jesus. Polycarp died a martyr's death because he confessed Jesus Christ as Deity (Lord) and would not recant; but he died with peace in his heart.

B. Paul's thanksgiving and prayer for his converts in Philippi. Chapter 1:3-11.

1. Reasons for his thanksgiving 1:3-8.

a. He is thankful for their fellowship in the Gospel (3-5). *I give thanks to my God* (He is mine[3] and I am His) *upon my remembrance of you* and yours of me; *always in each request on behalf of you all, forming* and expressing *that request with joy.* The aged Apostle enters into the presence chamber of intercessory prayer on their behalf, always with joy and gracious thanks in a spiritual rhapsody. (v. 5) One of the grounds of Paul's gratitude and thanksgiving is *for your fellowship* or common participation and sharing with me *in the Gospel* and its furtherance or promotion *from the first day,* by your cooperation in prayer, work and gifts, *until now.* They had sent messengers with gifts for his support four times, in Thessalonica (Thes. 4:5), in Corinth twice (Acts 18:5; II Cor. 11:7-10) and now in Rome (4:10-20).

b. The Apostle reflecting on their faithfulness (v. 6) was thankful also, *being "confident of this very thing itself, that He who began a good work in them will go on completing it up to the day of Christ Jesus,* when he will return again to earth. God does not begin a work and leave it imperfect and futile (Jowett). He will put the finishing touches to his work in them. Paul fully justifies next this confidence. v. 7. *Even as it is just that I,* I above all men, (emphatic)[4] *should think this on behalf of you all, due to my having you in my heart, as those who, alike in my imprisonment and in the defense* or vindication *and in the establishment of the Gospel* or development of its propagation and verification of its power in the believing, *are my copartners, all of you, of His grace* given to me in glorious privilege of suffering.

v. 8. Paul calls *God* to *witness how* he *longs for them* with a homesick affection *in the bowels of mercies* or very heart *of Christ.*

2. His prayer for them 1:9-11.

---

3. Personal pronoun more.
4. Emoi not moi (Moule).

v. 9. *And this I pray: that your love* in the fullest Christian sense, your love to God and the brethren, *may abound,* of which love he as one had experienced personal evidence, *yet more and more in the sphere of accurate* experimental *knowledge and in all manner of discerning insight* leading into or *resulting in your putting to the test the things that differ,* through a fine spiritual perception, sifting truth from error and the better from the best, and approving the true and best. This was all to the purpose *that they might form in themselves characters of single-heartedness,* sincerity and perfect openness toward the God of things as they are, being also *void of offense* in not stumbling themselves or causing others to stumble, until they shall come *unto the* great *day of Christ's judgment.* He prays that in that day they may have been *made full permanently of the fruit of* the God-kind of *righteousness,* which kind of righteousness they had received *through* the intermediate agency of *the redeeming grace of Jesus Christ* and must themselves cultivate in fruit bearing, *to the glory and praise of God,* the true end and aim of all our blessings and labors.

II. Paul's prison experiences in Rome and his feelings and outlook as related to the progress of the Gospel there. 1:12-26.

A. The effect of his prison experiences had resulted in a movement of progress and a promotion of the Gospel. 1:12-18.

1. His Christianity had been known throughout the Praetorian Guard (v. 12,13.) *I wish you brethren* in Philippi to *know that the things* which I experienced *resulted rather for the* cutting forward or *advancement of the gospel, so that my bonds,* after the manner of the military custody, *turned out to be evident,* of the character of being *in Christ* and not due to any political crime. This was true *in the whole Praetorian Guard* through Paul's being chained to a different soldier each day (vs. 12,13). The Philippian Christians were evidently under the impression that his imprisonment was a shackle to the Christian work of the apostle. On the contrary the Gospel was cutting its way forward *among* the soldiers and *all the other*[5] *Romans.* His bonds had become badges of honor and had won for him sympathy and had given him access to the soldier group to whom he became a friend and chaplain in fact, though assumed.

2. Another effect or result[6] was to embolden timid Roman Christians. 1:14-18.

v. 14. *The majority of the brethren in the Lord,* some of whom were timid, in view of the strenuous activities of Paul, which attracted much attention to the Christians *came now*[7] by Paul's *bonds to have more confidence* and fearless conviction, through the example of Paul's courage and his not being ashamed of his chain. They were animated to a willingness *to venture more* abundantly *in speaking the word of God more boldly,* even if they should have to suffer with the apostle as a consequence.

---

5. All the rest loipois pasin.
6. *Hoste* with the infinitive denoting result.
7. Were made, peroithotas.

3. Paul classifies these preachers vv. 15-18.

vv. 15-17 *Certain ones actually began to proclaim Christ because of their envy* of Paul, and a rivalry leading sometimes to open *strife, while certain others on account of their good will,* for the apostle are stimulated to greater evangelistic activity in *preaching Christ. Some indeed on account of love* for Paul announce the message of Christ, *knowing that Paul was set for the defense* through apologetics *of the gospel. Others* did their preaching *through motives of partisanship* and a factional spirit, propagating their own wrong interpretation of Christianity, *thinking to raise up in this way tribulation for Paul,* by separating his disciples from him, *and adding affliction to his bonds.*

v. 18. *What then? Only that in every way, whether in pretense or, in truth, Christ is proclaimed; and therein I rejoice and will go on rejoicing.*

B. Paul's outlook and feelings in relation to his present situation, he next makes known to the Philippian brethren. 1:19-26.

1. He was sure of the result of his hard experience, in the defense of the gospel.

vv. 19, 20 *For I know that this* experience *will work out, through your supplication and through the supply of the Holy Spirit* sent *by* (from) *Jesus Christ, in my salvation.* This was *according to* Paul's *earnest expectation and hope, "that in nothing I shall be put to shame,* by a miscalculation, resulting in disappointment, *but that by every kind of boldness*[8] in giving my testimony *as at all times also now Christ shall be magnified in my body whether through life or* through *death."*

2. Paul's feeling about his life at this time was one of peace whether he should continue in life or be taken by death.

v. 21. *For to me,* to continue *to live is Christ and to die is gain,* for death would usher him into a more

v. 22. blessed life still. *But if* he were to continue *to live in the flesh,* being acquitted before the Roman tribunal, *'this to me would issue in more fruit of work* for Christ, *then what I shall choose I do not know.'*

3. He was in a quandary between two things, vv. 23-26.

v. 23. I am *held in a suspense, in a quandary between the two things, having a personal desire to* lift anchor and *depart to be with Christ for that would be far better* ("by much more better").

v. 24. *But,* at the same time he recognizes that, *to abide in the flesh is more necessary,* and obligatory on him, *"on account of you."*

v. 25. and of this, *having become persuaded* and convinced thoroughly,[9] *I know that I shall remain* and *shall continue to remain by the side of all of you* as your comrade and helper *for your progress* (cutting forward) *and joy of the faith,* flowing from it, in loyal reliance and confidence in your Lord. This *is in order that your exultation may overflow in Christ Jesus* (their Messiah-Saviour) *in* me as a living link, *through my boldness* as a present example of

8. Instrumental case.
9. Perfect tense, pepoithōs.

the Lord's love to you when I shall be liberated by Jesus and sent back again *to you* in Philippi.

III. The Apostle exhorts the Philippian Christians to live a life worthy of the Gospel in unity and humility based on the example of Christ. 1:27-2:18.

A. He urges them to conduct themselves worthily as citizens of the Christian commonwealth, striving together in teamwork for the Gospel without fear of the adversaries. He reminds them that it was freely given to them not only to trust in but also to suffer for Christ and they should do so calmly 1:27-30.

1. Whether Paul should be restored to them or not he is

v. 27. supremely concerned that they should *order their lives as Christian citizens in a manner worthy of the unifying power of the Gospel of Christ.* This was to the end *that whether coming and seeing them or being absent he might hear* the news *concerning their circumstances that they were consistently and firmly standing together in one spirit and with one soul wrestling side by side against the obstacles* and enemies, *for the faith of the Gospel,* which

v. 28 embraces the truth of Christ. And they are *not to be scared in any way by their adversaries* out of this attitude of calm and courage. This refusal to be *fluttered* or frightened like a surprised bird or beast, *is an evidence of the eternal perdition of their adversaries and the eternal salvation of the faithful witnesses of Christ* and is a condition of conflict and courage which comes *from God.* The reason for all this counsel which he offers them is "*because there was freely granted to you the favor* and blessings, *on behalf of Christ not only to believe in him, but also to suffer for him* experiencing the *same* kind of *conflict,* as they should wrestle side by side for the Lord against such evil *as that which you saw in me* in Philippi when he founded the church *and which you are now hearing to be in me* in the prison in Rome.

B. The apostle exhorts them to non-partisan Christian unity and unselfish Christian humility laying down the bases of such unity in the objective blessings in Christ and in the fellowship and partnership of the Holy Spirit and also in the subjective appeal in Christian love and tender human sympathy of the brotherhood in the Lord. 2:1-4.

1. Paul had great joy in the Philippian church and begs these Christians who had been doing well to go on to even better things filling up his cup of joy to overflowing by the assurance that they are determined to live in holy harmony. He was slightly disturbed lest a partisan spirit should arise in this church as it had in others in Asia Minor and elsewhere. There had been some evidence of disharmony between two of the leading women of the church, Euodia and Syntyche (4:2) and in his concern, the writer adds to his fervent exhortation for unity of effort in the face of adversaries (1:29f) a further and more complete exhortation to unity and humility (2:1-4).

2. The grounds of the appeal to unity are expressed in four conditional sentences, assuming in each case that the condition is true to fact (v. 1). *If there is any* power of *exhortation* in your experiences *in Christ, if any incentive in* Christian *love* between you, *if partnership of the Holy Spirit* is a

reality in unifying the church, *if there are any tender mercies and* any *compassion in* human hearts of the

v. 2. brotherhood, as there surely is in each case,[10] then *fill up to the full my joy, in order that you may think the same thing* having the same mental attitude, *having the same love* in unison of affection, fellow-souls or *souls-together thinking the one*

v. 3. *thing* in a mind which is unity itself. Let there be *nothing in the way of factional* or partisan *strife,* nor in the way of selfish egotism *according to empty vainglory but in humble-mindedness* or lowliness of mind, *reckoning each the other*

v. 4. *better than themselves. Do not,* each circle or partisan group of you, *look to your own interests, but* each *to those of others also.*

C. Paul calls attention to the example of humility and self-sacrifice, witnessed in Christ's incarnation, resulting in his final exaltation. He emptied himself of his pre-existent glory and taking on himself the limitations of humanity, humbled himself even to a felon's death on the cross, being exalted by the Father as a consequence to the place of majesty and the universal worship and adoration of mankind and all intelligent creatures in the universe. 2:5-11.

v. 5. *Keep on thinking this same thing in you which was also in Christ Jesus,* reflecting the example of humility and self

v. 6. forgetfulness which you beheld in Him, *who, existing in the form of God, did not consider the being on equality with God* the

v. 7. Father *a prize to be held on to, but emptied himself* of his privileges of the glorious environment of heaven *taking upon himself* the limitations of humanity in his incarnation, making himself void or empty, by his own act, of the manifestation and exercise of Deity, as he had always experienced it in the heavens and *taking the form of a slave becoming* or entering into a state of being *in the similitude of men. . .* And *being found in the* guise or *pattern of man* he went further

v. 8. still and *humbled himself, becoming obedient unto death,* even

v. 9. *the death of the cross. Wherefore,* because of this act of voluntary and supreme humility, *God exalted him high up* above the state of glory which he enjoyed before the incarnation. This he did in his resurrection and ascension to glory and in *giving him a name which is above every name,* in order *that* in

v. 10. *the name of Jesus every knee should bow,* of all created beings, the celestial in the heavens, the terrestrial or those on earth, or those beneath the earth. Because Christ took upon himself humanity permanently, God gave him a name above every

v. 11. name, *that in the name of Jesus every tongue should confess in worship to his Lordship, to the glory of God.*

D. The Philippians are to follow this example of humility and work out their salvation, realizing the plan of God in their lives. 2:12-18.

---

10. First class condition affirming reality.

The Christian's connection with God brings great responsibility and resources and the apostle appeals to them on the basis of the fact of the incarnate Christ to rise to higher heights in a holiness of life.

v. 12. *So, my beloved ones, just as you always obeyed me,* obey me now, *not as in my presence only* and under my immediate contact *but much more in my absence* and depending more directly on your resources in Christ, *work out your own salvation* or spiritual development in spiritual safety, health and joy, *with fear and trembling* lest you should grieve the Eternal Love. Do not depend on me but look straight up to God (who is nearer than Paul could be).

v. 13. *For it is God who is energizing in your very inmost being in the springs of thought and will, both in your willing and in your carrying into effect His will, for His good pleasure's* sake (vs. 12,13).

v. 14. *Do all things apart from murmurings and disputings,* thoughts or utterances of discontent and self-assertion toward one another, grudgings of other's claims and contentions for

v. 15. your own, in order *that you may become,* what, in full realization you scarcely yet are, that is *unblameable and singlehearted,* because self-forgetting, *God's children* of unmistakeable likeness, and *blameless in the midst of a generation crooked and distorted, among whom you are shining as luminaries, in the world,* stars in a gloomy night, *holding out*

v. 16. the Gospel as the *word of* light and *life.* This will *afford me exultation in view of the day of Christ,* in anticipation of what I shall feel then — *that I did not run in vain nor toil in vain,* though I do not sigh over a hard lot or wish to suffer less on your behalf. *Nay even if I am being*

v. 17. *poured out* as a drink-offering *on the* altar of *sacrifice and* ritual *service of your faith,* as you in faith offer yourselves as a living sacrifice, *I rejoice and I go on rejoicing* with

v. 18. *you all* for your faith and sacrifices *and in the same way you too rejoice and will go on rejoicing with me* (2:14-18).

IV. Paul's Intended Plans and Movements. 2:19-30.

The Apostle Paul had a great love for people. He had many personal friends and also many other admirers whom he had never met. He loved his brethren and especially his fellow workers in the cause. Among those who were associated with him during the period of his imprisonment in Rome were Timothy and Epaphroditus, both of whom were very dear to him.

A. Paul had plans *already,* born out of prayer in the Lord. (2:19-24)

v. 19. *I hope in the Lord Jesus, to promptly send Timothy to you in order that I may be of good cheer, knowing your circumstances.* He hoped also that they might be gladdened by his presence later. He expected to be set free soon.

v. 20. *For I have no one (at hand) who is equal-souled,* or like-minded ,as well qualified as Timothy spiritually, *who will* take the responsibility, *genuinely,* even to the point of anxious *care for you* Philippian brethren.

v. 21. *For all of* those fellow Christians from whom I might choose workers at this time, *are* bent on and *seeking their own* interests *not those of Jesus Christ.*

v. 22. *But the proof* or test *of him* (Timothy) who passed through experiences with Paul at the time of the founding of the Church at Philippi (Acts 16,17), you *recognize,* that *as child with* (his) *father* in closest companionship *he did bondservice for the Gospel.*

v. 23. *So this one then I hope to send, immediately upon getting a clear view of my circumstances* relative to my trial.

v. 24. *But I feel sure through* my communion *in the Lord that I myself will speedily come* following this messenger of mine.

B. Paul refers to the mission, the illness and the recovery of Epaphroditus whom he is now sending back to them (2:25-30).

v. 25. *But I counted*[11] *it obligatory to send back to you* even now, in charge of this letter, *Epaphroditus, my brother* in the bonds of common sympathy, *my fellow-worker* in the cause, and *my own* Christian *fellow-soldier,* sharing with me the many common perils in the work of the Gospel. Epaphroditus was Paul's comrade in love, in work, in perils (Lightfoot). *But* he was also the messenger, *an apostle,* as in truth, also the *minister* of the Philippians to my *need* financial and spiritual.

v. 26. He was not as gifted as Timothy but Paul commends him warmly and praises the good work he has done. He states the reasons for urgency *in sending him on to you since he was suffering from homesickness for you all* at Philippi and *was distracted,* through overwrought feeling, *because* you Philippians *heard that he had fallen ill.*[12]

v. 27. And so it was, *for he did fall ill* and came *near to death. But God had mercy on him,* granting to him recovery in answer to prayers and *not only on him but also on me that I might not have sorrow upon sorrow,* sorrow for the loss of a good fellow-worker whom you would lose also in your effort for my benefit, and sorrow upon top of the sorrows of my prison experiences.

v. 28-30. *The more promptly therefore did I send him in order that seeing him again you might rejoice and I may be less sorrowful. Receive him therefore in* the sphere of *the Lord Jesus with all gladness, and hold such men* as he *in high esteem, because on account of the work of Christ* he was *at death's door, hazarding his life,* playing as it were the gambler with it *that he might supply your lack,* completing your loving purpose *in ministration* designed by you *for me.*[13]

V. Paul begins his final exhortations but pauses suddenly for an extended digression 3:1-4:9. *Finally my brothers:*

A. He exhorts them to be joyful Christians. Nowhere in his epistles does his mysticism shine out with more brilliance than here. His passion for likeness to Christ becomes the motive and goal of a chivalric holy quest.

---

11. Epistolary Aorist.
12. Ingressive Aorist.
13. Objective genitive.

v. 1. Paul's suggested *comprehensive and final* watchword for these and all Christians is; "*Rejoice* (be glad) *in the Lord.*"

Joy in the Lord has preserving power. The word joy occurs five times and rejoice eleven times in this brief epistle. *To write these things* of counsel *to you is not grievous for me and for you it is safe.*

B. In an extended digression, Paul warns them against the opposing errors of Judaism and Antinomianism, which were threatening them. 3:2-4:1.

1. Beware of Judaizers, for real Christians are the true spiritual circumcision. Paul contrasts the doctrine of works with the doctrine of grace as illustrated in his own experience (3:2-14). To write the same things about the Judaizing teachers which he had written to many others was not tiresome for him and for them it was safe. He calls attention to the power of joy in the Lord as a preservative against their errors. Also he repeats the warnings against Judaists for their safety.

v. 2. *Look out for the* unclean scavenger, *dog-like* false teachers, full of insolence and cunning. They had "dogged" the steps of Paul all over the Roman Empire. Dog was a word of frequent use among the Jews in speaking of Gentiles. These "dogs" were the "*evil-workers,*" working actively the wrong by teaching the false doctrine of salvation by works. These sacramental and ceremonial teachers were like hucksters selling in the street (2 Cor. 6:17) who expose the best fruits in the top layers in their baskets and conceal that which is rotten beneath. *Look out for the* Judaistic teacher who inculcates dependence on the *concision* or mere carnal circumcision *as a means of salvation,* because such false teaching has no value but becomes a mere "mutilation of the flesh," in which there is no spiritual value at all.

a. In his former life as a Jew, Paul could boast (3:3-6).

v. 3. For, as a Christian, the apostle declares that not the Judaists but *we* (*Christians*) *are the true circumcision.* He cites three reasons for his declaration: first, *we* (*Christians*) *are doing priestly service in a spiritual ministry to all peoples and spiritual worship to God, by the help of the Holy Spirit.* The second reason is that "*we are glorying in Christ Jesus.*" The third reason is that "*we have not placed our confidence in the* tribal, national and ceremonial prerogatives or *the fleshly character* of a legalistic selfrighteous life,

v. 4. *even though I myself,* considered from the point of view of religions, *am having confidence in the flesh.*

v. 5. *If anyone else thinks that he has ground of confidence in the flesh, I have more* ground for boasting than he. Paul sums up a few items of the basis for saying this: *With reference to circumcision, I was an eighth-day child.* I was a son of the Covenant coming *from the Israelitish race,* and not a proselyte. As to descent I am *of the tribe of Benjamin,* which gave to Israel Saul, her first king. I am *a Hebrew* by ancestry, and came *from a Hebrew home* where the Hebrew (Aramaic) and not the Greek language was spoken and where the ancient customs and manners of the Hebrews were loyally observed. *As touching the Law* of Moses and its observance I am *a Pharisee* and the son of a Pharisee.

v. 6. *In the matter of zeal* for the ancient faith of our Hebrew Fathers *I was a persecutor of the* Christian *Church,* and *as to the strict righteousness* of life dictated *by the Law* I am *found* ceremonially *blameless.*

b. But Paul turned his back on all these Jewish advantages and privileges that he might gain Christ (3:7-11).

v. 7. Before Paul's conversion he was accustomed to count up with miserly greed all these assets of his Hebrew heritage and accomplishments — the profits and advantages of race, religion and personal attainments. *But now* that I have experienced a spiritual new birth through the grace of Christ, *the things I once counted gain* and profit *I now count loss on account of Christ.*

v. 8. *But* he goes even further, *indeed, now, at least, also I do count* by this new-life standard of values, not merely the religious and racial values mentioned above, but *all things* literally and emphatically as *loss, because of the surpassing value of the excelling knowledge about* and acquaintance with *Christ Jesus my Lord.*

v. 9. "*On account of whom, I suffered the loss of all these things, and* so heartily as to *consider all of them as refuse to be* cast to scavenger dogs in the streets *or* as *dung* for the dung-heap. This is *in order that I might gain Christ.* But not only that attainment but *that I might be found in Him not having mine own righteousness, that* derived *from* the strict observance of *the law* as in the life of the Jew, *but the* God-kind of righteousness, which comes *through a vital faith in Christ, the righteousness* which is derived not from the law but *from God based on faith.*

v. 10. In order *to know Him* (through this faith relationship) in rich Christian experience, coming thus to understand *the power* which worked mightily *in His resurrection,* which works out in the experience of the Christian in his assurance of immortality, in his triumph over sin, as a pledge of the believer's justification, in an understanding of the dignity of the human body of the believer and its destined resurrection, and in the stimulating of the whole moral and spiritual being of the believer. Paul would also enter into intimate knowledge and *the fellowship* of his vicarious *sufferings becoming conformable to this death.* That deep experience of fellowship with Christ's sufferings on the cross and always before and after the crisis hour of the cross, comes through bearing daily the cross of vicarious suffering in His steps, and for His sake, in his strength. Growing in conformity to His death is a continued and progressive action in the direction of complete surrender to the participation in suffering with him on behalf of the world, in a daily dying for Him, thus filling up the measure of his vicarious sufferings for mankind.

v. 11. Paul is *thinking of the glorious resurrection* of true Christians, who fell asleep in Jesus, *and expresses a modest and devout hope of coming to share in it, without casting any doubt upon its future realization.* The conditional sentence is of a character to express humility but not doubt as to Paul's status as a believer in Jesus. *If by any means I shall attain to the resurrection from the dead.*[14]

c. The Apostle does not claim to have reached the goal of perfection but is racing on, with the out-stretched neck of a runner, with his face fixed toward the goal ahead and every nerve taut. vs. 12-14. Paul was keenly conscious of the possibility of misunderstanding as to this hope expressed, because there were some at Philippi who were claiming high sanctity and so affecting superior airs toward their brethren (Kennedy) with inevitable irritations and jealousies. The Antinominians, on the other hand, decried the reality of guilt for sin. Some modern evolutionists teach that sin is a mere animal inheritance, "nature red in tooth and claw," not yet shaken off. Perfectionists minimize their own faults while finding fault with and looking down upon their brethren, "not blessed with their perfect state." Paul positively disclaims perfectionism.

v. 12. *Not as though I had already received* the crown of accomplished glory *or have been perfected with a full-grownness in Christ, but I press forward if so be that I may lay hold on that, for which I was laid hold on by Christ Jesus.*

v. 13. *Brethren, I do not account myself to have seized that* crown yet. The Apostle felt a holy dissatisfaction with his spiritual attainments and eager longing for attaining loftier heights in Christ. So he adds: *But one thing*: *forgetting* on the one hand *the things behind and* on the other *leaning forward* as a runner on the home stretch *toward the things ahead,*

v. 14. *I pursue intently pressing down on the goal unto the prize of the upward calling of God* through the voice of his grace *in Christ Jesus,* coming down from the heights of glory and urging the Christian to come up thither.

2. Paul warns the Philippian Christains against Antinomianism and calls their attention to high moral standards in the Christian life, as citizens of heaven: 3:15-4:1.

v. 15. He starts out with the right point of view: *So let as many* of us *as are full-grown men* in Christ *be of this mind* or think this way. The Apostle is not contradicting his previous denial of absolute sinless perfection. "The mind mature Christians should have is that those who rest in Christ immovable for their acceptance and press forward in Christ persistently in their obedience, discover fresh causes constantly for humility and for progress in Him" (Moule). *And if in any respect ye are otherwise minded* about sinless perfection, *this also will God unveil unto you* so that you will come to understand the mind of the spirit about this matter. Paul was sure that the Spirit of God was speaking by him, which is a testimony to the truth of inspiration. It is not dogmatic self-satisfaction to say that sinless perfection is disclaimed here by Paul.

v. 16. *Only whereunto we have attained,* up to our full present light in the Gospel, *let us walk in the same* path of unchanging principles of faith, love and holiness with a watchful desire to cherish harmony of spirit and conduct (Moule).

---

14. The believer's resurrection.

v. 17. Keep your eye on the guide, *Brethren,* and *become imitators of me.* This Paul said, not egotistically. He was the founder of this Church at Philippi and their apostolic guide. *Watch also* in order to tread in the steps of *those who so walk, as you have* (me and my missionary helpers: perhaps Timothy and Epaphroditus) *us as a type* or model to guide you in conduct.

v. 18. *For many are walking around, of whom I have been accustomed to tell you, frequently,* when I was with you *and now also tell you, shedding tears* as I do so, that they are *the enemies of the cross of Christ,* the power of which upon the soul, they have not had a personal experience.

v. 19. *Of whom the end is perdition, whose god is their belly* or sensual appetites resulting in the degradation of their bodies, *and whose boast,* "that they see deeper and soar higher," *is* based *in their shameful conduct, who have a mind for material things* (on the earth) and wish to cover up their sin with the robe of a philosophic theory. Evolution, in like manner in modern times, accounts for sin as a degree in the upward development of the animal-man which will slough off in the process at a certain stage.

v. 20. But we Christians are a colony of heaven, *for our citizenship is in the heavenlies, from whence we await expectantly a Savior, the Lord Jesus Christ.*

v. 21. *Who shall transfigure the body of our humiliation* to be *conformed to the body of his glory,* thus preparing it for the eternal abode with Christ in heaven. This he will do in ways and manners inscrutable, *according to the energy of his ability* actually *to subdue to himself all things* that exist.

v. 4:1. *So, my brethren, beloved and longed for, my joy and my crown* of victory because you are citizens of heaven, have courage here on earth also, and *thus stand fast in the Lord, beloved ones,* holding on to your present certainties, your glorious Savior and your heavenly hopes.

3. Exhortation to two leading sisters in the church, Evodia and Syntyche, to heal their dissensions, and an appeal to all to live lives of joyfulness, of freedom from anxiety and in the pursuit of good aims. 4:2-9.

v. 2. *To Evodia I appeal and to Syntyche I appeal to be of the same mind in the Lord,* in the power of their common union in Him, laying aside their differences of feeling, born of self. These women were probably deaconesses in the church in Philippi, for women had a high position in the church (Lightfoot). It might have been an accidental friction between two energetic Christian women (Kennedy).

v. 3. *I* (Paul) (*even*) *beg you, true yokefellow,* perhaps Epaphroditus, Timothy or Luke (Robertson), rather than "ma chere epouse," *with Clemente* too of later fame, perhaps as Bishop of the church in Rome, *and my other fellow workers, whose names are in the Lord's Book of Life* in heaven, *help those women who wrestled along with me as* devoted and courageous *workers of the Gospel.* Paul carried the crime and distress of an unchristian spirit in these Christians into the very sanctuary of the heavenly peace to die there through the lovely and tactful intervention of these peacemakers. These women were spiritual athletes who had done worthy-work with Paul for which he was grateful.

v. 4. Turning now from the subject of unchristian dissensions, the Apostle strikes again the keynote of the epistle, that of Christian joy. He knew the joyous life in Christ, which surmounts every other mood, and brings serenity and calmness to the soul stayed on God (Robertson). It is in the Lord that we find the life that will stand the shock of all sorrow and sin. *Rejoice in the Lord at every time. Again I say rejoice.*

v. 5. *Let your forbearance* or gentleness which is selflessness, (which yields anything, only of self, for Christ's sake), *be known to all men.* This "sweet reasonableness" or mildness of disposition leads one to be fair and go beyond the letter of the law. Moderation should be advanced as a positive yielding or graciousness which takes the form of courtesy and should be made known to all with whom we have relationships.

v. 6. *The Lord is near,* in his continued presence with us in all our varied human life and experiences, to cheer, know, love, calm and beckon us on to follow in his steps. So *stop being anxious* we should never let ourselves be anxious with harassing care and solicitude, leading to brooding and pondering, as if we were alone from our Lord. Christ's cure for such worry and dread is to *Let your requests be made known unto God* coming into his very presence[15] and telling Him about them though He knows already. *By your prayer* in worship toward Him *and your definite*[16] *supplication* or petition to Him *accompanied by thankgiving,* for past blessing as a background for successful prayer, *let your requests be made known to God,* with perfect simplicity and detail, remembering that He bids us to pray (Moule).

v. 7. *And thus* through worshipful communion and trust in Him *the peace of God,* that inward tranquility of soul that is grounded in God's presence and promise *which transcends all understanding of the* intellectual powers or *mind, shalt,* according to promise *guard* safely as an armed sentinel of a garrison, *your hearts in all their* activities of the intellectual powers or *thoughts* with their consequent *emotions* leading to acts of the will, *in Christ Jesus.*

v. 8. Another element in a harmonious and joyful life of peace is to be found in high thinking. This is one of the things of finality in the Christian's experience — his thinking. In the stoic philosophy, prudence, temperance, justice and fortitude were the cardinal virtues. Paul does not attempt an all-inclusive list of Christian ideals, but presents two groups typical and illustrative of the Christian philosophy of life. *Whatsoever things are true;* resting on reality and aiming at reality as it answers to the nature of God (Robertson) and was revealed by and in Christ; *whatsoever things are honorable*: serious. sacred, self-respectful, reverend, producing reverence; *whatsoever things are right or just*: as between man and man, and man and God — these are fundamental and go to the roots of Christian right living; *whatsoever things are pure*:

15. *Pros ton Theon.*
16. Definite article.

stainless, chaste, unsullied, as clean words and clean deeds; *whatsoever things are lovely*: or amiable, gracious and kindly in manner, charming, attracting to themselves, calling forth love; *whatsoever things are of good report*: fair-sounding, in time with the standard of a truly Christian morality, sweet to speak of because prompting a noble tone of conversation — another beautiful triad of characteristics of the Christian ideal built upon the first. *If there is any virtue* at all, any excellence of ideal or character meriting the praise or moral approbation of the Christian; make such in any case the subject of careful reflection and of deliberate and prolonged contemplation. High thinking on the great and heroic virtues or ideas of moral excellence produces holy living, but a corrupted imagination genders moral turpitude. Virtue, such as merits the praise of Christians, is not the pagan self-grounded vigour, but the energy for right, founded in God (Moule).

v. 9. Paul adds a personal but not egotistic word of counsel for them to follow in their immaturity his example based on age and experience, seeking to realize the principles of his life in their practice. *The things you learned and received* as a revelation to you, *and heard* in my teaching *and saw in my example, these begin to do and go on practicing,* transmitting ideals into actual habits of life. "It is one thing to know and another to practice" (Browning). Paul even ventures that his life and example as an open book before them might help them to convert profession into performance, Christian ideals into true conduct. *And so* following this advice, *the God* who is the author *of peace* within and the giver of peace among men around *shall be with you* even though you are in the midst of a turbulent and tempestuous world. He will bring harmony and spiritual unity to you and through you in His church and in the world-order.

4. In gracious thanks for the collection, the apostle reveals in conclusion his secret of happiness and contentment in life. 4:10-23.

v. 10. Coming now to the conclusion of his letter he rings the key note again of joyful thanks. But, *I rejoice*[17] *in the Lord greatly* that *now at length* you *have blossomed*[18] *out again in your loving thought for me.* It was fine to be remembered again by old friends in this collection, although the Philippians had not forgotten but *were thinking*[19] *of him* all along, but the *opportunity had been lacking for* their *expression.*

v. 11. Paul would not have them get the idea that he was hinting for future favours and hastens delicately to say: *Not that I am speaking in respect to want, because I have come to learn*[20] through long experience *in whatever circumstances I am to be content.* Paul emphasizes[21] the fact that he had learned this lesson for himself: how to get on without some things. Paul had a manly independence in Christ who was his sufficiency, not Stoicism.

17. Epistolary constative aorist.
18. Second aorist active indicative.
19. Imperfect tense.
20. Cumulative aorist (Dana).
21. Use of *ego* for emphasis.

v. 12. *I know* both *how to be humbled,* running low as a river in a drouth, *and I know how to run over* as now with the fulness of your bounteous gift. *In everything* in particular *and in all things* of experience in life, I *have been initiated permanently*[22] *into the secret*[23] both how *to be full* (fed) *and* how *to be hungry,* both to run over and to run low or come short.

v. 13. This secret, in being ready to meet all the experiences of plenty and want, Paul found in Christ. *I am strong* in all things, *in Him who makes me able.* "I undergo all things since he himself strengthens me who is perfect man" (Ignatius). Having avoided any misunderstanding that he might be hinting for another gift, Paul extends courteous thanks and commends them for their gift to him.

v. 14. *You did well,* a good deed, *when you joined together in your participation with me in my affliction.* His appreciation of their gift is sincere.

v. 15. *But* (there was no need of this gift to assure him of their affection) *you Philippians know* and remember *in the beginning* of the work *of the Gospel. When I came from Macedonia* to go on and evangelize other parts of Europe in my second missionary tour *no other church shared with me in the matter of giving and receiving if not you only.*

v. 16. Because even while in Thessalonica *you both once and twice sent to* meet *my need.*

v. 17. By saying this, you must not think I am *seeking another gift, but* 'I *seek the fruit which is accumulating to your account.*'

v. 18. Paul is still concerned that they should not miscontrue his expression and adds, *But I have received in full* the discharge of your obligations in the gift now sent and *I am running over* with your bounty. *I have been filled up to the full receiving from Epaphroditus the things* (gifts) *from you, an odour of fragrancy, a sacrifice acceptable,* well *pleasing to God.*

v. 19. Paul now adds God's blessing: "And *my God shall supply every need of yours.* He has unlimited resources, and will make up to the Philippians from his infinite resources *according to his wealth in glory, in Christ Jesus.* They had filled Paul's cup to overflowing; his God would fill theirs up to the brim and over (Robertson).

v. 20. Now *to our God and Father be the glory* and praise for all like acts of fellowship of his children *forever and ever, Amen.*

v. 21-23. Paul bids them a fond farewell. He *greets every individual saint* or member of the church in Christ Jesus. *All the brethren* fellow-workers *with him* in Rome *join him in sending greetings.* So do *all the believers* in Rome *especially those of the household of Caesar. The Grace of the Lord Jesus Christ be with your spirit.*

---

22. Perfect tense.
23. The mysteries (cf. Mystery religions).

CHAPTER XXIII

The Epistles to the Colossians and to Philemon

Introduction

1. The exact time within the two years of Paul's imprisonment in Rome when he wrote the epistles to the Colossians and to Philemon is uncertain. We have followed Lightfoot and some others who placed the Philippian Epistle first, as being more akin to the Second Corinthian and Roman Epistles. Ephesians being a circular letter to be used in all the churches would seem to fit in best in the last place among the four letters of the Captivity. The most probable date of the writing of Colossians is A. D. 63 and the place after the evidence of research according to the best scholarship was Rome and not Ephesus.

2. The city of Colossae was located in the Lycus Valley about 150 miles east of Ephesus and something like the same distance west of Antioch of Pisidia. The site of the ruins of this town is about ten miles from that of Laodicea to the east and about the same distance from that of Hieropolis to the north-east. The Christian churches were founded in these three cities as a consequence of the work of Paul in the great metropolis of Ephesus during his three years' ministry there and were not founded by Paul personally. Converts from his work penetrated into those regions, and the natural expansion of evangelization in the provinces around Ephesus, through those who came in contact with the Gospel in Ephesus, accounts for the existence of these and other churches in this general region. Paul was deeply interested in this work of expansion from the strategically located city of Ephesus out to the east along the great thoroughfare which connected Ephesus with Antioch of Pisidia and the Galatian towns further to the east.

3. The Church in Colossae could not have been very large. Epaphras was the leading elder or pastor in the region or field of the three towns and was probably assisted by Philemon and Archippus. The same pastor with his helpers cared for the interests of the three mission churches. Paul was outspoken in his approval of the work of these brethren there and though he had not visited the churches personally was deeply interested in them (Colossians 2:1). They were invaded by Gnostics about the time of Paul's imprisonment and the pastor Epaphras made a trip to Rome to bear the greetings and perhaps a contribution from the churches to Paul and consult him about the inroads of the heretical teachers. That was the occasion of Paul's writing the letter to the Colossian Church in which he deals with the Gnostic heresy.

4. The Heresy of Gnosticism.

Greek Speculative Philosophy, coming down from the historic period two centuries before the time of Paul, attempted, as rationalists have ever been wont to do, to interpret everything in the light of and depending wholly on human reason. Greek philosophy had ever been concerned much about the origin and nature of the material universe. Some of these Greeks who had accepted Christianity, sought to interpret the teachings of Christ making use of their dualistic theory as to matter and spirit. They held that matter is inherently evil and spirit is essentially good. God, being good could not touch matter and hence the material universe, was created through a series of intermediate agencies called aeons, (emanations from God), who came in between God and matter. In order to make Christ fit into their system of philosophy they made of Him one of the Aeons. He was assigned the highest place among the aeons and was the logos (word) or highest expression of God, but was not himself God. Thus Christ, who was but an emanation from God or creation of God was not eternal. He in turn became the source of the second projection from deity and so the line of the aeons was extended to the final one called the Demiurge, who became the creator of matter. This whole system naturally subordinated Christ to the place of a mere creature and was a complete denial of His deity. Furthermore, the nature of man being both material and spiritual gave occasion to the theory that man's body being material is committed to evil or sin but his spirit being pure may win out through the right processes of thought and life, over the sinfulness of the flesh.

This heresy which blossomed out in its fullness in the second century can be traced back through the Epistle of Barnabas A.D. 120-130 and the writings of Ignatius A. D. 117, to the Johannian Epistles, A. D. 90-100, and on through the Epistles of Peter and Jude to the Pauline Epistles of Collossians and Ephesians. Intermingled with it in the Churches of the valley of Lycus are some vestiges of the principles of the Essenes (Colossians 4:13-16). This heresy of Gnosticism which Paul had to deal with in this epistle was a product of Hellenistic Judaism with a Palestinian tincture. He had been battling against the Judaists who were representatives of Palestinian Judaism and now he must meet heresy from another different and additional source.

The Colossian heresy was much higher up than the Pharisaic Judaism refuted by Paul in the Galatian Epistle. The problem for the Christian Greek Philosopher was to span the chasm between God who was pure and man who was sinful. He sought to do this by fabricating the theory of creation by the series of aeons. But no angel or spirit, one or many, being nearer God nor man, could reconcile the two (Lightfoot, *Com. Philippians and Collosians*, p. 113). Paul comes forward with the solution of the problem in his presentation of the nature, character and function of Jesus, the Messiah. Christ, and not the imagined Demiurge, was the intermediate agent in the creation of the material universe (Colossians 1:15-17), and the head of the Church, His body (Colossians 1:18). In him dwells all the Godhead bodily (Colossians 2:9) and he is above all the angels (Colossians 2:18). He being God and the only begotten son of God is the only mediator and alone can be the reconciler between God and man. His mediatorial function is not only in the creation of the material universe but also relates to men and their salvation in His Church, which is His Body. His cross is the at-one-ment of mankind with God. Jesus Christ is the head of His body which is the Church composed of the saved. It is through His mediation that we have communion, access, fellowship, with God. We pray in His name and can commune thus with the Father. This was known to be a common experience in the prayer-life of the Christian, moreover, on the basis of His real mediation in His church, Christians are justified in reasoning that His claim to be the Mediator in Creation is true. So the revelation of Jesus Christ as Mediator and Savior is complementary to the monotheistic doctrine of the Old Testament, presenting a transcendent Creator in whom evil is not inherent, along with free man as a fallen creature corrupted by sin, who must be reconciled to God and purified. The blood of Christ cleanses man from all sin and reconciles man and God.

The ethical error of the heretics was in putting the seat of sin in the material world without, instead of in, the human heart. This led the Gnostics to fence themselves about with negative prohibitions leading into asceticism. But these scrupulous restrictions failed to touch the springs of action in the human heart. Paul substitutes in the place of the ascetic idea the positive principle of personal communication with God through Christ, which kills the whole body of earthly desires and passions through the strong expulsive power of a new personal affection for God in Christ. Thus a vital faith in Christ is related to religious works as principle and practice. Vital faith is the surrender of self to Christ and is followed by and produces good works as an inevitable result.

In this exposition of the person of Christ, Paul is in perfect accord with other Apostolic writings as for example the Epistle to the Hebrews, written a few years later than the Colossian and Ephesian Epistles, and the Epistles and Gospel of John written a little more than a quarter of a century after Paul wrote. All of these writings present Christ as the intermediate agent in all Creation and the incarnate divine-human Mediator between God and Man.

Thus these Apostles opposed the Docetic Gnosticism which denied the reality of the humanity of Jesus (I John 1:1,3; II John 7) according to which Christ's body was an illusion, taken on to reveal himself to our senses. They also opposed the Cerinthian Gnosticism advocated by Cerinthus, a younger contemporary of the Apostle John. This form denied the identity of Jesus and the Christ. Jesus had the natural human life and Christ was the aeon which came upon Jesus at his baptism. With the Gnostics the *pleroma* or fulness was in the aeons but with Paul all the fulness of the Godhead dwelt in Christ solely.

The wrong views of the Gnostics about the Person of Christ led to asceticism on the one hand and to Antinomian license on the other. The advocates of the first taught that the imposition of ascetic rules and celibacy was the road to purification. This wrong conception has clung to historic Christianity down through the ages, in the celibacy of the priesthood, the folly of which Paul exposed. The Nicolaitans, on the other hand held that evil of sensuality in man, may be overcome by indulgence, excessive even to exhaustion. This theory reminds one of Freud's psychoanalysis sex complex of our times. Along with these errors running back to Epicureanism and Stoicism there was an admixture of the errors of Essenism and Oriental Mysticism.

To meet these errors of the Gnostics who exalted intellectuality or (Gnosis) knowledge, Paul urged *epignosis* or additional and more complete experiential knowledge. He presented Christ as the perfect propitiation, bringing peace and reconciliation between Man and God, as well as the *pleroma* or fulness of the God, superceding the imagined series of aeons supposed to be intermediate between God and matter as well as God and mankind. Christ had a real human body and shed his blood on the cross (Col. 2:3).

The revelation of God by Christ was historical in Jesus and adapted to the human understanding. He was deity, without which the beginning of Christianity could have no adequate explanation.

Content and Argument

In Colossae some of the Intellectuals who had come into the fold of Christianity brought forward speculative problems of Greek philosophic thought, as to the relation between spirit and matter in the constitution of the material universe and in the salvation of mankind. The flow of scientific and philosophic thought was forcing Christianity to further interpretation of its doctrines, in view of the current amalgamation of religions, in the unified political world heading up in Rome. The Gnostic teachers in Colossae sought to make a synthesis of Christianity with Judaistic and Pagan thought, which latter included the worship of angels along with Christ. Paul came to the help of the pastor, Epaphras, in Colossae, presenting Christ as the sole intermediate Agent in Creation and the only Mediator in Christianity, which was and is different from all other religions, not only in the degree of its ethical superiority but in its separate kind and character. Jesus is the Cosmic Christ as well as the mediatorial Savior of mankind.

These errorists were the "grevious wolves" to whom Paul referred when he was with the Elders from Ephesus in Miletus (Acts 20:29f). They were partly Judaistic but mostly Hellenistic in their background. Some were within the churches but they were allied to false teachers of the Pagan mystery cults then existent, of which there were many: the Eleusian mysteries, Mithraism, the vogue of Isis, and especially nascent Gnosticism, which was the most subtle of all in its attack, subordinating and compromising the person and work of Christ in a system of Greek Theosophy. Paul had to refute the arguments of these theosophists in his brief letter which as we see he did consummately.

Analysis and Paraphrase

I. Introduction 1:1-14.

1. Salutation of Paul and Timothy to the Colossian saints. 1:1,2. Paul always begins his epistles with a salutation identifying himself with his readers, as author, by an initial expression of his wish for them — the divine favor and Christian peace.

v. 1. *Paul,* commissioned messenger or *an apostle* sent *from Christ Jesus* and pertaining to Him, *through the will of God* divinely called to this work, associates *with* himself in his salutation, *Timothy, the brother* and beloved son in the faith, in this letter to the church in Colossae.

This is a plain statement of Paul's authorship, Baur and all his successors in criticism to the contrary. Objections to that authorship on any grounds, whether of the presence in it of Gnosticism, the language used, its advanced Christology, or others equally or less important have waned to a disappearing minimum before this sincere and humble, though positive statement of his divinely commissioned apostleship.

v. 2. *To the* holy ones, members of the church *in Colossae,* called out and 'set apart,' by the Christian calling, to become holy *and faithful,* because faith-filled, loyal and obedient, stedfast *brethren* or brothers, in the sphere of the redemptive work and their acceptance of it *in Christ.* The apostle, writing not from Ephesus or Caesarea but from Rome, on the occasion of the visit of Epaphras the pastor of the heresy-infected church in Colossae, this letter, which he is sending along by Tychicus, with that to Philemon, and the circular letter to the churches in the province of Asia, known as the letter to the Ephesians, expresses his greetings: *Grace,* the divine, though for man, unmerited favor, *to you and peace* or the divinely given and maintained tranquillity in the heart, which comes *from God our Father* in the peculiar and intimate relation which the twice-born have in his family, through their faith in and acceptance of Christ.

2. Thanksgiving for the progress of the Colossian brethren in the faith, in Christ, in their love for the brethren or saints everywhere, and in their hope from heaven, resulting in fruitfulness and development, which hope they learned through the faithful pastor and beloved fellow-servant Epaphras. 1:3-8.

v. 3. *We,* Timothy joining me, *give thanks,* in reality expressing them in prayer to *God, Father of our* divine *Lord, Jesus* our Savior, *Christ* our Messiah, and this expression is *at every time, when we are praying concerning you* as we do constantly.

vv. 4, 5. This thanksgiving is solidly based on their *hearing* in Rome the good news, which, as the brethren might infer, was brought by the loyal pastor Epaphras, "*about your faith* or internal trust centered *in Christ Jesus,* producing fidelity and steadfastness, *and* about *your* deeply spiritual, yearning brotherly *love which you have* and hold on to, *for all the saints* whatever their condition, position or disposition, because your love is not superficial or merely friendly

v. 5. but deep and abiding *on account of the hope, which is laid up* or stored up *for you in the heavens*, in the form of a reward which Christ the righteous judge shall give (II Tim. 4:8), the desire for which is one of the mainsprings for loving some saints who may be unlovely, with a Christian love which is unfeigned. About *which hope you* definitely *heard*[1] in or *by the word of the truth of the gospel* or the genuine and truthful good news preached to you by Epaphras your faithful pastor,

v. 6. Which *is present unto you*, coming into your midst, *even just as it is bearing fruit and increasing*, through its inherent energy and life-producing germ, externally with rapidity, *in all* the known Roman *world*, and demonstrating its inexhaustible reproductive power, *just as it* is *in your midst also, from the day* in *which you heard* by its annunciation in preaching *and recognized* with spiritual understanding *the grace of God* in his wonderful gift of salvation *in truth*.

v. 7. *Just as you learned* it *from Epaphras our beloved fellow-bond-servant*, just arrived in Rome with the good news from you, *who is faithful* for you, as *a minister of Christ on your behalf*,[2] who went to Colossae (on my behalf) for me as my representative to you while I was carrying on my work of the gospel in Ephesus,

v. 8. *Even the one who made evident to us*, both to me and my fellow-workers here, *your love* in the sphere of life *in the Holy Spirit* toward me, *whom you have never seen* yet regard as your friend and servant in the work of Christ.

3. Paul's prayer for the future advance and infilling of these saints with the additional and experiential knowledge, in all true wisdom and spiritual insight into the will of God, in order to an orderly and worthy walk, well pleasing to Christ, bearing fruit in every kind of good work and growing in the accurate knowledge of God; gaining thus full strength flowing out to them from God's self-revelation, resulting in a life of perseverance and patience, full of joy and thanksgiving to God who qualified us up to the adequate measure of possession of the inheritance of the saints in light. He it was who rescued us from the power of darkness and transferred us into the kingdom of the son of his love, in whom we have deliverance and the remission of our sins, and not through the mediation of the cosmic angels, as taught by the current heretics. 1:9-14.

v. 9. *On account of this* goodwill expressed through Epaphras toward us, *we also* in turn both Timothy and I *from the day in which we heard* of your faith, love, and hope, *do not cease praying* daily *on your behalf, and begging* definitely *that you might be filled* with the, *accurate knowledge of his will, in all wisdom and spiritual understanding* or insight into the will of God.

v. 10. *to the end that you should walk* in an exemplary conduct, *worthily of the Lord* Jesus, *unto every sort of* thing *pleasing* to Him, *in every kind of* good *work, bearing fruit*, as the good plant which has the life germ and reproductive

1. Aorist tense of denfinite actual occurrence.
2. Cf. Nestle's text.

power within, *and increasing* or growing outwardly in a continuous growth in *the accurate* and full experimental *knowledge about God,*[3]

v. 11 *being empowered* progressively and continuously, *with full* and varied *power according to* measure and character *of the might of His glory into a full,* willing, persistent and enduring *patience and longsuffering* of injustices and wrongs without complaint or bitterness, cowardice or despondency.

v. 12 Withal these graces are to be exhibited, *with joy, giving thanks to the Father who made you,* (as a loving Father would do *being himself sufficient or competent*[4] *to do so*) qualified *up to the measure* for the sharing *of the inheritance of the saints,* dwelling *in the* sphere *of light* of the heavenlies, which is their privileged place of abode and true lot here on earth, now, and more still hereafter (Ellicott).

v. 13. *Who rescued us for himself*[5] at the hour of our conversion *out of the power,* which is backed up by authority, *of the* thraldom of Satanic *darkness of* this heathendom *and transported us* as colonists, at that very time *unto the kingdom* and rule *of the Son of his love,* there to be settled as citizens in the Kingdom of the true light of the revelation of God's love, not like that claimed by the heretical teachers.

v. 14. *In* the sphere of the redemptive work of *whom we have the redemption or* deliverance already, *which* is exhibited *in the forgiveness of our sins,*[6] a logical result and real consequence of his work of redemption, wrought out by Him, which we realize in our experience when we accept Him by faith.

II. The preeminence of the Person and Work of the pre-existent Cosmic Christ in Creation, Providence, and also in Redemption, as Head of the universal Church. 1:15-20.

1. The person of Christ, as head of the universe, in creation. vv. 15-17.

He was the intermediate agent in the creation of all things, whether of the material universe, embracing all matter, or of the immaterial of intelligences, including all angelic principalities, powers and authorities, to which the false teachers would give the place of mediation in creation, instead of to Christ, the only Mediator.

v. 15. Paul turns away from his prayer at this juncture and glides into exposition of the vital theme, the Person of Christ, whom he presents as Divine, being the image of God, and the Creator and Sustainer of the Universe (vv. 15b-17).

v. 15 *Who* (Christ) *is the* very *image,* partaking of the exact character and nature *of the invisible God,* being Himself a person in the Godhead and thus revealing God to men, so that they might see him in Christ, and the unknowable should become known (Peake). Paul assumes the humanity of Jesus and at the same time affirms his deity, not as the angel-cult affirmed that Christ

3. Objective genitive.
4. Aorist active participle.
5. Aorist middle for himself,
6. Appositional phrase,

was *a son* of God, like his other creatures. Christ is here made by Paul the very image and embodiment of God (Robertson), possessing the very kind of character and nature that God has (M. Jones) and not such as the aeons were said to have, in the theory of the Gnostics. If Christ were not deity, Christianity itself would be a false vagary. This is a "reduced" Christianity of the 'Intellectuals', which Paul refutes, for Christ is *the first-born,* the pre-existent cosmic Christ, who had existence *before all creation,* whether of mere matter or of spiritual and intelligent creatures, including all angelic beings of whatever kind. Here the absolute preeminence, priority, pre-existence, and dominion over all creation are asserted.

v. 16. And the reason is adduced at once, *because in Him* (the) *"all things* of the universe", whether material or spiritual, *were created,*[7] *in the heavens,* the angelic myriads *and upon the earth,* whether things or men, *the visible and the invisible* as well, embracing all things, especially with reference to the things in the invisible world now under consideration, *whether thrones, or dominions, or principalities, or powers,* including all the supposed hierarchy of the Rabbinical system, if indeed such might exist, as the Gnostics supposed without proof, and even if they should exist, *all stand* permanently existent, *created*[8] *through Him,* the intermediate agent, *and for Him* as their end and destiny. Christ is the creative center and intermediate agent in the creation of all things, and the causal element accounting for their existence (Elliott). Creation of the universe was completed and is permanent and destined for Him as its head and goal.

v. 17. *And He is before* or prior to *all things* in time and rank, preexisting before they existed, *and in him all things* permanently *consist,* cohere or stand together, having Him as the center of their unity and as the sustaining support of their existence (Heb. 1:3). Christ is the center of the Cosmos (making it a universe through the power of His Cosmic will. This Christocentric philosophy of Paul surpasses Aristotle's understanding that God was the origin of the world and that it 'coheres through him *for us.*'

2. Christ is also preeminent as the Head of the moral creation in redemption, the Church, which is His body (vv. 18-20).

v 18. *And He*[9] *Himself is the Head of His body,* the church,[10] being supreme in the realm of the spiritual world and Lord of his church, governing the body as the head does being the source also of its life, energy, and power, *who,* in that He *is the Beginning,* having the priority both in time and rank in his relationship with the created universe, *the first-born from the dead,*[11] through His resurrection as the present living and reigning Christ, *in order that* He *may become himself preeminent*[12] *in all* things, the Head of the

---

7. Constative aorist passive.
8. Perfect passive indicative of *ktizō.*
9. Order of emphasis of the Greek text.
10. Appositional epexegetical construction.
11. Ablative case, idea of separation.
12. Present active participle, *protenōn,* of verb *protenō.*

Church in virtue of His Incarnation, Death and Resurrection, the basis of His just preeminence.

v. 19. *because in Him* (Christ), *he* (God) *was pleased*, and it was his goodwill *and pleasure to have all the plenitude* (pleroma) or fulness of the powers and attributes of God *to* permanently *dwell* or take up their abode, (Abbott).

v. 20 *and to reconcile all* the universe of men and things, *through Him*, as mediator, *unto Himself* (God), who himself needs no reconciliation but rather his creatures do, who are out of harmony with him, by *having made peace through the blood of His* (Christ's) *cross, through Him alone, whether the things upon the earth,* sinful men *or those* creatures, possibly fallen angels, over whom Christ triumphs in some way *in the heavens*, who instead of being mediators, as the false teachers in Colossae were teaching, would have, if such there be themselves, necessity of the sole mediator, Christ.

Paul discusses the preeminence of Christ, especially in view of the heretical teachings of some of the Christian leaders in the church in Colossae and the environmental background, the influence of which had contaminated their thinking with false Greek speculative philosophy and Oriental mysticism, mixed with Essenism and traditional Judaism. The ideas of nascent Gnosticism, with its false theory of creation and redemption, through a series of mediating emanations of the effulgence of Deity, gradually darkened, from Angelic beings and powers to the demiurgic shadowy creatures, tying the series on to matter inherently evil, resulted in angel worship, subordinating Christ to the series of angelic creatures and robbing him of his place and honor of sole Mediator.

Paul meets this heresy with a statement of the headship of Christ over the material universe and also over the moral and spiritual sphere. The unapproachable God is invisible but is revealed in the visible Christ, who is the express image and stamped-impress of his substance, thus revealing him to the senses of mankind and bridging the gulf between man and God. In His relationship, He is set forth over against the material universe, as the first-born Son; as the intermediate agent, and the goal of its creation, *preexistent before it in time and preeminent also in the dignity of rank, as well as being the center of its unity and bond of its providential upholding* (Mullins).

In His relation to the Church, He is head of the Body, and in virtue of His being the Beginning, He is its originator, the first-born from the dead, heading the procession of a great throng of those who through his redemptive work shall be raised. There is no need of a series of angelic beings to mediate in originating this new moral creation in which He is the sole mediator. All the plenitude of powers for this work of creation and providential upholding according to the good pleasure of the Father are summed up in Him. Through Him reconciliation is worked out by the shedding of his blood on the cross, effecting peace between men and God and meeting the needs of adjustment between God and all spiritual intelligences in the heavenlies.

III. The office or work of the Son in reconciliation illustrated, especially in the experience of the Colossians. 1:21-2:5.

1. Paul's doctrine of the Person of Christ having been stated,[13] he passes on to make application of it to his hearers and readers, who were once alienated and rendered personally hostile in their minds by evil works and are now reconciled in the body of His flesh through His death. 1:21-23.

v. 21. *And you at one time were in a continuing state of alienation from* God *and were hostile* toward God *in your mind,* intent and purpose, which found expression *in your*

v. 22. *works* which were emphatically *evil,*[14] *yet now He* (Christ) definitely *reconciled you, by or in the body of His flesh,* in a real incarnation, (the Gnostics to the contrary), *through* the intermediate agency *of His*[15] actual *death* on the cross, *to present you holy,* separated to God's service, *and without blemish and unreprovable before Him,* in His presence, now in an upright moral and spiritual character, and in the future judgment in a sinless purity.

v. 23. *if, indeed, you are abiding* or continuing *grounded and firm in your vital faith,* in Christ and His mediation *and are not shifting* continuously,[16] by the false teaching of supplementary, mediation of angels, instead of Christ's sole mediation, *from the* true *hope of the Gospel which you heard, which was preached*[17] universally *in all creation under the heaven, of which I, Paul, am become a minister.* The Christianity they had received from him was historic, missionary and universal in character.

2. The revelation of redemption, through human agency, in which Paul had a leading part through his ministry and sufferings, in carrying out the stewardship of the mystery of the Gospel. His anxiety on behalf of all Christians, especially the Colossian saints and the neighboring churches. 1:24-2:5.

a. Paul's joy in his ministry and sufferings. He found joy in his sufferings in his own body for the Body of Christ (1:24-29).

v. 24. *Now,* even though chained to a soldier, *I rejoice in my sufferings on behalf of you* Colossians and other Gentiles and *I am filling up to the full the "left-overs" of the tribulations* or afflictions *of Christ,* such as He suffered and such as His followers coming after Him must suffer, and I like the rest *in my flesh,* as my part *on behalf of His Body, which is the church.*

The 'remainder' of the suffering of Christ at any time is that which is lacking for the full establishment of God's Kingdom and the perfection of his people in that period and for the future. It is a form of mental anguish which the Lord felt on behalf of the Colossian Christians and which Paul in like manner felt.

v. 25. The sufferings of Christ on the cross, had an atoning value and were completed in His death, but in the suffering of Christ's followers there is no expiatory nature or value. Paul's suffering was on behalf of the church, "*of which,* he says, *I became a minister according to the stewardship of God's*

---

13. Periphrastic Perfect passive participle.
14. Position of article and adjective for emphasis.
15. Possessive use of definite article.
16. Present Middle participle, implying their voluntary action.
17. Aorist passive participle.

household the church, *which was given* or divinely commissioned *to me for you,* in your interests, *to fill full, the word of God* in carrying on its universal mission to all the peoples, but also the 'word of God,' which is the pure message of the Gospel, "uncorrupted by the false teachings of Gnosticism or other heresies."

v. 26, 27 *The mystery,* unlike those of the heathen mystery religions, which were confined to a narrow circle of men, is that 'love secret of universal salvation', *which has been hidden from the ages* (aeons) *and from the generations* gone, *but now was made manifest to his saints* in general, and not just to the apostles, but to all his saints,

v. 27. *to whom God willed* or wished *to make known, what is the wealth of the glory of this mystery* operative *among* the *Gentiles,* breaking down "all the barriers of race, nation, caste and sex," the revelation of the glorious fact of universal redemption, *who* (which) *is Christ in you,* dwelling in your hearts, and being the central fact of Christian redemption, *the hope* or pledge *of* future *glory* for you and all who trust in Him and His sole and effective mediation, in salvation.

v. 28. He is such a Christ as this of experience, history, hope and power, *whom we proclaim,* in contrast to one of intellectual exclusiveness, (such as the Gnostics present), *admonishing every man* to repent and turn from sin because of this gospel message, *and teaching every man* individually, until all are reached with full instruction, as to what they are to believe, *in all wisdom* offered fully and freely to all alike and to every man individually and in particular, to the end *that we might present every man* of you Christians *perfect* or full grown *in Christ,* in the end, and in absolute moral perfection or completeness before the tribunal of Christ, not sinless before that time as some would claim, but in the final judgment.

v. 29. *For which* goal or purpose *I also toil,* as an olympic wrestler in an agony of struggle, striving *according to his* mightily working *energy which works in me in power* (powerfully).

b. Paul's anxiety, on behalf of the unknown saints who had not seen his face, leading to his warnings against the false teachers of false philosophies. 2:1-5.

v. 1. *For I want you to know, how great a struggle I am having* in prayer *for you* my unvisited converts in Colossae, *and* for those *in Laodicea, and so many as* elsewhere, *have not seen my face in the flesh.* Paul had not visited the mission churches founded by Epaphras and others in the interior regions of the province of Asia, in the Lycus valley, being unable to do so.

v. 2. But he had been and was constantly[18] and anxiously striving for them in prayer *that their hearts,* including intellects, emotions and wills *might be* strengthened *or encouraged* to action, *having been knit together in* the bond of *love,* as the cells of the human body in vital helpful relationship, resulting *also* in united growth *into all the wealth* or riches *of full assurance* and con-

18. Present active indicative. *echō,* of linear action.

viction, coming from a complete intellectual grasp, through the use *of the understanding* or insight of a keen intelligence. They had need to use all their mental powers to come *unto the full knowledge* (epignosis) of *the* once hidden but now revealed *'mystery' of the God,* even *Christ,* unto this 'additional knowledge' of the mystery about Christ, who was the sum of the great love secret of God.

v. 3. *in whom are all the treasures of the wisdom* or contemplative reasoning *and* also *of knowledge* or apprehension, which is *hidden* or locked up except to the initiated. The Gnostic claimed instead that the secrets of salvation were 'locked up' in their esoteric writings about the angelic mediators, but the early Christians through Paul's instruction soon came to apply this term *apocryfoi,* apochryphal, to the false or spurious writings which were not inspired by the Holy Spirit.[19]

v. 4. *This I am saying* to warn you against any one who would lead you astray, *that no one may deceive you by* glib, *plausible speech* of 'specious argument or persuasive rhetoric' (Lightfoot), such as these Gnostic philosophers blandly use.

v. 5. *For even if I am absent in the flesh* or bodily, *still I am with you in the spirit, rejoicing and beholding* continually *your orderly array and the solid front of your faith in Christ.*[20]

IV. Having called their attention, with assurance of his confidence (vv. 4, 5), Paul charges the Colossians to abide in the truth of the Gospel as they had received it at first and not to be led astray by the strange philosophy of vain deceit, taught by the Graeco-Essenic heretics 2:6-15.

1. First, the apostle charges the Colossian saints to abide in the truth and walk in Christ loyally, rooted, built up and stablished in the faith. vv. 6, 7.

v. 6. I exhort you *then* that even in the same manner *as you received,* through Epaphras and others who preached to you, *Christ Jesus* the Messiah-Savior *as Lord,* above all principality and power and not as a mere mythical but the historical Christ, incarnated in the historical Jesus of Nazareth, now, *go on walking* in your daily life *in Him* as the road or way of your moral conduct.

v. 7. having been permanently *rooted*[21] in Christ as a tree in the good soil and *being built up*[22] continually and progressively upon and *in Him,* as a solid foundation, which also binds the church all together (Eph. 2:20), *and having been* as a result *stablished*[23] firmly *in your faith* in Christ, as your sole and supreme Lord, and in "the faith once delivered to the saints," *just as you were taught, abounding* as a natural consequence *in the giving of thanks* to Christ, which thanksgiving will be a good antidote to the false teaching of the Gnostic heresy.

---

19. Robertson, A. T., *Paul and the Intellectuals,* in loco.
20. Moffatt's Translation, in loco.
21. Perfect passive participle, *errizomenoi.*
22. Present passive participle.
23. Perfect passive participle.

2. They are warned positively against the current of false philosophy and reminded that all the plenitude or fulness (*pleroma*) dwells wholly in Christ, being communicated through Him; and also that the spiritual is the true circumcision, Christ having annulled the law of the ordinances and triumphed over all spiritual agencies however powerful. 2:8-15.

v. 8. Having "reiterated the need of adherence to the simple and sufficient faith in Christ,"[24] Paul warns the Colossians to be on their guard against false phlosophy. "*Look out lest there shall be*[25] *some one carrying you off*[26] *as booty,* kidnapping you for the purpose of seducing you from the true doctrine, in a captivity of error. There was evidently some person or more among the leaders in Colossae *who by means of philosophy* of a false type, of the godless kind, *of empty deceit,* trickery. Paul was not afraid of truth in any realm and is not here condemning 'knowledge and wisdom,' but warning against a philosophy which cuts God and the deity of Christ out. There is a true philosophy which grasps real truth as a whole and Paul was a philosopher in that true sense. But the philosophy of the false teachers in the Colossian church, was *according to the* wrong *traditions of* these mere *men,* passed on under oath as the esoteric exclusive knowledge, claimed by them. Paul says that this false philosophy was *according to the rudiments* or elements *of the world, and not according to Christ.* It was a mere man-made materialistic philosophy, smacking of the earthy, and based on the theories of the Gnostics "and of the Essenes their spiritual predecessors." There are traditions to all the realms of knowledge whether of science, philosophy, theology or other; but much of tradition is not true and much more is merely speculative or to be proven or verified. True science is verified by human experience, but false science and philosophy attack the bases of religious experience and must be met as Paul met this *by the test of fact and Christian experience.* Theories of the universe must leave place for God as personal Creator and for the deity and lordship of Christ. The recent discovery in the realm of the atomic background of the material world, leaves mankind helpless, except through the sovereignty of a loving God and the merciful mediation of Christ.

v. 9. The reason is found in the fact that *in Him* (Christ) *dwells* permanently *all the fulness* (*pleroma,* plenitude) *of the Godhead* or deity in *bodily* form, and even also in His glorified humanity upon the throne of the universe, the Docetic and Cerinthian Gnostic to the contrary.[27] Paul, writing under divine inspiration, was thus able to meet fully the heresy of the Docetic Gnostics, who denied the reality of the body of Jesus Christ, and that of the Cerinthian Gnostics, who denied the reality of the permanent incarnation of the Christ in the Man Jesus, both of which heresies flourished full-bloom in the second century, but were evidently existent in nascent germ in Colossae when Paul wrote this letter. He also thus destroyed the false philosophic

24. Moffatt, James: *Introduction to the New Testament* p. 151.
25. Future indicative makes more real and vivid than the subjunctive (Boise).
26. A definite person evidently meant.
27. Robertson, A. T.: *Paul and the Intellectuals,* p. 116.

basis which the heretics were laying in the Colossian church, and saved their Christian theology and ours. The Lordship of Christ rests upon His being the essence and not merely of the quality[28] of deity. He was manifested as deity in the incarnation in bodily form and bore the marks of his humanity when he arose from the grave and ascended to the Father.[29] The value of the relationship of Christ as Head of the church is in His deity, making Him the source or mediator of all spiritual things for His followers.

v. 10. *And you are already in Him made full.*[30] We are partakers of the divine nature by the new birth into the Kingdom; but we do not partake of the essence of deity as Christ did, *who is the head of every principality and power,* and center of all energy and life, as well as of control and government for his followers.

v. 11. *In whom also ye were circumcised with the circumcision not made with hands,* by the cutting of flesh from the body, but on the contrary, by *the Christ-Kind*[31] of spiritual *circumcision* that of the heart, *with the putting off* (and away) of the body of the flesh, the seat of sinful carnal passions. Thus Paul dealt with one of the practical errors growing out of the false theological tenets.

v. 12. *When you were buried with Him*[32] *in baptism* or immersion, a water-burial, "being plunged under the water, thereby declaring faith in the expiatory death of Christ for the pardon of past sins" (Thayer) and also of future sins as well, *wherein ye were also raised with him.* Baptism is according to Paul a symbol or picture of the death to sin and also of the resurrection to a new life in Christ. There is no sacramental efficacy in the ordinance of baptism, which is but a symbol of the reality of a death to sin and a resurrection to a new life, operating *through* or by means *of the faith in the working of God who raised Him* (Christ) *from the dead,* by his own energy.

v. 13. *and you* Gentiles *being dead* spiritually or morally, *in* (or by)[33] *your transgressions,* moral lapses, *and the uncircumcision of your flesh,* and thus alienated symbolically as well as really from God, *did he quicken together with Him*[34] *having* himself *graciously forgiven*[35] *us all our transgressions.*

vv. 14, 15. *Having blotted out* and so cancelled or taken out of the way *the bond against us* along *with the decrees,* which bond thus established was against us. We had signed this bond with our own assent of conscience with all the seals of decretal obligation; we were unable to pay *and He* (Christ) *has taken it out of the midst, nailing it to the cross.* The law of ordinances

---

28. Of the essence *theotōs* and not merely the quality, *theistōs.*
29. Phil. 2:5-11.
30. Periphrastic perfect passive, permanence and completion.
31. Subjective genitive.
32. Second aorist passive participle with associative instrumental autoi.
33. Either locative or instrumental makes sense.
34. Associative instrumental autoi with the verb compounded with sun.
35. Aorist middle participle.

was nailed to the cross, rent with Christ's body and destroyed with his death (Lightfoot).

v. 15. *Having spoiled the principalities and the powers* or authorities, *He made a spectacle of them openly triumphing over them in it* (the cross). These angelic powers, which according to Jewish traditions were the mediators in the giving of the law of Moses, were made hostile, in the teaching of the Gnostic teachers, toward the cross of Christ and his mediation. Here, Paul says Christ despoiled these angelic principalities and powers by stripping them of the worship which was being offered them by these false teachers and made a public show of them gaining over them a complete victory, through His atoning death on the cross.

3. Paul further warns the Colossian saints against being deceived by the empty forms and also against angel worship. 2:16-23.

a. They must not submit to the formal ritual observance of certain rules of abstinence, which are impotent as a means of curbing the evil tendencies of human nature. 2:16-17.

v. 16. Paul lays down the prohibition[36] against the imposition by the Essenic heretics. *Let no one therefore*, in view of the triumph of Christ over this false teaching, *judge you*, deciding for you, *in* respect to any act of *eating*[37] *and in drinking*, after the manner of their extreme Essenic asceticism, even going far beyond the Mosaic limitations as to food. In his plea for liberty Paul mentions not only diet (cf. Rom. 14:17, 21) but also the ritualistic rigor, *or in the matter* or category *of a feast*, such as the annual festivals of the Jews, *or* prescribing rules as to monthly sacred seasons, as *of a new moon or of sabbaths*, dictating as to the observance of a single sabbath.[38] The Sabbath was made on account of the human being not the human being on account of the sabbath (Mark 2:27). It is essential to man's physical and spiritual well being (Gen. 2:1-3) and might be any day in the week. The Christians honor Christ by using Sunday to get away from the legalistic idea, and celebrate His resurrection. Paul pleads for liberty of conscience and freedom from legalism and regimentation of religion.

v. 17. The reason for such admonition follows: *Which* things *are a shadow of the things to come;* These Mosaic distinctions were a shadow, *but the body*, substance and reality, *pertain to Christ* and are Christian.

b. Nor should they substitute the worship of angels in the place of loyal worship to Christ, the head of the Church (vv. 18, 19).

v. 18. They must beware of false teachers who would dethrone Christ, by exalting to the place of worship angelic mediators. *Let no one* assume the place or *act as umpire against you, wishing* to do it *in* an assumed attitude of *humility and in a* false substitution of *the worship of angels*, (as some substi-

---

36. Negative of prohibition with *me*.
37. Ending *sis* denotes act or action.
38. The plural *sabbata* was an effort to translate the Aramaic *Sabbathah* and means a single Sabbath or weekly sacred day.

tute the worship of so-called saints or human beings today), in the place of an exclusive worship of Christ. The affected humility is as false as its expression in angel-worship, much more "saint-worship" is blasphemous. It is equally wrong to put anything else, as the "laws of nature," in the place of one's worship of Christ. Such a person in his false attitude *is taking his stand on what he has seen, vainly puffed up by the mind of his flesh*, as the Gnostic devotees in their vain pride are puffed up with the idea of their superior knowledge (Abbott).

v. 19. *And not holding with a firm grasp the Head*, Christ *from whom all the body* or church *being supplied and compacted together, through the nerves* or joints *and bands* or ligaments, *grows with the increase of God.* The body severed from the head cannot grow.

c. On the contrary, they have died with Christ to these rudimentary rules of a self-imposed discipline which are of no value against the indulgence of the Carnal nature but tend to pamper it instead (2:20-23).

v. 20 *If ye died with Christ from the rudiments of the world*, as you surely did,[39] *why, as if living in* the sphere of *the world do you go on submitting yourselves to dogmas.*[40]

vv. 21, 22. *Handle not, nor taste, nor touch,*[41] *(all which things are to perish with the using), according to the precepts and doctrines of men*, probably about articles of foods prohibited and ceremonial observances without number.

v. 23. *Which things indeed have an appearance of wisdom*, as in the ascetic life, *and of lowliness of mind and in servere treatment of the body*, not (in) of any value against the indulgence of the flesh.

V. Exhortations to a practical application of the principle of the life, resurrected with Christ. 3:1-17.

1. A right relation with Christ in the resurrected life is the basis of proper conduct. 3:1-4.

v. 1. *If then ye were raised*[42] *together with Christ*, as you certainly were,[43] *begin and go on seeking habitually*[44] *the things above, where Christ is sitting on the right hand of God.*

v.2. *Set your mind*[45] *on the things that are above, not on the things that are upon the earth.*

v. 3. *For ye died*[46] *definitely and your life is hid* permanently[47] *with Christ in God.*

---

39. First class condition, according to fact.
40. Middle voice.
41. Aor. middle subj. second per. sing.
42. Aorist ind, act., actual occurrence.
43. First class condition, according to fact.
44. Pres. Imv.
45. Present Imperative, begin to do this and keep on doing it, if you have not already done it.
46. Aorist definitely.
47. Perfect tense, denoting permanence. 7 Aor. Imv.

v. 4. *When Christ*, who is *our life, shall be manifested, then shall ye also with him be manifested in glory.*

2. Enumeration of the vices to be put away from their conduct on the principle of death with Christ to sin. 3:5-11.

v. 5. *Put to death therefore* quickly *your members* which are *upon earth*, that is: *fornication, uncleanness, passion, evil desire, and covetousness, which is idolatry.* These are vices of the unchaste and voluptuous life of the heathen world. Christians must not harbor such but quickly put them away from their life and conduct.

v. 6. *On account of which* things *cometh the wrath of God* upon the sons of disobedience.

v. 7. *In which* things *ye also were accustomed to walk* beforetime *when ye were living*[48] *in such.*

v. 8. *But now do ye also put away all these* additional things: *anger, wrath, malice, railing, shameful speaking out of your mouth.*

v. 9. *Lie not one to another; seeing ye have put off*[49] *the old man with his doings.*

v. 10. *And have put on the new man, who is being renewed unto* accurate *knowledge after the image of him that created him*: (God's image).

v. 11 *Where there cannot be Greek and Jew*, no racial or national distinctions; *circumcision and uncircumcision*, ceremonial discrimination or dependence on mere ordinances; *barbarian, Scythian, bondman, freeman:*[50] *but Christ is all and in all.*

3. Enumeration of the graces to be put on in the resurrected life with Christ 3:12-17.

v. 12. *Put on therefore* promptly, *as the elect of God, holy and beloved, a heart of compassion, kindness, humility, meekness, long-suffering;*

v. 13. *forbearing one another and forgiving each other, if any man have a complaint against any; even as the Lord forgave you, so also do ye:*

v. 14. *And over all these things* put on *love, which is the bond* (or band which binds all together) *of perfectness* (full-grown, manhood in Christ).

v. 15. *And let the peace of Christ*, such peace as he demonstrated in his life, *rule in your hearts* (thoughts, feelings, desires) *to which also ye were called in one body; and be ye thankful.*

v. 16. *Let the word of Christ*, spoken and proclaimed by him, *dwell in you*, as a vital and living force, *richly in all wisdom, teaching and admonishing one another, with psalms and hymns and spiritual songs, singing with grace, in your hearts unto God.* Worship in song must be with grace and must be with a worshipful attitude to God.

v. 17 *And whatsoever ye do in word or deed*, do *all in the name of the Lord Jesus, giving thanks to God the Father through him.* All of life must be Christian, in a true Christian.

---

48. Imperfect, continued action.
49. Aor, part., definite occurrence.
50. No exclusion on account of different civilization or social status.

4. Special precepts in relation to the mutual obligations of the different members, and servants and masters, in the Christian family. 3:18-4:1.

v. 18. *Wives be in* habitual *subjection to your* own *husbands, as was fitting* ever since you became Christians, in the sphere of the life and character, in *the Lord.*

v. 19. *Husbands, love*[51] *your wives*, with a Christian love *and be not bitter against them.*

v. 20. *Children, hear obediently your parents in all things* (in the Lord) *for this is well-pleasing in the Lord,* where all relationships are holy.

v. 21. *Fathers, provoke* (or irritate) *not your children, that they be not discouraged* or disheartened.

v 22. *Servants* (slaves) *obey in all things them that are your masters according to the flesh, not with eye-service, as men-pleasers, but in singleness of heart, fearing the Lord.*

v. 23. *Whatsoever ye do, work heartily, as unto the Lord and not unto men.* The Christian slave is thus free, withal.

v. 24. *Knowing that from the Lord ye shall receive the recompense,* namely *the inheritance*: *ye serve the Lord Christ.* Nothing can prevent a slave from so doing.

v. 25. *For he that doeth wrong shall receive again for the wrong that he hath done*: *and there is no respect of persons.* Owners of slaves may well take heed to this!

Ch. 4:v. 1. *Masters, render unto your servants* (slaves) *that which is just and equal*: *Knowing that ye also have a Master in heaven.* To render what is just and equal would be to give the slaves liberty.

5. Precepts as to personal religious duties of the individual Christian in his devotional life and personal relationships. 4:2-6.

v. 2. *Continue steadfastly in prayer, watching therein with thanksgiving;*[52]

v. 3. *Withal praying also for us, in order that God may open unto us a door for the word, to speak the mystery* (love secret of salvation) *of Christ, on account of which I am also in bonds.*

v. 4. *That I may make it manifest, as I ought to speak.* This is the ministers' chief concern.

v. 5. *Walk,* in your conduct, *in wisdom toward those who are without,* the pales of salvation, *redeeming the time* (buying up the opportunity, making use of the opportune time).

v. 6. *Let your speech be always with grace,* an attitude of graciousness, *seasoned with* the *salt* of wisdom and good sense, *so as to know always how*[53] *it is necessary that you answer* each one. *Conclusion* in explanations about the teller, in personal salutations to various ones, and in final messages 4:7-18.

---

51. *Agapē,* Christian love, not mere human affection.
52. Instrumental with prep. *en.*
53. Present Inf. expressing habitual action.

a. Tychicus and Onesimus would report to them all about Paul and his affairs. vv. 7-9.

v. 7 *All my affairs, shall Tychicus make known unto you, the beloved brother and faithful minister and fellow-servant in the Lord,*

v. 8. *Whom I have sent unto you,*[54] in order *that you may know our estate, and that He may comfort your hearts;*

v. 9. *Together with Onesimus, the faithful and beloved brother* in Christ, *who is one of you* in Colossae. *They shall make known unto you all things that* are done here.

b. Salutations from fellow-workers vv. 10-14.

v. 10. Aristarchus my fellow-prisoner saluteth you, and (John Mark) the cousin of Barnabas (touching whom ye received commandments, if he come receive him),

v. 11 *And Jesus, who is called Justus, are of the circumcision: these only* are my *fellow-workers for the Kingdom of God, men that have been a comfort to me.*

v. 12 *Epaphras, who is one of you,* (having been their pastor) *a servant of Christ Jesus, saluteth you, always striving for you in his prayers, that you may stand perfect and fully assured in all the will of God.*

v. 13. *For I bear him witness, that he hath much labor for you and for them in Laodicea, and for them in Hierapolis.* He had pastored all three churches.

v. 14. *Luke, the beloved physician, and Demas salute you.*

c. Salutations to various persons and the church, and various messages vv. 15-17.

v. 15. *Salute the brethren that are in Laodicea and Nymphas and the church that is in their house.*

v. 16. *And when this epistle hath been read among you, cause that it be read in the church of the Laodiceans, and that ye read also the epistle from Laodicea* (probably the circular letter, Ephesians).

v. 17. *And say to Archippus, "Take heed to the ministry which thou hast received in the Lord, that thou fulfil it."*

v. 18. *The Salutation of me, Paul, with mine own hand. Remember* in your prayers *my bonds. Grace be with you.*

EPISTLE TO PHILEMON

"No longer as a slave, but more than a slave, a brother beloved" (v. 16).

Philemon, his wife and his son Archippus were converted under Paul's ministry in Ephesus. He became a zealous Christian, throwing his home in Colossae open as a place of worship for the church there, in its infancy. Archippus became a minister and fellow-worker of Paul later. In this household there existed slavery as in most well-to-do families at that time and one slave whose

---

54. Epistolary aorist.

name was Onesimus (meaning Profitable) turned out to be, not only unprofitable, but stole something from his master and ran away and hid himself in the wretched slums of Rome. The Phyrgian slave soon came to grief in the great city, and, like the prodigal, lost all he had. But having known something of Paul in Ephesus he made his way to the great-hearted apostle now in Rome, who dealt with him tenderly and won him to the gospel.

The monster Nero on the imperial throne enumerated among his cruel acts the carrying out of the ruthless silovian law, adopted by the Roman Senate about that time to protect the many heartless slave-owners from possible acts of vengeance of slaves against their masters. Nero ordered four hundred innocent slaves massacred, the occasion when Pedanius, a slave owner and senator, was slain by a slave who had been maltreated. The life of a slave in Rome was of little worth, especially at this time and Onesimus found protection with Paul and cleaved to him as his would-be servant, after he was converted.

But Paul knew he was a fugtive from the household of Philemon of Colossae and on the occasion of sending the letter to the Colossians by Tychicus he wrote a brief letter to Philemon and sent Onesimus back with Tychicus and the letter to his master.

Paul began the letter with the customary brief salutation (1-3) and a word of thanks for the liberality and goodness of this brother-in-the-faith and good friend. (4-7). He then reported the conversion of Onesimus the genuineness of which he had tested out. The slave who had become profitless to Philemon was now truly "profitable." Paul would have been pleased to retain Onesimus as his helper and companion but sends him back unto his owner, pleading that Philemon receive him back into his service. He offers to personally assume the obligation of the money the slave had stolen. Then he presumes to ask that Philemon prepare to receive him as his guest in his home on a brief visit he hopes to make soon in Colossae, and ends the letter with another exhortation and a blessing (8-22).

This brief letter of infinite charm, characteristically Pauline in its style and content is a window through which one may look in on the private life of Paul. How exquisitely courteous and refined in dealing with Philemon, how tender and solicitous about the converted slave, thus revealing the Gospel in which there is no difference — "neither bond nor free." Paul made no revolutionary attack on the institution of slavery but in one brief epistle undermined its whole fabric. This is how Christianity deals with vast social problems. Philemon forgave and took back him who had been his "profitless" slave, no longer as a slave but now as more than a slave, a brother beloved.

Paraphrastic Translation and Exegesis

1. Salutations vv. 1-3.

Paul a prisoner of Christ Jesus in *Rome and Timothy the brother* with me, *to Philemon* the dearly beloved *and our fellow-worker, and to Apphia our sister in* the faith, *and to Archippus our fellow soldier* in Christ *and to the church* which assembles *in thy house: Grace to you and peace from God our Father and the Lord Jesus Christ.*

2. *Thanks to Philemon.* vv. 4-7.

I give thanks to my God, always making mention of you at my prayer times, hearing of your Christian love and the faith you have towards the Lord Jesus *and in all the saints;* and my prayer is *that the fellowship* or sharing *of your faith may become effectual in the* accurate *knowledge of every kind of good which is in*[55] or among *us for* the benefit *of Christ. For I had great joy and comfort* when I heard of your *love, that the affections of the saints have been refreshed through you my brother.*

3. *Plea for the converted Onesimus* vv. 8-22, being encouraged.

Wherefore, though I have much boldness in Christ *to enjoin on* you *that which is befitting, yet on account of our* Christian *love, I rather exhort you, being* such *as I am, Paul an elder and now also a prisoner for Jesus Christ, I do exhort you concerning my child in the faith, whom I begat,* while preaching *in my bonds, Onesimus, the one who was once unprofitable to you but now both to you and also to me, useful,* whom I have sent[56] back to you in *his own person, that is, my very heart. Indeed I would gladly have kept him with me, that he might minister to me for you in these bonds which* are on account *of the gospel, but without thy mind I would do nothing, that* your *goodness should not be of necessity but of free will. For perhaps he was thus parted from you temporarily by God's providence, that you might regain him forever, no longer as a mere slave but more than a slave, a brother beloved. Indeed he is this to me most of all, and if to me so much more to you both in fleshly things and in the Lord? If therefore you regard me as a friend and companion take him to yourself as if he were myself. But if he has wronged you at all or owes you anything put that to my account. I, Paul, wrote it with my own hand, I will repay it, not to say to you that you owe to me even yourself besides: yea, brother, let me have joy of thee in the Lord: refresh my heart in Christ. Having confidence on thine obedience I write unto you, knowing that you will do even beyond what I say.*

4. *Paul requests hospitality and concludes.* v. 23f. *But withal prepare me also a lodging; for I hope that through your prayers I shall be granted unto you,* when I am liberated from prison.

Ephaphras, your pastor and my fellow-prisoner in Christ Jesus, salutes you; and so do Mark, Aristarchus, Demus, and Luke my fellow-workers.

The grace of our Lord Jesus Christ be with *your* spirit. Amen

---

55. Cf. Nestle's Text. v. 6.
56. Epistolary Aorist.

CHAPTER XXIV

The Ephesian Epistle (Circular)

Introduction

1. Authority and Genuineness.

THIS letter bears the imprint of Paul's style, vocabulary, and thought, and includes much of the content of the Colossian epistle written A. D. 63. It expands the idea of world-wide redemption in Christ, adding the explanation as to the manner of the revelation of this redemption to the Gentiles, through the instrumentality of Paul and the Church, the Body of Christ. The dignity of Christ as head of the universe in creation and of the Church in moral redemption is the theme of Colossians, while the dignity of the Church as the agent of revelation to the world is added in Ephesians in the presentation of God's plan of the ages for humanity.

Tychicus brought the letters to the Colossians and Philemon in Colossae and may have been the bearer of this circular letter at the same time (Ephesians 6:21). It was destined as it seems for the reading and use of all the churches in the Roman Province of Asia. The words "at Ephesus" (Ephesians 1:1) were not a part of the two oldest manuscripts (Aleph and B). Tychicus was sent by Paul from Rome on a mission of general information and encouragement to a number of churches including those of Ephesus, Laodicea, Colossae and possibly several others. Such being the case, the circular letter would, after being read in various churches, be returned to the central mother church in the great city of Ephesus, the capital of the Roman Province (Colossians 4:16 etc.), where copies would be made for distribution to all the churches of the region later. Ephesus would thus give its name to the epistle in the process of time, as was natural for convenience.

Paul wrote the letter in Rome and not in Ephesus or Caesarea as some critics would suggest. The lack of personal references in a circular letter would be the natural thing to expect. The very universal character of the epistle also with its grandiose sweep of the universe and the ages, would make irrelevant local application and reflections such as are found in Paul's previously written epistles.

External and internal evidence alike furnish much information as to the genuineness and authenticity of Ephesians. Very few critics today have any doubt about its Pauline authorship. The epistle was used by Clemente of Rome, (A. D. 96), Barnabas (106), Ignatius (115), Ireneus (175), Tertullian (190) and Clement of Alexandria (A. D. 195), all of whom gave their testimony.

2. Ephesus.

Ephesus was a great commercial metropolis, located on the main thoroughfare and trade route between Europe and Asia Minor. It was the Capital and most important city of the Roman province of Asia, being located on the banks of the Cayster river a short distance from the Aegean Sea. It was originally a sea-port, but at the time of Paul's ministry there mariners could not come up the river channel to the city, due to its becoming blocked by the deposits of silt in its bed. It was a free city with its own assembly and council, like that of Athens before the time of Paul, but its popular government declined under the Romans and the power passed into the hands of Roman officials, the chief of whom was the "town-clerk." The city was a center of culture being the home of the famous grecian painters Parrhassius, Appelles and other men of talent. It was also the center of the worship of the Greek Goddess Artemis, whose temple of marble erected there was one of the seven wonders of the world. There were also other remarkable architectural structures, as the vast amphitheater which would accomodate 50,000 spectators and two other outstanding buildings, later in the history of the city, the great Christian church dedicated by Justinian to St. John the Evangelist who lived in Ephesus after the destruction of Jerusalem, and the Mohammedan mosque, a specimen of Arabian-Persian architecture. The city of Ephesus after centuries disappeared and today the site is marked by extensive ruins and a nearby modern Arab village Aya Seluk, the *Holy Divine* (St. John).

3. The Church in Ephesus.

Paul founded the Church in Ephesus on his third missionary journey, while residing in the city for three years. He began his work of evangelization in the home of Aquilla and Priscilla. He had passed by there and made one brief stop on his return from his second missionary journey to Antioch of Syria. He was then invited and promised to return (Acts 18:19-21). On his arrival in Ephesus later (Acts 19:1) he stayed in the home of Aquilla and Priscilla who had improved upon the work of Paul's former brief visit, and together they founded the church. He later preached three months in the Jewish Synagogue, until fierce opposition arose, when he withdrew to the Lecture-Hall of Tyrannus nearby and carried on there for more than two years, in a ministry attended with marked results. The city was profoundly moved and the gospel spread through converts like Epaphras to many towns scattered over the regions round about. The magical arts suffered a great reverse as did the trade of the idol makers of the temple of the goddess Diana (Artemis). Tumultuous opposition arose and finally Paul was forced to retire from the city, leaving the church to carry on under the leadership of its own elders (pastors). The church which grew up was composed of both Jews and Gentiles, the majority of whom pertained to the latter group. Paul later placed Timothy in charge of the Church temporarily. John, the theologian, from his home in the city of Ephesus later carried on the work in connection with the seven churches in Asia to whom he wrote in the letters recorded in his Apocalypse. The Ephesian Church was the one which occupied the first place and attention of John for the long period of his ministry after the destruction of Jerusalem (A. D. 70).

4. General Character, Occasion, Place and Contents.

Renan, the French critic, called this letter *Une epitre banal* (a trivial epistle) but Samuel Taylor Coleridge, a subtle critic, pronounced it "one of the divinest compositions of man." Stalker calls the first three chapters "the profoundest thing ever written" and A. T. Robertson declares that this section "reaches the heights of Christian thinking and sounds the profoundest depths of truth." Most scholars who have studied and interpreted this epistle have been at one in declaring it the sublimest and most profound of all the New Testament writings. Paul leaves the vindication of personal authority, the polemical dealing with doctrines, and other elements found in his previously written epistles, and soaring bears us to the heavenlies in Christ in the eternities. (cf. Findlay, *Greek Expositor's New Testament*).

Ephesians start with some of the fundamental conceptions of Colossians, as that of creation and redemption, and leaving apologetic and controversial matter to one side goes on to a positive statement of those ideas expanded in his treatment of the practical method of their revelation to mankind. On the perfect work of Christ he seeks to build up the plan of the Church as an agent of revelation of this gospel to the nations.

The epistle is unified in structure and its plan is simple, the argument running the gamut of many great and beautiful ideas and remarkable conceptions. Paul introduces the epistle with his customary salutation and thanks to God for the rich heritage of Christians in transcendental blessings. He prayed for the Christians that they might understand these blessings.

The epistle is divided naturally into two main sections: one doctrinal and the other practical and hertatory. In the first section Paul presents the divine reality of redemption in Christ and in the second the practical consequences of that redemption (Dana). In the first section he enumerates the blessings of eternal election, predestination, adoption through grace in the Beloved, redemption and remission of sins through Christ's atonement and the revelation of the mystery of God's will in the oneness of the universe under one head in Christ, along with the moral oneness of the church under the sole mediatorship of Christ as the head, leading into the making possible the oneness of humanity as an ultimate goal. The universal sovereignty of the divine human head, Christ Jesus, excludes all aeons, principalities, and powers of the material and spiritual spheres in the universe, and merges the corporate unity of the church (Romans 12) in a larger conception of the supreme and sole Mediatorship and Lordship of the Divine-Human Head of the Church. The practical outcome of this universal redemption is in the creation of a new humanity through the spiritual revivification or new birth and the unification of Jews and Gentiles, doing away with their age-long division and estrangement, and building the two together in a living temple for the indwelling of the Spirit.

God's purpose and "plan of the ages" was to make a unified humanity. The secret of his age-long plan is clearly revealed in Christ and interpreted by Paul. The discord and strife in nature, the division in human society, the internal conflict in the heart-life of the individual all brought about by the willful transgression of mankind, are to be done away, harmonized and unified in Christ.

This is the ultimate purpose and plan of God for humanity and the second half of the epistle sets forth the part the church is to play in the program under the leadership of the Risen Christ and the Holy Spirit, proceeding from Him. The things of Christ: love, truth, and goodness, transcend all else, and represent God's eternal will in Creation and Redemption. For its realization through the Church Paul longs and on his knees prays to the eternal God.

To this end there must be unity in the Church (Findlay). There must be humility, meekness, forbearance, peace and all good brotherly relations. The cultivation of the Christ-life, discarding heathen vices, the practice of truthfulness and honesty, abstaining from corrupt conversation, bitterness, wrath, evil-speaking and malice; watchfulness against pagan forms of moral evil, sensuality and greed; reverent regard for all the proper relations in the Christian family and the maintenance of concord and peace in the church must be carefully learned and practiced. The Christian life is a warfare against the powers of Satanic darkness and calls for a complete panoply of defensive and offensive spiritual weapons with their constant use by the Christian. Paul closes this noble epistle with an exhortation and appeal to unceasing prayer and a final benediction in terms of grace and peace.

EXPOSITION OF THE EPISTLE

ANALYSIS AND PARAPHRASE

Address and Salutation 1:1, 2.

Paul, an apostle sent *from Christ,*[1] the divine Messiah, who was incarnated as *Jesus* the Savior of mankind, and pertaining[2] to Him, commissioned also *through the will of God* according to his wish, in address now *to the saints,*[3] *those being* (whether *in Ephesus* or elsewhere), set apart by God to be separated from sin, in holy living based on faith, *and* being *faithful*[4] and loyal *in* union with the *Christ Jesus.*

Grace, which is the free divine unmerited favor of God, *and peace,* a result of reconciliation between man and God due to faith in and union with Christ, and so proceeding both *from God our* gracious *Father and* the divine Son,

1. Ablative of origin.
2. Or genitive of possession.
3. Hagiois.
4. Pistois.

our Lord Jesus, and fellow-participator in the flesh, the *Christ,* who is the fulfillment of Jewish Messianic prophecy.

I. God's eternal plan and purpose of grace for his people and the world, expressed in merciful transcendent blessings heading up in redemption and realized through Christ. 1:3-3:21.

God provided this redemption independent of all human effort, contrary to both Judaistic and pagan conceptions of salvation by human merit and achievement, acting before the foundation of the world and in the atoning work of Christ, applicable and efficient in the reconciliation and transformation of men in human history.

A. Paul ascribes praise and thanks to God for these transcendent mercies and blessings which he enumerates. 1:3-14.

1. Mercy, predestinated by the Father, among the "all spiritual blessings" with which He blessed his people, in the choice of both Jews and Gentiles, from the foundation of the world, for perfecting with love. 1:3, 4.

v. 3. *Blessed,* praised *be the God, and Father of our Lord Jesus Christ,* who called him Father and taught us to so call him, *who himself* (God) *blessed us*[5] *with every* kind of spiritual benediction or *blessing* such as believers are privileged to enjoy *in the heavenly sphere,* already, *in Christ.*

v. 4 *Just as* his immeasurable and uncaused blessing was expressed in the fact that *he chose us in Him* at a definite moment,[6] not according to our works, but *before the foundation of the world* or universe (cosmos). The purpose[7] of God's choice of us in Him (Christ) was to be saints, set apart *to be* and become *holy and blameless before his face* and in his presence *in love,* being given this standing in the sphere of his love before we even had existence.

2. He predestinated us his saints to adoption, through Jesus Christ, for Himself, according to the good pleasure of his own will to the end of the praise of the glory of his grace, which he graciously bestowed on us in his beloved. Ch. 1:5, 6.

vv. 5-6. God in the sphere of his redemptive love *chose us out beforehand,* marking us as predetermined *for adoption* into his family *through* the intermediate agency of *Jesus Christ, for himself,* his very own to "serve and glorify Him forever." This was good in God the Father's sight being *according to the good pleasure* or resolve *of his will*[8] *unto the praise due to the glory of* his manifest character in *his grace, which he freely graced* or bestowed on *us,* compassing us with favors unmerited, *in his Beloved,* making us one with Him eternally. The blessed Father for his great love and grace blessed us in the sphere of his redemptive work and for the sake of his Beloved Son, who gave Himself in eternity that He might redeem us in time and become not only our Savior but our Lord, identifying himself with us in humanity that

5. Aorist, a definite occurrence.
6. Ibid.
7. Infinite to express purpose.
8. God's will (thělęma) which is his good wish or desire for every man.

we might be identified and identify ourselves with him in His holiness, through lives of constrained obedience and devoted loyalty and love. Thus law has been replaced by love, which is the motive power in the attaining to the standards of God in a holy and blameless life.

3. Mercy realized in the beloved son in whom we have also redemption through his blood, the remission of our sins, according to the riches of God's grace, which abounded to us in all wisdom and understanding, making known the secret of his will, to make all things head up in Christ, in whom we have the inheritance, according to the eternal purpose or plan of his will, that we might be destined for the praise of his glory. 1:7-12.

v. 7. *In whom,* (that is, Christ) *we have our redemption,* rescued from sin's bondage and bought up by Him from the slave-market of sin *through* the payment of the ransom price of *His own blood.* Thus it is that we have *the forgiveness of our trespasses,* the remission or taking away of our transgressions committed in deliberately stepping over the boundaries between right and wrong. This is all *according to the wealth of his grace,* "boundless in its resources and ungrudging in its bestowal."

v. 8. *Which he made to abound to overflowing to us* from the infinite resources of his love and *in* the sphere of *all wisdom and understanding,* enabling us to grasp and comprehend his purpose and plan in our redemption and cooperate in its application and execution in our salvation.

v. 9. This wisdom and understanding came to us *when he made known to us the mystery* or inside *of his will,* hidden for ages but now revealed *according to his good pleasure* in his Son.

v. 10. His gracious resolve *which he set forth*[9] *in Him* (Christ) with a view *to the economy* or orderly unfolding and appropriate stewardship *of the fulness of the* historical *ages,* the ultimate goal of this stewardship of the ages of history, in purpose and result,[10] is *to make all things head up in Christ, both those in the heavens* or in the eternal sphere of the action of God's grace, *and those upon the earth,* in the sphere of nature and of human affairs.

v. 11. *In Him,* who is the center and effective cause of unity in the things in heaven and upon the earth, is to be found also the unifying power and center of unity between man and God and *in whom we were made the inheritance,* so as to become "the Lord's portion," in purpose, when *we were foeordained, according to the purpose of the one working all things according to the purpose of his will.*

v. 12. This purpose is directed *to the end of our being* destined *for the praise of his glory,* so transformed in a spectacle before all intelligences as to win the admiration of all for our Redeemer, *we who had beforehand* anchored our permanent hope in the Christ.

This second step in the long paragraph covering verses 7-12 presents the work of redemption wrought out through the Son Jesus Christ in the incarna-

---

9. Second Aorist Middle, *protithemi.*
10. First Aorist Middle Infinitive.

tion. He redeemed us through his blood which was the price paid on the cross. The forgiveness of our transgressions, verifies the efficiency of the cross, through the peace, reconciliation, access and joy which come to us when we accept Him. This redemptive liberation of us from the bondage of sin overflows to us in the form of wisdom in the revelation of the secret of God's will and in prudence or workable understanding of the plan and purpose of God. His plan of the ages, was to sum up all things in Christ in the heavenly spiritual sphere and also in the earthly, restoring through universal salvation the world of men and nature unto God. This was the great love secret hidden for ages but now revealed in the redemption wrought out by Christ in his sinless life and atoning death on the cross.[11]

4. When you believed in the gospel of Christ you were sealed by the Holy Spirit, who is the pledge of God's inheritance in us and ours in Him. 1:13-14.

v. 13. *In Whom* (Christ) *also you when you heard the word of the* truth, the *Gospel of your salvation, in which also when you effectively believed, you were sealed by the Holy Spirit of Promise,*[12] through the bestowal on you of power and other spiritual gifts of the Paraclete, making you an actual possession or portion, belonging to the Lord and active for him.

v. 14. *Who* (the Holy Spirit) *is a pledge* or partial down payment[13] *of our inheritance, looking forward to the* completion of our deliverance or *emancipation* from all evil within the inheritance, which is to become the completely ransomed *property or possession* of God, *to the praise of his glory.*

In the profound expressions summed up: "in the wisdom and understanding" of the plan of redemption are; first, the infinite free will and sovereignty of God, manifested, though not completely understood by the saints, in the election and foreordination of the saints to adoption, and this before the foundation of the world. In the second place is redemption in the Beloved Son from the power and bondage of sin through the purchase-price of His blood (life) resulting in forgiveness and liberation to his chosen ones, destined through their acceptance of Him to become and be saints (*hagioi*). In the third place is the bestowal, as a foretoken and advance payment on the purchased property and possession of God in the saints, of the Holy Spirit's power and other spiritual gifts, clearly experienced (Mullins).

In general, all things, physical and spiritual, earthly and heavenly are embraced in the universal mediatorial work of Christ. That "all things" are to be unified in Him is the underlying thought of the whole epistle. This means that the evil forces of the universe will all be "summed up" through Christ, a part of an orderly system, subjected to the sway of God's will under the law of retribution.[14]

---

11. Cf. Mullins *Com. on Ephesians.*
12. "Long promised," Moffatt's Translation.
13. Pledge or partial down payment in a first installment.
14. Cf. Mullin's *Com. on Ephesians,* in loco.

B. Paul here digresses, to weave in praise for their faith, and prayer for a a more perfect knowledge on the part of the saints, who are the body of Christ, about Christ Himself who is their head. 1:15-23.

1. First, he declares that the basis and occasion for this praise (1:15-16) was that of *having heard of their faith in the Lord Jesus and their love for all the saints,* their brethren in Christ, he *does not cease giving thanks on their behalf, making mention constantly of them at his prayer times,* praying for them individually and collectively. Intercessory prayer on behalf of the saints in all the churches was a constant and most vital factor in all of Paul's ministry, an example devoutly to be followed!

2. He next declares the purpose (*hina* clause) and and definite aim of his prayers for them. 1:17-23.

v. 17. *In order that the God of our Lord Jesus Christ,* His Father, whom he worshipped being Son, *the Father of* the *glory* of the God-head, revealed to them in his glorious Son, *may give to you*[15] saints of the province of Asia, progressively more and more, *a spirit of wisdom and of revelation,* to be able to understand, through a growing insight, which he shall impart, *in* full, correct, and *accurate knowledge* (*epignosis*), the new things *about Him,* the ever-blessed Son, who is the head of His Body, the church.

v. 18. This wished[16] and prayed for end will be attained when God grants you the *illumination of the eyes of your heart,* in spiritual perception, *to the end that you may know what is the hope He had in calling you,* what *the riches* or wealth *of the glory of his inheritance is,* treasured up *in the saints,* a people for his possession (I Peter 2:9).

v. 19. *And what is the surpassing greatness of his power toward us who are believers,* working out our salvation, from the first until its final consummation in our perfection and beautification in eternity. This power is to be calculated *according to* the measure of the *energy of the strength of his might.*

v. 20. This energy is that *which he put forth in the Christ* (Messiah) *when he raised Him from the dead and seated Him at his right hand in the heavenly regions.*

v. 21. *Far up above all rule and authority and power and lordship,* all the ranks of the angelic and celestial beings, to whom the Gnostics had attributed the creation of the universe, yes, and *of every name that can be named,* with reverence and awe, *not only of this present earthly age* but *also in the coming age* of eternal life in the heavens.

v. 22. And put all things under his feet[17] (Psa. 8:6) in subjection, as in the consummation of this world-age it shall be and is looked upon by God as already done now (aorist tense). (Rev. 22:1) *Also he gave Him* (Christ) *as Head*[18] *over all things,* both as chief ruler with authority, and active motive Agent *in the church.*

---

15. Volative optative, *may give,* — Paul's wish for them.
16. Second perfect articular infinitive.
17. Timeless aorist.
18. Double accusative.

v. 23. *Which is His body, in all its several members unified* in Him, its real *Pleroma or fulness,* of grace, power, and glory, *of Him who is abundantly filling,* as the one who supplies, *all things in all* the saints or members of that Body. Thus Paul cuts up by the roots the Gnostic heresy of creation through a hierarchy of angelic Aeons, in which false system Christ was made the highest of Aeons in rank, but yet a mere creature, and therefore not the Son of God and divine. The deity of Jesus was thus denied by these Gnostic heretics.

Paul represents the relation between Christ and the church under the figure of that relationship in the human organism between the head and body.[19] The community of Christians is to be indwelt by the Spirit of Christ, as its real life principle. The Church must embody the mind and will of Christ in a vital unity of the organism. External organization to Paul is incidental to this vital organic relationship, an appropriate and consequent expression of it. Spiritual unity of all the followers of Christ is vitally important; organic union in external organization is incidental.

The church is the representative and direct manifestation of Christ to humanity. The Body must be under the control of the Head. The church must follow the direction of the Spirit of Christ. There is a true mysticism, not one of absorption, between Christ and the disciples, a relationship of inwardness, an indwelling, in the sense of the complete possession of the mind and will of the disciple and thus the control of the mind by Christ through His Spirit. This relationship of inwardness is one of faith which the disciple has in the Master, and in the divine response of the Lord to the faith of the disciple. The resources of the divine Lord are open to the prayer of the true disciple who is in Christ and has the Spirit of Christ in full control of his life. The divine response is never denied to the adoring faith of the disciple.[20]

All history is the working out of God's eternal purpose. His "plan of the ages" was to make men, who were the crown of his original creation, but who became perverted by the temptation and fall into sin and only those to be recovered through redemption in Christ and adopted into the Father-God's family as sons in the Beloved. Restoration of all things in nature and humanity in the sphere of and through Christ, is the key to the meaning of all history. This philosophy of history did not arise out of the cold logical deductions of Paul's mind but out of a vital life experience which was real in Paul and is real in all His saints. It goes down to the foundation of all our immortal hopes and reaches out to the ends of our eternal destiny.

Paul's prayer for the saints was that they might be given a spirit of wisdom and revelation, resulting in a fuller, deeper knowledge of God, that they might understand what they themselves were and what they possessed. He is encouraged to pray for them, from having heard of their faith in Jesus and

---

19. Romans 12; Ephesians 4:1-16.
20. Kennedy, H. A. A.; *Theology of the Epistles* pp. 147-152.

their love and confidence in one another as brethren. They needed the eyes of their hearts enlightened in order to obtain a clearer spiritual perception, through moral cleansing, obedient will, and intellectual perception, in order to be able to comprehend the *hope* God had in calling them and the hope wrapped up in their Christian calling, both of which covered the two eternities and included complete redemption and final glorification. They needed also to comprehend the riches of the glory of God's *heritage in his saints* who would be the means of demonstrating, as marvelous spectacles of his grace, to the universe of authorities and powers, good and evil, his manifold wisdom, grace, and power. The saints must come to comprehend also the transcendent greatness of God's inherent ability and power which has been demonstrated in the resurrection of Jesus and *His exaltation to the throne of the universe,* where He has a position above all the forms of authority and power, also over the present and future ages, and to whom all things are subjected in heaven and earth and in the church, His own body, of which he is the Head.

C. The gracious benefits of this redemption wrought out in Christ are witnessed to in the divine quickening of the spiritually dead and the effecting of the oneness of humanity by the abrogation, in and through Christ, of the law of commandments and ordinances, breaking down thus the wall of separation between Jew and Gentile, all races and nation through the power of the cross, making one humanity. 2:1-22.

1. And you (Gentiles) who were dead in trespasses and in your sins, God by His grace and on account of his love, made alive in Christ, and quickened and raised you up and exalted you with Him. 2:1-10.

a. The natural state of all men before regeneration is that of spiritual death. 2:1-3.

v. 1. *And you* Asian Christians, being at the time before your acceptance of Christ *dead* (corpses) spiritually, beyond all human power to restore, *in your trepasses,*[21] having fallen down from the line of true conduct *and in your sins,* having missed the mark of life's divine aim, as the archer misses the "bull's eye," *in which* sins *you at that time walked around* in a wrong path of conduct, which was *according to* or determined by *the age of this world,* or the character of the present age or times, in this temporal sensuous world *according to the prince of the power of the air,* the ruler in authority in the lower impure atmosphere of customs and fashions, who is the devil.[22] He is the originator *of the spirit now at work in the sons of disobedience,* who are, as you once were, alienated from the will of God. Both we the Jews, and you the Gentiles were in this condition of paralysis and death, corpses spiritually.

---

21. Locative Case, plural.

22. The ruler of the power of the air is the personal devil, Satan, whose existence Paul plainly referred to many times in his epistles. He heads the organized power of the unholy spirits, encountered by Jesus in the temptations in the wilderness and elsewhere, and against whom Paul warns us in many places: I Thess. 2:18; Rom. 16:20; I Cor. 5:5; 7:5; II Cor. 2:11; 11:14; Eph. 4:27; 6:11 et al.

Among which we all lived once in the desires of our flesh,[23] *following out the inclination of our appetites* and lusts in sinful self-gratification, *doing the* wishes or *desires of the fleshly appetites* which are the occasion of sinful choices and acts leading to a sinful disposition, *and of the mind* in which are harbored sinful imaginations and lusts. Thus the mind is drawn into the exercise of the fleshly appetities and the will executes the evil desires. (Mullins) In their natural state both Jew and Gentile equally were by nature the children of God's wrath. Being an Israelite and a member of the chosen race did not exempt the Jew from the necessity of regeneration, but he was *just like the rest* of men.

b. We were made alive freely through the grace of God in Christ that we his workmanship might afterwards be his devoted workmen in good works. 2:4-10. Paul here turns to the other side of the picture.

v. 4. *But our God being wealthy in mercy* according to his very nature, *on account of his* great (much) *love with which*[24] *he loved us* all, both Jew and Gentile.

v. 5. *even when we were dead* (spiritual corpses) *in the sphere* of *our trespasses* (responsible acts of transgression or falling away from the line of right conduct), *he quickened together with Christ*[25] (*by the grace* of God *you have been saved*)[26] and by that alone,

v. 6. *and raised us up with Him*, he in a physical and we in a spiritual, and yet-to-come-physical resurrection, *and made us to sit together with Him* our head, because it is all *in* the heavenly sphere of Him who is our redemption, *Christ Jesus.*

The resurrection power which raised Christ from being dead in Joseph's tomb, is that which raised us spiritually when we believed in Jesus. This power will also be operative in our final resurrection which with God is considered as if already done.[27] The same power has caused us already to sit down beside Christ on His eternal throne in the heavenlies. Thus Jews and Gentiles are already unified.

v. 7. The end in view in this gracious salvation for both Jew and Gentile is his own glory; *that he might demonstrate*[28] *for himself in the ages that are coming on* in the illimitable eternal future *the exceeding great riches of his grace in kindness* or benignity *upon us in Christ Jesus.* The achievements of

---

23. (Sarx) in many places in Paul's epistles means human nature as conditioned by the fall or the state of the unregenerate being in which the sin principle is dominant. This sin principle is potentially conquered for the life of the regenerate being, but must be expelled completely by faith in Christ and by putting off the old man.

24. Attraction of the relative from instrumental to accusative to agree with its antecedent.

25. Associative instrumental case.

26. Perfect passive Periphrastic Indicative.

27. Aorist future, of timeless aorist.

28. Final clause with (hina) and aorist middle subjunctive, for himself.

God's love in and through Christ will be on exhibition, as the most marvelous of all things in all the succeeding epochs and ages.

v. 8. *For* the reason for this great kindness, is found in his grace which Paul recites again in words which have come down as one of the clearest expressions of the evangelical faith, defining the plan of salvation. *For by grace have you been saved,*[29] *through* intermediate agency (*dia* with genitive) of *faith, and that*[30] act of being saved by grace through faith *is not of yourselves,* through your merits or efforts, it is *the free gift of God.* Grace is God's part; faith is yours, (Robertson)

v. 9. It is *not of* man's *works in order that none might glory.* There is no room for self-complacency. The fact so important is reiterated in further explanation: *For His workmanship we are,* and in no sense our own. Our works to save ourselves would avail nothing apart from his mercy and grace which are the real source and effective cause of our salvation, conditioned by our acceptance of it through faith as a free gift, *constituted in the* sphere of *Christ Jesus* by our union with Him, and destined *for good works which God prepared beforehand* even when he pedestinated us to adoption (1:5, 6) long before we were created or spiritually quickened, *that in them we might walk.*

Thus we have the explanation of gratuitous salvation set forth in unmistakable terms. It is an expression of God's grace. The rediscovery of this great fact was the source and sustaining power of the Reformation. There is great need today that Christendom should lead professed members of the churches to search their hearts with a recognition of the necessity of a clear experience of salvation by grace through faith, not a mere matter of form or church membership which so easily acquired through mere human contrivances apart from a real new birth through the Spirit, operated on the basis of a vital surrender of the life, by an understanding acceptance of Jesus Christ as Savior and Lord.

2. Reconciliation was wrought thus potentially in Christ between Jews and Gentiles. 2:11-22.

a. There had existed historically an irreconcilable division between Jews and Gentiles now recognized and declared by Paul. The apostle calls their attention frankly to the character of this division, that they may be humble and grateful to God. 2:11, 12.

v. 11. Wherefore you Gentile members of the churches in the Asian province *remember that once you the Nations* (*ethnei*) *in the flesh,* as far as the absence of circumcision, the sign of the covenant of Abraham is concerned, were and are *called the Uncircumcision by that* body of people the Jews, which is *called the Circumcision,* but which is merely *in the flesh wrought by hand.*[31] Gentiles "in the flesh" were as good as Jews circumcised only "in the flesh,"

---

29. In God's view of *fait accompli.* Perfect periphrastic tense denotes permanence.

30. The demonstrative pronoun *touto* refers to the whole matter including the grace of God and faith of man resulting in salvation.

31. Paul tactfully calls attention that the rite was not now spiritually used by the Jews as a valid sign of spiritual promises, but as a mere physical thing of little value.

a mere superficial rite in the practice of the Jews, but emphasized by them in their national separatism. It was different from spiritual circumcison. (cf. Phil. 3:2ff) But in any case *at that time were separated from Christ* the Jewish Messiah, prophesied to come, but the true, and not the traditional One. You were in permanent status of *being in alienation*[32] *from*[33] *the Commonwealth of Israel,* or outside of the theocracy of God's chosen people. In history, from the beginning of the race, the peoples were all contemplated alike, but all had lapsed from their original standing and must be restored by Christ. *You were strangers from the covenants of promise* made to Abraham (Gen. 9:6), Moses, and others, as representatives of the chosen race, in a peculiar sense, to be administered to the rest of the world. Such was your position in relation to revelation and its blessings and in your conscious experiences, "you were *without any kind of hope* and in the midst of a benighted existence without the light you now have in the face of Jesus Christ," *and* were *Godless,* in the sense of being in hostility toward God, *in the world.* They had, as heathen nations, gods, but not a true God. They must reflect as those who now had the light on what their former state had been, and consider the pit from which they had been dug.

b. But now they are on a different basis of fraternal equality with the Christian Jews in Christ Jesus, and the division of race is done away with in the cross. 2:13-18.

v. 13. *But now* it is not as it once was, *you are made nigh*[34] since your acceptance, *in Christ Jesus,* and pertain to the Commonwealth of the true spiritual Israel. This is a real relationship, established in the new covenant *in the blood of Christ,* and not a mere entrance into Jewry as proselytes.

v. 14. *For He Himself is our peace,* of both Jews and Gentiles, with God and all men, transcending nationality and race universally, *who made the two divisions of the race,* Jew and Gentile, *one,* a united race, *and broke down*[35] *the middle wall of partition* (between Jew and Gentile) as in reality in the Temple, when the court of Gentiles was once separated by a veil and wall impossible to be passed by the Gentiles on pain of death; but now no division between Jews and Gentiles existed in the church, having been done away by God's manifest providence in the coming of the Holy Spirit on both alike.

v. 15. The real wall between Jews and Gentiles was *the enmity.* This wall of partition, Christ *made null* — this personal and national prejudice and enmity — by fulfilling and thus nullifying the *Law of Commandments,* in the positive prohibitions, couched *in decrees.* This he did in his flesh, suffering on the cross for both Jew and Gentile alike *in order that*[36] *he might make the two, in himself into one new* (created) *man,* thus *making peace.*

---

32. Perfect tense.
33. Ablative as in case of other ideas of separation which follow.
34. Timeless Aorist.
35. Aorist Ind. Act. Part.
36. Final *hina* clause with first Aorist subjunctive expressing purpose.

v. 16. *And might reconcile both in one body* (the spiritual church) *to God through the* (intermediate) agency of *the cross, slaying the enmity in it.*[37] When two persons come repentant to God through Christ they cannot have enmity between themselves of a permanent nature. An end is put to it through their common Lord and one God.

v. 17. *And coming* from the cross *He preached peace to you Gentiles that were afar off and peace to those* (to the Jews) *who were near*, from having had the very oracles of God. The first word of Jesus when He came back to his apostles from the cross was, "Peace be unto you. As my Father sent me unto the world even so send I you into the world." They were sent on the same mission which had brought Him — the mission to *preach peace* between man and God and between men as brothers. This was then the foundation of peace "*because we both*, Jew and Gentile, *have* continued[38] having *access, in or by*[39] *one Holy Spirit to the Father.* Two led by the Holy Spirit must walk together in the same way.

c. The two branches of the race previously hostile can now be built together into a holy temple for the habitation of God, in the person of the Holy Spirit. 2:19-22.

Paul now seizes on a new figure of speech to get away completely from the old idea of division. Both Jews and Gentiles were to be built into a glorious holy temple, fitly joined together for a habitation of the Holy Spirit of God. He calls their attention to the fact (aorist tenses) that they had already as belivers been built together in the heavenlies with their brothers of other races.

v. 19. *So then* (accordingly therefore) *no longer are you foreigners,* without the rights of citizenship, and *sojourners* or dwellers just outside the family of God; *but you are fellow-citizens of the saints,* Abraham, Moses and David, descendents from whom came the Messiah, in the eternal city of God, in the spiritual church, in heaven and on earth. You are now *fellow-members of the family of God* (Rom. 8:29), having been born into this family spiritually "by grace through faith" in the Lord Jesus Christ.

v. 20. *Having been built*[40] *upon*[41] *the foundation of the apostles and prophets.* Paul here multiplies figures of speech to express the richness of the conception and make it clear. The marvelous figure of the spiritual Temple is wonderfully adapted to set forth the unified character of the spiritual church universal. Its foundation doctrines are to be found in the inspired writings of the apostles and prophets of the New Testament Churches. Also, *Christ Jesus being the chief cornerstone,* rejected as He was by the Jewish builders who crucified Him (cf. Matt. 21:42) but now become the primary foundation

37. Locative or instrumental (*en autoi*).
38. Present tense, linear action.
39. Locative or instrumental.
40. Aorist passive participle pointing to a point of time when this fact transpired.
41. *Epi* with the locative case.

stone at the angle of the structure by which the architect fixes a standard for the bearings of the walls and cross-walls throughout (Lloyd). He is the fulfillment and center of all the teachings of the apostles and prophets. Paul himself was of them (cf. II Peter 3:2) who built upon Jesus and no other foundation (I Cor. 4). Jesus is therefore the bond of structure which ties all the building together, like the layer of block-cement in the foundation of modern buildings.

v. 21. *In whom, every kind of building,* in its several wings, porticoes, and courts, *fitly framed together, grows* and is growing as the Gospel advances, *into a holy temple* or sanctuary for the manifestation of God, *in the Lord* Jesus, who is the center of the unity.

v. 22. *In whom also you* Gentile brothers, with all the saints, *are being built up together*[42] *for* (to form) *a permanent abode for our God*[43] *in the person of the Holy Spirit.*[44]

D. Paul's prayer is resumed, only to be broken by an extended digression and finished later. 3:1-21.

1. The Apostles was to go on praying for the Gentile brethren in the churches of the province of Asia. (v. 1).

v. 1. After the words "*I Paul*" he makes a long digression, only returning to his notable prayer for the readers at v. 14. He was diverted from the intended prayer, which he felt to be very important, after his presentation to them of the far-reaching idea and vision of a unified race, in the universal spiritual church.

2. So he pauses for an important digression to explain why he prays for them. 3:2-13.

To grasp the meaning of so great a conception they need special spiritual strength. But his words, "*the prisoner of Christ Jesus on behalf of you Gentiles*" had diverted him to make an explanation of his part in the program of God's "eternal plan of the ages," justifying the prayer for them, of which they were to have the record and from which to derive a large benefit. He had ever considered himself a bond-servant of Christ and now he thinks of himself as a prisoner for Jesus' sake, as they would readily agree on reflection since they surely must have heard.

a. He has a precious revelation — a love — secret (*mustarion*) to impart to them. 3:2, 3.

v. 2. *If indeed you did,* as he takes for granted,[45] hear of the *dispensation* or stewardship *of the grace* of God which was graciously *given to me for you to enter among you for labor.*

v. 3. *that according to divine revelation was made known to me the mystery* or secret which is my only qualification for preaching it *just as I wrote you above in brief words.*

---

42. Present passive indicative — linear action in progress.
43. Objective genitive.
44. Pneumati of Nestle, Capitalization correct.
45. Conditional Clause of first class; they did hear.

b. It is the secret which was hidden long ages but now is fully revealed to him for them — the secret or mystery of universal salvation and unification in Christ of Jews and Gentiles, and of God's eternal purpose to sum up all things in Christ, as head. 3:4-7.

v. 4. Whereby (looking to which) *you are able* having this information, *when you read this epistle, to perceive my understanding* or God-given insight *in the mystery,* secret *of our Christ, which* secret of divine purpose, was a long buried treasure.

v. 5. *In other generations,*[46] *not being made known to the sons of men,* either Jew or Gentiles, *as now it was unveiled to his holy apostles and prophets* of the churches of New Testament times *in the* revealing light of the Holy *Spirit.*

v. 6. The mystery made known was, *that the Nations* (Gentiles) *are fellow-heirs,* as members of God's family by the new birth, regeneration (Eph. 2:1-10), *and fellow-members of* and in the church, *the Body* of Christ, *and fellow-partakers of the promise in Christ Jesus through the Gospel,* including all the blessings of the Gospel to be enjoyed in the Messianic Kingdom on earth and in heaven, now and forever.

v. 7. *Of which* Gospel *I became* a deacon or *ministering servant according to the free gift of God's grace which was given to me according to the energy* or working force *of his power.* Paul attributed all his ability to carry on amid difficulties his work, to the divine call and sustaining grace of the Lord.

c. His special call and mission program included four things. 3:8-13.

(1) He was to preach to the Gentiles the unsearchable riches of Christ.

v. 8. *To me less-than-the-least of all the saints this grace was given, to herald to the nations the unsearchable* (untrackable) *riches of Christ.*

(2) He was to make known universally the many-sided grace of God. 3:9-11.

v. 9. *To turn the light on* so that any man might see *what is the stewardship of the mystery* (secret) *which has been hidden,*[47] as to God's eternal purpose or plan *from the ages past, in God, the Creator of all things.*

v. 10. As sovereign of all creation he had his own wise purpose in mind. There was perfect harmony between his work of creation and that of redemption. The purpose of Paul's difficult ministry as servant of the Lord was, *that there might be made known now to the principalities (governments) and authorities* of the angelic hosts *in the heavenly regions, through the* intermediate agency of the *church, the many-sided wisdom of God,*

v. 11. *according to His purpose or plan of the ages which He made in Christ Jesus our Lord.*

He had been given the grace of working with God in this stewardship of making known what the many-sided wisdom of God was in this demonstration of what He (God) could do in His gracious salvation of a ruined race. The

46. Locative of time.
47. Perfect passive participle.

wisdom of God manifested in the salvation of millions of individuals, each case of the vast multitude being entirely different from all the others, was as variegated as the leaves and flowers of all nature. What a spectacle, marvelous in its extensive and immense variety, and as wonderful in its eternal character in each separate person saved by grace!

(3) All may approach the throne of grace boldly. 3:12,13.

v. 12. All the infinite multitude of lost and ruined mankind, of which *we* are part, *have in whom,* (Him) Jesus Christ the Savior, *boldness* or freedom of utterance *and access* in confidence, introduction *through our faith in Him*[48] directly, to God's throne.

(4) The saints should be stimulated, knowing the divine purpose in the sufferings of Paul.

v. 13. *Wherefore I beg of you not to lose heart* and give way to the evil because of your sympathy for me *in my afflictions on behalf of you, which* very thing *is your glory.* In his vicarious suffering for them, Paul thought not on his suffering, but only that they might be strengthened and helped. Thus he closed the lengthy, but marvelous digression which had set forth his own responsible part in God's "plan of the ages," justifying and explaining to the full the marvels of God's grace to him.

3. The prayer of the apostle for his readers is now resumed and this time completed. 3:14-19.

Paul had a unique interest in the conversion of the Gentiles. Most of the members of the Asian churches were Gentiles and many of them had not seen Paul's face, but still they had heard of his special call to be the apostle to the Gentiles and that to him God made known the secret of the ages, so that the angelic and demonic powers were to witness the many-sidedness of the wisdom of the divine plan of the ages. The prayer is taken up just where he had left off, *toutou charin,* for this cause, and ends with the doxology. 3:20, 21.

a. Paul's attitude in the prayer. 3:14, 15.

v. 14. *For this cause, in view* of the unification of Jews and Gentiles (2:11-22) *I bow my knees* in the usual, but not necessary, attitude of the disciples of Jesus, *to the Father* (God), (but not in this place "Father of our Lord Jesus Christ" as the Latin Copies contain them in error).[49]

v. 15. *From whom every family* group *in the heavens and upon earth is named* or derives its name. All family life takes its cue from the family of God which embraces peoples of all races and nationalities. The whole race is to be one family when redeemed, when racial divisions shall have disappeared. The fatherhood of God is complementary to the brotherhood of man, which is and will be realized in the universal spiritual church. All is unified in the Father.

b. The objective in his petition. 3:16,17.

v. 16. The purpose and end for which he prays is, *that He* (God) *may give to you* believers *according to the riches of his glory* the resources of His nature

48. *Autou,* objective genitive.
49. Testimony of Jerome.

manifested to us: *to be made strong with* spiritual *power through* the mediating agency of *His Holy Spirit* of promise *in the* spiritual nature of the *inner man,*

v. 17. So *that Christ may take up his* permanent *abode, through faith, in your hearts.*

c. The comprehension of the incomprehensible riches of Christ. 3:18, 19.

v. 18. And *that* as a result, *being rooted in* the deep soil of the *love* of Christ and built or *grounded upon* its rock foundation, *you may achieve strength to grasp,* along *with all* the members of this family of *the*

v. 19. *saints, what is the length, breadth, height, and depth* or vastness, *and to know,* with an intelligence re-enforced by such a foundation, *what is the knowledge-transcending love of* and for *our Christ,* so that as a climax to the attainments of knowledge through love, *you may be filled unto all the fulness of our God.*

Paul wished for them great spiritual power, Christ permanently dwelling in their intellects, feelings, and wills a more intimate comprehension of Christ and His love for them, and the infilling of all the fulness of a gracious God. Thus the prayer, for the realization of the goal of redemption in, and through, and by means of the revelation of God's plan to all nations and in the marvelous transformations to be wrought out in the lives of individuals and of nations, a wonderful spectacle of the ages for the eyes of the myriads of the angelic hosts is concluded.

The doxology, wafting the prayer on the wings of praise to the courts of heaven was a fitting conclusion. vv. 20, 21.

v. 20. *But to Him who is able to do beyond all things,* vastly *beyond all we ask or understand,* of the wealth of His grace, *according to the power* of the Holy Spirit *which is already at work in us,*

v. 21. *to Him be the glory in the church* and by it, in its demonstration of the manifold wisdom of God, *and* much more, *in Christ Jesus,* who is the supreme gift of the Father, *unto all the generations of all the ages. Amen!*

Paul reassures his readers that the transcendent spiritual blessings, for which he had asked in the lofty prayer, which he offered for them, is easily within the power of God to give, and so he bursts forth at this juncture in a doxology of praise and thanks. He ascribes praise to God in words of sublime faith, in Him who is able to give far beyond all we ask or think in our prayers, in the sphere of the work of redemption in Christ Jesus, who is the bond of unity in all things and especially of the church, in, by, and through which the glory of His wisdom is to be demonstrated (Mullins).

II. Practical consequences of redemption through Christ, in the obligations, spirit and duties of the saints, members of the Body of Christ, the Church, 4:1-6:20.

A. Exhortation principally to spiritual unity. 4:1-24.

1. A practical view of spiritual unity in the Church. 4:1-16.

a. A worthy life in peaceful unity in harmony with the divine call, in all good brotherly relation. vv. 1-3.

In the last three chapters of this epistle to the believers in the province of Asia, Paul draws a picture of the Christian. He is a master artist and with a brush of great skill he adds touch after touch, a line here and a line there until the portrait stands forth, a masterpiece.[50] The whole life-character, conduct, activities, attitudes of the real Christian are seen, as we follow the artists' brush. We behold him as one who does not realize fully what he is or what he possesses. He must be one whose walk is that of humility, meekness, longsuffering. Character shines forth in his attitudes toward all men but especially toward his brethren in the Church and toward God the Father, Son and Holy Spirit. In his whole bearing he is one who recognizes his high and holy calling. He is diligent in the matter of his membership in the Body of Christ to preserve and promote harmony and spiritual unity. He avoids selfishness, self-seeking, self-assertion as the very enemies of his own soul and of spiritual unity and peaceableness in the Church. He seeks to employ his special gifts and talents divinely bestowed on him by the lord of glory, in the work of edification of the saints, to the building up of all, in the holy brotherhood of the Church.

In so doing he keeps within his own lane in the race for the mark of the prize of the high calling in Christ Jesus. Ambitious to excel, he is ready to recognize in his fellow members in the Body of Christ, their gifts, abilities and functions in the building up along with him of the Church and the Kingdom, the Bride of the Lamb, until she comes to the beauty of holiness and unflecked perfection in Him.

v. 1. *I exhort you therefore, I, the prisoner in the Lord,* whose captivity is evidently due to the work of the Gospel, appeal and earnestly beg you *to conduct yourselves in a manner worthy* and that morally, *of your life-calling, with which you were called,* when God spoke to your heart in the hour of your conversion to Him. I beg of you to ponder your lost condition before the time when you were called by God to Him who is the source of your eternal and infinite blessings in the heavenlies, now and forevermore.

v. 2. This exalted state into which you were called by God should not lead to any pride or self-exaltation, but on the contrary you should comfort yourselves *with all lowliness of mind* or modesty of opinion of yourselves *and meekness* or a willing submission and resignation in trial, in peace, beneath the will of God, *with longsuffering,* in an enduring spirit which outlasts the wrong suffered, without retaliation and without any burst of temper, but on the contrary *forbearing one another,* with liberal allowance for one another's frailties and mistakes, even when the brother hurts and wounds you, treating the offender consistently *in love* or with a lovely disposition which overlooks and depreciates the hurt. There is an active side of endurance which seeks to see the worth of others and get their point of view, forgiving and forgetting the wrong inflicted.

---

50. Cf. Bishop Moule, *Ephesian Studies,* p. 172.

v. 3. You must learn to bear, forbear and love in the community of the Church and also of the world, *giving diligence* or making earnest haste, *to preserve the* oneness or *unity of the Spirit,* which has been gendered in the common experience of the church community by the Holy Spirit. It should be conserved and promoted *in the bond of peace* with God and between one another as brethren, in the sphere of a common Lord Jesus and under the direction of the same Holy Spirit. This peace is the gift of God, dating from the hour of your acceptance of Christ, and should not be neglected or disregarded in daily practice in your contact with others.

b. In verses 4-6, Paul gives a beautiful and profound summary of all the causes or sources of spiritual unity and exhorts the readers to practice this unity in view of these sources of harmony. He enumerates the seven sources as: (a) One body (the church). (b) One Holy Spirit. (c) One Christian hope. (d) One Lord Jesus Christ. (e) One saving faith and also faith once delivered to the saints to be defended. (f) One baptismal ordinance, which is the door of the church. (g) One God and Father over, through, and in all.

v. 4. *One Body,* the mystical body of Christ (the spiritual universal church or kingdom), consisting of the regenerated and living members of the one Head (Christ), animated by *one* eternal (Holy) *Spirit,* who was instrumental in the regeneration of each individual member and now maintains the vital connection of each with Christ the Head, *even as you were called in one hope of your calling,* the same hope for both Jew and Gentile, which God had, in calling each one, and each had in his salvation, grounded in the same Christ, built around the same glorious life in Christ, to be realized through the same vital faith in the Common Saviour.

v. 5. *One Lord* Jesus Christ and he alone (no series of aeons): *one faith* or act of trust in Christ in order to salvation, both of Jew and Gentile; *one act of baptism,* the outward symbol of the death and resurrection of Jesus and more especially of the believer's death to sin and resurrection to newness of life, (Rom. 6:4) through the immersion of the body in and emergence from water, a burial and resurrection in symbol.

v. 6. *One God and Father of all* peoples alike, sovereign *over all* things and men, working *through all* to the carrying out of his will and *in* or *among all* to illumine, sustain, and fill up with his divine fullness.

We have here the mention of the three persons of the Trinity in the reverse order to the usual, perhaps as a suggestion of the present world order of God's active manifestation in the world. By three prepositions over all, and in all, and through all, Paul endeavors to show the universal sweep and power of God the Father in the lives of men. Here we have the unity of the Trinity in all their redemptive activities in the world, on behalf of mankind, as a basis and example for a unified church.

c. All the individual spiritual gifts of the one body should serve a unified brotherhood. There are many varied and differing gifts but one Lord who is the giver of all. 4:7-16.

(1). Each of our gifts was given by the Christ of the incarnation and victorious ascension and exaltation. vv. 7-10.

v. 7. *Unto each one* of us, the members of the Body of Christ (the Church), *was* definitely assigned or *given grace according to the measure of the gift of our Christ,* which is ideal and perfect in adaptation to the need of each worker and his uses for the Kingdom.

v. 8. Wherefore he (in the Scriptures) says: (Ps. 68:18) according to Paul's Rabbinical method of citation of slight variation from the exact form of the text and application of the text as an illustration of the victory of Christ over the grave, ascent to heaven, and bestowment of spiritual gifts on men. "*When he ascended up on high, He led the captivity of sin captive and gave gifts unto men.*"

v. 9. *But what is the, "he ascended," if not that he first descended to the nethermost region of the earth? The one who descended is himself the one who ascended far up above all the heavens in order that he might fill to the full all things.* Paul cites this Scripture to illustrate and explain the descent of Christ in the incarnation even to the nethermost region of death (Hades) to ascend later far up above all the seven heavens of the Jews, victoriously, in order that he might fill up to the full all things, He himself being the *Pleroma* or fullness.

(2). All these have for their common end, the edification of the Body of Christ, the Church, building up the individual and the Church. vv. 11-16.

v. 11. *And he himself gave some* to be *apostles,* especially gifted and endowed with the gifts of inspiration and with miracle-working power, but without succession; *and some prophets,* who were gifted with the abilities to tell forth and herald the message; *and some evangelists* who preached especially the gospel to the unconverted; *and some pastors and teachers,* frequently two functions in the same man. All these gifts were sometimes found in the same person, as for example in Paul himself. But there were many men and women with one gift in preeminence.

v. 12. The purpose of all this variety of differing gifts is *for equipment,* the adaptation and furnishing with equipment (*Katartismon*) *of the saints for the work of ministering, unto the end* and purpose *of the edification* or building up *of the Body of Christ.*

v. 13. *Till we attain, all of us, to the unity* or oneness *of our faith in and our accurate* and true *knowledge of the Son of God,* in whom we too are sons of the Eternal Father; and these ministries are to help us on in development *into a full-grown* (teleion) *man* in Christ and a matured humanity *even to the measure of the stature of the fulness* (Pleroma) *of Christ.* The goal is a mature church (body) even as the head, Christ is perfect — a goal of perfection humanly unattainable but which is set for us to strive toward.

v. 14. This high ideal of maturity of character should be striven for, *that we may be no longer infants in* our weakness and ignorance, *borne on billows and cast about* as driftwood *by every wind of false Gnostic teaching, by the dice-*

playing of religiously unscrupulous *men,* who *by their cunning* seek their own selfish ends, even *to the scheming of their deceit,* laying deliberate traps to subvert the believer and lead him away from Christ.

v. 15. Paul wishes to warn the Asian Christians against these false Gnostic teachers and urges *that they being followers of the truth* of the Gospel *in love* and sincere devotion to it, *might* without bitterness but avoiding the false teachers "*grow up wholly* in all respects in life and conduct, *into Him who is the head, Christ.*" That which genders harmony and spirituality is close union with Him.

v. 16. *Out of whom all the Body* of the Church, *getting* more and more *adjusted together* and better *compacted together through every joint* or nexus, which is a channel *for the* supply of life, power and direction from Christ, who is the head, *according to His energy* or working power, as *the measure of each part or member makes for the increase of the Body* as a whole in size and strength, *to* the end and purpose of *the upbuilding of itself in love,* which is the supreme element of its character.

The apostle starts out, in his discussion of the ministry in the Church and the ministering of the Church with a trinitarian background for unity in the Spirit, the Lord Jesus and the Father. He is showing how the Body of Christ is to be unified and edified for its work of ministering in the great work of carrying, to the world of humanity, the secret of the redemption in Christ, through their own accurate and experimental knowledge of the Christ himself.

The specialized ministry of a divinely chosen and spiritually equipped body of workers is to be divinely used in bringing the members of the body of Christ to a high standard of ministering service in the world-wide campaign, rather than to try to do all the work as a ministry and in so doing usurp the proper functions of the laity. There are distinct functions of apostles, prophets, evangelists, shepherds or pastor's and teachers but not the whole work of promotion of the kingdom and building of the church is to be done by these gifted specialized workers, who are themselves set to train and prepare the whole membership of the church for the vastly wider work of witnessing and thus evangelizing the world of unregenerate people, and building up in members and character the body.

Full maturity, in the absolute, can never be attained; but full-grown manhood in Christ in the relative sense is a goal to be sought perseveringly. Immaturity is widely prevalent in the character of the membership of the church.

Most of its members are mere infants and never reach adulthood. Here is the great service which the saints or members of the church must do for themselves and for each other through teaching, *training and fellowship in the* service. A sincere acceptance of the *full-orbed truth regardless of traditional or previous doctrine and practice* is a primary qualification for progress toward this goal. *Individual growth in contact with the Head is the road along which development must proceed and the goal and ideal is perfection in Christ.* It is *from Him that the supply flows out of every member of the Body.* The various members or parts of the Body must be *properly fit together that the supply may flow* through them by means of the active energy of each. *When all the parts perform their several functions properly it makes for the increase or growth* of the entire Body unto its building up of itself in love, the element in which the whole *process is carried on and the motive power behind all the activity.* (cf. Col. 2:19)

2. This spiritual unity should be separated morally from the unbelieving pagan world. 4:17-24.

a. The *terrible moral status of the pagan world pictured.* 4:17-19.

v. 17. *This then I say* over against my exhortation to you as to a life of humility, forebearance and unity (4:1-3) *and* solemnly declare or *testify* as a witness under oath and one *in the Lord,* and not just speaking an opinion of my own, *that you are no longer to walk* around or conduct yourselves as you formerly did as Gentiles *and even just as the Gentiles* (heathen peoples) *are accustomed yet to do in the vanity of their minds,* empty of all truth and principle and under false impressions and delusions.

v. 18. *They walk as those who have been and are darkened permanently*[51] in their understanding, involving the beclouding of both intellect and emotions in their mental and moral natures *and having been* alienated completely from the eternal life[52] of God, which is in Him and in believers to whom He imparts it, and which they possess *not because of the ignorance* of the life-producing truth, *which* ignorance *is in them and* which is due to the callous condition through hardening as if covered with a thick skin *producing a* spiritual *blindness*[53] *of their hearts.* Thus Paul traces the effects of habitual disobedience and resistence to the impressions of the Spirit of God, until the heart has lost the capacity to feel.

v. 19. Who being past feeling or capacity of sensitiveness to the moral impressions of the appeal of truth have turned themselves over once for all *to lasciviousness* or debauchery in lustful dissipation with scorn for all moral restraint, leading *into a working of all kinds of uncleanness* or impurity as a trade, such as the "white slave traffic," and that even *in greediness,* to make gain out of the prostitution of women or in the inordinate desire for sexual indulgences for themselves.

This dark picture of the moral conditions of heathen peoples in the time of Paul is almost unbelievable, but the truthfulness of it, nevertheless, is confirmed by the testimony of pagan writers of outstanding character and credence. In the Roman epistle (1:18-32) we have the same conditions reported by Paul more elaborately. The early apologists for Christianity also described these prevailing conditions in the pagan peoples, and history, even current history and observation, substantiates the extreme moral depravity of nations without the Gospel of Christ. Those Christians who excuse themselves for

---

51. Perf. Periphrastic passive participle indicating permanent status.
52. Ablative denoting separation.
53. Moulton's Translation.

inactivity in the work of universal evangelization and the work of Christian missions need to face the facts and conditions here depicted. One religion is not as good as another and the religion of Christ is the only one that has the power to moralize the pagan populations of the world, and even that must be withal the true Christianity of the Christ, who is the only Saviour of mankind, by His own claim. Christianity alone has salvation for man. "He was called Jesus because He was the only one who would save His people from their sins." Such is Paul's testimony also.

b. *The moral standard of the Church must be founded in the experimental knowledge* of Christ. vv. 20-24. *Here is the clarion call of Paul to the Church to come out from the world and be separate!*

v. 20. *But* in clear contrast to the lurid picture of pagan life (vv. 17-19) *you did not so learn*[54] *the Christ Messiah* when you met Him in your conversion experience of the new birth and forgiveness of your sins.

v. 21. If indeed you heard Him preached as I know you really did, *and were instructed in Him as to the truth as it is in Jesus* the real Christ and at the same time the real man, Jesus, the Gnostics to the contrary. "The lines of solid fact and spiritual reality meet nowhere but in Him, and divine Christ and the human Jesus." (Moule)

v. 22. Follows now a beautiful and striking contrast between the old sinful Gentile way of life and that of the regenerate man in Christ. This truth in Jesus refers in its application now to *your putting away* (once for all and quickly,[55] *your former manner of life, the old man* or nature of your unregenerate life of preconversion days *who is* decaying and *waxing corrupt day by day,* like an old garment or a decomposing corpse, *according to the* desires or *lusts of* moral *deceit,* lusts with which the imagination plays, and sinful habits of unregenerate days, now to be discarded.

v. 23. On the other hand the truth embodied in Christ Jesus enjoins that you *be renewed progressively* and continuously[56] *in the dominant spirit of your mind* becoming young again and youthful continually by constantly grasping and appropriating new truth.

v. 24. *And* that you *put on*[57] the brand *new man or nature,* product of the new birth, a new creature, *who after the pattern of the true God* has been *created in righteousness,* loyal and obedient to the will of God in a righteous conduct toward men *and in holiness* and *piety of the truth* as it is embodied in the Gospel of Jesus Christ.

"How different are the believing Gentiles from the unbelieving! Believers must beware of retaining anything of vanity, ignorance, or impurity of the old heathen life." (Dummelow, Ed.)

B. *Specific examples of this spiritual unity as related to moral rectitude in personal conduct.* 4:25-5:14.

---

54. Constative second aorist active indicative.
55. *Ei* with the indicative in a condition of the first class indicating reality.
56. Pres. Pass. Infinitive.
57. First Aor. Mid. Infinitive.

1. *Prohibitions* of *certain specific sins antagonizing spiritual unity*, in our mutual relations, 4:25-30.

Paul here makes a detailed application of the fundamental principle of right living. His catalogue of the prevailing iniquities in the longer section, 4:25-5:14, is appalling, including *lying, slander, quarrelsomeness leading to strife, dishonesty and theft, vulgarity, uncleanness, drunkenness, idolatry*, 'and *adultery*. He points out that their appreciation of the love of Christ manifested to them in his work of redemption should cause them to turn from such conduct. He delineates the cause for corrupt living and assigns it in part to their giving heed to erroneous teaching.

a. He appeals to them to live a worthy and noble life (v. 25).

v. 25. *Wherefore* in carrying out the program of putting off the old man and putting on the new, *having put away for yourselves* and on your own account decisively[58] the monstrous sin of lying or falsehood, the whole class of thought, speech and gesture which is classed properly as untruth, *speak the truth habitually, each individual of you with his neighbor*, to all men but especially to your Christian brother, because *we are* of the same organism, having the one head Christ and thus being *member one of another* mutually joined up in the same body with a sympathetic common lot in both pleasure and pain.

b. Next follows an *exhortation against wrath leading to strife*. (vv. 26,27)

v. 26. *You are permitted to be angry*,[59] *but do not go* on *being angry* thus nurturing a dangerous state of mind, which as righteous indignation against wrong is justified, and stop sinning and do not go on sinning.[60] Let not the sun go down upon your wrath or irritation, but make your anger *brief* and keep it under control so that your provocation may not lead to a permanent mental state of resentment.

v. 27. *And stop giving place to the devil*, giving away to temper[61] and anger. The devil is a calumniator, a slanderer, a great stirrer-up of strife, who 'throws across' many a hand-grenade in the form of accusation which explodes in a burst of enmity and strife. Uncontrolled anger is an "open door" to the devil and invites the destruction of spiritual unity, which is built up in Christ.

c. *Exhortation to leave off theft and cultivate work and charity* (v. 28).

v. 28. *Let the one habitually stealing* or a thief,[62] steal no more,[63] *stop stealing* and instead of robbing others *let him* show as a Christian his sincere and positive repentence, *by labouring hard with his own hands*[64] doing honest and good work, in order to accumulate, that *he may have* something to *contribute to the needy*, in worthy charity and help shared with those really in need.

---

58. Second Aor. middle of *apotithemi*, acting for yourselves decisively.
59. Permissive present imperative with the negative *me*.
60. Present imperative with negative *me*, of prohibition. (cf. Psa. 4:4, LXX).
61. Present active imperative of prohibition.
62. Present participle, linear action.
63. Present active imperative of prohibition.
64. Instrumental case.

d. Exhortation against corrupt or base and useless conversation, with an indication of the right use of words.

v. 29. *Let no base word* or speech tainted with moral decay, vulgarity as well as more avowed impurity (Moule) *issue or proceed out of your mouth* (Psa. 141:3) *but* on the contrary *whatever speech is good for edifying* or suitable to build up opportunely and appropriately, *that it may give grace to those who hear,* imparting a blessing.

e. Command to stop grieving the Holy Spirit by whom believers in Christ are sealed unto the day of complete redemption (v. 30).

v. 30. *Stop grieving the Holy Spirit of God,* paining Him with rebellious words and grievious deeds, *in whom you were sealed* as the purchased property for God's own possession, looking forward *unto* the day of consummated *redemption.* The Holy Spirit was sent by the Father and the Son as an earnest or pledge of the inheritance of God in the saints and he placed His brand on the believer in the work of the new birth.[65] The brand thus placed, marks the ownership of the property, as God's own possession. The Holy Spirit or third person of the Trinity is the instrument or agent in the branding. (cf. Eph. 1:13, 14). The work of a complete redemption will be perfect only when there is perfect conformity in the life of the believer to the will of God.

2. *Exhortations based on our relationship to Jesus the Head* of this spiritual unity. 4:31-5:14.

The apostle makes at this juncture a comprehensive appeal for them to abstain totally from the *sins of temper, tongue, and from acts and* habits which *destroy the unity and peace of the Church,* the home and the heart and for a life of patience and love learned in the fuller knowledge of Christ their head.

a. Become imitators of God in Christ-like love, putting to one side the sins of temper and tongue. vv. 31, 32.

v. 31. He enumerates another group of sins in addition, which oppose and destroy the ideal unity of the Body of Christ. *Every kind of bitterness of feeling* or resentful disposition and inward hardness of spirit against others; *and all wrath* (*thumos*), the boiling up of temper into passionate expression; *and anger* or indignation, which had risen gradually in wrath cooled down and became more settled (Thayer); *and clamour,* the loud outburst in a storm of anger; *and railing* in the use of abusive words of deliberate insult or as sometimes in "expressions of harsh and loveless criticism, politely and easily permitted," *let* these all *be* lifted up and quickly *taken away from you* as incongruous with first rules of Christian conduct (Moule); with all malice or badness of character, the native soil of unkindness from which sprung these miserable rag-weeds of careless anger and cruel words.

v. 32. ***And so become more kind to one another, gentle-hearted and tender, graciously forgiving each other, yourselves in solidarity, even as God in Christ***

---

65. The instrumental case, but might be construed as locative indicating also the sphere within which the sealing took place. Sinful words and deeds break up the unity of the spirit who is the informing and unifying agent in the body of Christ.

showed his divine favor in forgiving you. It was in the sphere of the work of redemption in Christ that God forgave your sins. It was all in God's mercy and grace. "The mercifulness of God forbids our being unmerciful to our brethren: become kind." (Dummelow). God, in Christ, the bond of union between God and man, forgives us our sins. In Him and through Him God comes to us and being in Him we inherit all the fulness of God's grace. (Mullins).

b. As God's own beloved children born into His family we are to imitate God, the example of our loving Father.

v. 1. *Become ye therefore* for your life as believers is one of becoming or growing and the example you are to contemplate is ever that of your perfect heavenly Father (cf. Matt. 5:45, 48), *imitators of our God* in a life of reverent humility, and especially forgiveness, *as* the loving Father's own *beloved children* (*tekna*), showing thus the family likeness. Imitation is one of the most fundamental of all principles of learning and there is no other example so pertinent to be imitated as the example of God the Father, exhibited in his love, which gave Christ to us; so we are to imitate him.

v. 2. *Walking around always* in your daily conduct[66] *in love* which is the spirit of seeking the welfare of others *just as our Christ did*[67] love us,[68] unlovely as we were in our lost estate, and gave himself over on our behalf an offering[69] and complete sacrifice[70] for us, thus setting the eternal standard for our love, for an odor of fragrance, a savor of repose and pleasing to God symbolic of restored peaceful relations between God and man.[71]

This injunction to imitation of God does not enveigh against the expiatory aspect of Christ's death which is taught by Paul in many other places in his epistles. (cf. 1:18-5:21; 22:23-26; Gal. 3:9-11).

c. The paragraph (vv. 1-5) continues the exhortation to purity and unselfish generosity which contribute to spiritual unity (vv. 3-5). A loving life is zealous for the purity exemplified in Jesus and forgets self in remembering others, not only meeting the wrongs done to one by others with loving forgiveness, in imitation of the Father's love and Christ's in His atoning for us; but in using every opportunity to cultivate in one's self the attitude of self-sacrifice in our love for the brethren and for "those who are without." Thus we may be in union with Him in the truest sense. And there is a warning added for cultivating the positive grace of thankful expression because the cultivation of the positive graces eliminates the negatives of spiritual unity, the sins of impurity and vice (v. 4)

v. 3. *But fornication*, a perilous growing and prevalent sin, the prostitution of one's body or committing of unlawful sexual vice, lightly regarded by heathen, but deeply perverse and sinful, *and all uncleanness* or impurity,

66. Present tense of linear action and customary conduct.
67. Aorist definite occurrence at the given time of his sacrificial offering.
68. *Hamōn* should be retained. (Vede Nestle's text).
69. Christ's own view of His atoning death (Matt. 20:28).
70. Here Psa. 1:6, Heb. 10:5.
71. The sacrifice of the Jews a symbol of submission.

widely prevalent in the first years of adolescense as well as adulthood, classed along with fornication and other sexual vices of sensuality among the sins of the soul against the body, *or covetousness* desiring to possess that which belongs to another, and here sexual greed directed toward the ruin of another's purity, *be never named* or ever mentioned, much less permitted to exist *among you as is seemly or becoming to saints,* who would be persons of moral purity. Such words even should be unfamiliar because of the lack of the reality of such sins, and if known should be used in unsparing condemnation of the evils they express. Keep away from such topics as lightly refer to these base sins lest they taint the imagination. The very mention of such things is positively prohibited to the Christian except in cutting criticism of them.

v. 4. *And filthiness and foolish words,* speech or talking in realistic manner about filthy subjects or in soulless "frankness" even about the intimate things of sexual character in married life, become attractive to the tainted imagination and tend to the cultivation of sensual lust. *nor jesting* in unclean bandiage or epigrammatic allusion to vice or in foul half-meanings which defile the conversation, as also many times a certain realistic type of literature, (Moule), *which things,* all of them, *are not fitting* or seemly to the man who once a sinner has been "set apart" for a saint to become saintly; *but rather giving of thanks,* a positive virtue which supplants and inhibits these vices of character and expression.

v. 5. The reason for such prohibition follows: *for this you know, recognizing by your own experience* (Robertson) *that every fornicator,* either the one who submits to it or, the one who perpetrates the foul offense against another, according to the eternal truth and principles of God and without exception, or *unclean man* whatever the form of this moral foulness or man who is ruled by *sensual greed which is* a form of *idolatry,* a dreadful and debasing worship of the creature, (cf. Rom. 1:20), or his own vile pleasure in the creature (Moule) *does not possess* as a matter of fact any *inheritance in the kingdom* of Christ and God, because he shows his unfitness for the kind of life and fellowship found in the kingdom. The idea of inheritance calls for certitude in character and conduct of the heir as a member of the family of God.

d. Be wide awake to the careful fulfillment of your duties and guarded against sharing in the unfruitful works of darkness. 5:6-14.

(1). Let no *false teachers deceive* you with empty words or speculative arguments (v. 6). Paul cautions the member of the Asian churches against being led astray by false teachers of error or any example of immoral living.

v. 6. *Let none deceive you with empty or vain words* about these sins just described as to their character and consequences. The Sophists tell you that these things are "natural", venial, "peccadillos"! But it is just these sins which incur God's wrath (Dummelow). Contrary to these sophisticated Gnostic teachers with their specious arguments, these sins are a horrible reality, and retribution is a tremendous law of inevitable consequence. God is righteous as well as loving and *on account of these things of sin the anger* (*orgē*) *of a just God is coming inevitable* and already boiling up in his wrath to pour over *upon the sons of the disobedience* to the Gospel.

(2). Do not become sharers in the unfruitful works of darkness but turn the light on that their evil may be reproved and exposed. 5:7 14.

v. 7. *Do not become fellow-sharers of them, participating* in these sins and approving their erroneous teaching. Paul adduces various incentives to a separate life out of the opposition between light and darkness. *For you were once as worldlings, darkness, but now as Christians you are light in the Lord.* Formerly their conduct made up of dark acts had resulted in character of the nature of darkness but now the contrary process should make them the light of the world (Matt. 5:12).

v. 8. *As children born of the light* of the Gospel truth, *walk around* in your daily conduct.

v. 9. *For the fruit of the light* of the Christian life is seen *in every kind of goodness* in thought, word and act, in good-will, benevolence and love toward all, and *in righteousness and truth,* conforming to the standards and laws of God in a holy life.

v. 10. *Putting to the test* and thus proving *what is well-pleasing to the Lord.* The rightness of their lives was to be tested and proven by whether God's manifest good pleasure was upon them. This would become evident not only to themselves but to others who also observed the blessing of God upon them.

v. 11. *And stop having fellowship with the barren or unfruitful works of darkness,* the actions and habits characteristic of and congenial to the life of sin, which are barren of any good harvest and end in sorrow and death. But do not only abstain completely from any sinful act yourselves but rather even reprove or expose them in others, bringing them to conviction by the light of the Gospel. Do not look with complacency upon them, but express by word and act your disapproval withal in a spirit of meekness and reverent fear, not in one of "I am holier than thou."

v. 12. *For the things done by them in secret, it is a shame even to speak about,* so vile and corrupting are their practices. The works of darkness should be exposed, but how? It cannot be done effectively by mere censors and denouncers, who are many times little better, if at all than those whom they denounce; but by the light of right living and loving example, with the setting forth of the truth of the gospel effectively.

v. 13. *But all things, when they are reproved or exposed, are made manifest by the light* of Christian life, and teaching. The nature of the evil becomes clear, and conviction of guilt and sin are secured. The light must be one of love and not of acrid criticism in a self-complacent attitude. *But all things when reproved are made manifest by the light; for everything that is made manifest is light.* Happy the believer whose life and truth acting together convict the world of sinners of the unfruitfulness of their works and attract them from the destruction of the darkness to blessedness and salvation of the light.

v. 14. *Wherefore* the Scripture of God says: *Awake, sleeping one,* from your drowsiness, *and Arise from among the dead about* you, and *Christ will make day dawn upon thee;* such were probably the words sung by the primitive Christians about the Christ, their Day-Star, and about those who, from the darkness of spiritual death, might shake themselves loose and arise to meet with glad acceptance this Dawn of a New Day, Christ, who makes a New Era and a New Humanity.

C. Wise and careful mutual subjection in relationships,[72] in the body of Christ 5:15-6:9. Having dealt now with the gross sins and license which were infecting and undermining the Christian life of the new churches of the Asian province, incident in part to the influence of a pagen environment of which most of the members had been an integral part before their conversion to Christianity, the apostle now turns to the positive side again and deals with the necessity of a wise and careful use by these saints, of their opportunities to cultivate spiritual exercises, activities and relationships. He presents as the remedy for and antidote against the moral plague, the grace of the Holy Spirit and his leadership in spiritual exercise, and the serious license exemplified in the habit of drunkenness which makes men sing a silly foolish jargon instead of the beautiful hymns of Zion, so sensible and so true.

1. Exhortation to carefully use their opportunities in spiritual activities and worshipful exercises. 5:15-20.

v. 15. Returning to his exhortation, the apostle says: *Look out* therefore strictly and be very careful *how you* conduct yourselves in your daily moral life, and *walk not as unwise but as wise buying up your opportunities* ;and

v. 16. thus *redeeming the time,* by making all the use of the events and circumstances of life that you can, for the sake of your Master, at the price of self-denial and aggressive strenuous work; *because the days,* in which you live in this sinful world *are evil* and you cannot let things drift carelessly in the important and difficult life of faith and endeavor.

v. 17. On account of this condition of the "market being full of trash" and of your need of wisdom in buying up the good, *stop being foolish* or without intelligence *and understand what the will of the Lord,* Christ *is.* It is surely an opportune time to buy up, as merchants of the King now, in the market of the world's revolutionary conditions the right ideologies and in the market of the closer world-relationships; an opportune time for expressing and insisting on Christian ideals. But it takes wisdom and courage too, and in dealing with these world problems of the kingdom it requires prayer and earnest seeking to understanding correctly and insist wisely on the right national policies as well as the highest moral standards in individual and social life. *Do not therefore become mindless* by careless forgetfuness *but be mindful* and intelligent *in understanding* with intuitive perception, through close communion in prayer and meditation in the word what God's will is.

v. 18. *And stop getting drunk with wine in which* there *is riot*; excess or or dissoluteness and debauchery. In such a condition of intoxication the

72. Dr. W. O. Carver, in his excellent treatise on Ephesians is responsible largely for the original mould in which the outline of this interpretation was first cast.

drinker breaks away from all the bonds of conscience and moral restraint. Drunkeness leads to all kinds of moral degradation and every form of impurity, with which it is commonly linked up.

On the contrary, be *filled habitually* to fulness in your spirits *with* the influences and discernment ministered by *the Holy Spirit.* The powers of reason and reverence are filled, not to say obliterated, in the man who is drunk with intoxicating beverages, but in the Spirit-filled man they are reenforced so as to be able to understand the will of the Lord. (cf. Prov. 23:31-35 RV). Total abstinence in relation to alcoholic drinks is the correct conduct; but none the less is the Christian to seek the "fulness" of the Holy Spirit because in the Spirit-led-life there is self-control, confidence, assurance and peace.

v. 19. As the exhilaration of the drunkard is given expression in the songs of riot and excess, so on the contrary the Spirit-filled Christians find expression for their inward joy and calm confidence in the Lord in *speaking to one another with psalms,* accompanied by the instrumental music of stringed instruments, *in hymns* of vocal rhythmic praise, *and in spiritual lyrical odes* of meditation in all forms of musical worship and praise, *singing and making melody* both vocal and instrumental, and at the same time real *in your heart* and heartily *to your* divine *Lord Jesus.* This "worship in song" must be internal in the heart, done heartily with the whole soul, and be audible "to one another" so as to be heard and understood and so lead and instruct the thought and it must be done in praise *to your Lord Jesus* the Risen Christ, who reigns in the whole universe now and forever. Christians must sing inwardly with the heart as well as outwardly with the lips. In this worship-picture we catch a glimpse of the heavenlies, where the sound of ethereal music fills all space.

v. 20. The mood of all worship is that of a thankful spirit and so these Christians are admonished; *giving thanks always,* at all times, and that is hard to do when one walks in the deep valley of sorrow and distress. And Christians are to be thankful for or *concerning all* things even to their afflictions and *on behalf of all* the activities and enterprises of the Kingdom and the people engaged in them. In this expression, which is unlimited[73] in its bounds, we find the universal character of Christian thankfulness. These thanks are to be rendered in the sphere of the name, character, or spirit *of our Lord Jesus Christ, to our God and Father* above all, as well as to our Lord Jesus, as the Son of God.

v. 21. This verse may well serve as the transition between the foregoing treatment of the exhortation to careful use of their opportunities in the general relationships in the church worship and other exercises (5:15-20) and the following exhortations to various classes constituting the fundamental institution of human society the family (5:22-6:9). Christians must not only be subject to God but *subjecting themselves to one another* in happy relationships with one another *in the reverent fear of Christ their Messiah,* who sits

73. The gender of *panton,* all, may be masculine or neuter referring to men or things.

upon the throne of the Universe and "whose eyes run to and fro in the earth." Happy in God's gracious blessing and joyful in worshipful service they are to "fear" to grieve the Lord Christ, and yield themselves in kindness to each others' claims, loved by and loving each as Christ loved them and loves them ever.

2. Exhortation to loving subjection to one another in the fear of the Lord in all the relationships in the Christian family (5:21-6:9).

In this topic the Apostle climbs higher still in his treatment of unity in Christ, reaching the Christian Home, which is *His Masterpiece in the* work of redemption of the human race. The human family is the symbol of Christianity, which is just one great family, as Christ taught. It is the most important and fundamental of all human institutions and was itself instituted by God the Creator *in the Garden of Eden in the beginning* of the race.

The truly Christian home is the school for the education of humanity *in the heavenly* mode of life. It is an *epitome of the New Jerusalem* society, that loves, worships and serves around the Eternal Throne. All phases of human duty and human hope are practiced and learned there. It is a 'Valerian spring' from which refreshing life-giving waters flow out to quench the thirst and refresh the souls of all who come in contact with it. It is a haven on a rock fortress where there is shelter from the storms of life. Here man may receive his foretaste of and training for the eternal home with God.

a. What first of all are to be the *relations between husband and wife* in the Christian family? 5:22-33.

(1) v. 22. The apostle first addressed the wives, connecting his exhortation with the participle "subjecting yourselves" in the transitional phrase (v. 20). *Wives subject yourselves* in line with the admonition to all Christians, but in a specialized way, *to your own husbands as to the Lord*, with reverent regard, consistent with the principles of Christ and in religious duty. Wives are not to subject themselves in any intimate manner to other men than their "own husbands," as is not infrequently seen in fashionable social circles today. The proper attitude to her own husband is a duty performed by the wife as unto the Lord and for His sake and honor.

v. 23. Follows then the beautiful analogy, *for a husband is the head of his wife as Christ is* (*the*) *head of his church*, which headship is a living union, where the two are "one flesh" and one body; but in this organic union as Christ is the head, so is man head in the human family and owes to his wife the same kind of love and loyalty, in the highest relationship of helpfulness and protection, possible. This is the statement of the Old and New Testament Scriptures. There is one essential and important difference in the relationship of Christ to his Church, beyond that of man to his wife, being as He is, *Himself the Saviour of the Body*, His Church. No husband can be savior, as Christ, in eternal salvation and providence; but man may represent symbolically Christ in being a good provider and protector for his family. He may thus save in a very important sense both the body and soul or spiritual well-being, at least, of his wife.

v. 24. But in spite of this difference, *as the Church subjects herself to Her Christ* as head with inmost love and highest reason so with full consideration of His transcendence, over man, *wives subject yourselves to your husbands in everything,* reserving supreme allegiance to Christ alone.

(2) Turning now to the husbands he admonishes and exhorts,

v. 25. *Ye husbands, love your wives, even just as Christ loved his Church and gave himself on her behalf,* with a supreme self-sacrificing affection, the fundamental and same condition the husband must fulfill if he is to exercise the same kind of authority of headship in the family, calling for the loving subjection of the wife. The husband may not be self-indulgent, capricious, and arbitrary, the oppressor of his wife, but on the contrary, her self-forgetting helpful companion and servant in the Lord.

v. 26. The purpose of Christ's love and devotion to His Church was *that he might hallow or sanctify her having cleansed her by the bath or laver of baptism in the water, in the manner and sphere of the word,*[74] or through acceptance of Christ by faith in the Word of the Gospel. If baptism is meant here, and it seems that it is the most obvious meaning, then it is symbolic of a complete cleansing as in the prenuptial bath of the bride.

v. 27. *That He himself might present to Himself the Church arrayed in glory,* and gloriously and beautifully clothed as the Bride, the Lamb's wife, to the Father, in the marriage feast of Heaven, as her 'savior from all sin and her Bridegroom, rejoicing over her (Isa. 42:5,) *as not having spot,* being purified by moral and spiritual cleasing from any spot on herself or her fleckless bridal vesture, by the laver of regeneration, in application of His cleansing blood and through sanctification's complete process as symbolized in the prenuptial bath. The baptism by immersion is symbolic of such complete cleansing of the whole personality of the regenerated one, who, would be free from sin and all guilt or any other consequence or wrinkle caused by age or decay or any of such things at all; but on the contrary *that she might be holy,* wholly consecrated, and morally pure from the positive side, *and without blemish;* free also from the negative side from all impurity or imperfectness and thus like the Bridegroom.

From the picture of the immaculate Bride, the Church in Heaven, when she shall be presented to the Father, Paul turns to remind the Christians of the Asian provinces, that this high goal of the Church's perfection is to be symbolized and set before the world through the Christian home.

v. 28. So with a love like that of Christ, the Bridegroom for His Church and Bride, the Christian *husbands are bound to love their wives just as their own bodies,* which, by the divine dictum they are, and as "one flesh." Christ gave His body as a sacrifice on behalf of His Bride through love and such must be

74. Some commentators find here a reference to the "Word" of the baptismal formula.

the love of the husband for his wife. Paul's ideal of marriage is the highest ever pictured, the would-be critics to the contrary. He was no ascetic and this picture in the Ephesian epistle is complete and independent of any local conditions in the light of which it must be interpreted (cf. I Cor. 7) as in Corinth. He who loves his own wife loves his own self, merged as the two are in physical, social, intellectual, moral life. They are joined together in spirit, soul, and body, and should be "set apart" to each other in a holy union of sinless human relationship which must not be polluted lest it be destroyed.

v. 29. *For no one ever* naturally *hated his own flesh but,* according to the law of self preservation *nourishes it* with food and physical culture so that it may grow up to maturity and soundness, *and cherishes it* with physical comfort, fostering it with tender care, studying and providing the means of doing so, just as Christ nourishes and tenderly comforts *the Church.* His love for the Church is not a selfish love, even if it is a self-love in the highest sense. The best and highest interest of the husband is to recognize his complete identity with the wife. What contributes to her welfare and betterment physically, mentally, morally and spiritually is best for him also. He cannot ascend the heights without her in a complete life. The two are one in interests and must work, think, and live in complete identity of interests and endeavor, if the final outcome is to be a finished and complete work. It is the husband's business therefore to nourish and cherish his wife and look to her comfort physically, and tenderly care for her mental and spiritual equilibrium and restful satisfaction, her social privileges and her opportunities, as he does his own.

v. 30 *For* remembering that *we* constitute the body of Christ and so *are* limbs or *members of His Body,* the Church, we should reflect that the same unity should exist in the Christian home magnified and intensified as an example of the very essence of Christianity and the test of the reality of the Christianity of the members of that unity. For we are "flesh of His flesh and bone of His bone" if we are true members of His body. And so the husband has to suffer if the wife suffers according to the law of physical and spiritual sympathy.

v. 31. *For this cause* (anti) (cf Luke 13:3) in order that a husband should realize this high goal of matrimony according to the eternal law of marriage, first laid down by God in the Garden of Eden, (Gen. 2:24), *a man shall forsake or leave his father and mother and shall be once for all joined or glued to his wife and the two shall be* progressively united and welded *into one* flesh and one life by the inevitable law of imitation and assimilation.

v. 32. *This mystery* or holy secret, which has been revealed in the Scriptures *is great but,* I speak in citing this facts *in reference to Christ and the Church,* also united in mystical union which like the union of husband and wife as one flesh (cf. Matt. 19:5, 6) is a revelation disclosed in the Gospel. Marriage is not a sacrament as averred by the Catholic creed and the word "mystery" cannot be justifiably translated "Sacrament" as in the Latin Vulgate. There is no magical, efficacy in marriage, but there is a real union of the physical, mental and moral life. Paul concludes his injunction as to the perfect marriage, to husbands and wives, by giving a practical application, of the high Archetype of the Lord Bridegroom's relation to His Bride and Church as an example of this holy matrimony between man and woman.

v. 33. Only (or nevertheless) *you husbands also, let each one of you,* as Christ does love His church, *begin and go on loving his own wife as himself, but* I enjoin *that the wife have reverent thought* not slavish but loving reverence or respect, *for her husband.* Subjection without loving reverence or respect would be servility (Dummelow). Having thus raised Christian matrimony from Paradise Lost back to Paradise Regained, as it was in the beginning and as instituted by God in the Garden of Eden, but higher still to the very courts of Heaven where we behold the Bridegroom presenting His Bride to the Father, that men and women understand the character and mission of the Christian home as a "little bit of Heaven" on earth and the only divinely originated social institution save the church, he turns to view another aspect of this Christian home.[75]

b. In the relations between parents and their children 6:1-4. Here is to be found the secret for the cure of the many evils which have attacked the home in the past, whose pagan traditions yet remain and perpetuate themselves in constantly recurring new forms. Here also we may learn to deal with the added problems of current worldly pagan influences and false philosophies and pschologies as well as the traditional social sins of forebears of generations past and a great accumulation of hereditary results both innate and social which play upon the home of the present. The *Ipse Dixit* of the Lord Christ, set forth in the words of His divinely inspired apostle, are here for our guidance and in the fewest and simplest words.

The character of the child will depend so much upon the harmony and unity between the parents and upon their proper conduct toward each other and toward the children. Only a miracle of God's grace can make the children what they should be, without that basis on which to build. But now we must come to the relations between the children and parents and see what the principles are for the proper training of the children.

v. 1. *You*[76] *children obey* with listening and attentive ears *your parents,* both father and mother, *in the* sphere of the will of the *Lord* and within the requirements of Christian duty and obligation, and that alone, *for this* kind of obedience *is right* or just and according to the laws of nature and God's revealed will. This is the vital, just, and eternal law and limit on the conduct of the child in the family. The relation of the parents and of the children to Christ constitutes a basis of just unity and holy rightness between the children and parents in the matter of the right use of authority in the parents and just obligation of attentive hearing and proper obedience of the children. Disobedience to parents is mentioned in the Bible as a formidable evil in

75. Cf. H. C. G. Moule, in loco.
76. Definite article, *the.*

human life (Rom. 1:30; 2 Tim. 3:2) and obedience has the reward of rich promise.

v. 2. *Honor thy Father and thy mother* (Ex. 20:12 & Deut. 5:16) *which is the first commandment* of the Ten, *with a promise* attached which stated as follows:

v. 3. *That it may be well* or become well *with thee* (or to thee[77]) *and thou shalt,* thus behaving, *live long* in the Promised Land or *upon the earth* reaping in the course of God's providence, peace and satisfaction from obedience to the first law of order of human society, made for the chosen race of Israel relative to the Promised Land, but applicable to all mankind.[78] There are many homes where the children do honor the law of God and recognize the value of true and loyal obedience; but it is without dispute that filial obedience in these times has been at a low ebb. A loving cordial and honoring freedom in the child is to be desired in the home but an excessive familiarity which leads to depreciation of the God-given authority and leadership of the parents is to be deplored at any time or any place. It is certain that there is always need for the firm and tender precept of the inspired word of Paul and the beautiful example of "subjection" of the boy Jesus in the home of Nazareth as the ideal and inspiration of children and parents alike as the divine directive in the Christian home. The appeal and instruction of the apostle to children is *in the Lord.* They are addressed as Christians or in virtue of being born into a Christian home where considered amenable to the principle embodied in the phrase "in the Lord." If the children addressed in the letter were actually Christians by understanding and accepting the Word of the Gospel, the appeal was certain applicable; and if they were not members of the Christian church, they were still responsible to their parents in the nature of the case, pertaining as they did to the social unit of the family, whose heads and authority were Christian.

v. 4. The apostle turns from his imperative admonition to the children to a negative prohibition to parents[79] followed by an equally positive command to bring them up in a Christian instruction and training. *And ye fathers,* heads of the family but including mothers as well (in the generic use of *pateres, do not irritate or provoke* with severity and with harshness, in the use of your parental authority, *inciting your children to anger* but with sympathy and love and, remembering your childhood days, deal with them with unselfish affection, and not with arbitrary unreasoning sternness, *bringing them up* nourished and educated *in the chastening discipline* which is pleasing to the Lord, using restraint and warning where needed, *and the admonition of the Lord,* which you (parents) have learned in the school of Christian experience.

---

77. Dative of advantage.

78. Moule, H. C. G., *Ephesian Studies* p. 384.

79. Present Imperative with negative *Mē*, of prohibition.

The parents have a responsible duty in the general education and particular training and guidance of their children but it must be done within the sphere of the Lord's will and wish and not dictated by the caprices of parents. It must be a firm discipline shot through with the nature of true parental love as deep as life and as far-seeing as eternity. This is Paul's brief summary for the moral education of the child. All the moral training must take its character from the relation of parents and children to the Lord. The instructions assume intelligence in the child enough to understand and believe and thus be received into the church; but in the case of all there is a moral and spiritual ideal for their culture and training. But all the ecclesiastical acts are on the voluntary choice which is the very basis of such relationship itself.

C. In the relationship between masters and servants 6:5-9.

The Christian home in the time of Paul in many instances had slaves who were bond-servants, and in modern times there are many servants of the labor of free choice or employees. The same Christian principles, which govern in the relationship of slaves to their lords or owners hold true in the case of employers and employed. Love must govern all relationships in the Christian home and a Christian society.

The Gospel found slavery in the world and in many cases it was a type characterized by cruelty on the part of masters or owners and hatred on the part of the slaves. Christianity undermined slavery in the Christian homes in the beginning as in the case of Philemon and Onesimus, by including the principle of a Christian democracy in the rights and privileges of the citizens in society. Paul did not seek to destroy slavery by revolution but by education on a Christian basis and social reform, generated from within man, through his religious regeneration through the new birth, by which all are brothers within the church, with equal rights and privileges in the Kingdom. In the relationship between Christian masters and slaves, and employers and employed there must be consideration in the one and fidelity and deference in the other.

v. 5. *Ye Christian bond-servants,* who have found your liberty and Lord in Christ, *obey* with attentive listening ears *your lords, masters, owners* (or employers), *according to the flesh,* who have control of your bodies but not your consciences which are free in Christ, *with fear and trembling* through reverence and concern to perform faithfully and in every particular your duty and obligation in the service *with singleness* or simplicity *of your heart* in honest desire without hypocrisy, as if the service were one being rendered to Christ Himself, sincerely and without any dishonesty or double dealing. Paul proffers these admonitions to slaves who were Christians, not approving of slavery but leaving the correction and uprooting of slavery with all its cruelties and wrongs to the silent working of the leaven of Christianity and its inevitable results in social reform and change. This would "bring liberty, fraternity and equality" in home, government and society at large, in the natural process of leavening in due time.

v. 6. *Not according to* the *eye-service* of those who work only when watched by their masters and thus *as men-pleasers* who have no higher motive than to please their human masters in order to curry favor *but as slaves or* bond-servants *of Christ* who really owns you, having paid the price of your redemption with his own blood. Thus in your service you should serve as *doing the will of God* and so interpreting your present status of life and service *from the soul* with cheerfulness and not under protest.

v. 7. *With good will* and not with resentment against your masters, owner or against society *but doing your service as to the Lord and not to men,* a faithful and obedient and therefore thorough work or service redounding to the glory of your spiritual master, who is Christ, and reacting in your favor with even the worst of masters or slave-owners.

v. 8. *Knowing* that each one, if he may *do anything good* at any time, shall *receive that same* thing *from the Lord* (Christ) according to the principles of a just and equitable compensation in the Kingdom of God; *whether he be bond or free.* The law of spiritual equity operates without regard to social class or economic status.

v. 9. The apostle next enjoins upon masters to practice the same principles in their dealing with the slaves or servants. *And you Lords, owners, masters or employers do the same things to them* observing the same principles and consulting their good as you expect that they shall render to you honest service for your good, forbearing or dropping *the threatening* which is so easy to those in power and not using compulsion or dealing with your slaves as mere chattels or property but on the contrary treating them as your brothers in the Lord, *Knowing that the Lord, of both you and them is in the heavenlies* or heavenly place, ruling and reigning forever, *and respect of persons,* for class, social, economic or other conditions, *does not exist,* is not nor ever will be *with Him.* So Paul concludes his exhortations to all the members of the Christian household as to their mutual relations and their relations to others who share with them in the common lot of the Christian Home, one of the main pillars of the new Christian Social order of a New Humanity.

And so concludes Paul with his divinely inspired artist's delineation the most beautiful picture of the home ever painted.

D. Final exhortation to a courageous struggle in the Christian life 6:10-20.

1. Seek the strength of the Lord in the spiritual conflict. v. 10.

The apostle began this epistle with a marvelous account of the "secrets" of eternal grace and love of the Father expressed in transcendent blessings to the saints in their election and calling, their redemption and regeneration in Christ, their sealing and santification by the Spirit. He is to close it, passing quickly from the glorious vision of the Christian home with its peace, its quiet and its security, to the fearsome field of battle, where we face the dark forces of an invisible foe with the hazards of defeat and a destruction not physical but spiritual and eternal in the balances of the conflict. The flare of the trumpet call, summoning us to the fierce battle sounds in our ears and the order from the supreme commander through His apostle to take each one his place in the line, fully armed and equipped to meet the strategies of a subtle enemy in mortal struggle, leaves no doubt in us that we must face the issue of life's real engagement in which He leads us on in the person of the Holy Spirit.

v. 10. *Finally, in respect of the rest be strengthened*[80] progressively *in the Lord*, the sphere within which we receive our strength, and be made strong *in the strength of His might* or unbounded power. What forces can conquer His power?

2. *Put on the whole armor of God.* 6:11-17.

a. The reason for this (vv. 11,12).

v. 11. Paul states the command, *Put on the whole or complete armor of God*, then he assigns the reason for the command, *that you may be able to stand*, hold your ground and not retreat or fall in the struggle, *in the face of the wiles*, deceits, cunning arts, stratagems trickery *of the devil* our real arch enemy.

v. 12. *For our wrestling* conflict is *not against blood and flesh* of mere men on a physical plane of the frail perishable *but against principalities*, fallen angelic or demonic rulers *against* demonic *authorities, against the potentates of the dark present world-order, against* the demonic *spiritual hosts* of evil *in the heavenly regions of* the air or high places of this earth. We are in a hand to hand struggle against the forces of evil, natural and supernatural and need the whole panoply furnished by God. There is no room for doubt as to the verity of these demonic forces and that they are striving against us, if we believe that Paul chronicled the mind of the Spirit through inspiration as well, as such existence is verified by our own experience in the struggle.

b. Different parts of the Christian's armor. vv. 13-17. In this hard warfare against the subtleties of these demonic enemies with a consummate organization, there was necessity of a complete spiritual equipment. The metaphor of the Christian soldier and his armor was familiar to Paul and especially now since he had been chained to a mail-clad warrior of the praetorian guard, a different one in turn, for months during the period of imprisonment in Rome. He was thus most intimately familiar with the different parts of the Christian panoply. In Paul's experience this spiritual struggle was a vivid reality and to seek and have the God-given armor for the conflict was of the greatest importance, to make victory sure.

v. 13. *On this account take up* quickly[81] *the whole* panoply or *armor of our God*, which comes from God, *that you may be able to* withstand the onslaught

30. Passive voices, present passive imperative.
81. Second Aorist active imperative, prompt action.

of these formidable foes in the evil day of temptation and terror *and having* accomplished or *done all things* in gaining the victory *to stand,* after the flight as victors on the field.

v. 14. *Take your stand* therefore[82] firm in your position of righteousness and your battle for the truth, *girding your loins round with a belt of truth* to hold together the mail armor for free movement (cf. Isa. 49:17) *and clothing yourselves with the breastplate of righteousness* of a sound character and holy life to cover the vital parts in the battle with your loyalty to His holy will and law.

v. 15. *And* having *shod for yourselves*[83] by binding the sandals under them in *preparation* or equipment for preaching *the Gospel of peace,* with that preparation derived from the Gospel itself, which produces peace with God in the heart and thought, through faith in Christ, the very best equipment for the Christian warrior of peace.

v. 16. *In all* situations and occasions, then *taking up the shield of faith,* looking to God, in reliance on your Lord, and so protected completely as the warrior in battle is protected by the large door-size shield which curves around his body giving protection on three sides, *you may be able with it to quench all the fire-tipped darts of the* evil one or *devil.* He is able with his flaming missiles, set on fire of hell, to inflame with anger and lust your hearts; but with the shield of faith to protect you, your work of extinguishing these deadly missiles may be safely carried on and completed.

v. 17. *And receive,* accept or take as it is offered you from God, *the helmet of your salvation,* which will serve as a helmet for your defense by covering your head and protecting that vital part in the midst of the conflict. This your salvation through faith in the Person of Jesus Christ, will be your deliverance in the crucial hour when savagely beset in the line of battle. You are to *receive also* the *short-sword* (*machairan*) used in trench warfare or line of battle, in hand to hand conflict, as a most deadly offensive weapon, *of the Spirit,* which is given by the blessed Holy Spirit and is *the eternal word of God.*

This is God's utterance of his spoken Truth, written down through inspiration by the Holy Spirit of his apostles and prophets, with which you will be able to meet Satan with the same answer given by Jesus, "It is written," to every temptation he may bring.

3. Making use of persevering prayer to maintain constant contact with the supreme commander and with the rank and file. 6:18-20.

The Christian soldier, thus equipped with armor, defensive and offensive, is to meet with courage, watchfulness readiness, the enemy, but his main help will be in keeping in communication with his commander through the heliography or "radio" connection of constant prayer. The Christian soldier

82. Ingressive aorist.
83. First aorist middle participle.

must not lose contact, in isolation, but in unity of movement the whole of the forces must move as one man through Spirit-led prayer.

v. 18. Stand therefore (v. 14) by means or through the intermediate agency[84] of every kind of form of *prayer* in worshipful approach to God *and* every definite request or *supplication to him* praying *in the* sphere and through the aid of the instrumentality of the Holy *Spirit* (cf. Rom. 8:27), and *unto this* same end *watching with every kind* of vigilant and wide-awake *perseverance* and definite supplication or *petition, on behalf of all the saints* thus maintaining connection, not only with the Lord, Commander, but with all their fellow-warriors, the saints, in the united conflict with the powers of evil.

v. 19. *And on behalf of me* in particular, I beg your intercessions, to the end *that I might be given word,* both in the content and in the effective delivery of the message of God's word, through the power of the Holy Spirit, representing the risen Christ my Lord, *to make known with boldness* and freedom *in the opening of my mouth, the mystery* or revealed secret *of the Gospel,* its world-wide scope and its universal application in the salvation of all peoples a secret long-hidden but at length revealed and

v. 20. *on behalf of which I am an ambassador* from the Sovereign Court of the Risen Christ, *in a chain,* though it be, and as a prisoner, *in order that I may in it,* the chain of imprisonment, with a great freedom, be able *to speak effectively,* the message *as I ought to speak it.*

So the apostle sends out by the radio connection of prayer to all the saints in the province of Asia and wherever he has borne the "message of the mystery," his call to a courageous "fight to the finish" in the warfare, 'not against blood and flesh' bidding them to "keep in touch perseveringly with Jesus" and follow the lead of His Holy Spirit in the united conflict. In the last word of greeting and benediction, he concludes:

4. Telling them that Tychicus will inform them about Paul vv. 21,22.

v. 21. The apostle is desirous to keep in touch with them. *But that you too,* as well as the brethren elsewhere, *may know the things* about me, my circumstances in the Roman imprisonment, *how I am faring* or getting on, *all things shall be communicated to you by Tychicus* your countryman and our *beloved brother and faithful minister in the* work and fellowship of *the Lord.*

v. 22. *Whom I am sending you for this precise purpose,* informing you at first hand, you may know of a certainty our *things* or *circumstances* in the Roman work and experience, *and that he may encourage, comfort and exhort your hearts.*

5. Apostolic blessings on all who love the Lord, vv. 23,24.

v. 23, 24. *Peace,* the Lord's gift to you all, the saints, based on your confidence in Christ and mutual harmony and helpfulness, *be to all the brethren,*

84. *Dia* with genetive denotes intermediate agency.

and love of the brethren to God supremely and *with or* accompanied by never diminishing *faith from God our Father*, the Father of our Lord Jesus, *and from the Lord Jesus Christ*, who is Head over all in Creation and Redemption and the sphere in which all blessings flow down to us from the Father. *Grace be with all them that love our Lord Jesus Christ in uncorruptness.* Grace is the beginning and the end of the epistle.

CHAPTER XXV

The Pastoral Epistles

I, Timothy, Titus, II Timothy

A. D. 65-68.

Introduction.

1. Historic Setting.

The whole trend of Paul's experiences in the two years of imprisonment in Rome, his expressions relative to his hopes, expectations and plans, together with the historic references of external evidences (Philippians 1:25; 2:24; Philemon 22), and the stubborn fact of the existence of the so-called Pastoral Epistles, point to the fact of his liberation at the end of his first trial. The reports of Agrippa and Festus, and the officer Julius, together with the influence of newly won friends, even in the imperial household in Rome, and the tactful handling of the situation by Paul himself, under divine help, "secured his acquittal", according to the testimony of Clement of Rome (Corinthians, Section 5), referring probably to Paul's visit to Spain. Eusebius (Eccl. Hist. 2:22) speaks of Paul's having set forth again upon the ministry of preaching after having defended himself, and that later he entered Rome a second time and there suffered martydom. He also states that during this second imprisonment Paul wrote II Timothy in which he speaks of his first defense and his impending death. The Muratorian Canon also refers to Paul's visit to Spain. Clement who wrote about thirty years after Paul's death says that he was "a herald both in the East and in the West" (I Clem. 5:6). To Clement the "limits of the West would be Spain." Other traditions also sustain this view.

Returning from Rome, the Apostle probably went first to visit the Churches in Asia and Macedonia. According to Lightfoot he visited Colossae and Laodicea, then came back up to Philippi. He next made his journey to Spain (II Timothy 4:10). Following that he returned to Ephesus (I Tim. 1:3), leaving Timothy in charge and going on to Macedonia where he wrote I Timothy. He next visits Crete and leaves Titus in charge and returns, passing by Miletus to Corinth, where he wrote the letter back to Titus. (II Tim. 4:20). Later he went to Troas (II Tim. 4:13), where he was arrested (II Tim. 4:20) and carried on to Rome. In the prison in Rome he wrote II Timothy. Later in A. D. 65-68 he was executed outside of Rome on the Ostian Way.

2. Authenticity and Genuineness.

The genuineness and Pauline authorship of these epistles have been attacked by some modern critics. From the first century to the nineteenth no one ever doubted that they were written by Paul except a few heretics like Marcion, Tatian and Basillides, who rejected them because the epistles would not fit into their system of thought. External evidence is strongly in favor of their authenticity. Among the witnesses are Clement, Polycarp, Ireneus, Tertullian and others. On the grounds of internal evidences Baur and Renan attacked the epistles on four counts: (1) The difficulty of finding a place for these letters in the life of Paul, as presented in the Acts and his own writings, (2) the large amount of peculiar phraseology, (3) the church organization indicated by these epistles, being later in history, (4) the erroneous doctrines of Gnosticism attacked in the epistles being of a later date. None of these accusations stand firm before the thorough examination of modern scholarship (Vide Plummer—Pastoral Epistles, pp. 4-9). Bishops and Elders were equals, not as in the second century. Paul's age and different circumstances would account for the difference in vocabulary. His style is essentially the same and not "entirely different" as E. F. Scott states (Literature of New Testament p. 193). He also uses the word *faith* as in the Galatian Epistle 5:22 (cf. I Tim. 1:12-17). It is harder to argue a *falsarius* who would assume the name of Paul and compose these letters than to admit any slight irregularity in style, vocabulary and doctrine in Paul's last messages of an aged apostle who was left to meet the last issue of his long life of service, practically alone.

I Timothy

In Macedonia, a second time now (Autumn of A. D. 67), Paul is greatly concerned about Timothy and the work in Ephesus and writes back to his "son in the faith" a letter (I Timothy) exhorting him to remain in Ephesus a while (I Tim. 1:3) instead of going on to other places, in his work of evangelist (II Tim. 4:5). Timothy was one of Paul's most beloved workers and was sent to Ephesus at this time for special reasons (cf. Acts 20:29ff). The heresy which Paul had combatted in the epistles written to Colossae and Ephesus during his first imprisonment in Rome needed reenforced refutation now, because false teachers continued their work of inculcating erroneous doctrines (I Tim. 1:3), using "fables and endless genealogies" of Gnosticism, with disputes, empty talk, and violent dogmatic affirmations. Timothy did not have robust health and was timid in disposition, so Paul exhorts him to firmness (I Tim. 4:12) and to "blow up the fire under the kettle" of the God-given talents and special spiritual gifts of his ministry. Looking back over his own life the aged Apostle thanks God for the privileges of his ministry in spite of his unworthiness (I Tim. 1:12-17) and desires that Timothy should fulfil the promise of his youth (I Tim. 1:18). He must live right and be studious (4:12, 13); be consecrated and watchful of his health (4:14f); and go on growing in knowledge and power. He must avoid the temptation to make money and seek pleasure (6:11). He must also "guard the deposit" and be faithful to his trust (6:20). Paul also dealt in his letters with the social problems which Timothy would meet in the church life and in the relationship the churches would have with the Roman State. Timothy had been disposed to resign the charge committed to him (in Ephesus) as he may have done once before when on a mission in Corinth, but Paul vetoed any such idea and encouraged him to go forward with the work there. How Paul loved this young preacher and yearned over his success in the difficult undertakings of the ministry! Timothy was strengthened and went forward to conquer and succeeded. He stuck by Paul to the last. Here are wise words from the greatest of all preachers to a young minister whom he loved dearly!

Analysis and Exegesis

Salutation Ch.1:1,2.

v. 1. *Paul, the* aged *apostle of Christ Jesus according* (in obedience) *to the* definite and authoritative *command of God our Savior,* from whom came, as the originator, our salvation, *and* equally a command *of Christ Jesus, our hope,* in its very substance and

v. 2. foundation,[1] *unto Timothy my true,* legitimate, born *child in the Christian faith; grace, mercy and peace,* I pray for you, *from God the Father and from Christ Jesus our* divine *Lord.* Timothy was with Paul, through whose ministry he was converted in Lystra, most of the time, from the beginning of the Second missionary journey the Apostle made, until the time of the writing of this epistle from Macedonia (circa) 67 A. D.[2] At this time he was pastoring the church in Ephesus. Paul twice summoned him to come to him in his second imprisonment[3] in Rome.[4] Tradition says he served as pastor (overseer) of the church in Ephesus and there paid the 'supreme price,' being beaten to death by a mob because of his arraignment of the idolatrous immorality of the worship of Diana.[5]

Paul seems to have foreseen the difficult problems that Timothy would have to meet and forewarned and prepared him in this First Epistle. He deals in this epistle first with the true function of the church, the proclamation of the Truth; and second, the chief function of the minister, the exposition of the truth within the church.

I. Paul appeals to Timothy to be faithful to his trust in defending the truth against the encroachments of error Ch. I:3-20.

A. The nature of the error 1:3-11. There was a group of false heretical teachers at work in Ephesus (1:4), of the Gnostic type. They made faith subordinate to reason, which smacks of modern rationalism. There teaching was also Jewish in character. The promoters of this heresy desired "to be teachers

1. Ellicott *Com.* in loco.
2. Plummer, Alfred, *Expos. Bibl. Past Epistles* p. 22f.
3. Ibid. p. 27f.
4. Cf. Second Timothy in loco.
5. Cf. Eusebius and (later) Nicephorus of the Fifth Century.

of the law." (v7) There teaching was of the nature of "empty talk" about the law. They "neither understood what they said nor whereof they affirmed" (vv 6,7). This error was a kind of synthesis of gnostic philosophy and legalistic Judaism. It was a fantastic heresy which was creeping into the churches of the province of Asia, centering about Ephesus its capital.

v. 3. *As I exhorted thee to tarry* longer *in Ephesus, when I was going into Macedonia* in order *that thou mightest charge certain* men (teachers) *not to teach a different* doctrine, than that taught by us,

v. 4. *neither to give heed to fables* (myths) *and endless genealogies,* such as those of the Jewish angelology and the Gnostic emanations or aeons, leading to no certain conclusions so do I now. These heresies are *such as lead to questionings* or controversies which have no conclusions or answers *rather than to a dispensation* or stewardship of God committed to us for development *in* the sphere of *faith.*

v. 5. But contrary to such endless discussions and disputings *the end* or aim *of the charge* or word of the true gospel communicated, *is one of* Christian *love* going out *from a* (clean) *pure heart and a good conscience and* sure *faith unfeigned,* and not hypocritical, to our fellowmen. The message transmitted by the heterodox teachers on the other hand consisted in quibbling subleties, the meaning of which they themselves did not understand.

v. 6. *From which things* of the true gospel, *some having swerved* in their aim *have turned aside into vain talking, wishing to be*

v. 7. *teachers of the law, though they understand neither what they are saying nor whereof they confidently affirm.* These false teachers did not even know the things they were stating and far less the subjects which they were assuming to explain.

v. 8. *Now, we know that the law of* Moses *is good* (beautiful) morally, *if any one* (teacher) *uses it lawfully* (in the right way). The false teachers used it improperly and applied it as obligatory in Christianity, ceremonies and all, as appendices or integral parts of the gospel.

v. 9. *Being aware of this, that the law is not made for a righteous man* who is within the number of those who are already justified and do not need to fulfil all its ceremonial requirements; nor is law intended for the morally good *but* for evil doers: *for the lawless* and *unruly, for the ungodly and sinners, for the unholy and profane, for the murderers of fathers and the murderers*

v. 11. *of mothers, for manslayers, for fornicators,* for *abusers of themselves with* men (sodomities), *for men-stealers,* (kidnappers), *for liars, for false-swearers,* who commit perjury, *and if there be any other thing contrary to the sound doctrine, according to the gospel of the glory of the blessed God, which was committed to my trust,* for them. This list of evil doers is surely Pauline, as also the teaching about the use and usefulness of the Jewish law of Moses, which is applicable universally in revealing and prohibiting sin in any form or character, in any person, 'saint or sinner.' But still it has no power to save the sinner and empower him to conquer sin.

B. Paul thanks God for the truth as he had experienced it in his long ministry 1:12-17.

v. 12. *I have thanks* in my heart *to him who gave me strength* within, that is, *Christ Jesus our Lord, for that, placing me in* his *service, he counted* on *me* as (trustworthy) *faithful.*

v. 13. *Though I was* (being) *before a blasphemer,* using stupid and injurious speech,[6] and a persecutor of the Christians[7] following them up to arrest, imprison and even secure their death; *and an insolent* person not only in words but in deeds of violence: *but I was pitied,* having mercy shown to me, *because being ignorant,* without the knowledge of Christ, *I did it* while *in unbelief* (sinful and wilful disbelief).

v. 14. *And the grace of our Lord* (Jesus) *superabounded, with faith and love,* both of Paul and especially of Christ, participating, *in* the sphere of *Christ Jesus.*

v. 15. *Faithful is the saying*[8] *and worthy of all acceptation, that Christ Jesus came into the world to save sinners; of whom I am* (first) *chief;* (first) not in time but in degree. The pre-existence of Jesus is here assumed, as also his mission as the Christ and Savior of all who accept him.

v. 16. *But, for this cause, I obtained mercy* (pity), *that in me as chief* or the worst of sinners, *Jesus Christ might show forth all* the utmost *longsuffering* which he has *for an ensample* (example) to follow, *for those about to rest their faith upon him* as a foundation, *for life eternal.* This rapturous thought led to the ascription of praise in v. 17.[9]

v. 17. *Now, to the King* (of the ages) *eternal, incorruptible,* who alone has immortality in himself and of himself, *invisible,* whom no man hath seen or can see, *the only* and true *God* (be) *honor and glory* (into the ages of the ages) *for ever and ever. Amen.*

C. The messenger of the truth bears a great responsibility and should be faithful to the truth. Ch. 1:18-20.

Returning from his digression relating to his own ministry, Paul adds to his command in the name of Christ to Timothy to resist heresy (v. 3) and to cultivate in himself and other Christians, love, flowing out from a pure heart, a good conscience, and a sure faith,[10] an additional charge to war a good warfare in the ministry. In order to reenforce his charge he cites the prophecies of the promise in connection with the choice of young Timothy, because of his good reputation in Lystra, Iconium and the surrounding region and the prophecies in connection with his ordination to the ministry. He further cites the examples of certain workers who had made shipwreck concerning the faith as a warning to Timothy (vv. 19,20).

---

6. *Blax,* stupid, *phēmē,* speech.
7. Cf. Paul going to Damascus Acts Ch. 9.
8. "All the revelation in Christ." *Ex. Gr. Test.* Vol. IV p. 98, Pros Timotheon A.
9. Boises *Notes* on the Epistles of Paul p. 509.
10. Ibid, pp. 506-508.

v. 18. *This charge* (command) which I have given thee (v. 3,5) *my child Timothy, I commit unto thee* as a sacred trust *in accord with the forerunning prophecies* or predictions[11] *which led to thee* on the occasion of thy choice and ordination, forecasting success and zeal in thy ministry. The purpose of my reminding you of those predictions is *that thou mayest by them* be stimulated and *war a good warfare* in the work of the ministry. The gift of prophecy in Paul was a special gift of the Holy Spirit enabling him to understand and expound divine mysteries with inspired authority and in communication with God fortell future events on occasion; but the chief object of the gift in the preachers of his and all times was for the conversion of sinners and building up of the saints. The predictions of a successful ministry for Timothy were based on the spiritual intuition and assured divine leadership of those who had participated in his ordination.

v. 19. *Holding* on to *faith* as a shield *and in possessing a good conscience,* the former of which cannot continue to exist without the latter. This was demonstrated: *which certain ones who having* deliberately *thrust from them* a good conscience *made shipwreck concerning the faith.*

v. 20. *Of whom is Hymenaeus,*[12] an insidious heretic and corrupter of Christianity *and Alexander,*[13] not identified with the coppersmith, who was not a Christian. These two were dealt with by the church under Paul's leadership: *whom I delivered to Satan* by elimination from the church *in order that they might be taught* by this disciplinary measure *not to blaspheme,* speaking evil of and defaming their Lord. They were heretics and wreckers of the faith and cause of true Christianity. The purpose of this severe discipline was their instruction and reformation,[14] and was not merely punitive but corrective.[15]

II Instructions of the Apostle to Timothy about church worship and organization. Careful attention to these foundational elements was the best way to combat the error of false teachings and guarantee sound doctrine. Ch. 2:1-4:5.

A. Worship: public prayers, one God and one Mediator; Christian living, in the right attitude toward God, with deep concern for the interests of the Messianic Kingdom on the part of both men and women in the church. 2:1-15.

1. The Second charge to Timothy was to teach members of the churches to use prayer and intercession. (vv. 1-8).

v. 1. *I exhort, first of all* (in the first place for importance) *that supplications,* (deēseis, expressions of needs), (proseuchas) *prayers* of personal devotion (enteuxeis) *intercessions* on behalf of others, (euxaristias) *thankgivings,* which should always accompany prayer of every form, *be made on behalf of*[16] *all men* (people).

---

11. Cf. C. J. Ellicott *Com. Tim.* p. 39.
12. Cf. 2 Tim. 2:17.
13. The Alexander of Acts 19:33 was a member of the church and was excommunicated.
14. Cf. Boise's *Notes* p. 510.
15. Cf. *Gr. Ex. N. Test.* in loco.
16. *Huper,* preposition very common in expressions of prayer of every type.

v. 2. *On behalf of kings and all that are in a high place* of authority, *in order that we may lead a tranquil and quiet life in all godliness* (piety) *and gravity.*

v. 3. *This is good and acceptable before the face of God, our Savior,*

v. 4. *Who wishes all men to be saved eternally and to come to the full,* accurate and experiential *knowledge of the truth.*

In verses 5-7 a summary statement is made of the gospel which Paul preached.

v. 5. Having stated that God's will is that all men should be saved he declares: *for there is* only *one God,* and *one mediator also between God and men,* himself *a man, Christ Jesus.*

v. 6. *Who gave himself a ransom* in exchange or instead of and *on behalf of all* men, *the testimony* to this great truth, to be borne, *in its own* peculiar and appropriate *times* or opportune seasons:

v. 7. *for which* purpose *I was appointed* at a definite time,[17] *a herald* (preacher) *and an apostle,* The false teachers of Gnosticism and Judaism denied the apostolic authority of Paul, hence his clear reference to his apostolic mission, as from God. *I speak the truth. I lie not* when I say I was appointed to this work and as *a teacher of the nations* (Gentiles) *in* the sphere of *the faith and in the truth,* belonging to the gospel.

v. 8. *I desire therefore that the men pray in every* (kind of) *place,* lifting *up* in the accustomed attitude of reverence *holy* (pure) *hands,* not soiled with wicked or impure deeds, *without wrath* (anger) *and disputing* as might occur in encounters with the heretical teachers. He wished that the men should take their religion seriously. One object of their prayers, singled out especially, was the rulers and those in high authority, a much neglected object in public prayers in the churches. It was not customary in primitive Christianity for women to occupy leading functions in the public worship.

2. A third charge to Timothy relative to Christian life in the church related especially to the women and deaconesses. Ch. 2:9-15.

v. 9. *In like manner,* I desire *that the women in* (comely) well arranged, *modest apparel, with shamefastness* (reverence) *and sobriety* (good sense). *adorn themselves;* and *not with braided hair, and gold* (ornaments) *or pearls* (costly jewelry) *or costly raiment* (fine, expensive dresses).

v. 10. *but, which becometh women professing godliness, by means of good works.* Decent dress must be combined with good works and godliness. Pursuing further the idea of propriety in conduct in the public services.

v. 11. *Let a woman learn in quietness with all subjection.* The great work of our Christian women of today in teaching, which is so manifestly blessed by the Lord, is not condemned by these inspired instructions of the apostle Paul. A woman who is truly adorned with godliness and good works will not be seen attired gaudily in worldly dress in her public worship and services. The beauty of the devoted personalities of Christian women is one of the

---

17. Aorist tense signifies a definite transaction (Robertson).

greatest lights in current Christianity. Ready humility to learn in quietness and to be subordinate to men, who should really lead, is one of their great virtues. Men, by neglect of aggressive leadership in the greatly imperative missionary campaign, oblige the women to assume assertive roles, where they would not, if the cause were not languishing for lack of leaders in public roles and functions.

v. 12. *But I permit not a woman to teach,* in public address *or to exercise dominion*[18] *over man but to be in quietness.* In matrimony women must not be enslaved but only subordinate. Many men do not measure up to the worthy and rightful headship given them in the order of creation in the headship of the family.

v. 13. Paul justifies his injunction on the ground of the Scriptural account of creation. *For Adam was first formed then Eve.* Christianity did not abrogate the primal law of the relation of woman to man. The second reason for Paul's injunction follows:

v. 14. *And Adam was not beguiled,* by the serpent, *but the woman was beguiled*[19] *and fell completely*[20] *into transgression* in the Garden of Eden.

v. 15. *But she shall be saved,* in the full New Testament sense *by her childbearing,* by thus fulfiling her destiny and acquiescing in all the conditions of woman's life,"[21] *if they* (gunaikes) *continue in faith and love and in sanctification, with sobriety* (good sense). Sin entered the race by Eve's transgression and the necessity of salvation followed. The giving birth to children was to become the salvation of mankind. The seed of the woman was to bruise the serpent's head. Womanhood was glorified in the birth of Jesus. Mary spoke of Jesus and called him her Savior. He is the salvation of woman in all the world from enslavement and all her ills.

B. Sound organization is a guarantee against undermining error. Ch. 3:1-4:5.

1. A fourth charge to Timothy:

Wisdom and spiritual guidance must be used in filling the official positions and functions in the church. The guidance of the Holy Spirit must be sought and allowed in this important function. Ch. 3:1-4:5.

A. Qualifications necessary in the official functions of Bishop (Pastor) and Deacon. Ch. 3:1-13.

1. The fourth charge to Timothy relates to the Pastor. The Bishop (Pastor) must have a good character, good home and good reputation[22] (vv. 1-7).

v. 1. *Faithful* (trustworthy) *is the saying* (the word), *if any man seeketh* (stretcheth forth his hand) *for the office of pastor* or bishop[23] (overseer), *he desireth a good work.*

---

18. Cf. C. J. Ellicott, *Com. I Tim.* p. 62f.
19. Aorist tense, definite occurrence.
20. Perfect tense gegonen denoting complete action and permanent result.
21. Cf. Ellicott I Tim. p. 54f.
22. Cf. H. E. Dana, *Life and Literature of Paul.*
23. Cf. Boises *Notes* p. 514, episcopos and presbuteros refer to the same office of pastor. He is not over the presbateroi.

v. 2. *Wherefore it is necessary that the bishop be without reproach, the husband of one wife,* not of more than one, if any at all, *temperate* or sober-minded, *orderly,* in his conduct, *hospitable* as one friendly toward strangers, *apt* or qualified *to teach;*

v. 3. *no brawler* addicted to drinking wine, *no striker* ready to use his fists, *but gentle*[24] (reasonable), *not contentious* ready for a fight, *no lover of money;*

v. 4. *One who ruleth well his own household* as the head of the family, *having his children in subjection* in the Lord *with all gravity.*

v. 5. (*But if*[25] *any man knoweth not how to rule his own house, how shall he be placed in care of the church of God*).

v. 6. *Not a novice* (new convert, Thayer), *lest*[26] *being puffed up* (wrapped in a mist of pride) *he might fall into the condemnation* (having its origin) *from the devil.* Paul here assumes the existence and insidious activity of a personal devil.

v. 7. *Moreover, he must have good testimony* (reputation) *from them that are without* (on the outside of the church), *lest he fall into reproach and the snare of the devil* (which is laid for him).

2. The fifth charge to Tinothy deals with the qualifications for deacons, which are much the same as those of the pastor, though the emphasis is more on the moral and religious and not so much on the intellectual side, as for the pastors. There should be a period of probation in the choice of deacons. (vv. 8-13).

v. 8. *Deacons in like manner must be grave* (sober), *not double-tongued* (ambiguous and doubtful in what they say), *not given* (or inclined) *to much wine, not greedy of*

v. 9. *filthy lucre* (avaricious); *having the mystery of the faith in a pure conscience,* without which there can be no clear view, no correct comprehension of the spiritual truths.[27] Spiritual unity in the common understanding of the Scriptures finds here its most serious impediment.

v. 10. *And let these,* chosen by the church for the diaconate, *first be proved* or tested out in a period of probation. Deacons should not be chosen as permanent members of the board until they shall have served, for a period, in probation; *then let them serve as deacons, if they be blameless.* The qualification is rather a moral than a highly educational one. The fitness for the office of bishop would call for a more obvious fitness, to be judged before special probation.

v. 11. Women (the wives of the deacons or perhaps deaconesses, *in like manner* must be grave, *not* (calumniators) *slanderers, temperate* (wineless), *faithful in all* things.

---

24. Cf. Phil. 4:5.
25. First class condition, according to fact.
26. Hina mē — that not.
27. Cf. Boise's *Notes* on Paul's Epistle p. 516.

v. 12. *Let the deacons be gentlemen*[28] husbands *of one wife* each only, governing well the children of their own households.[29]

v. 13. *For they who have served well* as deacons *gain for themselves a good standing* (degree) *and much boldness in faith, which is* exercised and experienced *in Christ Jesus.*

b. Warnings against errors which always threaten those in official positions 3:14-4:5. These warnings against error for the bishops and deacons were given in view of their great responsibilities with reference to the promulgation of the truth, because many in the church had departed from and perverted the truth, teaching that salvation was through a few ascetic formulas and ceremonies. There is great danger in the repetition of such history always. The preaching and teaching of the truth for the conversion of sinners and perfecting of the Saints is one of tremendous responsibility on the officers of the church. "The true function of the minister is that of the exposition of the truth in the church."[30]

v 14. *These things I write unto thee hoping to come unto thee shortly.* Paul was liberated and had visited Ephesus but was now in Macedonia, perhaps in Philippi. But he was arrested soon and imprisoned again in Rome, where he ended his active career, almost alone.

v. 15. *But, if I tarry long,*[31] *I am writing* in order *that you may know how men ought to behave*[32] *themselves in the household* or family *of God, which is the church of the living God, the pillar* adorning *and ground* supporting and constituting the foundation *of the truth.*

v. 16. *And* (confessedly) *without controversy* or discussion, *great is the mystery* (revealed secret) *of godliness* (godlike religious piety): that secret is the person of Christ: *Who was manifested in the flesh* (incarnated) *Justified in* the (his) *spirit* (being manifested sinless)[33] *Seen by angels* (messengers from heaven),[34] *Preached among the nations* (peoples) *Believed on in the world* (while incarnate and later.) *Received up in glory* (at the ascension).[35]

Ch. IV. vv. 1-5. After reciting the poetic expression of the creed of primitive Christians, Paul goes on to remind Timothy that there will be a falling away from this true doctrine by many within the pales of Christianity.

v. 1. *But the* (Holy) *Spirit sayeth*[36] *expressly, that in later times some,* of those who are in the churches, *shall fall away from the faith* in the Christ Jesus of the creedal hymn, *giving heed to seducing spirits and doctrines of*

---

28. Cf. andres vs. anthropoi.
29. The household included not only their own children but those of the household which included those of household servants.
30. Cf. Campbell G. Morgan, *Living Messages of the Books of the Bible,* Vol. N. Test. p. 49ff.
31. Condition of the third class with ean, general condition.
32. Present mid. infiinitive of anastrephō, behave oneself.
33. His challenge to his enemies: "who convicteth me of sin?"
34. Angels at his birth, at his death, at his ressurrection. But Christ also was manifested to the angel-messengers. the apostles and others after his resurrection.
35. This is a stanza of a Christian hymn sung in the primitive churches.
36. Paul here claimed inspiration.

demons. The false teachers are used of the devil. They denied both the humanity and deity of Jesus, some one, some the other[37]

v. 2. *by the hypocrisy of men that speak lies,* seared or *branded in their own conscience as with a hot iron,*

v. 3. *forbidding to marry and* imposing celibacy and *commanding to abstain from* certain foods which are eaten (foods, bromatōn) especially *meats, which God created to be received with thanksgiving by them that believe and know the truth.*

v. 4. *Because every creature of God is good, and nothing is to be rejected, if it be received with thanksgiving to God:*

v. 5. *For it is sanctified through*[38] *the word of God and prayer.*

III. The proper management of the affairs of the church and Timothy's relation to it. Chs. 4:6-6:19.

A. What Timothy's personal conduct should be. Again Paul charges Timothy that (4:6-16):

1. He must warn the church against error (vv. 6, 7a).

v. 6. *Putting the brethren in mind of these things, thou shalt be a good minister of Christ Jesus, nourished in the words of the faith, and of the good doctrine which thou hast followed* until now.

v. 7a. *But refuse* (have nothing to do with) *profane and old wives fables,* such as the imaginative stories of the like tales. They are not profitable for piety and so are profane being like the myths of the heathen, without any basis in reality.

2. That he should pursue spiritual attainments (7b-11)

v. 7b. *But rather exercise thyself for godliness* (piety).

v. 8. *For bodily exercise* (gymnastics) is *profitable for a little* (in a limited degree) *but godliness* (godlikeness, true religious culture) *is profitable for all things,* having (since it has)[39] *promise of the life which now is,* in this world, a full life physically, intellectually, morally and spiritually, *and of that which is to come,* the eternal life in the highest New Testament sense.

v. 9. *Faithful* (trustworthy) is the saying (declaration) *and worthy of all acceptation.*

v. 10. *For to this* end we *labour* (toil) *and are striving*[40] struggling as an athlete in a wrestling match), *because we have placed our hope*[41] completely and permanently *in the living God, who is the Savior of all men,* as a Preserver to some giving them life and breath and all things,[42] *but especially of the faithful,* who have anchored their faith in Christ and are set apart to Him, in a different and for higher sense. They are saved for eternity.

---

37. The Docetic Gnostics denied the humanity and the Corinthians the deity.
38. Dia with genitive, denotes the agency or means.
39. Causal use of the participle.
40. Present tense and progressive action.
41. Perfect tense of complete action and permanent result.
42. Cf. Acts Ch. 17.

v. 11. *These things command and teach.* So he ends this charge relating to the church and Timothy's personal conduct in relation to it.

3. Paul was insistent in his exhortation and counsel to Timothy about care as to his reputation (v. 12) and his development of himself in the ministry. Timothy must have been more than thirty years of age but he was occupying a position of great responsibility as pastor of the important strategic church in Ephesus. There were many other pastors in the province of Asia, older than Timothy, and he must be strong.

v. 12. *Let no man despise thy* youth; as it seems some did in Corinth, when Timothy went there on a mission from Paul some years before. There were some who were rebellious against Paul's apostolic authority and did not accept the offices of Paul's youthful messenger to them or heed his counsels. So Paul says: *but be* (become) *an ensample* (example or type for the faithful) *to them that believe, in word* (teaching or conversation), *in manner of life* (conduct), *in love, in faith, in purity* (Christian virtues and character).

v. 13. *Until I come give heed* diligently *to* the public *reading* of the Scriptures, *to exhortation and to teaching.*

v. 14. *Neglect not the gift that is in thee, which was given to thee through* the agency of *prophecy* (preaching) (accompanied by) *with the laying on of hands of the presbytery.* This public ceremony was like baptism but a symbol, and not magically in any way the means of conferring the inward grace. The divine appointment and setting apart to the ministry was an act of God, of Christ and of the Holy Spirit.

v. 15. *Take* diligent *care of these things, be continually in them, in order that thy progress* (cutting forward) *may be manifest unto all* thy fellow workers and the constituency of the churches. A leader has to be alive and aggressive. He must go ahead of the flock.

v. 16. *Give heed*[43] *to thyself* personally in spiritual growth *and to the teaching,* of the Gospel traditions and Scriptures, *continue* assiduously *in them; for doing this thou shalt save thyself* personally, securing thy spiritual development and leadership in the work *and those hearing thee* preach the word and give direction to the activities. This is exceedingly important for any preacher, especially the young men in the ministry.

B. As to the officers and dependants of the church. Ch. 5:1-25.

1. The paster must deal with the individuals as such. (vv. 1,2).

v. 1. *Do not rebuke an elderly man but exhort him as a father; the younger men as brothers;*

v. 2. *the elder women as mothers; the younger women as sisters, in all purity.*

2. He will need to have arrangements for the administration of charity to widows. (vv. 3-16). There seem to have been among the widows who were dependants certain ones who rendered service for the compensation received

43. Present imperative, go on improving yourself and your teaching.

from the church. They might have been deaconesses.

v. 3. *Honor widows that are widows indeed,* by giving them aid when necessary.

v. 4. *But if any widow hath children or grandchildren, let them* (the offspring) *learn first to show* filial *piety* or respect toward *their own family and to requite their parents, for this is acceptable in the sight of God.* Reverence (eusebeia) as filial piety is a duty of children and attending to parents in need does not interfere with duty to Christ.[44]

v. 5. *Now, she that is a widow indeed* (actually) *and* (left alone) *desolate, hath her hope set*[45] *on God and continueth in supplications*[46] expressing her personal needs *and in prayers* of personal devotion, and communion in the night and daytime.

v. 6. *But she that liveth riotously* giving herself to pleasure, in the enjoyment of sensuality *is dead* spiritually *while she liveth.* Such could not be aided or employed by the church.

v. 7. *And these things command, in order that they may be without reproach.*

v. 8. *But if any one does not take thought beforehand for his own* (relatives) *and especially for those of his household he has denied* permanently *the faith and is worse* in conduct *than an unbeliever.* He had more knowledge than an unbeliever and therefore his conduct is worse.

v. 9. *Let one be enrolled as widow* only *when she has become not less than sixty years of age, a one-man*

v. 10. kind of *woman* (a faithful wife of only one man), her character *attested by good works, if she has nourished children* (her own or others destitute of home), *if she has entertained strangers, if she has washed the feet of saints* (serving them in any humble way), *if she has furnished aid to persons in affliction, if she has followed close upon every kind of good work.*

v. 11. *But younger widows, refuse* to enroll in the list of those to be aided, and used as deaconesses, *for when they have become* (reckless) *wanton against Christ they desire to marry,*

v. 12. *having condemnation, because they have broken their first pledge of faith.*

v. 13. *And likewise they learn to be idle going from house to house; and not only idle but tattlers also, and busybodies speaking things which they ought not.*

v. 14. *I desire therefore that the younger* widows marry, *bear children, rule the household, give none occasion to the adversary* (devil) *for reviling.*

v. 15. *For already some are turned aside after Satan.*

v. 16. *If any woman that is a believer* has *widows, let her provide* for *them* a sufficient supply *and let not the church be burdened,* in order *that there may be a* sufficient supply *for those* who are *actual widows.*

---

44. Cf. Luke 14:26.
45. Perfect tense, indicating permanent character of her hope.
46. Perfect tense, permanent.

The writer, Paul, was accustomed to turn aside from his main subject in a digression. He did not have to do that in this case for his discussion of the pastor in his relation toward the constituency of his church was most naturally in order, in looking at the conduct of the pastor. Timothy was a young man comparatively and Paul would recommend to him the utmost care in dealing with all his workers old or young and especially in relation to the women of of his church in a large congregation. Among his women workers there were four classes more or less distinct. (1) The elderly widows alone in the world and dependent on the church. They could render a fine service in prayer for themselves and in intercession for others. (2) The widow with children and grandchildren could in most cases be supported by the children, but if in part, might, if helped, render some good service in the office of deaconess if adapted to such service. The children should be impressed with their duty in her support. (3) The widow who lived luxuriously for pleasure should not expect any support. (4) The actual widow who was deserving could be employed as deaconess if adapted to the work.

The deaconesses were not all widows by any means. They might be from the class of younger unmarried women or the married also. They were chosen and set apart by the church as the deacons were, taking upon themselves the same serious pledges and obligations. The instructions and injunctions of Paul later had a great influence on the status of woman in Roman society in reference to her dowry in a legal status in wills.[47] In the economy of Christian resources the church ought not to take on the burden of any who are not really destitute.

3. The right attitude toward elders or pastors and the responsibilities of such elders. 5:17-25.

a. Certain ones are to have the responsibility of teaching (v. 17) receiving remuneration for their services (v. 18). Cf. v. 1 also.

v. 17. *Let the elders who preside* and govern *well be counted worthy of double honor*: (esteem and compensation), *especially those* laboring hard[48] *in word* (preaching) and *teaching.*

v. 18. *For the Scripture saith, Thou shalt not muzzle the ox when he treadeth out the corn* (grain).[49] *And the laborer is worthy of his hire* or pay (wages).

b. The pastor-elders are to be held in high esteem (vv. 19-25).

v. 19. *Do not* (have the habit of receiving) *receive an accusation against an elder* (pastor), *except* (in the presence) (at the mouth) *of two or three witnesses.*

v. 20. *Them that sin* (go on sinning habitually) *reprove in the sight of all* the elders, *in order that the rest may have fear.*

---

47. Cf. H. E. Dana, *Life and Literature of Paul.*
48. Kōpiaō, toil.
49. Cf. Deut. 25:4; 24:15; I Cor. 9:9; Luke 10:7. Paul may have been quoting the Gospel tradition here because Luke's Gospel was written in 63 A. D. But he likely knew the teaching of Jesus when he wrote I Cor.

v. 21. *I* solemnly *charge* (conjure) *thee in the sight of God and Christ Jesus and the elect angels* (who will attend Jesus in his second coming) *in* order *that thou observe* (guard) *these things without prejudice* (prejudgment), *doing nothing by way of partiality.*

v. 22. *Lay hands hastily on no man,* (avoid such a habit), *nor be a partaker in the sins of others keep thysef pure* personally.

v. 23. *Be no longer a drinker of water* (exclusively), *but use a little wine for thy stomach's sake and thine often infirmatics.* The medicinal use of wine in a genuine and conscientious way only, is here justified. Timothy was delicate in health.

vv. 24. Paul warns Timothy against hasty and premature decision and action in relation to the matter of ordaining pastors, for the reason: *Of some men, the sins are* openly *manifest, going before* them *into judgment* (judicial trial) *but in some also they even follow.*

v. 25. *In like manner also there are good works that are manifest beforehand* (openly) *and those* (works) which are *otherwise cannot be hid* (always). "The discernment in mose cases as to good and bad candidates for the ministry is not difficult because men's conduct acts as a herald to their character."[50] In case there is serious doubt it is better to wait and allow an indefinite period of probation, at least. Sin, both that repented of and more that not repented of, must have its penalty; that repented of in this life and that unrepented of in both worlds.

C. Classes which present problems in the church. Ch. 6:1-19.

1. Servants (slaves). (vv. 1, 2). *Let as many as are servants* (slaves) *under the yoke* (of bondage) *count their own masters worthy of all honor that the name of God and the doctrine* (teaching of Christianity) *be not blasphemed* (evil spoken of). Paul's counsel to Christian slaves was not to run away nor to rebel against their masters but to use their Christianity as slaves to convert their masters and thus do away ultimately with the horrors of slavery if not slavery itself.

v. 2. *And they that have believing masters, let them not despise them,* because *they are brethren, but let them serve them the rather* than to be rebellious, *because those that are partaking of the benefit* of the good service *are believing and beloved.* Christianity accepts the social status as it is and changes it from the inside by heart change and not by superimposed methods of force. Slavery, such as Rome had has passed away almost. *These things teach and exhort* (habitually).

2. False teachers who demand liberal remuneration were a serious problem. Paul warns Timothy against such a wrong spirit. 5:3-16.

---

50. Cf. Alfred Plummer, *Expos. Bible* p. 170f.

v. 3. *If any one teaches*[51] *another* (different) *doctrine and does not give heed to sound* healthful *words,* even *those* words *of our Lord Jesus Christ, and to the doctrine which is according to godliness,*

v. 4. (piety), he is puffed up being enveloped in the mist of his own reasonings, *knowing nothing* for a certainty, *but being sick* or unsound in his mind *relative to questionings and disputes from which come envy, strife, blasphemies* (railings or injurious remarks), *evil* suspicions (under thoughts), or *surmisings,*

v. 5. (violent contentions) *wranglings of men corrupted in mind and bereft of the truth* (voluntarily),[52] *who think that godliness* (piety) *is a way of* financial *gain.* They do not know the difference between the gain of a love of godliness and the ungodliness of a love of gain. These teachers were self-interested and grasping. Improvement in social position and worldly prospects is not a pure motive for 'joining the church.' One must join Christ before joining the church.

v. 6. *But* true *godliness* accompanied *with* (contentedness) *contentment is great* spiritual *gain.*

v. 7. *For we have brought*[53] *nothing into the world,* when we were born and it is sure that *neither are we able to carry anything out* when we die.

v. 8. *And having food and covering,* or clothes and shelter *with these we will be content.*

v. 9. But they that are wishing to be rich fall into[54] temptation to do wrong, *and a snare and many foolish and hurtful lusts such as drown men in* the depth of utter *destruction and* irremedial *perdition.*

v. 10. *For the love of money is a root of all kinds* of *evils, which some* men *have reached out after and have been led to wander away from the faith and have thus pierced themselves through with many sorrows* (agonies, pains). Paul appeals to Timothy to avoid such a pitfall.

v. 11. *But you, O man of God, flee these things and follow after righteous*ness (dikaiosunēn) *godliness* (eusebeian,) *faith* (pistin), *love* (agapēn), *patience* (hupomonēn), *meekness* (praupathian).

v. 12. *Fight the good fight of faith,* and keep on fighting,[55] *lay hold on the life eternal, into which you were* definitely *called*[56] *and didst confess*[57] *the good confession in the presence of many witnesses.*

v. 13. *I charge thee in the sight of God who preserves* all things, alive and *quickeneth all things, and of Christ Jesus who before Pilate witnessed the good confession* laying down his life for us, *that thou keep the*

51. First class condition, according to fact or reality. Cf. Robertson *Word Pictures,* p. 591. There were certain false teachers doing this.

52. Middle voice, participle.

53. Perfect tense denoting completed action and permanent result.

54. Preposition *eis* with several accusatives describing a new sphere of life into which they pass.

55. Pre. imv. active, continuous, progressive.

56. Aorist passive, definite occurrence.

57. Ibidem.

v. 14. *commandment without spot, without reproach* (not open to reproach) *until the appearing of our Lord Jesus Christ* at his second coming, which (appearing)

v. 15. *he will make plain in his own times, who is the blessed and only Potentate, the King of Kings and Lord of lords:*

v. 16. *who only* (alone) *hath immortality, dwelling in light unapproachable, whom no man hath seen nor can see: to whom be honor and power eternal.* Amen.

3. The rich, who were likely few in the early churches, were a problem. They were proud and looked down on the poorer members. Paul recommended that they devote their wealth to the work of the gospel and philanthropy (6:17-19).

v, 17. *Charge them that are rich in this world, that they be not highminded nor set their hope on uncertain riches,* which take wings and fly away, *but on God who giveth to us richly all things to enjoy.*

v. 18. *That they do good* with their wealth, *that they be rich in good works,* humanitarian and philanthropic as well as more directly evangelical, *that they be ready to distribute, willing to communicate* (contribute).

v. 19. *Laying up* in store *for themselves* a *good foundation against* the *time to come, that they may lay hold on life which is real life indeed.*

v. 20. *O Timothy, guard that which is committed,* to thee, *turn away from vain babblings and oppositions of the* (gnostics) *knowledge, which is falsely*

v. 21. *so called, which some professing have erred concerning the faith. Grace be with you.*

PAUL'S LETTER TO TITUS

I. Introduction

1. Titus was one of the most valiant and trusted fellow-workers of Paul. The Apostle had been in Crete with him sometime during the period of his missionary activities visiting some of the churches in Asia and Europe, after his first imprisonment in Rome. He had been set free in his first trial under Nero and succeeded later probably in carrying out his visit to Spain. Titus was one of Paul's early converts and was with him in the victorious Conference of Paul and Barnabas, when Gentile liberty was won; himself, a Gentile convert, serving as a test case, when the Judaistic party in the Jerusalem church would have required him to be circumcised. Paul had stoutly refused to consent[58] and had won the approval of the apostolic "pillars of the church" in Jerusalem to Gentile Christian liberty on that occasion and Titus came in the latter years of Paul's labors to be very useful in the campaign in Europe and elsewhere. He was particularly efficient and greatly blessed

58. Cf. Acts 15:1-10.

in helping the Apostle when the church in Corinth was so torn up with partisan strife. He was sent there by Paul three times on special missions peculiarly difficult and succeeded. Paul did not have much time to spend in Crete, where the work had been established probably by "certain ones" who were in Jerusalem at Pentecost when Peter preached a memorable sermon and three thousand were converted. There were some persons from Crete present, and returning to their island home they took Christianity with them.[59] The Apostle left Titus in Crete to carry out a much needed reorganization of the work including a thorough indoctrination and disciplinary measures in the churches there.

2. The occasion, date and purpose of the letter. Paul had gone on from Crete to Corinth and later to Nicopolis in one or the other of which places he may have written the letter, in response to a letter received from Titus narrating the circumstances and conditions of the churches in Crete, as he had found them on a more thorough examination after Paul's departure. Both the Jewish and Gentile heretics were at work in Crete.[60] There had been a revival of rabbinism. Titus needed some instructions in his struggle against these heretics. Paul's letter was personal but dealt with church problems and would be used in its epistolary character in meeting and resolving those problems.

II Analysis and Exegesis

Salutation: 1:1-4

Paul presents himself in this rather long salutation as the authoritative bond-servant of God and apostle of Jesus Christ and states clearly that Titus is a true child of the faith having been converted under the Apostle's ministry. He is presented as Paul's appointed representative "for the establishment of faith in those to whom he was to minister." Titus in this capacity is to defend the gospel against the intrusion of error. This was his mission in Crete. He was to do a thorough work of reorganization and basic indoctrination and instruction in the churches.

v. 1. *Paul a* bond-*servant* (slave) *of God,* not a forger, *and* also *an apostle of Jesus Christ, according to the faith of God's elect* (for its establishment in the chosen ones of God) *and* with a view[61] *to the* full *knowledge of the truth which is according to* (designed for) *a godliness,*

v. 2. resting *upon a hope of life eternal, which God who cannot lie promised before times eternal.*

v. 3. *but in his own seasons* (opportune times) *manifested his word in the message, wherewith I was intrusted, according to the commandment of God, our Savior.*

v. 4. *To Titus my true* (born) child *according to* the common *faith* which is universal and has but one standard for all, without discrimination, whether Jew or Gentile.

---

59. Cf. Acts ch. 2.
60. Cf. Acts 2:11.
61. Cf. Robertson A. T. *Word Pictures,* Titus.

Grace and peace from God the Father and Jesus Christ our Savior.

1. The status of things in the churches in Crete called for sound organization, in view of the lack of discipline and corrupted character of the Cretan people and the corrupting immoral sophistries of false Jewish teachers. Ch. 1:5-16.

Organization

A. Official positions in the church must be carefully filled 1:5-9. Christianity had been spreading in Crete for some years when Paul left Titus there. Each Christian congregation must have an elder or person in pastoral care of it. As Paul's apostolic representative Titus was to give attention first to securing proper church officials. The word translated *appoint* is katastēsēs which was used in Acts 6:3 where the apostles instructed the congregation in Jerusalem to select for themselves seven men to serve tables and the apostles installed them in office. The qualifications required for elder (or bishop) were high as indicated in vv. 5-7.

v. 5. *For this cause I left thee in Crete in order that thou shouldest set in order the things that were wanting,* which were left unfinished on the occasion of my departure, *and appoint elders in every city as I gave thee charge,* when I was departing.

v. 6. *If any man is blameless,*[62] as surely in the case, *the husband of* only *one* wife, *having children* that are *believers, who are not accused of riot* or dissoluteness,[63] *or* of being *unruly.*

v. 7. *For the bishop* (or elder[64]) *must be blameless, as God's steward* which he is, *not self-willed,* pleasing himself, *not* soon *angry,*[65] *not given to* drinking *wine*[66] *no brawler* (quarrelsome) *no striker, not greedy of filthy lucre* (base gain)

v. 8. *but* on the contrary *given to hospitality* (a friend to strangers[67]) *a lover of* that which is *good, sober-minded* (wise in thought), *righteous* or just in conduct, *holy,* in accord with the law of God, *temperate* exercising self-control.

v. 9. *Holding to the trustworthy word in accordance with the teaching, in order that he may be powerful both to exhort in the doctrine which is healthful and to refute those who contradict,* the gain-sayers.

Discipline

B. There must be discipline, and warning against the false teachings, and also discipline of the church. 1:10-16.

62. Condition of first class, according to fact.
63. Cf. C. J. Ellicott *Com.* p. 192.
64. "Elder is the title oversight (Bishop) the function."
65. Not inclined to anger.
66. *Paroinon,* by the side of wine.
67. *Filozenon,* friend of the stranger.

Heretical teachers had caused great disorder and disturbance among the poorly instructed members of the Christian churches. Paul describes the character of those teachers and calls upon Titus to reprove them sharply. Their teaching was very seductive, being of the nature of shrewd speculation mixed with Jewish fables. The teachers themselves were motivated by base gain at the expense of the churches. They were void of purity, without faith and altogether wrong in their profession and practice, claiming to know God, but denying him by their evil works. That was a hard pastorate for Titus. But he always succeeded in the work he undertook for Christ and his great fellow-worker Paul.

v. 10. *For there are many unruly men, vain talkers and deceivers specially they of the circumcision.*[68]

v. 11. *Whom it is necessary to silence,* by stopping their mouths, *since they overturn whole households,* teaching things *which are not proper* or necessary to teach, *for the sake of disgraceful gain.*

v. 12. *A certain one of them,* (the Cretans), *a prophet of their own,*[69] *said, Cretans are always liars*[70] wicked *evil wild beasts, idle gluttons* (sensual gormandizers) or "slothful bellies" (Ellicott).

v. 13. *This testimony* of Epimonides *is true. For which cause,* that the national traits of the people of Crete are such, *reprove them* (the false teachers) *sharply,* with cutting words, *that they may be sound*[71] *in the faith.* The Cretan Christians were sick and the remedy should be severe that spiritual health might be restored to them.

v. 14. *Not giving* further *heed to Jewish fables and commandments of men who turn away from the truth.*

v. 15. *To the pure* in mind and heart *all things are pure; but to them that are defiled and unbelieving nothing is pure.* Paul is here referring to meats and drinks and the false ceremonial system which the Judaists wished to impose on the Gentile believers. *But they have been defiled* completely, *both their mind and their conscience.*

v. 16. *They confess* (profess) *that they know God, but by their works they deny him, being abominable and disobedient and* with respect *to every good work disapproved.*

II. Paul counsels Titus about the character of his teaching and administration of his instruction. Chs. 2:1-3:15.

A. In his teaching, conduct must be in conformity with a true faith. (v. 1-15). This must be true in his work among all classes and age-groups. The doctrinal foundation for right conduct is set forth clearly (vv. 11-14) followed by a solemn charge (v. 15).

---

68. Apparently Jewish Christians of the pharisaic type, tinged with gnosticism (Robertson *Word Pictures*, p. 600. Vol. Paul's Letter.

69. Epimenides of Cnossos. Here we have a quotation from a Hymn of Leus.

70. They claimed to have the tomb of Leus (Robertson).

71. Final clause with hina with pres. act. subj.

v. 1. *But you,*[72] in contrast to the seducing teachers *speak* always *the things which are fitting to a* (healthful) *sound doctrine* (teaching). This is to be true of his teaching of all classes and ages:

v. 2. that *aged men be temperate, grave, sober-minded, sound* or healthful *in* respect to *faith, in* Christian *love, in endurance,* readiness to stay under the load with patience,

v. 3. *that aged women likewise,* be *reverent in* their *deportment, not* (calumniators, diabolous, diabolic) *slanderers, nor enslaved to much wine, teachers of that which is good* and beautiful,

v. 4. *that they may train the young women to love their husbands, to love their children,*

v. 5. to be *sober-minded, chaste* (innocent), *workers at home, kind* (good), *subject to their own husbands, that the word of God be not blasphemed* or evil spoken-about.

v. 6. The younger men likewise exhort to be sober-minded.

The emphasis in vv. 1-6 is placed on conduct and moral precepts over against the emphasis of the false teachers, or silly superstitions as a substitute in the place of a godly life. Such teachers make religion a trade and the end sordid gain. Sobriety or sober-mindedness is a note which recurs through all these counsels. It manifests itself in discreet conduct and self-control, over indulgences of the lower sensual appetites of touch and taste and the higher appetences of the mind, of those who mistake religious feeling for the holiness of a righteous conduct. Sober-mindedness will keep Christians from being satisfied with themselves and disposed to magnify their accomplishments of the past and excuse their indifference to zeal for the present and future activities. The puffing up of the heart with egotism reduces the worker to a status of deadening complacency[73] and satisfaction with what he is.

vv. 7, 8. What Paul said about the younger men applied also to Titus as their teacher:

v. 7. *in all things showing thyself an ensample* (type) *of good works, in thy doctrine* showing *uncorruptness.*

v. 8. *gravity; sound speech* (discourse) *that cannot be condemned;* in order *that he who is of the contrary part* (opposite party) *may be* turned within and made to reflect *having nothing to say concerning us* that is *evil.*

vv. 9, 10. Paul always mentioned the class of Christian slaves, setting forth their status. *Exhort servants,* (slaves who had been converted to Christianity) *to be in subjection to their own masters*[74] *and to be wellpleasing to them in all things.* This was the best counsel to give to slaves even to those who suffered many cruelties and much injustice; *not gainsaying* or contradicting them,

72. Su, in position of emphasis.
73. Plumner, Alfred, *Expos. Bible.* Pastoral Epp. Ch. XXI.
74. Despotais, translated despot, an absolute ruler whose will was supreme for the slave.

v. 10. *not purloining* or pilfering, *but showing all good fidelity*, confidence in their masters and faithfulness in their service; in order *that they may adorn* (be an ornament to) *the doctrine*, (or teaching), *which* is *from God, our Savior, in all* things. The beauty of Christian life in a slave is one of the greatest proofs of the character of Christianity. In vv. 11-14 The doctrinal foundation for right conduct is stated clearly: the grace of God in redemption.

v. 11. *For the grace of God was manifested*, in the incarnation of Christ, bringing *slavation for all men*,

v. 12. *instructing us* with a disciplinary hand, in order *that denying ungodliness and worldly lusts we should live soberly, and righteously and godly in this present world* (age),

v. 13. *looking for the blessed* (happy) *hope*, a great motive power, *and appearance* (epiphony) *of the glory of the great God and our Savior Jesus Christ*.

v. 14. *Who gave himself for us* in order *that he might redeem*[75] *us from all iniquity and purify unto himself*[76] *for his own possession a people*[77] *zealous of good works*.

v. 15. Paul charges Titus: *Speak and keep on speaking*,[78] *and keep on exhorting and reprove* and *keep on reproving with all* and full *authority. Let no man despise thee*, but be courageous and firm.

B. Obedience to civil authority is also a (Christian) virtue which must be emphasized. Ch. 3:1-7.

v. 1. *Keep on reminding them* (the Christian Cretans) *to be in subjection* in inward disposition to *rulers*, (the superiors in the Roman government), *to authorities*, who are carrying out this rule, *to be obedient* in attitude and act, *to be ready unto*[79] *every good work*, that there may be peace and liberty, by a good example of obedience to law. A Christian must be a good citizen even if he should have to suffer injustice at times.

v. 2 *to speak evil* or injurious words *of no man; not to be contentious* but peaceful; to be *gentle, showing all meekness toward all men*.

v. 3. *For we also were beforetime foolish* without reflection, *disobedient* to all authority, *deceived*, wandering in error; *serving divers lusts and* sinful *pleasures, living in malice*, being bad in character; *and in envy*; being *hateful* and *hating one another*.

v. 4. *But when the kindness of God our Savior and his love toward man* (philanthropy) *appeared*, in the incarnation of Christ,

---

75. lutrōsętai, Aorist middle subj. the subject of the verb acting for himself.
76. Cf. Plumner *Com.* Titus pp. 263-269.
77. Cf. I Pet. 2:9, 10.
78. Present act. imperative, progressive continued action in all these three verbs of the charge.
79. Pros, up to.

v. 5. *Not by works* done *in righteousness which we did ourselves, but according to his mercy he saved us, through* or by means of the *washing of regeneration* being again *and the renewal* from *the Holy Spirit,*[80]

v. 6. *whom*[81] *he poured out upon us richly through the means of Jesus Christ our Savior.*

v. 7. in order *that being justified* (aorist) *by his grace we might* be made to *become heirs* of the riches of eternal salvation, *according to the hope of eternal life.*

c. Titus is charged to teach Christians (in Crete) the importance of maintaining good works. The practical application of true doctrine would counteract false teachings and foolish questionings. Titus should not be lax in dealing with the false teachers. Ch. 3:8-11.

v. 8. *Faithful is the* foregoing *saying* or statement about salvation (vv. 4-7), *and concerning these things I wish thee to affirm strongly, to the end that they who have believed in God*[82] may be thoughtful *to take the lead*[83] *in good works. These things are good and profitable for men.*

v. 9. *But avoid foolish questionings* (investigations) *and genealogies and strife and fightings* (contentions) *about the law; for they are unprofitable and vain* (empty).

v. 10. *A man who causes dissensions as* the *heretical* teachers, *avoid,*

v. 11 knowing *that such a man is perverted*[84] *and goes on sinning*[85] though, *being self-condemned.*

D. Conclusion referring to various historical matters about workers including Tychicus, Apollos, Artemas and Zenas.

v. 12. *When I shall send Artemas unto thee, or Tychicus* to take his place in his absence) *make haste to come to me in Nicopolis,* (in Epirus probably), for there I have decided to pass the winter.

v. 13. *Set forward Zenas the lawyer*[86] *and Apollos* on their journey diligently, providing the means *so that nothing may be wanting unto them.*

v. 14. *And let our* people *also learn to maintain good works for necessary uses, that they be not unfruitful.*

v. 15. *All that are with me salute thee. Salute them that love us in faith. Grace be with you all.*

II. TIMOTHY

1. The introductory observations on I Timothy and Titus give the historical setting of II Timothy also, lacking the addition of a few facts. Paul was

---

80. Ablative of source of this renewal of our natures.
81. Attraction of relative which is in neuter only because it refers to the neuter noun pronouns.
82. Perfect participle.
83. Thayer, Lexicon. Cf. R. V. to maintain.
84. Perfect middle, self-perverted, completely and permanently.
85. Present Ind. active, progressive and continued action.
86. Nothing more is known of him.

again in prison in Rome, having been arrested in Corinth, in Nicopolis where he had expected to spend the winter (Titus 3:12), or in Troas or Rome. The date of II Timothy is placed by some as early as the winter of A. D. 64-65 but was probably later in 66 or 67 A. D. On what charges he was arrested we do not know, but Paul had little hope of another release (II Tim. 4:18). It was perilous even to visit him now and all had left him save Luke (II Tim. 3:11). Onesiphorous was one who was not ashamed of Paul's chain and sought him out. Paul now faces death, but is not afraid, with the Lord (II Tim. 4:17). He is cold and needs his cloak (II Tim. 4:13) and asks Timothy that his manuscripts (books) be brought to him, bringing with him also John Mark (II Tim. 4:21). We do not know whether he reached Paul before the execution or not. This heroic and tenderly sympathetic letter, rich in personal details, makes a fitting close for his grand life. It was his Swan-song. (Robertson).

Analysis and Exegesis

Salutation 1:1, 2

v. 1. *Paul an apostle* sent *from*[87] *Jesus Christ through* the intermediate agency of *the will of God, according to the promise of life* eternal *which*[88] *is in Christ Jesus* both the Messiah and the Savior.

v. 2. *To Timothy my own*[89] *beloved child* in the faith, having been born spiritually under my preaching ministry in Lystra. We note a tone of tenderness in this salutation, an echo of the apostle's anticipation and expectation that the hour of his departure from life is rapidly approaching. *Grace, mercy and peace from God the Father and Christ Jesus our Savior.*

I. Paul thanks God for Timothy, his devotion reflecting his fine background, and his bright promise of a glorious future in the gospel ministry. He appeals to him (Timothy) to be faithful in defending the truth against the encroaching error 1:3-20.

A. Paul's thanks and prayers for Timothy. 1:3-5. He was thankful to God that Timothy had such a fine home-training which had meant so much in his faithful and faith-filled ministry of great devotion.

v. 3. *I have* in my heart a feeling of *gratitude*[90] *to God, whom I serve* in worship *from my forefathers, in a pure conscience, as unceasingly I have the remembrance of you in my supplications in the night-time and by day.*

v. 4. *longing to see thee, remembering thy tears,* when we last parted in Ephesus), *that I may be filled with joy.*

v. 5. *Having been reminded of the unfeigned faith which dwelt first, in thy grandmother Lois and in thy mother Eunice and, I am persuaded with a permanent conviction also* dwells *in thee.*

---

87. Ablative of source of his apostleship.
88. Use of the article as relative pronoun.
89. Techna is a child born into a family.
90. Charin, a feeling of grace, favor on his part as the recipient.

Paul's prayers for Timothy were the greatest help he could render from now on and he assures Timothy that they shall be constant and unceasing.

B. The apostle turns over to Timothy the "Trusteeship of the Gospel" in the great province of Asia, pointing out the difficulties he will meet and errors which will confront him. He will need to aquit himself as a strong man, stirring up all the gifts within him, bestowed by God when he was ordained to the ministry.

v. 6. *For which cause I put thee in remembrance that thou stir up the gift of God which is in thee through* the intermediate agency of *the laying on of my hands,* symbolically at the ordination. The act of laying on of the hands of the Apostle, as in the process of ordination now, was to symbolize the impartation of the Holy Spirit necessary to the work of the ministry into which Timothy was ushered at that time.

v. 7. *For God gave not to us a spirit of fearfulness, but of power, and of love and of discipline* (soberness). Timothy is to meet the difficult issues of his ministry in Ephesus with courage, love and a wise mind.

C. Paul gives as a basis for Timothy's faithful performance of the task, the power of the Gospel 1:8-10, and adds various illustrations of it 1:8-18.

v. 8. *Do not therefore be ashamed of the testimony of our Lord* Jesus *nor of me* (*his*) *prisoner* for his sake,[91] *but suffer hardship with the gospel according to the power of God;*

v. 9. *Who saved us and called us with a holy calling, not according to our works but according to his own purpose and grace, given to us in Christ Jesus before times eternal,*

v. 10. *but now made manifest through the* (epiphany) *appearance of our Savior Christ Jesus,* in his incarnation *who made death of none effect* (inoperative, R. V. demolished) *and brought to light, life and* (incorruption) *immortality, through* the intermediate agency of *the gospel.* Paul cites various illustrations of the power of this gospel: (1) In his own ministry (vv. 11-14). (2) In the examples of some who were not loyal in the ministry (vv. 15, 16), and (3) in the challenging example of Onesiphorus (vv. 16-18).

v. 11. *into which I was placed as a herald, and apostle and teacher,*

v. 12. *for which I am suffering even these things,* but even in my situation I am not ashamed, for I know in whom I have believed completely and permanently,[92] *and am persuaded* confidently *that he is able to guard my deposit* of soul and eternal life *unto that day.*

v. 13. *keep on holding the pattern of sound words* (health-giving words) *which you heard from me* in my preaching, *with faith and love in Christ Jesus.*

v. 14. *Guard the good deposit,* the pattern of sound words, *through the Holy Spirit who dwells* having his habitation *in us.*

Having presented the example of his own ministry, Paul next cites the il-

91. Objective genitive rather than subjective.
92. Perfect active ind of pisteuō.

lustrations of disloyalty of some workers which they had together observed in Asia.

v. 15. *This thou knowest, that all that were in Asia* of them who were with me in my first trial, *were turned away*[93] *from me; of whom two* deterrent examples *are Phygelus and Hermogenes.*[94]

v. 16. The stimulating example of Onesiphorus is refreshing and unique. (vv. 16-18) *The Lord grant mercy to the house* (household) *of Onesiphorus; for he oft refreshed me, and was not ashamed of my chain;*

v.17. *but when he was in Rome,* during my first imprisonment, *he sought me diligently and found me*

v. 18. (*the Lord grant to him to find mercy of the Lord in that day*), the great and final day of judgement; *and in how many things he ministered* to me and to the whole church *in Ephesus,*[95] *thou knowest very well.*

D. Paul appeals further to Timothy to be strong in his ministry because of his individual responsibility to the work of the gospel and to his fine family. Ch. 2:1-7. He should provide for a succession of loyal teachers.

v. 1. *Thou therefore, my* (own) *child be strengthened in the* sphere of *grace which is in Christ Jesus* (in his character and work).

v. 2. *And the things which thou didst hear from me* in my preaching, not only at your ordination but many times elsewhere, *among* and by means of *many witnesses, these same* commit thou *to faithful* and faith-filled *men, who shall be able* and competent *to teach others also.*

v. 3. *Suffer hardship* (afflictions) *with me as a good soldier of Christ Jesus.*

v. 4. *No one serving* as a soldier *in war, entangleth himself*[96] *in the affairs* of this[97] *life,* in order *that he may please him who enrolled him* in the army.

v. 5. Or to use also another figure: *if a man contend* as our athlete the (Olympic or other) games, *he does not win a crown for himself* and is not crowned, *unless he may have contended lawfully,* according to the rules of the game. Paul adds yet another illustration:

v. 6. *It is necessary that the husband* man *working be the first to* receive or *partake of the fruits.* It is right that he should be the first sharer. So Paul would guard the rights of the minister.

v. 7. Consider (put your mind on) *what I am saying; for the Lord shall give thee understanding in all things.*

D. Most of all, Timothy must be faithful in his ministry because of the example and sufferings of Christ 2:8-13.

V. 8. *Remember* habitually *Jesus Christ* and keep in rememberance the one, *risen from the dead;*[98] he was a descendant *from the seed of David* fulfilling

93. Second aorist passive of apostrephō.
94. About whom nothing more is known.
95. Locative case rendered by prep. *in* or *at.*
96. Pres. middle Indicative, subject acting for himself.
97. Definite article used as demonstrative.
98. Perfect passive participle, he rose and was raised permanently, not as Lazarus.

the mission of the Messiah of Jewish prophecy, *according to my gospel*, the same which was entrusted to me, which I preach.

v. 9. *In which* work of preaching *I am suffering hardship even to bonds as* if I were *a malefactor, but the word of God is not bound* (in bonds) but is running free.

v. 10. *Because of this I endure all things for the elect's sake*, in order *that they also may obtain salvation, which is in Christ Jesus, with eternal glory.*

v. 11. *Faithful is the* (word) *saying: For if*[99] *we are suffering with* him, as evidently we are, *we shall also live with* him. This is a precious assurance based on reality if indeed we are suffering for his cause, which should nerve every true worker for Christ.

v. 12. *If we are enduring* patiently the sufferings with him *we shall reign* with him in glory. What a spur is here to patient endurance! But on the contrary it is true also; *if we shall deny* him, *that one will also deny us.*

v. 13. *If we are faithless* and unbelieving, *that one remains always faithful*, for *he cannot*, being what he is, *deny himself*. He must be just and reward us when we are faithful but cannot reward us if we are unfaithful.

II. Paul warns Timothy of error exhorts him to defend the gospel truth well. Chs. 2:14-4:8.

A. The proper methods to be used in defending the truth. Ch. 2:14-26.

1. The positive and negative subject-matter of his instructions.[1] Timothy must defend the truth as verified and exemplified in his experience and correct the erring with sympathy and love and in loyalty to the gospel. (vv. 14-18).

v. 14. *Remind* them over whom you have charge *of these things* of the gospel which they heard me preach, *solemnly charging* them *in* the *presence of God, not to strive* (make war) *about words* or controversial teaching, which is *to no profit*, tending *to the subverting of them that hear.*

v. 15. *Make haste*[2] *to present thyself approved to God, a workman that needeth not to be ashamed, handling aright* (cutting the cloth straight according to pattern) *the word of the truth.*

v. 16. *But shun profane babblings* turning yourself away so as to avoid idle speculation and discussions of heretics; *for they will proceed further* (cut forward) *in ungodliness,*

v. 17. *and their word* (doctrine) *will eat as doth a gangrene*, a biting ulcer: *of whom is Hymenaeus*, before mentioned (I Tim. 1:20) *and Philetus*, unknown but of the same flock.

v. 18. *who concerning the truth of* the gospel, *have erred* missing the mark, *saying, that the resurrection has taken place already*, and thus *are overthrowing the faith of some.*

2. The true conception of the church in relation to all teachers true and false. (vv. 19-21).

---

99. Condition of the first class, according to reality.
1. Cf. *The Expositor's Greek Testament*. Vol. 4 p. 85.
2. Cf. R. V. Give diligence.

v. 19. *Indeed, the firm foundation of God,* which is his church *stands*[3] permanently, *having this seal: "The Lord knows them that are his own*[4] *and so let every one "who is naming the name of the Lord" depart from* (iniquity, injustice) *unrighteousness.*

v. 20. *Now, in a great house there are not only vessels of gold and of silver, but of wood and of earth* (earthenware): *some unto honor and some unto dishonor.*

v. 21. *If any man therefore purge himself of these* latter vessels to dishonor, *he shall be a vessel for honor, sanctified* (separated) *and* meet or useful *for the Master, prepared* or made ready *for every* kind of *good work.*

3. The personal preparation of the true teacher and how he must treat the erring. (vv. 22:26).

v. 22. *But flee*[5] and keep on fleeing from the lusts or evil sensuous desires *pertaining to* flaming *youth* but also all the insidious selfish longings of mind and heart *and* begin *and pursue* and keep on pursuing *righteousness, faith,* Christian *love, peace with them that call on the Lord out of a* clean (cleansed) or *pure heart.*

v. 23. *But foolish* (stupid) *and ignorant questionings* of false teachers who are uneducated and love speculation, *refuse* to hear or give attention to, *knowing,* as we do, *that they gender conflicts*

v. 24. *and* it is not for *the servant of the Lord* (ought not) *to strive but be* gentle (kind) toward all, apt and *skillful in teaching, forbearing,*

v. 25. *in meekness, correcting* or disciplining *them that set themselves in opposition, whether or not* (if perhaps) *at any time, God may give them repentence leading into a definite knowledge of the truth.*

v. 26. *and they may recover themselves*[6] (by becoming sober) *out of the snare or trap of the devil after having been taken captive by him* and led *into* that which is *his will.* This indicates the deplorable state into which a Christian might fall and yet be delivered by Timothy or any pastor using the divine measures recommended.

B. The nature of the error of these false teachers Paul explains. Ch. 3:1-17.

1 The practical shortcomings of the false teachers.[7] (3:1-9).

Ch. III

v. 1. *But know this, that in the last days,* a period of apostosy which Paul foresaw which for Timothy might be not too far away, *shall come grievous* or hard *times.*

v. 2. *For men shall be lovers of self* grasping selfishly, *lovers of money* (silver), *boastful, haughty* in showing off themselves, *railers,* speaking evil of others in blasphemy, *disobedient to parents, unthankful* or without gratitude, *unholy* in character and conduct regardless of law, human or divine

---

3. Perfect active, indicative of histēmi.
4. Cf. Numbers 16:5, 26, korah and his company.
5. Present imperative, begin to flee, if you have not, and keep on fleeing habitually.
6. First aor. active subjunctive of ananēpsō.
7. Cf. N. J. D. White, *Expos. Greek Test.* p. 84.

v. 3. *without* family or *natural affection, implacable* admitting of no truce with anyone, *slanderers,* like the devil himself who was a "slanderer from the beginning," *without self-control,* having lost that power of the will to control passion, becoming thus incontinent, *fierce, as an untamed savage,*

v. 4. *no lovers of good, traitors, headstrong* falling forward in recklessness, *puffed up* wrapped in a cloud of conceit, *lovers of pleasure rather than lovers of God,*

v. 5. *having a form of godliness but denying* by their conduct *the power thereof; from these also turn thou way.*

v. 6. *For of these are they that creep into houses and take captive silly women laden*[8] *with sins, led away by divers lusts, ever learning and never able to come to the* accurate and full *knowledge of the truth* of the gospel.

v. 8. *and like as James and Jambres* chief among magicians of Hebrew tradition, *withstood Moses, so these also withstand the truth; men corrupted in mind,* not standing the test but *disapproved* or *reprobate concerning the faith.*

v. 9. *But they shall not advance further* with their mischief and bad influence, *for their folly* (want of sense) *will be openly manifest to all men, as theirs* also (that of James and Jambres) *came to be.*

2. Paul recalls Timothy's spiritual background and history (a) circumstances of the beginning of his discipleship (vv. 10-13). (b) the person by whom and the scriptures on which his youth had been brought up. (vv. 14-17).

v. 10. *But thou didst follow my teaching,* (for Timothy was much in the company of Paul from the beginning of the second missionary journey); also *my conduct, my purpose* of the world wide evangelization, the *faith* in Christ, the *longsuffering* in many trials, *my* Christian *love, patience,*

v. 11. *persecutions,* everywhere, by false brethren especially and by others incited by them, *sufferings* of every type for the cause, illustrated in: *what things befell* me *at Antioch* of Pisidia in the first missionary journey, *at Iconium* where the Jews from Antioch had followed me to prevent my work, *at Lystra* where you first heard the message of the gospel from me and was converted: *what persecutions I endured,* in these places culminating as you know in my being stoned and left on the rubbish heap for dead by my enemies, whence you and others recovered my body to life and rescued me out of the hands of violence to send me on to Derbe, the next day; *and the Lord delivered me out of them all.*

v. 12. *Yea,* and it is true, that *all that would live godly* lives *in Christ Jesus shall suffer persecution,* as it shall ever be.

v. 13. *And evil men and imposters shall go on waxing worse and worse, deceiving and being deceived.*

v. 14. *But, do thou abide in the things which thou hast learned and hast been assured of, knowing of whom thou hast learned them.*

---

8. Perfect passive participle, complete and permanent state.

v. 15. *And that from a babe thou hast known* from thy mother Eunice and grandmother Lois, *the sacred writings, which are able to make thee wise unto salvation through faith which is in Christ Jesus,* the only Savior.

v. 16. Every Scripture (or all Scripture) *inspired of God is profitable for teaching, for reproof* or the refutation of error, *for correction* (setting straight) *for instruction in righteousness,*

v. 17. in order *that the man of God* may be *complete, thoroughly furnished*[9] *unto every good work.*

C. A final appeal to Timothy for loyalty. 4:1-6. The heretical teachers were aggressive and their teaching insidious but God was behind the gospel messenger and he must be faithful and loyal to the utmost and meet aggression with alert defense and positive effort. Paul passes to Timothy the torch of gospel light to bear on courageously reminding him that the end of Paul's career is near. Ch. 4:1-8.

v. 1. *I charge thee before the face of God and of Jesus Christ who shall judge the living and the dead, and also* in view of *his* final *appearing* or coming *and his* present *kingdom,*

v. 2. *preach the word, stand by in times opportune and* also when the *times are not favorable, reprove* by testing, *rebuke* by placing the blame upon the one in error, *exhort,* comforting and begging, and do all these things *with all patience and teaching.*

v. 3. *For the time will be* (come) *when they will not endure* and hold up under *sound* and healthful *doctrine* in your teaching, *but having to get their ears tickled,*[10] *will heap to themselves* popular *teachers after their own* lusts or desires.

v. 4. *and will turn away their ears* (hearing) *from the truth and will turn aside to the myths* or legends.

v. 5. *But be thou sober in all things, suffer hardship, do the work of an* evangelist, (fill up to the full) *fulfil thy ministry.*

v. 6. *For I am already being offered up,* poured out as a libation upon the altar *and the time of my departure is come.*

v. 7. *I have fought*[11] *a good fight,*[12] like a wrestler in the strenuous wrestling match in the Olympic games. *I have finished* and ended my (race) *course, I have kept*[13] (guarded) *the faith,* as a sacred trust.

v. 8. *Henceforth, there is laid up* (safely) *for me, a crown of righteousness* that is a proof of the righteousness by faith in Christ, *which the Lord the righteous judge will give* freely *to me in that day* of final awards; *and not only to me but also to all* those *who love his appearing.*

D. Paul's conclusion of his personal message to Timothy. Ch. 4:9-22.

v. 9. *Make haste to come to me as quickly* as you can;

---

9. Perfect passive participle of exartizō.
10. Present middle (causative) participle of knetho. C. Robertson's *Word Pictures.*
11. Perfect middle, subject acting and complete action with permanent result.
12. Azōna — it had been a struggle indeed.
13. Perfect tense again meaning he had completed his life work of the ministry.

v. 10. *for Demas* wilfully *forsook* (deserted) *me,* because *he loved the present world.* Paul was in prison and Demas had a business excuse, which took him away *and* he went to *Thessalonica; Crescens* Paul sent perhaps *to Galatia* and *Titus* on some errand for the apostle *to Dalmatia* (of Illyricum). Paul was anxious to keep in touch with all the new work established there, and no reproach is attached to the going of these two.

v. 11. *Only Luke is with me.* (He must have left some record of the work of Paul after the first imprisonment. It could have been lost). *Take Mark and bring him with thee; for he is useful to me for ministering.* Mark had made good in his ministry.

v. 12. *But Tychicus I sent to Ephesus.*

v. 13. *The cloak which I left in Troas with Carpus, bring when thou comest and the books, especially the parchments.*

v. 14. *Alexander, the coppersmith did me much evil: the Lord will reward him according to his works:*[14]

v. 15. *Of whom be thou aware; for he exceedingly withstood our words.* He had probably been in Rome at Paul's defense in his first trial or have opposed Paul's work elsewhere.

v. 16. *At my first defense no one came* forward with me to take my part, *but all forsook me; may it not be laid to their account.*

v. 17. *But the Lord stood by me and strengthened me,* in order *that through me the message might be fully proclaimed; and that all the Gentiles might hear and I was delivered out "of the mouth of the lion,"* (Nero had sat as his judge).

v. 18. *The Lord will deliver me from every evil work and will save me into his heavenly kingdom* (in the heavens): *to whom be the glory forever and ever. Amen*

v. 19. *Salute Priscilla and Aquilla and the house* (family) *of Onesiphorous.*

v. 20. *Erastus abode* (remained) *at Corinth; but Trophimus I left at Miletus sick.*

v. 21. *Make haste to come before winter. Eubulus saluteth thee, and Pudens and Linus and Claudia and all the brethren.*

v. 22. *The Lord be with thy spirit. Grace be with you.*

Thus ended the literary contribution of the most wonderful apostle and greatest interpreter of Jesus. Criticism has attacked his glorious letters which have stood as a Gilbraltar in the midst of the froth and foam of its tides. His example shines out across the centuries as a great luminary reflecting the image of the Son of God whose "bond-slave" Paul counted it his greatest privilege to be.

---

14. Ps. 28:4; 62:12 a citation in black type in the Greek text. Paul did not invoke such action of the Lord.

Bibliography

Selective Bibliography

ACKNOWLEDGEMENTS: According to the author's method, the Greek texts of both Nestle and Westcott & Hort have furnished the basis for deciding the order by paragraphs for the paraphrastic type of exposition verse by verse, used in this treatise. The field covered herein is the whole of Paul's Epistle, one by one, cast upon the background of a careful study of the life of their author and the environmental conditions of his work. Careful exegetical outlines of the epistles, made with the help of the greatest commentaries and other exegetical works, based on the Greek text, were laboriously wrought out and used in class-room work throughout the long professorial service of the writer in theological seminaries where he worked during many years. These outlines served as the tested framework upon which to build the expository treatment in detail by sections, paragraphs and verses. They are constituted so that they embody the gist of content and are a web of contextual nature which aids correct interpretation of each individual verse. The selective process has been employed in presenting the bibliography, omitting many of the works consulted in the years of teaching, the bibliography being limited to a shorter list more vitally used as helps to come at the clearest possible interpretation, reflecting the inspired message of the Spirit through the Apostle Paul. A bibliography merely suggestive of some of the most important works consulted is to follow. To the authors whose names are mentioned, and to others used, the writer of this treatise gives hearty thanks for the help rendered in getting at a more complete mastery of the biography of the great Apostle to the Gentiles and his vital messages in his letters to the churches, as well as of the incomparable history of the founding of those churches, written by Luke, whose picture of Paul is naught less than the most skillfully artistic painting of the greatest interpreter of Jesus, by an inspired hero-worshiper and disciple of the great man, Saul of Tarsus, alias Paul, the Apostle to Gentiles.

The author wishes to gratefully acknowledge the help of the New Orleans Baptist Theological Seminary for loyal cooperation in getting the MS typed, and of various members of his own family in the readings of proofs and particularly in help rendered in the editing of the MS, by a son, who is finishing his language work in Yale this year in preparation for mission work in China.

I Grammars on New Testament (Koine) Greek in the Light of Historical Research:

A Grammar on New Testament Greek by Robertson, A. T. (1914).
Other *Grammars of the New Testament Greek* by various authors as Winer (1822) revised by J. H. Thayer (1873), Frederick Blass, translated into English by J. H. Thayer (1911), Buttmann, A. (1895), Moulton, J. H. (1906), Robertson, A. T. and Davis, W. H. *A Short Grammar* (1931), Dana H. E. and Mantey, J. R. *A Manual* (1936). Lexicons: Thayer, J. H., *A Greek-English Lexicon of the New Testament* (1889), Winer, G. B., *A Grammar of the Idiom of the New Testament* (1897), et al.

II Texts:

Nestle, E. (revised, 1927)
Westcott and Hort (revised edition, 1936).

III Versions:

English: *Authorized, King James.*
The American Revised.
Other versions as those by Moffatt, Montgomery, Weymouth, Williams, Twentieth Century.
Revised Standard Version.
Latin Vulgate (Vatican Edition) (1892); Almeida (in Portuguese) et al.

IV Biographies and some general works on St. Paul and his Epistles:

Life of St. Paul (Hand Book), James Stalker (1912).
The Life and Epistles of St. Paul; Conybeare and Howson (1894).
Life and Works of St. Paul, Farrar, F. W., (1879).
The Story of Paul, Bacon (1904).
Student's Life of Paul, Gilbert G. A., (1899).
Paul the Missionary, Taylor, W. M. (1902).
Paul of Tarsus, Glover T. R., (1930).
Epochs in the Life of Paul, Robertson, A. T. (1909).
Life and Letters of St. Paul, Smith, David (1920).
St. Paul, Nock, Arthur D., (1938).
The Life and Literature of Paul, Dana, H. E. (1937).
Harmony of the Life of St. Paul, F. J. Goodwin (1895);
Student's Chronological New Testament, Robertson, A. T. (1904).
The Man Paul, Speer, Robert E., (1900).
The Life and Teachings of St. Paul, Garvie, A. E. (1910).
The Apostle Paul and the Modern World, Peabody, (1923).
St. Paul and His Interpreters, Schweitzer, Albert, (1912).
Paul and Paulinism, Moffatt, James, (1940).
The Apostle Paul, Sabatier, A., (Ed. Findlay, G. G.).
Jesus and Paul, Bacon (1921).
The Life of Paul, Robinson, B. W., (1918).
The Meaning of Paul for Today, Dodd, C. Harold (1921).
St. Paul, A Study in Social and Religious History, Deissmann (1912).
Paul the Interpreter of Christ, Robertson, A. T., (1921).
Paul, Renan (Portuguese Ed.).
The Faith of the New Testament, Conner, W. T. (1938).

V Introductions and General Exegetical Treatises:

The Environment of Early Christianity, Angus, S. (1910).
The Mysticism of Paul the Apostle, Schweitzer, A., (1929).
The Literature of the New Testament. Scott E. F., (1932).
The Pauline Epistles, Shaw R. D., (1904).

The Jewish People in the Time of Jesus Christ, Schürer, (1891).
Christian Beginnings, Enslin, M. S., (1938).
Pauline and Other Studies, Ramsay, W. M.
Studies of Paul and His Gospel, Garvie A. E., (1911).
The New Testament World, Dana, H. E. (1937).
In the Steps of St. Paul, Morton H. V., (1943).
The Testimony of St. Paul to Christ, Knowling, R, J. (1905).
The Acts of the Apostles, Foakes-Jackson, (1931).
Introduction to the Literature of the New Testament, Moffatt, James.
Introduction to the Acts of the Apostles, Stifler, J. M., (1892).
A Man in Christ, Stewart, James, (1940).
Jewish Christianity, Dana, H. E. (1937).
The Religious Quests of the Graeco-Roman World, Angus S.
The Teaching of Paul in Terms of the Present Day, Ramsay W. M. (1913).
Judaism and St. Paul, Montefiore, (1915).
The Cities of Paul, Ramsay, W. M.
The Church in the Roman Empire, Ramsay W. M. (1893).
Light from the Ancient East, Deissmann, A. (1909).
Essential Christianity, Angus, Samuel (1939).
World Christianity, Van Dusen, H. P., (1926).
Christian Missions in Today's World, W. O. Carver (1942).

VI Some Basic Works in Exposition:

Texts in Greek and Versions, Lexicons.
Word Pictures, Robertson, A. T., *Acts, Epistles of Paul* (1931).
Boises' Notes on the Epistles of Paul, Wood, N. E., (1896).
The Expositor's Greek Testament (on all Epistles).
The International Critical Commentary (all epistles).
Cambridge Bible for Schools and Colleges (all epistles).
The Acts of the Apostles, Carver, W. O., (1916).
The Nature of the Early Church, Scott, E. F., (1941).
St. Paul the Traveler and Roman Citizen, Ramsay W. M. (Ed. 1912).
The Earlier Epistles of St. Paul, Lake, (1915).
The Acts of the Apostles, Morgan, G. C., (1924).
New Testament Moods and Tenses, Burton E. D., (1893).
Various Commentaries, on certain epistles as for example, The Expositor's Bible.
Various individual Commentaries not in Series cited in the above lists, on certain epistles, as Moule on Ephesians, Romans.
Biographical and *general works on Paul's Life and Letters* used constantly as background material, various not cited above.

Scriptural Index

OLD TESTAMENT

NEW TESTAMENT

General Index